1994

Freedom and Tenure in the Academy

Freedom and Tenure in the Academy

William W. Van Alstyne, Editor

DUKE UNIVERSITY PRESS   *Durham and London 1993*

Library of Congress Cataloging-in-Publication Data
appear on the last printed page of this book.
Previously published as volume 53, no. 3 of *Law and
Contemporary Problems* journal, Summer 1990. New
material for this volume includes the Introduction by
William Van Alstyne and the chapter by Judith Jarvis
Thomson and Matthew W. Finkin.

CONTENTS

156, 522

INTRODUCTION

Three decades ago, the first professional journal symposium dedicated to academic freedom was published at Duke University.[1] With the publication of this new volume in 1993, the Duke University Press extends that tradition through this new, more wide-ranging work. The authors represented in this collection know their subject extremely well. What they have to say speaks directly to questions of academic freedom in the mixed conditions in higher education in the United States. In brief compass, these are the various subjects they address.

Professor Walter Metzger of Columbia University provides the first chapter in this original symposium with his detailed review of the history of the 1940 Joint Statement of Principles on Academic Freedom and Tenure. His exploration of the 1940 Statement is a logical place for this volume to begin, though not every reader will even have known of this Statement, much less see why it ought to lead off a book of this sort. So perhaps a few words by way of background will help.

This Joint Statement, agreed to and published by the Association of American Colleges (AAC) and the American Association of University Professors (AAUP) in 1940, was a development culminating more than a decade of discussion over revisions to prior statements on academic freedom, the earliest of which was published by the AAUP in 1915, when the country was divided over entry into World War I. Despite all the changes in higher education since 1940, the Joint Statement has remained unchanged since that time. And, while many interested in the subject of academic freedom may not be familiar with the 1940 Statement, it has in fact held an influential position in setting a baseline for institutional practices for the last half century.

As of 1992, the Joint Statement had drawn the endorsement of more than 130 national learned societies and professional associations. In a number of public and private colleges regulated by collective bargaining arrangements, either partial or complete incorporation of the 1940 Statement has made its provisions controlling between the parties. In a large number of contested court cases, where there was no specific contract or other provision governing the case, its general standards have been drawn upon to provide a princi-

---

1. See *Academic Freedom: The Scholar's Place in Modern Society*, 28 L & Contemp Probs (Summer 1963) (Hans W. Baade and Robinson O. Everett, eds).

pal source of the common law of the profession, so to govern these disputes. Beyond these considerations, its own supplemental interpretive case law, developed over decades through several hundred published case reports of Committee A of the AAUP (Committee on Academic Freedom and Tenure), has served as an interpretive aid to the profession as well as a unique record of the controversies over academic freedom during periods of political upheaval in colleges and universities in the United States. And the 1940 Statement has, on occasion, been utilized in the constitutional decisions of the Supreme Court.

In light of all this, it is surprising that Professor Metzger's skillful, close review of the origins of the 1940 Statement is in fact the first full and complete examination that has ever been provided of the 1940 Statement itself. It is all the more welcome on that account. His article is particularly valuable for bringing a long overdue inquiry to bear on a number of the Statement's most troublesome clauses, including several that read less like statements of first principles than as mere settlements or ambiguous compromises, as in some measure they were. The long-standing difficulties that parts of the 1940 Statement have ever since presented for universities and for the AAUP itself are not glossed over by Metzger. Rather, there is nothing glossed over in any of Metzger's elegantly written work.[2]

The second selection in this symposium parallels Metzger's work, but it examines a different kind of baseline measuring academic freedom in the United States. As the 1940 Statement of Principles has provided one kind of baseline for academic freedom and tenure in higher education, the Constitution's first amendment and fourteenth amendment clauses on free speech and on due process have provided a different kind of baseline guiding the ultimate hard law ("higher law") treatment of these same subjects in the courts. To be sure, the United States Constitution, unlike some more recent constitutions, says nothing specifically about "academic freedom."[3] And neither of the two due process clauses in the Constitution was framed with any sense of how either one might or might not apply in academic life. Yet, as these clauses have worked out in practice, both sets of clauses have yielded a great deal of enforceable protection in the twentieth century, however surprising this might seem. Professor Van Alstyne reports on this evolutionary path of the law, tracing the extent to which academic freedom has been accepted into domestic constitutional law, in *Academic Freedom and the First Amendment in the Supreme Court of the United States: An Unhurried Historical Review.*

Judith Thomson's shorter essay that appears next in these materials is the first of three highly topical pieces that follow these longer, introductory reviews. Her attention immediately turns to a much more sharply focused con-

---

2. The inclusion of the full 1940 Statement (in Appendix B) will serve the reader well in following Metzger's narrative of its politics and passage. For readers with a still deeper interest (and for comparison), the original General Declaration of Principles of 1915 is also included (in Appendix A).

3. See, for example, Article 5 of the Basic Law of the Federal Republic of Germany (Grundgesetz für die Bundesrepublik Deutschland von 23 Mai 1949 (BGBl.I, BGBl.III Nr. 100-1) (Sec. 1 protecting a general freedom of speech; Sec. 3 separately and expressly protecting freedom in art, science, research, and teaching).

troversy that has been felt recently in complaints that universities and various academic departments need a good deal of shaking up. Whether in a new university or an old one, it has been frequently observed, it is still obvious that someone or some group must in the first instance decide what is worth studying, who is best qualified to provide instruction, and what lines of research or publication are most suitable to pursue. The faculty usually claim the main prerogative on these matters, based on a superior claim to know—to know the relative promise or lack thereof of a certain proposed field of study, and to know who may be most promising to provide useful insights that might be brought to bear. Even supposing it is the faculty (rather than the administration, trustees, students, or someone else) who tend to make the greater number of these decisions, however, and even supposing they—the incumbent faculty—strive for what they deem to be detachment in making judgments of academic worth, they will still be operating according to some embedded views of their own as to what good work consists of, and what criteria of competence and of professional relevance count. But, if so, what inevitably must any such system tend to produce? The recurring radical critique is that any such system simply tends to perpetuate an entrenched status quo, disfavoring the unorthodox and the new, and defeating the very notion of the idea of a university where intellectual diversity and new ideas may germinate in the culture of academic freedom.

The observation offered in this critique is that the installation, promotion, and tenuring of only those satisfying only such criteria as characterize the incumbent faculty's judgments—of what counts as "relevant" work and what counts in being a "competent" candidate—make the system self-sealing (literally self-proving of its own criteria). The incumbent faculty was itself selected and advanced by prevailing notions of "relevance" of subject matter interest and prevailing notions of "competence" to do suitable work. Accordingly, each succeeding generation of faculty may tend to be quite indistinguishable from the last generation. The structure of the system itself thus makes it more or less impervious to change. Professor Thomson, Professor of Philosophy at the Massachusetts Institute of Technology, looks at this critique quite closely. Without blinking it away, she raises sharp questions of what it amounts to in the end, and what alternatives one might deem to be better. She does so in this altogether timely review, provocatively titled *Ideology and Faculty Selection*.

Robert O'Neil, the former President of the University of Virginia and current Director of the Thomas Jefferson Center for the Protection of Free Expression at that distinguished university, turns his own attention to a related modern area of academic freedom. The focus of his brief article is the arts on campus, freedom of expression, and judgments of academic worth. What of academic freedom and freedom of expression here? Colleges and universities frequently maintain artists in residence, with or without faculty status. Studio classes encourage varieties of student self-expression in dance, dramatic production, sculpture, and the plastic arts. Public foyers, as well as sheltered galleries, commonly display student works and all manner of seemingly odd productions as diverse in their own way as Picasso's *Guernica* is different in its way, say, from Robert Mapplethorpe's explicit homoerotic photographs. And criteria of "competence" or of "excellence" in these matters seem to many to be far less susceptible to any consensus of disciplined judgment than in those across the way, in physics, biochemistry, or even history and literary studies. Academic freedom and first amendment issues haunt this subject, most especially in the matter of what goes on display, what kinds of works taxpayers can be expected to tolerate in the colleges and universities they support, and who determines the latitude of what passes for art.

Despite expected quarrels over these matters, however, no one denies (or at least it is difficult to imagine such a denial) that the arts even now—as always—frequently do reflect an awesome gift of insight unique in enlarging the space of the mind. Professor O'Neil assuredly is on firm ground in beginning his review with the proposal that "[s]urely the first amendment ought to protect the artist's creative process and product as fully as it protects the spoken and printed word." Assuming that it does, however, just how does that play out on campus, together with academic freedom concerns? O'Neil's useful provisional overview is nicely reflected in the fourth essay in this collection, *Artistic Freedom and Academic Freedom.*

As though the uneasy status of the graphic arts on campus were not a sufficient subject by itself to test one's boundaries of freedom of expression and academic freedom, Professor Rodney Smolla confronts the tumult of offensive expression, political correctness, and so-called "hate" speech in looking at those boundaries still again. As the author of several works on the first amendment, as well as Director of the Institute of Bill of Rights Law at the Marshall-Wythe School of Law, he is thus well qualified to take the measure of recent events. A growing number of institutions have instituted campus speech codes to curb incidents of obnoxious, intrusive, and crude incivility on campus. On a related front, federal requirements applicable to any institution receiving any form of federal assistance (which means virtually all institutions) appear to mandate antiharassment regulations. Some of these regulations take the form of policing what one says in the classroom and what students may say about one another or about their views of particular groups on campus. Inevitably, a number of incidents have wound up in the federal courts. More soberingly, faculty now fear the cloying effects of conformist attitudes of political correctness backed by speech codes with an apparatus of investigation and accounting before nonfaculty boards of review. Professor Smolla's sharp reflections on these matters are crisply composed in his welcome essay, *Academic Freedom, Hate Speech, and the Idea of a University.*

David Rabban, a legal historian at the University of Texas, breaks away from the topics examined by Thomson, O'Neil, and Smolla to return to a larger academic freedom concern. The object of his quite elaborate review is previewed in the title of his article, *A Functional Analysis of "Individual" and "Institutional" Academic Freedom Under the First Amendment.* It takes but a very few words to say what this difficult subject is about. Universities face outward and face inward. When they face outward, they have sometimes not yielded to outside authority. Rather, they have sometimes resisted and, in doing so, have invoked

academic freedom in their own defense, so to maintain a strong reputation
for institutional integrity from external demands that would have them yield
their standards of faculty appointment, their standards for student admission,
or their commitment to free and open research. In going to court in just this
fashion, moreover, they have often been admired for not succumbing to these
external pressures, and thus for protecting the academic freedom of their faculty, students, and staff. When they face inward, however, they may likewise
face academic freedom claims against themselves, and so the question arises
as to what they may then tend to do about these, i.e., claims asserted against
them by their own faculty or their own students instead. As Rabban notes in
his introduction, in this case, something quite startling tends to take place.
"Increasingly," he notes, "administrators and trustees have invoked constitutional academic freedom not as an additional layer of protection for professors
against the state, but as a bar to judicial review of claims against universities by
professors alleging institutional violations of individual academic freedom."

Just what does one make of this latter development? And just what may
it portend? Are we now to be faced with choosing between two claims or two
rival theories of academic freedom? Is academic freedom "institutional," such
that the larger competition of ideas is best served by a protected pluralism of
very different kinds of colleges and universities, each entitled to put into place
whatever rules and standards it sees fit to adopt for itself and thus each constituting something of a law unto itself? Or is academic freedom "individual,"
such that faculty and students, regardless of the institution they find themselves within, are entitled to some commonly respected freedoms of critical
inquiry, expression, and dissent, without fear of dismissal at the unreviewable
discretion of the institution that finds them unacceptable according to its own
notions of what it wishes to allow? The point of departure for Professor Rabban's reflections on this large subject is a provocative essay by J. Peter Byrne,
who earlier noted the divergence in usage between academic freedom as an
institutional imperative rather than as a source of some individual claims.[4] The
Byrne article put its stress on institutional autonomy as the proper focus of
academic freedom ("institutional academic freedom"). Rabban's article is the
first comprehensively responding to Byrne's thesis. Both Byrne and Rabban
are assuredly well worth a serious reader's time.

This very sort of clash—between institutional claims and individual claims
of academic freedom—is concretely brought to the fore in the next contribution in this work, the article by Michael McConnell of the University of Chicago
law faculty, on *Academic Freedom in Religious Colleges and Universities.* And a
better "test case" can scarcely be proposed. Even the 1940 Joint Statement of
Principles recognized the inevitable tension that doctrinal commitments would
pose for religious institutions confronted with routine decisions of faculty appointment and curricular control. Here, at least, McConnell suggests, the fair
claims for "institutional academic freedom" of a religious school against its

---

4. J. Peter Byrne, *Academic Freedom: A "Special Concern of the First Amendment,"* 99 Yale LJ
251 (1989).

own faculty's possible assaults on its doctrines, were faced up to. As McConnell explains, the 1940 Statement appears to concede that "religious schools are entitled to depart from" secular standards of academic freedom, "so long as [such schools] clearly announce their intention to do so in advance." What is fairly required is not that a religious school yield its faith-bound commitments in structuring courses, in making appointments, or in reviewing what gets taught, and by whom. It ought to be enough, McConnell suggests, that each such institution openly declare the model of faith, morals, and epistemology within which its own vision of higher learning is offered, bearing in mind that this leaves alternative (secular) institutions free to pursue their different vision of teaching or study, in turn. McConnell draws added vitality for his reflections on this topic by noting that the Constitution itself acknowledges the special protection owing the free exercise of religion—a protection certainly extending to religiously affiliated schools and colleges. He faults the AAUP for having "repudiated the limitations clause of the 1940 Statement de facto," even while "wallow[ing] in standardless ambiguity de jure." And he offers a very spirited defense of the value of religiously committed colleges at least to be left alone in an otherwise dessicated secular age.

Professor McConnell's article is the best critical review thus far to appear of AAUP censure practices affecting religious colleges in the United States. It is paired with a response from Professors Judith Thomson and Matthew Finkin.[5] The reader is likely to find these two well-matched selections among the most absorbing and well written of all the essays presented in this work.

"[D]oes academic tenure reinforce academic freedom? Of course it does." So begins the next-to-last selection in this collection, jointly authored by Simeon Baldwin Professor Ralph Brown of Yale and Dr. Jordan Kurland of the AAUP, on *Academic Tenure and Academic Freedom.* But at what price, they also rightly ask? And if tenure is deemed a sine qua non of academic freedom, what does that say to the junior faculty for whom tenure is typically not even considered during their first half-dozen years? The junior faculty, it may be suggested, is the faculty most likely to be innovative, and most likely to offer some real contrast with the senior faculty. Yet they are at risk of nonrenewal by the senior faculty. So, wherein is the fairness of that? And why should a system ("tenure") lock institutions into virtual lifetime contracts with faculty when it must be obvious that they may not remain as good as others who are subsequently available to replace them, yet who are foreclosed from being considered absent someone's retirement, resignation, or death? Moreover, now that the Congress of the United States has presumed to forbid universities to set any age for retirement, even a generous uniform mandatory retirement age for its faculty (e.g., seventy or seventy-five), doesn't this "uncapping" make tenure an utterly unaffordable dead weight on university payrolls? Aren't there sensible ways of protecting academic freedom by means other than tenure systems? These are

---

5. Judith Jarvis Thomson and Matthew W. Finkin, *Academic Freedom and Church-Related Higher Education: A Reply to Professor McConnell.*

but some of the excellent questions addressed in the Brown-Kurland article that takes a fresh look at this perennial debate. And, concluding these reviews of academic freedom and tenure, Professor Matthew Finkin of the University of Illinois law faculty brings his specialty in labor law to bear in his highly instructive review of *Academic Freedom and Tenure in the Vortex of Employment Practices and Law.*

William W. Van Alstyne

Freedom and Tenure in the Academy

THE 1940 STATEMENT OF PRINCIPLES ON ACADEMIC FREEDOM AND TENURE

WALTER P. METZGER*

I

In the field of American higher education, prescriptive dicta concerning academic conduct seldom exhibit much staying power. Some are meant to be ephemeral, to answer a transient public criticism with an immediately placating response. Some are designed for longer duty but are quickly reduced by the swift pace of events to a remnant of a changing *geist* and then to a relic of a forgotten past. Especially short is the life expectancy of pronouncements on the proper scope of academic freedom and the proper terms of employment of faculty personnel. On such subjects, the collective expressions of academic groups, especially if they seek improvement on a global scale, seem to pass from birth to eternal rest at the speed with which American foundations finance academic conferences with similar agendas or one edition of the *Chronicle of Higher Education* is followed by publication of the next.

One of the arresting features of the 1940 Statement of Principles on Academic Freedom and Tenure[1] is its exceptional durability. Compared with the high infant mortality rate of its species, its ability to stay alive for as long as fifty years stacks up as a Methuselah accomplishment. That it stayed alive during the *last* fifty years makes its longevity all the more remarkable. Born to an academic world that was relatively small, self-contained, and stable, it came of age in a world that had grown immense, delocalized, and volatile. Nevertheless, except for the reinterpretation in 1970 of certain illegible or outmoded passages, it has managed without amendment to take these transforming years in stride. It has weathered any number of roller coaster swings: the rise and fall of McCarthyism, the flow and ebb of student riotousness, and the feasts and anticipated famines of college student enrollments. It has survived the quickening of academic trends that had been set in motion prior to 1940, such as the steady decline in the share of material

---

* Professor of History, Columbia University.

1. *1940 Statement of Principles on Academic Freedom and Tenure* ("1940 Statement"), in *Policy Documents and Reports* 3 (AAUP, 1984) ("*1984 AAUP Red Book*"); see Appendix B, 53 L & Contemp Probs 407 (Summer 1990). All references to the 1940 Statement in this article are to the text that was written in 1940, the historic text, and not to the text edited in 1990 to remove gender-specific references. Contrast 1940 Statement, in *Policy Documents and Reports* 3 (AAUP, 1990) ("*1990 AAUP Red Book*"). This is done in a Rankean spirit—to record the event as much as possible *wie es eigentlich gewesen ist.*

and human resources going to the private sector of American higher education and the rise in the public sector of multicampus universities under statewide systems of control; it has survived the initiation and acceleration of trends that had hardly been sighted before 1940, such as the spread of faculty unionism and the rise of the federal government as a major academic rule-giver and financier. If it deserved no other praise, the 1940 Statement would merit admiration for its hardiness in the face of incessant, often rapid, sometimes convulsive, change.

But it is not on this ground alone that we who are academics find it praiseworthy; were we inclined to honor mere persistence, no matter how marginal or vestigial, we would pay homage to the vermiform appendix. As it happened, this holdover from another era, far from paying for the gift of life with loss of function, has added to its significance as it aged. During the first two decades of its existence, it secured the endorsement of no more than a handful of learned societies and academic administrative associations. During the 1960s, it gained the backing of as many as sixty-five such legitimizing bodies; during the 1970s, when stock-taking on academic freedom and, especially, academic tenure came into vogue, it suffered but one organizational defection and picked up thirty-five new subscribers; during the 1980s and early 1990s, as though to demonstrate that its charms were ageless, it added thirty-four new endorsers to the list.[2] Moreover, as time wore on, more and more colleges and universities (they have not been counted but they are surely numerous) saw fit to incorporate bits and pieces of it into their regulations, or by reference or quotation to embrace it whole. In the field of law, it seems not to have had much of an impact until the 1970s, when a spate of contested academic discharges on grounds of financial exigency led lawyers and judges to use it as an authoritative guide to academic usage on that subject; thereafter, it would be paid the compliment of citation when the courts sought to explicate other terms of faculty employment contracts.[3] Only with respect to professional self-regulation may it be said that the 1940 Statement did not put on weightiness late in life, and this is because, to the American Association of University Professors ("AAUP"), the chief nonlegal monitor of academic freedom and tenure in this country and the co-author and primary user of this document, it was of signal importance from the very start.

Even its celebrants will admit that the 1940 Statement has not been a hit in all academic quarters. A roll call of its endorsers would disclose the conspicuous absence of the American Council on Education, the Association of American Universities, and several other prominent members of the academic administrative establishment. In institutions where the reflexive

---

2. *1990 AAUP Red Book* at 7-10 (cited in note 1).

3. In the four-year period, 1972-1976, a computer search by then AAUP staff counsel David Rabban found that the 1940 Statement and documents based on it figured in forty-nine federal court decisions. It played a prominent role in state court decisions during this period as well, starting with the landmark case of *American Association of Univerity Professors v Bloomfield College*, 129 NJ Super 249, 322 A2d 846 (1974), aff'd, 136 NJ Super 442, 346 A2d 615 (1975).

cautiousness of the house attorney is allowed full sway, allusions to the 1940 Statement in bylaws and handbooks may be accompanied by a boilerplate reserve clause disclaiming any legal obligation to adhere to some or any of its terms. And in institutions, highly visible but still quite few, where universal limited-term appointments are the rule, the 1940 Statement has obviously been ignored or recanted. But these evidences of standoffishness or opposition are not surprising: one does not expect everyone in this fractured and diverse domain to give unreserved consent to anything. What is surprising is that support for the 1940 Statement cuts across so many internal divisions. These include divisions between administrators and professors, first and foremost; divisions between public and private, church-connected and independent, teaching-oriented and research-oriented institutions; and finally, divisions between the specialist profession of the "discipline" and the ecumenical profession of the "faculty"—the two academic professions that both liberate their overlapping memberships by sanctioning dual loyalties and oppress them by generating counterpulls. When and if the time comes to write the funeral address for the 1940 Statement, the fair memorialist will stress, not that it went just so far, but that it bridged so much.

II

IL NOME! IL NOME!

All in all, the fifty-year record of the 1940 Statement gives us abundant cause to salute it for its vitality—a virtue greater than mere endurance—and to pay tribute to its growing usefulness—a rare accompaniment to advancing age. But what *is* this thing we so proudly hail? To what works, seemingly unrelated, does it have a cognate connection; from what works, superficially alike, does it really stand apart? At first glance, an easy answer to the question of identification, which always shades into a question of classification, would seem to be ours for the asking. Ordinarily, objects that are hard to categorize are also hard to utilize and hence are unlikely to be roundly praised. In this case, however, the generic identity of a much-used object has proved elusive. Like Elsa plighting her troth to the cryptic Lohengrin, American academics and others have embraced the 1940 Statement without knowing its family name.

On this score, those who know it best and love it most—the leaders of the AAUP—may offer limited enlightenment. Around a decade ago, Ralph S. Brown and Matthew W. Finkin, veteran members of the AAUP's national Committee on Academic Freedom and Tenure, widely known as Committee A, described the 1940 Statement as the "Bible" and "Constitution" of their organization and, by extension, of the entire American academic profession.[4] These level-headed law professors were not descending into flights of utter fancy; some broad affinities do exist between this creation of their microcosm

---

4. Ralph S. Brown, Jr. & Matthew W. Finkin, *The Usefulness of AAUP Policy Statements*, 59 Educ Rec 30 (1978).

and those two world-historic masterpieces. Like the Book of Books, like the federal Constitution, the 1940 Statement does satisfy a hunger for standards of goodness and justice that are less fickle than those favored by contemporary opinion, more universal than those available to local wisdom, and more disinterested than those promoted by partisans in fighting dress. In addition, these analogies help to bring out qualities in the work that might be missed in a casual perusal of it. Likening the 1940 script to Holy Scripture calls attention to the aura of sacrosanctness it has acquired within the AAUP over the years. These are secular precincts; nevertheless, when it performs its work of the guardian variety, Committee A incants the words and phrases of the 1940 Statement with a reverence usually reserved for the hymning of a doxology, and the AAUP Washington staff ponders its every word with an exegetical skill that invites comparison with that of gospel hermeneuts and Talmudic scholars. In the same sense, there is something to be said for likening the handiwork of 1940 to the magnum opus of 1789. The comparison underscores the symbiosis between rules and cases; in both instances, the norms embodied in a governing text help tell rights from wrongs in specific controversies, while the clarifying factuality of specific controversies refreshes the normative commands of the governing text. And this comparison may highlight aspects of the 1940 Statement that would otherwise go unremarked, such as its sectional structure, its enumerated subparts, its extreme succinctness, and the fact that its words and phrases have but one definitive interpreter.

But no one seriously supposes that these flamboyant figures of speech can put the "what-is-it?" question to rest. Obviously, it would strain comparison to the snapping point to imply that there was anything Biblical about the literary style of the 1940 Statement: anyone who has read the dry, spare prose of this two-page document (five pages counting footnotes and interpretive commentary) does not have to be told that it fails to capture the sublimity of the Book of Genesis or the lyricism of the Book of Psalms. Given their way with words, the authors of this document, had they undertaken to rewrite the Pentateuch, would probably have called it the 1200 B.C. Statement on Divinized Administrative Policy Affecting Certain Classes of Israelite Personnel! Here, perhaps, hyperbole is too blatant to be misleading. But in the analogy between the 1940 Statement and the Constitution, the exaggeration is sufficiently muted to foster a false impression. Brown and Finkin sought to convince the courts that the contractual obligations of the institutional subscribers to the 1940 Statement were defined by the AAUP's later interpretation of its elliptical language, especially its one-sentence reference to terminations of faculty employment for financial reasons. To drive home the point that the original verbiage should be read in the light of the AAUP's subsequent constructions, they hit on a metaphor they were sure every judge would appreciate. "In its form and language," they and their confreres wrote in an AAUP amicus brief, "the 1940 *Statement* resembles a constitution. Like other 'constitutions', [it] has generated 'legislation'—

supplemental statements and recommended institutional regulations—and 'judicial' interpretations—reports of investigations into cases involving potential departures [which] supply a gloss that helps define its meaning."[5]

Judges, as it turned out, were not all that appreciative of this kind of artful reasoning by analogy. In the immediate case, the court ruled that the AAUP's version of the 1940 Statement lacked legal effect because it was formulated after the execution of the faculty employment contract referring to that document;[6] in other cases, judicial resistance to the AAUP's approach centered on the status differential between a widely endorsed professional statement and a unilateral reading of it by one of its authors.[7] Apparently, no one took exception to the forensic use of the 1940 Statement as a violation of its original intent—yet this, to the historian, if not the lawyer, is a crucial point. Those who wrote the 1940 Statement put their words to paper long before academic freedom had entered the protective folds of the first amendment and some time before academic tenure had acquired strong advocates on the bench or many statehouse friends. Their animating assumption was that the defense of these professional goods would have to lie outside the law, in the perfection of the policies and practices of institutions of higher learning. Their aim was to elevate academic conduct to a high uniform standard; their means—an inventory of "do's" and "don'ts"—reflected their belief that, since the law allows academic institutions to be run like so many extraterritorial enclaves imposing rules of their own devising on the native population, the only way to achieve that elevation was through moral, not legal, prodding. That the words they concocted for that purpose might be used to affect the outcome of courtroom battles seems to have been furthest from their minds. This inference can be drawn from the authors' failure to consider the legal implications of their language in their writing conferences, from the fact that very few of the conferees had legal training, and from the unlawyerly frequency with which undefined and vague terms were preferred for the flexibility they afforded to words that were well defined and clear. In time, the courts would become more accommodating to the concerns of academic employees, and the 1940 Statement, as indicated, would become a litigatory resource. But, as a rule, the original function of an object, and not its later adaptation, is better able to tell us what it is. Instructed only by the AAUP's gifted metaphorists, one would hardly suspect that the 1940 Statement was put on earth not to reinforce legal claims, but to provide a feasible substitute for them.

If we cannot rely with complete confidence on the closest friends of the 1940 Statement to define it, may we rely on the work itself to spill the beans? Undoubtedly more can be learned from a scanning of the text than from insightful but extravagant analogizing. But the text does not speak for itself,

---

5. AAUP's Brief as Amicus Curiae at 31-32, *Scheuer v Creighton University*, 199 Neb 2d 618, 260 NW2d 595 (1977).

6. 199 Neb 2d at 630, 260 NW2d at 600.

7. See, for example, *Browzin v Catholic University of America*, 527 F2d 843, 847-48 (DC Cir 1975).

as one soon discovers when one looks in its body for confirmation of the promise of its title. The authors of this document did not call it a "statement *on* academic freedom and tenure"; they called it a "statement of *principles* on academic freedom and tenure." The use of this intermediating word was not a slip of the drafting pen. One group of participants, hoping to fashion a document that would enscribe convictions rather than hard and fast regulations, and that would invite trustee approval rather than adoption, thought the insertion of a nicely general and uncoercive word like "principles" would do the trick; the other group, with quite opposite intentions but also fearful that many trustees would resist anything that smacked of central code-writing, went along. "Principles," which is to say, fundamental credenda, not practical rules, are what the 1940 Statement tells us it is about.

Up to a point, the document lives up to its own billing. Certainly, its preamble, like most preambles, sticks to a high level of abstraction. Its four annunciatory declarations—that institutions of higher education exist not for themselves but for the "common good"; that academic freedom is "essential" to that purpose; that academic tenure is "indispensable" to academic freedom no less than to academic job security; and that "academic freedom carries with it duties correlative with rights"—are presented not as policies to be enacted but as articles of faith to be professed. And most of the next section on "academic freedom" is also filled with pithy propositions of lofty sweep. Here the authors recorded their belief that academics were entitled to three kinds of freedom, each corresponding to a major function or activity: "freedom in research and in the publication of results"; "freedom in the classroom in discussing (the teacher's) subject"; and "freedom from institutional censorship" when the teacher "speaks or writes as a citizen." Reiterated in Committee A reports, institutional regulations and legal briefs, these three axiomatic dedications to principle would become extremely familiar to American academics over the years. This is not to say that they ever became altogether platitudinous or even entirely noncontroversial. If it is now almost universally agreed that academic freedom is essential to a university, the one grace the institution may not lose without losing everything, it is far from obvious to everyone that academic tenure is academic freedom's needed handservant. And though most who do these conceptual mappings divide academic freedom, like Caesar's Gaul, into three main parts, some insist that good logic would divide it into only two (freedom to teach and freedom to do research, arguably the only professionally relevant freedoms, with citizen or extramural freedom ceded to the large neighboring country of ordinary civil liberties),[8] and a few would divide it into four (the three that go with the

---

8. For views in favor of a two- rather than three-ply definition of academic freedom, see Stephen R. Goldstein, *Academic Freedom: Its Meaning and Underlying Premises in the American Experience*, 11 Israel L Rev 52 (1976); William W. Van Alstyne, *The Specific Theory of Academic Freedom and the General Issue of Civil Liberties*, 404 Ann Am Acad Pol & Soc Sci 140 (1972). For views against the displacement of extramural freedom, see Thomas I. Emerson & David Haber, *Academic Freedom of the Faculty Member as Citizen*, 28 L & Contemp Probs 525 (Summer 1963). For institutional autonomy as a feature of

faculty's roles plus one attached to the students' status)[9] or even five (all of the four individual academic freedoms, along with institutional academic freedom, also known as institutional autonomy).[10] It would by no means be true to say that, where the 1940 Statement is couched in the rhetoric of principles, it gives itself over to trite deliverances or empty gab.

But a good part of the 1940 Statement is *not* couched in the rhetoric of principles. Some matters are first flung into the conceptual air and then brought back to earth by the gravitational pull of quite concrete concerns. In the academic freedom section, the authors could not resist interspersing mundane operational details with canonical pronouncements under each of the three subheadings. In the last section on academic tenure, their interest in the particulars of policy emerged full force. They did start this section by distinguishing between the "principle" of academic tenure (which they reduced in one sentence to the precept that faculty members should be retained indefinitely, if they are retained at all, after a period of probation) and the implementation of academic tenure (to which they gave over the rest of the section, stressing the importance of a trial period of fixed duration and a dismissal procedure in accord with specified elements of due process). To avoid the appearance of legislating in detail for governing boards jealous of their prerogatives, the authors characterized the second as merely representing "acceptable academic practice," that is, as a recommended but not obligatory interpretation of the principle, which alone required universal assent. But distinctions do not live on tag words alone, and it was not lost on some of these wordsmiths that a failure to follow the only modus operandi elaborated or even mentioned in this section would be taken as a failure to abide by the principle as well. At all events, in the cauldron of actual cases, "may" did dissolve into "must," and adherence to the tabular and judicial niceties of tenure became as requisite to the AAUP guardians as commitments placed on a more conceptual plane. In sum, the 1940 Statement manages to combine what it advertises and in part displays as a set of principles with what it never labels but in fact promotes as a set of rules. Alas for tidy categorizing! In this respect, the 1940 Statement is not a pure strain but a crossbreed, one part theorist's exercise and one part operator's manual, a kind of elephant with stripes.

Or is it a horse of wholly different color? In the 1940 Statement, each passage entitling faculty members to a different kind of academic freedom is followed by a clause or sentence introduced by "but" and laden with

---

academic freedom, see J. Peter Byrne, *Academic Freedom: A "Special Concern of the First Amendment,"* 99 Yale L J 251 (1989).

9. See Philip Monypenny, *Toward a Standard for Student Academic Freedom*, 28 L & Contemp Probs 625 (Summer 1963); *Developments in the Law—Academic Freedom*, 81 Harv L Rev 1045, 1128 (1968).

10. See Comment, *Testing the Limits of Academic Freedom*, 130 U Pa L Rev 712 (1982). The geography of academic freedom can be configured in all sorts of ways. For a three-part definition that brings together public school teachers fighting government control, professorial teaching and research freedom, and institutional autonomy, see Mark Yudof, *The Three Faces of Academic Freedom*, 32 Loyola L Rev 831 (1987).

messages to faculty members admonishing them to do right things. Without more knowledge of the authors' intentions than the text supplies, one cannot tell whether each freedom was granted on condition that the precepts conjoined to it were obeyed, or whether each series of "shoulds" sets the outer boundary of a freedom that was, up to that edge, granted to every faculty member unconditionally, or whether, indeed, the postscripted materials were neither meant to be quids that paid for quos, or markers that described the scope of privileges, but merely words to the wise that the recipients of each entitlement were asked to live by but could with impunity ignore. Nevertheless, though the 1940 Statement leaves their status quite unclear, these exhortations to professional good behavior do suggest to some that the document finds its closest parallel to the Principles of Medical Ethics of the American Medical Association, or the Canon of Legal Ethics of the American Bar Association, or the attempts by a host of other professions to raise the ethical standards of their members by code and, in consequence, by deed.

The 1940 Statement may have the makings of a professional code of ethics, but it says too little on that subject to have the typical markings of one.[11] Most professional codes pay close attention to how professionals should behave toward one another: calls for mutual civility, strictures against undercutting, comments on the proprieties of referral—these concerns with professional comity bulk large in undertakings of this kind. By contrast, the 1940 Statement totally ignores the etiquette of peer relationships (with one exception—it gives a modest amount of instruction to faculty members called upon to judge the professional fitness of their own colleagues). Again, most professional codes dwell on the obligations of the professional practitioners to society, enjoining them to render gratuitous services to the needy, to maintain a high level of training, and to prevent quackery and chicane from taking root. The 1940 Statement, in a barrage of "shoulds," does refer to the obligations of academics in their role as citizens. But the obligations it refers to are not owed to the public; they are owed to the academics' institutions, which supposedly stand to suffer the displeasure of the public when these obligations are contravened. Finally, all but radical sociologists and deep-dyed cynics would agree that one of the hallmarks of professionalism is its unequivocal, if not wholly selfless, devotion to the best interests of the client. A code of professional ethics that failed to disavow conflicts of interest, specify fiduciary responsibilities, or put in other good words for altruism, would strike the cynics as curiously candid and others as unworthy of its name. With one ambiguous exception, however, the 1940 Statement ignores the professional-client relationship. It does say, ostensibly on behalf of

---

11. In a vast literature, the following works on professional codes of ethics are particularly relevant to this discussion: *The Ethics of Professions and of Business*, 101 Ann Am Acad Pol & Soc Sci (1922); *Ethical Standards and Professional Conduct*, 297 Ann Am Acad of Pol & Soc Sci (1955); Carl F. Taeusch, *Professional Ethics*, in Edwin R. A. Seligman, ed, 12 *Encyclopaedia of the Social Sciences* 472 (Macmillan, 1954).

students, that faculty members in their classrooms should avoid "controversial discussion unrelated to their subject," but this single piece of proclient moralizing hardly touches on the worst teaching offenses and itself embodies a dubious pedagogy. Further evidence that the 1940 Statement does not belong in a conventional ethological box lies in the fact that in 1966 the AAUP adopted a separate Statement on Professional Ethics that covered all the professional relationships given short shrift a quarter of a century before.[12]

Obviously, a document so full of "shalts" and "shalt nots" does bear the imprint of the ethicist's imagination. What makes this document so hard to place is the "thou" to which that imagination is addressed. The commandments of the 1940 Statement are not aimed exclusively—or even primarily—at the academic professional; they are aimed, with the noted exceptions, at the academic professional's employer. As here defined, academic freedom denotes a set of functional zones in which faculty members may express themselves, free from the dictates of their institutional employers. These "no trespassing" signs are not turned against the external power of the state or church (as they are on the European continent, where the *studium* engaged in a historic battle against the *imperium* and *sacerdotium*), nor does this kind of zone defense serve to restrain professorial insiders, who are painted as the rightful possessors, and not as the potential deprivers, of academic freedom rights. Similarly, as here defined, tenure is a set of rules designed to remove from the dismissal process the arbitrariness and intolerance that institutional authorities may be able to display in legal safety. Although the concept of judicialized tenure also requires faculty members to adhere to due process when they are cast as judges, there is no doubt that the 1940 Statement holds trustees and presidents mostly responsible for institutionalizing forbearance and fair play. In addition, the material costs of tenure rules (such as the award of at least a year's salary to a teacher dismissed for reasons other than moral turpitude) are billed to the institution's treasurer, and the transmutation of all these injunctions into policy requires enactment by the institution's governing board. If one were to persist in regarding the 1940 Statement as a code of ethics, one would have to admit that it is a strange one—a managerial code that, for some mysterious reason, takes pains in one of its parts to salt in some professional ethics too.

Somewhat strange it may be, but the 1940 Statement is not so unusual that it bears no illuminating likeness to other things. To place it in its class, one

---

12. *Statement of Professional Ethics*, in *1990 AAUP Red Book* at 75 (cited in note 1). This statement was revised by its AAUP author in 1987. In addition, the association has addressed particular ethical problems (such as resignation of faculty members, conflicts of interest in government research, rights and freedoms of students, faculty responsibility in campus demonstrations, plagiarism, and discrimination). Where possible, these pinpointed comments attempt to draw their authority from words in the Ur-text, the 1940 Statement, especially from the declaration that academic freedom "carries with it duties correlative with rights." But the AAUP made sure that none of the above ethical issues that were lively at that time, such as the proper protocol for faculty resignations, got into the 1940 Statement itself.

must turn from metaphors that are offered tongue in cheek and textual clues that may be misleading to the nominative possibilities opened up by history— the legislative history of the document and the occupational history of the profession. The legislative history, which begins as far back as 1915, tells us that the 1940 Statement may profitably be studied as a *pact*; the occupational history, starting with the crisis of the Great Depression, tells us that the 1940 Statement may be helpfully understood as the prompter of a great *reform*. In romantic opera, the quest for hidden names ends in a denouement of divulgence, after which the curtain abruptly falls. In this paper, *pact* and *reform* are not given as climactic revelations designed to forestall further inquiry. But they may be taken as identification tags without which this Pimpernel is likely to remain damnably elusive.

III

PACT

It is common knowledge that the 1940 Statement was co-authored by representatives of the AAUP and representatives of the Association of American Colleges ("AAC"), an organization composed of undergraduate academic institutions and run by their top administrators. This knowledge, however, has not commonly excited much curiosity—and it should. Why, it is reasonable to ask, did the only organization in America dedicated to the advancement of academic freedom and tenure need administrators to help them tell the world how this might best be done? Why did the AAUP professors share writing honors with an organization of college presidents, whose institutional interests and personal belief systems were not likely to be wholly consonant with their own? If it is true that in such matters opposites attract (though sworn enemies surely would not), why did the AAUP join with only one segment of the executive set—the part affiliated with the AAC? And, to come to the point of this questioning, what does the 1940 Statement owe to the fact that it is a pact and what to the identity of the pact-partner?

One thing is clear: the leaders of the AAUP did not go looking for co-authors because they were at a loss for words. On the contrary: from the moment of its creation, the association was in the hands of academics who proved to be the nation's most effective expositors of the meaning of academic freedom and most eloquent advocates of desirable tenure rules.

In 1915, the infant AAUP set up a committee of distinguished professors, chaired by the Columbia economist, E.R.A. Seligman, and captained by the Johns Hopkins philosopher, Arthur O. Lovejoy, to prepare a treatise on academic freedom and tenure that would clarify and justify concepts long considered in many lay and academic circles as dubious or arcane. The document that emerged after a year of deliberation—a twenty-page Declaration of Principles, also known as the Seligman Report—was instantly acclaimed by AAUP members as a work of seminal significance; gradually it would acquire in wider circles the reputation of a minor classic.[13] As would be true of its descendant a generation later, the word "principles" in its title did not quite accurately describe its contents. In this case, the term was a misnomer, not because the authors commingled policies and precepts (insofar as they were rule minded, they relegated what they called "practical proposals" to a clearly marked appendix), but because, despite the obvious need for brevity, they refused to reduce their value judgments to a few unargued propositions. Theirs, they felt, was to reason why, and their reasoning, which borrowed from intellectual history and social philosophy as well as from practical ethics, was intended to provide a rationale founded on a coherent, if not elaborately embroidered, theory.

Utilitarian in temper and conviction, the theorists of 1915 did not view the expressional freedoms of academics as a bundle of abstract rights. They regarded them as corollaries of the contemporary public need for universities that would increase the sum of human knowledge and furnish experts for public service—new functions that had been added to the time-honored one of qualifying students for degrees. Still, although they tied this functional defense of academic freedom to the new gnostic missions of the academy, they ransacked old stores of philosophy to make their case.

The marketplace libertarianism of J. S. Mill is evident in their contention that truth is never finally possessed but must be endlessly discovered, and that error is best corrected not by the pre-emptive use of power but by the competitive play of minds. The Pauline notion of stewardship lurks in their insistence that the governing boards of private academic institutions, like the governing boards of public ones, are not vested with the prerogatives of owners but are burdened with the obligations of fiduciaries, and that they are ultimately accountable not to gift givers or taxpayers, but to the whole society, a trust relationship that extends not only to the society in being but also to the society in prospect, to a posterity that has as yet no voice. The Coleridgean idea of clerisy, intermixed with "new class" claims stretching back to the Comtean Enlightenment, can be detected in the authors' assertion that academic professionals, by virtue of their special gifts and training, possess the ability to make veridic judgments in their disciplines that the laymen who appoint them lack, and that they should therefore be free of lay interference when they act as resident agents for their specialties and counselors to society

---

13. *General Report of the Committee on Academic Freedom and Academic Tenure*, 1 AAUP Bull 17 (December 1915) ("1915 Declaration"); see Appendix A, 53 L & Contemp Probs 393 (Summer 1990). When presented to the AAUP's January 1916 annual meeting, this document bore a leaden title, which dropped out of sight before it could get into the swim of history. It came to be called the Seligman Report in deference to the chairman who composed its first draft, though with greater justice it might have borne the name of Lovejoy, who made major substantive and linguistic changes in the text. It also came to be called the "1915 Declaration of Principles," a rubric that covers nine-tenths of the text and all its analytic contributions, although the authors used that heading to refer only to its first section. In this article, the latter title will be used. In referring to the "authors" of this document, this article alludes not to Seligman and Lovejoy alone, but to the members of the committee, most of whom passed on drafts and some of whom (especially Franklin Giddings of Columbia, and Frank A. Fetter and Howard C. Warren of Princeton) made important contributions to it.

on call. And a medley of Shakespearean and Galilean quotations could be heard in their repeated warning that academics must be and must seem to be dispensers of the results of their own independent investigations rather than vehicles for the opinions of their paymasters, an appeal to the scientists' conscience that echoed the precept, "to thine own self be true." No matter where they originated, these functional arguments had a common terminus: it is for society's sake, not for their own sakes, that professors must be academically free; professors can be academically free only if those in charge of universities concede that the latter must not, as corporate bodies, have truths to speak for or errors to suppress.

The idea of institutional neutrality—the view that a university cannot put the stamp of its approval or disapproval on a disputed truth-claim and still be faithful to its social trust—was of such critical importance to these authors that they highlighted it in almost every paragraph, though they did not refer to it by that name. Lest institutional neutrality seem too bloodless an idea to rise to sine qua non importance, they resorted to colorful figures of speech to describe it. They likened the operation of the neutral norm to the separation of executive and judicial powers at the federal level: "with respect to the conclusions reached and expressed by them," university teachers should be understood as "no more subject to the control of trustees, than are judges subject to the control of the President," and "trustees are no more to be held responsible for, or to be presumed to agree with, the opinions and utterances of professors, than the President can be assumed to approve of all the legal reasonings of the courts." To this end, too, they utilized another domestic image, one drawn from higher education. A university, they wrote, should be "an intellectual experiment station, where new ideas may germinate and where their fruit, though still distasteful to the community as a whole, may be allowed to ripen until finally, perchance, it may become part of the accepted intellectual food of the nation and of the world." The authors well knew that academic governing boards in this country were under no legal compulsion to treat their institutions as inviolable refuges for seedling thoughts. They hardly had to be told that the constitutional law of the land and state laws on academic incorporation safeguarded the right of churches to found colleges that would propagate their version of religious truth, that the tax laws were too undeveloped to favor charity for propaedeutics over charity for propaganda, and that ideological dismissals from private and even public institutions were not usually redressible in the courts. They believed, however, that they could take cognizance of these legal realities without deferring to them. Any university, they wrote, "which lays restrictions upon the intellectual freedom of its professors proclaims itself a proprietary institution, and should be so described whenever it makes a general appeal for funds; and the public should be advised that the institution has no claim whatever to general support or regard."

The theory of academic freedom erected on these foundations allowed the authors of the 1915 Declaration to redesign the interior spaces of academic freedom, heretofore drawn to German specifications that had never been fully in touch with American academic life. These theorists had no room in their blueprint for *Lernfreiheit* or student freedom; only faculty members were to be the beneficiaries of their call for trustee restraint. They expanded the boundaries of *Lehrfreiheit* to include not only the freedom of the faculty to teach and do research without fear of censorship—the German two-part convention—but also the freedom of the faculty to talk and write about matters outside their certified area of competence and unrelated to their professional duties. This was the first authoritative enunciation of the trinitarianism that in 1940 would emerge in barer form. Their stated reason for tacking on extramural speech was a circumstantial one: the AAUP had found that professors were more likely to be punished for expressing unpopular ideas in a public forum than for anything they said in the classroom or did in the lab. They were also concerned that the denial to academics of the rights of citizens would make it difficult to attract able people into the profession. They had an implicit but compelling third reason, and it was derived from the logic of institutional neutrality. From a neutralist perspective, it did not much matter whether a governing board, speaking for a university, quarreled with an opinion by an expert or a nonexpert, or with an opinion voiced in a public arena or somewhere else: what mattered was that the board, on a mooted issue, had breached its social trust by compelling the institution to take sides.

Finally, the 1915 Declaration opened a new chapter in the history of academic tenure, by fitting it out with a new working plan, a series of concrete proposals concerning the acquisition and dispossession of tenure citizenship that, when refined and broadly adopted, would represent a very great reform. In this, too, the Declaration was more than a mere beginning but was a fount.

For an organization still in swaddling clothes, this polemical and analytical tour de force, magisterial in tone and yet plainspoken, at once familiar and original, was not only a gift it gave to a larger cause but an invaluable testimonial to its own precocity. One might suppose, therefore, that its leaders had an institutional interest in not rushing into a collaborative sequel that would compel it to share credit with outsiders and dim the luster of a bright debut. But, in fact, no sooner was the Declaration received by AAUP members with much self-applause than the leaders sought to use it as a scaffold for a joint venture with administrators, a follow-up that could be engineered only at the expense of infant vanity. Their reasons for doing so are instructive; they help explain why their followers in 1940 did not simply write what pleased them or bid for fame exclusively in their own words.

More than anything else, an unanticipated change in the planned activities of the association convinced its leaders during its natal year that going it alone would not carry them very far. In 1915, much to their surprise, Lovejoy, Seligman, and company were inundated by calls for help from faculty members on far-flung campuses who alleged that they were or were about to be dismissed because of their spoken or written views. Despite the empty treasury of the neonate association and their own chronic shortage of free time, this dutiful, unhappy few decided to respond to every seemingly meritorious SOS, not by taking the faculty member's complaint at face value, but by visiting the site of the proposed offense, nosing out the facts, interviewing all the parties, trying if possible to set things right, and then, if need be, exposing uncorrected wrongs.[14]

No program could have been better designed to reveal to the AAUP the disadvantages of being the sole source of support for the doctrines set forth in its Declaration. Even as they conducted their investigations, negative reviews of that work began to appear in conservative newspapers and administration journals. Much of the criticism was aimed at what was seen as its self-serving character. The editorial writers of the *New York Times* dismissed the professors' argument for professorial talkativeness and trustee reticence with a characteristic sneer: " 'Academic freedom,' that is, the inalienable right of every college instructor to make a fool of himself and his college by . . . intemperate, sensational prattle about every subject under heaven . . . and still keep on the payroll or be reft therefrom only by elaborate process, is cried to all the winds by the organized dons."[15] Others were more given to condemn it than deride it for its alleged one-sidedness. To the chancellor of Syracuse University, it seemed only fair that if professors were free to act on their "conscience and conviction," then trustees should be granted the freedom to fire them on their own conscientious and doctrinal grounds—a fairness doctrine that equated the right to express opinions with the right to banish them.[16] And always in these organs someone could be counted on to make the worst accusation of bias—to call the document the manifesto of a professors' trade union, a description meant to be disparaging and regarded by the AAUP members of that period as demeaning.[17] Still, it was one thing to encounter the ex parte argument when it appeared in journals of opinion, where it could not take immediate effect and could eventually be answered by a stinging letter to the editor, and another thing to confront it during a campus investigation, where it could serve to deny the AAUP access to the

---

14. See Walter P. Metzger, *The First Investigation,* 47 AAUP Bull 206 (1961); Walter P. Metzger, *Origins of the Association: An Anniversary Address,* 51 AAUP Bull 229 (1965).

15. *Quotations: The Professors' Union,* 3 School & Soc'y 175 (1916), quoting the New York Times.

16. *Is the College Professor a 'Hired Man'?,* 51 Literary Digest 65 (1915).

17. See Lightner Witmer, *The Nearing Case* 68-69 (B.W. Huebsch, 1915) (reprinted with a new foreword, Da Capo Press, 1974), quoting *The Professors' Union,* a February 1914 editorial that appeared in the University of Pennsylvania *Alumni Register.* George Cram Cook, an academic socialist, berated "academic workers" for failing "to consider seriously the only line of action likely to lead to their independence . . . . The 'union' is capable of taking 'professor' out of the category of the ridiculous." George Cram Cook, *The Third American Sex,* 1 Forum 455 (1913). But Professor George A. Moore, the Harvard theologian who refused to associate himself with the new professorial organization because "[f]or the sake of a profession which I esteem I regret seeing it—pardon the word—unionized," gave expression to more typical sentiments. Letter, George A. Moore to Arthur O. Lovejoy (1915) (presented by Lovejoy to author in October 1960, and since merged with the files of the AAUP under the "Lovejoy 1915" heading). (This article cites repeatedly to archival documents in files possessed by the AAUP. All subsequent references to these materials will bear the notation "AAUP files.")

administration, defeat AAUP efforts at mediation, and justify refusals to redress abuses cited in AAUP reports.

This peripatetic vanguard tried in a number of ways to secure a reputation for impartiality. One device employed by Lovejoy—to compose reports that would live up to the highest standards of judicial poise and objective scholarship—would serve as a model for later generations seeking to gain the confidence of both administrators and faculty members in divided houses. Another Lovejovian technique was to publish findings that did not vindicate the faculty complainant; for reasons rooted in the dynamics of a membership organization, this way of disowning the slogan, "my coprofessional right or wrong," did not set a lasting precedent. A third stratagem, which the visitation squads quickly saw the need for but which was beyond their power to effect, was to induce high-ranking and influential administrators to affix their seal of approval to doctrines that had become covered with professor fingerprints. Promising to rid the concepts of freedom and tenure of the taint of faculty class bias, while opening local rejectionists to the charge that they did not represent the sentiments of their own administrative class, this stratagem would appeal to every cohort of AAUP frontline caseworkers from that day to this.

The founding generation saw an added advantage in turning what started out as a solo enterprise into a joint one. In the spring of 1917, the new part-time secretary of the AAUP, H. W. Tyler, launched what became a long campaign to lure academic presidents to a conference that would endorse the spirit and main provisions of the 1915 Declaration in a formal statement. The crowning benefit of such a get-together and such a compact, according to this Massachusetts Institute of Technology professor of mathematics, would not be simply to strengthen the hand of the association when it answered the calls of faculty members in distress; even more significantly, it would reduce the number of occasions in which faculty members were likely to be distressed. "So far," he wrote, "we have been dealing with the individual institutions . . . . If we have now reached the point where we can deal with a whole class of institutions at once, we may be in a position to win a campaign instead of a battle."[18] He was convinced that presidents in league with professors would do more to persuade governing boards to abide by proper policies than anything a small society of professors could do alone, and all the elected officers agreed that saving one institution at a time was a Sisyphean task that they hoped an entente with presidents could lift from AAUP shoulders. In later years, the institutionalization of case investigations and the increase in AAUP resources would take the edge off the latter reason for reaching out. No one in 1940 would have recommended a pact as a labor-saving device. But the belief that an act of legislated prevention was worth more than a pound of (often delayed, sometimes only marginally helpful) cure was shared by both leadership generations, as was the desire to devise a statement on

18. Letter, H. W. Tyler to Frank Thilly (March 26, 1917) (miscellaneous AAUP files).

academic freedom and tenure that would be fit for framing in every academic board room. The two leadership generations had a further link in the person of Tyler, who would remain in office for eighteen years and would twice strive to make the foreign policy initiatives launched in the natal period bear fruit.

In one important respect, however, AAUP diplomatists in different times were taxed with different missions. When Tyler first broached the idea of a pact, representative groups of presidents and professors had never met to discuss professional issues on any stage wider than that of a particular campus, nor had the twain ever met, even at the local level, to agree on terms of employment through collective bargaining. Venturing into a void, the early leaders had to grope for answers to the most elementary questions. Who in the heterogeneous camp of college and university presidents would be suitable pact-partners? What items in the 1915 Declaration could be safely dropped or traded off, and what items should be deemed nonnegotiable? Whose drafted understanding of academic freedom and tenure should be used as the basis for discussion and be allowed to inform the final text?

By the time the next generation tried its hand, these questions had been answered for it. Its predecessor had identified the one presidential body willing to collaborate with the AAUP, had created an agenda for discussion that could be modified but not ignored, and had reached an agreement with the other side. This agreement, known as the Conference Statement of 1925, would be the going treaty for AAUP members who came late to this foreign service. Their task was not to write on an empty tablet; it was to revise what had already been written. Since they sought to amend, not replace, a co-authored work, the later leaders felt obliged to reopen negotiations with the same administrative body and not try to play the field. In short, where the first generation was awash with options, the second generation was pinned down by givens.

One can better understand what the AAUP of 1937-1940 was up to when one sees how the AAUP of 1915-1925 made up its mind. To the question of who should be invited to the parley, Tyler had a ready answer: he proposed that delegates from every national association of administrators should be invited in order to secure the broadest possible consensus. He did not fear that the AAUP would find itself in the overwhelmed minority in such a come-one, come-all assembly: "My expectation is that we should find the presidents as a class quite amenable to friendly treatment, and that those who might be otherwise inclined would be very much influenced by the collective action of their associates."[19] Tyler's sanguineness elicited a troubled response from colleagues that revealed a deep strain of antiadministration feeling in the AAUP's collective personality. Pointing out that none of the major administrative associations had embraced the 1915 Declaration and that one indeed had been strongly hostile to it, the president of the association, Cornell philosopher Frank Thilly, thought it more likely that "our friend, the

---

19. Id.

enemy" would use the occasion to build "a solid front against us" than that it would respond to AAUP blandishments and break ranks. Lest the wisdom of the 1915 Declaration be trampled under by a hostile phalanx, he urged that the AAUP join hands with individual administrators, not associations, and, among individuals, only with proven friends.[20]

Among the founders, Thilly's antipresident animus did not rank as the most extreme. One of the earliest sponsors of a professorial association was the well-known Columbia psychologist, J. McKeen Cattell, whose chafing encounters with his own domineering president, Nicholas Murray Butler, had convinced him that the whole apparatus of presidential power should be dismantled, leaving a duumvirate of faculty members in control and lay boards in support, along the lines of the Oxbridge universities. Legally, in America, the governing board was the fountain of academic authority; historically, it had been the conduit through which pressures hostile to the faculty had been passed on to professors and sometimes amplified. Nevertheless, Cattell and the syndicalist faction that supported him lavished an invective on the deputy that they seldom visited on the source.[21]

Needless to say, if most of the early leaders had been of this persuasion, a pact with academic presidents would have been not just unpalatable but unthinkable. But most of Tyler's colleagues were (to borrow a phrase from English history) Whigs, not radicals: that is, they were protective, even though they could be highly critical, of the current monarchy (read presidency). As senior professors at major universities who were also pre-eminent figures in their respective disciplines, the founders had too-ready access to their own presidents to see them as devils incarnate and were themselves on too many short lists of candidates for presidencies to think well of abolishing that post.[22] In the 1915 Declaration, it should be noted, they took aim at the transgressions of governing boards and ignored the managerial revolution that was shifting responsibility for personnel decisions from the legal governors of universities to their on-site agents. But if Whigs were not radicals, neither were they Tories, that is to say, loyal adherents to the party of the King. It was no accident that the AAUP was founded, not by the overworked and underpaid junior members of the profession, nor by their unrenowned seniors toiling away in the humblest places, but by an academic *corps d'elite* positioned in the cynosure institutions. Such professors were haughty enough to take affront at presidents who sought the deference due to royalty and secure enough to take on presidents who treated faculty criticism of their policy or person as a kind of *lèse majesté*. Nor was it an accident that the first self-defining act of the association was the passage of a constitutional provision declaring administrators ineligible for membership; this reflected a

---

20. Letter, Frank Thilly to H. W. Tyler, (March 31, 1917) (miscellaneous AAUP files); Letter, Frank Thilly to H. W. Tyler (April 7, 1917) (miscellaneous AAUP files).

21. James McKeen Cattell, *University Control* (Science Press, 1913).

22. See John Dewey, *Faculty Share in University Control* (with comments by Arthur O. Lovejoy) in Association of American Universities, *Journal of Proceedings and Addresses of the Seventeenth Annual Conference* 27 (Association of American Universities, 1915).

deep professorial desire to create a professional space unconstrained by presidential presences. In Whiggish hands, pact-making would be burdened by the ambivalence of professors who sought out partners they were ready to look down on, who respected the presidential breed for being organizationally powerful but disdained it for being too often petty and tyrannical and intellectually second-class. These contradictory feelings, which for special reasons subsided in 1925, would rise up again in the second round when AAUP professors with a touchy professional *amour-propre* met a number of presidents they needed to win over but could not stand.

Tyler never abandoned his belief that "the more the merrier" was the right prescription for a treaty conference, and in 1925 he would go through the motions of acting on it. But the weight of leadership opinion did not subscribe to his motto, "blessed are the pactmakers, for to them all presidents are the children of God." The dominant view in the association fell between Thilly's and Tyler's. There was scant support for an invitation list so restricted that like would be sure to commune with like and no speaker would fear to be contradicted. At every parliamentary opportunity, the *eminences grises*, Lovejoy and Seligman, coaxed their colleagues into passing resolutions calling for "joint actions with other *organizations*."[23] If it were done 'twere well it were done collectively—this was clear to those who measured the weight of a formal agreement reached by the emissaries of two estates and ratified by their respective governments against that of a harmonious exchange between like-minded people in one field of work who happened to occupy different posts. On the other hand, the word "other" did not imply the word "all." While many would have doubtless taken any organization's show of willingness to attend as strong proof that it deserved to be asked, most had a fairly clear idea of which presidential group, if it came, would be a godsend, and which, if it stayed away, would not be missed.

From all accounts, the early AAUP leaders, had they been forced to choose one and only one set of collaborators, would have picked the presidents of the elite research universities with major graduate schools, the institutions that belonged to the then exclusive Association of American Universities ("AAU"), formed around the turn of the century. Since these presidents were also *their* presidents, one might suspect that the "our crowd" mentality of the privileged was here at work. But in professor-president relations, closeness did not invariably make the heart grow fonder (as the founders' own frequent brushes with presidents over budgets and policies, prides and precedents, amply demonstrated). Something other than mere propinquity—something taken from recent academic history—seemed to have done more to color their affections. As a group, the AAU presidents had been prominently identified with the secularization of American higher education, a major wellspring of academic freedom on these shores. Although the first stirrings of hostility to

---

23. E. R. A. Seligman, *Address of the President: Our Association—Its Aims and Its Accomplishments*, 8 AAUP Bull 90, 108 (1922); Stenographic Record of Eighth Annual Meeting of the AAUP (1921) (AAUP files).

sectarianism arose in the colonial colleges, and the first programmatic separation of college from church can be traced to the Jeffersonian era, the most dramatic victories of academic secularism were not scored until the latter part of the nineteenth century, when the presidents of certain old patrician colleges and the presidents of new establishments breathed into life by tycoon wealth labored to turn their institutions into universities comparable to Europe's research powerhouses. In 1915, AAUP memories did not have to stretch far back to recall that the architects of these transformations—the presidents of Harvard, Johns Hopkins, Chicago and the like—had been in the forefront of the battle to defend institutional neutrality against attempts by conservative religious forces to keep the Darwinian sciences at bay and to bar the critical study of the Bible. Clearly, the authors of the 1915 Declaration had in mind the attempts by antievolutionists and fundamentalists to institutionalize a godlier biology and a literalist interpretation of the Word when they dwelled on the functional necessity of free scientific inquiry within ideologically uncommitted universities.[24] They quoted administrators sparingly, but they quoted with particular relish one titan recently retired from the Harvard presidency who said that any governing board that would make "arbitrary" use of the dismissal power to "exclude from the teachings of the university unpopular or dangerous subjects" was—he used no softer word—"barbarous."[25] In these elevated quarters and on these well-defined topics, the AAUP could well believe that professors and presidents would indeed be friends.

In more recent years, to be sure, some doubts had arisen about whether the successors to the Charles W. Eliots, Andrew D. Whites, and Daniel C. Gilmans were as inclined to resist political and economic pressures as those worthies had been to withstand religious ones—the recent dismissal of the nonrevolutionary Marxist, Scott Nearing, from the Wharton School of the University of Pennsylvania was a worrisome investigated case in point.[26] But there were grounds for optimism on this score as well. In 1916, A. Lawrence Lowell, Eliot's replacement as Harvard's president, made headlines by refusing to discipline a professor for his pro-German utterances, a refusal that threatened to cost the university the loss of a large bequest from an irate alumnus.[27] Lowell's justification for restraint—a university that takes

---

24. The character of the contribution of the presidents of major universities to the secularization of American higher education in the latter part of the 19th century is suggested by the following: Andrew Dickson White, *Autobiography* (Century, 1905) (2 vols); Hugh Hawkins, *Charles Eliot, University Reform, and Religious Faith in America, 1869-1909*, 51 J Am Hist 191 (1964); Thomas Wakefield Goodspeed, *A History of the University of Chicago: The First Quarter Century* (Chicago, 1916); Winton U. Solberg, *The Conflict Between Religion and Secularism at the University of Illinois, 1867-1894*, 18 Am Q 183 (1966); Daniel Coit Gilman, *The Launching of a University* (Dodd, Mead and Co., 1906).

25. 1915 Declaration at 23-24; Appendix A at 395 (cited in note 13), quoting a 1907 address from Harvard president Charles William Eliot to the New York chapter of the Phi Beta Kappa Society.

26. *Report of the Committee of Inquiry on the Case of Professor Scott Nearing of the University of Pennsylvania*, 2 AAUP Bull 127 (1916).

27. Abbott Lawrence Lowell, *Annual Report to Harvard Corporation, 1916-17*, quoted in Henry Aaron Yeomans, *Abbott Lawrence Lowell, 1856-1943* 311-12 (Harvard, 1948).

responsibility for deciding what professors may not say thereby assumes responsibility for everything professors do say, and a wise university would refuse the first responsibility in order to relieve itself of the second—struck a blow for institutional neutrality that the AAUP would find very much to its liking. Thereafter it would argue in the Lowell manner that the tactic of mutual dissociation (the professor disavowing any claim to speak for the university, the university refusing to censor or condone what he says) is the proper way to enforce the neutral principle, the best means to the desired lack of corporate ends.

Whether AAU presidents were as likely to endorse the AAUP's position on academic tenure as they were on academic freedom was probably regarded as a more open question. But the 1915 Declaration did suggest that the same institutional characteristics that made academic freedom a functional necessity were likely to make academic tenure an operative reality. While its authors hoped to establish their kind of tenure system everywhere, they made it clear that the AAU universities, large enough to maintain an array of specialties beyond the ken of lay and administrative nonspecialists, sophisticated enough not to stand petty watch over speech in the lecture hall and classroom, and ambitious enough to encourage the faculty to live a double life wedded both to their science and their university, provided the best available environment for healthy tenure practices and was thus a training school for potential pact-partners *sans pareil*.

The initial affinity of the early AAUP leaders toward one administrative association was matched by their initial antipathy toward another. Left to their own preferences, the AAUP leaders would not have chosen to treat with the presidents of denominational colleges, whose very existence posed a challenge to the neutral principle; nor with the presidents of small undergraduate colleges with very sheltered student bodies, whose regimen more closely resembled the supervisory strictness of a school than the strategic leniency of a university; nor with the presidents of low-level traditional liberal arts colleges, where the curriculum was too abecedarian and faculty members too often jacks-of-all-trades to give laymen much opportunity to honor academic expertise. Since institutions of these sorts were then conspicuous in the Association of American Colleges, that organization was at once perceived by leading members of the AAUP as the home of some of its worst natural enemies: the clerical president who administered doctrinal tests to incoming or resident faculty; the patriarchal president who treated faculty members as sojourners in his house who were expected to resign whenever he determined they should go; the provincial president who knew little of matters beyond his teacup world.

The AAUP's negative impression of the AAC was strongly colored by an article that appeared in the AAC *Bulletin* two years after its founding. In 1917, its newly formed Committee on Academic Freedom and Tenure of Office, set up as a counterfoil to Committee A and composed mainly of presidents of religious colleges, issued an extensive review of the 1915 Declaration that was thoroughly out of sympathy with its arguments and alarmingly out of touch with the norms of accurate reportage. Not at all unwilling to place faculty members at the mercy of vague creedal requirements and an inquisitional spirit, the AAC committee asserted that "[a] man who accepts a position in a college which he has reason to believe is a Christian institution" may not claim under academic freedom "the right privately to undermine or publicly to attack Christianity," even if the behavioral or confessional demands of the institution had not been specified prior to appointment. With regard to academic tenure, the Committee opined that the key question raised by the 1915 Declaration was whether "any association of university professors [should be allowed to] compel a corporation to retain in office for an indefinite time one who is manifestly unfit for that particular place." No one acquainted with the 1915 Declaration solely through this misreading of it would suspect that it proposed not to maintain the manifestly unfit but to make unfitness manifest through certain probative procedures. Finally, the committee could not resist inveighing against the "mischief-makers," "vexels," and "impossible persons" on the faculty who were tolerated by trustees and would be cashiered by any "well-organized corporation."[28] It was this obtusely hostile review that led Thilly to estimate the chances of the AAUP prevailing over a melange of presidents to be about as good as those of the early Christians emerging triumphant from the lions' pit. It prompted even the tolerant Tyler to remark that the AAC institutions were "the very ones which, on account of their size and local quality, were most in need of reform" and to predict that they would be slow "to accept a progressive policy in advance of the large institutions in the Association of American Universities."[29]

To paraphrase a Scottish poet, the best-laid schemes of mice and academic men gang aft agley. The AAUP sought out the AAU, but the AAU did not reciprocate. The journal of the AAU took no notice of the 1915 Declaration; an AAUP questionnaire on items in that report sent out to AAU presidents elicited few replies; the staff of the AAU did not warm to Tyler's approaches. Its unresponsiveness may have been due to a number of factors: to its preoccupation with graduate education and other concerns of the disciplinary professions not directly implicated in current academic freedom and tenure issues; to its belief that among its constituent members academic freedom was a paradise already gained and that tenure held no advantage over informal gentlemen's agreements; or—perhaps this was the most potent reason—to its perception that as the oldest and most Brahmanic of administrative associations, it would not add to its dignity or repute by hobnobbing with a newly-arrived, untested association of professors drawn in all likelihood from the malcontents on the faculties of the very institutions it served. By contrast, the AAC took the pronouncements of the organized professors very seriously,

---

28. Committee on Academic Freedom and Tenure of Office, *Report of Committee*, 3 AAC Bull 49-55 (April 1917) ("AAC Report").

29. Letter, H. W. Tyler to Frank Thilly (April 3, 1917) (miscellaneous AAUP files).

witness the speed with which it set up a committee to deal on a parallel, if not equal, footing with the formidable Committee A and the space it devoted in its *Bulletin* to a rebuttal of the latter's work. Moreover, even in blustery opposition, its freedom and tenure committee paid oblique tribute to the professors from Johns Hopkins, Columbia, and Wisconsin by referring to them as "excellent men in responsible positions"[30] who were somehow offering bad advice, and by treating the 1915 Declaration as an encyclical that had to be solemnly refuted before it could be comfortably defied. The probable explanation for this attitude is that the AAC, as the sole administrative organization that concentrated on the cross-disciplinary problems of college teaching, was especially sensitive to the views of the sole ecumenical association of college teachers. Also, by virtue of the fact that it was as parvenu as the AAUP and a lot less snobbish than the AAU, the AAC probably regarded dialogue with well-placed professors, even if hostile, as a way of moving up, not stepping down. From these early signs, a clever prognosticator would have bet that the AAUP would eventually get not the pact-partner it wanted, but the pact-partner that wanted it.

That required foresight: for some years the leaders of the AAUP lived with the disquieting thought that they might not find any pact-partner at all. Certainly, as long as they bristled at the AAC's adverse review, they would not be cheered by the flattery of its attentiveness. But then the AAC changed its mind, or, rather, changed the membership of the Freedom and Tenure Committee, and the reconstituted committee changed its mind. In 1922, that committee issued a second report that in effect repudiated the first one. It described the 1915 Declaration as "highly important" (its new chairman called it "monumental").[31] It urged all colleges and universities to safeguard academic freedom, which included recognition by the institution that a faculty member in speaking and writing upon subjects beyond the scope of his own field of study is entitled to the same freedom and responsibility as attached to all other citizens. It endorsed the principle of tenure to the extent of urging that faculty members who had demonstrated their competence and compatibility to the satisfaction of the institution should receive a long-term or indefinite appointment, and that the termination of such an appointment for cause should be preceded by a hearing on charges. It held that religious colleges could require faculty members to adhere to creeds but distanced itself from its precursor by insisting that such requirements be made known to candidates for positions before they sign on. It introduced a number of exceptions and qualifications into its statement that sapped the protective strength of a number of provisions in the AAUP Declaration, but it displayed none of the sodden animus that had defaced the committee's review of that document five years before.[32]

---

30. AAC Report at 49 (cited in note 28).
31. Association of American Colleges, Record of Annual Meeting 79 (1922).
32. Charles N. Cole, *Report of the Commission on Academic Freedom and Academic Tenure*, 8 AAC Bull 94-103 (March 1922).

This rejection of the antagonistic past was the work of Dean Charles N. Cole of Oberlin College, who along with the distinguished educational historian, Charles F. Thwing, president of Western Reserve University, and Dean Roy C. Flickinger of Northwestern University, had replaced presidents of church-related colleges on the committee and had altered its temperamental and ideological balance. The committee turnover signalled that the AAC, which had started out as a meeting-ground for the heads of the smallest and most parochial private colleges in the country, had begun to gather in the presidents (and, importantly, the deans) both of private liberal arts colleges with regional and national reputations and of sizeable private universities with strong undergraduate divisions—a small but growing and influential minority of personalities of secular bent and broad horizons. And the policy turnabout suggested that cosmopolitan AAC presidents might have more in common with cosmopolitan AAUP professors than they had with provincial AAC presidents, and that an interorganizational alliance might well be built on this break in executive ranks.

These were indeed glad tidings to the officers and secretary of the AAUP, who had gone through the years of unwanted isolation with increasing pessimism. It did not take long for them to perceive that formal collaboration was a possible outcome of improved rapport.[33] But it did take some time before habitual mistrust yielded to unaccustomed friendliness. The AAUP had reasons to be wary: the old guard was still ensconced in the governing councils of the AAC; the new guard failed by a long shot to endorse the whole 1915 Declaration. The reborn AAC also had grounds for cautiousness, not least of which was the danger that a meeting with the AAUP, following upon its endorsement of what were thought to be pro-AAUP sentiments, would not sit well with members to whom that very acronym was a provocation. Gradually, each side assured the other that it had much to gain and nothing to lose from a detente. At the 1923 annual meeting of the AAC, Dean Cole delivered a ringing defense of academic tenure (far from protecting "all college teachers not disqualified by gross misconduct," it is "a policy by which teachers of tested competence, character and loyalty are lifted above the plane of annual, biennial or quinquennial appointments and put into the position of trusted partner appointed without term"),[34] and thereby indicated that a joint conference would not waste its time debating AAUP first principles. For its part, the AAUP let it be known through the chairman of Committee A, Professor H. F. Goodrich of the University of Michigan Law School, who met with Cole at Ann Arbor to resolve outstanding differences, that it would be willing to accept the 1922 report, with minor amendments, as a preliminary draft and basis for discussion, and would not press for the Seligman moon if

106,522

33. Executive Comittee Actions, May 26, 1923 (AAUP files); H. F. Goodrich, *Annual Report of Committee A*, 10 AAUP Bull 71, 74-75 (1924).

34. Charles N. Cole, *Report of the Commission on Academic Freedom and Academic Tenure*, in 1923 AAC Proc 127-28 (1923).

that was likely to produce an unratifiable document.[35] Finally, as a historian of diplomacy might put it, they had taken enough confidence-building steps to agree on the date of a summit meeting.

In the historical preface to the 1925 Conference Statement, it is recorded that the American Council on Education ("ACE"), a coordinating agency for higher education established in 1918, invited the AAUP, the AAC, the AAU, the Association of Governing Boards, the Association of Land Grant Colleges, the Association of Urban Universities, the National Association of State Universities, and the American Association of University Women to a conference in Washington from which a succinct collective agreement on the principles of academic freedom and tenure emerged.[36] The facts are correct, but this way of recounting them hides the truth.

The idea of gathering under one umbrella so large a part of the infinite variety of American higher education was the brainchild of H. W. Tyler, who had remained wedded to the hope that such an assembly, like a league of nations, would covenant to abide by a common code, and who found a way at last to act on that hope when, as the AAUP's representative on the ACE, he succeeded to its rotating presidency. The council resolution he put forward authorized the issuance of invitations only when the AAUP and the AAC decided that the time was ripe for it, a proviso that left no doubt about who was really throwing the party. The conference, which lasted no more than one full day, made few changes other than stylistic ones in the distributed draft, and those changes were not of large importance.[37] The discussion was lively, but it was kept within bounds by Tyler, who chaired the conference. Once, when the representatives of the women's association raised such questions as whether good teaching could be objectively measured or productive scholarship clearly assessed, he shunted those hardy perennials of academic discourse to a subcommittee, which never reported. Given the provenance and management of this affair, it was hardly surprising that only the AAC and the AAUP took pains to adopt the final statement.[38] The second

35. Memorandum of Charles N. Cole and H. F. Goodrich (April 9, 1924) (Committee A memoranda, AAUP files).

36. *Principles and Proceedings Governing Academic Freedom and Tenure*, 18 AAUP Bull 329 (1932).

37. 1925 Conference Records (AAUP files).

38. The Conference Statement did not have easy sailing through the governing bodies of the AAUP. To answer criticisms, Tyler and others promised that a second conference would soon be held to rectify the defects of the first conference statement, but refused to risk sending the document to the local chapters for their approval. Letter, H. W. Tyler to AAUP President, A. O. Leuschner (January 31, 1925) (1925 Conference folder and Council Letters 1925-26 folder, AAUP files); letter, H. W. Tyler to A. O. Leuschner (May 6, 1925) (1925 Conference folder and Council letters 1925-26 folder, AAUP files). At the 1926 annual meeting of the association, the delegates expressed their "general approval" of the 1925 Statement, but added that "[i]t is understood that the [provisions of the 1925 Statement] are to be interpreted as far as this Association is concerned in the light of its previous declarations on academic freedom and tenure . . . ." Record of Annual Meeting of 1926 (AAUP files). Lovejoy headed off the possibility of an outright rejection by reminding the members that the AAUP did not start from a "clear field" but from a document already adopted by the AAC and that the AAUP team had decided to agree "not necessarily to all that might be desired but a minimum standard sensibly in advance of what is as yet generally accepted by the administrative authorities of American colleges." Id. The AAC adopted the 1925 Statement handily, recognizing it

Treaty of Washington, unlike the first (and slightly more famous!) conference of that decade on international naval disarmament, did not concert the views of all the major powers. It was an AAC-AAUP affair through and through, and the others were merely extras placed in seats to lend the *mise en scène* an air of fullness. A decade later, when the prime movers of the 1925 conference decided that the pact had serious flaws and should be revised, neither suggested that the various groups once assembled in Washington should be brought together again. Neither saw any point in repeating what had been mostly a charade.

*****

What difference did it make that the 1940 Statement was the result of a second try at pact-making by the AAUP and AAC, and not a product of the AAUP alone? The difference can be roughly measured by comparing the AAUP's unalloyed work in 1915 with the co-authored statements that came after, taking due account of the changes the 1915 Declaration might have undergone if its single parent had tried to bring it up to date. For orderly analysis, it may help to distinguish differences attributable to the period in which these works were written ("signs of the times") from those attributable to differences that would have appeared in any period ("genre effects"). Further, where the aria and the two duets disagree, it may be helpful to distinguish disagreements based on discrepant omissions ("agenda gaps") from disagreements resulting in head-on collisions ("confrontations"). Finally, it may pay to speculate on what might have happened if the AAUP had found a different pact-partner ("what if?"). Two caveats: (1) the uncovering of discrepancies between AAC and AAUP positions should not obscure their large area of concurrence; (2) it should not be automatically assumed that whatever is clever, useful, or prescient in the 1940 Statement was put there by the professors, and that everything flat, unprofitable, and regressive is there because the presidents could not be moved.

A.   Signs of the Times

Neither the AAC nor the AAUP ever sought to compose an exhaustive, detailed list of the shortcomings and misbehaviors that would give an academic institution sufficient cause to dismiss a faculty member. The presidents' group declined to do so out of deference to the diversity and desired autonomy of institutions; for the same reason they tried to avoid mandating a uniform dismissal procedure. The AAUP did not hesitate to impose uniform procedures on that disorder Americans were pleased to call a system of higher education. But it did share the substantive shyness of the AAC: except insofar as it agreed that an infraction of an etiquette of public speech were institutionally punishable[39] it consistently refused to itemize the

---

as, for the most part, the handiwork of its own committee. Association of American Colleges, *1925 Records of Annual Meeting*. A few years later, however, the presidents of small colleges would also begin to voice strong opposition to the 1925 Statement.

    39.   See generally Part IIE.

grounds on which professors might be dismissed. Its primary reason was that a "criminal code" approach, as it came to be called, could lead to the proscription of so many specific actions, and applied with so much literalness, that little room would be left to judge the motives of the affected teacher or to take into account in the final reckoning his professional record as a whole. For different reasons, the two associations agreed to employ an inexplicit phrase of art—"professional unfitness"—to serve as the *quod erat demonstrandum* of a dismissal hearing, and to leave to local experience the definition of which particular falls from grace merited condign punishment.

Still, if the AAUP took a firm stand against a precise and exhaustive specification, it did manage in the 1915 Declaration to identify in general terms a few charged offenses that justified a dismissal hearing and a few verdicts that merited dismissal without notice. These *en passant* references to "what" on the way to a more thoroughgoing consideration of "how" set the precedent for a similar kind of indirect and partial enumeration of punishable offenses in the first president-professor pact. In 1915, the AAUP had alluded to "habitual neglect of assigned duties," "grave moral delinquency," and "professional incompetence" as valid grounds for terminating the appointment of a tenured professor. In 1925, the AAUP and the AAC, in the same by-the-way manner, mentioned, as before, "professional incompetence" and "gross immorality," but added a new capital offense—"treason." The last offense was regarded as so egregious that, along with "immorality," it could, merely by being charged, result in a summary dismissal if the facts were not in dispute.

As soon as he read the document, the distinguished first President of the AAUP expressed a grave concern. John Dewey let Tyler and Lovejoy know that he found the acknowledged possibility of a dismissal for treason both gratuitous and dangerous. "If a person were convicted of treason, naturally the connection with the university would cease, as it would were he convicted by the courts of any other crime." But if treason were given a popular interpretation, the charge of this offense "might be employed in cases similar to those arising during the late war to justify the dismissal of teachers whose views on national policy were contrary to the patriotic sentiments of the time." For once, Lovejoy, who had been at the Washington conference as a member of the AAUP's four-man delegation and had been as usual the dominating intellectual force among his peers, seemed defensive, if not abashed. He had not fought to strike the troubling word, he told his philosophical colleague, "because it had occurred in the resolutions of the Association of American Colleges . . . and because the representative of that Association feared . . . he would have great difficulty in getting the revision approved at the meeting of that body . . . if the word had been cut." He would have preferred to see the word omitted, but only "if this could be done without sacrifice to the rest of the agreement, which as a whole seems to constitute a great advance." Tyler also recalled that the decision to let "treason" stand, though opposed by other participants as incautious, was made in deference to a higher prudence—in order to appease a governing body made up of presidents with fixed ideas.

There was more to it than that. The conference minutes, though sparse, do not suggest that this issue received long or hot discussion, and the retrospective statements of the conference members do not suggest that they had swallowed a bitter pill. Tyler was nonchalant: he thought the word "would probably do no real harm," though he did not say why he doubted that those who cried "treason" would make the most of it. Lovejoy was argumentative; he tried to convince Dewey that there was nothing to fear, first, because the members at the conference all agreed that the term should be interpreted in a strictly legal sense, and, second, because if it were interpreted in such a way as to force out a mere political dissenter, the teacher "would have very good grounds for a damage suit."[40] These arguments were not worthy of that forensic master: "treason," however understood by the discussants, was not defined in the document and thus could be anything in the eye of an uninformed beholder; playing with fire is hardly made more safe by the hope that burns will be compensated later on. A plausible explanation for Lovejoy's weak retort is that, unlike his recovered peer, he had not yet regained the robust libertarianism that had deserted him during the Wilsonian "Great Crusade,"[41] and that, when national loyalty was at issue, the lingering symptoms of war psychology, dovetailing with a desire not to rock the conference boat, kept him from acting at his semantic best. And if in the mid-1920s Lovejoy still needed more time to recuperate from the illness of superpatriotism, it is likely that many presidents other than those who belonged to the AAC, and many members of the AAUP apart from its principal founder, had at least as far to go.

In the years that immediately followed, treason was seldom if ever charged against a faculty member to effect a dismissal, doubtless because faculty members could be dismissed more expeditiously by stretching the elastic in "immorality" and "incompetence." But the reference to "treason" in the first AAC-AAUP pact would become increasingly objectionable to professors and administrators alike, especially in the New Deal period when the campus mood grew conspicuously less conservative and when the House Un-American Activities Committee began to give the pursuit of subversives a bad name. More than the weightier matters that drove the AAUP and the AAC back to the conference room, this oddity, which became an eyesore, served as a constant reminder of the need to revise the 1925 Statement, and the revisionists of 1940 would agree to expunge it before they agreed on anything else.

40. Letter, John Dewey to H. W. Tyler (April 1, 1925); Letter, A. O. Lovejoy to John Dewey (April 13, 1925); Letter, H. W. Tyler to John Dewey (April 7, 1925) (all in 1925 Conference folder, AAUP files).

41. See A. O. Lovejoy, Edward Capps, & A. A. Young, *Report of Committee on Academic Freedom in Wartime*, 4 AAUP Bull 29 (February-March 1918) (report mostly written by A. O. Lovejoy).

B.   Genre Effects

The literary goal of AAUP-AAC collaboration was to reduce the complexities of academic freedom and tenure to a capsule statement that could be read at a glance, be readily understood, and be acted on with despatch. Accordingly, the collaborators sacrificed explanation to synopsis and leisurely argument to dicta tightly phrased. Accordingly, too, most of the philosophy of the 1915 Declaration was parked outside the 1925 and 1940 Statements, as were all the images and turns of phrase for which the draftsmen could find no succinct equivalents. What are here called "genre effects" are the substantive differences between single-authored and double-authored words that can be laid not to conflicts in collaboration but to the sheer need to epitomize.

Chief among the ideas lost in compression was the norm of institutional neutrality, the keystone in the AAUP's primal theory of academic freedom. Faint traces of that norm can be found in the 1925 Statement by a reader willing to endure the eyestrain of detecting traces. For example, the academic freedom section alluded to what *institutions may not do*, not to what *faculty members may do*; instead of offering three helpings of largesse, the administrative signatories of this document agreed to three self-denying ordinances. Another trace of the neutral norm can be found in the 1925 wording of the Lowell principle. Faculty members were admonished "to take pains, when necessary, to make it clear that they are expressing their own views, and not those of the institution" because it had to be "clearly understood that an institution assumes no responsibility for views expressed by means of its staff." By 1940, even these weak residues of 1915 had disappeared. Uncomfortable with the Seligman *façon de parler*, the authors of the 1940 Statement elected to put the case for academic freedom in a positive, not a negative, fashion: ergo, they spoke of faculty entitlements instead of institutional forbidances. In addition, they gave up the idea that dissociation was an institutional desideratum and thus converted the rump statement—a faculty member "should make every effort to indicate that he is not an institutional spokesman"—into little more than a plea for good public manners.

Finding no phrase that explicitly upholds the essentiality of the neutral norm, the wielders of the 1940 Statement have been spared the difficult task of drawing lines between permissible and impermissible institutional partisanship. They have not been called upon, for example, to distinguish an *educationally* neutral institutional policy (not necessarily desirable and arguably impossible) from a *politically* neutral institutional policy (arguably always possible and even imperative). Nor have they been required to draw distinctions between regulations regarding the time, place, and manner of free expression, which minister to institutional convenience and play no favorites, and regulations that are demonstrably discriminatory in intention or effect. Had it been studded into the text, the demand that the academic corporate body be unopinionated might well have over-taxed the interpretive and operational skills of Committee A. But out of sight has a way of becoming out of mind, and code-enforcers have paid a price for not remembering what the essayistic first generation wrote and later epitomizers failed to capture. Their amnesia has doomed the 1940 Statement to irrelevance on a host of lively academic freedom issues, ranging from academic investment decisions made under ideological pressure to the ideological biasing of departments through patterns of appointment that shut out significant schools of thought.[42]

This nonremembrance of things past has played havoc with attempts by the AAUP and others to grapple effectively with the "limitations clause," the only provision in the 1940 Statement that touches on the compatibility of individual academic freedom with institutional religious or other doctrinal tests. The words of this provision come from an every-day vocabulary— "limitations of academic freedom because of religious or other aims of the institution should be clearly stated in writing at the time of the appointment"—but they vibrate with mystery and ambiguity when read without the 1915 master key.[43]

For all their deep-seated secularity, the authors of the 1915 Declaration did not challenge the right of a religious college to exist. Nor did they undertake to rid the academy of all religious tests. Why were they so permissive where, in the light of neutralist theory, it might be expected that they would be stern? In part, discretion dictated forbearance. The pluralist tradition in religion, sanctioned by centuries of American experience, argued not only for freedom of worship but for freedom to proselytize as well; the laissez faire tradition in education, secured by the constitutional immunization of private colleges from state encroachments, protected the proselytical college and permitted enrollments in mundane subjects in those colleges to count for conventional academic degrees. Not contesting the right of an academic institution to indoctrinate students in its sponsor's faith, the founders felt that they could hardly contest its right to make adherence to that

---

42. The campus turmoils of the 1960s set loose a wave of fresh analyses of the norm of institutional neutrality. *Neutrality or Partisanship: A Dilemma of Academic Institutions*, 34 Bulletin of the Carnegie Endowment for the Advancement of Teaching (1971); Alan Montefiore, ed, *Neutrality and Impartiality: The University and Political Commitment* (Cambridge, 1975). From that time on, the interest of American academics in the issue of academic neutrality has not lacked for controversies on which to feed. See Derek Bok, *Beyond the Ivory Tower* (Harvard, 1982); W. Todd Furniss and David Gardner, eds, *Higher Education and Government: An Uneasy Alliance* (American Council on Education, 1979); Alan Pifer, *Beyond Divestment—The Moral University*, 38 AAHE Bull 3 (May 1986). One indication of how distant the AAUP has been from this concern is that not one of the forty-six statements it promulgated either alone or with others between 1963 and 1990 so much as touches on it. See generally *1990 AAUP Red Book* (cited in note 1). Only recently, with regard to the persistently troubling "limitations clause," has the norm of institutional neutrality made a significant reappearance in an AAUP journal. Matthew W. Finkin, et al, *The Limitations Clause of the 1940 Statement of Principles*, 75 Academe 52 (September-October, 1988).

43. In 1967, an AAUP committee set up to re-examine the limitations clause referred to the 1915 assertion that restrictions on the academic freedom of professors were incompatible with academic freedom. It concluded, however, that the 1940 agreement allowed it to improve on the application of these restrictions but otherwise tied its hands. *Report of the Special Committee on Academic Freedom in Church-Related Colleges and Universities*, 53 AAUP Bull 369 (Winter 1967).

faith a condition of membership in its faculty. Perhaps if the major universities founded by churches, such as Harvard and Chicago, or the distinguished colleges established by sects, such as Amherst and Carleton, had continued to catechize their faculties, the AAUP would have felt obliged to launch a frontal attack on this classic form of institutional non-neutrality. But in 1915, although the academic landscape was filled with small denominational and Catholic colleges, almost every academic institution of wealth and consequence had relinquished any confessional requirement they had ever had, and it seemed that the quest for endowments and reputation, not to mention the appetites stirred by the pension gifts offered to nondenominational colleges by the Carnegie Foundation for Teaching, would lead the great bulk of the lagging institutions to follow suit. There seemed to be no need to tilt at formidable traditions when the historical trend and all the high examples seemed perfectly able to do the trick.

But in 1915 the AAUP would not countenance an attempt by an academic "instrument of propaganda" (in whatever cause, be it for socialism, the protective tariff, or religious dogma) to parade itself as a home for academic freedom or call itself a true college or university. "Concerning the desirability of the existence of such institutions, the committee does not desire to express any opinion. But it is manifestly important that they should not be permitted to sail under false colors." Honest advertising was the obvious program for institutional neutralists who viewed religious tests as the enemy of academic freedom but did not want to be dictatorial or quixotic in opposing them.

To cut down on the deceptive use of religious tests, the authors of the 1915 Declaration insisted that all institutions of a sectarian or partisan character should make this fact known to candidates for academic positions before clinching their appointments. The timing of this disclosure struck the AAUP as important for several reasons. Applied before the bargain was struck, a religious test would give applicants the information they needed to make an informed career decision; divulged afterwards, it could take unsuspecting faculty members by surprise. Furthermore, the young AAUP supposed that a precursive religious test would help the college define its true character not only to the job-seeker, but to the public, the profession, and perhaps itself. Conversely, it assumed that the posterior religious test, applied within the sanctum of a college, would serve such nefarious purposes as helping one religious faction seize control of the institution from another or give a president an excuse for ousting an otherwise entrenched faculty foe.[44] The AAUP had not said, however, that a forerunning religious test was

---

44. One early case, predating the formation of the AAUP, was investigated and reported by Lovejoy and a small committee on behalf of several disciplinary societies. *Case of Professor Mecklin, Report of the Committee of Inquiry of the American Philosophical Association and the American Psychological Association*, 11 J Phil, Psych & Sci Method 67 (1914) (case of Mecklin and Lafayette College). For some early AAUPers, the dismissal of Willard Fisher from Wesleyan University on vaguely religious grounds pointed to the danger of letting administrators hide a disreputable reason for dismissing a teacher in a presumably more reputable creedal bunker improvised for the occasion. "Willard Fisher Case" folder (1915) (AAUP files) (donated by Donald L. Kemmerer); "Fetter Draft of Report on

tantamount to no religious test. When the AAC first offered its opinion on this subject in 1917, it had defended the appropriateness of all religious tests, whether administered before or after an appointment. When it spoke in 1922 for the second time, it took the position that an academic institution has every right to prescribe an orthodoxy, but that it may not, consistent with academic freedom, do so ex post facto. In the glow of the rapprochement, the AAUP welcomed this much accommodation to the neutral principle and did not press the point that, while it found some religious tests more palatable than others, it regarded all religious tests as inimical to academic freedom.

The 1925 Statement recorded the AAC's second thoughts, not the AAUP's first thoughts, on this subject:

> A university or college may not impose any limitation upon the teacher's freedom in the exposition of his own subject in the classroom or in addresses and publications outside the college, except in so far as the necessity of adapting instruction to the needs of immature students, or in the case of institutions of a denominational or partisan character, specific stipulations in advance, duly understood and accepted by both parties, limit the scope and character of instruction.[45]

Hardly deserving of a prize for literary clarity, this convoluted sentence could be reconstrued as follows: (1) provided it makes its doctrinal demands crystal clear in the original terms of employment, an academic institution may impose such demands with the permission of the AAC and the AAUP; (2) once they agree to adhere to doctrinal demands that have been nominated in the bond, faculty members who later change their minds, and are on that account dismissed, can expect no succor from the AAC or the AAUP; (3) although the end of the sentence speaks of limits only on instruction, the beginning speaks of limits on outside publications and addresses too, and so it may be supposed that the institution is allowed to discover a punishable apostasy in every mode of expression; (4) denominational or other partisan institutions that obey this prescription for open dealings are not violating the rules of academic freedom, but are rather qualifying for a narrow exemption provided for under those rules; hence, they may claim to have academic freedom when they limit it only in these sanctioned ways. Yet more concisely: there is nothing wrong with an opportune religious (or other doctrinal) academic test.

In the course of the next decade, the AAUP had an opportunity to learn from field experience that an antecedent religious test was filled with defects. For one thing, no religious test, early or late, was likely to be confined to specific articles of belief. In a Protestant milieu, where theology tended to dissolve into piety, a dogmatic core was hard to isolate; in a Catholic milieu, where matters of faith were authoritatively decided, so too were matters of morals, and the two were authoritatively intertwined. The AAUP saw great

Fisher Case" (1915) (donated by Frank W. Fetter) (AAUP files); *Summary Report of the Committee on Academic Freedom and Academic Tenure on the Case of Willard C. Fisher of Wesleyan University*, 2 AAUP Bull 119 (1916).

45. AAUP, *1925 Statement of Principles on Academic Freedom and Tenure*, 18 AAUP Bull 329 (1932) ("1925 Statement").

dangers to personal freedom in this interlinking of creed with conduct. Religious communities often failed to distinguish the spiritually essential from the culturally familiar; behaviors deemed innocuous in some religious settings, such as dancing, drinking, or marrying someone who had been divorced, could be seen in another as steeped in sin.[46] When the AAUP tried to draw a line between valid doctrinal demands and invalid behaviorial coercions, it appeared to set itself up as the arbiter of true religion, which was an awkward presumption, to say the least. For another thing, the leadership of religious colleges all too often lacked the stability and continuity necessary to make preappointment promises binding. Two kinds of academic institutions were likely to administer tardy religious tests; those torn by internal conflicts within the parent church, and those shuttlecocking between past and present, appealing to new nonreligious constituencies while trying to hold on to older religious ones. Divided and traditional religious colleges grew faster than had been predicted in 1915, so that it seemed that before the 1925 Statement could ameliorate the problem of religious tests, historical trends were likely to exacerbate it.

If anyone on the AAUP negotiating team burned to rewrite the 1925 passage on religious tests in order to reclaim institutional neutrality as a root idea, this desire escaped the recorders of the 1940 negotiations. Pact-writers on a second round have a natural reluctance to open up settled issues to fresh debate; the adage about not stirring up sleeping dogs has a special relevance for workers in this genre. For the second round, the AAUP and the AAC came in with drastically altered texts on only a few topics, and the topic of religious tests was not one of them. To prepare the ground for their conference with the presidents, the AAUP asked its legal counsel, John M. Maguire of the Harvard Law School, to improve on the first agreement, the inescapable starting point for discussion. Treating this more as a rewording than a rethinking assignment, Maguire split the overpacked sentence into its component parts, shifted all but one part to other regions of the text, eliminated the cumbersome syntax of what remained, and emerged with what, after some amendment, would come to be known as the "limitations clause."[47]

---

46. The Bethany College-Croyle case, Committee on Academic Freedom and Academic Tenure, *Report of Enquiry into Conditions at Bethany College*, 5 AAUP Bull 26 (May 1919) (case of H. I. Croyle), was the key case from a religious college before 1925. In it the AAUP was unable to decide whether the professor had been fired because he taught the Bible from "the modern point of view" or because he flouted social conventions. Similar uncertainties afflicted treated but unreported religious college cases before the pact. Case file, Mercer College-Fox (1924) (AAUP files); Case file, Missouri Wesleyan-Reed (1925) (AAUP files). The 1925 distinction between acceptable and unacceptable religious tests was not of much help to the AAUP. What was murky about the proper grounds for dismissal from a religious college before 1925 did not become clearer afterwards. Some administrators of religious colleges would take advantage of the religious exemption to effect a quite secular end, such as ridding themselves of professors who were thorns to them personally. See Academic Freedom and Tenure, Committee A, *Report of the Sub-Committee of Inquiry for William Jewell College*, 16 AAUP Bull 226 (1930) (case of Ryland Fleet).

47. The heavy flow of religious college cases coming to AAUP attention after 1940 as a result of changes within Protestant and Catholic higher education gave the limitations clause a salience to

In some respects, Maguire editorialized more aggressively than he had planned and came closer to the AAUP's original intent than he knew. He indicated in his stripped-down sentence that any expressional constraint due to an institution's "religious or other aims" was indeed a "limitation of academic freedom" and remained such even if it took the better of several possible forms. He uncoupled the reference to religious tests from the reference to teaching technique, thereby avoiding the suggestion that a demand for intellectual conformity on the part of mature adults and the protection of the sensibilities of callow youth were much alike. He inserted the requirement that institutional limitations on free speech should be clearly stated "in writing" (the 1925 Statement had merely asked for a clear bilateral "understanding"); this reflected a growing awareness that oral agreements are notorious breeders of misunderstandings, and that intramural conflict can be resolved more readily when documents, rather than merely memories, are used to evaluate conflicting testimony. Finally, by altering the format of the sentences to avoid stating a prohibition followed by an allowable exception, he did something to escape the inference that the AAUP and the AAC had gotten into the business of issuing indulgences to religious colleges provided they were careful about when they showed their stripes.

But without the arguments for institutional neutrality to light his way, the drafter of the limitations clause did not do enough. Reshuffling words without adding explanations (the compressed genre did not admit of explanations), he still left many readers with the impression that academic freedom and religious tests could reach a modus vivendi through candid employment contracts drawn up and signed at the proper time. Simply as a practical matter, the post-1940 reliance of the AAUP on the prophylactic power of this device would often prove to be misplaced. Though the limitations clause made no direct attempt to reduce the scope of religious tests (it spoke of religious "aims," not just of religious "credenda"), it was hoped that the "in writing" requirement would be helpful in this regard, that the very act of composition would compel college authorities to record the crux of required belief and eschew demands for adherence to nonessentials. Unhappily, as the litigation virus began to work its way into academic life, and employment contracts came to be written with the understanding that they might one day be construed in court, the precursive religious test became more likely to reflect the studied subtlety of the college lawyer than the artless musings of the religionist. Far from inspiring forthrightness and restraint, the "in writing" rule put a premium on ambiguity that left plenty of room for post hoc administrative construction. Literary craftsmanship descended to literary craftiness when faculty candidates at the appointment gate were asked to pledge "faithfulness to the spirit of a Christian college" or "adherence to the

---

administrative spokesmen and AAUP investigators it had not had in its earlier formulation. It should be borne in mind, however, that easily half of the complaints brought by faculty members in religious colleges alleged mistreatments that had nothing to do with religious tests and did not spark controversy over the meaning of the limitations clause.

standards of the Church" (the details to be entered later).[48] In the typical situation, very broad primary legislation was enacted at the threshold, and later, when the situation warranted, an expedient secondary legislation filled in the gaps.[49]

Had it been completely free to speak its mind, the AAUP would surely not have put everything it had to say about religious tests into an elliptical "limitations clause." On its own, in a more pliant format, it might well have taken fresh pains to insist that academic freedom, though in part the child of religious consciences, was historically the enemy and is logically the antithesis of religious tests. Drawing on twenty-five years of case experience, it might have concluded that prevenient religious tests were not clearly superior to sequent tests given without early warning, if only because their vagueness and overbreadth could just as well turn them into surprise attacks against faculty members. With room for exploration, it might have asked whether academic freedom is less offended when religious tests are administered selectively—to theologians but not to physicists, to coreligionists but not to gentiles, to clerics in the sponsoring church but not to ordinary communicants[50]—or

---

48. Before 1940, the AAUP occasionally found itself embroiled with administrators who claimed that a by-law reference to the "Christian" character of the institution adequately warned would-be faculty members of the dogmas they were expected to profess. See H. D. Wolf & Newman I. White, *Report on Converse College*, 20 AAUP Bull 434 (1934) (case of Peter Carmichael). After 1940, the AAUP could use the limitations clause—especially its demand for written prespecifications—to argue that so vague a description was no substitute for precise doctrinal demands. This approach put the AAUP in the strange position of advocating more rather than less prior restraint. Never quite satisfied that the early warning had been clear, specific or exhaustive enough, the AAUP would sometimes turn the limitation clause to the advantage of the complainant. In one case, it claimed that a college's designation of itself as "an instrument of witness for the Presbyterian Church" did not sufficiently warn the faculty member that acceptance of the divinity of Christ was required. Case file, King College-Marshall (1974) (AAUP files). In another case, it argued that a priest who is not told before appointment that he will forfeit his position if he resigned from the priesthood may not be dismissed for doing so later on without violating the limitations clause. William P. Berlinghoff & Rodger Van Allen, *Academic Freedom and Tenure: Seton Hall University (New Jersey)*, 71 Academe 28 (May-June 1985) (case of Leonard Volenski). Interestingly, when institutions did state their creedal restrictions with great specificity (these tended to be highly sectarian and insular institutions), the AAUP could not bring itself to approve. In one religious college case, a strong argument against the front-loading logic of the limitations clause emerged when an AAUP team confronted a close-to-perfect example of a proprietary institution. See C. William Heywood, *Academic Freedom and Tenure: Concordia Theological Seminary (Indiana)*, 75 Academe 57 (May-June 1989) (case of Alvin J. Schmidt).

49. Often enough, the "secondary legislation"—the precise offense for which the deviater from the general limitation pays a price—is stated very generally too. In some AAUP cases, especially those that emanate from small women's colleges run by religious orders, the charge of creating a "scandal" is said to justify a dismissal under the 1940 Statement. The charge of "scandal," one AAUP investigating committee wrote, is "not susceptible to common and specific definition. To the President of Saint Mary's College and to some others, it meant bad public manners. To others, it meant inaccurate or volatile or ambiguous discourse. To still others it meant bad publicity. It meant everything and it meant nothing." John P. McCall, Walter D. Mink & Bernard F. Reilly, *Academic Freedom and Tenure: St. Mary's College (Minnesota)*, 54 AAUP Bull 37, 42 (Spring 1968) (case of Richard Caldwell).

50. Nothing in the 1940 Statement suggests that the same limitations must apply to all members of the faculty of a religious college. The AAUP has never rebuked a Protestant institution for screening its theologians but not its Latinists for correct belief, or a Catholic institution for applying stricter restrictions to Catholic faculty members than to non-Catholic faculty members, or for discriminating against apostates—*provided* the restrictions are specified beforehand in the terms of appointment. This permitted selectivity of restraint undercuts one of the chief arguments for

when the college finds greater culpability in heretical teaching than it does in heretical research, or in academic than in personal nonconformity.[51] Without an imperative need for tact, the AAUP might have repeated what it had written in 1915—that it challenged, not the right of missionary institutions to exist, but their right to conceal their character by pretending to be true colleges or universities—and it might have used the epithet "proprietary" to counter their claim to general public support. Finally, free to think things through for itself, the AAUP, forswearing the desire to enlist for combat duty against every religious college in the country, might yet have concocted rules of engagement that would have allowed it to do battle within its means. But the genre to which the AAUP was committed did not encourage such reflections and elaborations.[52]

In 1970, a committee established by the AAUP and the AAC to clarify nebulous or puzzling passages in the 1940 Statement noted that "[m]ost church-related institutions no longer need or desire the departure from the principle of academic freedom implied in the 1940 Statement, and we do not

---

precursive tests, for if what a religious institution stands for may vary from one discipline to another, or one privately bargained contract to another, it can hardly stand for anything clear and unmistakable in the public eye. On the other hand, since the proviso itself applies across the board, the AAUP has been able to hold that all academics, including priests under the discipline of a hierarchic church, are entitled to its protection.

51. The limitation clause appears in the paragraph concerned with freedom of teaching, which would seem to argue that it refers only to communications in the classroom. In general, the AAUP has taken the position that it may apply to publications as well. See Frank R. Kennedy & Donald C. Bryant, *Academic Freedom and Tenure: Mercy College*, 49 AAUP Bull 245 (1963) (case of Austin Shelton, Jr.). Whether the limitation clause applies to "private" or "nonprofessional" faculty behavior is an open question. In a recent case, the AAUP determined that the wedding of a divorced member of a Catholic university faculty was too unrelated to the issue of professional fitness and too squarely within the zone of private conduct to be subject to institutional discipline under the 1940 Statement. Jose M. Sanchez & Paul H. Walter, *Academic Freedom and Tenure: The Catholic University of Puerto Rico*, 73 Academe 34 (May-June 1987) (case of Jeannette Quilichini Paz). But this has not been a rigorously maintained position, probably because it puts the AAUP in the uncomfortable position of drawing the boundaries of religion, and also because this approach really bypasses the limitation clause, whose concern is not with professional fitness but with religious compatibility.

52. On its own, the AAUP might have arrived with the following position:

We hold these truths to be self-evident, that every doctrinal limitation imposed by an institution upon a faculty member as a condition of employment is incompatible with the principle of academic freedom, that this incompatibility remains whether the limitation is applied to applicants for, or to present holders of, academic appointments, is framed in vague or specific terms, or is promulgated with or without faculty consent, and that an institution that imposes such a limitation and that claims to safeguard academic freedom is engaging in a form of deception that should be exposed and reproved. Nevertheless, it is our view that the existence or even punitive application of limitations does not call for an AAUP vote of *censure* unless it is attended by other departures from good practices, such as a failure to acquaint the faculty member of those limitations before appointment or a denial of due process in the course of terminating the appointment.

Judging from a recent case, the discriminative use of the censure instrument as a way of avoiding close combat with every proselytic college while holding fast to the AAUP patrimony under pact conditions may be in the cards. See Bertram H. Davis, Richard G. Hider & Schubert M. Ogden, *Academic Freedom and Tenure: The Catholic University of America*, 75 Academe 27 (September-October 1989) (case of Charles Curran); *Report of Committee A 1989-1990*, 76 Academe 32, 32-33 (September-October 1990) (Committee A's recommendation to censure Catholic University). For a critical view of this approach, see Michael W. McConnell, *Academic Freedom in Religious Colleges and Universities*, 53 L & Contemp Probs 303 (1990).

now endorse such a departure."[53] This comment signified that, after thirty years on the books, the limitations clause could still be authoritatively interpreted as endorsing a departure from academic freedom—an exegetical defeat the AAUP could not have desired but did contribute to. Further, the comment assumed that the "endorsement" had been so overtaken by changes in the attitudes of religious colleges that it had lost its constituency and hence had lost its point.[54] As it turned out, that assumption was premature. The liberalizing trend in American Protestantism and the modernizing breezes that blew through the Roman Catholic Church from the Second Vatican Council were destined to be countered by the resurgence of Protestant fundamentalism and papal opposition to Johannine reforms. As a result, there remains to this day no dearth of administrators of religious colleges who take comfort in the 1940 Statement's presumed assurance that they can eat their academic freedom cake and have it too.[55] Until this moment, the AAUP has continued to apply the limitations clause in part because it recites everything in the 1940 Statement as a mantra, but mostly because it can squeeze droplets of faculty protection from the view that, unless it is premeditated and preannounced, a religious test may not validly take effect.

C.   Agenda Gaps

History is full of telltale omissions, of dogs that solve mysteries when they do not bark. In this connection, the revealing omissions have to do with topics included in the 1915 Declaration that did not gain entry into the 1925 or 1940 Statements, and topics emphasized in the later documents that had simply been ignored before. A few examples:

In 1915, the founders of the AAUP, filled with a blossoming sense of professional self-importance, sought to enhance the power and influence of faculty members in the governing of their institutions. Because of the great diversity of policy-making mechanisms in academe and the widely disparate

---

53.   AAUP, *1970 Interpretive Comments*, in *1984 AAUP Red Book* at 5 (cited in note 1).

54.   Stenographic Record of the Joint Meeting of the AAUP and AAC to Reconsider the 1940 Statement at 64-77 and passim (February 26-27, 1969) (AAUP files).

55.   Taking advantage of the limitations clause is not the only way in which this result can be achieved. The comment of a New York Supreme Court judge in a case involving the challenged appointment of the philosopher Bertrand Russell to the City College of New York shows that it can also be achieved by definitions. "Academic freedom" he wrote, "does not mean academic license. It is the freedom to do good and not to teach evil." *Kay v Board of Higher Education of the City of New York*, 173 Misc 943, 951, 18 NYS2d 821, 829 (Sup Ct 1940). This definition has had special resonance in Catholic higher education. As Catholic Duquesne University once put the same idea: "Academic freedom, like all things finite, has its limitations . . . . The truth confines the human intellect within limitations that connote true freedom—freedom from error . . . ." After this definition there followed sixteen "don'ts," the violation of any of which would constitute grounds for terminating a tenured apointment. They included giving support to any idea that undermined the "stability" of family life and any idea that fostered "materialistic Communism." Policies and Regulations Concerning Appointments to the Faculties of Duquesne University (1940) (AAUP files). Many academics in Catholic institutions now take strong exception to a definition of academic freedom that equates it with compulsion to tell the "truth," but this means that the AAUP liberal definition of academic freedom has found protagonists in what had once been a wholly unpromising sphere, not that it is certain to prevail there.

opinions in their own ranks about whether these mechanisms should be retained, dismantled, or reformed, the founders said nothing in their academic freedom essay about faculty participation in the *legislative* processes of their universities. They did, however, dwell on faculty participation in the *judicial* processes of their universities, and on this matter they exhibited very strong guild complexes. They made a lasting contribution to this aspect of academic governance when they proposed that the faculty, as a body, should judge the validity of dismissal charges leveled against any of its members: this was a key application of the concept of peer review. They made a contribution that lasted through the 1925 Statement when they proposed that the reappointment and nonreappointment of junior faculty should always be effected with the advice and consent of a relevant body of senior faculty. And they made a contribution that would have an exceedingly short life span when they proposed that, on academic freedom issues, the faculty body convoked to weigh dismissal charges should be not only the court of first impression but the court of last appeal. In 1915, these guildsmen argued that "in matters of opinion, and of the utterance of opinion . . ., [lay] boards cannot intervene without destroying, to the extent of their intervention, the essential nature of a university . . . ." They made the same point with regard to professional ethics: "[i]t is . . . inadmissible that the power of determining when departures from the requirements of the scientific spirit and method have occurred, should be vested in bodies not composed of members of the academic profession."[56] On these subjects, the authors of the 1915 Declaration were Manichean; "lay" meant partisan, self-interested, and uninformed; "professional" meant nonpartisan, disinterested, and knowledgeable.

The 1925 Statement incorporated two inventions of prewar professional self-assertiveness: the call for peer review of charges against permanent faculty members, and the provision for faculty consultation in the employment or disemployment of junior faculty personnel. But aside from these carry-overs (plus an ambiguous reference to a faculty magistrate to screen charges based on public speech offenses, discussed in Part IIE), the spirited professionalism of 1915 was not retained. Not a trace remained in the 1925 Statement of the lay versus professional conceit that filled the pages of the Declaration. In the pact statement, all cases in which the professional fitness of a faculty member was brought into dispute, including those involving academic freedom, were to be decided finally by the lay governing board. With this tethering of professorial ambition to the realities of campus power, the faculty hearing ceased to be a symbolic re-experiencing of the medieval *consortio magistrorum* and became more an advisory instrument of the institutional authorities.

In 1940, what might be called the deguilding of the idea of academic freedom and tenure went a good deal further. This Statement retained the

---

56. 1915 Declaration at 38, 34; Appendix A at 404, 402 (cited in note 13).

notion of an independent faculty hearing, strengthened by due process innovations and weakened by an "if possible" qualification. But the involvement of full and associate professors in the retention and nonretention of instructors and assistant professors dropped out of the program of these treaty-writers, along with the faculty watchdog in public speech cases that the 1925 Statement had contrived. Meanwhile, no attempt was made to revive the conclusionary faculty verdicts called for in 1915 or the pledge that the local faculty would police the conduct of its own.[57] There were two reasons for this now very wide agenda gap. One was that the professional had come to speak more in the voice of the white-collar employee than in the voice of the medieval master. The other was that the bid for faculty autonomy had to yield to the facts of campus hierarchy, or presidents and professors would never have been able to agree.

An agenda gap, it should be noted, may be caused by an early as well as a late omission. The authors of the 1915 Declaration totally ignored the threat posed to academic freedom and tenure by the problem of financial exigency. This was hardly because all the academic institutions they knew were prosperous. Given the decades-long tendency of the institutional population to grow faster than the student population and the large number of private academic firms with weak endowments and in chronic need of more paying guests, the AAUPers of 1915 must have been aware that pinched institutional budgets were a common fact of academic life. Perhaps they thought it *infra dignitate* to dwell on so crass a thing as cash. This may seem hard to credit today, but they did eschew materialism in the fashion of their day when they thought it "undesirable" that persons "should be drawn into the profession by the magnitude of the economic rewards it offers," and when they used up all the letters of the alphabet save the last one before they would deign to establish a committee on professorial salaries. Probably their main reason for not mentioning institutional economic privations is that they just did not believe it had much to do with freedom and tenure deprivations. They may well have been too sheltered to understand that an administration, merely by crying poverty, could have all the pretext it needed for removing permanent faculty members without hearings, and for making ideological or personal enemies walk the plank.

Oddly, though professors were not disposed to guard against the deceptive uses of financial exigency, their presidential partners of some years later were. On this issue, pride of first authorship belonged not to the idealists of the AAUP but to the realists of the AAC:

> Termination of permanent or long-term appointments because of financial exigencies should be sought only as *a last resort*, after every effort has been made to meet the need *in other ways* and *to find for the teacher other employment in the institution*. Situations which make *drastic* retrenchment of this sort necessary should *preclude expansion of the staff at other points at the same time*, except in extraordinary circumstances.[58]

---

57. 1940 Statement at 3-4; Appendix B at 407-09 (cited in note 1).
58. 1925 Statement at 329 (cited in note 45) (emphasis added).

In other words, the termination of a long-term appointment for other than proven cause had not only to be *justified* but in fact *necessitated* by straitened circumstances. The action had to be patently last ditch, although this did not mean such dismissals were impossible; if the financial crisis could not be alleviated by other means, the axe could fall. In instructing financially strapped institutions to find alternative employment for their deposed faculty members, this provision further implied that a budget is not an iron givenness but is a reflection of human interests and desires within relatively broad or narrow resources constraints, and that even relatively tight budgets usually leave margins for choice. Many years later, the AAUP, in its own Recommended Institutional Regulations, would add a stiff definition of financial exigency, an order of execution more protective of tenured than of nontenured faculty members, and temporary recall rights for the victims of retrenchment, to the tactics devised in 1925 to head off disingenuous claims to penury.[59] Still, it was remarkable that the constructive skepticism of the presidents should have gone that far that early. They asserted in effect that faculty members should not be treated by colleges and universities in financial distress the way workers in automobile factories were treated by companies with lagging sales. They used the word "drastic" to describe an institutional action that blighted academic careers and hopes: anyone who would have preferred a cooler adjective, such as "regrettable" or "unfortunate" would have been quarreling with a principled position, not disputing words.

The 1940 Statement was written during the last years of the Great Depression, and many of its key tenure provisions bore the mark of those prolonged hard times. On the issue of financial exigency, however, it was strangely unresponsive to a reality that, one might have supposed, should have brought that issue into high relief.[60] Although they performed wholesale surgery on no other part of the 1925 Statement, the framers of the second pact elected to eliminate the entire paragraph designed to block the removal of tenured faculty members for trivial or specious pocketbook reasons. In its place they inserted a laconic sentence: "Termination of a continuous appointment because of financial exigency must be demonstrably

---

59. *Recommended Institutional Regulations on Academic Freedom and Tenure* §§ 4(c)-(d), in *1984 AAUP Red Book* at 23-25 (cited in note 1) (adopted by AAUP in 1976) ("RIR").

60. Up to the point where it resumed negotiations with the AAC, the AAUP had received a handful of complaints over terminations said to be caused by financial pressures but had responded to them rather perfunctorily. Once a president, in reply to an AAUP opening inquiry, stated that he was compelled by the state of the institutional budget to terminate tenured appointments, and no other reason for the action suggested itself, the AAUP either washed its hands of the case or published a brief statement of fact. 1930 case folder, *Hiram College-DuBois*; 1931 case folder, *Transylvania College-Maney et al*; 1931 case folder, *Morningside College-Overton*; 1931 case folder, *Texas Christian College-Glaze* (all in AAUP files). When it did publish a report critical of the administration in a financial exigency case, the AAUP did not avail itself of the protective tools made available to it in the 1925 Statement. 1931 case folder, *Texas Christian-Smith et al* (AAUP files); *Report*, 19 AAUP Bull 472-76 (1933); *Illinois Wesleyan-Bennett*, 20 AAUP Bull 447-49 (1934). In general, the attitude of the association seemed to be: money problems are acts of God and it is pointless to question or revile them; if some nonmonetary causal factor gives us leave to criticize the administration, let us do so; if not, let us advise our complainants to accept their fate.

bona fide." If not quite retreat to 1915's blankness, since the call for a demonstration of good faith *was* a sign of concern, the replacement sentence was much less mindful than the 1925 provision of the parlous relationship between security of academic tenure and claims of financial exigency. True, it did assert that such claims had to be bona fide or else the dismissal of tenured professors on those grounds would be invalid. But it did not define the degree of economic hardship needed to authenticate a claim of financial exigency, and without an *in extremis* standard any financial strain, any budgetary squeeze, could plausibly justify an executionary act.[61] But financial strains and budgetary squeezes are the usual lot of dependent institutions that can generate only a part of their working revenues, of nonmarket institutions that cannot pass on all their costs to final purchasers, and of eleemosynary institutions that always try to do more than they can afford. Accordingly, the exigency provision in the 1940 Statement threatened to let a chronic condition extenuate departures from tenure rules, and thus convert what was intended as an exception into what could very well become the rule.

Moreover, shorn of the objective tests of "good faith," the 1940 provision could be said to require nothing more than a sincere economism, which is easy enough to assume and very difficult to belie. On the strength of this provision, it could be argued that a department induced by the tunneled numerology of cost accountants to lop off professors teaching classes with low enrollments, or a school instructed to save money by ousting expensive senior faculty to improve its balance sheet, were acting in an economic spirit and thus presumably in "good faith."[62] This road easily led to the philistine

---

61. In RIR 4c, a bona fide financial exigency is defined as an "imminent financial crisis which threatens the survival of the institution as a whole and which cannot be alleviated by less drastic means" than the termination of one or more tenured appointments. RIR (cited in note 59). Perhaps no deliverance from the AAUP has struck administrators as more wrong-minded and unrealistic. They ask, is there no room in the AAUP scheme of things for prudent planning, that is to say, for a rational response to anticipated, though not yet present, ills? Must the ship be almost at the point of capsizing before it may lighten its weight by trimming its tenured crew? Must things get markedly worse before steps may be taken to make them better? The general AAUP response has been that anything less than an *in extremis* standard would pose a profound threat to academic tenure and academic freedom. One administrator records the view that a "financial exigency begins, not when a school is bankrupt, but when it has significant difficulty in supplying additional positions to departments in the ascendency." Ralph S. Brown, Jr., *Financial Exigency*, 62 AAUP Bull 5 (1976). Were this definition to prevail, and tenured faculty could lose their jobs to finance expansion as well as to effect contraction, tenure would become a nullity for all seasons. A court rules that a financial exigency exists when there is an "urgent need . . . to restore the financial ability of a college to provide from current income . . . the funds necessary to meet current expenses, including debt payment and sound reserves, without invading or depleting capital." *Lumpert v University of Dubuque*, (#39973, Iowa state district court unreported, 1974). This was to say that the claims of tenure were to be subordinated to the claims of benefactors who wish to keep their bequests intact, to the claims of creditors who may be as varied as the local stationers and local fuel company, and to the squirreling instincts of trustees who may wish to turn surpluses into nest-eggs against the day when deficits might appear. It should strike no one as surprising that the AAUP looked askance at a definition that put the claims of tenure at the very end of a line that stretched around the block.

62. According to the AAUP gloss in RIR 4c, to be validly claimed, a financial exigency must threaten the survival of the institution "as a whole" and not just one or more of its subcomponents. In a multi-campus system, this would mean that the entire system would have to be on the verge of bankruptcy before any campus could be exempted on financial grounds from the rule that tenured faculty members may be dismissed only for adequate personal cause established in a due process

assumption, widely shared in the more Westinghouse reaches of academe, that tenure rested provisionally on teacher productivity and student fads.[63]

What were they thinking of—those representatives of the AAUP and AAC who traded a strong statement on financial exigency for a weaker one? Their thinking is not fully disclosed by the skimpy conference record on this subject, but an article by President Henry M. Wriston of Brown University, a powerful figure on the AAC team and the author of the replacement sentence, increases our ability to read their minds.[64] In 1940 as in 1925, the professors left it to the presidents to decide what, if anything, should be said about financial exigency. Their persistently phlegmatic attitude may be explained in part by the fact that the Great Depression took a much lighter toll on the senior faculty, to whom the exigency exception alone applied, than on the junior faculty, who were always vulnerable to ejection for unstated reasons. This fact convinced Wriston that tenured professors had less to fear from a shrinking fisc than from spurious financial arguments used by administrators who were trying to run for cover. It had been his experience, he wrote, that presidents would rather blame the discharge of a faculty member on the limitations of the budget than on the limitations of the faculty member, the former being almost always present and the latter being almost always painful. Wriston regarded this kind of disingenuousness, even if motivated by kindness, as inimical to sound personnel practices, and it was to stiffen the backbone of his colleagues that he plumped for a bona fide clause. But this explanation does not explain everything. Wriston was well aware that plots against tenure

---

hearing. Getting boards and administrators to agree, especialy in the public sector, has proved to be a difficult and even perhaps a futile task for the AAUP. But the alternative—to accede to attacks on tenure by the simple expedient of starving certain institutions in a system through managerial decree—is even more unappealing. RIR (cited in note 59). For AAUP cases that raise the whole-part issue, see *City University of New York: Mass Dismissals Under Financial Exigency*, 63 AAUP Bull 60 (1977); *University of Idaho*, 68 Academe 1a (1982); *The State University of New York*, 63 AAUP Bull 237 (1977). The courts have not been friendly to the AAUP argument that financial exigency in a subcomponent is but another word for inefficiency, that is, the less than optimal use of personnel—and that this should not be a valid basis for rescinding tenure. *Scheuer*, 199 Neb 2d at 624, 260 NW2d at 601. David Fellman, *The Association's Evolving Policy on Financial Exigency*, 70 Academe 14 (1984).

63. RIR 4c allows for irregular dismissals when a program or department of instruction is discontinued for primarily educational reasons. RIR (cited in note 59). This second exception was not covered or even contemplated by the financial exigency clause of the 1940 Statement. Committee A reasoned that an institution should not be barred by the rules of tenure from dropping an educationally unworthy program—an engineering school that had become technologically outmoded, a department of linguistics that had lost its stellar cast and could not replace it, an undergraduate program in journalism that had become a patent waste of the students' time. If tenure positions are forfeited as a result, the AAUP was prepared to live with it, although the association enjoined the institution to make "every effort" to find a "suitable alternative position" for every tenured professor thus displaced. This was a large concession to quality on the part of the AAUP, and it had the capacity to cause mischief in several ways. For one thing, the "program" could be so small that its excision was tantamount to a dismissal of one individual without due process safeguards. *Browzin*, 527 F2d at 849. For another thing, institutions have interpreted this exemption as permitting them to *reduce* a program in the interest of economy without a showing of financial exigency, an interpretation that subverts the educational aim of the discontinuance clause and negates the RIR effort to define financial exigency.

64. Henry M. Wriston, *Academic Freedom and Tenure*, 25 AAC Bull 110 (1939). This article is an invaluable source of information about what transpired in the conferences up to that point, seen from a president's perspective.

could be hatched by the business mentality in academe. In the same article, he argued that "the displacement of a [permanent] teacher should not be done merely as an 'economy' move, but [only] because of a *genuine emergency* involving *serious* and *general* retrenchment."[65] This comment leaves two questions searching for an answer: Why, if Wriston was willing to define financial exigency so rigorously in an article, did he not do so in the 1940 Statement? And why, if a president could see the point of 1925's protective clauses, did the professors, who had more to gain from them, not lift a finger to retain them in the next negotiating round?

D. What If?

Every discussion so far under "genre effects" and "agenda gaps" points to effects attributable to the pact; there has been little explicit assessment of the contributions of the pact-partners. But the company the AAUP chose to keep doubtless did help shape the document it agreed to. The influence of the presidential participants can be seen in many parts of the 1940 Statement, but perhaps nowhere is it more luminously displayed than in the cautionary language in the academic freedom section. It is here that one especially feels bound to ask "what if?"—what if the AAU and not the AAC had joined hands with the AAUP in 1925 and 1940?

Under "freedom of investigation," the working draft of the AAC in 1925 read as follows: "a university or a college may not place any restraint upon the teacher's freedom in investigation unless restrictions upon the amount of time devoted to it becomes necessary in order to prevent undue interference with teaching duties, *which are the primary function of the college instructor.*"[66] Probably because Lovejoy's scissors went to work, the last nine words were snipped from the final draft. But they held the key to the AAC presidents' thoughts. Ever since the late nineteenth century, when scholarly and scientific inquiry was first incorporated into the roles academics were expected to perform, there had developed a growing library of complaint about the tendency, in this wedding, of the entrepreneurial activity of research to foster faculty neglect of the institutional obligation to teach. The notion that scholarship was the vile seducer and teaching the slighted spouse became canonical among traditional educators in the undergraduate institutions before World War I and among progressive educators afterwards, and it probably had a resilient appeal to presidents of AAC teaching-centered colleges, who were fond of proclaiming that marital fidelity in professional matters was their stock in trade.[67] The 1915 authors had made no such charge against research; if anything, they personally believed that the sin of infidelity went the other way, that grading too many freshman papers and

---

65. Id (emphasis added).
66. First Draft, 1925 Statement (Maguire files #10, AAUP files) (emphasis added).
67. The strong survival of an antiresearch ethos has been documented by Laurence R. Veysey, *The Emergency of the American University* (doctoral dissertation, University of California at Berkeley, 1961), especially in chapter four.

doing too many household chores drew faculty members away from their truest love, sustained inquiry. And it is probable that *their* presidents, toward whom the published and publicized research of faculty members wafted the sweet smell of success, did not share the view of their collegiate brethren that writing books and conducting experiments were comparable to acts of adultery.

By 1940, the AAC presidents had become less touchy on this subject. Using a Maguire redraft that sought "only to improve the language" and again did somewhat more, they agreed to a milder formulation of their old position: "the teacher is entitled to full freedom of research and in the publication of the results, subject to the adequate performance of his other duties." This setting of faculty priorities seemed sufficient to safeguard the institution's interest until Tyler, drawing on his MIT experience, suggested an additional proviso: "but research for pecuniary return should be based upon an understanding with the authorities of the institution." Apparently, the idea that faculty research could be a means of institutional as well as individual self-advancement had not fully dawned on the world of the colleges, or else the presidents would not have needed a professor to remind them that the vamp that made them so uneasy could be required to help pay their bills.[68]

Was there not more to be said about freedom of inquiry at that time? In 1940, academic research was on the threshold of wartime and postwar transformations. Some problematic aspects of that looming future could even then be glimpsed. If academic "big science" had not yet reached the Brookhaven scale of costs, it had sufficiently soared over the Edisonian scale of 1915 to offer portents of academic freedom and tenure threats soon to come. Already academic statesmen were wondering in print how freedom of inquiry could be protected in the face of large-scale federal support, classified military research, security clearances for academic personnel, and the hugger-muggeries of the national police. The handwriting on the wall also pointed to serious tenure problems. Although the number of full-time researchers without teaching responsibilities would not explode until after the war, it was already large enough to raise the question of whether full-time researchers on soft money should be eligible for tenure citizenship and, if not, how professionalism could be squared with the predestinarianism doctrine that nothing certain academics do can ever earn them salvation. The leaders of the AAUP, who, as before, were associated with major research universities and were still distinguished figures if not lions in their disciplines, might well have examined these issues with presidents from the AAU, which was a less exclusive organization than before, but still consisted of the leading research centers. Even if they could not have found common ground on emergent issues, they might well have made headway against long familiar issues

---

68. Maguire redraftings of the 1940 Statement, 1940 Statement folder (AAUP files). These revisions of the 1925 Statement would be modified at many points when they were taken up by the negotiators, but so much of their structure and verbiage survived that they are indispensable to a reconstruction of the evolution of the final text.

touching on the ethics of academic research, such as the propriety of concealing knowledge to protect a prize or patent, or of accepting gifts for research from special interests with ideological ambitions, or of conducting experiments under academic auspices that could be harmful to the environment or human subjects. To some degree at least, the thinness and brevity of the commentary attending "freedom of investigation" can be laid to the inexperience and lack of interest of the AAUP's actual interlocutors.

One can also find indications under the heading of "freedom to teach" that matters might have taken a different turn if the AAU and not the AAC had joined with the AAUP. In 1915, the Seligman contingent devoted a thoughtful paragraph to the problem of the unseasoned student in the college classroom who may be vulnerable to culture shocks. They did not offer a clear directive to the academic teacher on this matter. On the one hand, they warned the teacher to be especially on guard against "taking unfair advantage of the student's immaturity by indoctrinating him with the teacher's own opinions upon the matters in question . . . ." On the other hand, they held it to be the teacher's duty "to give to any students old enough to be in college a genuine intellectual awakening," and they supported this position with the aphorism that "it is better for students to think about heresies than not to think at all . . . ." In the end, they left the issue up to the "pedagogical wisdom" of the individual instructor convinced that, on this delicate ice, heavy-footed codifiers should fear to tread.[69]

The AAC presidents felt no such inhibitions. In the draft they brought to the 1925 Conference, they treated the presence of immature students not as an argument for sensitive teaching but as an exception to instructional freedom. A university or college may not impose any limitation "except in so far as the necessity of adapting instruction to the needs of immature students . . . limit the scope and character of instruction." They felt so strongly about the danger of pedagogical domination that they devoted a separate paragraph to it: "No teacher may claim as his right the privilege of discussing in his classroom controversial topics outside of his own field of study. The teacher is morally bound not to take advantage of his position by introducing into the classroom provocative discussions of irrelevant subjects not within the field of his study."[70] The AAUP, perhaps more than half-agreeing, did not demur.

"What if?"'s can no more be proved than can any other fling of the imagination, but it is hard to believe that the presidents of Chicago, Johns Hopkins, and Columbia, accustomed to mature graduate students and urban if not always urbane undergraduates, would have pictured their own classrooms as stages on which faculty Svengalis sought to seduce the minds of student Trilbys. And it is also hard to believe that they would have remained quite as eager as their collegiate counterparts to tell academics how to teach even after they stopped drumming up this melodramatic classroom plot. In 1940, again working with one of Maguire's supposedly minimal redrafts, the

---

69. 1915 Declaration at 35, 36; Appendix A at 402-03 (cited in note 13).
70. 1925 Statement at 329, 330 (cited in note 45).

AAC presidents agreed to drop all reference to the problem of student immaturity—apparently their own colleges were running out of students who could be scared out of their wits by a new idea. They thus abandoned the view that the innocence quotient of the audience should determine the amount of freedom a teacher should enjoy. But they did not relinquish all their apprehensions about the don's capacity to mesmerize and mislead. Without much argument from the AAUP, they continued to insist that academic teachers should stick to their subjects. For a time, the word "controversial" dropped away (as did "provocative"), but then the former was restored by the committee on style. The final version read: "The teacher is entitled to freedom in the classroom in discussing his subject, but he should be careful not to introduce into his teaching controversial matter which has no relation to his subject."[71]

A total break with the past would have been more clarifying than this softer recapitulation of it. Not making clear what at root was objectionable—the controversialism or the digressiveness—the authors left it up to their readers to decide whether a wandering teacher would be in bounds if he provoked no classroom argument, and whether an arrant polemicist would be safe if he but stuck to his original syllabus. In 1970, the AAUP-AAC committee on interpretation stated that the intent of this passage had not been to discourage controversy but to "underscore the need for the teacher to avoid persistently introducing material which has no relation to his subject."[72] According to this interpretation, the controversialist, the intellectual provocateur, and the Devil's advocate would all be safe, and only the irrepressible meanderer, no more beloved by presidents in the AAU than by those in the AAC, would run afoul of this admonition. It had taken many years and some fancy exegetical footwork to efface the stamp of the small college from this part of the 1940 Statement.

It may also be argued that a different cast of presidential characters would probably have written different cautionary lines for the passages on extramural freedom. The legislative history of these passages throws unique light on the important question of how all of these stated admonitions were to be enforced, and for this reason it will be given a somewhat closer look.

E. Confrontation

In marked contrast with the swift and harmonious exchange of views that cemented the 1925 Statement, the deliberations leading to the 1940 Statement were prolonged, volatile, and acrimonious. Not counting a series of informal meetings called by the AAC to protest the AAUP's handling of freedom and tenure cases, the two associations met officially four times between 1937 and 1940 to hammer out a revised freedom and tenure statement. Again and again the enterprise came to the verge of foundering:

---

71. 1940 Statement at 3; Appendix B at 407 (cited in note 1).
72. 1940 Statement at 5 (cited in note 1).

Henry Wriston reported after the third encounter that "[t]here has never been a meeting when we did not think we might have to adjourn and throw up the task."[73] In October 1938, the conferees did reach an agreement that embraced the substance of the AAUP's positions on several issues. The AAUP council promptly approved it, but the AAC board of directors turned it down, objecting to concessions it interpreted as capitulations. It would take two more years before a meeting of presidents and professors would produce a meeting of minds and an outcome that both organizations would accept.

Why, after the smooth delivery of the first agreement, did the second one have such a painful birth? Part of the answer lies in the difficult personalities of the second group of accoucheurs. After a lapse of a half-dozen years, the AAC freedom and tenure committee was revived in 1934 with an entirely new cast of characters. The dominant figures on the new committee, now called a commission, would for some years be the presidents of relatively small colleges who picked bones with the AAUP using blunt utensils. The commission chairman, President J. L. McConaughy of Wesleyan University, had a grudge against the professors' association for what he regarded as its persistent maligning of the administrations of small colleges, and he was determined to do everything he could to make it stop.[74] After proposing a joint national tribunal to hear and judge faculty grievances in place of the unreliable Committee A (a prevision of binding arbitration which most of his fellow presidents had no use for), he tried to get the AAUP to agree that it would not undertake to investigate a case, publish a case report, or censure an administration without first securing AAC (which was to say, his own) consent.[75] Presuming that the AAUP had given him that veto power, he proceeded to pepper it with peremptory demands that this or that impending case be dropped because he had ascertained that it was wholly without merit, and that this or that administration be removed from censure because he had heard from its president's own lips that it had not erred. When the AAUP

---

73. Wriston, 25 AAC Bull at 111 (cited in note 64).

74. The strained relations between the AAUP leaders and the new AAC Commission leaders are detailed in correspondence that can be found in Committee A case folders, arranged alphabetically by name of institution, for the period 1933-1938; the Maguire files, which were donated by Maguire to this author and were then deposited in the AAUP files; and the 1940 Statement folder. This correspondence, too voluminous to be cited extensively, provides the background for these personality analyses.

75. The first face-to-face meeting in November 1935 between Maguire and Mitchell, representing the AAUP, and McConaughy, representing the AAC, was explosive. The latter was reportedly livid in his complaint that college presidents had not been fairly treated by Committee A and that the AAUP was more sympathetic to universities than to colleges. Only the mollifying presence of President Wriston of Brown and Chancellor S. A. Capen of Buffalo kept it from ending in a rift that would have doomed any further negotiations. Maguire memo on the New York preliminary meeting in November 1935, 1940 Statement folder (AAUP files). "I felt that the representatives of the AAUP were in an incomfortable position because they were guests, were much outnumbered, were encountering men who have the authoritarian habit, and were subjected to a concerted attack which had been prepared in advance." Letter, John M. Maguire to Walter Wheeler Cook and others (December 10, 1936) (Maguire files #10, AAUP files).

balked, McConaughy threatened to sever diplomatic relations with it, which would have meant putting an end to renegotiating talks.[76]

For years Secretary Tyler had thought that a well-intentioned group of presidents might play a useful mediatory role in the early stages of a freedom or tenure case, and a number of AAUP leaders had toyed with the idea of joint investigations and of case reports over double signatures. But McConaughy, whom even his own colleagues described as tactless and overbearing,[77] managed to get everybody's backs up and deal the idea of cooperative investigation a mortal blow. The Virginia astronomer, S. A. Mitchell, who as President of the AAUP had usually been accommodating toward administrators, told this thunderer of ultimatums that his organization would not accept the AAC's dictation. Walter Wheeler Cook, who took Tyler's place as part-time secretary in 1934, found in McConaughy's effort to hold the pact negotiations hostage to the success of his importunings proof that the replacement of the all-faculty Committee A by a two-headed constabulary or judiciary would be a suicidal form of unilateral disarmament.[78]

If McConaughy roiled the negotiations with his imperious temper and leaden ear, President W. C. Dennis of Earlham College, the only AAC delegate to attend all the drafting sessions, burdened the conference with a lawyer's analytic mind put to the service of obsessive negativism. Dennis was troubled by so many issues, both those under review and those long settled, that one can only conclude that he was characterologically inclined to look for trouble. Starting out with the apprehension that church-related colleges, if they adhered to the principle of academic freedom, might have to sanction the "use of profanity" (the bemused Carlson replied that a little "cussing" would not do students abiding harm), Dennis wound up with a more general concern about the viability of faculty hearings in small colleges and the soundness of exempting the extramural utterances of faculty members from institutional constraint.[79] It was he who persuaded the AAC Board to reject the agreement reached in 1938, and it was to keep him from submitting yet another minority report that the other participants at the final meeting expended all the politique energy they could command.

It is a commentary on the schizoid character of the AAC that even while it was attracting more presidents from large urban universities than ever before it allowed this sensitive commission to come under the sway of presidents

76. Letter, J. L. McConaughy to S. A. Mitchell (December 17, 1935); letter, J. L. McConaughy to H. W. Tyler (February 1, 1936) (threatens to break off negotiations unless DePauw College was removed from the censure list) (Maguire files #10, AAUP files). 1933 case folder, *De Pauw College-Huffered*; 1935 case folder, *Culver Stockton College-Graham* (all in AAUP files).

77. Letter, John M. Maguire to Anton J. Carlson, reporting Wriston's evaluation of McConaughy (April 17, 1937) (Maguire files #10, AAUP files).

78. Letter, S. A. Mitchell to J. L. McConaughy (February 12, 1936); letter, H. W. Tyler to J. L. McConaughy (February 10, 1936); letter, Walter Wheeler Cook to H. W. Tyler (February 10, 1936) (Maguire files #10, AAUP files). 1936 case folder, *Coe College-Ogburn* (AAUP files).

79. Remarks of W. C. Dennis (Notre Dame educational conference under the auspices of the AAC, October 1936), 1940 Statement folder (AAUP files); Carlson report on that conference to Himstead and others (October 22, 1936) (Maguire files #10, AAUP files).

who, if not quite the 1916 cohort redivivus, were too set in their provincial ways and too suspicious of the AAUP ever to be confused with the fraternizers of 1925. This is not to say, however, that the AAC had a monopoly on rigidity, querulousness, and confined perspectives. In 1936, just as the redrafting process got underway, the AAUP chose Ralph E. Himstead to be its first full-time general secretary. That appointment marked the beginning of the modern history of the AAUP—a history that includes the routinization of initial charisma, a significant growth in membership and influence, a near-debacle during the McCarthy period, and a renaissance under new leadership after that. More immediately, the arrival of Himstead had the effect of worsening the already bad personal chemistry of the meeting room. A thin-skinned law professor from Syracuse University, where he had come to detest its authoritarian president, Himstead had less tolerance for the vanities and insults of that breed than did most of his better-connected, less-embattled colleagues.[80] Inevitably, the correspondence between the new general secretary and the Wesleyan president grew so heated that calmer heads among AAUP leaders, fearful that this fire might consume the budding negotiations, proposed to scan the letters sent from Washington to Middletown and, if necessary, hose them down.[81] Himstead's negotiating skills were noticeably poor when McConaughy was in the chair or even in the room. It was no coincidence that he began to reveal a talent for give-and-take only after McConaughy left the AAC Commission and Wriston took the gavel and, with the help of S. P. Capen, the worldly chancellor of the University of Buffalo, set the tone.

On most matters dealt with by the 1940 Statement, the two camps were not at each other's throats. It is simply not the case that the professors fought for freedom while the presidents fought for restrictions, or that one side believed in tenure while the other side did not. Many differences that cropped up in discussion were over nuances of phrasing and were resolved without personal animosity. But two issues could not be readily resolved, and it was these issues that invited testy egos to do their worst. One issue concerned the AAUP's proposal that all probationary periods be of a standard

---

80. Of all the AAUP leaders, Himstead was the least enthusiastic about renegotiating the original pact with the ACC. "Personally I am sorry that it was suggested at our March conference that we consider revising our tenure rules . . . I doubt whether at this time we can come to any agreement with McConaughy's committee . . . ." Letter, Ralph E. Himstead to Anton J. Carlson and others (October 23, 1936) (Maguire files #10, AAUP files). Even after the negotiations began, after strong urging from Carlson of the AAUP and Wriston of the AAC, he remained a persistent advocate of caution and delay. The reason was not just his profound antipathy for McConaughy and his sort; he also feared that the local chapters, then in the throes of a periodic attempt by the rank and file to wrest decisional authority from the Washington Office, would interpret the negotiations as consorting with and giving comfort to the enemy. He was resolved to tell the members as little as possible about the progress of meetings; indeed, he did not reveal that a revision of the 1925 Statement was their purpose until a new agreement was actually reached in 1938. Ralph E. Himstead, *Report of the General Secretary*, 23 AAUP Bull 570 (1937). Letter, Ralph E. Himstead to Walter Wheeler Cook (December 2, 1937), Cook folder, 1937-1943 (AAUP files).

81. Letters, John M. Maguire to Anton J. Carlson (April 17, 1937), and Anton J. Carlson to John M. Maguire (April 20, 1937) (Maguire files #10, AAUP files).

as well as a fixed duration; more than a technical follow-up to 1915 or 1925, this was a transformative idea that went far beyond contemporary personnel practice. The second issue involved the AAC's desire to subject the public utterances of academics to institutional discipline; this too contemplated a leaping change, but less into the untrod future than into a partly transcended past. Both issues, it should be noted, created divisions within the AAUP and the AAC as well as between them. This was a saving grace, for strictly two-sided confrontations would have been a recipe for polarization and paralysis.

The authors of the 1915 Declaration gave a seemingly contradictory answer to the question of how freely faculty members might express themselves in public forums on matters not related to teaching or research. On the one hand, still in touch with the religious roots of their calling and eager to protect the good name of their profession, they insisted that academics reach a limiting line of professional propriety long before they reach the boundary between legally protected speech and libelous, seditious, or obscene utterances. They thought it "obvious" that faculty members in their role as citizens should abide, not by the maximalist doctrine that anything goes if it is within the law, but by the realization that they had a "peculiar obligation to avoid hasty or unverified or exaggerated statements, and to refrain from intemperate or sensational means of expression." On the other hand, opposed to any suggestion that academic teachers, like many schoolteachers, had to shed their constitutional liberties when they passed through the campus gate, they maintained in the very same paragraph that "it is neither possible nor desirable to deprive a college professor of the political rights vouchsafed to every citizen." (They left open for discussion the question of whether academic social scientists would risk their reputation for disinterestedness if they ran for public office or managed a political campaign.[82]) They thus faced the problem of reconciling two opposed ambitions—to hold the academic professional to high standards of public conduct and to secure for the academic professional the ordinary right to free speech.

It is instructive to note how the authors of the 1915 Report chose *not* to solve this problem. They did not attempt to distinguish between the form of expression (which would be subject to demands of public etiquette) and the content of expression (which for freedom's sake would be best left alone). Indeed, they explicitly rejected this stock approach to the reconciliation of liberty with respectability: "It is . . . in no sense the contention of this committee . . . that individual teachers should be exempt from all restraints as to the *matter* or the *manner* of their utterances . . . ." Nor did they contend that academic freedom, even under constraints, bestows more freedom on faculty members than other citizens customarily receive, since it displaces no legal civil liberty, yet offers protections from economic penalties that may elsewhere repay dissent. With a keen eye for the argument that would be

---

82. 1915 Declaration at 37-38; Appendix A at 404 (cited in note 13).

most appealing to the public, they preferred to stress the sacrifices professors volunteer for and not the preponderating privileges they retain.

The 1915 solution was to make all strictures against professionally unbecoming public speech matters for professional, not lay, enforcement. To the greatest degree possible, they urged that the etiquette of academic public speech be "self-imposed." Coming from homogeneous social and cultural backgrounds, these AAUPers could believe that most faculty members would conduct themselves properly in public even when left entirely on their own. Where self-enforcement proved insufficient, they thought a canon of decent discourse could be "enforced by the public opinion of the profession"—that is, by fear of collegial disapproval.

Had they said no more, they would have made freedom of extramural utterance practically coextensive with legally defined freedom of speech, since professional admonitions would have been merely precatory. But the founders of the AAUP, like the founders of the nation, were too pessimistic about the moral perfectibility of human beings to trust the task of human betterment wholly to personal upbringing and communal pressure. They conceded that "there may, undoubtedly, arise occasional cases in which the aberrations of individuals may [have] to be checked by definite disciplinary action."[83] By saying this, they admitted that what faculty members say and write in off-campus settings and during their off-duty hours may in principle be used against them in institutional trials looking to their dismissal. But if the institution could take cognizance of a faculty member's public speech in a disciplinary hearing, and if the faculty member is not protected by a rule of evidentiary exclusion, would the faculty member not be "deprived of political rights vouchsafed to other citizens?" The authors of the 1915 Declaration answered that irrepressible question by rehearsing the key articles of their guildist faith. Such a deprivation would occur, they wrote in effect, if *lay* governing boards were to judge a faculty member guilty of unprofessionalism in public discourse. But it would not occur if such judgments were rendered by the profession itself, which was to say, by the local faculty. Did history not teach that when colleagues are their brothers' keepers, personal vendettas, party dogmas, and petty tyrannies are very likely to result? The 1915 authors made no mention of the dangers of collective oversight. They sought only to convince the governing boards that anarchy would not ensue if they steered clear of extramural utterances and let the faculty police that zone. They pledged

> that the profession will earnestly guard those liberties without which it cannot rightly render its distinctive and indispensable service to society, [while] it will with equal earnestness seek to maintain such standards of professional character, and of scientific integrity and competency, as shall make it a fit instrument for that service.[84]

This was one place in the 1915 Declaration where epiphany supplanted explanation.

---

83. 1915 Declaration at 38; Appendix A at 404 (cited in note 13).
84. 1915 Declaration at 39; Appendix A at 405 (cited in note 13).

The 1925 Statement compressed this convoluted issue into two brief sentences:

   (a) A university or college should recognize that the teacher in speaking and writing outside of the institution upon subjects beyond the scope of his own field of study is entitled to precisely the same freedom and is subject to the same responsibility as attach to all other citizens.

   (b) If the extra-mural utterances of a teacher should be such as to raise grave doubts concerning his fitness for his position, the question should in all cases be submitted to an appropriate committee of the faculty of which he is a member.[85]

In all probability, these formulations, which came from the AAC presidents, were quite pleasing to the Lovejoy team. The AAUP had been agreeably surprised by the strong support given by the presidents to the principle embodied in (a). What was said in (b) contained one key idea in the 1915 Declaration—that extramural speech enjoyed no absolute immunity from the prosecutorial reach of the institution—and was half supportive of another—it agreed that the faculty should be the first to pass judgment in public speech cases (though it said nothing about whether or not that judgment would be the last). Conspicuously missing was sentence (c)—a list of speech offenses that faculty members were told they must assiduously avoid. Instead of reiterating the prohibitions of 1915, the 1925 Statement simply said that whenever anything said or written in the public sphere raises "great doubts" about the speaker's or writer's "fitness for his position" it may spark a disciplinary action. As a member of the committee on style, Lovejoy had an opportunity to refurbish the text in the course of polishing it, but he chose not to add the monitory furniture of 1915. His reason seems obvious enough. Uninhibited about using terms like "sensational," "hasty," and "unverified" as finger-waggings at members of the profession who would be the sole judges of their sweep, the leaders of the association shied away from doing so in a pact that left the faculty with no exclusive jurisdictions or conclusive verdicts, and that would have allowed emotion-laden terms of uncertain meaning to be used as lethal tools by governing boards and administrations. And at that time the AAC presidents did not insist on enumerating the punishable improprieties of faculty public speech.

But in a later day they would. During the next decade, the vituperations and petty conspiracies of cellular left-wing politics, along with attempts by the American Federation of Teachers ("AFT") on certain campuses to organize and mobilize the resentments of junior faculty, gave some administrators a bad case of jitters. These were mostly big-city, east and west coast aggravations; elsewhere, many administrators found that faculty public speech, strident in the best of times, had been made more so by the provocations of the Depression. By the mid-1930s a number of AAC presidents were convinced that the failure of the 1925 Statement to specify certain speech acts as unconscionable was a flaw in urgent need of correction. The Commission on Academic Freedom and Tenure owed its revival to this

---

85. 1925 Statement at 330 (cited in note 45).

particular dissatisfaction with the old agreement, and its agenda for the first formal meeting with the AAUP, held on its initiative, had mainly this revisionary end in view.

Most AAUP leaders held a different view—they thought it had become more necessary than ever to protect the citizen in the academic. The passing years had only reaffirmed what the founders had discovered: that academic freedom was most vulnerable to attack not in the laboratory or the lecture hall but in the civic forum. The association had had to deal with relatively few cases of alleged infringements on freedom of research, in part because researchers communicating with fellow researchers were seldom overheard or, if overheard, were not easily understood; in part because scholars and scientists whose discoveries disturbed the peace were likely to be rewarded for doing so, and winners of Nobel Prizes were not apt to complain to the AAUP. The association had dealt with more cases involving attacks on freedom of teaching, especially in proselytical colleges, but these, too, were relatively infrequent, probably because happenings in the classroom were almost as shielded from outside observation as were occurrences in a confessional. But extramural utterances—in earshot of unfriendly listeners, seldom in need of decoding, generally unsupported by the authority of the chair or the panache of a learned discipline—did not have the same protective covers yet could stir up the most potent foes. Most of the cases handled by Committee A up to that time had been academic tenure cases, pure if not always quite so simple; of those that were academic freedom cases, the vast majority were extramural freedom cases; in that group, the typical cause of an academic freedom violation was the dismissal either of a faculty member accused of riling an important public and thus bringing the institution into disrepute or else of a faculty member held to be insubordinate by administrators who equated loyalty to Alma Mater with subservience to themselves. Any proposal by the AAC presidents to strengthen the hands of administrators in an area where academics were so exposed was bound to make the AAUP leadership uneasy. "I fear our friends in the Association of American Colleges have in mind to find some way to cut down freedom of expression, especially off the campus," Cook wrote to Carlson. "We must watch our step and not allow anything of that kind to happen."[86]

The AAUP had read the intentions of their old partners correctly. The AAC delegates came to the first meeting with the AAUP in October 1937 with a stack of fresh proposals. They would repeat sentence (a) of the 1925 Statement, which applied only to academics speaking and writing outside the classroom and their own field of study. But they proposed to lay down new restrictions for teachers doing other things:

> The teacher speaking and writing on his own subject outside the classroom should do so soberly and seriously, not for notoriety of self-advertisement, under a deep sense of responsibility for the good name of the institution and the dignity of his profession.

---

86. Letter, Walter Wheeler Cook to Anton J. Carlson (October 28, 1936), 1940 Statement folder (AAUP files).

Or, as an alternative:

> In statements on his specialty outside the classroom the teacher's loyalty to the institution may necessarily curb the "freedom of speech" enjoyed by the citizen who is not an employed teacher.

Several closings to these pronouncements were suggested by the presidents:

> [T]he teacher in speaking and writing outside of the institution upon subjects beyond the scope of his own field of study is entitled to . . . the freedom [of] other citizens, [but he] should speak or write with the restraint and good taste of a scholar, recognizing that the public will judge the institution by his utterances [and should understand that extramural freedom] is not an aspect of academic freedom.

Or else:

> Even when faculty members make it clear that they are expressing their personal opinions the institution to which they belong will be held responsible for what they say.

In this flurry of new language, the 1925 provision for a faculty screening mechanism in public speech cases was brushed aside. Without actually saying so, the presidents left no doubt that enforcement of these stern commands should be an administrative responsibility.[87]

The AAC presidents had not reasoned very cogently on this issue: why should faculty members be under tighter constraints when they speak in public about something they have studied than when they deliver opinions on matters beyond their ken? But clearly, this issue inflamed them more than any other; on no other did they go to the trouble of formulating alternatives to the standing text, let alone do so with incendiary language. The AAUP representatives at this initial session (Himstead, Carlson, Cook, Tyler, Maguire, and Laprade, a Duke historian who had just become chairman of Committee A) sensed at once that the presidents had launched a groping assault on one of their bastion principles. They were not about to agree that extramural freedom should be separated from academic freedom, especially when the purpose of that divorce was to give institutional loyalty a higher value than freedom of expression. But they chose to avoid a head-on collision over words that had been offered provisionally, and more as fulminations than as polished prose. They proposed that their own Maguire, whose editorial skills had already been put to work on other parts of the academic freedom section, should try his hand at this troubling part, and all agreed that he should reconcile conflicting viewpoints in a sense-of-the-meeting note that would be entered retrospectively into the minutes. That tall order would have fateful consequences.

Then in his tenth year of service to the AAUP, Maguire had been hired by Tyler as a part-time legal consultant to assist the association in a threatened libel suit that did not materialize, and had stayed on as adviser to Committee A and as the secretary's alter ego. After Tyler's departure from the secretary's office, Maguire had been called upon less often to lend a helping hand. With the arrival of Himstead, who had a notorious incapacity to delegate authority

---

87. Typescript, AAC on "Academic Freedom," 1940 Statement folder (AAUP files).

and who thought that two lawyers on the premises were twice the desirable number, Maguire had moved to the outskirts of AAUP leadership. He did, however, retain the aura of someone who carried the best traditions of the AAUP in his head, and it was as keeper of the collective memory that he was called on to perform rewriting chores. Until he turned to the extramural freedom issue, no one in the AAUP questioned his efforts, but on that issue, Maguire turned out not to be on the same wavelength as many of his colleagues.

Maguire was, to the nth degree, a gentleman of the old school, a person convinced that there were certain things the civilized members of society simply did not say or do, and that the university, as the epitome of civilization, had special reason to contain speech within acknowledged chalk lines. Moreover, although he quarreled as a civil libertarian with the presidents' seeming indifference to the spectre of censorship, he shared their discomfort with the inflammatory rhetoric of academics on the political left and with the militant behavior of certain adherents to the AAUP's union rival. Just before he took on his rewriting assignment, he and other AAUP leaders had been accused by a left-wing faction on the AAUP Council of dragging their heels in the investigation of a *cause célèbre* of that period—the dismissal from Yale of an outspoken radical, Jerome Davis—and of helping to fashion a case report that whitewashed the administration of that University.[88] The accusation was in fact unfounded: Maguire's influence had waned before the Davis case arose. But what Maguire thought of the likes of Davis suggests where he might have come out if he had been more involved. "While my training has been liberal," he told this author in 1961,

> I must confess to fundamental conservative impulses. Were I president, with Professor Davis a member of my faculty, I am sure that his performance would arouse my resentment. To me it seems impossible that a man who talks and writes so much can be thoroughly careful, sound and wise. But, of course, one of the functions of a university is to suffer fools patiently.[89]

The emotions stirred up in him by the Davis affair—a genteel aversion checked only in part by a persevering tolerance—probably had not subsided when he cocked his pen at the extramural freedom text.

Maguire took as his point of departure the presumption that a faculty member in the role of citizen does not shed the obligations and responsibilities he assumes in the role of teacher or investigator. A customer in a millinery shop tries on but one hat at a time, but to Maguire, "the college or university teacher is *at once* a citizen, a member of a learned profession and an officer of an educational institution." This three-in-one image was a new one, though Maguire might have thought it went far back. The 1915 Declaration did assume that statements made by faculty members in all three roles could acquire material significance in hearings designed to test their

---

88. 1936 case folder, *Yale University-Davis* (AAUP files).

89. Interview with John M. Maguire (January 22, 1960) (verbatim record of five tapes in possession of the author).

professional fitness, but there was a difference between denying that categorical immunity attached to speech on certain topics or in certain forums and asserting that no academic role ever eclipses or displaces any other. Giving evidentiary value to all academic verbal acts in an internal hearing did something to undermine the dictum that academics were entitled to "precisely" the same freedom as other citizens, but positing a multiple persona that merged all academic roles and attendant responsibilities made that dictum much harder to sustain, and, rather than cling to a foolish inconsistency, Maguire let the dictum go. This did not mean that he drew no distinctions between civic and professional expressions. He did write that, when a college or university teacher "chooses to speak or act as a citizen, he should be absolutely free from professional or institutional censorship." These words might seem to preserve half the 1915 loaf, retaining the idea of institutional neutrality but rejecting the idea of guild control. In fact, they accomplished little; no sooner was the principle stated than it crumbled under the ethical baggage carried by the two other coterminous roles.

> But [the faculty member's] special position in the community imposes special obligations . . . . As a man of learning, he should never forget that the public may judge his whole profession by his utterances. As an educational officer, he must remember always the public inclination to identify him with his college or university and the unusual influence which his status gives him. Hence we must at all times be scrupulously accurate, must exercise appropriate restraint and good taste, and must make every effort to indicate that he is not an institutional spokesman, but expressing individual views. The price of freedom is perpetual personal responsibility for the welfare of his college or university, and of his profession.[90]

Having to be conscious of these obligations "at all times," the academic could not be entitled to special protections at some times; the everlasting "man of learning" and "educational officer" made hash of the idea of a special civic role.

Who was to enforce these stirring, omnipresent admonitions? Maguire did not say, in so many words. But his silence on this crucial point was eloquent. He broke with the Seligman past when he refused to hold that his admonitions were mostly to be enforced by the pressure of colleagues or a peer constabulary. He took issue with the 1925 Statement when, like the AAC presidents, he made no provision for a faculty screening mechanism. What, then, remained? He did not say "no" to the idea that the enforcement of this admonitions should be entrusted to individual consciences. But he would have had to have written a vigorous "yes" to give anyone the impression that his confidence in the faculty's inner moral light went that far. Maguire shared the founders' cold-eyed realism about the foibles of academics without sharing their romantic infatuation with guild control. Accordingly, although he would have been the last to urge lay boards and administrators to turn themselves into a thought police, he did not believe that their intervention in public speech cases would violate the natural order of things. If anything, he thought that a hard and fast statement designed to bar such interventions

---

90. Maguire draft, 1940 Statement folder (AAUP files).

would be both unnatural and futile. He told his colleagues that he dropped the 1925 provision for a faculty committee in speech cases because it "could be interpreted as requiring an administration to accept the decision of the [faculty] committee. That does not seem reasonable to me."[91] If this struck him as unreasonable, so too did the idea that an administration should accept the self-serving judgments of individual faculty members. Maguire's colleagues, and then the presidents read the spaces between his lines as holding that the ultimate disposition of speech cases should rest with the academic authorities, and the reticent author would never claim that he had been misunderstood on this point.

Circulated among the AAUP leaders, Maguire's draft touched off a cannonade of criticism seldom heard in this clubby sphere. Former secretary Cook, likely to pound hard when his free speech ardors were aroused, was extremely agitated. He declared that the list of admonitions abounded in ambiguous terms ("poor taste" indeed!); that effective political action was designed to arouse strong emotions and should not be held to a standard of "scrupulous accuracy"; that the verb "must" suggested binding rules of conduct rather than words of caution, the latter being the most that the monitory language of the treaty should imply.[92] Himstead, still feeling his way on these issues, was subdued, but Ralph Dewey, his assistant, described the Maguire draft as "question-begging, obscure as to meaning and . . . dangerous to the profession." Some feared that the list of admonitions would improve the weaponry of college presidents who sought to remove difficult professors and were looking for any stick, while others feared that it would arm administrators and professors specifically against the raucous radicals, and that the AAUP's enemies on the left, accusing it of collaboration, would have a field day at its expense. Maguire returned fire by arguing that "if we [are] to get anywhere in having a new statement adopted, we must thoroughly convince the presidents . . . of our willingness to assume responsibilities and [should not] ignore the weight of their opinions in the interest of inconsiderate faculty members." Cook pounced on this argument: "I am not speaking of the inconsiderate faculty members, but of the good men, like Laski, Frankfurter and Green, who would suffer" from the censorship Maguire would impose. Carlson defended Maguire's draft with the argument that it sought to do for professors what doctors and lawyers had done—that is, lay down norms of professional good behavior. But Tyler, breaking with his old friend on this issue, put his finger in the weakness in that analogy—the medical and legal professions had the power to discipline their own members, while Maguire handed over that crucial power to administrators.[93] Maguire got the worse of this heated argument. He would remain a member of the

91. Letter, John M. Maguire to associates (October 23, 1936) (Maguire files #10, AAUP files).

92. Letters, Walter Wheeler Cook to Ralph E. Himstead (October 12, 1937); Ralph E. Himstead to John M. Maguire (November 16, 1937); Ralph Dewey to Ralph E. Himstead (October 28, 1937) (all in AAUP files).

93. Letters, John M. Maguire to Ralph E. Himstead (November 18, 1937); Walter Wheeler Cook to Ralph E. Himstead (December 1, 1937); Anton J. Carlson to Ralph E. Himstead (November 3,

association for another decade, but his reputation among his colleagues would not recover from their criticisms, and he would never be called upon again to interpret basic AAUP philosophy.

It would be logical to suppose that Maguire's critics received his contribution with thanks, dropped it into the dead letter file, and promptly forgot all about it. What actually happened tells us why history is not a branch of logic. First of all, the Maguire draft, while it could be repudiated, could not be buried. It belonged to the meeting as a whole, and it was entered, as promised, on a record distributed to everyone, including the AAC presidents, who sang its praises. Second, because of the long intervals between all the meetings and the press of business at the next meeting, a year elapsed before the Maguire draft came up for consideration *en banc*. This delay gave the AAUP time to ask itself whether it had more to lose by renouncing the draft (with the possibility that this would lead to a split that would destroy the conference) or by doctoring it so as to retain most of its words but weaken its effect. The AAUP negotiators decided on the second course, reasoning that progress on the vital tenure front justified a prudent pullback on the academic freedom front, provided the retreat did not turn into a rout. Third, they refined the Maguire admonitions to the point where they could convince themselves they improved on any that had appeared before. Where the AAUP founders had placed themselves high above the hurly-burly of public life by expressing their dislike for "hasty" and "exaggerated" public utterances, and the AAC presidents' plea for the "serious" and the "sober" read like an ode to gloom or a temperance tract, the words Cook and Carlson chose seemed less cranky and more precise. This is the version that would wind up in the final text:

> Hence [the college or university teacher] should at all times be accurate, should exercise appropriate restraint, should show respect for the opinions of others, and should make every effort to indicate that he is not an institutional spokesman.

To be sure, these adjectival changes, though more than cosmetic, did not change Maguire's basic thrust. But the editors did find a way to alter the thrust without defacing the entire text. In President Wriston's view, once it was agreed that verbal conduct was a proper target of academic legislation and that guild regulation of that conduct could not work, the only escape from undesirable institutional censorship would be unconditional self-enforcement. Consequently, he suggested that the AAUP add the following sentence to the Maguire draft: "The judgment of what constitutes fulfillment of these obligations should rest with the individual." The AAUP jumped at the suggestion, not only to take the threat out of the text with one swift move, but to cut all the Gordian knots into which the issue of extramural freedom had been for so long entangled.[94]

1937); H. W. Tyler to Ralph E. Himstead (November 11, 1937), all in 1940 Statement folder (AAUP files).

94. Letter, Mark Ingraham to Ralph E. Himstead (January 27, 1940), attributed the self-enforcement proposal to Wriston. See Wriston, 25 AAC Bull at 115-16 (cited in note 64).

Put on the table at the third meeting held in October 1938, the amended AAUP draft drove a wide wedge between AAC locals and cosmopolitans. To President Dennis and his small-college allies—E. J. Jacqua, President of Scripps College and Meta Glass, President of Sweet Briar College—the idea that faculty members should be the final judges of their own indiscretions seemed dangerous and absurd. Like the AAUP professors, they too drew lessons from case experience—from tales of faculty members antagonizing potential donors with tactless comments, dispensing insider information so as to embarrass their institutions, exploiting colleague and student discontent to foment rebellion—and they very much doubted that the boors, the snitchers and the malcontents would be able to recognize, let alone reform, themselves. Dennis, the ringleader of the opposition to the AAUP on the issue of self-enforcement, fastened on the idea of setting up a nationwide external tribunal, perhaps made up of representatives of the AAC and the AAUP, to take jurisdiction over cases in which academics were accused of speech improprieties in public forums. He thought this would be a statesmanlike middle way between the folly of trusting faculty members to guide their own tongues and pens, and the danger of allowing administrators to serve as a board of censors. Wriston was withering in his opposition to this idea. He argued that most presidents, like himself, were too preoccupied with their own problems to go fishing in the troubled waters of other presidents; he pointed out that the verdict of an external tribunal would have to be carried out by local campus authorities, so that the whole scheme was really tantamount to institutional enforcement, albeit in several steps. Most of all, he took exception to the argument that faculty members were by character incapable of speaking with decorum and good sense. "It is with the individual that responsibility rests in other professions," he would write. "So let it be with us."[95] Wriston and Capen, plus a solid AAUP contingent, carried the day for self-enforcement. With this controversy and the long-pending tenure issue resolved, the conferees were able to agree on the entire package, and the so-called 1938 Statement was sent to the governing boards for ratification.[96]

Dennis could not sway the negotiating conference, but he did prevail at the highest level of the AAC. It is unclear just why the AAC board of directors took such strong exception to the self-enforcement sentence. Dennis tried to convince them that the sentence as it stood would debar not only institutional discipline but also administrative criticism of untoward speech. It is hard to imagine that the logic of this argument—giving one group the right to judge requires another group to seal its lips—won over many board members. More likely, those who had not been privy to the conference discussions and had to deduce intents from texts found the juxtaposed ideas in this passage

95. Wriston, 25 AAC Bull at 115-16 (cited in note 64).
96. Report of Joint Conference of Representatives of Association of American Colleges and American Association of University Professors on Academic Freedom and Tenure (October 17-18, 1938). Minutes of the Meeting of October 17-18, 1938, 1940 Statement folder (AAUP files).

troubling. Faculty members who promised to be on good behavior and who then insisted that they must decide whether they kept their promise might well have seemed to be more than a little disingenuous. Faculty members who conceded that the reputation of their college hung on their every wink and whisper but who would not let the college take actions in its own defense might well have appeared to be playing games with words. By combining Maguire's high-flown pledges with a growled "don't tread on me," the AAUP seems to have leased the worst of several worlds, seeking two desiderata in a way that appeared duplicitous, hoping to placate but sounding arrogant, and in the end seeming too clever by half. It was not easy to cut Gordian knots with a single swipe of a rusty sword.

A year after their first accord was rejected, the AAC and the AAUP met again to try to salvage a project on which they had lavished so much time and energy. Wriston and Capen did not attend the November 1940 meeting; Carl Wittke, dean of Oberlin College and a former chairman of Committee A, and W. O. Tolley, president of Allegheny College, replaced them as spokesmen for what might be called the permissive position on extramural freedom; Dennis came to hold forth as mulishly as before on his pet project. The AAUP delegation included two standbys, Carlson and Cook, who had some of the fight knocked out of them by the debacle of two years before; a number of newcomers who left no mark; and Himstead, now three years into his term of office and much more self-confident than before. Himstead had not taken a strong position on the extramural freedom issue, in part because he did not follow all its sinuosities, but mostly because he rated this issue distinctly secondary to the issue of tenure, on which he was determined to take an unyielding stand. Without clear ideas about how to break the impasse but determined to do it, he stumbled on a solution halfway into the final session:

DENNIS: All I ask is that there shall be some impartial tribunal to try the case of a professor who acts so foolishly that he risks his usefulness . . . . I do not want a man to be an absolute judge in his own case.

HIMSTEAD: If a professor's utterances are a reason for dismissal . . . we already have a provision [under the tenure rules] for an institutional hearing.

DENNIS: Isn't that reserved for a professor who kills somebody . . . ?

HIMSTEAD: No. If a member of your faculty would start making speeches advocating free love, you have provisions for handling it right here in the [tenure and due process] section of the Statement.

DENNIS: If you agree to that, there is nothing between us.[97]

The two retired to put their newfound harmony into treaty language, and they returned with a set of interpretive comments that would be pinned to the 1940 Statement as a footnote to its paragraph on extramural freedom. At the core of these comments lay Himstead's breakthrough concession:

if the administration of a college or university feels that a teacher has not observed the admonitions [the reference was to the Maguire *piece de resistance* as amended] and believes that the extramural utterances of the teacher have been such as to raise grave

---

97. Minutes of the Joint Conference of Representatives of the Association of American Colleges and American Association of Professors on Academic Freedom and Tenure at 22 (November 8, 1940), 1940 Statement folder (AAUP files).

doubts concerning his fitness for his position, it may proceed to file charges under Paragraph (a) of the section on Academic Tenure.

To administrators who did avail themselves of the judicial machinery of the tenure system, Himstead and Dennis addressed these warnings: "[i]n pressing such charges the administration should remember that teachers are citizens and should be accorded the freedom of citizens"; "in such cases the administration must assume full responsibility" and the AAUP and AAC "are free to make an investigation." The conference unanimously endorsed this compromise, and one of the great stumbling blocks in the way of ratification by the AAC governing board was removed.[98]

Afterwards, many AAUP members and officials would be uncertain about just what the pact-partners had agreed to. One extramural freedom case in particular would show that what had been settled in script had not necessarily been settled in many minds. In 1960, the Board of Regents of the University of Illinois dismissed Leo F. Koch, an assistant professor of Biology, for writing a letter to a student newspaper condoning premarital sexual intercourse between consenting students (Himstead's hypothetical curiously come alive!). To convince the AAUP investigators and the academic world that Koch's academic freedom had not been violated by its action, the board came up with findings that tracked the 1940 Statement: Koch, it held, had not adhered to the standards of "accuracy," "restraint," "respect for others," and dissociation from his institution prescribed by that code for extramural utterances, and he could thus be validly discharged after a due process hearing for not living up to his academic responsibilities. The AAUP team of investigators, headed by Professor Thomas I. Emerson of the Yale Law School, plus every member of Committee A, agreed that the Illinois administration had not accorded Koch adequate due process; for this reason, the association voted for censure. But a sharp internal division arose over whether any institutional sanction—even the relatively mild one of a reprimand, which had been recommended by a faculty hearing body—could be imposed on Koch under the 1940 Statement. Professor Emerson, taking vigorous exception to the view that only "responsible" extramural utterances were protected under the insigne of academic freedom, considered the passages in the 1940 Statement so marred by backing and filling as to be almost meaningless. Several members of Committee A, calling attention to the postulate that academics should be accorded the freedom of citizens, argued that the 1940 Statement did not sanction occupational punishments for allegedly untoward public speech. But a majority of the committee, after reviewing the history of failed attempts to find alternatives, concluded that the interpretive footnote plainly did say that a failure to adhere to the verbal standards laid down for extramural utterances could be used by an administration as a ground for dismissal.[99]

---

98. Footnotes, 1940 Statement, *1984 AAUP Red Book* at 4-5 (cited in note 1).
99. *The University of Illinois, Report of the Ad Hoc Committee*, and *Academic Responsibility; Statement of the Ad Hoc Committee in the* Koch *Case*, 49 AAUP Bull 25-43 (1963).

From a yet more distant perspective, it seems abundantly clear today that the Committee A majority in the Koch case was correct. Thanks to Himstead's late-hour concession, the 1940 Statement did permit the regents of a university to enforce its exhortations through regular disciplinary procedures. And more than Himstead realized, his conversion had broad consequences. For one thing, by admitting that extramural utterances could be grist for the ordinary mills of academic discipline, Himstead stripped them of the unique credentials they had held in AAUP's eyes since 1915. Nor was their privileged position restored by anything agreed to in the footnote. The warning that the AAUP reserved the right to intervene in such cases was no more than a fig leaf: the AAUP was free to intervene in any kind of case and few believed that an administration would be intimidated by the AAUP's threat to loose the fateful lightning of its terrible swift sword. The other warning—that administrators pressing charges should accord faculty members the rights of citizens—was at most a plea for judicial leniency, not for prosecutorial restraint, since it was designed to accompany rather than deter a disciplinary action. For another thing, if the words uttered by professors in a civic context are punishable, a fortiori so too are words spoken in their classrooms. As clarified by Himstead, the admonitions of the 1940 Statement were thus not just right-sounding but empty; they were precepts without teeth.

To the academic freedom purist, the AAUP may seem to have suffered an ignominious defeat through this compromise. In reality, this long-time defender of academic freedom actually scored a number of victories, though these do not leap to the eye of the perfectionist. First of all, it headed off an attempt by the presidents to detach extramural freedom from its academic freedom moorings. This may look like a Pyrrhic victory to those who think that the civic utterances of academics find a safer haven in the first amendment to the Constitution than in a spongy professional norm. But even today it may be doubted that the law is the citizen-academics' shepherd who invariably sees to it that they shall not want, and it is certain that untying the triadic bundle in 1940 would have weakened the professional defenses of academics whose public words came back to haunt them in a disciplinary action on their home grounds. Secondly, the AAUP's concessionary posture may well have done more for academic freedom in the long run than would the less-yielding stance it at first preferred. In the world of the Henry Wristons, academic freedom was a cultural familiar in need of little explanation and no apology, but in the large expanse of academic America represented by E. C. Dennis, it was still a cultural stranger, tolerated for its reputation but eyed with puzzlement and mistrust. The formulations the AAUP came up with—the role analysis, the monitory language, the enforcement give-back—should be read not simply for their noetic meaning, but as placating gestures designed to acculturate academic authorities to a concept they still regarded as somewhat alien. And it seems safe to conclude that its words did have that designed effect, that academic freedom did find a comfortable home in all corners of the nation, precisely because it did not embolden faculty members to do their worst or utterly shackle academic administrations.

Finally, as a practical matter, Himstead's key concession—that the machinery set up to test charges of professional shortcomings and misdemeanors may be used to test a charge of irresponsible public utterance too—did not put extramural freedom at significantly greater risk than before. Indeed, Himstead was confident that invoking this procedure would lessen the frequency of such prosecutions. His deprivileging of civic utterances, like the waiving of conclusive faculty verdicts and the general decline of a guild esprit, did contribute to the slide toward ordinariness that is so prominent a part of this story. But "ordinary" in this instance did not imply "routine." Even as the two associations were locking horns over constraints on extramural freedom, they were engaged in a parallel conflict over the reform of academic tenure. The further judicialization of the dismissal process, one of the key reforms Himstead urged upon the presidents, promised to deter wrongful punishments for civic speech as well as to discourage the wrongful use of that instrument for other ends. If Himstead took concession to be the better part of valor in the freedom area, he did so largely because he assumed it would be made innocuous by a breakthrough he hoped to accomplish somewhere else.

IV

Reform

In the mid-1930s, an AAUP survey of a representative sample of American academic institutions, 125 in all, revealed that close to half of them appointed all their faculty members on an annual basis. Mostly in the public sector and largely concentrated in the South and West, these thoroughgoing annualists were not all cut from the same cloth. Some of them clung to the Draconian practice, common in public institutions during the nineteenth and early twentieth centuries, of vacating all positions at the end of every year and reappointing only those former incumbents who could pass a de novo test. Most of the others renewed the appointments of their faculty members, especially those of high professorial rank, with little re-evaluation, and sometimes as a matter of course. But all of them, whether or not they were engaged in the vascular opening and closing of positions, did keep all of their faculty members on short-term, renewable appointments, and so could be labelled, even by the definitions of that time, as lacking a system of tenure.[100] The rest of the 1930s sample—mostly Eastern and private institutions, together with the flagship public universities of the Midwest and West— generally offered all faculty members at the rank of full professor (and quite often the rank of associate professor too) an appointment that bore no date of expiration and was variously termed "continuous," "indefinite," or

---

100. Malcolm W. Willey, *Depression, Recovery and Higher Education* 80-81 (McGraw Hill, 1937).

"permanent." By definition, such an appointment was continued without having to be explicitly renewed; in many places, such an appointment would not be discontinued unless a serious dereliction, rather than a somewhat reduced level of performance or an inability to meet a raised level of expectation, came to light. But seldom was it understood that such an appointment could not be terminated unless the holder of it had been formally accused of an offense, the accusation had been weighed in a campus hearing, and the accuser—invariably the administration—had carried the burden of proof. And hardly ever did it mean that charges intended to bring about the termination of such an appointment had to be heard by a committee of the affected teacher's peers, which would judge their veracity and seriousness. Did academics so appointed have tenure prior to 1940? Surely so ancient an idea as tenure did not wait until well into this century to make its first American appearance. Tenure as a well-grounded expectation—that is to say, as a deservedly confident belief that one's appointment would be allowed to continue until resignation or retirement—was real enough: it fed on a variety of authoritative signals, informal understandings, personal ties, and calming precedents. Tenure as a retrospective fact—in other words, long incumbency—was not uncommon, thanks to the salubriousness of the academic work environment as well as to the issuance of nonexpiring employment contracts. But tenure as we know it today—as a set of due process rights that go with the acquisition of a certain status, everyone being eligible for that status after serving a fixed number of years—did not exist or else existed only in seed even in the mainstream universities. There is much to be said for what may be called "premodern" tenure. A deeper sense of security may well be imparted by the trust formed in face-to-face relationships than in the distrusts embodied in formal rules. But *Gemeinschaft* works better than *Gesellschaft* only when it is not severely tested—in the interstices of human crises, so to speak. Once the members of a community have a falling out and the sentimental bond is broken, the separated parties are likely to rue the lack of clarity, rationality, predictability, and formal justice that are the gifts of modern tenure rules.

Overall, there were many more assistant professors and instructors than full and associate professors among the faculty members surveyed in the 1930s. Where it was presumed that the dignity of a senior professorship forbade the periodic testing of its incumbent, it was also presumed that the inexperience or as yet unfulfilled promise of a junior faculty member warranted appointments of short duration—three years at the most, one year as a rule. Superficially, it would appear that a majority of the junior faculty members in institutions practicing premodern tenure were on all fours with every faculty member in institutions without tenure, in that they too could be turned out of office by inaction (when their contracted-for time ran out) and sub silentio (without a finding of cause or even a required explanation). But those who lived the low-rank life in places that gave tenure to their high-ranked members faced an opportunity and experienced a frustration not known to their undifferentiated neighbors. The presence of two classes of tenants in the house of learning, one elevated by rank above the other and therefore spared the periodic threat of eviction, had the potential of turning the lower floor into a proving ground from which qualified persons could be lifted out of insecurity on the elevator of promotion. But few institutions of higher learning set a limit on the number of times short-term leases could be renewed, or fixed a particular moment in the employment cycle when those found meritorious would rise to their just deserts. As a result, a system was created in which teachers of lesser rank, appointed time and again, could compile as many years of service as their higher-ranking colleagues without ever gaining surcease of the pain of temporariness or an end to bouts of springtime nervousness when contract renewal time came round.[101]

These flaws in the American tenure system were not disclosed to the AAUP for the first time in the 1930s; they had been evident to it since its founding, indeed they had done much to precipitate its founding. And the AAUP had wasted no time in advancing practical solutions. In 1915, the Seligman authors, concerned about the lack of judiciality in the dismissal process, proposed that all eligible faculty members "should be entitled, before dismissal, to have the charges against them stated in writing in specific terms" and—a major demand—that they should receive a "fair trial" on those charges before a judicial body composed of their institutional peers. "At such trial," they went on to say, "the teacher accused should have full opportunity to present evidence"; in cases where the charge was professional incompetence, they were to be able to introduce the testimony of departmental colleagues and fellow specialists from other institutions. But not everyone was eligible for such a hearing—not by a long shot. To the founders, the only faculty members entitled to peer-run hearings before dismissal were the holders of permanent appointments (the rest received refusals of reappointment, not dismissals), and the only faculty members

---

101. This overview of the status of academic tenure during the negotiation and the adoption of the 1940 Statement is based on a number of national surveys: an incomplete though suggestive survey conducted by W. W. Cook for the association in 1931, 18 AAUP Bull 255-57 (1932); stenographic minutes of Council discussion of that report, Council Minutes (AAUP files); Wildred M. Mallon, *Faculty Ranks, Tenure and Academic Freedom*, 39 Nat'l Catholic Educ Ass'n Bull 177 (1942); Loya Metzger, Professors in Trouble (doctoral dissertation, Columbia Univ, 1978) (study of institutions with and without written rules of tenure during the 1930s); Cecil Winfield Scott, *Indefinite Teacher Tenure: A Critical Study of the Historical, Legal, Operative and Comparative Aspects* (Columbia Univ Press, 1934); National Education Association, *Tenure Policies and Procedures in Teacher's Colleges* (NEA Press, 1943); Paul Clare Reinert, *Faculty Tenure in Colleges and Universities from 1900 to 1940* (St Louis Univ Press, 1946). For a brief history of academic tenure, see Walter P. Metzger, *Academic Tenure in America: A Historical Essay*, in William R. Keast, ed, *Faculty Tenure* 93 (Jossey-Bass, 1973). For surveys that followed the framing of the 1940 Statement and that may measure changes it may well have helped to bring about, see Clark Byse, *Tenure in American Higher Education: Plans, Practices and the Law* (Cornell Univ Press, 1959); Martin A. Trow, *The Distribution of Academic Tenure in American Higher Education* (Carnegie Commission on Higher Education, 1972); W. Todd Furniss, *Faculty Tenure and Contract Systems: Current Practice* (ACE Special Report) (July 27, 1972); Paul Dressel, *A Review of the Tenure Policies of Thirty-One Major Universities*, 44 Educ Rev 243-53 (July 1963); Frank Atelsak, *Tenure Practices at Four Year Colleges and Universities* (ACE, 1980).

entitled to permanent employment were professors, associate professors, and "everyone above the grade of instructor . . . after ten years of service."

These proposals were in direct response to the state of affairs uncovered by the first investigations. To counter the claim of one private university that a veteran assistant professor had no more right to a formal hearing than the merest tyro in that rank, the Seligman authors argued that after a while—after a long while—the disability that ordinarily attached to a low professorship should cease to exist. Several public universities claimed that they were legally incapable of making contracts for longer than the time period covered by legislative appropriations; to this the Seligman group replied that governing boards could make long-term commitments which, if not legally enforceable, would nevertheless be morally binding. In many cases on the first year's docket, a president's word in the trustees' ears was the sum of the dismissal process. Responding to this immediate reality but drawing on very distant, even medieval, precedents, the Seligman group proposed that a faculty hearing body be interposed between administration and governing boards to break into and monitor their auricular communications.[102]

But this generation of AAUP leaders was too locked into the assumptions of their time to propose deeper-going reforms. For one thing, beyond insisting that specific charges be put in writing, that relevant evidence should be introduced and that the proceeding be "fair," they had nothing to say about how the faculty should conduct a dismissal hearing: without further elucidation, they left it to the judgment of scholars to set the rules for such proceedings. Their low interest in procedural instruction was a reflection of their high degree of professional self-romanticization. They simply took it for granted that faculty members were equipped by career-long training to weigh evidence with abundant care and treat their colleagues justly. Significantly, they called for "fairness," a quality hard to define but evident to gentlefolk when they saw it, and not for "academic due process," a phrase of later coinage, which mimicked the methodology of the courts.

Similarly, the 1915 criteria of eligibility for the judicial benefits of tenure, though obviously at odds with blanket denials of tenure, did very little to relieve the blocked mobility that could beset a two-tier system. The conventional wisdom of 1915 held that faculty rank, a sure testimonial of current merit, should be the key determinant of eligibility for tenure. The founders did not fundamentally disagree. They proposed that all full and associate professors should be given a permanent appointment regardless of their length of service; that it should take as many as ten years before a statute of limitations could be invoked to offset the inconsequence of an assistant professorship; and that this veterans' bonus should not be extended to instructors, who under their proposals were allowed to labor indefinitely in that lowly grade.

---

102. 1915 Declaration at 41-42; Appendix A at 405-06 (cited in note 13).

Even in this undeveloped state, the reforms with which the young AAUP became identified met with considerable resistance. Before World War I, administrative opposition centered on the role reversal implicit in a faculty hearing of dismissal charges. Calling on the president to be a charge-maker rather than a discharge-maker, the AAUP was asking that he place himself on a level with the professor he accused and play the part of a humble adversary before a faculty clad in judicial robes. This was asking a great deal at a time when the academic executive ego was not exactly of the shrinking kind.[103] After the war, some experts in industrial work psychology held that job security hurt productivity and that everyone, even professors, performed better when pressured by market threats.

All the more, then, was the AAUP gratified by the AAC's measured acceptance of parts of its tenure program. The AAC team headed by Dean Cole had signalled that there would be no attack on the principle of tenure at the Washington conference—and there wasn't any. Both sides readily agreed that "[i]t is desirable that termination of a permanent or long-term appointment for cause should regularly require action by both a faculty committee and the governing board of the college." "Desirable" fell a good deal short of "necessary"; still, the AAUP had reason to be pleased that presidents, who might have insisted that their wishes in the matter of dismissals should be treated as foregone conclusions, consented to any faculty intermediation at all. Beyond this, the two sides took a small step toward making the dismissal process more judicial when they agreed that "in all cases where the facts are in dispute, the accused teacher should always have the opportunity to face his accusers" before "all bodies that pass judgment upon his case." In this acknowledgement of the importance of confrontation, the idea of academic due process for the first time glimmered.[104]

Glad that their worst fears were pleasantly disappointed, the AAUP leaders were not disposed to lament their unsuccesses. In reviewing their handiwork before the AAUP council, they passed over the fact that they had ducked the critical issue of tenure eligibility. The 1925 Statement referred to "temporary" or "short-term" appointments, which could be terminated merely by giving timely notice, and "permanent" or "long-term" appointments, which could be terminated only for cause and after a full-dress hearing. It said nothing, however, about what entitled a faculty member to pass from one state to the other. The AAC presidents had no desire to make tenure one of the privileges of rank, possibly because they feared that so many faculty members had been paid in the psychic currency of title in lieu of the coin of the realm that the linkage would result in massive and unanticipated enfranchisements. The AAUP professors made no move to link academics'

---

103. For examples of presidential resistance to peer review in dismissal cases, see Andrew S. Draper, *The University President*, 97 Atlantic Monthly 35 (1906); C. R. Van Hise, *The Appointment and Tenure of University Professors*, 12 AAU J Proc 61-62 (1910); Merle Curti, 2 *The University of Wisconsin; a History, 1848-1925* 43, 55-56 (Univ of Wisconsin Press, 1949).

104. 1925 Statement at 330, 331 (cited in note 45).

status to years of service, probably because they thought it unprofessional to award a high honor to mere longevity. Thus, both sides could derive some satisfaction from a statement about "being" that ignored the question of "becoming."[105]

The Great Depression brought the AAUP to a turning point in its thinking about tenure reform. Unlike later downturns in the American academic economy, this unprecedented one did not, even in its most severe early years, cause the dismissal of many tenured faculty members. The chief economies exacted at the expense of their group came from cuts in nominal salaries (in deflationary times this did not produce a commensurate cut in purchasing power), slower rates of promotion from associate to full professor, and attrition. It was hard to tell whether the paucity of dismissals was attributable more to the protections of tenure than to the professional and social standing of the tenured. There was no doubt, however, that without the armor against adversity provided by a permanent appointment, the less well-established junior faculty could be naked before the storm. To be sure, hard times did not take their worst toll on this group by contracting their ranks. Too many institutions held on to inexpensive low-level beginners to allow their demographic profile to change dramatically. But many short-term contracts did run out and were not renewed, and these were bound to have chilling demonstration effects for all. Throughout the country, the competition for nontenure positions tended to turn new Ph.D.s into scramblers for openings that demanded heavy workloads at cut-rate pay, and turned the currently employed into supplicants for continued favor. In times of relative prosperity, external opportunity could take the edge off internal discontents. During the Depression years, this safety valve went seriously out of kilter: for some time, both the vacancy rate at lower rank levels and the rate of tenure promotion sank sharply; afterwards they rose somewhat but did not return to former levels.[106]

The plight of the academic underclass during the Depression gave the AAUP a strong compassionate reason for reopening negotiations with the AAC; that it and the AFT were vying at this time for the affections of that constituency gave it a pragmatic sanction for doing so as well. Still, when they first met with the AAC presidents after the onset of the Depression, the AAUP professors were not yet ready to recommend a radical change of course. Maguire's reworking of the 1925 agreement still treated transience and permanence as categories without connective tissue. A tentative restatement

105. The AAC presidents wanted to allow for renewable contracts of considerable duration as a third option between transience and permanence: the AAUP used a syntactic form ("or" rather than "and") that accepted long-term appointments only as a possible alternative to short-term and permanent ones but did not accept them as a standing *tertium quid*. The AAUP professors did not force the issue, apparently convinced that even a static statement on eligibility rebuked the idea that an entire faculty might properly consist of temporary help, and in this way did tenure a good turn. But this formulation surely did not give the untenured army in tenure-granting places a good turn: for all these pact-writers had to say, permanent temporariness could continue to be their lot.

106. Willey, *Depression, Recovery and Higher Education*, chaps 2-3 (cited in note 100).

of the AAUP's position drawn up by Cook and used as a working draft for the next two meetings moved away from 1925 but could not shake the major presuppositions of 1915. It called for the tenuring of everyone in the upper professional ranks and everyone in the ranks below who had put in more than a certain number of years of service. This two-variable set was rife with complexities and complications, which the conferees puzzled and battled over for some time.[107]

It took the AAUP general secretary almost two years fully to convince his colleagues that tenure should be completely divorced from rank and tied exclusively to years of service. It had not been obvious to Himstead that an award given once or twice in a lifetime and almost never repossessed was a more accurate gauge of academic merit than the repeated votes of confidence implied in a string of reappointments. What did become obvious to him was that no criterion of eligibility other than a temporal one offered the junior members of the profession so many ramified and vital protections. The program of tenure reform that became his passion had a logic to it, which can be laid out in enumerated steps:

1. AAUP investigators often ran up against the administrative contention that old hands on unrenewed term appointments gained nothing from their length of employment that would entitle them to a dismissal hearing. This argument often served to frustrate an inquiry into underlying administrative motivations and sometimes helped administrations side-step censure. Himstead was quick to see that the best way to counter this argument was to uphold the principle that tenure rights accrue to faculty members after so many turns of the service clock and do not depend on the institution's contract and promotion policies. Destined to be called "de facto tenure," this way of liberating the tenure rights of veterans from the explicit say-so of the institution would become, after 1940, an indispensable tool of AAUP case analysis.[108]

2. A promotion in rank had the quality of an impromptu act; a completed work period had the quality of a rite of passage. Himstead was not the first to call this period a "probationary" one; that word, in limited academic use, was drafted into the formal AAUP vocabulary by Cook, who may have borrowed it from the Protestant ministry or from the federal civil service. Later, a few academic critics, half-facetiously mistaking its etymology, would complain that the term was rather too suggestive of the suspended sentences meted out to persons convicted of minor crimes or of the time spent in Coventry by students required to atone for high jinks or low grades. But Cook's associates

107. 1937 Cook Draft, 1940 Statement folder (AAUP files).

108. Nothing did more to focus AAUP attention on the importance of a time standard for tenure than the negative reception of its report on the *Yale University-Davis* case (see note 88). In it, the association had ruled that an associate professor with thirteen years of service was not entitled to a dismissal on hearing charges simply because the institution had not seen fit to promote him to tenure. Lovejoy, who was still watching out for his baby now grown up, thought this was a posture the organization dare not continue to hold. "We must decide upon what *we* regard as a justifiable period during which a teacher may be recognized *by us* as on probationary status." Record, 1937 Annual Meeting (AAUP files).

thought "probationary" was an inspired loan word, admirably suited to describe the character, timing, and purpose of one segment of the employment stint. The word suggested that this period was a time of trial, not a time for coasting; that its aim was to give the novitiate the opportunities of an internship and the institution the benefits of a second look; that it was to start close to the individual's arrival and end after a finite amount of time; that it should be regular and calculable, not capricious or ad hoc. Himstead's contribution to the development of the probation concept was to stress its helpfulness to the probationer. For him, the chief benefit of this device was not that it gave the institution a chance to check its gate evaluation of recruits with knowledge acquired from closer observation, but that it gave flesh to the hope that the journeymen years of academics would be treated as pretenure years and not as a collection bin for cheap, submissive, and unhopeful labor. He hammered away at the Cook proposal because he feared that any opening of a second road to tenure through the discretionary award of title prizes would diminish the use and usefulness of the probationary scheme.

3. Not alone among his colleagues but with an inimitable doggedness, Himstead insisted that the number of years anyone could spend in probationary service should be fixed at a single maximum that would apply to every college and university in the country. The root of this ambition was not an abstract devotion to common standards (had he made a fetish of uniformity, he would also have insisted on a universal minimum) but a practical desire to shore up his program of reform at its potentially weakest points. An unending probationary period would not be a probationary period but a career-long purgatory; even an open-ended probationary period could threaten to devour most of a faculty member's working life. The fixed star in Himstead's constellation of beliefs was that the welfare of the academic profession as well as the peace of mind of the persons in it required vigilance against the evil of permanent transience. The obvious countermeasure was to cap the number of probationary years. When the presidents proposed that each institution set the cap as it saw fit, Himstead led the AAUP's resistance to the proposal, his principle objection being that a forest of probationary periods of different lengths, all equally valid, would make it impossible for the organized profession to criticize an overrun or even define excess. At the start, Himstead, like most of his colleagues, thought that five years on probation was just right; in the course of the negotiations, he went up to six; in the climactic last meeting, to appease the pact-partners, he accepted seven. He found no cabalistic magic in any of these numbers—five, six, or seven all had the desirable property of falling between the very few years of probationary service advocated by the teachers' union and rejected by the AAUP as amounting to instant tenure, and the founders' double-digit standard, which would have alienated from the AAUP most academics under thirty or thirty-five.[109] For Himstead, the important thing was to establish a

---

109. Not every AAUP leader thought that any intermediate number would do. Cook believed that "every time we add a year, it puts us at a greater disadvantage with the teachers' union."

broadly accepted, fixed, and universal limit to the number of years an academic professional could work in an academic institution without the protections of academic tenure, and for this purpose, while extreme numbers were to be avoided, a number of numbers would do.

4. It was not lost on Himstead that lasting impermanence could be the lot of academics even if every institution were to limit its probationary period to five, six, or seven years. A faculty member who undergoes a trial period runs the risk of being tried and found wanting—or at least unwanted. Under the constraints of the proposed reform, a negative judgment reached (with due notice) close to the end of the permitted time period would have the inescapable effect of compelling the individual to pack up and go. And then what? To try again somewhere else and, that failing, try again? The vision of junior faculty members wandering like so many Ishmaels from one academic institution to another, serving as probationers in one place until their allotted years were up and then being hired as beginners in another, was disturbing to the leaders of the AAUP, and to no one more than Himstead. The answer they came up with (it was necessarily a formulaic answer) was to provide that all the years a person spent in the profession were to count as probationary years of service in the current institution, although by mutual agreement no more than three years need be so credited. Included in the 1940 Statement, the carryover credit provision added another computation to the time-counts featured by a modern tenure system. The seven-year rule would become broadly accepted (except in some of the highest reaches of academe), but the notion that probationary years spent at institution X were fungible with probationary years spent at institution Y, when each institution is morally certain that it is superior to the other, was to live a troubled life.

5. Most of the conceptual differences between Himstead and his colleagues were worked out before the important October 1938 meeting with the presidents; one difference, however, was not. This had to do with the acceptability of the policy of "up or out," a short-hand used to describe the systematic refusal by an institution to retain and thus grant tenure to a terminal probationer it does not think highly enough of to promote. Himstead became deeply alarmed when he learned that Harvard and Yale, in a major remodeling of their tenure rules begun in 1938, welded the principle of tenure after a period of probation to the practice of automatic extrusion barring a coincident rise in rank.[110] Such a policy, he lamented, would cause high turnover among the younger faculty, since their ranks were overcrowded and the finances of academic institutions did not permit much population growth at the top. He surmised that the expellees from Harvard and Yale would not find it difficult to land new positions, but he dreaded to think of

---

Wriston and Capen, as anti-union as any of their colleagues, agreed, and beseeched their colleagues not to press for the highest possible number lest a battle be won but a war be lost. Minutes of the Joint Conference, October 1938 (AAUP files).

110. *Academic Tenure and Promotion in a Situation of Increasing Equilibrium*, papers presented by Dean George H. Chase of Harvard University and Dean Edgar S. Furniss of Yale University, in Association of American Universities, *42nd Annual Conference*, 98-106 (Univ of Chicago, 1940).

what would happen to the refugees from such a policy if it were generally adopted by colleges and universities and they could not count on being resettled by trading on the reputations of their past employers. For him, the proper policy was "in or out": at the end of the probationary period, faculty members may stay with tenure or else leave, but if they stay they may do so at as low a rank as instructor and with no advance in pay. He tried to get colleagues to agree and he wanted the negotiated draft to show that "up or out" was "not in harmony with our principles."[111] A number of his confreres begged to disagree. "What difference does it make to our Association," asked Mark Ingraham, if Harvard's authorities "don't want anybody they cannot promote?" "We are interested in the probationary period," not in the grounds for judging tenure-worthiness after that course is run. Laprade noted that, under their new rules, Harvard's authorities were "forcing themselves to make up their minds in a much shorter time [eight years] than they ever did before" and were thus meeting a critical AAUP objective. Arthur N. Holcombe, Professor of Government at Harvard and a council member, tried unsuccessfully to budge the general secretary by dilating on the AAUP-ishness of the new rules and by emphasizing that the President of Harvard, James B. Conant, had just been appointed to the AAC commission where the AAUP could depend on his being a force for good.[112]

The text of the 1940 Statement shows that this disagreement ended in a stand-off. "After the expiration of a probationary period, teachers or investigators should have permanent or continuous tenure . . . . Notice shall be given at least one year prior to the expiration of the probationary period if the teacher is not to be continued in service after the expiration of that period." These words do not prohibit "up or out": if the institution wishes to clothe tenure with the trappings of title (or a jump in monetary compensation or a more ample fringe), it is entirely at liberty to do so. But neither do these words prohibit or even discourage "in or out"—Himstead's concession to frugality in the interest of security. Institutions that would justify tenure quotas on the ground that they could not afford to pay for more tenured professors would have themselves, not the 1940 Statement, to blame.

Amid these efforts to reform the rules of tenure, where did the AAUP's pact-partners stand? No one should be astonished to learn that the AAC presidents were taken aback by the unfolding of a blueprint for tenure reform that went far beyond the 1925 Statement and the limited amendments to it that had been broached in the early sessions, or that they raised objections to it, one serious enough to threaten the negotiations. But to anyone acquainted with the contemporary discourse on this subject, it is striking that at no time did the AAC presidents, whether of the McConaughy or the Wriston wing, call the concept of tenure itself into question. One would hunt in vain

---

111. Ralph E. Himstead at the AAUP Council meetings of December 1939 and April 1940, Council Stenographic Records and Council Letters (1940) (AAUP files).

112. Letter, Mark Ingraham to Ralph E. Himstead (February 4, 1939), Ingraham folder; Council Stenographic Records, April 1940 (AAUP files).

through the transcripts of these meetings for a reference to tenured professors as "deadwood" or to the equation between aging and decaying that reflects the cultural gerontophobia latent in that warehouse metaphor. One would conduct a futile search for a presidential comment to the effect that universal short-term contracts, permitting periodic review and easy discharge, were needed to weed out the indolent or incompetent and prevent the hangers-on from going slack. One would occasionally find a worried estimate of the institutional cost of this or that tenure feature, but one would not find a single attempt to lay the distortions of the academic labor market or the low rate of academic productivity at the door of tenure. This was not the silence of persons too filled with loathing to enter into argument or too resigned to an evil to try to fight it; by every indication the presidents regarded tenure as beneficial and the arguments in favor of it as beyond debate. Their unanimity on this fundamental point suggests that they reflected no eccentric predilection; the executive folk wisdom of that day taught them many times over that in the faculty's easy removability lay the intrusive governing board's opportunity, and that being able to cite the obstacle of tenure enabled a president more safely to refuse to carry out its meddlesome command. The importance of this concurrence with the AAUP over fundamentals cannot be overestimated. It is safe to say that tenure would never have taken root in this country if the presidents had not been able to see the good of it, and that it would be moribund today, despite subsequent constitutional and legal developments in its favor, if they did not have strong self-interested and disinterested reasons for keeping it alive.

The AAC criticized the AAUP's new tenure plan not for its faulty philosophy but for its lack of flexibility. Maintaining flexibility in tenure matters had always been one of the AAC's primary objects in these negotiations. In the early discussions, before the AAUP's initiative completely parted company with the past, the presidents again attempted to counter the stark alternative of transient or permanent, nontenured or tenured, by introducing an intermediate category.[113] During the next phase, as the AAUP plan gathered Himstead touches, the presidents looked for ways by which the tenure timetable could be bent by administrative discretion to meet individual contingencies and varying institutional needs. By October 1938, however, Wriston and his coterie of major university presidents had been persuaded that the AAUP plan should be supported and that the goal of greater flexibility, except on small numerical details, should be renounced. This defection had two effects: it cast the small college presidents, Dennis as usual in the lead, in the role of intransigents and spoilers with regard to tenure as well as extramural freedom, and it created a coalition of inflexibilists capable

113. Interestingly, in the early rounds of negotiations, Wriston joined McConaughy in proposing three statuses: permanent or continuous; temporary and probationary; and more than temporary but not permanent (which would entitle the recipient to a very long period of notice). Minutes of the Joint Conference, January 1938; letter, Mark Ingraham to Ralph E. Himstead (April 1, 1938) (Ingraham folder, AAUP files). Wriston had a change of heart which he explains in *Academic Freedom and Tenure*, 25 AAC Bull 110 (cited in note 64).

of winning on a hands-up vote. The tenure section of the 1938 agreement, while not as hard-set as Himstead would have wished (it advertised itself as no more than "accepted practice"), rejected all softening amendments: in a succinct paragraph, it called for a maximum period of probation of six years, universal adherence to that maximum, credit of up to three years for probationary service rendered elsewhere, and two clear-cut statuses—that of probation and that of tenure—within the ranks of every regular full-time faculty.[114]

This stiff-backed version of tenure reform, like the self-enforcement clause in the academic freedom section, did not survive the hostile review of the AAC Board of Directors. The board read the paragraph as proposing to confine academic administrations to a straitjacket and acted to delete it. In its place it submitted a demand for flexibility as bold as any that had been heard before: "Each institution should define with great care the probationary period and notify every appointee of its precise length and terms." Although these words implied no forsaking of either the principle of tenure or the idea of probationary periods, they caused deep consternation among AAUP leaders. Ingraham thought that they foreshadowed a return to the dependency of tenure on rank, since they treated the probationary service requirement so open-endedly; Carlson felt that if the fitness or unfitness of a person who had withstood the rigors of the Ph.D. could not be demonstrated after six years of scrutiny, "our junior faculty, and the principle of academic freedom, to the extent that it derives from tenure" will be "sacrificed to administrative sloth. . . ." Himstead was beside himself. He believed that the presidents had sounded a bugle call of retreat that would take the profession back to "the anarchy prevailing before 1925." He accused Wriston of not holding up his side of the bargain—"we accept a limit of propriety in free speech; why don't you recognize tenure?"[115] The alarmists turned out to be mistaken: the desire for flexibility, absent any deeper animus, had the power to delay, but not to kill, reform. At the November 1940 meeting, the AAUP got all the presidents to agree to the reinstatement of the 1938 language in return for tacking on an extra year to the probationary period and a written promise that the 1940 Statement would not be applied retroactively. And this time, the board of directors did not object.

Inflexible tenure reform ultimately won out in these negotiations for the same reason that it prevailed quite independently at Harvard and Yale and made a convert of the president of Brown—it offered vital benefits to the institution that flexible tenure reform would have scotched. One of these benefits was quality control. By requiring the institution to come to a definitive tenure decision at a time certain, an inflexible policy gave fewer hiding places to the academic bent for equivocation and procrastination

114. 1938 Statement in 1940 Statement folder (AAUP files).
115. Letters, Anton J. Carlson to Ralph E. Himstead (November 2, 1940); Mark Ingraham to Ralph E. Himstead (January 27, 1940); Ralph E. Himstead to Council (April 12-13, 1940); Ralph E. Himstead to Henry M. Wriston (February 2, 1940) (all in 1940 Statement folder, AAUP files).

always likely to be exhibited when hard personal decisions were called for. By replacing the old two-track system with a single track leading to an inescapable fork, an inflexible policy reduced the likelihood that anyone, after appointment, would go long unnoticed or become a fixture of an institution without having first been judged. Judged in comparison with whom? The 1940 Statement did not say. The report of the Harvard arts and sciences faculty that helped set up its stringent tenure rules praised the opportunity they afforded to judge probationers not only in the light of their own performance or that of other Harvard probationers, but in comparison with everyone at a similar stage to whom Harvard might offer an appointment. Not every academic institution would suppose that every tenure match was Wimbledon, that every player was seeded, or that every competitor was world class. But the idea did filter down to more average institutions that control of faculty quality could be enhanced by unflinching tenure reform, and this realization was reflected in the eventual dying down of AAC small-college resistance. Inflexibility held out another benefit: it promised to cut the high cost of institutional compassion. Rather than throw their unpromotable instructors and assistant professors into the cold Depression market, Harvard had let them stay on, year after year, acquiring the sort of de facto tenure Himstead did not contemplate—that born of institutional tender feelings. But the financial cost of sheltering large numbers with dismal prospects was high, and the qualitative cost of tying up funds for quasi-charitable purposes was incalculable. On the other hand, unpostponable stay-or-go decisions, coming up like clockwork, could be just what the doctor ordered—a purgative solution to a problem of overcrowding that could be administered without remorse. Ironically, Himstead's rigidity, conceived as the salvation of the junior faculty, could in the same scheme of things serve to cast off the junior faculty, and the AAUP, for all its efforts on behalf of the academic underprivileged, would later be hard pressed to convince them that it deserved their love.

The last part of the tenure reform program inscribed in the 1940 Statement concerned procedures for dismissing tenured faculty. Still wedded to the principle of faculty hearings, the AAUP persuaded the AAC to reaffirm it (here the presidents did insist on one gesture to flexibility—faculty hearings only "if possible"). This time, no longer persuaded that justice would be done if only faculty members were asked to do the judging, the AAUP also sought and received the assent of the AAC to a number of procedural guidelines. The 1940 Statement repeated the demand for written charges, which the teacher should have an opportunity to rebut, and added the right of the accused both to the presence of an adviser who might act as counsel and to a stenographic record of the proceedings that would be complete and accessible to all parties. These were not only the first steps toward judicialization that would ever be taken by these bodies: in 1958, the AAUP and AAC would agree to preliminary hearings, limited cross-examination, explicit findings on every charge, and a formal way of articulating the medial judgment of the faculty with the trustees' final review. Still, the 1940 Statement's steps may be said to mark the true birth of academic due process in this country.

V

CONCLUSION

Is the future of the 1940 Statement bright? One can find a multiplicity of reasons for supposing that its days are numbered. It has stepped on the toes of so many potential academic supporters—the libertarians who deplore its stand on freedom, the unionists who believe arbitration should be substituted for peer review, the many who expect more of it than it delivers and would wish it had said less on many counts—that one may wonder whether it will hereafter find anyone to befriend it. It is so out of touch with critical developments in the academic profession, such as the immense increase in the number of part-timers drawn from the casual labor market, and it is so out of sympathy with some of the current devices of academic management, such as nontenure tracks and rolling short-term contracts, that one may wonder whether the combination of a postmodern academic work force and a premodern administrative mentality will not finally do it in. But then one may also wonder how it was that these antagonistic forces, some of which are not of recent vintage, did not kill it off long ago. The possibility should not be dismissed that the 1940 Statement will endure because it serves the enduring interests of the academic profession and the academic enterprise, not to perfection, but better than anything else in existence or readily imaginable.

ACADEMIC FREEDOM AND THE FIRST AMENDMENT IN THE SUPREME COURT OF THE UNITED STATES: AN UNHURRIED HISTORICAL REVIEW

WILLIAM W. VAN ALSTYNE*

I

INTRODUCTION

In 1940, the American Association of University Professors ("AAUP") and the Association of American Colleges ("AAC") put forth their 1940 Statement of Principles on Academic Freedom and Tenure.[1] In the half century since its original issuance, the 1940 Statement has become well known in higher education in the United States, and its principles of academic freedom are widely observed. It has been incorporated expressly or by reference into many faculty handbooks in American colleges and universities, endorsed by more than one hundred national learned and professional associations, and relied upon in a number of state and federal courts. It is, overall, the general norm of academic practice in the United States.

As a general legal proposition, however, the 1940 Statement is an example of very soft law. Generally speaking, the 1940 Statement is not policed by courts. Rather, it is policed principally by Committee A of the AAUP[2] and by publication of AAUP's ad hoc committee investigation case reports in the AAUP's professional journal. And while this may understate the 1940 Statement's influence in some respects (for example, as when a university has adopted it and made it part of the faculty's contractual guarantee), the 1940 Statement is certainly not hard law in the ultimate sense one differently associates, say, with the first amendment to the Constitution with its general protection of free speech. That fixed constitutional provision, even if limited

---

* William R. Perkins Professor of Law, Duke University School of Law; Past President and General Counsel, American Association of University Professors.

1. *1940 Statement of Principles on Academic Freedom and Tenure* ("1940 Statement") in *Policy Documents and Reports* 3 (AAUP, 1984) ("*1984 Red Book*"); see Appendix B, 53 L & Contemp Probs 407 (Summer 1990).

2. For an explanation of the function of Committee A, see generally Louis Joughin, ed, *Academic Freedom and Tenure: A Handbook of the American Association of University Professors* (Univ of Wis Press, 1967).

to acts of government, as it is,[3] is at the opposite end of the legal order from the precatory law of the AAUP and AAC. In comparison with the soft law of the 1940 Statement, the first amendment is hard law indeed. The 1940 Statement instructs institutions of higher education respecting the kind of disposition they ought, in the opinion of the Statement's sponsoring and endorsing learned societies, to take toward academic freedom. As already noted, however, the 1940 Statement generally requires affirmative institutional action of some sort to carry its provisions into legal effect (for example, incorporation by reference into college or university bylaws, into letters of faculty appointment, or collective bargaining agreements). No such step is required in respect to the first amendment, of course. The Bill of Rights, including the first amendment, is quite different from the 1940 Statement. The first amendment is, after all, part of our fundamental law. Compliance, therefore, is not optional; its protections are enforceable in every court in the United States.

Even so, the first amendment is in its own way very much like the 1940 Statement: the first amendment's immediate use value is in large measure derived from the case law that has grown up around it, as has happened also with the 1940 Joint Statement and Committee A. What the courts understand the first amendment to say, rather than what one may otherwise suppose it provides, tends necessarily to occupy the main ground in working through its various applications and use. Given the role courts have occupied in the American constitutional order at least since *Marbury v. Madison*[4] was decided in 1803, the case law of the first amendment provides the basic, though not exclusive, road map in tending to guide first amendment disputes. The AAUP's Committee A case law (that is, the very large body of published case

---

3. The first amendment provides: "Congress shall make no law respecting an establishment of religion, or prohibiting the free exercise thereof; or abridging the freedom of speech, or of the press; or of the right of the people peaceably to assemble, and to petition the Government for a redress of grievances." As suggested by its language, the first amendment is not addressed to the states. The Supreme Court confirmed that impression in 1833. *Barron v Mayor and City Council*, 32 US (7 Pet) 243, 247-51 (1833) (The Bill of Rights was proposed and ratified as a set of affirmative restrictions on the national government only; it has no application to the states.). With the ratification of the 14th amendment in 1868, arguments came to be advanced that the 14th amendment incorporated some of the protections the Bill of Rights had furnished against the national government as restraints equally binding thereafter on the states. (For one recent and elaborate review of this subject, see Michael K. Curtis, *No State Shall Abridge: The Fourteenth Amendment and the Bill of Rights* (Duke Univ Press, 2d ed 1987)). In 1925, the Supreme Court accepted that view in respect to the first amendment, in dicta. *Gitlow v New York*, 268 US 652, 666 (1925). In 1931, the identification of the full free speech and free press clause to the due process clause of the 14th amendment was employed by the Court to hold invalid a state law. See *Near v Minnesota*, 283 US 697, 701-33 (1931). See also *DeJonge v Oregon*, 299 US 353, 356-66 (1937). Since that date, the 14th and first amendments have been treated by the Supreme Court as framing parallel, binding restrictions on the national and state governments, although neither by itself applies to private entities not operating as agencies of the state.

4. 5 US (1 Cranch) 137 (1803). *Marbury* affirmed the Supreme Court's pivotal role in applying the Constitution, much as Bishop Hoadley had addressed the pivotal role of judges in England in his sermon preached before the King in 1717 ("Whoever hath an absolute authority to interpret any written or spoken laws, it is he who is truly the lawgiver, to all intents and purposes, and not the person who first spoke or wrote them."). See William B. Lockhart, et al, *Constitutional Law: Cases—Comments—Questions* 1 (West, 6th ed 1986).

reports that used to appear in the *AAUP Bulletin* and that now appear in the AAUP's publication *Academe*) has functioned informally in an equivalent fashion in respect to the 1940 Statement. This informal case law has provided specific clarification and application of that fifty-year-old, two-page declaration. Roughly speaking, albeit of course at a much softer level of authority, Committee A has provided the guiding case law of academic freedom identified with the 1940 Statement comparable to that provided by the Supreme Court.

However, there is no reason a priori to expect these two bodies of case law to share any substantial common ground. Rather, the more reasonable assumption would be that the Supreme Court case law of the first amendment and the informal Committee A case law of the 1940 Statement would move along separate, even if roughly parallel, paths: the first dealing with large matters of free speech, government censorship, and government power to punish what people say, the second dealing with academic freedom as a tight bundle of interests distinct unto itself. In fact, however, this is not quite true. Rather, while the first amendment and the 1940 Statement are indeed differently grounded, their case law has tended very substantially to overlap. In fact, a large portion of the previously purely soft law of academic freedom has found a niche in the hard law of the Constitution through the usages of academic freedom in the Supreme Court. It is this process we shall shortly follow in an unhurried review.

Beyond this major, largely post-World War II development, moreover, the Supreme Court has also taken some of the values narrowly represented in the 1940 Statement and expanded upon them in a variety of ways. For example, the 1940 Statement addressed itself to academic freedom as an imperative in higher education. Consistent with some trends in first amendment case law, however, academic freedom has secured some purchase for public school teachers as well. As a different example, whereas "academic freedom" is defined in the 1940 Statement as the "[f]reedom of *teaching*" (and of faculty research and faculty extramural activities of certain kinds),[5] some Court decisions speak of academic freedom in respect to students, and not solely those who teach. As still a third example, although academic freedom is usually treated (in the 1940 Statement) as a matter of individual freedom, usually that of individual teachers to address matters of professional interest without threat to their jobs,[6] some Court decisions apply a first amendment notion of academic freedom much more corporately, that is, to the university or the college as an entity. The university, it is thought, may claim a certain corporate academic freedom to set its own institutional course—in

---

5. Of which more mention will be made later on. See, for example, note 112 and accompanying text.

6. The standard dictionary definition is of this sort. See, for example, *American Heritage Dictionary* 70 (Houghton-Mifflin, 1985) ("academic freedom" defined as: "Liberty to pursue and teach relevant knowledge and to discuss it freely without restriction from school or public officials or from other sources of influence").

curriculum, in admissions, in appointments—sheltered from government to some degree as a matter of constitutional (academic freedom) right.

Conversely, however, even in respect to these examples, the pathway of academic freedom's definitional development has tended to be a two-way street; in some measure these developments have taken place equally within the AAUP as within the doctrines of the Supreme Court. So, for instance, while the AAUP has not attempted to police its newer Joint Statement in the same case law investigating-and-reporting manner Committee A employs for the 1940 Statement (its resources are too limited to do so), the AAUP nonetheless did help fashion a Joint Statement on Rights and Freedoms of Students in 1967.[7] So, too, the AAUP has involved itself in matters of institutional academic freedom and diversity, and has appeared a substantial number of times to support the claims of first amendment academic freedom by public school teachers. The AAUP's own notions of the varieties of academic freedom, like the notions of the Supreme Court, have become more complex over time. Indeed, the AAUP's *Policy Documents and Reports*, the "*Red Book*" (its collection of basic policy statements and documents), addresses a far broader range of subjects than those just touched upon. The *Red Book* currently collects 179 pages of policy statements and documents: 177 pages more, that is, than the original two-page 1940 Statement presumed to do. The phrase "academic freedom" has thus become one of extended usage for the AAUP as well as for courts interpreting and applying the first amendment during the past half century or so.

Nonetheless, it is principally the latter—the usages of academic freedom in the Supreme Court—we mean to trace, rather than the formulations of the AAUP. To do that most usefully, however, we do not begin with the Supreme Court's modern decisions, but with its past decisions. Not by chance, they are linked to the origins of the AAUP.

II

LINKING ACADEMIC FREEDOM TO THE FIRST AMENDMENT: A SHORT, HISTORICAL SKETCH

A

At the turn of the twentieth century, the first amendment was virtually in a state of pre-history so far as academic freedom was concerned. Indeed, academic freedom to one side, the first amendment had no real immediate significance for free speech in general, never mind anything more specialized or arcane as *Lehrfreiheit* ("freedom to teach") or *Lernfreiheit* ("freedom to learn"), in the United States.

The first amendment had no general bite in 1900 because of the American judiciary's extremely cramped view of the amendment's scope. Despite its unqualifiedly strong language ("Congress shall make *no* law abridging the

---

7. AAUP et al, *Joint Statement on Rights and Freedoms of Students*, in *Policy Documents and Reports* 153 (AAUP, 1990) ("1967 Statement"); see Appendix C, 53 L & Contemp Probs 411 (Summer 1990).

freedom of speech or of the press"[8]), the amendment was deemed to furnish no more than fig leaf protection from anything other than certain kinds of governmentally imposed licensing or permit systems. In a word, the amendment applied almost solely to some few forms of prior restraint.

The prevailing Supreme Court jurisprudence of the first amendment amounted to little more than a restatement of William Blackstone's eighteenth century *Commentaries on the Laws of England*,[9] predating the Constitution and the first amendment. Blackstone, summarizing the common law of the eighteenth century, reported approvingly that restrictions on speech having any bad tendency in the view of public authority were quite commonplace. Other than restrictions involving some sort of press licensing system of the sort abandoned in England in 1691, Blackstone noted, it was thought to be pretty much up to Parliament and the customs of England to decide what kinds of speech might or might not be allowed. In a word, *the* freedom of the press (and so, too, of speech) was its freedom from having to satisfy crown censors. It was not a freedom from criminal or civil sanctions, imposed after the fact in light of the scandal of one's actual remarks.

Most judicial interpretations of the first amendment adhered sedulously to Blackstone—they enacted Blackstone's *Commentaries* into constitutional law. The usual judicial assumption was that *the* freedom of speech and of the press that the first amendment protected from abridgments by Congress was merely that freedom familiarly allowed at common law and nothing more. This view is accurately captured in a much-quoted dictum by Justice Holmes, writing for the Supreme Court in 1907: "[T]he main purpose of such constitutional provisions is 'to prevent all such *previous restraints* upon publications as had been practiced by other governments,' and *they do not prevent the subsequent punishment of such as may be deemed contrary to the public welfare*."[10] This extremely narrow interpretation of the first amendment (and, incidentally, equally of the fourteenth amendment—it is the latter that is applicable to the states), left the amendment practically useless. And so far as academic freedom might be an issue as a subset of freedom of speech, there was even more to be discouraged about.

The additional source of discouragement developed separately from a strand of constitutional analysis specially applicable to employment relationships, including public employment (that is, employment by the state). All employers were deemed to be unconstrained by the Constitution insofar as they might require that one suspend one's freedom of speech as a

8. Compare, for example, US Const, 4th amend (forbidding only *unreasonable* searches and seizures). In most constitutions that contain free speech and free press clauses, the rights are heavily qualified. See, for example, article 100 of the Norwegian Constitution (second oldest after the United States Constitution, adopted in 1814) (freedom of publication protected unless it expresses "contempt of religion [or] morality," in which case it is not).

9. See Edward Christian, ed, Blackstone's *Commentaries*, Book 4 (*Of Public Wrongs*) 150-53 (Robert H. Small, 1825).

10. *Patterson v Colorado*, 205 US 454, 462 (1907) (first emphasis in original; second emphasis added).

condition of holding an appointment or job. The *law* (that is, the body of constitutional law applicable to this subject) was only too clear: when a speech restriction limiting what one might say or write was set forth in advance as a condition of one's employment, it was not thought to raise a first amendment question at all. One was free to accept the position or not, on the terms offered; if one accepted, one was accordingly bound.

This view, too, is reflected in a case decided by Holmes in 1892, while he was still serving on the Massachusetts Supreme Court. Dismissing the appeal of a New Bedford policeman who had been fired following some public remarks critical of how the department was run, Holmes drew a distinction that was to have a lasting effect:

> The petitioner may have a constitutional right to talk politics, but he has no constitutional right to be a policeman. There are few employments for hire in which the servant does not agree to suspend his constitutional right of free speech, as well as of idleness, by the implied terms of his contract. The servant cannot complain, as he takes the employment on the terms which are offered him.[11]

Holmes hedged only trivially on the distinction. In dicta, he suggested that if the conditions thus imposed incidentally to public employment were unreasonable in some extreme sense (that is, that the conditions seemed utterly gratuitous), the courts might intervene on substantive due process grounds. Seldom, however, would that extreme instance be deemed to have occurred; indeed, Holmes gave no example of what he had in mind.

Plainly, these views and precedents would leave any claim of mere academic freedom stranded as a constitutional matter; indeed, they left freedom of speech stranded at large. And, in fact, these views of the first and fourteenth amendments carried over for decades into the twentieth century, as a large number of cases would show.

Blackstone's bad tendency test held sway under the first amendment until well after World War I.[12] The add-on employment *waiver* rationale was applied by the courts until well after World War II.[13] It will serve our purpose here to note one famous case particularly on point—the original Scopes Monkey Trial case[14] in which Clarence Darrow and Arthur Garfield Hayes argued quite vainly on the constitutional issue in the Tennessee Supreme Court in 1927.

At issue in *Scopes* was whether John Scopes, a Tennessee public high school teacher, could be fined or jailed for teaching "any theory that denie[d] the story of the divine creation of man as taught in the Bible," in violation of a state statute governing his conduct as a teacher in the Tennessee public schools.[15] Could he discuss the theory that man may have developed not all

---

11. *McAuliff v Mayor of New Bedford*, 155 Mass 216, 220, 29 NE 517, 518 (1892).

12. For a useful review, see generally David M. Rabban, *The First Amendment in Its Forgotten Years*, 90 Yale L J 514 (1981).

13. See, for example, *Bailey v Richardson*, 182 F2d 46 (DC Cir 1950), aff'd by an equally divided Court, 341 US 918 (1951).

14. *Scopes v State*, 154 Tenn 105, 289 SW 363 (1927).

15. 154 Tenn at 108, 289 SW at 364. The statute, incidentally, was not limited to public school teachers. Rather, it applied to "*all the Universities*, Normals and all other public schools *supported in*

at once in perfect form, as a creation of God, but over time, from earlier life forms through the cumulative effects of mutation, reproduction, and natural selection, as Darwin had proposed? The statute gave fair warning that he could not. Violations, moreover, were punishable as a crime (apart from providing grounds for dismissal). Scopes was duly convicted and fined following a full jury trial.

Scopes' criminal conviction was in fact reversed in the state supreme court because of a technical sentencing error committed in the trial court; since Scopes agreed to leave the state, there was no subsequent reprosecution or appeal. But in reversing, the Tennessee Supreme Court left no doubt about the futility of arguing any constitutional objections to the act, whether as applied to a public school teacher or to a state university professor:

> [Scopes] was under contract with the State to work in an institution of the State. He had no right or privilege to serve the State except upon such terms as the State prescribed. His liberty, his privilege, his immunity to teach and proclaim the theory of evolution, elsewhere than in the service of the State, was in no wise touched by this law.
>
> The Statute before us is not an exercise of the police power of the State undertaking to regulate the conduct and contracts of individuals in their dealings with each other.[16] On the other hand it is an Act of the State as a corporation, a proprietor, an employer. It is a declaration of a master as to the character of work the master's servant shall, or rather shall not, perform. In dealing with its own employees engaged upon its own work, the state is *not hampered* by the limitations of . . . the Fourteenth Amendment to the Constitution of the United States.[17]

Between the general bad tendency test on the one hand, and the additional doctrine represented by *Scopes* (that the state is not hampered by the fourteenth amendment in directing the work of its appointees and staff), very little by way of protected free speech was left unaccounted for, to say nothing of academic freedom as such. To be sure, as we have noted, *private* schools and *private* universities (that is, those not receiving public monies) could choose to provide for something roughly called "academic freedom," if they wished. That would be up to them.[18] But even insofar as it was up to them, obviously the issue would turn on trustee tolerance—to control or not control what its faculty might do—and nothing else. It was not a matter of first amendment law.

---

whole or in part" by public funds. Tennessee Anti-Evolution Act, 1925 Tenn Pub Acts 27 (emphasis added).

16.   If the statute had been extended to reach teachers in private schools and private colleges, however, it is not clear they would have fared any better than Scopes in a free speech claim. Remember that at this time the first amendment standard of judicial review would require the court to examine the restrictive state law solely under the prevailing bad tendency test. Under that test the state would need to show only that some not unreasonable view of public welfare would be advanced by forbidding such teaching, whether or not it was acceptable to the private school or college. But see *Meyer v Nebraska*, 262 US 390 (1923), and *Bartels v Iowa*, 262 US 404 (1923) (further discussed in notes 24-33 and accompanying text).

17.   *Scopes*, 154 Tenn at 109-12, 289 SW at 364-65 (emphasis and brackets added).

18.   Under the prevailing bad tendency first amendment test, however, and despite the dicta of the Tennessee Supreme Court, even this statement may be too broad. See the brief discussion in note 16.

B

Throughout this period, however, significant developments in shaping academic freedom nonetheless took place. What academic freedom required was some compelling justification, at least as a strongly defensible professional imperative in higher education, even if (perhaps especially if) there was no immediate prospect of finding support in hard law.

Part of that case had already been made over decades, indeed over centuries, of course; in some measure academic freedom was already reflected in the practices of a number of institutions in the United States. Part of it was developed with a new spirit from the impact of writings such as John Stuart Mill's already classic *Essay on Liberty* [19] published in 1859, whose chapter on "Liberty of Thought and Discussion" would eventually also influence the Supreme Court. Part could be (and was) adapted from earlier sources (for example, "The Areopagitica,"[20] Milton's essay of 1643, urging the usefulness of permitting "truth and falsehood" to grapple without press censorship), and even earlier discourses on the freedom of the mind as well.

But freedom of the mind and freedom of speech had always had their limits, as Milton as well as Blackstone noted (and approved), including limits public bodies enacted for reasons they deemed socially worthwhile. If writings such as Mill's were felt to be interesting and provocative, many also thought them naive and oblivious to other interests that might more dearly matter. To many, moreover, there seemed little reason to grant academics more latitude than anyone else. As Glenn Morrow was to explain years later:

> The justification of academic freedom cannot be based merely on the right to freedom of thought and expression enjoyed by all citizens of a liberal society, for academic freedom implies immunity to some natural consequences of free speech that the ordinary citizen does not enjoy. . . . The justification of academic freedom must therefore be sought in the peculiar character and function of the university scholar [if it is to be found at all].[21]

In the general view of freedom of speech, one will recall, the bad tendency test was applied. Insofar as trustees, philanthropists, and others concerned with colleges and universities—whether private or public—might feel a duty to disallow teaching, research, or publication contrary to common notions of truth, faith, order, and good taste, nothing in general legal philosophy or first amendment jurisprudence provided any reason for self-restraint. There was, that is, very little reason to accept any self-denying ordinance of noninterference, whether one was a legislator or a trustee. To stand aloof in either role might merely imply an effete indifference to the public good. Viewed this way, noninterference would constitute the irresponsible stance.

An answering rationale needed to come, as Morrow suggested, from an enlarged notion of what one deems to be the public good of a university,

---

19. See Philip Wheelwright, ed, *Jeremy Bentham, James Mill, J.S. Mill: Selected Writings* (Doubleday, 1935).

20. See Don W. Wolfe, ed, 2 *Complete Prose Works* (Yale Univ Press, 1982).

21. Glenn R. Morrow, *Academic Freedom*, in David L. Sills, ed, *International Encyclopedia of the Social Sciences* 4, 6 (MacMillan & Free Press, 1968).

whether public or private: that is, of what a university should be doing, and what defines the duties (never mind the rights) of its faculty. Borrowed only partly from English universities, the developments being shaped gained ground in the United States more substantially from the example of particular German research institutes, in which a number of American scholars received their graduate education and in which *Lehrfreiheit* was already an established and familiar term.[22]

A faculty, especially a research faculty, is employed professionally to test and propose revisions in the prevailing wisdom, not to inculcate the prevailing wisdom in others, store it as monks might do, or rewrite it in elegant detail. Its function is primarily one of critical review: to check conventional truth, to reexamine ("re-search") what may currently be thought sound but may be more or less unsound. Its purpose is likewise to train others to the same critical skills. Such a faculty inquires—as an obvious sort of example—whether original and seemingly authoritative sources have been mistranslated or misunderstood. Such a faculty likewise labors to enlarge the field of experimental data and to make itself useful by publishing the results. It seeks through its own sets of disciplines and conventions to examine its own culture's characteristics as well as those of other societies, past and present, even as an outsider would be prepared to examine them, that is, without special affection or predisposition of the sort likely to cloud the integrity of the work. Its successes in these endeavors are the measure of its chief work, and also of its most important social assignment. This is what a professional faculty is meant to do. Much like the office of devil's advocate within a church (that, while faithful, desires also not to confer sainthood unrigorously and so charges someone to check itself from error), universities are licensed truth-hunters defined and bound by academic freedom. As Arthur Lovejoy (a founder of the AAUP in 1913) observed in the 1930 edition of the *Encyclopaedia of the Social Sciences*, the ultimate social good of a university "is rendered impossible if the work of the investigator is shackled by the requirement that his conclusions shall never seriously deviate from generally accepted beliefs or from those accepted by the persons, private or official, through whom society provides the means for the maintenance of universities."[23]

---

22. See Richard Hofstadter & Walter P. Metzger, *The Development of Academic Freedom in the United States* 377-407 (Columbia Univ Press, 1955); Charles Franklin Thwing, *The American and the German University: One Hundred Years of History* ch 3 (Macmillan, 1928); Leo Rockwell, *Academic Freedom: German Origin and American Development*, 36 AAUP Bull 225-36 (1950). "'*Lehrfreiheit*' meant that associate and full professors, who were salaried government officials working in universities supported by the state . . . could determine the contents of their courses and impart the findings of their inquiries without seeking ministerial approval or fearing ministerial reproof." Matthew W. Finkin, *On "Institutional" Academic Freedom*, 61 Tex L Rev 817, 822 (1983), quoting Walter P. Metzger.

23. More than a half century later, in the spring of 1988, the House of Lords adopted a bill defining academic freedom in a manner closely fitting Lovejoy's rationale ("academic freedom" proposed for the protection of teachers as "freedom within the law *to question and test received wisdom*, and to put forward new ideas and controversial or unpopular opinions, *without placing themselves in jeopardy of losing their jobs* or privileges") (emphasis added). David Walker, *In a Rare Rebellion, British Lords Demand Academic-Freedom Law*, in Chron Higher Educ A1, A43, col 3 (June 1, 1988). Compare

C

Before this claim of vocational freedom could be coupled with the first and fourteenth amendments, however, a number of things needed to change. For one thing, the flaccidness of the prevailing first amendment bad tendency test would require overhaul, as would the master/servant metaphor. These changes eventually did occur (we shall shortly note how and when), but before they did, a separate development in constitutional case law took hold. We turn first to this sidebar development before resuming the tracery of first amendment doctrine in the Supreme Court. We do so because the first *serious* Supreme Court protection of what one might now consider academic freedom did not arise out of the first amendment at all. Rather, it came from the judicial application of pre-existing legal doctrines. The partial deliverance of academic freedom came at the hands of an activist, conservative Supreme Court defending private options against the state.

In 1920, a number of midwestern state legislatures moved to stem what they regarded as the regrettable tendency of youngsters from immigrant families to learn and speak only a foreign language rather than English. Iowa and Nebraska were among these states, and each by general statute in 1919 forbade any school instruction in any language other than English before the eighth grade.

The two cases reaching the Supreme Court testing these laws differed from *Scopes*, however, in that the Iowa and Nebraska laws did not limit the teaching restriction solely to the public schools; rather, they mandated English-only instruction in all *private* schools as well. Both cases in fact involved criminal conviction of men who taught reading German in private Lutheran schools: Robert Myer in Nebraska and August Bartels in Iowa.[24] The *Scopes* rationale, dismissing Scopes as a mere employee confined to do the state's work on such terms as the state might decide (as master to servant), did not apply. Rather, the cases were as *Scopes* might have been had Scopes been a teacher in a private school, proceeding exactly as the school employed him to do, though not as the state legislature wished.

The Nebraska and Iowa statutes were not impugned on grounds of interfering with Meyer's or Bartels' first or fourteenth amendment freedom of speech, however. Nor is it easy to see how they might have been cast as free speech claims, since neither Meyer nor Bartels was affected other than as a teacher, that is, as a person for hire, furnishing foreign language instruction,

---

Lovejoy's definition in Edwin R. A. Seligman, ed, 1 *Encyclopaedia of the Social Sciences* 384 (Macmillan, 1930):

> Academic freedom is the freedom of the teacher or research worker in higher institutions of learning to investigate and discuss the problems of his science and to express his conclusions, whether through publication or in the instruction of students, without interference from political or ecclesiastical authority, or from the administrative officials of the institution in which he is employed, unless his methods are found by qualified bodies of his own profession to be clearly incompetent or contrary to professional ethics.

24. See Teaching of Foreign Languages in the State of Nebraska, 1919 Neb Laws 249; Iowa Language Act, 1919 Iowa Acts 198; *Meyer*, 262 US at 397; *Bartels*, 262 US at 409.

albeit in a privately operated school. As of the date of these cases, moreover, the Supreme Court had not even held that the first amendment necessarily applied to the states as distinct from its application to acts of Congress. *That* decision, identifying freedom of speech as a specific *liberty* equally protected against state action by the fourteenth amendment, did not come until 1925, incidental to a political sedition prosecution, *Gitlow v. New York*.[25] Even after *Gitlow*, the Court still continued to apply the mere bad tendency test.[26]

The free speech clause was not relied upon in either case; neither did Meyer or Bartels successfully challenge the statutes on the ground that they interfered with the free exercise of religion, even though the laws dictated instructional practices of religious (Lutheran) schools. In the particular circumstances, however, it was difficult to make a free exercise claim, for in neither case was it alleged that giving or receiving instruction in German was a requirement of Lutheran faith.[27]

The emphasis in both *Meyer* and *Bartels* was, rather, on substantive due process principles generally.[28] The Court summed up the collective effects of the Iowa and Nebraska statutes: their restriction against any private school offering any program of foreign language instruction to any student prior to the eighth grade; their antivocational restriction of teachers like Meyer and Bartels, now cut off from fulfilling teaching contracts willingly entered into by the private schools; their effective foreclosure of families from choosing *any* school able to teach their children anything in their own language before the eighth grade. And to what end? Certainly not as a necessary means of assuring an adequate facility in English, since that might be done by less draconian means.[29] The unnecessary excess of the states' laws, merely in order to assure basic English literacy,[30] was deemed to be unwarranted by any

---

25. 268 US 652 (1925).

26. In brief, in *Gitlow* the Court did make the connection firming up the equivalence of 14th and first amendment protection; but the majority nonetheless affirmed the particular defendant's criminal conviction (by applying the first amendment's mere bad tendency test).

27. As a matter of historical interest, the first case presenting such an additional and successful claim of "free exercise" of religion did arise a few years later in *Pierce v Society of Sisters*, 268 US 510 (1925), where the Court relied partly on the religious freedom clause to invalidate the particular state law. In *Pierce*, the Court held that parents cannot be compelled to enroll their children in public, rather than parochial, schools providing additional religious instruction—assuming only that the parochial school meets reasonable minimum state educational and safety standards.

28. See also *Farrington v Tokushige*, 273 US 284, 298-99 (1927) (*Meyer* and *Bartels* applied in behalf of private schools similarly restricted in a federal territory, Hawaii, citing the due process clause of the fifth amendment and treating it substantively the same as the due process clause of the 14th amendment, in *Meyer*.).

29. Note that the laws altogether closed off an entire area of learning freedom (*Lernfreiheit*) at a single stroke. The statutes did not seek their objective affirmatively, for example, by providing that children be suitably tested for English and given remedial instruction if found deficient. Rather, they operated by forbidding any foreign language instruction prior to the eighth grade, *period*, whether one already was well versed in English or not. See 1919 Neb Laws 249; 1919 Iowa Acts 198 (cited in note 24).

30. Following so shortly on World War I, these laws were also very possibly driven in part by an anti-German animus and not solely by an unalloyed solicitude for the educational welfare of immigrant family children.

proper police power interest. The Court reversed the criminal convictions of Meyer and Bartels.

Meyer and *Bartels* mark an important first boundary in our review of academic freedom. They do so by distinguishing between what the state may decide to do in its own financing (that is, its administration of public, tax-furnished educational resources) and what it may not necessarily forbid at large. The foundation of the decision was not the first amendment, but the cases are still vital to the autonomy (and academic freedom) of private universities and schools.[31]

Principally, the Court relied upon the 1905 case of *Lochner v. New York*,[32] in which it had likewise intervened against police power claims of the welfare state. *Lochner* was a decision that many regarded as both infamous and wrong (Holmes dissented in *Lochner*, but then he also dissented in *Meyer* and in *Bartels*). Perhaps it was, yet its standard of judicial review is critical in *Meyer* and well worth taking into account.

In *Lochner*, the Supreme Court invalidated a New York law forbidding employment of persons in private commercial bakeries for more than ten hours each day. The Court struck down the law as a violation of the right of employees and employers to decide such matters for themselves At the time it was decided, *Lochner* was widely condemned as a judicial embrace of social Darwinism. In subsequent decades, moreover, judges practically vied with one another in denouncing its allegedly procapitalist view of the due process clause of the fourteenth amendment.[33] What is relevant about the *Lochner* reference in *Meyer*, however, is the strong view it reflects respecting the role of the judiciary in applying the fourteenth amendment to protect private choice and personal liberty from the general tendency of the public welfare state. Absent that strong view of the Court's role in protecting private liberty under the fourteenth amendment, neither *Meyer* nor *Bartels* would have been decided as they were. Rather, the criminal convictions of Meyer and Bartels would have been sustained, exactly as Justice Holmes voted to do.

Although the measure of judicial review in *Meyer* ("activist" or "interventionist" review, as it is sometimes dismissively described) was drawn from *Lochner*, it would be a mistake to consider *Meyer* merely as of a piece with *Lochner*, that is, as an example of the social Darwinist thought that had already

---

31. See also the interesting thesis of Robert Bork in his book, *The Tempting of America: The Political Seduction of the Law* 47-49 (Free Press, 1990) (proposing a first amendment perspective for *Meyer v Nebraska* insofar as the state law may have sought "to prevent the teaching of ideas not officially approved"). A noted conservative nominee to the Supreme Court, Judge Bork was opposed because his professional views of correct constitutional interpretation would repudiate the Supreme Court's jurisprudence of "substantive due process," and therefore presumably leave state governments unimpeded in enacting laws of the sort held invalid in *Meyer*. As his brief comments on *Meyer* may suggest (in this lengthy book replying to his critics), depending on the perspective one brings to the first amendment as a separate and sometimes subtle constraint on government power to induce academic conformity, the assumption may have been quite unsound.

32. 198 US 45 (1905).

33. See generally Robert G. McCloskey, *Economic Due Process and the Supreme Court: An Exhumation and Reburial*, 1962 Sup Ct Rev 34.

led the Court to invalidate a large number of economic and social regulations in general. Aspects of *Meyer* have endured long after the demise of *Lochner*. They have developed separately, as a major element in academic freedom cases in the United States, though the *Lochner* profile of judicial review (in second-guessing economic regulations) under the fourteenth amendment has generally been abandoned by the Court.

The continuing issue foreshadowed in *Meyer* is the issue we noted earlier: what useful constitutional limitations are there, if any, that constrain government from superimposing its will on educational institutions to prescribe who shall (or shall not) be admitted, what shall (and shall not) be studied, and who may (and may not) teach in private as well as in public institutions? *Meyer* by no means settled that large question. It did, however, take the question seriously, that is, the Court submitted it to active, toughminded, substantive due process review. Moreover, at one place in its brief opinion, the *Meyer* majority turned to the point directly. It noticed the similarity of the laws at issue to the authoritarianism laid down in Plato's *Republic*: classifying the young, removing each from any family preference respecting their education, and rearing them in the image of (that is, for the best needs of) the state. In terms of academic freedom, *Meyer v. Nebraska* is even today a front-line constitutional case.

Indeed, *Meyer* is worthy of immediate juxtaposition with an earlier case in which its strong reasoning was not applied, *Berea College v. Kentucky*, decided by the Supreme Court in 1908.[34] The decision affecting Berea College reflected no Court "activism." The state was allowed to have its way.

In the legislation that precipitated *Berea College*, the State of Kentucky asserted a police power interest "to preserve race identity" (the words are the state's own; I quote from the summary of its argument before the Court).[35] It legislated that interest, first, by providing for racially separate public schools, then, as to private schools and colleges, by providing that each could admit either white or negro students, but not both.

As in *Meyer*, counsel for Berea College did not address the state law as applied to the *public* schools. What the state might do in structuring public education was not at issue (nor could it have been at the time, given the state of equal protection law prior to *Brown v. Board of Education*,[36] still nearly a half century away). Rather, the college stressed its separate claims as an educational institution: to determine its own policies, unprepossessingly, as it wished. It likewise stressed the claims of the teachers who chose to teach there, and of its students, who evidently preferred to enroll there, not despite but because of what it was. In short, in all salient respects, the college's position was strikingly similar to the position later (and successfully) advanced in *Meyer*. In modern terms, it would be called a strong *institutional* academic freedom claim: an institutional freedom to provide such standards of

34. 211 US 45 (1908).
35. Id at 51.
36. 349 US 294 (1954).

admission, curriculum, and instruction as the faculty and college feel most worthy to offer those willing to seek its education, notwithstanding the state's wish to compel it to conform.

In *Berea College*, unlike *Meyer*, the Supreme Court gave the college's fourteenth amendment appeal short shrift. It sustained the state law, requiring Berea College to admit student only on the terms the state suggested, or to close its doors. As in his dissent in *Meyer*, Justice Holmes agreed, altogether consistently with his dour general view that neither the first nor the fourteenth amendment meant very much.

Berea College did, however, yield a dissent that is worth quoting. Justice Harlan (with Justice Day concurring in his dissent) took strong exception to the majority's weak view of the fourteenth amendment. His dissent in *Berea College* reads this way: "I am under the opinion that in its essential parts the statute is an arbitrary invasion of the rights of liberty and property guaranteed by the Fourteenth Amendment against hostile state action and is, therefore, void."[37] Harlan then went on to say:

> The capacity to impart instruction to others is given by the Almighty for beneficent purposes and its use may not be forbidden or interfered with by Government— certainly not, unless such instruction is, in its nature, harmful to the public morals or imperils the public safety. . . . If pupils, of whatever race—certainly, if they be citizens—choose with the consent of their parents, or voluntarily, to sit together in a private institution of learning while receiving instruction which is not in its nature harmful or dangerous to the public, no government, whether Federal or state, can legally forbid their coming together, or being together temporarily, for such an innocent purpose.[38]

At the same time, Justice Harlan distinguished the difference of public schools on the then conventional rationale: "Of course what I have said has no reference to regulations prescribed, for public schools, established at the pleasure of the State and maintained at the public expense."[39]

Even given its date (and the general state of fourteenth amendment law of that time), *Berea College* was a devastating decision. What the state insisted on in respect to admission and educational practice in public schools and colleges, the Court held, it could impose on others, foreclosing them from pursuing their own educational principles and ethical norms. This was not the judicial philosophy reflected in *Meyer*. Indeed, between the very different attitudes toward state power reflected by *Meyer* and by *Berea College*, there is no common principle obviously at work. *Meyer* provided an outpost of professional and institutional academic freedom Berea College was altogether denied. We shall have occasion to return to the general theme of *Meyer*. In the meantime, we need to pick up where we were.

---

37. 211 US at 67.
38. Id at 67-68.
39. Id at 69.

D

To recapitulate briefly, we had noted, first, that successful academic freedom claims did not develop naturally or easily as an incident of early twentieth century first amendment doctrine. Rather, they developed largely without benefit of the first amendment, generally under private auspices and in response to the vacuum of doctrine associated with the first amendment as hard law. Second, we noted that beginning in 1913, the AAUP sought to gain some purchase against the law by pressing forward with the idea of the university as an institution necessarily characterized by academic freedom, in other words, in which academic freedom is inseparable from academic work. From then on, the AAUP sought to advance this characterization of higher education in the United States. And in significant measure, that effort succeeded, even while the law of the Constitution tended to lag behind.

Nevertheless, even in the 1920s, two constitutional developments (additional to *Meyer*) did take place in the Supreme Court, each of which was to have major effects we will trace to the present. The first was the development of the doctrine of "unconstitutional conditions"; the second was the defection of Justice Holmes (and Justice Brandeis) from the bad tendency test in favor of a more robust view of the first amendment.

1. *The Collateral Doctrine of Unconstitutional Conditions.* The basic doctrine of unconstitutional conditions is straightforward. Professor Tribe states it succinctly: "The . . . doctrine of 'unconstitutional conditions' holds that government may not condition the receipt of its benefits upon the nonassertion of constitutional rights *even if receipt of such benefits is in all other respects a 'mere privilege'*."[40] The doctrine appears full-blown originally in a 1926 Supreme Court opinion by Justice Sutherland, *Frost & Frost Trucking Co. v. Railroad Commission*:

> It would be a palpable incongruity to strike down an act of state legislation which, by words of express divestment, seeks to strip the citizen of rights guaranteed by the federal Constitution, but to uphold an act by which the same result is accomplished under the guise of a surrender of a right in exchange for a valuable privilege which the state threatens otherwise to withhold. . . . It is inconceivable that guaranties embedded in the Constitution of the United States may be thus manipulated out of existence.[41]

The doctrine thus holds that government may not exploit its leverage with citizens or other persons with whom it comes into contact; it may not trade off waivers for scarce opportunities or goods it happens to control. In a word, government may not act to buy an estoppel of constitutional rights.

On its face, the doctrine strongly counters the employment waiver rationale Justice Holmes relied upon in the New Bedford policeman's case in

---

40. Laurence H. Tribe, *American Constitutional Law* 681 (Foundation Press, 2d ed 1988) (emphasis added).

41. 271 US 583, 593-94 (1926). The phrase appears in a number of earlier cases, including *Doyle v Continental Ins. Co.*, 94 US 535, 543 (1876) (Bradley dissenting) ("[T]hough a State may have the power . . . of prohibiting all foreign corporations from transacting business within its jurisdiction, it has no power to impose unconstitutional conditions upon their doing so.").

which Holmes suggested the policeman could take the job on the terms offered or turn it down, but not have it both ways.[42] Sutherland's position puts an end to that view, basically once and for all. The doctrine of unconstitutional conditions simply cuts through the policeman's agreement. It relieves him of all inappropriate terms. It does so by superintending the bargain directly; it voids any and all unconstitutional terms of the government's deal. One cannot be discharged for failing to honor a condition that should not have been presented in the first place. The doctrine frees the individual to test the substantive validity of the terms themselves; it puts the government to the test of justification and disallows the defense of contract per se.

The *Frost* case was more of a piece with *Lochner* than with academic freedom or first amendment rights: it dealt purely with business interests and an effort by a state to impose conditions of public service in exchange for a valuable advantage the state threatened otherwise to withhold (the use of state highways and roads).[43] But *Frost* has had a modern career more significantly associated with the first amendment, and its rationale bears directly on public teachers and state university personnel. Thus, although not itself an academic freedom case, *Frost* assuredly supplies an important link in this unhurried review.

An excellent example of the application of *Frost*, though not one involving academic freedom in any strict professional usage, is provided by *Pickering v. Board of Education*, a unanimous 1968 Supreme Court decision.[44] The contrast *Pickering* provides with *New Bedford* and *Scopes*[45] is instructive of the change that dates from the *Frost* case, decided in 1926.

The case was brought by Marvin Pickering, a high school teacher in Will County, Illinois. In 1964, he had sent a signed personal letter to a local newspaper. The letter was highly critical of the way the Board of Education and the district superintendent of schools had handled proposals to raise new revenue for the schools. The Board then reviewed Pickering's continuing suitability in light of his letter, in a due process hearing, and concluded that his publication of the letter was " 'detrimental to the efficient operation and administration of the schools of the district.' " It directed that he be dismissed.[46] The case was thus similar to the *New Bedford* case. The outcome in the Supreme Court was not.

The Supreme Court rejected the *New Bedford* rationale. Insofar as the state supreme court's affirmance of Pickering's dismissal seemed partly to turn on the notion that Pickering's teaching position could be circumscribed by the

---

42. See note 11 and accompanying text.
43. *Frost*, 271 US at 589; see also notes 32-33 and accompanying text.
44. *Pickering v Board of Educ. of Township High School Dist.*, 391 US 563 (1968). See also *Perry v Sinderman*, 408 US 593 (1972); *Givhan v Western Line Consolidated School Dist.*, 439 US 410 (1979); *Mt. Healthy City School Dist. Board of Educ. v Doyle*, 429 US 274 (1977); *Rankin v McPherson*, 483 US 378 (1987). But see *Connick v Myers*, 461 US 138 (1983).
45. See notes 11, 14 and accompanying text.
46. *Pickering*, 391 US at 564-65.

requirement that he refrain from adverse public comment on the local public school administration, the Supreme Court simply demurred:

> To the extent that the Illinois Supreme Court's opinion may be read to suggest that teachers may constitutionally be compelled to relinquish the First Amendment rights they would otherwise enjoy as citizens to comment on matters of public interest in connection with the operation of the public schools in which they work, it proceeds on a premise that has been unequivocally rejected in numerous prior decisions of this Court.[47]

The Court thus enabled Marvin Pickering to object that such a compelled agreement was void as an "unconstitutional condition." The case fits neatly within the analysis we have previously derived from Justice Sutherland's opinion in *Frost*.

Nevertheless, the doctrine of unconstitutional conditions, helpful as it is and significant as it has been, has also been misunderstood even in subsequent decisions of the Supreme Court. The confusions that have grown up around it result partly, though not entirely, from the wishful belief that it solves more problems than it does. Its limitation is simply a variation on the maxim that water rises no higher than its original source. Concretely, the doctrine does not instruct one in understanding whether a specific condition is unconstitutional; rather, it requires the government to show adequate justification for what it presumes to do, and to make that showing "on the merits." In brief, the doctrine declares that any answer of the sort that the petitioner (whoever the petitioner is) agreed to or at least had notice of the restriction, is never sufficient to carry the government's case. The government must defend the constitutionality of the condition on its merits, and not on the ground that it bought the right to impose the restriction.

To restate the doctrine slightly differently, it means that government cannot exempt itself from the constitutional restraints that otherwise apply to its actions merely because, were one to treat the same matter as one of private party contractual agreement, a *private* party would be relieved of any further obligation to continue to furnish work or pay if the other party willfully failed to observe the conditions openly attached in advance. The main point of the doctrine is that government is never a private party. Its arrangements, whatever they are, are always circumscribed by restrictions in the Constitution. These restrictions apply irrespective of the form in which the government acts, whether it acts as an employer, or as a seller or buyer of goods. They apply when it acts as administering agency of a public university, or as a provider of state or federal funds. They apply when it determines who can teach and who cannot.

In part, moreover, the doctrine of unconstitutional conditions is also a variant of two other closely related doctrines in American constitutional law regarding unconstitutional purpose in the actions of government. The point often appears in the form of a judicial statement that "what government is forbidden to do directly, it is equally forbidden to do by indirection."

---

47. Id at 568.

96

Sometimes it is put in terms of "the purpose and (intended) effect" of the government's act. And sometimes it is put, even as Sutherland suggested in *Frost*, that the government has acted to do one thing "under the guise" of doing something else.[48] In the end, it comes to the same point.

Specifically, the word "guise" in the Sutherland quotation does suggest that the government is in fact acting by indirection (by some manipulative means—to adopt contract terms, waivers, contractual submission and the like) in order to achieve an end it is not entitled to seek. The very idea is thus one of overreaching for a degree of control over others the government is not otherwise permitted to assert consistent with the first amendment, but which overreaching, incorrigibly, it continues to pursue.

But this valuable point to the doctrine is also subject to its own misunderstanding if one inflates it to mean that whenever the government acts, it is always deemed to act solely for some ulterior end and never from any bona fide concern linked to the position one holds that might be sufficient to sustain the conditions attached. Such a conclusive presumption of improper purpose cannot be and in fact is not maintained in the courts. To the contrary, if the government can show a bona fide concern fairly linked to the position and the condition in question, the condition may not be a guise for anything else and may not be unconstitutional at all. Rather, if shown to be warranted by the circumstances, the condition will be sustained. Such a condition is not an unconstitutional condition. If it needs a name, moreover, there is an obvious one: call it a constitutional condition, instead.[49]

Under these circumstances, whatever the conditions are (and, to be sure we have not as yet said what they may be in any particular case), it will necessarily follow that one must comply with the condition or be prepared to go elsewhere. Moreover, that such conditions may have been nonnegotiable from the outset may itself make no difference at all. Obviously the government is not required to trade what it need not yield; so its

---

48. 271 US at 593.

49. Consider the following example. Suppose that the Supreme Court holds that mere membership in the Communist Party or the American Nazi Party (or any other party) cannot be outlawed. Suppose a state legislature, unimpressed by the Court's view that one's choice of political affiliation is protected by the first amendment, and determined to make such affiliation as difficult as it possibly can, adopts an act making ineligible for any employment by the state—including as a state university or public school teacher—any person holding membership in the proscribed parties. The statute fits Sutherland's description of a guise in the *Frost* case and should be held invalid. According to our stipulation of its purpose, the legislature seeks the destruction of political parties it considers a social menace. Forbidden to act directly, it has proceeded toward the same end indirectly, by withholding "a valuable privilege" from anyone not "surrendering" his or her constitutional right. The statute is invalid under the *Frost* doctrine.

Suppose, however, one stipulates a different objective, namely, a concern solely for national security in respect to highly classified secrets. And suppose one substitutes a statute narrowly drawn to that end. It is not obvious that a restriction on some such kinds of access determined in part by one's political affiliations would necessarily be held unconstitutional. Of course it is possible that this statute, too, is but a guise, that is, that the claim of national security concern is a legislative fraud. Nevertheless, absent very strong evidence to that effect, it is not likely to be presumed so and, if not presumed so, such an act, narrowly drawn, may be constitutional despite its marginal effect in discouraging certain political affiliations that are otherwise a matter of first amendment "right." Compare *United States v Robel*, 389 US 258 (1967); *Wieman v Updegraff*, 344 US 183 (1952).

unwillingness to bargain over such matters (whatever they are) is neither here nor there. The matter is, indeed, at an end.

In substance, then, the doctrine of unconstitutional conditions helps police government actions without necessarily dictating how any particular case will come out. It does so, first, by enabling the petitioner to attack the condition, rather than being treated as having waived any objection to it; and second, by then putting the government to a suitable burden of having to prove a bona fide—constitutional—objective sufficient to sustain the condition as applied to the petitioner in the manner the government proposes, or otherwise give it up. But while these are crucial benefits of the doctrine (otherwise, government could simply buy up every constitutional right by estoppel), they are ultimately inconclusive in deciding real cases. The government may be able to carry its burden of justification for the condition. The question returns us to the first amendment. What justifications are sufficient to sustain restrictions on one's speech against first amendment objections, in one's relations with government? What is the basic first amendment test? What must government show? And how does that requirement of a showing finally bear on academic freedom?

2. *From "Bad Tendency" to* New York Times v. Sullivan *via the Dissenting Opinions of Holmes and Brandeis: The Emergence of "The Central Meaning" of Free Speech.* Mr. Justice Holmes, who served on the Supreme Judicial Court of Massachusetts for twenty years and then served on the United States Supreme Court for thirty more, has been brought into this essay at every turn of the discussion. Always, until now, however, he appears as judicial bête noir, always he votes against each constitutional claim, personifying in each instance the most skeptical, narrow view of constitutional rights. In each case we have looked at thus far—*Frost* and *Berea College* as well as *Patterson, New Bedford, Lochner,* and *Meyer*—Holmes voted to sustain the state's regulation against every constitutional claim. And, quite obviously, he seems never to have championed first amendment rights.

How can it be, then, that Holmes nonetheless came to be canonized as one of the greatest Justices ever to have served on the Supreme Court? Partly, indeed perhaps largely, because his view of the first amendment—and of the central meaning of freedom of speech—fundamentally and finally changed.[50] Holmes was almost certainly the most philosophically inclined judge ever to occupy a seat on the Supreme Court. And, after two decades on the Court, he began to write altogether different kinds of epigrams than the sort he had authored in 1892; new epigrams very much like these: "The United States may give up the Post Office when it sees fit, but while it carries it on the use of the mails is almost as much a part of free speech as the right to use our

---

50. See David M. Rabban, *The Emergence of Modern First Amendment Doctrine,* 50 U Chi L Rev 1205, 1303-20 (1983); David S. Bogen, *The Free Speech Metamorphosis of Mr. Justice Holmes,* 11 Hofstra L Rev 97 (1982).

tongues."[51] How different this sounds from the earlier, dismissive talk of "privileges" that government may subject to such conditions it sees fit to impose. Just so, here is another paragraph from a similar Holmes dissent written near the end of the same decade, in 1928: "[I]f there is any principle of the Constitution that more imperatively calls for attachment than any other it is the principle of free thought—not free thought for those who agree with us but freedom for the thought that we hate."[52] There is obviously a stronger commitment to free speech in this passage than in Holmes' earlier, somewhat disdainful, remarks.

Here is Holmes again in his most famous dissent in 1919, in *Abrams v. United States*:

> [T]he best test of truth is the power of [a] thought to get itself accepted in the competition of the market. . . . That at any rate is the theory of our Constitution. It is an experiment, as all life is an experiment. . . . While that experiment is part of our system I think that we should be eternally vigilant against attempts to check the expression of opinions that we loathe and believe to be fraught with death, unless they so imminently threaten immediate interference with the lawful and pressing purposes of the law that an immediate check is required to save the country. I wholly disagree with the argument . . . that the First Amendment left the common law as to seditious libel in force.[53]

And here is Holmes dissenting (still again with Brandeis) in 1925: "If in the long run the beliefs expressed in proletarian dictatorship are destined to be accepted by the dominant forces of the community, the only meaning of free speech is that they should be given their chance and have their way."[54] One even reasonably attentive to Holmes will see something new in passages such as these. In significant ways they will eventually lend strong support to academic freedom as well. But, more generally, Holmes suggests that *any* idea (including one that would reorganize the government as a proletarian dictatorship and terminate the Constitution itself) is as fully protected as any other. The first amendment itself does not take sides.

Holmes now philosophically resigns himself to the obvious in a larger sense: life must settle for proxies of truth. Indeed, life can only provide proxies as truth, each in turn being perpetually subject to displacement by other ideas that become more compelling proxies of truth, each proxy simply being whatever seems most correct to each of us, tested in comparison with alternatives equally unrestricted in their availability to us—an availability it is one function of freedom of speech to assure. The notion of bad tendency as a justification to restrict the availability of an idea threatening the status of

---

51. *Milwaukee Publishing Co. v Burleson*, 255 US 407, 437 (1920) (Holmes dissenting). Compare *Lamont v Postmaster General*, 381 US 301 (1965). (*Lamont* is an important case that takes Holmes' suggestion seriously; it holds that an Act of Congress burdening certain political mail violates the first amendment, despite the plenary power vested in Congress. Incidentally, *Lamont* is worthy of special remembrance; it is the first case ever to strike down an Act of Congress on first amendment grounds. Id at 305.)

52. *United States v Schwimmer*, 279 US 644, 654-55 (1928) (Holmes dissenting).

53. 250 US 616, 630 (1919) (Holmes dissenting). Surely Holmes' position has moved from his 1908 view that the first amendment did little more than enact the common law whole.

54. *Gitlow*, 468 US at 673 (Holmes dissenting).

institutions, groups, established wisdom, or values through speech cannot survive this view of the first amendment. The status quo must always defend itself. The notion of bad tendency as a justification to restrict the availability of an idea is gone.

Within this central vision of the first amendment, the bad tendency test gives way under the Holmes rationale. The matter is further explained sharply in a later dissenting opinion by Justice Rutledge in 1944:

> It is axiomatic that a democratic state may not deny its citizens the right to criticize existing laws and to urge that they be changed. And yet, in order to succeed in an effort to legalize polygamy[, for example,] it is obviously necessary to convince a substantial number of people that such conduct is desirable. But conviction that the practice is desirable has a natural tendency to induce the practice itself. Thus, depending upon where the circular reasoning is started, the advocacy of polygamy may either be unlawful as inducing a violation of law, or be constitutionally protected as essential to the proper functioning of the democratic process.[55]

The net of it is, then, that the natural tendency of one's freedom to present what is currently thought hateful and wrong as actually quite desirable and right, to induce breaches of law by those to whom the appeal is communicated—some of whom may then break the law as it is—is *not* enough to enable the state to chill or to punish the person making the case. Under this very strong view, even predictable increases in violations of existing laws, traceable to the efficacy of the criticism of the law, cannot be expensed to the critic of the existing law or of the prevailing social ethic, even though the lawbreakers themselves may still be punished. It is a social cost of free speech in a democratic state.

In so suggesting, moreover, Justice Rutledge was but elaborating usefully on an abrupt point made eighteen years earlier, in *Whitney v. California*, by Brandeis (who joined Holmes in the various dissents quoted above): "The fact [alone] that speech is likely to result in some violence or in destruction of property is not enough to justify its suppression."[56] This, indeed, is very strong stuff. It is also, however, the meaning of free speech in the United States. From this point and this principle, all modern doctrines descend. It is, moreover, not necessary to review a lengthy series of subsequent cases to illustrate the principle. One case most especially, *New York Times Co. v. Sullivan*,[57] decided by the Court in 1964, shows in a single decision how greatly results have changed.

Sullivan was an ordinary civil libel proceeding brought in the Alabama state courts. False statements referable to Mr. Sullivan as a city commissioner in Montgomery, Alabama, had appeared in a political advertisement published by the *New York Times* (the advertisement solicited funds for a political cause). The text of the advertisement contained factual exaggerations about Sullivan's actions as city commissioner and about the extent of his participation in certain civil rights confrontations in Montgomery. The

---

55. *Musser v Utah*, 333 US 95, 101-02 (1948) (Rutledge dissenting) (citations omitted).
56. 274 US 357, 378 (1926) (Brandeis concurring).
57. 376 US 254 (1964).

statements were deemed defamatory per se under the Alabama common law of libel, consistent with the state judge's instructions, and the jury awarded $500,000 in general damages in favor of Sullivan and against the *Times*.

Sullivan might have been reversed under the Supreme Court's then-existing first amendment doctrine.[58] But the Supreme Court by-passed alternative grounds for reversing the judgment and proceeded to rewrite libel law in the United States. Directing its attention to the centrality of free speech and political issues in the United States, the Supreme Court held that, up to a certain point, even *false* press reports that may damage the public standing of a public official may be immune from civil or criminal redress. Indeed, the Court went on to hold, neither factual falsehood, nor actual harm (loss of job, shunning by the community), nor even lack of reasonable care in ascertaining the actual facts prior to publication, nor all in combination will necessarily be sufficient for a successful libel action. The first amendment, the Court held, not only disallows criminal prosecution of the publisher,[59] but also bars a law providing for personal, civil redress. To overcome that bar, according to the Court's opinion in *Sullivan*, the plaintiff must meet a new (first amendment) standard of scienter. Specifically, as determined in a later case, *St. Amant v. Thompson*, the plaintiff must establish by evidence of convincing clarity that the defendant actually knew the factual statements were false and published them despite that knowledge or, at a minimum, published them as true even though the defendant "in fact entertained serious doubts as to the[ir] truth. . . ."[60] Negligent failure to check for falsehood is not enough. *Sullivan* grants a first amendment immunity to standards journalists themselves would regard as professional malpractice. In this respect most especially, it is a remarkable case. Moreover, the first amendment rule *Sullivan* announced has since been extended to other figures who attract political interest and its implicit risks of parody and of withering, sometimes cruel, ridicule, as well as of defamation.[61] *Sullivan* has cut a wide first amendment swath through the law of torts, particularly libel and defamation.

---

58. There were several grounds on which the Supreme Court might have reversed without announcing the rule it did. Specifically, for example, the amount awarded by the jury bore no relationship to any evidence of actual damage to Sullivan's public standing in Montgomery, nor was there evidence of mental anguish or community shunning (no such specific evidence was required in cases alleging libel per se). Moreover, Sullivan was not mentioned by name in the advertisement, nor did the *Times* itself do anything other than publish the advertisement, that is, it had no direct hand in the advertisement's original preparation, nor did it represent anything on its own behalf as a source of news. Any award beyond purely nominal damages under these circumstances might well have been regarded as foreclosed by the first amendment. No broader issue need have been reached.

59. The first amendment assuredly does apply to bar such prosecutions. See, for example, *Garrison v Louisiana*, 379 US 64 (1964).

60. *St. Amant v Thompson*, 390 US 727, 731 (1968) (decided subsequent to *Sullivan* and adding to its reasoning).

61. For its most recent extension and application, see *Hustler Magazine, Inc. v Falwell*, 485 US 46, 56 (1988) (political advertisement parody depicting televangelist fictitiously as a drunken and incestuous hypocrite, held absolutely protected by first amendment regardless of emotional distress publisher may have meant to cause and was determined in fact to have caused). *Hustler* holds that the first amendment protects a right of political ridicule virtually absolutely. *Hustler* is also a highly important terminal case in a very long historical line; it ends the last possible vestige of any valid law of seditious libel in the United States.

Underneath, however, *Sullivan* is of a first amendment piece with the Holmes-Brandeis-Rutledge quotations we have abstracted from cases going back to the 1920s. The overall lesson is that neither the bad tendency, nor the "clear and present danger," nor yet the actual fact of some proximately resulting harms—even harms foreseeable to the author, the parodist, or the speaker as of the moment he or she looses her words on paper or sends them out into some public or private audience—will necessarily bring the utterer athwart of the law. Whether it will do so depends on what one sees to be the resulting cost to free speech. In *Musser,* Justice Rutledge's insightful dissent explored this concept of cost in a general way through the compelling example of speech advocating polygamy.[62] In *Sullivan,* the Court likewise pursued the concept of costs to free speech and developed still an additional step: "That erroneous statement is inevitable in free debate, and that it must be protected if the freedoms of expression are to have the 'breathing space' that they 'need . . . to survive' [seems obvious]."[63] Thus, in the Court's view, even factual misstatements, including some that may be quite damaging to public officials or to other public figures, nonetheless receive a qualified first amendment immunity. Without extending our case law examples much further, perhaps we can now see where these first amendment trends will lead.

In the 1950s, Judge Learned Hand proposed a first amendment formula that tried to catch some of the developments we have rather casually reviewed. His formulation is useful as a general statement, and far removed from the original, bad tendency test. Even so, it needs careful reading; it is often misunderstood. Here is the general formulation Hand suggested: "In each case [courts] must ask whether the gravity of the 'evil,' discounted by its improbability, justifies such invasion of free speech as is necessary to avoid the danger."[64]

Judge Hand's formulation is usually read as though it were a simple tort law formula for judges to apply. It is taken to say that if (but only if) one has fairly discounted the gravity of the evil to be avoided by the improbability of its likely happening as a result of someone's speech, so as not to exaggerate the need for the restraint on speech and so as not needlessly to interfere with speech, one may then invade free speech, albeit only to the extent necessary to avoid the danger.[65]

---

62. See note 55 and accompanying text.

63. 376 US at 271-72 (citations omitted). Critics of *Sullivan* (and there are many) do not disagree with the basic statement. Rather, the quarrel is whether the scienter standard exceeds any proper first amendment need, that is, that at least with respect to commercial publishers including newspapers, liability for negligent failure to check for falsity would be the appropriate line for the first amendment to draw where the plaintiff carries his or her burden under every other standard provided in *Sullivan* itself.

64. *Dennis v United States,* 341 US 494, 510 (1951), citing opinion of Judge Learned Hand in *United States v Dennis,* 183 F2d 201, 212 (2d Cir 1950).

65. Alternatively, implicit in the formula is the suggestion that where for some reason the measures taken to avoid the evil fail, but if the test is otherwise satisfied, the law may provide appropriate redress for the actual harm that ensued.

However, this reading goes too fast and takes too much for granted. One must read Judge Hand's statement more carefully. Judge Hand was framing a larger, harder question, and he did not say what the answer would necessarily be: courts must additionally ask whether X danger of Y evil justifies such invasion of free speech as may, admittedly, be necessary to avoid the danger; there is no implicit assumption that it necessarily will.

Moreover, from what we have reviewed thus far, it should now be apparent that the answer to Judge Hand's unanswered question turns out to be quite complicated under first amendment doctrine today. The short answer is that sometimes it will, but sometimes it won't, as the Court's holding in the *Sullivan* case illustrates, as Rutledge's example in *Musser* implies, and as the Brandeis quotation in *Whitney* declares. The answer is it won't, if the invasion leaves freedom of speech "too little space in which to breathe"—too little space to enable people to speak passionately for their beliefs or to seek through their speech to transfigure society, regardless of the direction they would try to take it by the political effects of their ideas and their appeals. In the hard law of the first amendment, the central meaning of first amendment in the United States today is found in the far greater substantiality of this constitutionally sheltered "breathing space" than was once provided. In the decades since 1907-1908 and *Patterson*,[66] constitutional doctrine has moved very far (farther than most Americans themselves understand) from the bad tendency test.

E

As an interlude to our discussion thus far, now that we have a more current and different grasp of freedom of speech under the first and fourteenth amendments,[67] we can easily see how freedom of speech fits some fairly standard cases of the sort we already touched upon. We are now in a much better position than we were a few pages ago to examine how such cases might come out on the merits when reviewed in the Supreme Court since these changes occurred.

An excellent case for such an examination is *Pickering v. Board of Education*,[68] our earlier case involving Marvin Pickering, the letter-writing high school teacher, which was decided in the Supreme Court just four years after *New York Times v. Sullivan*. Pickering's difficulties, one will recall, arose from the critical letter he wrote to a local newspaper, commenting on recent school bond measures that had failed despite strong and well-publicized school board endorsement and support.

Pickering's letter identified him as a local teacher, although he declared in the letter—albeit complainingly—that he was writing only "as a citizen, taxpayer and voter, and not as a teacher, since that freedom has been taken

---

66. See note 10 and accompanying text.
67. Bearing in mind that, since 1925 the first and 14th amendments have been treated alike in respect to free speech.
68. 391 US 563; see note 44 and accompanying text.

away from the teachers by the administration."[69] His letter harshly criticized the board's public representations made to encourage voter support for the bond issues; it suggested that some of them were untrue or at least misleading. His letter also argued that some past uses of funds were not in keeping with their original representation, for example, that more had been spent for athletics than for education, contrary to what had been said by the board. Overall, moreover, his letter laid a large portion of blame for the failure of the bond issues on the board and the school administration itself. Some specific statements in his letter (for example, on the cost of school cafeteria lunches) were false, although there was no suggestion that Pickering either knew or thought them to be inaccurate.

Previously, we limited our review of *Pickering* to a single, preliminary point, namely, a *New Bedford*-type claim made by the board in the state court that so long as Pickering continued to work as a public employee with notice that he did so under the constraint of forbearing from criticizing the schools, he could not complain of being terminated once he was shown in a fair hearing to have dishonored that condition. Under this view, recall, it was up to Pickering to determine the acceptability of the tradeoff; he could quit whenever he found it unacceptable, but he could not ignore it and expect to be kept on. We already noted the Court's rejection of that proposition under the *Frost* rationale. But we also noted something else: that the doctrine of unconstitutional conditions is often inconclusive of real cases; it begs the question of whether some conditions are not necessarily unconstitutional at all. Thus, a concrete example—regarding access to classified information— was furnished in a passing footnote to make the point plain.[70] Noting this inconclusiveness, we returned to the main track of first amendment doctrine. We return, re-examining *Pickering*, to see the final result reached under substantive first amendment law.

Pickering's letter identified him as a teacher. Moreover, he wrote about matters affecting the public schools about which readers might assume he was particularly well informed. In places, his letter was factually inaccurate. It was also sarcastic, insinuating, and rude. It was not addressed quietly or internally to make helpful or constructive suggestions to the elected members of the board. Rather, it was released into the local newspaper for its general ventilative effect. To be sure, there was no evidence of its community impact.

---

69. *Pickering*, 391 US at 578. Pickering's complete letter appears in the Appendix of the case, id at 575. As to his latter statement, the Supreme Court concluded that he had some factual basis for it to the extent that the Teachers Handbook required prior submission to a school principal and triplicate copies to a publicity coordinator in advance. Since the letter elsewhere indicated that this was the basis for Pickering's claim (that "freedom has been taken from the teachers by the administration"), the Court held that readers were merely invited to judge for themselves, that is to say, that the statement was clearly offered as Pickering's opinion, rather than as a revelation of false facts. Id at 570-71.

70. See note 49 (Access to highly classified information may be denied on considerations of national security, and even one's political affiliations that cannot be forbidden may nonetheless be taken into account in granting or withholding such access in certain circumstances, depending upon the degree of perceived serious risk.).

Nonetheless, were there no suitable grounds for the board to expect something better of a teacher in Marvin Pickering's position? In *Pickering*, the Court first held—as we might expect—that a rule forbidding any teacher or other school employee to comment publicly on any matter affecting the local schools without administrative permission would be an unconstitutional prior restraint under the first amendment. Assisted now by *Sullivan* and our review in the preceding section, we can now go much further, however, and see how the result for Pickering was substantially more favorable than when weaker views of the first amendment prevailed. Specifically, here is how matters went.

The opening emphasis of the opinion is on the public subject matter of Pickering's letter: school taxes, referendum bond measures, and popular voting at scheduled elections, the stuff of the democratic process itself.[71] Such public political speech, the Court insists, is highly protected overall; one cannot, as a condition of being a teacher, be forbidden to address such public issues publicly on the claim that school interests would be better served by a nonpartisan silence. Moreover, the critical, rather than neutral or supportive, tone of Pickering's views is "unequivocally reject[ed]" as providing grounds for his dismissal;[72] the first amendment does not allow the school board to require that he speak only favorably or neutrally, whether of itself or the alleged need for school bonds, as a condition of speaking at all.

Next, that Pickering was not merely critical in what he wrote but was also unpleasantly insinuating toward the board was treated by the Court as insufficient grounds to fire him for his public or professional incivility. "In these circumstances," Justice Marshall said, "we conclude that the interest of the school administration in limiting teachers' opportunities to contribute to public debate is not significantly greater than its interest in limiting a similar contribution by any member of the general public."[73] Thus the board could not seize upon Pickering out of frustration that, in their view, his letter did not represent them fairly or treat them courteously, though their feeling might itself be an understandable and even warranted reaction in light of the letter's tone. The board's interest in requiring general fairness, or even civility, was

---

71. *Pickering*, 391 US at 564-68. In contrast, a subsequent case, *Connick v Myers*, 461 US 138 (1983), draws a bright-line distinction that puts public employees at risk for voicing internal work-related grievances principally related to their own status. Under *Connick*, the employee may be fired, without recourse at all under the first amendment, by those of whom or to whom they complain. The Court's desire to seek some de minimis limit on "mere internal complaint" cases (as it is inclined to call them) is understandable, but the line drawn by *Connick* is not. The difficulty with *Connick* is that its first amendment line is arbitrary and indifferent to any particularized facts as well as to the severity of the restriction at risk (dismissal). *Connick's* lesson is that public employees who may have a just complaint may be fired with impunity by the very person already abusing them simply for speaking about the matter, even assuming their complaint is entirely true. Indeed, they may be fired because it is true. In respect to academic personnel, moreover, since it is obvious that both general and specific "workplace conditions" are constitutive elements of getting work done in a literal sense, academic freedom itself implies the protection of some prerogative to speak about such matters. See, for example, Matthew W. Finkin, *Intramural Speech, Academic Freedom, and the First Amendment*, 66 Tex L Rev 1323, 1335-45 (1988).

72. *Pickering*, 391 US at 570.

73. Id at 573.

too insubstantial under the circumstances (that is, as the court noted, "not significantly greater than its interest in limiting a similar contribution by any member of the general public").[74] The connection between the letter and Pickering's possible professionalism or lack thereof as a teacher (how he conducted himself in the classroom) was wholly speculative. The Court likewise noted that Pickering did not personally work for the board itself.[75]

Finally, the Supreme Court protected Pickering despite his factual mistakes, pursuant to the *Sullivan* rationale. As in *Sullivan*, the Court noted some margin of error is inevitable in such matters. The Court held that to cite Pickering's mistakes as creating the risk of dismissal when venturing into local, public, political debate would provide too little breathing space under the first amendment. The board could seek correction of the factual mistakes by recourse to the newspaper columns Pickering used. It could not, however, dismiss Pickering. In short, Pickering's free speech claim prevailed.

Pickering is thus an excellent illustration of how things have changed since 1908, and of how much stronger the first amendment has become in a general way. It is now but a very short step to fit academic freedom within the first amendment. We turn at once to see how it was done.

F

Academic freedom made its first express Supreme Court appearance in a dissent by Justice William Douglas, a former academic, in a 1952 case, *Adler v. Board of Education*.[76] With Justice Black concurring in his dissent, Douglas invoked "academic freedom" three times, in a specific, first amendment usage. He also gave the phrase a distinguishing identity for general legal use.

At issue in *Adler* was a New York statute providing for the disqualification and removal from public employment of any person espousing the use of violence to alter the form of government in the United States. The act (the Feinberg Law[77]) also provided that membership in any listed subversive group would constitute prima facie evidence that the person possessed the disabling trait. It further provided for disclaimer oaths and other detailed inquiries, as well as investigative hearings.

The majority of the Court sustained the statute from facial attack. In the main, it relied on the still-lingering right-privilege distinction, harkening all the way back to 1892; for that reason, the majority position was not to last. Fifteen years later, the right-privilege rationale no longer sufficed as a prop in the Supreme Court, and *Adler* was substantially overruled.[78] Our interest is, correspondingly, limited to the Douglas dissent.

---

74. Id.

75. So the result might have been different had Pickering been an employee of the Board. Later cases press this point rather hard.

76. *Adler v Board of Educ. of the City of New York*, 342 US 485, 508 (1952) (Douglas dissenting).

77. 1949 Laws of State of New York ch 360.

78. See *Keyishian v Board of Regents*, 385 US 589, 605-06 (1967), discussed at notes 107-08 and accompanying text. ("[C]onstitutional doctrine which has emerged since [*Adler*] has rejected its major premise. That premise was that public employment, including academic employment, may be

Justice Douglas voted to hold the Feinberg law unconstitutional. His overall approach was of a piece with *Meyer* and *Bartels*, two cases we have previously reviewed.[79] In *Adler*, however, Douglas expressly drew on the first amendment to shelter academic freedom. In *Meyer*, as we noted, the protection of academic freedom was merely an incident of substantive due process review. The analytic similarities of the cases—the majority opinion in *Meyer* and the Douglas dissent in *Adler*—are nonetheless striking.

In *Meyer*, the Court found fault, not with the stated object sought by legislature (to assure English literacy in youngsters regardless of the school in which they were enrolled), but with the means. Similarly, Justice Douglas did not find fault with the *stated* object of the Feinberg Law.[80] Rather, he argued, the fault also lay with the means. In *Meyer*, the objection was that the device used by the legislature to achieve a proper end was unconstitutionally excessive. A similar objection, in Douglas's view, was equally applicable in *Adler*.

Douglas wrote that if the state did not mean to "raise havoc with *academic freedom*,"[81] it must confine itself to limiting certain specific acts endangering public safety or putting public education at unfair risk. But the Feinberg Law, he insisted, was not so confined and was, rather, prejudicially restrictive in respect to those it disabled from teaching and excessive in how it would necessarily affect others as well. Declaring that "[t]here can be no real *academic freedom* in [the] environment" of exclusion and of teacher fear generated by the Feinberg Law,[82] Douglas found fault with it in two intertwined respects. The first was that the per se employment disqualification of persons from academic appointment in any public school based on what they might espouse as individuals was inconsistent with one of the concerns of academic freedom because it eliminated a nonrandom,

---

conditioned upon the surrender of constitutional rights which could not be abridged by direct governmental action. . . . *[T]hat theory was expressly rejected in a series of decisions following* Adler." (citations omitted and emphasis added)).

79. *Meyer*, 262 US 390; *Bartels*, 262 US 404; see notes 24-34 and accompanying text.

80. The "*stated* object" is deliberately emphasized because, given the broad manner in which the statutes in *Meyer* and *Adler* were drawn, the question of what the legislature in each case actually meant to do is unclear. In *Meyer*, as discussed in note 30, there was reason to believe the legislature may have been acting only partly in good faith, that is to say, to improve English literacy but also to suppress the German language. The statute was efficiently drawn to do both. In *Adler*, there is the same double effect (improve national security but also suppress Communists) and possibly some of the same mixed legislative motives as well (in *Adler*, as in *Meyer*, the statute seems drawn to do both). So the problem in each case, commonplace in civil liberties litigation, is in large part this problem of double effects and the corresponding problem of how best for the judiciary to confine legislatures to legislate appropriately, limiting their legislation only to constitutionally permissible ends. The majority in *Meyer* and Douglas in *Adler* confronted this problem directly. But neither Holmes in *Meyer* nor the majority in *Adler* did. The general judicial approach since *Adler* is to subject statutes affecting first amendment rights to strict scrutiny, with no favoring assumption to the legislature that the breadth of the statute was required by the circumstances; rather, the necessity for such breadth must itself be shown to the satisfaction of the court. (For an oft-cited reference on the general role of judicial review and heightened scrutiny in first amendment cases, see *United States v Carolene Products Co.*, 304 US 144, 152 n4 (1938)).

81. *Adler*, 342 US at 509 (emphasis added).

82. Id at 510 (emphasis added).

ideologically specific cohort from further consideration as teachers in any public school.[83] So sweeping an exclusion, in Douglas's view, raised a serious academic freedom, first amendment concern.[84] Additionally, the statute also operated as a source of intimidation to other teachers. "[The] system of spying and surveillance [provided for by the statute] with its accompanying reports and trials cannot go hand in hand with *academic freedom*," Douglas argued, taking into account the full apparatus of the Feinberg Law.[85] "It produces standardized thought, not the pursuit of truth."[86] The problem of the Feinberg Law in this view was that it bore down threateningly on all teachers in the New York system. It would, in Douglas's view, compel teachers within the system to steer a wide course to keep from triggering the trip wires of the New York law. It was far different than a statute directed to acts of professional misconduct. Its chilling effect, lest one draw attention to oneself (for example, by the nature of the subject, the materials one might assign, or how one might propose to examine the subject in class), was obvious and substantial, in Douglas's view.[87] A more narrowly crafted law was required to avoid the costs to academic freedom.

The Douglas dissent in *Adler* is notable beyond the fact that the phrase "academic freedom" appears for the first time in direct first amendment usage. Douglas also employed academic freedom as a distinct, identified subset of constitutional first amendment concern. He does not dismiss it as merely parasitic on a standard free speech claim. Within the framework Douglas provides, moreover, there remain almost no problems left to give it recognizable shape within standard first amendment law.

G

Later in the same term, Justice Felix Frankfurter (like Douglas, also a former academic) provided a concurring opinion that nearly completes the identification of academic freedom protection as a subset of first amendment

---

83. Id at 508-09.

84. The concern is that the exclusion self-selects all of a certain incidental political disposition just as, say, a Soviet exclusion of all individuals holding pro-capitalist attitudes from teaching eligibility would do, within their system, in an opposite way. This is an *academic* wrong, moreover, in that it is not merely an alternative way of framing a standard, personal free speech claim.

85. *Adler*, 342 US at 510-11 (emphasis added).

86. Id at 511.

87. This may, incidentally, be a suitable place to note the connection of the 1940 Statement of Principles on Academic Freedom *and Tenure* (emphasis added) with Justice Douglas's position in *Adler*. Teachers perpetually subject to nonrenewal, by mere notice that their services are no longer required by the institution, may be kept on their toes by the uncertainty of reappointment from year to year. But the lack of tenure also undercuts academic freedom in a serious way; as did the law in *Adler*, albeit in a different fashion, the system presses teachers to steer away from any possible trip wire that might put them out on the street. Thus, the AAUP regards tenure, following a probationary period (up to seven years), with dismissal thereafter for cause as determined in some kind of pretermination academic due process hearing, a vital safeguard to academic freedom itself. (The alternative, in a manner of speaking, is a system that keeps those who teach on their knees.) See William R. Keast, *Faculty Tenure* (Jossey-Bass, 1973); Fritz Machlup, *In Defense of Academic Tenure*, 50 AAUP Bull 112 (1964); William W. Van Alstyne, *Tenure: A Summary, Explanation, and "Defense,"* 57 AAUP Bull 328 (1971); Ralph S. Brown & Jordan E. Kurland, *Academic Tenure and Academic Freedom*, 53 L & Contemporary Problems 325 (Summer 1990).

law. In *Wieman v. Updegraff*,[88] the Supreme Court reviewed a state statute requiring compliance with a broad disclaimer oath as a condition of public employment.[89] Frankfurter concurred in the decision holding the statute unconstitutional under the fourteenth amendment, but he wrote separately to say why the statute was invalid as applied to teachers in particular, apart from its unconstitutional effect on the associational rights of other public employees.

The statute applied to all persons seeking or holding public jobs. The particular case before the Supreme Court, however, had been brought on appeal by several state college faculty members. Justice Frankfurter held that the oath requirement was too broad to be sustained as to them in particular. His opinion, with Douglas concurring, marked out tightened boundaries limiting state control of public school and university faculty, on a specialized rationale. Frankfurter's objections in *Wieman* were based on vintage academic freedom premises, absorbed into first and fourteenth amendment law.

Closely tracking Douglas's opinion in *Adler*, Frankfurter used the same constitutional analysis to the state law at issue that Douglas had applied to the Feinberg Law. Here, as in *Adler*, the first objection was to the winnowing effect of the disclaimer oath on the pool of eligible appointees for public school or state university teaching. The oath's exclusion was a coarse means of checking legitimate public interests in determining professional competence or on-the-job integrity. At the same time, it was bound to have a parochializing effect downstream, shaping the scope of academic freedom as a practical matter. Related, but equally substantial, in Frankfurter's view, was the additional dampening effect of the oath on the remaining (already narrowed) field of academic personnel. The point is the same as the one Douglas emphasized in *Adler*: the intimidating effect of the regulation on all remaining academic personnel. Both branches of Frankfurter's objection are quickly noted in the following few words:

> [T]he Fourteenth Amendment protects all persons, no matter what their calling. But, *in view of the nature of the teacher's relation to the effective exercise of the rights which are safeguarded by the Bill of Rights and by the Fourteenth Amendment*, inhibition of freedom of thought, and of action upon thought, *in the case of teachers* brings the safeguards of those amendments vividly into operation. Such unwarranted inhibition upon the free spirit of teachers affects not only those who, like the appellants, are immediately before the Court. It has an unmistakable tendency to chill that free play of the spirit which all teachers ought especially to cultivate and practice.[90]

Significantly, Frankfurter added an observation that warrants close attention: "The functions of educational institutions in our national life and the conditions under which alone they can adequately perform them are at the

---

88. 344 US 183 (1952).

89. The oath eliminated from any public employment any person affiliated with any listed subversive organization, whether or not the disqualified person was aware of whatever it was that made the organization subversive when he or she joined. The "[i]ndiscriminate classification of innocent with knowing activity," the Court held, cut too wide and arbitrary a swath. On that ground it was held invalid under the due process clause of the 14th amendment. Id at 191.

90. Id at 195 (emphasis added) (Frankfurter concurring).

basis of *these* limitations upon State and National power."[91] What are "these" limitations? Obviously, they are those that he had just addressed: first and fourteenth amendment limitations on state and national power to narrow the width of academic eligibility or chill the professionalism of public school or public university faculty in performing their proper work.

What underlies *these* limitations? "The functions of educational institutions . . . and the conditions under which alone [academic personnel] can adequately perform them," Frankfurter insisted.[92] What functions? — "*The*" functions include critical *educational* teaching functions, as Frankfurter understood those functions, of course.

Frankfurter's operating premises all sound very familiar by 1952, the date of his opinion, in terms of the general case already long since made *outside* the Constitution (till now), to explain the imperatives of academic freedom. But in *Wieman*, Frankfurter concretely linked that case finally into the hard law of the first and fourteenth amendments as well. He soundly located in these amendments a strong set of constitutional restrictions on state and on national power in establishing and operating public educational institutions. Frankfurter's position in *Wieman* was no different with respect to public educational institutions than the Holmes dictum in the 1920s and Holmes's discussion of the post office.[93] The government may give up the post office whenever it likes, Holmes had said, but may *not* presume to run it however it pleases, because, while the post operates, its use by each of us on fair first amendment terms is virtually as critical as the free use of our tongues. So, equally, Frankfurter suggested in *Wieman*, the government may give up public education whenever it likes, yet *not* conduct it other than according to conditions of academic freedom *so long as it stays in the business of education*. The premises of the first amendment require the protection of academic freedom in the structuring of state universities and public schools.

Five years later, Frankfurter reiterated and filled out these thoughts in *Sweezy v. New Hampshire*, decided by the Supreme Court in 1957.[94] *Sweezy* arose out of investigative hearings conducted by the New Hampshire Attorney General pursuant to state legislative directives under the New Hampshire Subversive Activities Act.[95] It is of a piece with *Adler, Wieman*, and a dozen other cases pulling and hauling at the first amendment during the 1950s when disloyalty investigations, oath requirements, and new employment restrictions loomed large.

New Hampshire Attorney General Louis Wyman had subpoenaed Paul Sweezy to answer questions including several inquiring into specific lectures he had given at the University of New Hampshire. At the hearings, Sweezy freely described himself as a "classical Marxist" and a socialist; he also

---

91. Id at 197 (emphasis added).
92. Id.
93. *Burleson*, 255 US at 437; see notes 51-54 and accompanying text.
94. 354 US 234 (1957).
95. NH Laws 1951 ch 193; now NH Rev Stat Ann, 1955, ch 588, §§ 1-16.

testified that he had never advocated the use of violence as a means of altering any government in the United States. However, Sweezy declined to divulge what he had discussed in his lectures at the university. He was cited for contempt and jailed until he would comply.

The majority opinion of the Supreme Court in *Sweezy* is only of passing interest, because it ultimately turned on a rather narrow ground. The Court noted that the questions asked of Sweezy skated very close to first amendment concerns of free speech and academic freedom (Chief Justice Warren's observations were strongly supportive of *both* kinds of first amendment claim).[96] Then, however, the opinion moved away from that discussion to hold that there was insufficient evidence in the record to sustain the claim that the legislature wished the Attorney General to pursue its inquiry in the manner he had pressed against Sweezy. That being the case, the Court held, Sweezy's refusal to answer was not clearly in contempt of anything the legislature might have sought, so treating Sweezy as in contempt was a denial of due process of law. Justice Frankfurter (with Justice Harlan joining him) concurred in the result, but not in Chief Justice Warren's reasoning. Frankfurter's position required that the case turn on the substantive academic freedom first amendment claim Sweezy had advanced. Finding the state attorney general authorized by the state legislature to have proceeded as he did, Frankfurter went directly to the sole remaining question: did the first amendment shield Sweezy's refusal to answer questions probing the contents of his university lecture? Frankfurter and Harlan held, on first amendment academic freedom grounds, that it did.

The Frankfurter opinion extended his opinion in *Wieman* on academic freedom. In several respects it also anticipated the *Sullivan* holding about first amendment imperatives of adequate "breathing space." His point in *Sweezy* was not that teachers may never be required to account for their teaching; it was that the social imperatives of academic freedom operate through the first amendment to require close judicial superintendence of such inquiries because of their implicitly chilling effects. Thus, he held, only compelling need will excuse such an inquiry when it is pursued by political agencies, even including authorized committees of the state legislature and even when the university is one the state operates and funds.

The test Frankfurter proposed (and which he held had not been met in this case) was as follows: "Political power must abstain from intrusion into this

---

96. Chief Justice Warren's opinion did expressly invoke "academic freedom," and he distinguished it from general first amendment rights of political expression. "We believe that there unquestionably was an invasion of petitioner's liberties in the areas of *academic freedom and* political expression . . . ." *Sweezy*, 354 US at 250 (emphasis added). He also declared that "[t]he essentiality of freedom in the community of American universities is almost self-evident," and that academic freedom has a student, as well as a faculty, aspect: "Teachers and students must always remain free to inquire, to study and to evaluate, to gain new maturity and understanding; otherwise our civilization will stagnate and die." Id. Then, declaring that "[w]e do not now conceive of any circumstance wherein a state interest would justify infringement of rights in these fields," Warren nonetheless abruptly broke off the discussion ("[b]ut we do not need to reach such fundamental questions of state power to decide this case") and moved to another basis to decide. Id at 251.

activity of freedom, pursued in the interest of wise government and the people's well-being, *except for reasons that are exigent and obviously compelling.*"[97] The phrase, "except for reasons that are exigent and obviously compelling," is *not* the usual standard an inquiring legislative committee need meet under the first amendment in order to overcome a first amendment-based refusal by a witness properly subpoenaed to respond to its questions.[98] Frankfurter's standard is significantly more stringent, as he was at pains to acknowledge. His justification was a continuation of his concurrence in *Wieman*. It was directed to the social functions of universities and to the first amendment corollary of academic freedom that Frankfurter regarded as constraining the government when academic freedom is at stake:

> When weighed against the grave harm resulting from governmental intrusion into the intellectual life of a university, such justification [as might ordinarily suffice in other settings] for compelling a witness to discuss the contents of his lecture appears grossly inadequate. . . . These pages need not be burdened with proof, based on the testimony of a cloud of impressive witnesses, of the dependence of a free society on free universities. This means the exclusion of governmental intervention in the intellectual life of a university. It matters little whether such intervention occurs avowedly or through action that inevitably tends to check the ardor and fearlessness of scholars.[99]

Quoting at the end of his opinion from what, in 1957, he rightly called "perhaps the most poignant"[100] statement on academic freedom yet to appear anywhere—a searing Statement of Remonstrance by The Open Universities in South Africa against their own government's actions—Frankfurter added the following:

> A university ceases to be true to its own nature if it becomes the tool of Church or State or any sectional interest. A university is characterized by the spirit of free inquiry, its ideal being the ideal of Socrates—to follow the argument where it leads. . . It is the business of a university to provide that atmosphere which is most conducive to speculation, experiment and creation. It is an atmosphere in which there prevail the four essential freedoms of a university—to determine for itself on academic grounds who may teach, what may be taught, how it shall be taught, and who may be admitted to study.[101]

Returning to the case at hand, Frankfurter acknowledged that the particular intrusions posed by the limited questions Sweezy had been asked might seem minor and unthreatening, but insisted they were not. The overall chilling effect in the circumstances would be major, even if immeasurable. The justification given for the intrusions was neither exigent nor compelling under the circumstances. So, he held, considerations of first amendment academic freedom precluded Sweezy from being held in contempt. With Justice

---

97. Id at 262 (emphasis added).

98. Compare *Sweezy* with *Braden v United States*, 365 US 431 (1961) and with *Wilkinson v United States*, 365 US 399 (1961) (contempt convictions for refusing to answer legislative investigative committee questions upheld against first amendment objections, the standard of judicial review as applied not being as stringent as that required in *Sweezy*).

99. *Sweezy*, 354 US at 262.

100. Id.

101. Id at 262, 263, quoting *The Open Universities in South Africa* 10-12 (a statement of a conference of senior scholars from the University of Cape Town and the University of Witwatersrand).

Harlan, he joined in the reversal of Sweezy's contempt conviction specifically on this ground.

In the dicta of the Chief Justice in *Sweezy*, and more concretely in the passages we have reviewed in *Sweezy*, *Wieman*, and *Adler*, distinct principles of academic freedom were linked directly to the protections of the first and fourteenth amendments. In academic life, the first amendment had come around.

III

ELABORATING THE USAGES OF "ACADEMIC FREEDOM" IN THE SUPREME COURT

A. (1957-1967)

Within the decade following *Sweezy*, 1957-1967, a half-dozen decisions in the Supreme Court worked at the edges of the *Adler*, *Wieman*, and *Sweezy* doctrines expressly relating first amendment developments and academic freedom. Five of these cases principally involved public colleges and universities. The sixth touched public schools as well. The trend of the cases yielded a strengthened first amendment philosophy within the Court. Four of the six cases elaborated on academic freedom within the special protection of the first amendment. Only the first of these cases, *Barenblatt v. United States*,[102] briefly faltered from Frankfurter's strongly stated position in *Sweezy*, although another also substantially bypassed a generalized academic freedom claim even while providing relief on an alternative ground. The other four moved strongly to verify claims of academic freedom marked out in first amendment metes and bounds.

Barenblatt v. United States, the first of these cases, was decided by a closely divided Court, five-to-four, in 1959. In *Barenblatt*, Justice Harlan wrote for a bare majority in sustaining a federal misdemeanor conviction of a former University of Michigan teaching fellow who had been prosecuted for contempt in refusing to answer questions during a public session of the House Committee on Un-American Activities. Several of the questions were directed to his possible knowledge of alleged Communist Party activities at educational institutions, including some seeking to determine the extent of his participation, if any, in Communist Party activities. Unlike *Sweezy*, none of the questions pressed him on any particular teaching or studying in which he may have been engaged, and the issue of academic freedom appears hardly to have been engaged.

Justice Harlan, finding the committee duly authorized to investigate the general subject, and finding also that the committee had reason to think the witness might have information pertinent to the inquiry, sustained the demand for answers against Barenblatt's first amendment objection. The

---

102.   360 US 109 (1959).

majority opinion made no reference to academic freedom except as a footnote mention from an amicus brief filed by the AAUP.[103]

The dissent by Justice Black also yielded no useful focused discussion of academic freedom. Rather, the Black dissent launched an excoriating first amendment attack on the House committee generally. The case was adjudicated in generalized free speech terms.[104] *Barenblatt* proved to be quite uneventful in the long run, either to extend Frankfurter's discussion in *Sweezy* or to cut it off.

Four years later, in *Yellin v. United States*,[105] a similar contempt conviction of a witness who had declined to respond to questions—some of which bore on the witness's activities while at the University of Michigan—was overturned in the Supreme Court. Even so, the new five-to-four majority on the Court, though it held oppositely from *Barenblatt*, also deflected any academic freedom issue even more completely than the *Barenblatt* Court had done. The case overall is probably a better example of the Court still struggling to find its feet. The sole mention of "academic freedom" reported in the case went largely unaddressed. The case was disposed of in the noncomplying witness's favor, but on narrow procedural due process grounds.[106]

In contrast, in 1967, the New York Feinberg Law (previously upheld in the *Adler* case) was struck down on its face on substantive first amendment grounds in *Keyishian v. Board of Regents*.[107] Moreover, the emphasis was not only once again centered on the first amendment; but the outcome also turned specifically on the professional effects of the law, that is, on its effects on teachers. The state law's requirement of an annual subversive-action

---

103. Id at 130 n29. The AAUP amicus brief (October Term, 1958, No 35) argued that first amendment imperatives of academic freedom do not privilege teachers from accounting for their work, but suggested that the standards endorsed by Justice Frankfurter in the *Sweezy* case had not been fulfilled by the Committee, thus, that the contempt sanction ought not be sustained. Justice Harlan did not appear to dispute the point as established in *Sweezy* (he had, after all, joined Frankfurter's opinion in *Sweezy*); rather, his opinion implies that the issue was not necessarily engaged by the facts before the Court.

104. That is, the dissent, like the majority opinion, was occupied with the role of the House Committee on Un-American Activities overall and its broad threat to lawful dissent and political affiliation *generally*, rather than with the particular facts of the *Barenblatt* case. Justice Black did cite *Sweezy*, id at 139-40, as requiring proof of a compelling need before the committee could brush over a witness's first amendment interests; and he did conclude that no sufficiently compelling need had been established by the committee, but it was a secondary reproach at best. For a fresh view of *Barenblatt* generally, see Harry Kalven, *A Worthy Tradition* 497-531 (Harper & Row, 1st ed 1988).

105. 374 US 109 (1963).

106. Id at 124. In *Yellin*, the witness was asked a number of questions in public session concerning his activities as a student at the University of Michigan and why he had provided no reference to having been at the University when he later applied for a steel-mill job. In declining to answer this and several other questions, Yellin read a statement in which he claimed privilege partly on grounds of academic freedom, id at 140, but the objection is neither elaborated on nor further addressed by the Court. Rather, the majority of the Court held that Yellin could not be held in contempt for refusing to answer questions in any *public* session because a request that he had submitted to be heard solely in *executive* session had not been referred to the whole committee for consideration and voted on as provided by the committee's own rules. In short, the Court held that such procedural protections of witnesses, such as the Committee Rules, could not be ignored by the committee, even assuming the rules could be repealed or revoked at will.

107. 385 US 589, 609, 610 (discussed in note 78).

disclaimer affidavit, the scope of the required affidavit, and the heavy accompaniment of enforcement machinery laid in place for proceeding against those accused of taking the oath falsely, were held to be unconstitutional as applied to state university or public school teachers.

The analysis of the first amendment academic freedom abridgments of the Feinberg Law was undertaken by Justice Brennan in *Keyishian*. Overall, the analysis is of a piece with that of Justice Douglas in *Adler*, except that now it represented a *majority* position in applying the first amendment. Writing for a new majority, moreover, Justice Brennan placed the protection of academic freedom within the *core* of first amendment concerns and not at its margins. The paragraph in which he did so would be quoted repeatedly by the Court during the next twenty years:

> [A]cademic freedom . . . is of transcendent value to all of us and not merely to the teachers concerned. *That freedom is therefore a special concern of the First Amendment*, which does not tolerate laws that cast a pall of orthodoxy over the classroom. . . . The classroom is peculiarly the marketplace of ideas. The Nation's future depends upon leaders trained through wide exposure to that robust exchange of ideas which discovers truth out of a multitude of tongues, [rather] than through any kind of authoritative selection.[108]

In holding the law invalid as applied to those in public education, *Keyishian* marks an important rite of passage. What *New York Times v. Sullivan* had meant in respect to journalism in the United States—a landmark first amendment decision *providing professional breathing room for critical journalism—Keyishian* forcefully represents in respect to academic freedom, including the academic freedom of those holding appointment by the state.

Later in the same term in *Whitehill v. Elkins*,[109] the Court voided a Maryland disclaimer oath on similar grounds. The Maryland act required teachers to swear as a condition of public university appointment that the oath taker was not engaged "in one way or another" (sic) in acts seeking the overthrow of the state or national government by force or violence.[110] False swearing was made punishable as perjury. The opinion for the Court holding the requirement void was by Justice Douglas. He concluded that the oath act (and a section providing for the dismissal of those found on reasonable grounds to be subversive[111]) was too broad to be consistent with the first amendment obligations to secure adequate protection of academic freedom in public education.

---

108. Id at 603 (citations and quotation marks omitted, emphasis added). For examples of the steering effect of the Feinberg Law the Court found to conflict with academic freedom, see id at 601 ("The very intricacy of the plan and the uncertainty as to the scope of its proscriptions make it a highly efficient *in terrorem* mechanism. It would be a bold teacher who would not stay as far as possible from utterances or acts which might jeopardize his living by enmeshing him in this intricate machinery."). The opinion also draws heavily from Frankfurter's concurring opinions in *Wieman*, 344 US at 194-98, and *Sweezy*, 354 US at 255-67, in explaining the full first amendment rationale.

109. 389 US 54 (1967).

110. Maryland Subversive Activities Act, Art 85A Md Code Ann §§ 1, 11, 13 (Michie 1969), repealed by Acts 1978, ch 257.

111. Id at § 14.

As in *Keyishian, Sweezy, Wieman,* and *Adler,* moreover, Douglas's first amendment analysis focused on the law's impact on teachers and professors.[112] As an example of the law's objectionable steering effect, Douglas observed that a faculty member, once having taken the oath, would need to avoid attending any international conference whose auspices were not totally known to him, simply from fear of drawing an investigation upon himself as having violated his oath.[113] After quoting extensively from *Sweezy,* Douglas framed the dispositive objection this way:

> The continuing surveillance which this type of law places on teachers is hostile to *academic freedom.* . . . The restraints on conscientious teachers are obvious. . . . That very threat [posed by the breadth of the disclaimer oath] may deter the flowering of academic freedom as much as successive suits for perjury.[114]

And, finding the breadth of the disability unwarranted because any proper governmental concerns with security or with professional integrity could be composed by more narrowly drawn rules not imposing these *in terrorem* effects on academic freedom, the Court held the Maryland statutes void.

In *Whitehill,* Douglas thus employed the reference to academic freedom as a reference to an understood, settled first amendment shield against the state in its superintendence and control of public education, much in keeping with his views dating from *Adler,* as well as in keeping with Justice Brennan's *Keyishian* opinion in the same term of the Court. The proper fit, identifying academic freedom with the first amendment, was made. The measured protection of academic freedom from hostile state action had become a settled feature of first amendment law.

Intermediately during this decade (1957-1967), moreover, two other cases were resolved by the Supreme Court in which "academic freedom" appears, although less centrally than in either *Keyishian* or *Elkins.* Both cases also resulted in holding state statutes invalid on first and fourteenth amendment grounds. The more relevant of the two cases, *Baggett v. Bullitt,* decided in 1964,[115] had been brought by sixty-four members of the faculty, staff, and student body at the University of Washington, who sued for declaratory judgment and injunctive relief from two state laws, the first of which applied to all public employees, and the other only to teachers. The latter required a broad affirmative oath "by precept and example [to] promote respect for the

---

112. That is, the objectionable effects are those bearing on the affected persons' professional work as teachers (the "academic freedom" effects of the law). The obverse side of the same regulatory coin would be the objectionable "free speech" effects of the law, that is, the extent to which, insofar as one becomes a teacher subject to the disclaimer oath, one must then steer clear of political associations and activities others remain free to pursue. For an elaboration of the distinction, see William W. Van Alstyne, *The Specific Theory of Academic Freedom and the General Issue of Civil Liberty,* in Edmund Pincoffs, ed, *The Concept of Academic Freedom* (Univ of Texas, 1972). For an example of a federal regulation limiting first amendment rights of public employees but clearly not implicating academic freedom, see *United States Civil Service Commission v National Ass'n of Letter Carriers,* 413 US 548 (1973) (congressional restriction of civil service employees from certain forms of active personal involvement in political campaigns, upheld).

113.   389 US at 60.

114.   Id at 59 (emphasis added).

115.   377 US 360 (1964).

flag and the institutions of the [United States and the] State."[116] The companion statute, applicable to all public employees, imposed a broad disclaimer oath denying that the employee was a "subversive person," defined as one who knowingly joins or knowingly remains a member of any group that "advocates, abets, advises, or teaches any person" seeking to alter the form of state or national government by force or violence.

As neither statute had yet been construed by the state supreme court, Justices Harlan and Clark thought the case premature. In their view, the statutes were open to a narrow interpretation that might disarm them of any undue chilling effects. Writing for seven members of the Court, however, Justice White disagreed and held the statutes void in light of their immediate impact on those required to take and abide by the oaths. Moreover, the examples Justice White gave of the objectionable downstream effects likely to be generated by the statutes were examples of professional, anti-academic freedom steering effects,[117] as distinct from ordinary anti-free speech effects. Significantly, too, in voiding the acts, Justice White noted:

> Since the ground we find dispositive immediately affects the professors . . . and the interests of the students at the University in academic freedom are fully protected by a judgment in favor of the teaching personnel, we have no occasion to pass on the standing of the students to bring this suit.[118]

This passing remark merits more than a few words of its own. Students were not subject to either of the statutes, that is, students were not subject to any oath or other constraint under either statute. Yet students had presumed to appear as parties in interest to have both statutes declared void. What was their standing to do so? It was certainly not to stand in for the faculty (several faculty were already plaintiffs in the case). But the students claimed a separate (albeit related) standing because of what they alleged to be the direct effects of the laws on their own academic freedom. That is, the students claimed that the faculty would be inhibited by *in terrorem* effects of the oath from giving a full professional account of themselves in educational relationships with the students. Their claim as students was that it was not constitutionally permissible for the State of Washington to attempt to structure their education by putting the faculty under duress to compromise their professional interaction with students. Taken on its own terms, their claim of learning freedom was straightforward and strong. Justice White did not treat it as frivolous. To the contrary, his point is that since the academic freedom interests of the students were vindicated through the judgment in favor of the faculty plaintiffs, it was not necessary to determine whether the students could

---

116. 1955 Act, Wash Laws 1955, ch 377, 1931 Act, Wash Laws 1931, ch 103.

117. 377 US at 369-72 (examples include a faculty editor's reluctance to edit any scholarly journal with articles by Communist scholars from apprehension of appearing to act inconsistently with his oath; a reluctance to consult with such persons or attend a convention or present a paper with such persons present; an inhibition in class on any critical treatment of existing institutions, as inconsistent with the separate oath committing one affirmatively to promote respect for such institutions by precept and example).

118. Id at 366 n5.

have successfully maintained the action even if no faculty had been willing to come forward (perhaps from fear of targeting themselves).[119]

The student academic freedom claim, so identified in *Baggett*, albeit obliquely, is notable. It is not in tension with the claim of academic freedom advanced in the same case by the affected faculty. Rather, the two are exactly consistent in seeking an educational environment in which the good faith critical professional skills of the faculty are not foreclosed by hostile state action from being available to the students in the manner of instruction they receive and their professional interaction with the faculty. We shall shortly see several other cases where the argument is taken up (it might usefully have appeared much earlier, for example, in *Scopes*). The last case we note between 1957 and 1967, however, was not litigated along such lines.

At issue in the remaining case of this period, *Shelton v. Tucker*,[120] decided in 1960, was an Arkansas statute[121] requiring every teacher in each state-supported school or college annually to submit a list of all organizations in which the teacher had held membership or to which the teacher had contributed financially during the preceding five years, as a condition of continuing eligibility for (re)appointment each year. A number of noncomplying public school teachers and state college faculty members sued to have the requirement enjoined. Unlike any of the cases thus far reviewed, the requirement assailed in *Shelton* simply sought the requested information; that is, it did not probe the teaching of the faculty, impose any sort of disclaimer oath, or render anyone ineligible on grounds of any particular affiliation (knowing or otherwise). Nonetheless, on a closely divided (five-to-four) vote, the Supreme Court struck the statute down on first amendment overbreadth grounds.

Four Justices, including Frankfurter, found nothing facially amiss with the state requirement. In certain respects, moreover, the generality of the annual reporting requirement was arguably a point in its favor; the requirement did not imply that only certain affiliations or some affiliations more than others might trigger additional investigation and inquiry. Nor did it steer one away from certain groups, causes, parties, or political action groups.

For Justice Frankfurter (joined by Justices Harlan, Whittaker, and Clark), this was enough to conclude that the suit was premature. In the event that any public school or state college faculty members might be able to show subsequently that any of them, after complying, were not renewed in the course of annual review because of hostile use by school administrators of the information disclosed as an incident of the required annual listing, it would be

---

119. The claim, in first amendment terms, is entirely as appropriate for the students to assert in this kind of setting as an equivalent claim brought on behalf of students to contest the racial assignment of teaching staff also affecting the conditions of the education the state chooses to provide. For an example of just such a claim, see *Rogers v Paul*, 382 US 198 (1965). And for an insightful general discussion, see Henry P. Monaghan, *Third Party Standing*, 84 Colum L Rev 277, 297-304 (1984).

120. 364 US 479 (1960).

121. Second Extraordinary Session of Ark Gen Assembly of 1958, Act 10.

timely then, and not earlier, to check the statute's application on strict first amendment grounds. Since, however, the comprehensive disclosure requirement was on its face relatable to at least some few uses that might be entirely proper (for example, some kinds of organizational affiliations or contributions could provide grounds for concern arising from apparent conflicts of interest, or at least furnish reason for inquiry), the teachers could not claim a first amendment right to associational secrecy. For Justice Frankfurter, in brief, the teachers' claims went too far. In defending his position, moreover, Frankfurter also made the following observation: "If I dissent from the Court's disposition in these cases, it is not because I put a low value on academic freedom. . . . It is because that very freedom, in its most creative reaches, is dependent in no small part upon the careful and discriminating selection of teachers."[122] The majority, in reaching the opposite conclusion on the main issue, was not overall at odds with Frankfurter's general view. Rather, the majority emphasized that the lack of any tenure system under Arkansas law put every teacher at fresh risk each year, with no burden on a nonrenewing school to do more than send notice that the services of a given teacher were no longer desired without obligation to say why. Against the factual background of recent massive resistance to desegregation in Arkansas, and the expressed anxiety of the plaintiffs that in these circumstances the disclosure laws would intimidate teachers affected by them to abandon membership and financial support for certain voluntary organizations such as the National Association for the Advancement of Colored People rather than face the risk of covert retaliatory use of the information they would be required to supply, the majority held that the state's interests in forced disclosure were insufficient to sustain the requirement on its face. They regarded the requirement as too indiscriminate. Emphasizing the lack of confidentiality, the lack of procedural protections (that is, tenure), and the general atmosphere of public hostility, and quoting elaborately from *Wieman* and from *Sweezy*, the Court struck down the Arkansas statute. Principally, however, the emphasis of the decision is more of a piece with the opinion in *Pickering*, since its stress is on the rights of those who teach not to be put under duress to forego ordinary political rights of association and citizen speech. Only secondarily is *Shelton* an academic freedom case.

B. (1968-1978)

Nine cases in the Supreme Court report usages of "academic freedom" in constitutional litigation during the eleven years bounding 1968-1978. As in the preceding section, not all are equally germane. But part of what one gains from an unhurried review is some clearer sense of what counts as an academic freedom interest, as against an ordinary (albeit strong) free speech concern as such. So it is not useless to see some instances of the distinction at work, as in

---

122. 364 US at 495-96.

some measure we already have. As we have already had occasion to notice, moreover, there are instances in which both descriptions of the interest at issue may be opposite.[123]

Some of the cases decided during this period are separately interesting, moreover, in reporting constitutional usages of academic freedom entangled with other constitutional clauses and issues. As one example, two cases measure the extent to which conditions of academic freedom or the lack thereof may limit the extent to which church-affiliated schools and universities may or may not receive direct fiscal support disbursed by the state. As a different example, the last case we consider here, *Board of Regents of The University of California v. Bakke*, draws on a claim of academic freedom in attempting to reconcile a state university admissions policy with the fourteenth amendment. The issue addressed by the Court in *Bakke* is the extent to which public universities may use race as a partial determinant of who shall attend the state university, claiming the power to do so as a valid exercise of academic freedom. But we begin with something much more obviously connected to the first amendment, the Court's 1969 decision in *Tinker v. Des Moines School District*.[124] *Tinker* was a major decision arising under the first amendment, importing free speech rights onto the premises of public schools in a manner and to an extent not previously secured in any decision by the Supreme Court.

At issue in *Tinker* was a claim brought on behalf of three public high school and junior high school students (respectively sixteen, fifteen, and thirteen years old). Through their parents, who warmly supported their children's actions, they sued in federal court to forestall school penalties from being imposed upon them following their suspension for defiance of a school district rule forbidding armbands from being worn on campus. The plaintiffs' position was that the rule was an unwarranted restriction on their rights of personal and political expression. That the restriction was limited to the premises of the school, they insisted, did not mean that it should therefore be sustained. Rather, plaintiffs argued, absent some justification more compelling than a flat policy preference to disallow such activity on school grounds, the rule ought to be seen as an impermissible prior restraint on their rights of free speech. By a majority of seven to two (Justices Black and Harlan dissenting in separate opinions), the Supreme Court agreed.

Writing for the majority, Justice Fortas held that the first amendment did apply directly to the public school premises, that is, that no *cordon sanitaire* could be thrown up around it forbidding political expression on the premises by those in attendance during the school day. This first holding was a major step by the Court, quite similar in respect to students, to *Sullivan* in respect to the press. No previous case had gone so far. Then, advancing to the particular facts of the case, Justice Fortas held that the activities of the students (wearing black armbands on school grounds during the school day as

---

123. See, for example, note 112 and accompanying text.
124. 393 US 503 (1969).

a personal, silent expression of reproach of U.S. engagement in Vietnam) were not subject to school restriction beyond that reasonably necessary to keep them from disrupting the program and activities of the school. Justice Fortas concluded that the scanty record did not reveal sufficient evidence of anything the school board might have relied on stronger than an "undifferentiated"[125] anxiety of adverse reaction to the students' behavior, and that this was simply not enough under the circumstances. The lower court decision was reversed.

In practical effect, the Supreme Court granted the plaintiffs a declaratory judgment entitling them to talk politics on their high school or junior high school campus—even by wearing armbands—in the absence of identifiable clear signs of adverse effects that might justify more tailored restrictions by the school administration.[126] In the course of his wide-ranging opinion (two Justices concurred only narrowly), moreover, Justice Fortas wrote aggressively in criticism of student speech-restrictive public school board policies at large. He prefaced his analysis with the following passages, which came to be much quoted in other cases:

> First Amendment rights, applied in light of the special characteristics of the school environment, are available to teachers and students. It can hardly be argued that either students or teachers shed their constitutional rights to freedom of speech or expression at the schoolhouse gate. This has been the unmistakable holding of this Court for almost 50 years.[127] . . . In our system, state operated schools may not be enclaves of totalitarianism. [S]tudents may not be regarded as closed-circuit recipients of only that which the State chooses to communicate. They may not be confined to the expression of those sentiments that are officially approved.[128]

Some of the Court's phrases in these passages fit well with strong academic freedom claims (for example, "[i]n our system, state-operated schools may *not* be enclaves of totalitarianism . . . students may *not* be regarded as closed-circuit recipients of only that which the State chooses to communicate").[129] They fit well, that is, with several points we have already derived in relating student and faculty academic freedom from *Baggett, Keyishian*, and cases of a like sort. They match up strongly also with other portions of our general review: that like the post, the state may give up public education when it chooses; but while carrying it on, the state is not sole master of what students are free to learn, whether on their own initiative or in interaction with those free to teach.

---

125. Id at 508.

126. It is likely that a restriction on carrying one's political insignia into the classroom might well have been sustained, though a campuswide ban per se fails.

127. This was not entirely true. Indeed, *Tinker*'s significance was that it established for the first time that, in some measure, public school premises cannot be restricted as a forum for political expression by students. Since *Tinker* there has been some erosion, though *Tinker* has not been overruled. See, for example, *Bethel School District No. 403 v Fraser*, 478 US 675 (1986) (student disciplined for off-color remarks as part of campus campaign speech on behalf of another student; *Tinker* heavily qualified). See also *Hazelwood School District v Kuhlmeier*, 484 US 260 (1988) (principal's unilateral and substantial censorship of student-managed, faculty-supervised newspaper sustained, 5 to 4).

128. *Tinker*, 393 US at 506, 511.

129. Id at 511 (emphasis added).

Still, allowing for all this, *Tinker* is not focused on academic freedom,[130] certainly not in the profile that has thus far stretched from *Adler* through *Keyishian*, *Whitehill*, and *Baggett*. Rather, *Tinker* represents a strong first amendment judgment by the Court respecting general free speech claims by students during hours of compulsory attendance at publicly run schools, rather than anything more subtle. It is an example of a strong view of general first amendment free speech rights in an open society, but not more.[131]

Four years after *Tinker*, in 1972, the Court reviewed a related first amendment claim by a group of college students in *Healy v. James*.[132] A chapter of Students for a Democratic Society ("SDS") had applied for official recognition as a student organization at Central Connecticut State College ("CCSC") in 1969. That status was sought in order to qualify the organization to place announcements of meetings or rallies in the student newspaper, to post notices on campus bulletin boards, and "most importantly"[133] (to quote Justice Powell), to use campus facilities for holding meetings. Recognized groups already included the Young Republicans, Young Democrats, Young Americans for Freedom, and the Liberal Party. Despite a six-to-two vote by the college Student Affairs Committee (four students, three faculty, and the dean of students) recommending approval, the college president disapproved the group's application.

The student organizers sued in federal district court to enjoin, on first amendment grounds, the president's refusal. The president defended his decision on the basis that a line should be drawn disallowing campus status "to any group that 'openly repudiates' the College's dedication to academic freedom,"[134] which, arguably, SDS did. SDS chapters had been involved in episodes of trashing and disruption at some other colleges. In the SDS view, colleges as well many other social, economic, and political structures in the United States were rigged against the interests of the poor. SDS was itself skeptical and contemptuous of the conventional view of academic freedom, a view they regarded as protecting the status quo. Influenced strongly by Herbert Marcuse's writings (for example, *Repressive Tolerance*[135]), many SDS members believed that prevailing first amendment doctrine was itself vicious

---

130. The sole actual mention of academic freedom in *Tinker* is a footnote reference to a law review note, Note, *Academic Freedom*, 81 Harv L Rev 1045 (1968) (using the phrase in its title). 393 US at 506 n2.

131. The dissenting opinion by Justice Harlan is useful in elaborating this point. Id at 526. Also, in saying that "*teachers* [do not] shed their constitutional rights to freedom of speech . . . at the schoolhouse gate," id at 506, Justice Fortas is correct in the sense the *Pickering* case shows. The dictum may seem to go further, however, and to imply that public school teachers may also use school premises as the students used them, for example, to wear political armbands; but that is doubtful (nor would academic freedom necessarily embrace the idea). Rather, it is likely a public school rule forbidding teachers to wear political armbands or buttons during working hours on school premises or in classrooms would—and should—be sustained.

132. 408 US 169 (1972).

133. Id at 176.

134. Id.

135. Robert Paul Wolff, Barrington Moore, Jr. & Herbert Marcuse, *A Critique of Pure Tolerance* 80-117 (Beacon Press, 1969).

because it enabled entrenched elites to exploit others by perpetuating a myth of an open marketplace of ideas, which the elites dominated for their own ends. SDS did not agree that moral people should tolerate the free circulation of evil ideas; rather, moral people should act to disrupt their presentation when necessary to prove they were no longer acceptable in the classroom or anywhere else.

Despite all this, however, in seeking recognition at CCSC, the SDS chapter had actually filed an unprepossessing statement of educational purposes. When pressed for further information as to whether they might engage in interrupting classes, they replied only that their action would "be dependent upon each issue."[136] The president decided that this was not adequate and disapproved their request. After still further campus hearings on the question of recognition (hearings mandated by the district court), the president renewed his disapproval on grounds that recognition of the SDS chapter would be "contrary to . . . orderly process[es] of change" and would present a "disruptive influence" to the college.[137] The district court sustained the president. The court of appeals affirmed the district court. The Supreme Court unanimously reversed in an opinion written by Justice Powell.

In his opinion, Powell quoted *Tinker* and declared: "At the outset we note that state colleges and universities are not enclaves immune from the sweep of the First Amendment. [W]e break no new constitutional ground in reaffirming this Nation's dedication to safeguarding academic freedom."[138] Then, after noting that the student organization had complied with the college's filing requirements and that the president's adverse decision operated as a prior restraint under the circumstances, Justice Powell placed the burden of justification on the college and held that it had not been met. Any risk of disruption or intimidation was inchoate, not sufficiently clear nor present to justify refusing to allow the chapter to form and meet on campus. The philosophy of the organization, even assuming it countenanced violence and disruption, "affords no reason" for disallowing it to persuade others of the truth of its point of view, so long as it in fact operated on campus in an orderly fashion, even as the Young Democrats or Young Americans for Freedom already did.[139] Powell's statement was exceedingly strong in applying the first amendment. It virtually repeated the position Holmes and Brandeis had taken a half century earlier as a general first amendment rule: "Whether petitioners did in fact advocate a philosophy of 'destruction' [is] immaterial. The College, acting here as the instrumentality of the State, may not restrict speech or association simply because it finds the views expressed by any group to be abhorrent."[140]

---

136. *Healy*, 408 US at 173.
137. Id at 179.
138. Id at 180 (citations omitted).
139. Id at 187.
140. Id.

Concern with respect to actual acts of disruption or actual acts of intimidation, or with respect to acts to deprive others of their opportunity to speak or be heard, is entirely proper, Powell declared firmly for the Court. But, quoting from *Tinker* again, Powell held that definite actions, or at least discernible threats of such actions, must materialize to warrant sanctions by the college, including revocation of recognition. A ban of the organization in advance of *any* untoward activity or *any* specific threat could not stand, consistent with the fourteenth amendment's application of the first amendment to the state college.

At the end, Powell hedged only in one respect. The decisions of the lower courts were reversed, but the case was remanded for further proceedings to determine whether the SDS group would express a minimal willingness to be bound by such campus regulations as the Court had already indicated the college might maintain and strictly enforce (against disruption, invasion of classrooms, or interference with other speakers, for example). The Court thus left the possibility open that the group might be banned if, notwithstanding a request to do so, it declined to submit a statement of willingness to be bound by the valid rules that the college maintained for the protection of academic freedom and for general order on campus.[141]

Healy, even more than *Tinker*, is an exceptionally strong first amendment decision, albeit confined to *state* colleges (as *Tinker* is confined to public schools). Neither implies that unaffiliated outside groups may willy-nilly wedge themselves onto public school or state college premises. On the other hand, neither case (certainly, not *Healy*) permits the college to draw a sharp line according to the ideological auspices of student groups free to claim campus breathing space of their own up to the point of actual threats, acts of intimidation, actual acts of disruption, or interference with the educational program or rights of others on campus, as both cases are at pains to say. A concurring opinion by Justice Douglas carried the point even farther than did that by Justice Powell. Douglas defended the radical heterodoxy of student groups as a check even as to the faculty itself:

---

141. Extracting such a commitment to observe the rules necessarily puts groups such as SDS under a strain. In the circumstances, the act of making such an affirmative expression is inconsistent with the group's view that such rules are not entitled to respect (because, in SDS's opinion, they constitute a parliamentary façade by means of which dominant classes maintain elite control). It may be argued that refusal to express acceptance of such rules may not be sufficient grounds to ban the group, though enforcement of the rules would be utterly sound. The problem is akin to a pledge of allegiance test. Compare these two statements:

    (a) In applying for recognition on campus, we accept and agree to observe all college rules applicable to recognized student organizations;

    (b) In applying for recognition on campus, we acknowledge that the College has a set of rules applicable to recognized student organizations, and we understand that we will not be regarded by the College as exempt from them.

The second form effectively records the fact of notice of the rules; it makes clear that recognition in no way implies waiver by the college of its rules. The first form, requiring acceptance of the rules, however, seeks a concession respecting the accepted legitimacy of the rules; somewhat like a "pledge of allegiance," it is more doubtful on that same account.

Some [of the faculty] have narrow specialities that are hardly relevant to modern times. History has passed others by, leaving them interesting relics of a bygone day. More often than not they represent those who withered under the pressures of McCarthyism or other forces of conformity and represent but a timid replica of those who once brought distinction to the ideal of academic freedom.[142]

At least passingly related to *Tinker* and to *Healy*, moreover, is *Jones v. State Board of Education*,[143] denied review in the Supreme Court in 1970. At issue in the case was a petition for certiorari, brought by a state college student who had been suspended by the college. He claimed it was done solely because he distributed a campus pamphlet for the Student Nonviolent Coordinating Committee ("SNCC"), urging a student registration boycott—an activity he claimed the first amendment protected. After hearing oral argument, the Court dismissed the petition for lack of sufficient evidence in the record regarding the actual basis of the student's suspension (it appeared in the course of oral argument before the Court that he may have been suspended for having lied to the campus disciplinary committee rather than for having distributed the pamphlet). So, technically, the case altogether washed out. But one Justice, Douglas, filed a dissent.

Douglas did not relate the student's actions to academic freedom (the phrase "academic freedom" actually appears solely in the student's pamphlet, reprinted in the case), but his opinion treats those actions as protected by the first amendment nevertheless. That the pamphlet statements may have been "ill-tempered and in bad taste," or "even strongly abusive,"[144] Douglas says, may not on those grounds enable the state college to have the pamphleteer suspended or dismissed. On the other hand, Douglas insisted, "[t]his does not mean that free speech can be used with impunity as an excuse to break up classrooms, to destroy the quiet and decorum of convocations, or to bar the constitutional privileges of others to meet together in matters of common concern."[145] In brief, the Douglas opinion does not break new ground, but it does represent a very strong view of student-citizen, on-campus free speech.

Tinker, Healy, and *Jones* are, in sum, strong first amendment cases. All treat students as possessing assertable first amendment rights *on campus*. All involve student engagement in some conspicuous form of personal political expression. In many respects, their parallelism to *Sullivan* and *Pickering* is quite complete: they are animated by a strong first amendment breathing space rationale extended in three dimensions at once.

The first dimension is in the holding that the first amendment disallows public authority to cordon off public school or public college premises by any strict limitation restricting students in attendance to "educationally germane" speech alone; it appears specifically in the Court's express, reiterated proposition that students need not leave their involvement in general political

---

142. *Healy*, 408 US at 196-97.
143. 396 US 817, cert dism, 397 US 31, reh denied 397 US 1018 (1970).
144. 397 US at 33 (Douglas dissenting).
145. Id at 33-34.

debate at the school gate.[146] The second dimension of the breathing space rationale is that the extent to which the first proposition holds true is more substantial than one might have supposed, in both a procedural and in a substantive sense. So, the cases suggest, procedural limitations (for example, those generally concerned with time, place, and manner of on-campus expression) must not sweep wider than reasonably warranted in order to avoid *material* kinds of interference with the orderly campus environment. Both *Tinker* and *Healy* (and certainly Douglas's dissent in *Jones*) strongly so suggest. Substantively, the rules may generally not pick and choose "acceptable" philosophies to be presented on campus through student on-campus expression; nor, evidently, may common forum advantages of operating on campus (for example, as a recognized student group) be withheld because of misgivings associated with a particular group's ideological bent or because of strong public disapproval. Third, these propositions evidently hold, in some degree, even in respect to quite young persons (for example, in *Tinker*, one of the students was only thirteen). While it may be doubtful whether these first amendment beachheads involve student academic freedom in any ordinary understanding (that is, compare these cases with the academic freedom student claim in *Baggett*), one may rightly pause in thinking the matter through. They do assure students of some right to fashion what is in some loose sense a constitutionally protected cocurriculum on campus—the teaching agendas and learning experiences of their own actions—carried on in a manner that may well influence the official curriculum as well. Obliquely, therefore, if not directly, they do secure a kind of anarchistic student academic freedom under first amendment auspices one might be mistaken to discount or dismiss.

Two years after the dismissal of certiorari in *Jones*, the Court denied certiorari in a case in which Justice Douglas again dissented, *President's Council v. Community School Board*.[147] The case is an inconclusive forerunner to an address by the full Court of the same issues in 1982,[148] but Douglas's dissent is noteworthy because it bears intimately on his exceptional views in *Healy* and *Jones*. It also virtually completes the twenty-year cycle of Douglas opinions on the larger subject, beginning with his seminal dissent in the 1952 *Adler* case, the first explicit use of academic freedom in the Supreme Court.

President's Council had been commenced in federal district court by a combination of plaintiffs: a junior high school principal, a librarian from one of the affected schools, and several parents suing for themselves and their children.[149] Their object was to secure a mandatory injunction ordering the

---

146. *Tinker*, 393 US 503.

147. 457 F2d 289 (2d Cir 1972), cert denied, 409 US 998 (1972).

148. *Board of Educ., Island Trees v Pico*, 457 US 853 (1982); see notes 237-49 and accompanying text.

149. Had the publisher and author joined the case as plaintiffs, the additional issue would have been joined whether *their* freedom of speech and press interest—to reach willing readers—was violated by the state action interposed by the school board's banishment of the book from public school library shelves. (To frame the issue in this way is not to imply a certain answer, but it may

school board to return a particular book[150] to the school library shelves, from which the school board had ordered it removed.

Noting that the book remained available to those students presenting a written request by their parents, the court of appeals (in affirming the district court's dismissal of the case) held that the alleged violation of academic freedom was no more than "miniscule" (sic), if real at all: the court regarded the whole matter to be much too trivial to "elevate this intramural strife to first amendment constitutional proportions."[151] Dissenting from the Supreme Court's subsequent denial of certiorari, however, Douglas strongly disagreed:

> Academic freedom has been upheld against attack on various fronts. . . . The first amendment is a preferred right and is of great importance in the schools. . . . Are we sending children to school to be educated by the norms of the School Board or are we educating our youth to shed the prejudices of the past, to explore all forms of thought, and to find solutions to our world's problems?[152]

Douglas left it quite unclear whose academic freedom (presumably that of the students?) had been abridged. We shall see later, in the Court's treatment of the 1982 *Pico* decision, what became of this species of dispute when it was more fully discussed. The first amendment importance of the dissent is that Douglas regarded the school board action as reviewable at least to see whether the state was acting through its public school system to restrict the availability of ideas out of a community preference for insulating conventional wisdom from critical appraisal (albeit in the form of a particular book on the library shelf rather than in the form of the remarks of a classroom teacher); it is not at all clear that he was wide of the mark in voting to have the Court take a closer look at the case. Indeed, his dissent is related in this respect to a major Supreme Court case of this same period, *Epperson v. Arkansas*,[153] decided in 1968.

Epperson was a reprise on *Scopes*; it dealt with a virtually identical state criminal statute, adopted in Arkansas the year after the Tennessee court had sustained the Tennessee act. Like that act, the Arkansas statute forbade

> *any teacher* . . . in any University, College, Normal, Public School, or other institution of the State, which is supported in whole or in part from public funds . . . to teach the theory or doctrine that mankind ascended or descended from a lower order of animals [or to use any textbook] that teaches the [same theory or doctrine].[154]

Notwithstanding this statute, a public school teacher, Susan Epperson, did assign such a textbook for use in her high school biology class; she sued in state court for a declaratory judgment to determine whether she could use the

---

provide an additional first amendment link with the other plaintiffs asserting compatible interests in lifting the ban.)

150. Piri Thomas, *Down These Mean Streets* (Knopf, 1967).
151. 457 F2d 289, 292 (2d Cir 1972).
152. *President's Council*, 409 US at 999-1000 (Douglas dissenting).
153. 393 US 97 (1968).
154. Ark Stat Ann §§ 80-1627 to 1628 (1960 Repl Vol). Note that just as was true of the Tennessee statute, the restriction also applied at the university level. That being so, any suggestion that the statute merely meant to shield especially young children from emotional conflict (between subjects addressed in school and family loyalties) would seem entirely farfetched.

textbook without threat of discharge or criminal prosecution. The state chancery court, responding to the numerous U.S. Supreme Court decisions we have previously canvassed, held that the state could not "restrict the freedom to learn, and restrain the freedom to teach" by categorical criminal law censorship of this sort, even within its own schools and colleges.[155] As it was to turn out, however, *only* the state chancery court's opinion applied first amendment-academic freedom as the principal basis for decision; somewhat ironically, and altogether anticlimactically, neither the state supreme court nor the U.S. Supreme Court did.

The state supreme court gave the entire case short shrift. In a two-sentence per curiam reversal of the chancery court, the state supreme court treated the state as free to set the terms of teaching and learning in public schools and public universities as it wished (just as the Tennessee Supreme Court had done in the 1920s); it peremptorily upheld the restriction as "a valid exercise of the state's power to specify the curriculum in its public schools."[156] In brief, the Arkansas Supreme Court treated the teachers as confinable in their classroom coverage exactly as the state legislature preferred; correspondingly, the dependent freedom of the students, in their interactive learning relationships with the teachers, was implicitly cut off as well. *Epperson* thus went to the Supreme Court as an excellent first amendment academic freedom case. The case was as strong—perhaps stronger—than that joining the issues we noted in *Baggett v. Bullitt*,[157] albeit drawn in the setting of secondary education, rather than in state colleges and universities.

In the Supreme Court, Justice Fortas (writing for six members of the Court) initially addressed the case in strong first amendment, academic freedom terms. He invoked *Keyishian*[158] and *Shelton v. Tucker*[159] to settle the full relevance of the first amendment to the classroom. He likewise referred to *Meyer*,[160] describing it as a case in which "the Court did not hesitate to condemn under the Due Process Clause 'arbitrary' restrictions upon the freedom of teachers to teach and of students to learn."[161] But, having set up the case in these strong, promising terms, Justice Fortas then deflected the actual decision into a narrower channel. He concluded that it was not necessary to strengthen the constitutional constraint upon the powers of the state government to operate public schools and universities as it wished, even though the state attorney made virtually no effort to defend the law (he more or less desultorily adhered to the state supreme court's view that no defense

---

155.   393 US at 100, quoting unreported opinion of Chancery court.
156.   242 Ark 922, 416 SW2d 322 (1967).
157.   377 US 360. See note 115 and accompanying text.
158.   385 US 589 (1967).
159.   364 US 479 (1960).
160.   262 US 390 (1923).
161.   *Epperson*, 393 US at 105. This was, however, slightly careless of Justice Fortas; *Meyer*, it will be remembered, dealt with an effort to restrict German language instruction in *private* schools, not (merely) public schools, as here.

was needed—that is, that the state could do as it liked as to its own schools and colleges—a view clearly incorrect under pre-existing Supreme Court decisions). Rather, Justice Fortas concluded, whatever valid reasons a state might adduce in some circumstances, to justify the way it has allocated scarce educational resources or has taken into account the age of students (for example, the appropriateness of reserving some subjects to higher age groups), no such considerations accounted for the categorical, across-the-board exclusion at issue. Instead, Fortas held, the Arkansas statute had no purpose other than to serve the interests of the dominant religious faith of the region by forbidding public classroom instruction inconsistent with its tenets.[162] A legislative preference merely to protect a dominant religion is disallowed as contrary to the first amendment's establishment clause. Accordingly, the court struck down the Arkansas statute specifically on that ground.[163]

The decision in *Epperson*, however, was weakened by the surprising concurrence filed by Justice Black (surprising because, along with Justice Douglas, Black had been most forceful in the long list of academic freedom cases and regulations in the 1950s and 1960s). In Justice Black's view, the statute was void only because the state supreme court had left it uncertain whether a teacher was "forbidden to mention Darwin's theory at all or [was forbidden only] from contending that it was true."[164] If the statute meant to prohibit any mention, then, while it might be valid as thus understood, the state court needed to make clear the extent of the statutory prohibition, in order that teachers not be made to guess. For Black, therefore, the vice of the

---

162. Id at 107. Note, again, that the statute applied uniformly to public higher education as much as to secondary education in Arkansas, thus—on its face—proposing no distinction in respect to secondary education, that is, no basis for crediting a rationale applicable to the one level of schools vis-á-vis the other, since the legislature made no such distinction at all. The foreclosure of any academic presentation respecting evolution of the species (like the equivalent banning of books, journals, or other publications containing like material through the mails) should be the easiest kind of first amendment case under these circumstances. Of course, to the extent that the restriction was also enacted because those having the power to do so wanted the topic and materials suppressed as a set of blasphemous ideas, Fortas was not wrong to fault the statute separately under the establishment clause. (The case is no different in that regard than the use of state power to forbid the publication or republication of Galileo's telescopic evidence tending to confirm Copernican astronomy; that the ban is limited to state-supported educational institutions should make no difference at all.) For a recent and excellent review of blasphemy and the first amendment, see Robert C. Post, *Cultural Heterogeneity and Law: Pornography, Blasphemy, and the First Amendment*, 76 Calif L Rev 297 (1988).

163. There is and can be no doubt that the First Amendment does not permit the State to require that teaching and learning must be tailored to the principles or prohibitions of any religious sect or dogma. . . . In the present case, there can be no doubt that Arkansas has sought to prevent its teachers from discussing the theory of evolution because it is contrary to the belief of some that the Book of Genesis must be the exclusive source of doctrine as to the origin of man. . . . No suggestion has been made that Arkansas' law may be justified by considerations of state policy other than the religious views of some of its citizens. . . . The law's effort was . . . an attempt to blot out a particular theory because of its supposed conflict with the Biblical account, literally read.
393 US at 106-09. Justice Fortas's sole usage of "academic freedom" appears in footnote citations of law journal titles (id nn10, 13).

164. Id at 112 (Black concurring).

law was its threat of criminal sanctions against one who might guess wrong; putting teachers at risk in that way was unfair—a denial of due process.

At one point, Justice Black made an unexceptionable observation that teachers may not, as a matter of constitutional right, commandeer the classroom in whatever way suits their fancy.[165] At another point, however, he veered very much in the direction of moving all the way from that undisputed basic proposition virtually to the rhetoric of the right-privilege distinction the Court had long since rejected:

> I am . . . not ready to hold that a person hired to teach school children takes with him into the classroom a constitutional right to teach sociological, economic, political, or religious subjects that the school's managers do not want discussed. . . . I question whether it is absolutely certain, as the Court's opinion indicates, that "academic freedom" permits a teacher to breach his contractual agreement to teach only the subjects designated by the school authorities who hired him.[166]

As though to underscore the extreme implications of Justice Black's view (and to separate himself from them), Justice Stewart authored a separate, one-page concurring opinion. Stewart distanced himself from Justice Black by declaring that he believed it would violate the first amendment's free speech clause (not merely the establishment clause) for a state statute to forbid public school teachers "so much as to mention the very existence of an entire system of respected human thought" (he expressly includes "Darwin's theory"); he then wrote that "since Arkansas may, or may not, have done just that, I conclude the statute before us is so vague as to be invalid under the Fourteenth Amendment."[167] To restate his proposition accurately, had it been clear that the statute did forbid any mention of Darwin's theory in the treatment of subjects to which it would be relevant, Justice Stewart would have held the statute invalid on *that* account—not for vagueness (Justice Black's sole objection) but for unconstitutional *overbreadth* (an objection Black evidently would not have endorsed). And that objection, consistent with the pre-existing case law of the Court on academic freedom and the first amendment, certainly seems correct.

Indeed, in a roundabout but nonetheless instructive fashion, two principal cases decided by the Court during this decade strongly confirm Justice Stewart's position in *Epperson*. The earlier case, *Tilton v. Richardson*,[168] was decided in 1971. It reviewed the substantive constitutionality of an act of Congress providing for capital construction grants for which private as well as public colleges and universities were eligible; the grants were targeted for specified kinds of campus buildings and facilities such as classrooms, science laboratories, and libraries. The immediate question was whether religiously affiliated colleges could participate in these grants despite the first amendment provision respecting the separation of church and state. In a closely divided vote, five-to-four, the Supreme Court held that they could.

---

165. Id at 113.
166. Id at 113-14.
167. Id at 116 (Stewart concurring).
168. 403 US 672 (1971).

Significantly, in sustaining the constitutional eligibility of the particular religiously affiliated colleges and universities at risk in the case, Chief Justice Burger, writing for the majority, expressly used academic freedom as the constitutional litmus test: whether despite the formal governance of certain colleges by religious bodies, they were nonetheless "characterized by an atmosphere of academic freedom rather than religious indoctrination" such that they compared favorably with other eligible institutions in that respect and ought not be characterized as primarily agencies of a church.[169] So, at various points in his opinion, the Chief Justice noted that non-Catholics were admitted as students,[170] that non-Catholics were members of the faculty,[171] that the schools "introduced evidence that they made no attempt to indoctrinate students or to proselytize,"[172] that none required attendance at religious services,[173] and that the theology courses "are taught according to the academic requirements of the subject matter and the teacher's concept of professional standards."[174] In elaborating on these observations, he went on:

> [T]hese four schools subscribe to a well-established set of principles of academic freedom and nothing in this record shows that these principles are not in fact followed. . . . Although appellants introduced several institutional documents that stated certain religious restrictions on what could be taught, other evidence showed that these restrictions were not in fact enforced and that the schools were characterized by an atmosphere of academic freedom rather than religious indoctrination. All four institutions, for example, subscribe to the 1940 Statement of Principles on Academic Freedom and Tenure endorsed by the American Association of University Professors and the Association of American Colleges. . . . Many church-related colleges and universities are characterized by a high degree of academic freedom and seek to evoke free and critical responses from their students.[175]

In the related case decided five years later, *Roemer v. Maryland Public Works Board*,[176] the same requirement was (nominally) applied. The case involved a taxpayer challenge to a state funding program under which private colleges within the state might apply for state financial aid equal to 15 percent of the per-student amount provided to the state college system. Writing for a plurality of the Court, Justice Blackmun first observed that more than two-thirds of the eligible private colleges had no religious affiliation (the point of his observation being, presumably, to negative any suggestion that the program was but a disguised effort to support religious institutions). Then, as to those having such an affiliation, he noted, each was characterized by a "high degree of institutional autonomy," none received funds from or reported to the Catholic Church, and "[e]ach college subscribe[d] to, and abide[d] by, the 1940 Statement of Principles on Academic Freedom of the American Association of University Professors."[177] Again, the proposition

---

169. Id at 681.
170. Id at 686.
171. Id at 687.
172. Id.
173. Id.
174. Id at 686.
175. Id at 681-82, 686.
176. 426 US 736 (1976).
177. Id at 755-56.

was that these are appropriate expectations a court or a public agency would use to measure the constitutional eligibility for state assistance of private colleges and universities. Moreover, no member of the Court in either case entertained the proposition that *state* schools, controlled directly by government, could somehow be exempt from these standards of academic freedom when private schools seeking public help would not be. Nor is there any logical reason to explain why state schools should be exempt. In this sense, then, Justice Stewart's view in *Epperson* also seems entirely sound, even treating *Epperson* as a straightforward academic freedom case.[178]

As in *Tilton* and *Roemer*, express reference to the 1940 Joint Statement of Principles (or, rather, an interpretative report of the 1940 Statement by Committee A) also appeared in an additional Supreme Court case decided during this period (1968-1978), reviewing a faculty member's first and fourteenth amendment claims. The case, *Board of Regents v. Roth*,[179] was in part a reprise of the *Pickering* case. As in *Pickering*, the terminated faculty member sued for reinstatement on grounds that his termination (at the Oshkosh campus of the University of Wisconsin) was prompted by his public criticism of the university administration—criticism that, consistent with the Court's decision in *Pickering*, he believed could not be used to affect his appointment. The district court concluded that it was unnecessary to reach a decision on that question (unlike *Pickering*, where the basis for the school board's action was a matter of record, in *Roth* the regents did not admit that the faculty member's public criticism was a consideration in their decision; the burden thus fell on Roth to show that it was). Rather, the court held, Roth's status on the faculty as a tenure track appointee sufficiently distinguished him from a one year visitor or other kind of ad hoc contract appointee such that some kind of intramural procedure prior to his effective termination was

---

178. The dissents in *Tilton* and *Roemer* did not disagree with the discussion in the text. Rather, the dissents took strong exception to the majority's conclusions respecting the evidence used to describe the private schools as truly satisfying the Court's own criteria. 403 US at 689 (Douglas dissenting); 426 US at 769-72 (Brennan dissenting); id at 772-74 (Stewart dissenting). And, at least in *Roemer*, the dissents seem to have the better of the argument by far. For example, in *Roemer*, Justice Stewart noted that in *Tilton* the Court found from the record positive evidence that "the theology courses were taught as *academic* subjects," id at 773-74 (emphasis added); no such positive evidence was produced in *Roemer*; further, in *Roemer*, all members of the religion or theology faculty at two of the colleges were Catholic clerics—a point making the absence of positive findings (in respect to the teaching of those courses) additionally disturbing. As far back as our discussion of the *Adler* case, see notes 76-87 and accompanying text, note was taken of different (albeit often related and synergistic) ways in which the state itself might offend the first amendment in respect to faculty staff and academic freedom: not merely by direct command, or by chilling rule, as in *Epperson* on the one hand and as in *Adler* on the other hand, but also by preshaping a faculty that is nominally otherwise fully protected in its academic freedom. Stewart correctly identifies this issue, in *Roemer*, in this way: "Recognition of the academic freedom of these instructors does not necessarily lead to a conclusion that courses in the religion or theology departments at the five defendant [institutions] have no overtones of indoctrination." Id at 774. The point is the obvious one, that is, the staffing criteria of the college may already have done their work.

179. 408 US 564 (1972). See also *Perry v Sindermann*, 408 US 593 (1972) (*Roth* applied, faculty member's aprofessional speech activities held to be protected by the first amendment, and case remanded to determine whether quasi-tenure status was sufficient to trigger 14th amendment fair hearing pretermination due process rights). In *Roth*, the express, favorable reference to the Committee A Report appears at 408 US 579 n17.

required in order to protect his academic freedom. The case advanced to the Supreme Court to consider the procedural issue separately. The Supreme Court then divided in three ways at once: one Justice (Douglas) agreed with the district judge's reasoning and result; two (Brennan and Marshall) would have gone even further to require hearings; and five voted, instead, to reverse.

In substantially agreeing with the district court, Justice Douglas reached a set of conclusions urged in an amicus brief the AAUP filed in the case.[180] The brief's emphasis was essentially in two parts. The first part noted the hazard to academic freedom implicit in any peremptory power of the Wisconsin regents to nonrenew a faculty member's appointment without explanation. The second part noted that while tenure track appointees are necessarily at risk in some ways that tenured faculty are not at risk, they are also unlike one-year visitors or fixed-term contract appointees. Appointment on a *tenure* track implies a more ongoing relationship than a simple term contract. The vast majority of tenure track first-year appointment contracts are routinely renewed precisely because the relationship is at this stage usually still ongoing; it would be odd if tenure track appointees typically were nonrenewed after a single year. This pattern held within the University of Wisconsin system—almost no one other than Roth on tenure track appointment was nonrenewed as early as he. The AAUP contended that the protection of the academic freedom of these faculty members required that before their tenure track status was ended, some procedural protection should be available, just as the district court had held.[181] The Douglas opinion agreed. His own emphasis, moreover, was explicitly keyed to substantive first amendment academic freedom concerns.[182] But the majority reversed the district court, and remanded the case for retrial.[183]

To be sure, the majority in *Roth* cast no retrospective doubt on its long line of cases protecting academic freedom as a subset of first amendment rights. Nor did it retract anything from its *Pickering* (free speech) line of cases. Even though Roth's speech may have been more involved with citizen-interest speech than with his teaching, research, or professional participation within the university, the Court left no doubt that insofar as his nonrenewal was improperly based on either sort of consideration, he could prevail in his action, once he proved his claim. But the Court detached that means of protecting his academic freedom—by suing and by proving affirmatively in court the improper basis of the regents' action—from the claim that his tenure track status entitled him to something more from the university than an

---

180. AAUP's Brief as Amicus Curiae, *Board of Regents v Roth*, 408 US 564 (1972) (No 71-162).

181. See Procedural Standards in the Renewal or Nonrenewal of Faculty Appointments, 56 AAUP Bull 21 (Spring 1970). See also *Roth v Board of Regents*, 310 F Supp 972, 979-80 (WD Wis 1970) ("Substantive constitutional protection for a university professor against non-retention in violation of his First Amendment rights . . . is useless without procedural safeguards."). (The AAUP position was that such substantive constitutional protection was not "useless," but that it was nonetheless incomplete under the circumstances.)

182. 408 US at 579-84 (Douglas dissenting).

183. Id at 579.

unexplained pink slip, if academic freedom was not to be put unfairly at risk for persons in his position. Despite the AAUP's firm agreement with Roth, the Court held that this claim came up short as a matter of fourteenth amendment due process law. Effectively, the Court chose to regard Roth as though he had been a one-year or other term appointee and not on the tenure track at all, who had simply not been asked to stay on, despite the AAUP view that this kind of comparison elides an essential difference and falsifies a critical distinction in status and expectations.[184]

Given the Court's approach in *Roth*, however, this particular subject remains a significant area of professional concern; the Constitution has come around less than one might have hoped.[185] Procedurally speaking, academic freedom remains caught in a crevice of vulnerability. To the extent that public sentiment prefers that those who teach shall be appointed only pursuant to an indefinite series of closed-end contracts, each (in theory) entirely new and terminal unto itself, without doubt the effect is necessarily one of inhibiting any professional departure from uncontroversial methods and substance, lest one find oneself out on the street with only a problematic right to sue. *Roth*, in recognizing no distinction between such appointees and tenure track faculty, widened that crevice even more. Given the common-sense basis on which such faculty might have been distinguished from strict term appointees (from whom they are in fact substantively distinguished in general educational practice), and given also the Court's general express emphasis on academic freedom as a core first amendment concern, *Roth*

---

184. In the AAUP view, tenure track appointees are by category and definition differently situated as an ordinary legal matter than closed-term appointees, visitors, or, indeed, faculty at institutions having no tenure system at all (for example, faculty all of whom never have anything more than each annual dead-end contract, regardless of how many such previous dead-end contracts each might already have had). Specifically, one who is appointed to a tenure track position in an institution embracing a tenure system is receiving assurance by the appointment that, absent some perceived deficiency in his or her professional performance, the expectation of appointment renewal and eventual review for tenure is objectively reasonable. This, ordinarily, is what appointment to the full time faculty on the tenure track means. (Exceptions qualifying that understanding are ordinarily few in number, for example, institutionwide financial exigency or a serious decline of enrollment in the department or discipline of one's specialty such that nonrenewal could occur though one's own work was considered to have gone very well.)

185. Despite *Roth*, moreover, the Court has not applied its logic uniformly since 1972. See, for example, *Cleveland Board of Educ. v Loudermill*, 470 US 532 (1985); *Arnett v Kennedy*, 416 US 134 (1974). (Both cases are, as noted by the dissents in each, indistinguishable from *Roth*; the status furnished the public employee was described conterminously with the procedures laid out in advance for ending that status, which procedures the public employer sedulously followed, exactly as in *Roth*. Nevertheless, in *Loudermill* and in *Arnett*, the Court declined to treat the due process clause as self-referentially limited. It held, rather, that whatever due process the due process clause itself would require would have to be provided even if it was more than the state had promised.) Perhaps part of the problem in *Roth* was the apparent failure of the AAUP adequately to stress to the Court the substantial difference between tenure track and simple term contract academic appointees. Even so, the total case law in this area is simply not consistent, even within itself, since *Roth*. (For four different discussions, see Richard A. Epstein, *Unconstitutional Conditions, State Power, and the Limits of Consent*, 102 Harv L Rev 4, 70-73 (1988); Stephen F. Williams, *Liberty and Property: The Problem of Government Benefits*, 12 J Legal Stud 3, 27 (1983); William W. Van Alstyne, *Cracks in "The New Property": Adjudicative Due Process in the Administrative State*, 62 Cornell L Rev 445 (1977); Frank I. Michaelman, *Formal and Associational Aims in Procedural Due Process*, in J. Roland Pennock & John W. Chapman, eds, *Nomos XVIII* 126 (New York Univ Press, 1977)).

remains an anomalous exception in the sweep of the cases we have reviewed. One reasonably could have expected it to come out the other way, even as the district court supposed.

In contrast with *Roth* and its concern with academic freedom and due process where an individual faculty member's position was in question is *Regents of the University of California v. Bakke*,[186] a highly publicized case decided in 1978. It is also the last case within the 1968-1978 period of review in which an express usage of "academic freedom" appears. The judgment in the *Bakke* case was determined by a single Justice, Lewis Powell, in an opinion in which no other member of the Court joined.[187] At issue in *Bakke* was an admissions policy at the medical school of the University of California at Davis. Bakke had applied and been refused admission in 1973 and 1974, though his academic qualifications were substantially greater in every objective category than those averaged by thirty-two other students who had been admitted but with whom Bakke was never compared.[188] Under the policy approved by the medical school faculty, he was not permitted to be compared with any of them for admission only because he was not American Indian, Asian, chicano, or black. The reason for disallowing such direct comparison, moreover, proceeded from the same baseline explanation: few, if any, of those insulated from comparison with Bakke might have been deemed more qualified than he, had direct comparison been made. Since the faculty deemed it unacceptable for Bakke to be considered more qualified, no such direct comparison was to take place. In the faculty's view, it would have undermined its affirmative

---

186. 438 US 265 (1978).

187. Four members of the Court voted to affirm the entire state supreme court judgment for Bakke and also forbidding the university to consider race or ethnicity in admitting students, under Title VI of the Civil Rights Act of 1964, 42 USC § 2000a-3 (1988). Four other members would have reversed the entire judgment rendered in the California Supreme Court, excluding Bakke from being admitted. Justice Powell alone found that the judgment below was half correct and half incorrect, a position that thus put him in charge of the actual outcome of the case, pursuant to an opinion in which he wrote for no one except himself. (For another rare instance of a 4-1-4 vote, in which the opinion written by the Justice who announced the judgment for the Court also received no concurring votes, see *Oregon v Mitchell*, 400 US 112 (1970) (sustaining an act of Congress insofar as it set the minimum voting age for federal elections at 18, but not sustaining it as applied to eligibility to vote in state or local elections).) (*Oregon v Mitchell* is separately notable for another reason; it is the only Supreme Court case since 1936 holding an act of Congress unconstitutional for lack of substantive constitutional enacting power, which has not yet been overruled by some other case.)

188. Bakke's science grade-point average ("GPA") was 3.44 and his overall GPA was 3.46. For 1973, the average science GPA of 16 other students was 2.62 and their overall GPA average was 2.88; for 1974, the second year of Bakke's application, the science and overall GPA average of the new group of 16 was even lower, respectively, 2.42 and 2.62. The disparities in the four categories of MCAT scores were still more dramatic: on the verbal component of the MCAT, Bakke was in the 96th percentile, the average for the 16 was in the 46th (1973) and 34th (1974); on the quantitative component, Bakke was in the 94th percentile, the average of the group was in the 24th (1973) and 30th (1974); on the science component, Bakke was in the 97th percentile, the average of the group was in the 35th (1973) and 37th (1974). Bakke did least well on the general information component of the MCAT, placing in the 72nd percentile. But the average of the group was, in respect to the same general information component of the same MCAT each year far below that (the 33rd percentile in 1973, the 18th percentile for 1974). These figures are all taken from a table presented in the Powell opinion in the case. 438 US at 277 n7.

action plan for Bakke to have been evaluated on the same terms with the other thirty-two students.

Four Justices concluded that this scheme violated Bakke's federal statutory right to equal consideration without regard to race, a statutory right applicable to admission to any program funded in whole in or in part by federal funds.[189] The fifth, critical, vote was cast by Justice Powell. Unlike the other four Justices, however, Powell rested his decision squarely on the fourteenth amendment and not on the act of Congress alone. Noting that the fourteenth amendment applied directly to the Davis medical school (a state institution), Powell found none of the university's explanations satisfactory to justify its separate racial dual-track admissions practices as against the constitutional guarantee of equal protection of the laws. Accordingly, on that fourteenth amendment basis, he concurred with the four Justices who affirmed the judgment Bakke had received in the California Supreme Court. Allan Bakke's own overall comparative qualifications could not be dismissed by a racially closed system that put so substantial an admissions premium on not being white. The fourteenth amendment would not countenance closed racial reserves.[190]

Even so, in Justice Powell's view, to the extent that the medical school faculty's policy on admissions might rest on a good faith judgment of a *professional* sort, reflecting the same kind of academic judgment pursuant to which a faculty member might determine how most usefully to address a given subject, or what line of attack to take on a research project, or even which textbook to use, then some judicial deference might, on that ground, be due. In elaborating on his suggestion, Justice Powell's usage of "academic freedom" in the *Bakke* case was not at all strained; in fact, it was consistent with the Court's own prior usages of academic freedom.[191] And he developed his point both strongly and well.

Concretely, Justice Powell suggested, if the ethnicity (or the race) of candidates for admission were in the faculty's professional opinion relevant

---

189. USC §§ 2000a-3. (The Act generally forbids racial discrimination in programs assisted by federal funds.)

190. *All* applicants were eligible for eighty-four places within the regular admissions process under the Davis plan. Assuming, however, one were unsuccessful within that nondiscriminatory pool of applicants, one might nonetheless be eligible for any of sixteen set-aside places, but only if one qualified by a specified racial trait. Within the latter (racially restricted) pool, one would then be compared only with others likewise eligible and not with persons like Bakke. The comparative qualifications of applicants like Bakke would matter only if, once the special, racially restricted process of admission were concluded, one or more of the sixteen places had still not been filled (because too few minimally qualified persons had been within that pool in a given year). Then the other, left-out applicants (such as Bakke) might have some possible second chance. In Powell's view, this racially exclusionary admissions track could not be justified insofar as it discounted Bakke's qualifications down to zero vis-à-vis those considered within that track, though Powell did not hold that race could play no role at all. In the latter respect, he differed from the four Justices who ruled strictly on the basis of Title VI. His reasons for differing, bearing on academic freedom as they do, are provided in the text. See notes 195-99 and accompanying text.

191. The phrase is employed three times in the Powell opinion; the most relevant discussion appears at 438 US at 311-15, citing and relying on *Sweezy* and *Keyishian* as the judicial precedents most forcefully on point.

136

simply in the same manner as, say, their place of residence or their difference in undergraduate academic major—as attributes relevant to consider in the dehomogenization of what would otherwise constitute an unduly "look-alike, think-alike" cohort of first-year medical students—its consideration might not be excluded from the admissions process. Indeed, in Powell's view, its unique exclusion as having no constitutionally permissible relevance for academic admission would unnecessarily frustrate a good faith professional resolve to construct a learning, teaching, and research environment in which useful *Lehrfreiheit* and *Lernfreiheit* are expected to occur.[192] Finding no absolute fourteenth amendment requirement for its nonconsideration for any purpose whatever, Powell voted to reverse that portion of the state supreme court's judgment that held that race must be ignored by any public or publicly supported university. Because, on the other hand, Bakke never received any consideration in respect to his comparative attributes, talents, skills, and background vis-á-vis those who were favored by the Davis racial set-aside plan, Justice Powell also voted to affirm that part of the judgment holding that Bakke had been unfairly excluded from such opportunity for comparative consideration.[193] A proper program "treats each applicant as an individual," consistent with the equal protection clause, Powell insisted, even when it allows proper institutional academic freedom judgments to be given breathing room on their own account:

> [An integrated program] treats each applicant as an individual in the admissions process. [Within such an integrated program, t]he applicant who loses out on the last available seat to another candidate receiving a "plus" on the basis of ethnic background will not have been foreclosed from all consideration for that seat simply because he was not the right color or had the wrong surname. It would mean only that his combined qualifications, which may have included similar nonobjective factors, did not outweigh those of the other applicant. His qualifications would have been weighed fairly and competitively, and he would have no basis to complain of unequal treatment under the Fourteenth Amendment.[194]

---

192. The argument is similar to (but more carefully developed than) that submitted by the AAUP in its amicus brief in the case, which is summarized as follows:

> Many institutions of higher education, especially graduate and professional schools, receive more applications from candidates who are qualified, i.e., able to successfully complete the course of study, than the institution can admit. [Under these circumstances] an institution may validly conclude that the quality of the educational experience for all students is enhanced by considering as one factor in the admission process the racial diversity of the class selected. Accordingly, the AAUP will suggest that a faculty, in exercising its experienced judgment, may identify a nontrivial number of qualified minority students for admission to assure the optimal educational experience for the entire class selected.

AAUP's Brief as Amicus Curiae at 2-3, *Regents of the University of California v Bakke*, 438 US 265 (1978) (No 76-811).

193. Since, moreover, the university was unable to show that Bakke would have failed of admission even had he not been disqualified from comparison with all sixteen of the favored students both in 1973 and in 1974, pursuant to a proper integrated admissions program (which in Powell's view the Davis plan clearly was not), the state court judgment enjoining the school from refusing to enroll him was entirely proper in Justice Powell's view of the case. Accordingly, he voted to affirm this part of what the state supreme court had done. In brief, Bakke prevailed individually and the plan was enjoined.

194. *Bakke*, 438 US at 318.

That the point was a serious point, and not a specious or lightly conceived suggestion, was attested by the strong footnote he added:

> The denial to respondent of this right to individualized consideration without regard to his race is the principal evil of petitioner's special admissions program. Nowhere in the opinion of [the four justices voting to sustain the program as it was] is this denial even addressed.[195]

Powell's use of "academic freedom" in *Bakke*, and his quotation of the dictum by Justice Frankfurter from the *Sweezy* case,[196] represent no departure from the usages of academic freedom we have examined. When Powell writes of academic freedom as "long . . . viewed as a special concern of the First Amendment,"[197] his emphasis remains constant at all times. To gain purchase through the first amendment, the decision in any academic freedom case, whether individual or institutional, must still rest—as Frankfurter noted—on *academic* and not on some other grounds. It is all the same, moreover, whether the decision pertains to "who may be admitted to study" rather than to "who may teach," or "what may be taught," or "how."

So, for instance, suppose the selection of a given textbook were made by a given teacher or university professor because of a desire to befriend the particular publisher whose text one concedes to be poorer than that provided by other publishers, but whom one nonetheless felt a passionate desire to befriend.[198] This is not a selection made on academic grounds. Accordingly, it should receive no first amendment academic freedom deference. Rather, one will need a reason of a different sort to defend a given textbook selection[199] on academic freedom grounds, for example, that one believes the text is superior in some respect over alternative choices (whether or not others agree), or that its presentation is more lucid than that of alternative books (again, whether or not others agree), or, though not necessarily "better" in either of these respects abstractly, its perspective is more illuminating and best fits one's design for the course. Implicitly, Powell is saying all the same things in *Bakke*. He voted to reverse that part of the state court judgment disallowing *any* consideration of race in state university admissions practices; he did so on limited first amendment, academic freedom grounds. In limiting the decision, and in tightly circumscribing the university's procedures, he also sought to take due account of Bakke's equal

---

195. Id at 318 n52.

196. " 'It is the business of a university to provide that atmosphere which is most conducive to speculation, experiment and creation. It is an atmosphere in which there prevail "the four essential freedoms" of a university—to determine for itself *on academic grounds* who may teach, what may be taught, how it shall be taught, and who may be admitted to study.' " Id at 312, quoting *Sweezy*, 354 US at 263 (emphasis added) (see note 101 and accompanying text).

197. *Bakke*, 438 US at 312.

198. Perhaps because the publisher had opposed the war in Vietnam and the faculty, or a majority of the faculty, also opposed the war in Vietnam. Perhaps because the publisher had contributed money to a prolife organization or, conversely, to Planned Parenthood, and, again, the faculty also favored that social cause. Perhaps because the author is one's nephew—or niece. The range of nonprofessional (and also of unprofessional) reasons is nearly inexhaustible.

199. —Whether the defense (that is, the explanation) one means to provide is to the institution, to one's students, or, indeed, to the author or publisher of an alternative book.

protection claims. Whether one thinks the opinion ultimately correct or not, the Powell opinion in *Bakke* remains to this day one of the most well-disposed treatments of "academic freedom" one can find in the cases that have adverted to that freedom in the Supreme Court.

C. (1979-1989)

In the first of the dozen cases reporting a usage of "academic freedom" in the most recent decade of Supreme Court adjudications, *Cannon v. University of Chicago*,[200] the reference to academic freedom also appears in an opinion by Justice Powell. In marked contrast to *Bakke*, however, *Cannon* presented no constitutional issue. Rather, the case turned on differences of attitude toward academic freedom in matters of statutory construction and the extent to which concerns for academic freedom may influence the interpretation of a law.

In enacting Title IX of the Education Amendments of 1972, Congress provided that no person could on the basis of sex be "subjected to discrimination under any education program or activity receiving Federal financial assistance."[201] The act provided expressly for agency enforcement of this provision. It did not, however, create private causes of action. Nonetheless, a majority of the Court held that such actions, though not given explicit congressional authorization, would be deemed authorized by Title IX. It was on this point that the case had gone to the Supreme Court.

In dissent, Justice White took issue with the majority. In his view, Congress had deliberately chosen not to provide for such private suits but only to require that recipient institutions answer to the appropriate disbursing agency.[202] Justices Blackmun and Powell joined in Justice White's dissent. Justice Powell, however, wrote an additional thirty-page dissent to underscore the extent of his disagreement with the majority's view, and his dissent expressed concern for academic freedom.[203] In Powell's view, insofar as universities would now need not only to satisfy government agencies of their compliance with the act (as Congress had intended) but would need also to take care not to invite private suits, they would be under duress to alter standards, not because the standards were inappropriate, but simply in order to forestall such suits. To be sure, Powell did not doubt Congress's power to authorize such suits. However, absent a clear expression from Congress, the Court itself ought not "revise the balance of interests struck by the legislation."[204] To do so was to ignore the costs to academic freedom, for example, by hindering a university's ability to set academic standards in good professional faith, uncompromised by an additional anxiety of threatening suits.[205]

---

200. 441 US 677 (1979).
201. 20 USC § 1681(a) (1988); see generally 20 USC §§ 1681 to 1683 (1988).
202. *Cannon*, 441 US at 718 (White dissenting).
203. Id at 730 (Powell dissenting).
204. Id at 748 n19.
205. May fear of private suits adversely affect one's decisions on the merits of things? Justice Stevens briefly considered and dismissed this concern as "speculation." Id at 709. Compare the

Powell's concern for academic freedom in *Cannon* was of a piece with Justice Frankfurter's opinion in *Sweezy v. New Hampshire*.[206] An individual teacher (as in *Sweezy*) or an institution (as in *Cannon*) can be substantially compromised at the margin of professional judgment when the alternative is to risk an encounter with a very high-voltage fence. If one's sole concern is that the fence stimulate a suitably strong aversive reflex, of course, one will not mind; indeed, one may be inclined to say, "the higher the voltage, the better this fence!" In Powell's view, this was pretty much the majority's approach in *Cannon*.[207] But, for Powell, it is just this reasoning that also made the decision even more obviously incorrect. The higher the voltage, the greater the fear and so the greater the loss of the margin of the useful field now newly abandoned nearby the fence. The majority of the Court might see that loss as of little consequence. But so to suppose, and so to decide the case absent a clear congressional requirement to do so was in a larger sense seriously inconsistent with the Court's own prior decisions since 1957. Unavailing in *Cannon*, Powell's opinion was nevertheless well within the tradition Frankfurter marked out beginning with *Sweezy*, and influential with the Court in cases such as *Keyishian* and *Bakke* as well.

In contrast with *Cannon*, the issue in *Regents of University of Michigan v. Ewing*[208] concerned the substantive due process claim of a student dropped in his sixth year from the University of Michigan Medical School and refused readmission on academic grounds after failing a major written examination— a two-day test administered by the National Board of Medical Examiners, successful completion of which was required to receive his degree. The student, Scott Ewing, did not dispute the requirement of the examination nor the requirement of its successful completion to secure a degree. He did not deny that he had failed to achieve the university's minimum passing score for the test. But he observed that others who had failed the same examination

---

general reflections of Judge Learned Hand: "After now some dozen years of experience I must say that . . . I should dread a lawsuit beyond almost anything else short of sickness and death." Learned Hand, 3 *Lectures on Legal Topics, Association of the Bar of the City of New York* 106 (Macmillan, 1926). Academics, like others, may do a great deal to avoid sickness or death, nor are they known to be braver than Learned Hand in fearing a lawsuit.

206.   Indeed, in his discussion of academic freedom, Powell explicitly drew from and relied upon Frankfurter's opinion in *Sweezy*. 441 US at 747-48, citing Frankfurter in *Sweezy*, 354 US 234; see also text accompanying notes 94-101.

207.   Ten years after *Cannon*, in *University of Pennsylvania v EEOC*, 111 S Ct 577 (1990), the Court also rejected any claim of qualified confidentiality of tenure review files under subpoena demand of the EEOC. The AAUP filed an amicus brief endorsing a qualified privilege, akin to that generally recognized when grand juries subpoena a reporter's notes, and relying on *Sweezy*. AAUP's Brief as Amicus Curiae, *University of Pennsylvania v EEOC*, 110 S Ct 577(1990) (No 88-493). Two federal courts of appeal had agreed (although two others had not), and each had directed federal district courts to review EEOC subpoenas of academic tenure review files of confidential peer review materials by standards of scrutiny derived from Frankfurter's opinion in *Sweezy*. Purporting to distinguish *Sweezy* on the basis that the inquiry in that case went to the content of teaching, whereas here it went to the determination of professional qualification (though why that difference should be thought to matter is nowhere explained), the Court rejected the claim. *University of Pennsylvania*, 110 S Ct at 585-87. The tenor and decision in *University of Pennsylvania* are more at odds with *Sweezy* than any other single case to come from the Supreme Court during the past thirty-five years.

208.   474 US 214 (1985).

had been permitted to retake the examination rather than being dropped. Indeed, it appeared that he was the first student ever to be dropped rather than being permitted to try again. To be sure, his scores were the lowest in the history of the program, and the medical school had provided a hearing that reviewed his whole academic career and not simply his examination score. (From any point of view, therefore, *procedural* due process was easily satisfied in the medical school's handling of his case.[209]) But in Ewing's view—and in the view of the federal court of appeals that reviewed the trial record of the case in the district court—there was nothing in the record that provided any reasonable basis for the apparent harshness of discontinuing Ewing's medical school career. On that basis, the court of appeals had reversed the district court's dismissal of his case.[210]

The Supreme Court unanimously disagreed with this disposition. In respect to substantive academic judgments within universities, the Court declared:

> When judges are asked to review the substance of a genuinely academic decision . . . they may not override it unless it is such a substantial departure from accepted academic norms as to demonstrate that the person or committee responsible did not actually exercise professional judgment . . . . Added to our concern for lack of standards (there are none obviously provided by the Constitution or elsewhere according to which judges or juries can say what norms of academic competence are suitable or unsuitable for any university as such) is a reluctance to trench on the prerogatives of . . . educational institutions and our responsibility to safeguard their academic freedom, "a special concern of the First Amendment."[211]

Only where the faculty can be shown to have abdicated its responsibility to make judgments on academic grounds (that is, only when it does "not actually exercise professional judgment") does it forfeit the protection the first amendment provides.[212] *Ewing*, with *Keyishian*, Frankfurter's opinion in

---

209. Whether the school might have been faulted had it not provided such a hearing incident to a student's dismissal for academic (rather than disciplinary) reasons was thus not at issue in *Ewing*. In all likelihood, however, no particular kind of intramural review of the kind provided Scott Ewing would be held to be required as a matter of constitutional right. (In an earlier case, the Supreme Court expressed substantial reservations on the point. See *Board of Curators, University of Missouri v Horowitz*, 435 US 78 (1978).) Where, in contrast, a student's standing in a public university is put in jeopardy because of an infraction of the rules (such as stealing, harassment, drinking, plagiarism, or campus disruption), predecisional intramural procedural due process is much more likely to be deemed constitutionally required. See, for example, *Dixon v Alabama State Board of Educ.*, 294 F2d 150 (5th Cir 1961).

210. In conventional 14th amendment constitutional terms, Ewing's complaint was one of substantive due process, that is, the alleged lack of any sufficient substantive reason for depriving him of his "property" interest in his status as a student in good standing in a state university. Of course, the case may also be seen as one affecting a student's substantive academic freedom in the same sense as discussed in *Baggett v Bullitt*, 377 US 360, that is, the continuing freedom of one within the university to continue to study, to learn, and to interact with the faculty, assuming satisfactory work as determined in good professional faith. See, for example, 1967 Statement at 142; Appendix C, 53 L & Contemp Probs at 412 (cited in note 7) ("Student performance should be evaluated solely on an academic basis, not on opinions or conduct in matters unrelated to academic standards.").

211. *Ewing*, 474 US at 225-26. The standard adopted and applied by the Court in *Ewing* was put forward in virtually the same terms in the amicus brief of the AAUP. AAUP's Brief as Amicus Curiae, *Regents of University of Michigan v Ewing*, 474 US 214 (1985) (No 84-1273).

212. See also Justice Powell's strongly supportive view adopting essentially the same standard on matters of evaluating persons for appointment or tenure, in *Hishon v King & Spalding*, 467 US 69, 80

Sweezy, and Justice Powell's opinion in *Bakke*, is among the Court's strongest first amendment-based decisions articulating the meaning of academic freedom in higher education.

With two exceptions, both addressed to the scope of academic freedom in public secondary education, the balance of decisions reporting a usage of "academic freedom" in the Supreme Court during this most recent decade are but slight refinements on earlier themes.

Such a refinement is furnished by *Widmar v. Vincent*,[213] decided by the Court in 1981. *Widmar* provided a reprise on *Healy v. James*[214] and raised anew the scope of constitutional protection afforded student groups on public university campuses. Unlike *Healy*, however, *Widmar* did not involve a refusal to "recognize" a particular student organization, such as a refusal to permit it to meet on campus, post notices, solicit members, and have the same on-campus privileges as any other student organization could claim. At issue, rather, was a board of curators rule forbidding a particular use of university buildings or university grounds regardless of what group might be involved. The use of such buildings or grounds for "religious worship or religious teaching" was forbidden, and the board of curators believed this restriction was required by a clause of the Missouri Constitution.[215] Cornerstone, a student organization of evangelical Christian students from various denominational backgrounds at the University of Missouri at Kansas City, found itself altogether frustrated by this use restriction. Effectively, the restriction denied them any use of university buildings for the very sort of meetings and activities they were most committed to provide as a group.[216] Lacking any other recourse against the rule, Clark Vincent and other student

---

n4 (1983) ("Courts of Appeals generally have acknowledged that respect for academic freedom requires some deference to the judgment of schools and universities as to the qualifications of professors, particularly those considered for tenured positions."). See generally Judith Jarvis Thomson, *Ideology and Faculty Selection*, 53 L & Contemp Probs 155 (Summer 1990).

213.   454 US 263 (1981).

214.   408 US 169.

215.   *Widmar*, 454 US at 263. The Missouri constitutional provision was worded similarly to, but somewhat more far-reachingly than, the provision in the first amendment that forbids any act of Congress "respecting an establishment of religion." Mo Const, Art I §§ 6, 7; Art IX § 8. In *McCollum v Board of Educ.*, 333 US 203 (1948), the Supreme Court had held that this clause in the first amendment was equally applicable to the states through the 14th amendment and was violated by a religious "released-time program" in a public school, which co-ordinated religious instruction by religious teachers using school classrooms during the regular school hours. (The fact that students were nominally not compelled to attend, but might instead remain in a regular classroom while the released-time religious classes met, was held to be of insufficient significance.) Compare *Zorach v Clauson*, 343 US 306 (1952) (similar plan sustained, five-to-four, when the released students met religious classes off school premises, even if those not opting into the program were kept in a study hall at the public school). In *Widmar*, even supposing that the 14th amendment might not bar a state university from permitting sectarian religious activities on campus when sponsored by a student group permitted use of campus facilities on the same terms as every other student group, the board of curators believed that the Missouri Constitution nonetheless forbade such use of public facilities. 454 US at 265.

216.   "A typical Cornerstone meeting included prayer, hymns, Bible commentary, and discussion of religious views and experiences." Id at 265 n2. The meetings were also generally open to other students to attend, part of the purpose being to win adherents to Cornerstone's religious commitments. Id.

members of Cornerstone sued to enjoin Gary Widmar (the dean of students) and the university's board of curators from enforcing the rule against them. In the Supreme Court, as well as in the court of appeals, their claim prevailed on first amendment grounds. Justice Powell, writing for the Court in *Widmar*, said that even supposing that Cornerstone sought "to win . . . converts"[217] in its meetings on campus (as well as to realize its members' shared religious enthusiasms), the point provided no sensible distinction from what the Court had already decided in *Healy* and *Tinker*. Common rules of time, place, and manner governing on-campus facilities, consistent with standards reviewed in *Healy*, would apply to Cornerstone as to any other on-campus group,[218] but not a content-censoring restriction, which, in the Court's view, the curator's rule, even if adopted under requirement of the state Constitution, obviously was. *Widmar*, moreover, is not reasoned on the basis of the free exercise clause but on more generalized freedom of speech principles. *Widmar* is thus of a piece with the strong holding in *Tinker*, Powell's holding in *Healy*, and Justice Douglas' opinion in *Jones v. Board of Education*.[219]

A concurring opinion in *Widmar* by Justice Stevens[220] makes a point not in disagreement with Powell's majority opinion, but qualifying it in a manner anticipating his own applied usage of "academic freedom" in *Ewing*. Stevens expressly referred to "academic freedom" to disallow intrusive judicial review of institutional procedures for handling disputes in allocating university space. In Stevens' view, the first amendment may shelter on-campus free speech and meeting rights of students at public institutions. Even so, he insisted, where such groups seek use of facilities, the first amendment does not require suspension of institutional opinion respecting their relative academic worthiness—at least in mediating competing demands, if not in judging their general "right" to be on campus. Rather, the first amendment specifically protects academic value judgments reflected in institutional mechanisms established to determine priorities of use where not all requests can simultaneously be granted. In Stevens' view, institutional discretion of this sort is not different in kind than the sort Powell embraced for the Court in the *Bakke* case. It is correspondingly entitled to a strong measure of academic freedom respect in the courts.

Stevens offered an example: suppose one group requests use of a room to show Disney films, and another requests its use to present *Hamlet*. Must the conflict be resolved by, say, flipping a coin or by some other equally

---

217. Id at 269-70 n6.

218. See id at 276. An additional cautionary note is sounded in regard to student activities otherwise protected by the first amendment when conducted in ways that "substantially interfere with the opportunity of other students to obtain an education." Id at 277. But allowable regulations of this sort are themselves merely an example of uniform rules of time, place, and manner (for example, rules suitably drawn to avoid harassment of others by regulating the time, place, and manner of holding one's meetings or otherwise seeking to win support for one's general views), and not a ban based on the unwelcomeness of certain ideas.

219. *Jones*, 397 US 31. See also 1967 Statement at Part IV; Appendix C, 53 L & Contemp Probs at 413-15 (cited in note 7).

220. 454 US 277, 278-80.

impersonal mechanism, lest some other basis be thought to infringe on the first amendment claims of both groups? Stevens suggests not. If the decision is to prefer Disney to *Hamlet* (Stevens uses this contrast deliberately), and for the reason that *Hamlet* is already well covered in standard courses whereas "the genius of Walt Disney" has not previously been given any airing at all, then, though the decision is made on this basis of comparative academic worth rather than some other more "neutral" basis (for example, as to who applied first), the first amendment shifts its center of gravity to protect the decision from intrusive judicial review.[221] In this respect, the usage of "academic freedom" reflected in Stevens' concurrence in *Widmar* is of a piece with the position he reflected in *Ewing* as well.[222]

In a case arising between *Widmar* and *Ewing*, involving faculty rather than students,[223] a different usage of "academic freedom" appears. A Minnesota law imposed an obligation on the state board governing the state community college system to "meet and confer" from time to time with faculty on matters of educational policy. It imposed a similar obligation equally on the administration of each college. At the same time, however, the same law also forbade either the state board or any community college administration to permit any faculty member to appear in such meetings other than as a designee of whatever professional association (that is, union) had gained exclusive representation rights for collective bargaining purposes, even though these meetings were in no sense collective bargaining sessions but were meant to address other kinds of issues. The effect of the law, combined with the practice of the faculty union, was altogether to exclude nonunion

---

221. See id at 278-79 (Stevens concurring) ("Judgments of this kind should be made by academicians, not by federal judges . . . ."), citing *Sweezy*, 354 US at 261 (Frankfurter concurring), and *Bakke*, 438 US at 312, and repeating the quotation that "[a]cademic freedom, though not a specifically enumerated constitutional right, long has been viewed as a special concern of the First Amendment." 454 US at 279.

222. Yet despite Justice Stevens' insightful and supportive endorsement of academic freedom in this usage, that is, protecting such allocative decisions from judicial review, one may doubt that the analogy to *Bakke* or *Ewing* properly holds in cases of this sort. Why? Because in respect to *these* groups, each involving no institutional endorsement or sponsorship (*Widmar* and Cornerstone is an example), their presence on campus owes nothing to judgments of academic connection; accordingly, neither should their requests about times and places to meet. Consider a case similar to that which Justice Stevens proposed. Suppose it is not a case where a student group rehearsal of *Hamlet* (for its own amusement) competes for reservation of an unused room with a student group request to reserve the same room to view Disney films (for its own amusement). Rather, a reservation request by the Federalist Society is followed later the same day by a competing request for the same room at the same time by the Student Gay-Lesbian Alliance. On Justice Stevens' view, the latter request, though second-arriving, may be given priority if done on the basis of an academic (rather than a political) judgment. What would such a judgment consist of? Presumably it might be merely a judgment of just the kind Stevens used: federalism perspectives are already well covered in the standard curriculum, whereas gay-lesbian perspectives have not been equally featured. From the decision-maker's position, this may seem reasonable enough. From the perspective of the rejected group, however, it seems supererogatory (as well as suspect). Losing the room on such grounds to some university event or university sponsored activity is one thing. Losing it to another group no different from itself (in that it is equally an unsponsored group and, like this group, merely pursuing its own agenda on campus) on some notion of superior academic timeliness about the other group's agenda, is another. It puts the university's thumb on a scale where arguably it does not belong at all.

223. *Minnesota State Board for Community Colleges v Knight*, 465 US 271 (1984).

faculty members who wished also to be heard on matters of educational policy (for example, what should be taught). Such faculty might still attempt to communicate their views informally—by writing personal letters[224]—but they were barred from speaking in the only formally required regular meetings. Several of the adversely affected faculty sued to enjoin this restriction on first amendment grounds. The federal district court held that this restriction, running as it did to these overall "meet and confer" meetings and not more narrowly (for example, to specific collective bargaining negotiations alone), unfairly curtailed the first amendment academic freedom of those faculty members not electing to be union members to be heard on matters of equal professional concern to them as academics.[225] However, the Supreme Court reversed, albeit in a closely divided vote.

Writing for the Court over a dissent by Justices Powell, Stevens, and Brennan, and a partial dissent by Justice Marshall, Justice O'Connor put the decision reversing the lower court principally on the basis that, had there been no state law requiring such meet and confer sessions, plaintiffs could not have compelled the holding of such meetings. This being so, in her view, they had no better basis for complaint here. Insofar as the state wished to provide for such meetings by way of an extended opportunity for the union to communicate its concerns on general matters (leaving others to the informal recourse they already enjoyed), there could be no sensible constitutional objection. Going beyond the needs of the immediate case, however, O'Connor also added the following passages, at once both clear and bleak in rejecting an entire category of professional academic freedom first amendment claims:

> To be sure, there is a strong, if not universal or uniform, tradition of faculty participation in school governance, and there are numerous policy arguments to support such participation. See American Association of Higher Education—National Education Association, Faculty Participation in Academic Governance (1967); Brief for American Association of University Professors as Amicus Curiae 3-10. But this Court has never recognized a constitutional right of faculty to participate in policymaking in academic institutions. . . . Even assuming that speech rights guaranteed by the First Amendment take on a special meaning in an academic setting . . . there is no constitutional right to participate in academic governance.[226]

Though concurring in the particular judgment in the case, Justice Marshall expressly disassociated himself from this part of the Court's majority opinion.[227] Writing separately in dissent, Brennan explained for himself,

---

224. Id at 277 n4.

225. *Knight v Minnesota Community College Faculty Ass'n*, 571 F Supp 1, 7-12 (D Minn 1982). In an amicus brief, the AAUP agreed with this view. AAUP's Brief as Amicus Curiae, *Minnesota State Board for Community Colleges v Knight*, 465 US 271 (1984) (Nos 82-898 and 82-977). See also *Madison Joint School Dist. v Wisconsin Employment Relations Comm'n*, 429 US 167 (1976) (holding that a state law effectively forbidding a nonunion teacher to address an elected school board in a general meeting of the school board open to the public, without the union's permission to do so, violated the silenced teacher's personal first amendment rights; AAUP amicus brief supporting the claim on first amendment-academic freedom grounds).

226. *Knight*, 465 US at 287-88.

227. Id at 293 (Marshall concurring) ("Such participation is . . . essential if our academic institutions are to fulfill their dual responsibility to advance the frontiers of knowledge through

"why, irrespective of other grounds, principles of academic freedom require affirmance of the District Court's holding,"[228] namely that in his view:

> [The f]irst amendment freedom to explore novel or controversial ideas in the classroom is closely linked to the freedom of faculty members to express their views to the administration concerning matters of academic governance. . . . The freedom to teach without inhibition may be jeopardized just as gravely by a restriction on the faculty's ability to speak out on such matters as by the more direct restrictions struck down in *Keyishian* and in *Epperson*. In my view, therefore, a direct prohibition of some identified faculty group from submitting their views concerning academic policy questions for consideration by college administrators would plainly violate the principles of academic freedom enshrined in the First Amendment.[229]

An additional dissent separately added by Stevens (and joined by Justices Brennan and Powell) strongly endorsed Brennan's perspective. As a consequence, the contrast within the Supreme Court in *Knight* could not have been more pronounced. The majority saw the case as simply a matter of meetings that need not have been provided for in any event, and insofar as they were provided they furnished an opportunity for substantial faculty representation albeit limited to designees of the faculty's own professional group. The dissent viewed the same statute, however, as working a serious and unwarranted restriction on some faculty members' opportunities to be heard on matters of academic substance as part and parcel of their own academic freedom, disadvantaging them solely on the basis of their individual decisions not to become union members although still obliged to pay full dues. Unaffected by the Court's decision in *Knight* are such meetings as are required to be held for general public purposes.[230] Unaffected, too, may be the assurance that faculty submitting professional concerns through correspondence and other channels may still claim a strong measure of first amendment academic freedom protection. Still, the majority's dicta as well as its holding in *Knight* significantly diminish a university faculty because of the distinctly managerial view of academic institutions to which the O'Connor opinion strongly yields. Among decisions of the past decade, *Knight* is one of two[231] that have leaned against the course Justice Frankfurter originally set for the Court in *Sweezy*, three decades ago.

Knight is nonetheless also a useful transitional case in moving to the last three decisions completing this unhurried review of usages of academic freedom and the first amendment in the Supreme Court. What makes it so is the character of the colleges engaged in the litigation. *Knight* concerned two-year community colleges, which are not quite four-year public baccalaureate degree institutions nor advanced degree research universities on the one hand, nor public primary or secondary schools on the other. We have not

---

unfettered inquiry and debate . . . and to produce a citizenry willing and able to involve itself in the governance of the polity . . . .") (citation omitted).

228. Id at 295 (Brennan dissenting).
229. Id at 296-97.
230. See *Madison Joint School Dist.*, 429 US 167.
231. The other is *University of Pennsylvania*, 110 S Ct 577.

hitherto noticed a great deal turning on such matters,[232] but the distinction becomes more important as our review nears its end.[233]

Some of "the functions of educational institutions in our national life" to which Justice Frankfurter made reference in *Wieman v. Updegraff*[234] are of a sort more easily associated with universities than with public schools, for example, functions of critical scholarship and research. The tasks of primary and secondary schools are at once much more mixed and substantially more instrumental than those of colleges or universities. The age of the student, the requirement of attendance, the standardization of teacher credentialing, the structured inculcation of basic skills, and other factors describe a very different milieu. The importance of these schools is not diminished by these observations. Far from it.[235] They nonetheless serve in a cautionary fashion, distancing the environment of public schools from universities. Academic freedom plays out somewhat differently in the milieu of primary and secondary public education.[236] It is drawn in principally as a constitutional check against state tendencies to misuse powers of educational command to censor materials or instruction, but it plays out much more ambiguously and without the same breadth of reach.

An example of the difference is offered by the 1982 decision of the Supreme Court in *Board of Education v Pico*[237] The case arose after a local

---

232. For example, although *Sweezy* involved a state university (rather than a community college or a local public school), the strong statement by Frankfurter emphasized "the nature of the teacher's role" and the importance of disallowing "unwarranted inhibition upon the free spirit of teachers" (that is, it was not limited to "professors" or to those with doctorates). Moreover, several of the more significant cases were public school rather than higher education cases (for example, *Adler* (disqualification from public school teaching of persons with certain political affiliations), *Pickering* (public expression by teachers), *Scopes* (public school course content restrictions) and *Epperson* (same)).

233. See, for example, *DiBona v Matthews*, 220 Cal App 3d 1329, 269 Cal Rptr 882 (1990), cert denied, 59 USLW 3402 (1990) (community college administration's cancellation of drama class held to violate first amendment, suit brought by the drama instructor and an enrolled student; court rejected the comparison of community college with high schools in measuring the protected range of drama instructor's professional discretion to determine course content, locating it more closely in keeping with the fuller range of academic freedom in colleges (than in high schools) and noting: "Defendants have cited no authority—and we are aware of none—which would allow a college or university to censor instructor-selected curriculum materials because they contain 'indecent' language or deal with 'offensive' topics." Id at 1346-47, 269 Cal Rptr at 893).

234. 344 US at 197; see notes 88-92 and accompanying text.

235. Indeed, it is primary and secondary education (not universities) that was the immediate reference of the Warren Court when it noted: "In these days, it is doubtful that any child may reasonably be expected to succeed in life if he is denied the opportunity of an education." The quotation is, of course, from *Brown v Board of Educ.*, 347 US 483, 493 (1954).

236. In *West Virginia State Board of Educ. v Barnette*, 319 US 624 (1943), the Supreme Court struck down a state law requiring public school children to participate in daily pledges of allegiance to the American flag. It did so on the ground that such compulsory expression of political belief under state direction was inconsistent with the broad protection afforded by the first amendment from forced recitation of political beliefs one may not share, and that even grade school children may constitutionally resist such exercises despite the ambitions of the state (including a democratic state) to inculcate patriotism by this means. Id at 634-42. Perhaps surprisingly, Justice Frankfurter dissented. Id at 646. Plainly, his views on the "functions" of public schools, and his views of the "functions" of universities, were not all the same. For a recent thoughtful review of such matters more generally, see Amy Gutmann, *Democratic Education* (Princeton Univ Press, 1987).

237. *Board of Educ., Island Trees v Pico*, 457 US 853 (1982).

elected school board in Island Trees, New York, ordered the removal of nine specified books from all high school and junior high school libraries in the district. Suit was brought in federal district court on behalf of several students. On first amendment grounds they sought an injunction against the school board's removal decree insofar as it affected the libraries at the schools in which they were enrolled. But the constitutional basis for their suit was far from compelling.[238] Some of the books were seriously controversial; their suitability for youngsters (in comparison with university students[239] or community college students) was by no means obvious. Nor could it easily be argued that, even so, they might well serve to cultivate values of tolerance and a mutual appreciation of positive differences in a free democratic society— themes the Court had stressed as consistent with the proper educational function of public schools. To the contrary, the books might be thought to convey destructive images and crude, offensive stereotypes.[240] To be sure, the first amendment might well not permit a *general* ban on the availability of such books to minors merely on that account, but no restriction on what these students could buy, read at home, or borrow from a public library was involved here. Nonetheless, the students prevailed, at least partially. On first

---

238. Since only students were suing (no teacher, librarian, book publisher, or author claimed ground for relief), the case shaped up quite unpromisingly, as a claim asserted by public school students to have their first amendment view of material suitable for a school library prevail in opposition to the view of the school board of the district in which they resided. Viewed this way, the case seemed weak. The district court granted summary judgment to the school board. 474 F Supp 387 (ED NY 1979). Fortunately for the plaintiffs, however, the board had acted against recommendations of its own appointed parent-teacher book review committee in respect to seven of the nine books it ordered removed. In rejecting the committee's recommendations, moreover, the board had declined even to say why. Portions of the plurality opinion for the Supreme Court substantially relied on these facts in determining what deference was due the judgment of the school board. 457 U.S. at 874-75. Additionally, as the case proceeded in the courts, the action seeking reinstatement, or reshelving, of the books was strongly supported in amicus briefs filed on behalf of the National Education Association, the American Library Association, the Authors League of America, and P.E.N. American Center. See id at 855. So the actual array of interested parties in securing first amendment limits on school library book-removal practices by politicized school boards was in fact very substantial, putting the case in a stronger light.

239. A critical first amendment distinction of this kind is made in the dissent illustrating the constitutional difference (of role and function) members of the Court tend to attribute to universities as distinct from public schools. See id at 915 (Rehnquist dissenting) (expressly distinguishing universities from public schools in just this way). See also note 236 (views of Justice Frankfurter on the same point).

240. By way of example, Justice Powell provided seven pages of excerpts from some of the books as an Appendix to his dissent, 457 US at 897-904. They included such passages as these: "There are white men who will pay you to fuck their wives. They approach you and say, 'How would you like to fuck a white woman?' 'What is this?' you ask. 'On the up-and-up,' he assures you. 'It's all right. She's my wife. She needs black rod, is all. She has to have it. It's like a medicine or drug to her. I'll pay you.' " Eldridge Cleaver, *Soul on Ice* (quoted at id at 897); "What do you think goes on in the wagon at night: Are the drivers on their knees *fucking their mothers?* . . . . 'Who else would do anything like that but a mother-fucking Zhid?' . . . . 'No more noise out of you or I'll shoot your Jew cock off.' . . . 'You cocksucker Zhid, I ought to make you lick it up off the floor.' " Bernard Malmud, *The Fixer* (id at 898-99); " 'I wonder if sex without acid could be so exciting, so wonderful, so indescribable.' . . . . 'Another day, another blow job . . . . If I don't give Big Ass a blow he'll cut off my supply.' " Anonymous, *Go Ask Alice* (id at 899).

148

amendment grounds, albeit on a close five-to-four vote,[241] the Court granted them an opportunity to put the school board's actions on trial in federal district court, with a fair possibility of getting some of the books put back.

The success of the case essentially turned on evidence in the record that at least some of the books[242] had been removed because of a desire to suppress information and perspectives reflected in these books not supportive of political and social doctrines the board members and their most active constituents sought personally to advance through their control of public schools. Removal of the books from all of the district's public school libraries may have been ordered, in short, " 'not in the interests of the children's well-being' " but rather for the purpose of establishing those political views " 'as the correct and orthodox ones for all purposes in the particular community.' "[243] The strategy was to "contract the spectrum of available knowledge"[244] by banning books presenting views other than those the board members wanted to prevail in the larger community.[245] There being evidence of this design in the record of the case, then, as the court of appeals had held, the plaintiffs " 'should have . . . been offered an opportunity to persuade a

---

241. The case utterly divided the Supreme Court, producing seven separate opinions, and a majority on no opinion. Id at 899. See the description provided in the Supreme Court Reporter's remarkable headnote to the case:

> BRENNAN, J., announced the judgment of the Court and delivered an opinion, in which MARSHALL and STEVENS, JJ., joined and in all but Part II-A(1) of which BLACKMUN, J., joined. BLACKMUN, J., filed an opinion concurring in part and concurring in the judgment, *post*, p. 875. WHITE, J., filed an opinion concurring in the judgment, *post*, p. 883. BURGER, C.J., filed a dissenting opinion, in which POWELL, REHNQUIST, and O'CONNOR, JJ., joined, *post*, p. 885. POWELL, J., filed a dissenting opinion, *post*, p. 893. REHNQUIST, J., filed a dissenting opinion, in which BURGER, C.J., and POWELL, J., joined, *post*, p. 904. O'CONNOR, J., filed a dissenting opinion, *post*, p. 921.

Id at 854-55.

242. Among the nine books targeted for removal from the high school library were Kurt Vonnegut, Jr.'s *Slaughterhouse-Five*, Desmond Morris's *The Naked Ape*, and Langston Hughes, ed, *Best Short Stories of Negro Writers*. Id at 856 n3. All have figured prominently in public school book-banning litigation. See, for example, *Parducci v Rutland*, 316 F Supp 352 (MD Ala 1970) (reinstating a high school 11th grade English teacher after dismissal for insubordination in refusing to discontinue use of Vonnegut's *Welcome to the Monkey House*). This case is especially noteworthy insofar as the federal judge, Frank Johnson, wrote explicitly that the teacher's professional interest was that of "academic freedom," as a first amendment-protected freedom, and held that the action of the school principal and school board "constituted an unwarranted invasion of her First Amendment right to academic freedom." Id at 356.

243. *Pico*, 457 US at 860-61 n16, quoting opinion of Judge Sifton, 638 F2d 404, 417 (2d Cir 1980) (reversing the grant of summary judgment in favor of the board). By way of example, the Court quoted from statements made by several board members such as this: " 'I am basically a conservative in my general philosophy . . . . *I feel that it is my duty to apply my conservative principles to the decision[s] . . . in which I am involved as a board member and I have done so with regard to . . . curriculum formation and content and other educational matters.*' " Id at 872-73 n24 (emphasis added). A deposition of another board member acknowledged that he voted to remove one of the books because of its "anti-Americanism," such as the failure of the book to *omit* mention that George Washington was a slaveholder. Id at 873 n25. "That [including mention that Washington did own slaves] is one example of what I would consider anti-American," the board member said. Id.

244. Id at 866, quoting Justice Douglas in *Griswold v Connecticut*, 381 US 479, 482 (1965).

245. See discussion and examples in notes 240, 243.

finder of fact that the ostensible justifications for [the school board's] actions
. . . were simply pretexts.' "[246]

Pico was, by any fair judgment, an important first amendment (and
academic freedom[247]) decision, albeit perhaps less so for the decision it
reached than for the decision it avoided. Decided on the grounds identified
by the Court, it stands for an orthodox general first amendment principle, in
no way peculiar to public education: public agencies, local school boards not
excepted, may not attempt to "contract the spectrum of available knowledge"
when the object to be served is to try to restrict freedom of information just
because the information is of a kind others might draw upon to question or to
dissent from the views that that public agency[248] thinks it best for the public,
or some subset of the public, to entertain. Understood this way, there is really
nothing extraordinary here. Justice Robert Jackson put the basic relevant
proposition quite well half a century ago, and probably no one has much
improved upon it since:

> The Fourteenth Amendment, as now applied to the States, protects the citizen
> against the State itself and all of its creatures—Boards of Education not excepted.
> These have, of course, important, delicate, and highly discretionary functions, but
> none that they may not perform within the limits of the Bill of Rights. That they are
> educating the young for citizenship is reason for scrupulous protection of
> Constitutional freedoms of the individual, if we are not to strangle the free mind at its
> source and teach youth to discount important principles of our government as mere
> platitudes.[249]

Indeed, not the worst way of testing *Pico*'s own limited holding is to ask what
one would say had the Court decided the case in favor of the school board.
Were a school board to be regarded as unreviewable in designating only such
books as it approved as "suitable" for public school library use, how could

---

246. 457 US at 860, quoting (with approval) the approach reflected in the court of appeals, 638
F2d at 417. *Pico* thus had a strong, direct link to *Ewing*, reviewed in the text accompanying notes 208-
12. Here, in *contrast* to *Ewing*, there was strong evidence that the board was not actually exercising a
good faith judgment at all. Moreover, so far as there had been a review of the particular books on
general grounds of educational suitability (a review that appeared to have been made in good faith),
that review had reached much different conclusions as to most of the books. See note 238.

247. And *Pico* is an "academic freedom" case, reaching (as it does) the conditions inside
educational institutions, the contents of their libraries, student opportunity of access, and
professional staff judgment in their selection and use, albeit decided on limited first amendment
grounds. In *Pico* itself, moreover, faculty academic freedom was also implicated directly and not
merely indirectly by the school board's directive ordering removal of the books, especially since the
directive also forbade any curricular use of the same books. See *Pico*, 457 US at 858 ("As a result [of
the board's actions], the nine removed books could not be assigned or suggested to students in
connection with school work."). Among the plaintiffs' complaints in the case was a complaint quite
the same as that which we examined originally in *Baggett*, 377 US at 360, that the school board action
infringed on the range of the student's own educational interaction, because the restrictions on those
who taught affected as well those who wished to learn. See *Pico*, 457 US at 862 n18 (describing the
board actions as "restrictions upon [the teachers'] ability to function as teachers in violation of
principles of academic freedom.").

248. Or, rather, those politically able to dominate that agency, which must then merely stimulate
competition among community groups, in turn, as to whose views shall control. Compare the
opinion of Justice Jackson in *Barnette*, 319 US at 641: "It seems trite but necessary to say that the
First Amendment to our Constitution was designed to avoid these ends by avoiding these
beginnings."

249. Id at 637.

one reconcile *that* rule of law with the first amendment or with any genuine academic freedom in public schools, and what kind of rule of law would such a rule be? This is, however, roughly the alternative the majority of the Court in *Pico* believed it was confronted with, given evidence in the record of the assumptions the school board entertained of its prerogatives as well as how it acted on those assumptions. There is little reason to suggest that the Court was anything other than correct.

Although *Pico* dealt with a removal of books from public school libraries, it is strongly of a piece with cases such as *Epperson v. Arkansas* and *Scopes v. Tennessee*, though *Epperson* and *Scopes* were instances of classroom rather than library censorship. In each, political decisions were at work deliberately to "contract the spectrum of available knowledge" within the public school. In each instance, the restriction was sought in order to insulate the ideological status quo from the distress that is always at risk when academic freedom is tolerated at any level of education, whether it is applied to certain subjects, to certain books, or to certain teachers. *Scopes* and *Epperson* merely furnished clear examples. But *Pico* was also, as the Court properly reviewed it, essentially the same sort of restriction one step removed.

Scopes and *Epperson* had dealt with efforts not to ban academic access to books by modern social anti-establishmentarians such as Kurt Vonnegut or Langston Hughes, but rather to suppress teaching of Charles Darwin's work— even a century after his original field studies had taken place. And, quite remarkably, soon after *Pico* the Supreme Court made still another return to Charles Darwin and academic freedom in public schools. It did so in 1987, a date coincidentally marking the bicentennial of the Constitution, twenty years after *Epperson*, decided in 1968. The case providing the occasion for a further review of this seemingly endless feud between science and religion is *Edwards v. Aguillard*.[250] With *Scopes* having served as the beginning of our unhurried review, it is altogether fitting that *Edwards v. Aguillard* should itself serve as our end.[251]

---

250. 482 US 578 (1987).

251. For the sake of completeness (that is, in reporting usages of "academic freedom" in the Supreme Court), however, mention should be made of one other case in the Supreme Court adverting to academic freedom during this most recent decade, *Memphis Community School Dist. v Stachura*, 477 US 299 (1986). *Stachura* was a private civil action brought in federal court by a public school teacher of life sciences after she was suspended by a local school board without a hearing (albeit with pay). The board had suspended her in hasty response to a local uproar based on inaccurate reports about two films she had used in her seventh-grade class on human growth and sexuality. Both films in fact had been provided by the local health department and approved by the high school principal; so, as it happened—unsurprisingly when due process is ignored—the teacher was suspended even while conducting her class altogether unexceptionably, that is, exactly in the manner she was authorized to do. Stachura was hastily reinstated the following fall semester albeit only *after* she had filed suit against the school board and its members. Though reinstatement was thus no longer at issue, she pressed forward with claims for money damages and fared quite well at trial; the jury awarded her $275,000 in compensatory damages and $46,000 in punitive damages. Significantly for our purposes, in sustaining her claims as stating proper causes of action, the federal district court described her first claim as a claim seeking damages for the violation of her right to

The original legislative anathematizing of Darwin from all of public education in Tennessee, we recall, was sustained in 1927 on the master-servant view of teachers in public schools. Indeed, in *Scopes*, the Tennessee Supreme Court held that in respect to tax-supported publicly administered schools and universities[252] the state was simply "unhampered" by the fourteenth amendment in deciding what was to be taught by those whom it paid. By 1968 and *Epperson*, however, as we have already noted, the decisional law of the first amendment had dramatically changed. The strong protection of professional academic freedom within public universities and also in some measure in ordinary public schools had come to be accepted in the Court, reported in its own usages of academic freedom beginning in the 1950s, in the course of holding invalid a large number of state restrictions chilling professional teaching and research. *Epperson* itself vindicated that freedom in assuring a high school biology teacher that she could address Darwin in her classroom, despite the state's legislated ban.[253]

Even so, despite the Court's decision in *Epperson*, the ancient contest had not yet run its course. In 1982, the Louisiana legislature enacted a true Hobson's choice. If natural science were taught, then the teacher must teach "creation-science"[254] as well. Teachers could be relieved of the duty to

---

"academic freedom." (Her other claim sought damages for a violation of her right to due process, that is, for failure to provide a fair hearing before the complaints against her were acted upon.) The court of appeals agreed and likewise described the school board's action as one violating her "academic freedom." *Stachura v Truszkowski*, 763 F2d 211, 215 (6th Cir 1985). It is just this point that makes the case appropriately mentionable here: the Supreme Court also used the same term unexceptionably in describing her right. See, for example, id at 302, 309 (use of the term "academic freedom"). *Stachura* is thus a helpful case, marking the identification of teaching freedom-academic freedom—in first amendment law.

But the matter is not dwelt upon here, because the case was accepted for review in the Supreme Court only to consider a different point: not to decide whether Stachura's academic freedom was protected by the first amendment, but, granting that it was, to determine how damages were to be measured when it is violated by a local school board and its members. The Court agreed that every form of damage to Stachura (including mental anguish, damage to reputation, lost income and/or lost teaching opportunities) could figure in the jury's award, including punitive damages as well. It rejected the idea, however, that additional damages could be awarded on some jury divination of the intrinsic money worth of a constitutional right per se, an award the district court had allowed. The case, though a fair argument can be made that such an award is not inappropriate, is nonetheless unremarkable in its treatment of that feature of claiming damages.

252.   Recall that the Tennessee statute involved in *Scopes* and the Arkansas statute involved in *Epperson* applied to all public colleges and state supported universities as well as to public schools. See notes 14-18 and accompanying text.

253.   As we observed, see notes 153-67 and accompanying text, the Court held that insofar as the banishment of Darwin from the public school (or university) was done to serve interests of a dominant religion, it was invalid under the first amendment on that account. Nevertheless, *Epperson* also stood for a stronger rationale. The concurring opinion by Justice Stewart, as we noted, was not restricted to a limited establishment clause rationale. In *Pico*, moreover, *Epperson* was identified with *Keyishian* and other academic freedom cases in the Supreme Court. See, for example, 457 US at 853. Justice Brennan also described *Epperson* as a case affirming the duty of courts to intervene where "essential to safeguard the fundamental values of freedom of speech and inquiry." *Pico*, id at 870, quoting *Epperson*, 393 US at 104.

254.   "Creation-science" was defined in the statute itself as a belief regarding origins, whether of chemical elements, galaxies, organisms, species (including man) and all else, that they "were created ex nihilo and fixed by God." See Creationism Act, La Rev Stat Ann § 17:286.1-286.7 (West 1982). See also *Aguillard*, 482 US at 596 ("[T]he largest proportion of superintendents interpreted creation science, as defined by the Act, to mean the literal interpretation of the Book of Genesis.").

provide instruction in "creation-science," that is, *only* by abstaining from teaching what the legislature called "evolution-science." The choice, therefore, was to teach each with the same vigor and attention as the other, or to teach neither.

The case challenging the Louisiana act was brought in federal district court by a coalition of teachers, parents, and students. That court, as well as the court of appeals, meticulously reviewed the legislation, and both concluded that the actual point of the act was to regulate public school curricula strictly in behalf of religious interests. The act plainly meant to compel teachers either to stay away from discussing evolution[255] or, failing that, to offer Bible explanations (called "creationism") as part of ordinary science, to be inculcated as of equal validity. The court of appeals struck the act on the same basis as the Arkansas statute had been held invalid in *Epperson*, that is, as a violation of the establishment clause. The Supreme Court agreed.[256] In doing so, it added that nothing in its decision should be taken to "imply that a legislature could never require that scientific critiques of prevailing scientific theories be taught."[257] But it also registered its firm agreement with the lower courts that this act was not an act of that permissible sort.

In deciding *Aguillard* as it did, moreover, the Court also expressly addressed the meaning of academic freedom in public education. It undertook to do so because the Louisiana act purported on its face to have been enacted not to restrict but rather to protect academic freedom—the academic freedom of students.[258] In response, noting how the act was meant to work concretely, and agreeing with the elaborate court of appeals' review of the very question of how academic freedom would in fact be affected, Justice Brennan quite unremarkably concluded: "The Act actually serves to diminish academic freedom by removing the flexibility to teach evolution without also teaching creation-science even if teachers determine that such curriculum

---

255. The principal sponsor of the law expressly stated as his own strong preference that teachers say nothing, thus achieving the effect of the law that was invalidated in *Epperson*. See references and quotations at 482 US at 587.

256. *Aguillard v Treen*, 634 F Supp 426, 428 (ED La 1985) aff'd, *Aguillard v Edwards*, 765 F2d 1251, 1257-58 (5th Cir 1985); see 482 US at 593-94 (discussion by Justice Brennan). See also 482 US at 602 (Powell concurring, noting that the material expected to be used in teaching "creation-science" was expected to come essentially from the Bible as the written word of God, and from materials supplied by "research" centers in which membership itself, however, required that "a member must accept 'that the account of origins in Genesis is a factual presentation of simple historical truth.' "); id at 609 (White concurring) ("[T]he teaching of evolution was conditioned on the teaching of a religious belief. Both courts concluded that the state legislature's primary purpose was to advance religion and that the statute was therefore unconstitutional under the Establishment Clause.").

257. Id at 593.

258. The effort of the Louisiana legislature to describe the act in these terms, moreover, is itself extremely instructive of the extent to which the legislature was aware how much conditions had changed since *Scopes*. Sixty years earlier, there would have been no need at all to explain or to account for whatever the legislature decided on such matters. (That, after all, was the essence of *Scopes*.) Now, however, given the changes in constitutional doctrine and the virtual certainly of a first amendment challenge, there was felt need to say something to put a proper face on the matter at hand. Choosing the explanation of solicitude for "student academic freedom" (learning freedom) was the best thought the legislature had.

results in less effective and comprehensive science instruction."[259] The court of appeals had taken the same approach, namely that "[a]cademic freedom embodies the principal that individual instructors are at liberty to teach that which they deem to be appropriate in the exercise of their professional judgment. . . . Although states may prescribe public school curriculum concerning science instruction . . . the compulsion inherent in the Balanced Treatment Act is, on its face, inconsistent with the idea of academic freedom as it is universally understood."[260] The Act, in brief, actually denied one kind of academic freedom to students insofar as it denied them learning freedom in the specific sense of *access to* and the *benefit of each teacher's best professional, good faith judgment, understanding, and skills*. It operated in its own way as the Act reviewed and held invalid in *Baggett v. Bullitt*.[261] It also operated in the same manner here as another statute would operate were it to require that one teaching astronomy either propose no science descriptions at all or propose Ptolemaic (earth-centered) models as viable science alternatives to Copernican ideas, that is, to require "balanced treatment" of earth-centered astronomy for the same reason as "creation-science" was required here (to confirm "God's plan" according to the Bible).

To be sure, *Aguillard* was not unanimous and it did divide the Supreme Court, albeit not by any very close vote. What is more useful about *Aguillard*, as a fair way of completing this unhurried review of academic freedom and the first amendment, however, is not anything in the division of the Court.[262] Nor is it anything that separates it or its useful observations on the meaning and content of academic freedom from its discussion and decisions in *Sweezy*, *Baggett*, *Keyishian*, *Ewing*, *Pico* and others that lend strong encouragement and support to academic freedom, whether in universities or in public schools. It is useful, rather, because overall its treatment of that freedom is in keeping with these other cases and because it, too, tends to report a far better understanding of the first amendment imperatives for academic freedom than characterized the empty doctrines of American constitutional law when Scopes was a teacher in Tennessee. Today, on the 50th anniversary of the Joint Statement of Principles and the 200th anniversary of the Bill of Rights, despite *Aguillard*, it would still be quite incorrect to suggest that the protection of academic freedom is now reasonably secure. Assuredly it is not. Still, a

---

259. 482 US at 586 n6. See also discussion, id at 588-89. The court of appeals had taken the same approach, namely, that

> [a]cademic freedom embodies the principle that individual instructors are at liberty to teach
> that which they deem to be appropriate in the exercise of their professional judgment. . . .
> Although states may prescribe public school curriculum concerning science instruction . . .
> the compulsion inherent in the Balanced Treatment Act is, on its face, inconsistent with the
> idea of academic freedom as it is universally understood.

765 F2d at 1257.

260. 765 F2d at 1257.

261. 377 US 360; see notes 115-19 and accompanying text.

262. The case came into court untested in actual application, enabling Scalia (for himself and Chief Justice Rehnquist) to suggest possibilities of legislative face-saving interpretation, that is, interpretations as might not impose more than trivially upon those subject to its "balanced treatment" provisions, according to which it could then be sustained.

number of things have come out nearly right, and the jurisprudence of the first amendment is vastly better than it once was.

IDEOLOGY AND FACULTY SELECTION

JUDITH JARVIS THOMSON*

I

The first statement on academic freedom by the then-new American Association of University Professors ("AAUP") was its 1915 Declaration of Principles,[1] which said that a university

> should be an intellectual experiment station, where new ideas may germinate and where their fruit, though still distasteful to the community as a whole, may be allowed to ripen until finally, perchance, it may become a part of the accepted intellectual food of the nation or of the world.[2]

The purposes for which our society establishes such institutions are, as the declaration said, threefold: the advancement of knowledge, the provision of higher education for students generally, and the training of specialists in the various professions. Such institutions therefore play a crucial, central role in the nation's cultural and economic life, for it is in them that the nation's future is born. To the extent to which they do not welcome new ideas, their threefold purposes cannot be well accomplished, and the future that grows out of them is stunted. As the AAUP's later 1940 Statement of Principles on Academic Freedom and Tenure put the point, in brief: "Institutions of higher education are conducted for the common good [,which] depends upon the free search for truth and its free exposition."[3]

But on some views, institutions of higher education are failing to serve as intellectual experiment stations: they are charged with behaving like homes of orthodoxy, reaction, and conventionality. Feminists complain that institutions of higher education are dominated by male-inspired conceptions of what constitutes good scholarly work, and that the content of teaching makes women's lives and women's work at best invisible. Feminists are joined by scholars in Afro-American Studies in complaining that the literary canon these institutions place before their students is at best arbitrarily restricted to the products of white males—I say "at best arbitrarily," since on some views the canon is a product merely of white male bigotry. Some people complain that the philosophical canon these institutions place before their students is improperly restricted to the products of Western philosophy, totally ignoring

Copyright © 1990 by Law and Contemporary Problems
* Professor of Philosophy, Massachusetts Institute of Technology.
1. AAUP, *Declaration of Principles (1915)*, reprinted in L. Joughin, ed, *Academic Freedom and Tenure: A Handbook of the American Association of University Professors*, App. A, at 157-76 (Univ of Wisc Press, 1969) ("1915 Declaration"); see Appendix A, 53 L & Contemp Probs 393 (Summer 1990).
2. 1915 Declaration at 167-68; Appendix A at 400 (cited in note 1).
3. *1940 Statement of Principles on Academic Freedom and Tenure*, in *Policy Documents and Reports* 3 (AAUP, 1984) ("*1984 AAUP Red Book*"); see Appendix B, 53 L & Contemp Probs 407 (Summer 1990).

the East; and some complain that even within Western philosophy, it is nowadays not possible for nonanalytic philosophical work to get a hearing on campus.

From a different direction come complaints to the effect that left-wing politics and commitments now dominate college and university faculties, and that institutions of higher education are behaving like homes of left-wing orthodoxy, so that conservatism cannot get a hearing on campus. From yet another direction come complaints that colleges and universities are the homes of relativism and nihilism, and that serious work aimed at discovering and teaching moral and political truths is made unwelcome there.

This kind of complaint—and I have mentioned only a small sample—is not new. Some twenty and thirty years ago the orthodoxy complained of was right-wing: it was charged that colleges and universities were not opening their doors to the ideas of the left, and that Marxist economics and Marxist social theory could not get a hearing on campus.

It is of interest that the 1915 Declaration went directly on to say:

> Not less is it a distinctive duty of the university to be the conservator of all genuine elements of value in the past thought and life of mankind which are not in the fashion of the moment. Though it need not be the "home of beaten causes," the university is, indeed, likely always to exercise a certain form of conservative influence. For by its nature it is committed to the principle that knowledge should precede action, to the caution (by no means synonymous with intellectual timidity) which is an essential part of the scientific method, to a sense of the complexity of social problems, to the practice of taking long views into the future, and to a reasonable regard for the teachings of experience. One of its most characteristic functions in a democratic society is to help make public opinion more self-critical and more circumspect, to check the more hasty and unconsidered impulses of popular feeling, to train the democracy to the habit of looking before and after.[4]

But this obviously cannot be understood as supplying a rationale for the rejection of new ideas. The authors of the declaration said "a reasonable regard for the teachings of experience," not a willful refusal to be open to new experience, and the passage is best understood as a prescription that the university should not flutter in the winds of changing current fashion, which is entirely compatible with the prescription that the university should not allow itself to be dominated by the orthodoxy of a past fashion.

Complaints that institutions of higher education fail to welcome new ideas have to be taken seriously, since we all suffer in the long run to the extent to which they fail to do so. The wide attention such charges generate in the public at large is testimony to public recognition of that fact. I will not even try to assess the correctness of any of these complaints, either those being made nowadays or those that were made some twenty and thirty years ago. The AAUP's Committee A on Academic Freedom and Tenure has only recently begun to confront these issues directly,[5] and what I take on is the

---

4. 1915 Declaration at 168; Appendix A at 400-01 (cited in note 1).

5. Committee A's current interest was triggered by an inquiry it received in 1984 from a law school professor. Committee A responded briefly to the general question this letter raised in *Some Observations on Ideology, Competence, and Faculty Selection*, 72 Academe 1a (January-February 1986), and

modest task of asking, on the one hand, whether it might not be useful to make some distinctions, and, on the other hand, whether anything useful can be said at a very general level about what kind of defense against such charges is available—when it is available. I will focus on an institution's selection of new faculty, not reaching the further questions that arise when what is in the offing is reappointment or the award of tenure.

II

Faculty selection calls for decision at two levels. There is, first, the decision about which field (area, discipline, specialty) to hire *in*; once the first decision has been made, there is, second, the decision about which candidate in the relevant area to hire.

We are a college, and an alumna offers us funds for an endowed chair, the field of expertise unspecified. What shall we devote the chair to? Well, what are our needs, and which is most pressing? We look around us and conclude that our offerings in history are weak, particularly in American history. On the other hand, while we have three faculty members in philosophy, we have no one who is trained in Greek philosophy. But it is also true that we have no department of computer science; we could devote the chair to that field and divert funds from mathematics and classics to contribute to the building of the new department. And so on.

A decision on this matter rests on three kinds of judgment. In the first place, there is the obvious question of cost. Any appointment, at any level, imposes costs on the institution, and I do not mean merely the opportunity costs of forgoing someone or something else. Building a new department of computer science, for example, would be a very expensive affair, requiring both additional new faculty and an investment in equipment and laboratory space. Even expanding our offerings in American history might not be without further cost: it would, at a minimum, require expanding the library's holdings if the person appointed specializes in a different area from those of the faculty members who currently teach American history here.

In the second place, and more interesting for present purposes, we may need to ask ourselves the deep question what kind of institution we are. What really is our educational mission? What are we trying to do for those who are currently our students? What do we want to be able to do for those we would like to encourage to become our students in the future? What we see as our needs will be constrained largely by our views about the answer to this question, even if we do not find ourselves provoked into asking it explicitly.

Largely, but not wholly; for there is an in some ways still more interesting third question that lurks here: which fields are themselves worthy of long-term investment? This question is immediately relevant for a university in

to the specific question about law schools in its report for 1985-86, *Report of Committee A, 1985-86*, 72 Academe 13a, 18a-19a (September-October 1986). The present article may be regarded as ruminations on the issues dealt with in those two policy statements.

light of its direct commitment to the advancement of knowledge. But the question arises even for four-year colleges, since the question whether work in a field is of scholarly importance, and, if so, of what kind, bears on the question in what way, and therefore whether, an investment in it would contribute to the college's fulfilling its educational mission. Fields within academic disciplines, and even academic disciplines as a whole, wax and wane in interest over time. Forty years ago, linguistics was a quiet enterprise, tucked into the average school (if on campus at all) in its department of English or foreign languages and literatures; nowadays it thrives on campuses across the country in departments of its own. Even more striking has been the stunning growth of computer science on campuses. By contrast, departments of education have shrunk, and at some schools have disappeared altogether. When it looks at its offerings and asks itself what it needs, a school cannot avoid making a judgment about which fields are worth investing in, given its purposes.

In the case of some fields, the answer is easy. "Look," we might be told, "astrology is booming nowadays: all manner of new ideas are being developed. And doesn't the AAUP say that an institution of higher learning should be an experiment station, where new ideas may germinate?" We may be excused if we do not regard ourselves as obliged to supply germination space for what goes under the name "new ideas in astrology."

Why may we be excused for this? Because it is obvious that there is no future in those new ideas.

But there is something worrisome about this reply. Isn't "it is obvious that there is no future in those new ideas" the very voice of the defender of an orthodoxy?

No one, in fact, worries about the absence of astrology in college and university offerings: no one charges them with being homes of orthodoxy in light of their not including it. But suppose someone did. It pays to ask what we could reply in defense of ourselves. Astrology should, after all, be an easy case, and attention to it should therefore help us to see what is in question in harder cases.

So let us suppose that we are the college's committee, charged with recommending to the college at large a disposition of the new chair. We decide to begin with an open house: everyone is invited to come in with suggestions. Someone who attends the open house suggests that we devote our chair to astrology. In our later, private, discussions, we trouble to vote on all suggestions, and we vote against astrology. Word of this gets out, and the friend of astrology requests a hearing before us, at which he says, "New ideas . . . AAUP . . . germination space . . . defenders of orthodoxy!" What do we reply? Well, we say that there is no reason at all to think that the planets and stars influence the ordinary lives of ordinary people. Sometimes what an astrologist predicts does, in fact, happen: my horoscope for last Wednesday said that I would meet a tall, dark man that day, and I did. But, on the one hand, what an astrologist predicts very often does not happen, and, on the other (even more important) hand, there is no reason to think that it is because of events in the heavens that an astrologist's predictions turn out to be true when they do.

What we do, in short, is to put it to the friend of astrology that astrology does not meet even the minimal standard an enterprise must meet if it is to count as a science, namely that there should be reason to believe that its theories explain the truth of its predictions when they are true.

But the friend of astrology is not without a reply. Most likely he will make a variety of allegations of fact that would, if true, give reason to believe that it *is* because of events in the heavens that an astrologist's predictions turn out to be true when they do. If he takes this line, he is arguing that astrology really does meet the standard we said that an enterprise must meet if it is to count as a science.

Alternatively, he may argue that this standard should be rejected: that it is neither here nor there whether astrology meets this standard, because an enterprise need not meet it in order to count as a science. This reply is less likely, however, since it is the respectability of the label "science," interpreted as *we* interpret that label, that friends of astrology would like the enterprise to be thought to deserve.

Let us postpone consideration of those two possible replies. We should now look rather at the following third possible reply that he might make: "Prove it!" It is important to stress that this reply will not do at all.

To begin with, could we prove that astrology fails to meet the minimal standard, and therefore is not a science? Perhaps you could, but I can't. I can't even do much in the way of formulating an argument. I believe that the motions of the heavenly bodies do not influence the everyday affairs of ordinary people, but on what ground do I believe this? My believing it is a product of a vague, loose conception of how the world works and of what causality involves and requires, picked up over the years from experience (which includes some snippets of science I have become acquainted with), and there is nothing I can produce in the way of compact, clear argument for my belief. Perhaps one of my colleagues in our physics department could do better than I can (I am, let us suppose, a member of the English department), but I say only perhaps, because demonstrating that the motions of the heavenly bodies do not influence the everyday affairs of ordinary people is not a task that the average physicist has ever thought of carrying out, and it is not obvious how he or she is to do so.

Does that mean that I acted improperly in voting against astrology? I should think not. To suppose it does is surely to indulge in excessive high-mindedness about what responsible decision-making requires. Since my belief really did issue from a conception of how the world works, acquired from past experience, I need not be capable of proving that there is no future in astrology in order to have acted responsibly in rejecting it.

Indeed, it would have been irresponsible for me to have acted otherwise. For what were my alternatives? To abstain from voting? To suggest we flip a coin? To suggest we turn the decision-making over to some other person or group? None of these alternatives would have been as good. As a member of the committee, I was under a duty precisely to bring my past experience to bear on, among other questions, the question what fields are worth investing in. Given my past experience, I would have failed in that duty if I had refrained from voting against astrology.

The friend of astrology is now before us, however, at the hearing he requested, and we *can* reverse ourselves. But if, in reply to our assertion that astrology fails to meet the standards required of a science, he merely says "Prove it!", there is no ground for complaining of our behavior if we do not reverse ourselves. If he gives no reason to think we were mistaken when we first took our vote, everything remains as it was. His saying "Prove it!" can on no view be thought to shift the burden of proof to us.

The point here is worth stress: new fields, indeed, new ideas generally, have the burden of proof. And it might be worth noting also the connection between this point and that "conservative influence" the 1915 Declaration said the university is likely to exercise. By its nature, as the declaration says, a university is committed to caution, and to "a reasonable regard for the teachings of experience."[6] We fail to display that reasonable regard if we suppose that we are not entitled to act on beliefs based on past experience unless we can prove them true. No doubt some of those beliefs may be mistaken, and I will draw attention to an example shortly; it is fair to say, more strongly, that none of those beliefs is immune to revision later. But in the absence of reason to think revision is called for, responsible decision-making does not merely allow, but calls for relying on them.

As I said, however, it may be that the friend of astrology will not say "Prove it!": he may instead make the first or second replies to which I draw attention. On the one hand, he may make allegations that would, if true, give reason to believe that it *is* because of events in the heavens that an astrologist's predictions turn out to be true when they do. On the other hand, he may argue that that standard should be rejected: he may argue that an enterprise need not meet that standard in order to count as a science. Whichever line he takes, he is picking up the burden of proof, and there will then be room for debate about whether he is carrying it. I do not say that he cannot (I do not suppose that astrology is self-contradictory); I say only that he must.

A second important point is that he has not carried his burden of proof by virtue of saying just anything at all. (For example, he has not carried it if he has offered us in evidence of the powers of the stars only that they sing to him at full moon.) His carrying the burden requires his producing what we—given our past experience—can see to be reason to revise our beliefs. For what is in question is whether *we* would be acting responsibly in refusing to reverse ourselves—not whether an all-knowing God would, but whether *we* would.

---

6. See note 4 and accompanying text.

This means that our acting responsibly in refusing to reverse ourselves is entirely compatible with our being mistaken.

New ideas have occasionally been rejected by the respectable academic audiences to whom they were first presented and later turned out not merely to have been right, but to be of the greatest scholarly importance. Perhaps the most striking recent example is the discovery by Barbara McClintock of transposable genetic elements in maize. She first presented that work in the early 1950s, but was met at the time by bewilderment and therefore lack of interest, and it was not until many years later that the importance of the work was recognized: she received the Nobel Prize for it in 1983. The example is particularly striking because Dr. McClintock was not a struggling young graduate student in the early 1950s; she was by then a distinguished biologist who had in 1944 become the third woman elected to the National Academy of Sciences, and in 1945 served as president of the Genetics Society of America. How could the ideas she presented in the early 1950s have been so roundly rejected at the time? An academic career is built on a battery of deep intellectual commitments, and it is arguable that the respectable biologists who rejected her ideas were being improperly (because excessively) protective of their own commitments: accepting her new ideas would have required a major revision in those commitments.

It is also arguable, however, that there was no impropriety in the rejection of those ideas, and that the ideas simply were at the time too new and unconventional to be absorbable into the biology of the time. Absorbing a body of new ideas into a science requires finding theoretical room for them: theoretical connections must be made between the new and what it is important to preserve of the old—and what it is important to preserve of the old becomes clear only when those connections are made.[7]

What we learn of, of course, are the instances in which the initially rejected new ideas finally came to prevail. It is certainly possible that other new ideas have sunk without a trace because their discoverers did not have the self-confidence and stamina (to say nothing of the funds) to carry on with their work despite rejection.

But the question is, what conclusion should be drawn from actual examples such as that of McClintock, and the possibility of other, equally

---

7. Stephen Jay Gould also suggests that McClintock's own personal style may have contributed to the rejection of her ideas:

> McClintock has always worked for herself and in her own way, never tailoring her efforts to win acceptance, or even to promote understanding among those who might need a little extra prodding or clarity to appreciate an unconventional notion. [S]he never did all she could to promote her chances in the admittedly tough battle for acceptance and understanding of transposable elements.

Stephen Jay Gould, *Triumph of a Naturalist*, reprinted in Stephen Jay Gould, ed, *An Urchin in the Storm: Essays About Books and Ideas* 164 (W.W. Norton, 1987). Gould's *Triumph of a Naturalist* is a review of Evelyn Fox Keller, *A Feeling for the Organism: The Life and Work of Barbara McClintock* (W.H. Freeman, 1983). That a scientist has to work to get his or her new ideas accepted stems from the fact that the new has the burden of proof. And see note 8.

I am indebted to Mary C. Potter for the McClintock example and the reference to Gould's essay.

important, new ideas that were mistakenly dismissed and did not in the end prevail? It could hardly be concluded that the assessment of new ideas—for example, in deciding which to fund further research on—should be taken out of the hands of currently respected experts and turned over to people outside the field. With the best will in the world, currently respected experts may get things wrong; outsiders might be so far lucky as to get things right, but if they do then that *is* mere luck.

It is not easy to say what constitutes making such assessments with, as I put it, the best will in the world. It is easy enough to say that the assessment must be made with due care, and not on grounds irrelevant to scholarly values. Obvious examples of assessments made on grounds irrelevant to scholarly values are those based on the sex, race, or politics of those who profess the new ideas. Again, a person who makes a negative assessment of new ideas because their coming to prevail would result in his or her losing status—his or her position of distinction in the field and the research funds it attracts—is also, obviously, making the assessment on grounds irrelevant to scholarly values. But it is likely to be a delicate matter whether an assessment really is being made on irrelevant grounds, for academics are rarely conscious villains: where nonscholarly values are at work, this is likely to be unconsciously or only semiconsciously so.

Moreover, love of one's own commitments may not issue merely from love of one's own status, and there is much that is good in it—compare that "conservative influence" to which the 1915 Declaration drew attention and the fact that the new has the burden of proof.

This connects with one source of the difficulty of defining due care. It won't do to say that the degree of care required is in proportion to the importance of the purpose for which the assessment is being made. Time itself is a scarce resource, and the degree of care that is due is surely a function not merely of the importance of the task for which the assessment is being made, but also of what the assessors take to be the degree of inherent implausibility of the new ideas and the time it would take to investigate whether their attribution of implausibility is mistaken. This is among the reasons why the absorption of new ideas in science may be sluggish, and the more sluggish, the more unconventional the new ideas are: replicating the work that issued in the new ideas, and then studying their further implications, takes time, and the scientist's colleagues need to be convinced that the time would be spent profitably.[8]

There is such a thing as excessive love of one's own commitments, of course, even where what lies behind it is concern for the truth and not merely for status, but the signs of it are likely to be delicate. I have in mind the thinking of people who know of data that appear to conflict with their theories, but do not take seriously enough the task of confronting the data.

---

8. And this is among the reasons why the scientist has to work at the enterprise of getting his or her new ideas accepted. See note 7.

(How seriously is seriously enough? That is hard to say. There are times when it is right simply to plow ahead, hoping that the apparent conflicts can be sorted out later.) Or the thinking of people who know of data that appear to conflict with their theories, and construct excessively ornate procedures for squaring the data with the theories. (There *are* epicycles in nature; which postulated epicycles are excessively ornate?) I talk here of "data," but scientists are plainly not the only ones who may behave in this way: any academic may.

It is clear, in any case, that while the new has the burden of proof, and the proof required is proof to the assessor, the assessor must exercise due care and must make his or her assessment on scholarly grounds, without excessive love for his or her own commitments. But having carried out that duty is compatible with having reached the wrong assessment.

I began by inviting you to imagine that we are a committee charged with making to the college a recommendation as to the disposition of its new chair, and I pointed to the fact that doing so will involve our asking ourselves which fields are worthy of a long-term investment. Asking about a field differs only in degree from asking about a new idea, for a field is just a set of more or less tightly interconnected ideas that generate a set of research programs and a methodology for carrying them out. So, similar conclusions hold of our enterprise. It pays to mention, however, in light of the considerations just attended to, that we must be sure to have among us members who possess some expertise in the fields available to us for choice, or who are capable of advising us of ways to acquire it in what we can see to be hard cases.

Astrology is an easy case. Our principled defense against the charge that in rejecting it we have refused to welcome new ideas and behaved like defenders of an orthodoxy lies in nothing more arcane than the fact, if it is a fact, that we have exercised the appropriate degree of care in assessing it, and have made our assessment on scholarly grounds, without excessive love of our own commitments. What marks astrology as an easy case is the fact that— given our own past experience—the appropriate degree of care is no care at all. We are entitled to dismiss it out of hand.

I am sure you think the same holds of creationism. What about feminist epistemology? Some people think that is not a field of study at all, but mere politics masquerading as theory. Some people think that the ideas central to Marxist economics, or for that matter, central to supply-side economics ("voodoo economics"), have no more place on a campus than do those central to astrology. The same point holds if committee members vote against giving these ideas a place on campus: they have a principled defense against the charge that they are refusing to welcome new ideas and behaving like defenders of an orthodoxy to the extent to which they have made their assessment in the way I described.

III

The people I just mentioned think that those ideas have no place on campus at all: they would not have them among their offerings even if unlimited funds were available. Why so? Why not live and let live, so long as there is no shortage of funds? Where, as at most colleges and universities, the faculty as a whole has a major say as to the academic program its school offers, and decides to whom the school's degrees will be awarded, the faculty stands behind its school's offerings to this extent at least: it certifies that (in its view) the program is academically respectable.[9] If we think that astrology or feminist epistemology or Marxist economics (or what you will) are not academically respectable enterprises, we will not want them included in our school's offerings at all: we will not want a student's courses in those subjects to count toward the degrees our school awards.

Others, however, may think that those enterprises do have a place on campus, but not at the cost of forgoing other enterprises. That is, they may be quite content with the thought of work in those areas counting toward the degree, but think that—given limited funds—the school has other, more pressing needs.

Decisions made on this kind of ground are familiar enough. We might be entirely content, perhaps even happy, with the thought of our college acquiring an anthropologist, a teacher of Greek, a specialist in Chinese history, even a specialist in the history of astrological literature, while also thinking that what we need more pressingly is a computer scientist, a specialist in Greek philosophy, or a specialist in American history.

It might be worth making a distinction here. We may consider some subjects to be of great inherent interest and importance, and reject them *only* on the ground that, given our educational mission, it is less important for us here at Such and Such College that they have a place on campus. Anthropology, for example. Or the history of astrological literature. (We might even think that a study of that literature could shed fascinating light on the history of culture and of science.) In rejecting those enterprises, we imply nothing invidious about work done by those engaged in them. Our rejection issues wholly from a conception of our educational mission and of what is required for carrying it out.

We may consider other subjects to be of some inherent interest and importance, and reject them on mixed grounds: on the one hand, the belief that they are of less general interest and importance than other enterprises, on the other hand, the belief that, given our educational mission, it is less important for us to have them on campus. Marxist economics, perhaps. Or feminist epistemology.

---

9. It is often said that an institution of higher education must be neutral, placing itself on neither side of a disputed claim to truth. The underlying thought here must surely be right. But what exactly *is* the underlying thought? Colleges and universities do, after all, quite properly declare themselves on the substantive question of what constitutes work worth giving academic credit for. See also note 14 and Part VIII.

Our views about the relative interest and importance of the various fields are like our views that this or that (putatively) scholarly enterprise is not a scholarly enterprise at all: we have a principled defense of them just to the extent that we have exercised due care in arriving at them, and have made them on scholarly grounds, without excessive love of our own commitments.

Similarly, for our view about our educational mission. Are we defenders of an orthodoxy—an orthodoxy here about what our institutional aim should be—in refusing to alter it so as to make room for enterprises not currently on campus? We may have a similarly principled defense of our refusal to do so.

Discussions of this kind are fairly common on campuses. Swings in views of the relative importance of scholarly disciplines do take place; compare the shifts I mentioned in views about the importance of linguistics and education. But discussions about educational mission have become even more common in the last forty years and have captured the attention not merely of the faculty and students on campus, but of the wider public as well. During the 1950s people said "Tighten up!" (Remember Sputnik.) During the 1960s people said "Loosen up!" During the 1980s people said "Tighten up!" I am sure that throughout the nineties people will be saying both: loosen up here and tighten up there.

It goes without saying that reasonable people both on and off campus will disagree with the conclusions we reach at Such and Such College, whether about assessments of fields or educational mission. And different schools— even different schools that hope to attract similar student bodies—will therefore offer different programs. But that can hardly be regarded as ground for complaint; quite to the contrary, it is a sign of health in the nation's educational system that it allows for these differences. I may think your views on such matters grossly mistaken, idiotic in fact, and you may think the same of mine; we should both welcome the variety in institutional programs that grows out of our differences.

IV

Having decided which field to invest in, a school is then confronted by candidates for its position, and each will have a battery of attitudes and beliefs. Hiring decisions are very strongly affected by the candidates' attitudes and beliefs, and there is room here for yet another charge of refusing to permit entry to the new.

Of course a candidate's attitudes matter: they matter because they bear on how he will behave on campus, which itself matters because it bears on his suitability for the position the school wishes to fill. To the extent to which we have reason to think a candidate feels contempt for blacks or Jews or women, for example, we have reason to think he will not behave fairly with others, whether students, colleagues, or anyone else the holder of the position will have to deal with. This point is not limited to what are most commonly thought of as prejudices. Consider, for example, arrogance and impatience. Sneering at and humiliating students may not be *the* worst of academic sins, but on most views it is among the worst; sneering at and humiliating one's colleagues is something they may be willing to put up with in exchange for sufficient brilliance, but it is risky, given the need for cooperation in carrying out the department's work. Indeed, the department's joint work may not be the only thing that suffers from the presence of the excessively arrogant: bullying and intimidation can chill independent thinking, especially in the less secure junior members of the department.[10]

An attitude that we have reason to think will cause unacceptable behavior on campus may be, as we might put it, belief-driven. What I have in mind is the possibility that a candidate's contempt for Jews, for example, issues from his believing that Jews are greedy and dishonest. (Of course it may instead be that the belief is attitude-driven, or that attitude and belief developed together, circling round and reinforcing each other.) That the attitude is belief-driven in no degree protects it, however: if the candidate's attitude gives us reason to think he will behave unacceptably on campus, then the fact that his attitude is belief-driven makes his harboring it no less reason to think so. That is so even if the belief that drives his attitude is true.

For another kind of example, consider the candidate who makes clear that he feels contempt for those who hold certain views widely accepted in the field. His contempt might be—indeed, is likely to be—belief-driven: he is likely to feel it because he believes that the views are grossly mistaken. The belief that drives his contempt might cut more deeply: he might believe not merely that the views are grossly mistaken, but that the very standards that are commonly thought to justify them are the wrong standards. Or the belief that drives his contempt might cut more deeply still: he might believe not merely that the views are grossly mistaken, not merely that the standards thought to justify them are the wrong standards, but that it is a gross mistake to think that there *can* be standards for the acceptability of views in the field. This does cut more deeply, for it says that those in the field are mistaken not only in thinking that reasoning in such and such a way is rational, but in thinking that there are any constraints of rationality at all governing the field—one who believes this believes that no assertion in the field can be any better supported by reason than its negation can, and that the only "good" argument in the field is the argument that convinces, there being no room for the further question whether anyone ought to be convinced by it. We might give the name nihilism to this belief.

Those who work in the natural sciences may wonder how anyone could put himself forward as a candidate for a faculty position in a field—how anyone could wish to spend his life teaching and conducting research in a field—if he is a nihilist about the field. But if they feel puzzled, that just shows they have

---

10. Paul Carrington draws attention to the importance for academic freedom itself of an institutional ambiance that encourages intellectual risk-taking, and to the need for mutual respect and restraint in generating that ambiance. See Paul D. Carrington, *Freedom and Community in the Academy*, 66 Tex L Rev 1577 (1988).

led sheltered lives. Nihilism is a going concern in the humanities, in literary theory, for example, and in philosophy.

It is also a going concern in legal theory. Some years ago, Dean Paul D. Carrington argued that those who profess "legal nihilism" have "an ethical duty to depart the law school, perhaps to seek a place elsewhere in the academy,"[11] and I think it plausible that what he had in mind by "legal nihilism" is a belief about law of the kind I pointed to, namely the belief that no assertion in the law can be any better supported by reason than its negation can.[12] The people he had in mind are members of the Critical Legal Studies movement, and many of them do appear to hold this belief.[13]

Suppose the candidate for our position does feel contempt for those who think there are standards governing reasoning in the field, and that his contempt is belief-driven by nihilism about the field. The fact that his contempt is belief-driven does not protect it, even if nihilism is true. If, for example, we have reason to think that his attitude will issue in unfair treatment of others, or in bullying or intimidation, we have, to that extent, reason to think he is not suitable for our position.

V

Are there any beliefs such that a candidate's having them by itself disqualifies him? We need to distinguish. In the first place, it might be said that some beliefs are such that anyone who holds them may be expected to *behave* in unacceptable ways on campus. Some people think that those who believe that communism supplies the truth about political, economic, and social matters would not engage in or allow students to engage in free inquiry. (Some think the same of those who believe that anticommunism supplies the truth about those matters.) Some think that those who believe that blacks are

---

11. See Paul D. Carrington, *Of Law and the River*, 34 J Legal Educ 222, 227 (1984). It was this article that provoked the law professor's inquiry about the AAUP's position on the use of ideological considerations in faculty selection at law schools. See note 5.

12. I say only that this is plausible, for some things Carrington says suggest that he meant something different by "legal nihilism." He does say that "the nihilist" professes "that legal principle does not matter," id at 227, which suggests that my interpretation in the text above is correct. But he also says that the people he has in mind cast doubt on the idea "that legal principles actually influence the exercise of power," id, which is not the same—you might well think that some assertions in law are better supported by reason than their negations are, while at the same time thinking that those in power have acquired and retained their power by something other than reason. A historical thesis is one thing, a thesis about the nature of law quite another. But I do not think this unclarity unique to Carrington: I think it may be fair to say that some members of the Critical Legal Studies movement have not themselves always been sensitive to this difference.

13. Here, for example, is Robert W. Gordon:

[B]ecause [law] is founded upon contradictory norms, its principles cannot constrain a single set of outcomes even if intelligently, honestly and conscientiously applied. In contract law, for example, there is *always* a legitimate argument for maintaining one party's freedom of action and a contrary argument for protecting the other party's security; for every argument for enforcing the deal . . . there is a counter-argument for voiding the deal.

Robert Gordon to Paul Carrington, in *"Of Law and the River," and Of Nihilism and Academic Freedom*, 35 J Legal Educ 1, 2 (1985) (emphasis in original). That counterarguments are always available is not an interesting thesis, so I take Gordon to mean something stronger, namely that equally good counterarguments are always available. See id.

on average genetically inferior to whites in intelligence would behave dismissively toward blacks on campus. Some think that those who accept nihilism would engage in bullying and intimidation.

Again, some think that the holders of this or that belief would use their classes as opportunities for proselytizing on matters extraneous to the subject, or would omit material which the department requires its students to become familiar with.[14]

On the other hand, these expectations—all of them—may just be false. For example, it is entirely possible for a person to believe that blacks are on average genetically inferior to whites in intelligence without behaving dismissively toward blacks on campus. For another example, someone who is a nihilist about a given field may treat those he thinks deluded with great respect; and he may be happy to dwell on their work in all suitable detail in his classes, if only because the more worthy the work of the people one is criticizing, the more impressive one's demonstration of their mistakes.

There *are* closer cases. What, for example, of those who believe that only the politically acceptable are entitled to freedom of speech on a college or university campus? Doesn't their holding that belief give us reason to think they would try to prevent, and incite others to try to prevent, the politically unacceptable from speaking on campus? Yes; and I think we may take them to have the burden of explaining why we should not think they would. All the same, explaining away the appearance is possible: for example, their belief might be a matter of political theory and not something they have any intention of acting on or of inciting others to act on.

I can think of no belief a candidate might hold that is by itself *conclusive* reason to think he would misbehave on campus. Further reason to expect misbehavior, arising from other features of the candidate than his beliefs, is required if he is to be rejected as unsuitable on the ground of how he would act if he joined the faculty.

It is arguable, however, that the holders of certain beliefs may rightly be expected to try to produce effects on students of a kind we should be concerned about. Consider the nihilist about ethics, who believes that no moral judgment can be any better supported by reason than its negation can. On his view, the only "good" argument for a moral judgment is the argument that convinces, there being no room for the further question whether anyone ought to be convinced by it. Aren't we entitled to expect such a person to try to dampen, even extinguish, his students' interest in what makes a moral

---

14. See William W. Van Alstyne's amusing imaginary interview of an enemy of sociology (the candidate calls it "bullshit on stilts") who applies for a university's position in sociology, Van Alstyne communication to the Committee on Academic Freedom and Tenure of the AAUP, in *"Of Law and the River,"* and *Of Nihilism and Academic Freedom,* 35 J Legal Educ 20 (1985). We certainly do not think institutional neutrality requires that it be open to each member of a department to include in or omit from his or her classes whatever he or she wishes. Typically, the members of a department jointly fix on the material that must be attended to by a student who concentrates in the department's discipline. They thereby jointly declare themselves on the substantive question of what constitutes work worthy of a certification of competence in the discipline. See note 9.

argument really be good (as opposed to merely convincing)? Yes, because the nihilist about ethics precisely thinks that interest misguided.

The question is, however, whether trying to produce this effect is behaving unacceptably. Bullying and intimidation, misuse of classroom time, and incitement to interfere with political speech on campus are clear improprieties, but trying to dampen a student's interest in what makes a moral argument really be good (as opposed to merely convincing) is no impropriety if the nihilist about ethics is right, and there therefore isn't anything that makes a moral judgment really be good (as opposed to merely convincing). Moreover, it is no impropriety even if the nihilist is mistaken; if the nihilist is mistaken then he will have acted no more objectionably than has a scientist who in good faith, but mistakenly, dampens a student's interest in certain questions in biology or physics.

It might pay to stress too that the nihilist about ethics need not also be an amoralist, by which I mean a person who believes that no conduct is morally right and no conduct morally wrong. The nihilist about ethics may hold quite firm moral views: he may think much conduct morally right and much morally wrong entirely consistently with thinking (at the metaethical level) that his own moral views are not a product of reason. So the fact of his nihilism is not only not conclusive reason to think he will try to cause his students to act badly if it suits their fancy to do so, it is not even good reason to think he will try to do this.

Can things be thought otherwise in a professional school? What of the candidate for a position in a law school who is a legal nihilist? Does it make a difference that the position is in the university's law school as opposed to the university's department of philosophy? Dean Carrington suggests that it does.[15] He suggests that the legal nihilist will dispirit his students, even disable them for the work for which they are being trained, and perhaps even encourage them to behave dishonestly in their later legal practice. He says that if a university takes on the responsibility of training professionals, it also accepts a duty to constrain teaching that will impede their capacity to do honorable professional work, so that while legal nihilism may well have a place elsewhere in the university, there is no room for it in a law school.

The charge that the legal nihilist will make dishonorable people of his students is surely overdrawn. The legal nihilist might also be an amoralist, but he need not be. Indeed, the particular legal nihilists who are Dean Carrington's targets are certainly not amoralists: they do have strong moral views—their work is positively drenched in moral indignation. The legal nihilist may well be a nihilist about ethics; according to some views of the relation between law and morality, it is not tenable to think morality rests on reason while law does not. But even if the legal nihilist *is* a nihilist about ethics, that is compatible with his rejecting amoralism.

_____

15. Carrington, 34 J Leg Educ at 227 (cited in note 11).

However, there isn't nothing in the charge that the legal nihilist will dispirit his students if he succeeds in convincing them of the truth of legal nihilism. For them to become convinced of the truth of legal nihilism is for them to become convinced that writing a brief and arguing a case are like writing commercials for soap powder: what counts is only whether you can construct an argument that will get the relevant audience to buy what you want them to buy. That leaves plenty of room for students to be trained in the skills required for selling their products successfully, so there is no reason to think their becoming convinced will disable them from the practice of law. But incoming law students typically think better than this of the profession they wish to become members of, and those who do will be dispirited. Some may even drop out.

Still, entering students in all parts of a university bring with them views it will dispirit them to discover the falsity of, and the fact that the discovery will dispirit them just is not by itself ground for their school to protect them against it—whether their school is the university's division of arts and sciences or one of its professional schools. If legal nihilism is false, then the students who are dispirited by it are mistakenly dispirited. But it can no more be thought proper for a professional school to protect its students against the possibility of mistaken dispiriting than for a biology or physics department to protect its students against the possibility of a similar mistake.

In short, nihilists cannot in general be rejected by reason of the effects they will try to produce in their students. Individual nihilists may rightly be expected to behave unacceptably on campus, not on the sheer ground of their being nihilists, but rather on the ground of whatever about them besides their nihilism gives reason to believe that they will behave unfairly, or will bully or intimidate, or misuse the classroom, this being possible in the case of non-nihilists as well.

VI

I asked whether there are any beliefs the having of which might by itself disqualify a candidate. We have considered the possibility that some beliefs are such that anyone who holds them may be expected to *behave* in unacceptable ways on campus. A second possibility is that some beliefs are such that we have good reason to think anyone who holds them is *intellectually* less than fully competent to occupy the position we wish to fill. This is surely true. Suppose a man applies for our position in mathematics and tells us at his interview that he's discovered a frightful mistake made by mathematicians: strictly speaking, $7 + 5 = 13$, and it's just good luck for us if our bridges don't fall down. He may be disqualified as a candidate on that ground alone. No doubt an institution of higher learning should be an intellectual experiment station, but some new ideas are self-contradictory.

A slightly less weird possibility is the candidate for our position in modern European history who tells us at his interview that there was no Holocaust. We may well think this belief absurd, but it is not self-contradictory.

What is of interest in my description of this candidate is that the position for which he is a candidate is in modern European history. What if it were in chemistry? There would, presumably, be an impropriety in our dismissing his candidacy for a position in chemistry on the sheer ground of his believing there was no Holocaust. Why? Because his having that belief, however absurd we think it, presumably does not by itself show that he is less than intellectually competent to fill a position in chemistry—it does not by itself show anything about his ability to do research and teaching in chemistry. The fact that a candidate for a position in modern European history believes there was no Holocaust is another matter: we may well think that fact does give us ground for suspicions about his competence *as a historian*, for we may well think it shows he is incompetent at assessing historical evidence.

It is of course logically possible that he is right, for as I said, the idea that there was no Holocaust is not self-contradictory. (Contrast the belief that 7 + 5 = 13.) Moreover, it is logically possible not merely that he is right (as a matter of good luck), but also that he has good reason to believe that there was no Holocaust, good reason that we simply do not know of, indeed good enough reason to outweigh our reasons for believing that there was one, reason of a weight such that if we knew of it, we too would believe that there was no Holocaust. We may well think this highly unlikely, but it might be true. The question of his competence to occupy a position in history is therefore not conclusively settled by the fact that he believes there was no Holocaust. What his competence turns on is his reasons for holding that belief—his ability to justify it.

His ability to justify it *to us*. For what is to be said here is exactly the same as what is to be said in connection with the prior decision about what field to hire in: it is in light of our past experience with and in history that we must assess his competence for the position, that being exactly what a hiring committee is charged with doing. And we have a principled defense of our assessment just to the extent that we have exercised due care in arriving at it, and have made it on scholarly grounds, without excessive love of our own commitments.

The same holds for the varieties of nihilism. It is, after all, possible for the members of a given law faculty to think that legal nihilism, while no danger to the souls of the students, is nevertheless an absurd view, a person's holding of which is good reason to suspect him of intellectual deficiencies. (It is, after all, possible that they think, on the basis of careful study of the literature, that the arguments offered for legal nihilism have been dismal at best.) On some views, they should nevertheless invite a legal nihilist to join their faculty in order that this lively and active school of thought be presented to their students, and who more vividly to present it than a proponent of it? Perhaps they should. But it seems to me not at all obvious that they must. They might think that their educational mission is best carried out if they arrange for the presence in their offerings of all currently lively and active schools of legal thought, including those they think profoundly wrong—subject only to financial constraints. But must they think this? Or again, they might be modest: they might say to themselves, "Well, *we* are convinced it is profoundly wrong, but who are we? Maybe we are the ones who are profoundly wrong." But on any view of the matter, this modesty not only may but must have its limits. A faculty not only may but must settle on what constitutes student work that will earn the school's degree.

VII

We have canvassed two kinds of grounds on which a candidate's beliefs might give us reason to reject him. On the one hand, there is the reason his beliefs might give us to think he would misbehave on campus. There is no denying that some beliefs give reason to think this, but I suggested that the belief itself is not conclusive: the expectation of misbehavior may just be mistaken, and further evidence is required if the conclusion is to be justified. On the other hand, there is the reason a candidate's beliefs might give us to suspect him of intellectual incompetence. There is here too no denying that some beliefs do give reason to think this, but I suggested that (self-contradictory beliefs apart) the fact of having the belief is not itself conclusive: the attribution of incompetence may just be mistaken, for incompetence lies in the candidate's reasons for holding the belief and not in the mere fact of his holding it.

Is there some further, third, kind of ground on which a candidate's beliefs might give us reason to reject him? I think not.

What makes this a difficult question, however, is the school sponsored by a particular religion. Suppose we are a school of theology within a Catholic university, and a candidate presents himself for our position in metaphysics and tells us he is an atheist. Or for our position in moral theology and tells us he believes there is nothing per se wrong in contraception or homosexuality. Will it do for us to reject him on ground of the sheer content of his beliefs?

Schools of theology can, and I think always do, say more than just "Look at the things he believes!" In the first place, we may think the candidate's holding those beliefs is reason to suspect him of intellectual deficiencies and thus of incompetence. Perhaps we think it perfectly clear to the eye of natural reason that there is a God and that contraception and homosexuality are per se wrong; and perhaps we think that the reasons the candidate offers us for rejecting these views are dismal at best. If so, then we are not rejecting him on ground of the sheer content of his beliefs.

Alternatively (or also), we may think his holding those beliefs is reason to expect him to misbehave on campus—we may think that he will misuse his classroom or refuse to present material we require our students to learn. But this expectation is suspect unless something more is forthcoming, for we would stand in need of reason—reason beyond the fact of his having those beliefs—for thinking that he in particular will misuse his classroom.

More interesting is the fact that we may expect him to dispirit, and not merely to dispirit but positively to disable our students. If our educational mission includes the training of Catholic priests, then if we hire this candidate, and he succeeds in convincing the students of his views, he will have rendered them incapable of engaging in an enterprise for which it is our educational mission to train them. This is a more serious charge than can be brought against the legal nihilist: if hired by the law school and then successful in his teaching, the legal nihilist will dispirit but not disable his students. I said that entering students in all divisions of a university bring with them views it will dispirit them to discover the falsity of, and that the fact that the discovery will dispirit them just is not by itself ground for their school to protect them against it, whether their school is the university's division of arts and sciences or one of its professional schools. But what of *disabling* our students? How could it not be open to us to reject those who would positively impede our carrying out of our educational mission?

This argument from disabling invites the reply that the educational mission of training priests had therefore better not be carried out within a university that lays claim to a place in the community of higher education. But is that right? Is it unacceptable for a university to lay such a claim if it has carved out an isolated corner within its walls for the training of priests? Even if it is in respect of all its other divisions a university like any other? (It is an interesting question why a religious group would want its priests trained within what is otherwise a university like any other. Why not operate independently, next door to the university? But I am sure that this question is not unanswerable.) On the other hand, what if the isolated corner were instead reserved for the training of propagandists for the advantages of a protective tariff?[16] Does just anything go in just any corner, so long as its purpose is openly declared, and it is so far isolated as not to infect the rest? Or is religion special? I fancy that religion *is* special: that the university that carves out a corner for training priests does not show the disrespect for what a university is that is shown by the university in whose corners anything goes that can get itself funded. But I leave open what an argument for this view might look like.

What is plain, however, is that an argument from disabling would be markedly harder to make if the candidate I described were applying for a position in the university's division of arts and sciences as opposed to its school of theology. Students do not in general seem to be disabled by becoming convinced that there is no God or that there is nothing per se wrong in contraception and homosexuality. They will certainly be disabled from being Catholics if they become convinced of these things; but it is hard to see how a university could be thought to have a place in the community of higher education if its educational mission includes training its students to be Catholics.

16. I borrow this example from 1915 Declaration at 159; Appendix A at 394 (cited in note 1).

These issues are difficult, however, and I have wished only to draw attention to them because they are so obviously among the issues that arise for us if we take the 1915 Declaration seriously.[17]

VIII

I have been concerning myself with ideological grounds for decisions on initial faculty selection, and have said nothing at all about procedures for making those decisions. In particular, I have throughout spoken of "we," and have left open who this "we" is. It is plain enough, however, that the faculty has a central role in such decisions, both in deciding about fields and in deciding among candidates: quite apart from the fact that the existing faculty may well be thought to have rights to a strong voice on such matters, there is the instrumental fact that faculty decision-making is likely to further the institution's purposes best. As I said, outsiders may be lucky enough to make successful choices, but if they do then that *is* mere luck.

However, an interesting problem arises at the intersection of the question what we are to think of ideological grounds for the decision-making and the question who is to do the decision-making, and I think it pays to have just a brief look at it. What I have in mind is a problem that can arise when there is ideological inbreeding in a department. Imagine an extreme case. The Department of Dee at Upscale University is in Upscale's Division of Humanities, and all of the department's members profess adherence to X-ism, which is a particular movement within the discipline. (I hardly need say it is not for no reason that I suppose Dee to be a humanities subject.)

We can connect this with our topic if we suppose that Dee Department has a position to fill and that, after going through Upscale's established search procedures, it has just recommended to the appropriate institutional committee that Dr. Bloggs be appointed. Lo and behold, Bloggs is yet another X-ist, and the supporting letters in his dossier are all from X-ists.

I am sure that this situation is already likely to make an administrator feel nervous. But with what justification? We can suppose it quite clear that there has been no bad faith in the department's decision-making: the members have throughout exercised due care, and have made their past and current decisions on scholarly grounds, without excessive love of their own commitments. They simply are convinced of the truth of X-ism: all anti-X-ism in the discipline they would give you reason to think absurd, and all in the discipline that bypasses X-ism they would give you reason to think benighted. Now, while academics generally believe that ideological diversity is a good

17. For some recent discussion of these issues within the AAUP, see Subcommittee of AAUP Committee A, *The "Limitations" Clause in the 1940 Statement of Principles*, 74 Academe 52 (September-October 1988); Leon Pacala, *Comments*, 74 Academe at 57 (September-October 1988); William Van Alstyne, *Comment*, 74 Academe 58 (September-October 1988). See also the case report, Investigating Committee of Committee A, *Academic Freedom and Tenure: Catholic University of America*, 75 Academe 27 (September-October 1989); *Comments from Counsel for the Administration of the Catholic University of America*, 75 Academe 39 (September-October 1989); Michael W. McConnell, *Academic Freedom in Religious Colleges and Universities*, 53 L & Contemp Probs 303 (Summer 1990).

thing in a department, I know of none who would be prepared to license administrative enforcement of diversity on a department over its good-faith assurances that its ideological stance is correct.

Other things being equal, of course, for what if X-ism is a battery of astrological theories? As I said earlier, it is the institution as a whole that awards the degrees on the recommendation of its faculty, and the faculty not only may but must take a stand on what student work is worth its degrees. So let us suppose that X-ism is not a battery of theories for the study of which Upscale's faculty would be prepared to refuse academic credit out of hand. Then given the facts so far described, there seems to be nothing for the administration to do about the situation. In particular, nothing in the way of assessing Bloggs' candidacy by any procedure other than that normally followed at Upscale.

There is another way in which other things may fail to be equal, however. For let me now add some further details. Dee Department's graduate program has been sliding downhill steadily in the national rankings, despite healthy financial support from the university; no member of the department has won a major national fellowship in over a decade; the department has been receiving fewer and fewer applications to its graduate program and has been forced to accept more and more of them in order to fill its teaching assistantships; and it has been having increasing trouble finding teaching positions for its Ph.D.s who wish to teach. Members of the Dee discipline outside Upscale explain this phenomenon in this way: "The place is riddled with that loony X-ism! Upscale's X-ists are good X-ists, as X-ists go, but there's nowhere of interest that X-ists go."

How do the members of Upscale's Dee Department explain the phenomenon? *They* say in complete good faith that it issues from an anti-X-ist orthodoxy out there in the discipline, which prevents X-ism from getting a fair hearing; X-ism (they say) is fifty years ahead of its time.

Why wasn't the situation attended to by the administration before things reached this pass? Let us suppose that Upscale has no visiting committee system and has a long tradition of allowing its departments a considerable measure of autonomy.

Must Upscale allow this situation to go on indefinitely? It won't do to reply that X-ism may after all be the truth about the discipline and that X-ism may really be fifty years ahead of its time. Any body of theory that is not self-contradictory (including astrology) may turn out to be true. What makes trouble for the idea of taking action is not that X-ism may be true, but that the members of Dee Department are in good faith convinced that it is.

On the other hand, Upscale surely need not allow the situation to go on indefinitely. It is arguable, more strongly, that Upscale's administrators ought to intervene, and that they would be failing in an important administrative responsibility if they allowed Dee Department to carry on, business as usual.

The question what the administration can properly do is obviously a hard one. The question is no less hard if the administration is able to get non-Dee faculty cooperation in acting to constrain Dee Department. Faculty members cherish departmental autonomy, but they also place a high value on the status of their institution and therefore on the respectability of its programs; so non-Dee faculty members may themselves be no less ready than their administration to act improperly against Dee Department. But I think we cannot deny that *some* course of action must be open to Upscale.

Does this commit us to the view that an administration may take action on substantive grounds? I think the answer may be yes. For I suggested that ideological inbreeding in a department is not something that would by itself justify administrative intervention, and what I think triggered the thought that some course of action must be open to Upscale's administrators is what I added when I told you that Dee Department has been sliding down the public disciplinary hill, and that those in the discipline at large attribute the phenomenon to its members' X-ism. But how could adding that have made the difference? I think it *may* be only by way of its having given reason to think that X-ism is mistaken. For if the phenomenon could plausibly be explained in some way other than by appeal to a mistake in X-ism—if, for example, the phenomenon could plausibly be explained by personal prejudice against X-ists—then wouldn't intervention be unacceptable? But to intervene on the ground that there is good reason to think X-ism mistaken is to intervene on a substantive ground.

In any case, suppose the administration does intervene and that X-ism does not merely shrink at Upscale but gradually dies out as the current members of Dee Department retire. It might turn out that X-ism later takes over the discipline. Then X-ism really was ahead of its time! And Upscale's administrators have themselves made the mistake. It is worth stress that this no more shows they acted improperly in intervening than a similar mistake would show the faculty had acted improperly in making the kinds of decisions we looked at in earlier sections. Neither administration nor faculty is under a duty to be right, only to make a serious and fully responsible effort to be.[18]

---

18. I am grateful to Mary C. Potter and William W. Van Alstyne for comments on an earlier draft.

ARTISTIC FREEDOM AND ACADEMIC FREEDOM

ROBERT M. O'NEIL*

I
INTRODUCTION

The Cincinnati, Ohio, jury surely did the right thing by rejecting obscenity charges against Contemporary Arts Center Director Dennis Barrie following the exhibition of Robert Mapplethorpe's photographs.[1] Yet a different outcome at that trial might have forced higher courts to consider to what degree the fine arts enjoy protection under the first amendment, an issue that has been curiously neglected in the evolution of freedom of expression. First amendment protection of artistic expression and several related questions affecting both free expression generally and academic freedom in particular deserve more attention than they have received. These questions are the focus of this article.

The article addresses academic and artistic freedom from three perspectives. Part II discusses the constitutional status of an artist's freedom to create. Part III analyzes an artist's freedom to display or perform his or her works, particularly in college and university facilities. Part IV explores complex questions of freedom in funding for the arts—including, of course, the perplexing (and now partially resolved) debate over content restrictions on grants from the National Endowment for the Arts.

II
FREEDOM TO CREATE

Surely the first amendment ought to protect the artist's creative process and product as fully as it protects the spoken and printed word. Legal scholars and practitioners of the arts have consistently assumed that art is

---

Copyright © 1990 by Law and Contemporary Problems

* Professor, University of Virginia; Director, Thomas Jefferson Center for the Protection of Free Expression.

1. See Kim Masters, *Art Gallery Not Guilty of Obscenity: Cincinnati Jury Clears Mapplethorpe Exhibition of All Charges*, Washington Post A1 col 4-6 (October 6, 1990). The obscenity charges were not unexpected. Shortly before the opening of the Mapplethorpe exhibit in early April, 1990, the Contemporary Arts Center sought an injunction against threatened prosecution, but a federal judge declined to intervene. An arrest was made for violation of the Ohio obscenity laws soon after the show opened, although law enforcement officers were ordered by federal courts not to interfere with the continued display. The show went on as scheduled, with record crowds, while director Barrie awaited the criminal trial that occurred in late September and October. *State v Mapplethorpe*, 90-CRB-11699A (Cincinnati Dist Ct October 5, 1990).

"speech."[2] But that assumption needs closer examination; the state of the law is less clear than these scholars assume. Artists familiar with the current state of the law are right to be uncomfortable. One scholar who recently reviewed the cases summarizes current doctrine with a realistic sense of resignation:

> Artistic expression has been assigned derivative and second class status in the views of many first amendment thinkers, the Supreme Court, and other courts. [F]rom a first amendment perspective the ideal kind of expression is political discourse, and all other kinds of expression, including artistic expression, are accorded lower degrees of first amendment protection depending on their similarity to political expression.[3]

To test this conclusion, an independent review of the scope of first amendment protection for artistic expression is in order. In pursuing the constitutional question, "Is art protected?," it is necessary to bear in mind a logically antecedent question: "What is art?" Courts are not comfortable defining art. One recalls Justice Holmes' stern warning at the turn of the century: "It would be a dangerous undertaking for persons trained only to the law to constitute themselves final judges of the worth of pictorial illustrations."[4] Moreover, the very nature and concept of art is changing rapidly—with credit (or blame) to Andy Warhol and other pioneers of new forms of creative expression.[5] In fact, much of what shocks many viewers about current art is more its novelty than its inherently abrasive content. Thus it becomes progressively more difficult even for art critics, let alone judges, to determine "what is art,"[6] and this article will focus instead on the more familiar question of whether art is protected.

The search for sources of constitutional protection of artistic expression is not fruitful. Curiously, the Supreme Court has never defined precisely the scope of first amendment protection for the creative and performing arts.[7] There are, however, several sources from which to glean useful hints. Nearly forty years ago, for example, in *Burstyn v. Wilson*,[8] the court considered the constitutionality of a New York statute permitting the banning of motion pictures on the ground they are "sacriligious." In striking down the statute, the Court held without dissent that "expression by means of motion pictures is included within the free speech and press guaranty of the First and Fourteenth Amendments."[9] In so holding, the Court explained:

> It cannot be doubted that motion pictures are a significant medium for the communication of ideas. They may affect public attitudes and behavior in a variety of ways, varying from direct espousal of a political or social doctrine to the subtle

---

2. See, for example, Zechariah Chafee, *Free Speech in the United States* 545-46 (Harvard Univ Press, 1941).

3. Sheldon H. Nahmod, *Artistic Expression and Aesthetic Theory: The Beautiful, the Sublime and the First Amendment*, 1987 Wis L Rev 221, 222.

4. *Bleistein v Donaldson Lithographing Co.*, 188 US 239, 251 (1903).

5. See Note, *Post-Modern Art and the Death of Obscenity Law*, 99 Yale L J 1359 (1990) (authored by Amy M. Adler).

6. See Andrew Grundberg, *Art Under Attack: Who Dares Say That It's No Good?*, New York Times B1 col 3-4 (November 25, 1990); Leonard D. DuBoff, *What is Art? Toward a Legal Definition*, 12 Hastings Comm & Ent L J 303 (1990).

7. See generally Nahmod, 1987 Wis L Rev 221 (cited in note 3).

8. *Joseph Burstyn, Inc. v Wilson*, 343 US 495 (1952).

9. Id at 502.

shaping of thought which characterizes all artistic expression. The importance of motion pictures as an organ of public opinion is not lessened by the fact that they are designed to entertain as well as to inform.[10]

Arguably that judgment, or at least its logic, went beyond film, and carried full constitutional protection to all artistic media.[11]

Additional, if somewhat oblique, insight comes from cases inquiring into obscenity. During the three decades since the Court first sought to define obscenity and review procedures for its suppression,[12] the Justices have stressed that judgments "in the area of freedom of speech and press . . . must always remain sensitive to any infringement on genuinely serious literary, artistic, political or scientific expression."[13] A particular work can be found obscene only if it lacks, inter alia, "serious . . . artistic . . . value."[14]

These criteria compel consideration of the artistic qualities of works claimed to be obscene. As the outcome of the Mapplethorpe trial seems to suggest (since much sympathetic and apparently persuasive testimony related to the artistic qualities of Mapplethorpe's work),[15] that mandate alone may have considerable value to the fine arts community. It may even be that when a given work is found to be "art," it cannot also be held obscene; the very notion of constitutionally unprotected art may be logically untenable—at least as far as obscenity is concerned. The same is not true under the newer child pornography laws recently sustained by the Supreme Court;[16] much material that may violate these laws may also have considerable artistic merit, leaving unclear the relationship between the status of art and other exceptions to the first amendment. In any event, obscenity cases, because they do not address the issue, fail to provide any direct support for declaring that art is speech for constitutional purposes. Their language sharpens the inquiry for finding obscenity, but surely does not resolve the central issue.

Justice William O. Douglas, apparently alone on this as on many topics, once addressed constitutional protection of art directly. Dissenting in a 1960 case involving quite different matters, he argued that "the actor on stage or screen, the artist whose creation is in oil or clay or marble . . . are beneficiaries of freedom of expression."[17] Yet even Justice Douglas never found the opportunity to apply these precepts to vindicate an artist's claim of free expression.

---

10. Id at 501.

11. Later cases involving film review boards seemed to qualify that protection. See *Times Film Corp. v City of Chicago*, 365 US 43 (1961).

12. See *Roth v United States*, 334 US 476 (1957) (first attempt of Supreme Court to define obscenity).

13. *Miller v California*, 413 US 15 (1973).

14. Id at 22-23.

15. Isabel Wilkerson, *Obscenity Jurors Were Pulled Two Ways*, New York Times A12 col 4-6 (October 10, 1990).

16. *New York v Ferber*, 458 US 747 (1982) (sustaining New York criminal statute that prohibits persons from knowingly promoting sexual performances by children under the age of 16 by distributing material that depicts such performances).

17. *Poe v Ullman*, 367 US 497, 514 (1960) (Douglas dissenting).

Artists can also turn for support to *Southeastern Promotions, Ltd. v. Conrad*,[18] a first amendment case that comes close to addressing protection of artistic expression. In holding that a city could not exclude from a public auditorium performances of the rock musical "Hair," at least not without fairly elaborate procedural safeguards, the Court felt called upon to discuss briefly the nature of the activity the city authorities had summarily barred.[19] The arbitrary and subjective basis the city gave for barring the musical would have sufficed, said the majority, "only if we were to conclude that live drama is unprotected by the first amendment—or subject to a totally different standard from that applied to other forms of expression."[20] No member of the Court argued that rock musicals should be so viewed. Yet this dictum suggesting that the first amendment protects artistic expression was not without an important limitation: "Each medium of expression, of course, must be assessed for first amendment purposes by standards suited to it, for each may present its own problems."[21] This addendum offers at least some basis for the artist's fear that creative and performing arts enjoy less than the full protection afforded the spoken and printed word.

Even in the lower courts, the case law is surprisingly meager, and the judicial views are in less than perfect accord.[22] As recently as 1988, a federal appeals court sustained the removal of Richard Serra's "Tilted Arc" from Manhattan's Federal Plaza.[23] In so doing, the court would do no more than concede that "artwork, like other non-verbal forms of expression, may under some circumstances constitute speech for first amendment purposes."[24]

So grudging a view of the creative arts is not unique. An earlier federal appeals court upheld the removal of controversial art from gallery space in a state university student center.[25] The judgment reflected, in major part, the court's disparaging view of the paintings that provoked the dispute. Without deciding what degree of deference judges ought in principle to give to works of art, the court found the claim for protection weak in part because "there is

---

18.   420 US 546 (1975).

19.   Id at 569-72. A ruling in favor of the show's promoters would have required the Court to do no more than fault the city's shoddy procedures; glaring deficiencies in the way requests for auditorium space were handled made it unnecessary to decide whether or not the proposed use of the facility was clearly entitled to first amendment protection.

20.   Id at 557.

21.   Id, citing *Burstyn*, 343 US at 503.

22.   See, for example, Ralph E. Lerner & Judith Bresler, *Art Law: The Guide for Collectors, Investors, Dealers and Artists* 315-23 (Practicing Law Institute, 1989).

23.   "Tilted Arc," commissioned and underwritten by the General Services Administration, was installed on the Federal Plaza in downtown Manhattan in 1981. It was an arc of steel 120 feet long, 12 feet tall, and several inches thick. It soon became an object of intense public debate and criticism because of its enormous size, and because it was designed to rust over time. After a public hearing in 1985, at which the sculptor was allowed to explain his views on the piece, the GSA decreed its removal, though insisting it "made no judgment whatsoever concerning the aesthetic value of the Tilted Arc." The removal order was ultimately sustained. See *Serra v United States General Services Admin.*, 847 F2d 1045, 1048 (2d Cir 1988); Richard Serra, *Art and Censorship*, 14 Nova L Rev 323 (1990); Richard Serra, *Tilted Art Destroyed*, 14 Nova L Rev 385 (1990).

24.   *Serra*, 847 F2d at 1048.

25.   *Close v Lederle*, 424 F2d 998 (1st Cir 1970), rev'g 303 F Supp 1109 (D Mass 1969). For the facts of the dispute and lower court decision, see text accompanying notes 48-49.

no suggestion that, unless in its cheap titles, plaintiff's art was seeking to express political or social thought."[26] The court then compared the paintings before it to campus speaker bans, which in its view "involve a medium and subject matter entitled to greater protection than plaintiff's art."[27] The implication seems clear and is consistent with the scholarly view cited earlier:[28] art that conveys a political message or theme stands markedly higher in the constitutional order than art that is "merely art," however great its critical acclaim or its aesthetic appeal.

For example, a federal district court assessing a controversial sculpture stated that "the art form involved in this case constitutes speech within the meaning of the First Amendment and thus is entitled to constitutional protection"[29]—a statement that drew its principal support from the broad protection espoused in *Southeastern Promotions*. Moreover, the challenged sculpture embodied a primarily political message—in fact, political caricature of a kind that may be entitled to protection almost without regard to the medium of expression in which it appears.[30]

The Seventh Circuit, however, has been less willing to distinguish political and nonpolitical art. Several years ago, Judge Richard Posner observed that "freedom of speech and of the press protected by the first amendment has been interpreted to embrace purely artistic as well as political expression . . . unless the artistic expression is obscene in its legal sense"[31]—although the court went on to hold that an artist could not resist a state college's relocation of his controversial art works from a highly visible campus gallery.

One can find a few other references to the constitutional status of artists and their works, but they are essentially cumulative. There seems to be a fairly firm consensus that art that conveys a political message is fully protected. Works whose merit is "exclusively artistic" sometimes fare less well. Such a dual standard may find little historic or philosophical support,[32] but has proved remarkably durable and quite hard to dislodge.

Neither artists nor constitutional scholars concerned about the arts should take much comfort from the way this issue has been addressed. While no court has squarely rejected first amendment protection for the creative and performing arts, that fact offers small solace indeed—especially in view of the protection that seems to have been extended to such less ennobling media of communication as nude and topless dancing.[33] The arts, and those who

---

26. Id at 990.

27. Id.

28. See note 3 and accompanying text.

29. *Sefick v City of Chicago*, 485 F Supp 644, 648 (ND Ill 1979).

30. See, for example, *Yorty v Chandler*, 13 Cal App 3d 467, 91 Cal Rptr 709 (1971).

31. *Piarowski v Chicago Community College*, 759 F2d 625, 628 (7th Cir 1985).

32. Indeed, there is very early evidence of an assumption that artistic expression was of a rather high order and thus arguably entitled to protection. Zechariah Chafee cites a declaration of the Continental Congress in 1774 that basic freedom would include "the advancement of truth, science, morality and arts in general." Chafee, *Free Speech in the United States* at 545 (cited in note 2).

33. See, for example, *Schad v Borough of Mt. Ephraim*, 452 US 61 (1981).

create and study them, deserve better in a society whose liberty is centrally tied to artistic as well as political expression.

One might simply continue to assume that, when and as necessary, the arts will get their due. Suggestions to the contrary are relatively few, and appear only in dicta[34]—though, for that matter, even the sympathetic statements seem to accompany judgments adverse to the artist and thus represent largely Pyrrhic victories. Alternatively, one could hope that litigation of these issues will eventually compel the courts to address an issue that has too long been left to implication. If, for example, the director of Cincinnati's Contemporary Arts Center had been convicted on obscenity charges for displaying the Mapplethorpe photographs, higher courts in Ohio would have been forced to appraise the medium of expression and to define much more clearly the extent of first amendment protection to which it is entitled.

Anything less than full first amendment protection for the arts seems anathema. To limit full protection to "political" speech would create an anomaly; a political cartoon with modest artistic value or a crude political sculpture would be fully protected, while an internationally recognized work of fine art would not be. Moreover, such a distinction would imply that even the finest and most widely acclaimed work of art makes little or no contribution to civic life or to the values served by democratic self-government. To that suggestion, Alexander Meikeljohn has given the most persuasive answer:

> [T]here are many forms of thought and expression within the range of human communication from which the voter derives the knowledge, intelligence, sensitivity to human values: the capacity for sane and objective judgment which, so far as possible, a ballot should express.[35]
>
> . . . .
>
> [The] people do need novels and dramas and paintings and poems, "because they will be called upon to vote."[36]

III

FREEDOM TO PERFORM AND DISPLAY WORKS OF ART

On the issue of the artist's right to display and perform controversial works, there is more direct law, and the results seem a bit more consistent. Yet here, too, the guidance provided by these results is less clear than the historic importance of the creative arts warrants.

A. The "Performance" Cases

Perhaps the easiest cases have been those arising on a college or university campus. Two recent cases involve a film[37] and a play.[38] In both cases, state college officials cancelled the performances on the basis of off-campus

---

34. For example, *Close*, 424 F2d at 990.
35. Alexander Meikeljohn, *The First Amendment Is An Absolute*, 1961 Sup Ct Rev 245, 256.
36. Id at 263 (quoting Professor Harry Kalven).
37. *Brown v Bd. of Regents*, 640 F Supp 674 (D Neb 1986).
38. *DiBona v Matthews*, 269 Cal Rptr 882 (Cal App 1990).

criticism of their content. In each case, the courts held firmly in favor of the right to hold such performances, and thus added importantly to the stature of the performing arts.[39]

Brown v. Board of Regents involved a film scheduled to be shown at a theater in the art gallery of the University of Nebraska at Lincoln. The film in question was "Hail Mary," the most recent film directed by Jean-Luc Godard. Its most controversial feature—that which evoked the charge of blasphemy— was a contemporary picturing of the birth of Christ. Protest against the film came from persons outside the campus, including a state senator who berated the theater director because some of her constituents thought the film sacrilegious or blasphemous. The director's superior bowed to this external pressure and cancelled the showing. A group of would-be viewers of the film promptly took the issue to federal court.[40]

The immediate result may well be less important than the reasoning and the broader implications for freedom of artistic display and performance within the academic community. In assessing the dispute, the court relied on a recent Supreme Court decision regarding the removal of books from school libraries, *Board of Education, Island Trees Union Free School v. Pico*.[41] In *Pico*, the Supreme Court established firm and protective first amendment principles on that subject.[42] The Court noted that the academic setting of *Brown*, in fact, made bowing to external political or religious pressure even less acceptable: "Even if the cause had been only the fact of controversy . . . cancellation would not have been justified, because action taken by an arm of the state merely to avoid controversy from the expression of ideas is an insufficient basis for interfering with the right to receive information."[43]

Several factors may, however, modify the scope of this important decision. First, regardless of the content of the film, its artistic merit, or its message, the reason given for the cancellation was highly suspect. Thus the court might simply have concluded that a state university had no business banning any activity arguably protected by the first amendment in response to such pressures; such a holding would have avoided consideration of the degree of protection the film warranted. Second, film as a medium of expression had by this time received a substantial measure of first amendment protection.[44] Thus, such a decision upholding the right to show a controversial film may not extend fully or easily to forms of expression litigated less frequently. Finally, the religious content or theme of the film may have afforded a measure of constitutional status that would not necessarily attach to art treating other themes, or to art lacking such a focus or message.

---

39. *Brown*, 640 F Supp at 681-82; *DiBona*, 269 Cal Rptr at 890-91.
40. *Brown*, 640 F Supp at 676-78.
41. 457 US 853 (1972).
42. Id at 871.
43. *Brown*, 640 F Supp at 679.
44. *Kingsley International Picture Corp. v Regents*, 360 US 684 (1959).

The other case[45] examining freedom of performance occurred later and potentially provides more protection to artists. A California junior college theater instructor chose for his class a play that treated race relations in a highly charged fashion. It included "a flurry of racial slurs and epithets"[46] just before a black police officer fatally shot a white suspect on stage. Community pressure, here too fueled partly by religious groups, caused the college administration to cancel performance of the play, even as a class exercise. A group of prospective playgoers sued to enjoin the ban.

In preventing the administrators from cancelling the performance, the court relied on the basic principles of *Brown*: strong community pressure would not justify banning from the campus controversial ideas, values, or views, even when embodied in an artistic medium rather than in lecture or newspaper form. The court also noted that the inappropriateness of the ban was even clearer here than in *Brown*, because cancellation of the play went to the heart of a college course, rather than simply limiting the extracurricular offerings of a campus theater.[47]

B. The "Display" Cases

Although these performance cases are consistent, and help to broaden protection of the arts, the same cannot so readily be said of cases involving exhibitions in university galleries. An early example, *Close v. Lederle*,[48] involved removal by the University of Massachusetts at Amherst of an art exhibit from the student union. The exhibit, the work of a junior faculty member, was originally welcomed, but later was deemed by the university administration to be "inappropriate" after complaints about its presence in a heavily travelled corridor. The faculty member claimed the removal violated his first amendment rights. The district court was sympathetic, and ordered the administration to reinstate the exhibit.[49] The court held the university art gallery to be a public forum. Since the artist had complied with the procedural rules for use of the forum, and since there was nothing "inappropriate" in the paintings, the judge found the removal of the paintings to be a violation of the artist's first amendment rights. Yet the court of appeals reversed, in part because of the view that wholly artistic expression deserves less protection than political expression.[50] But the reviewing court also paid exceptional deference to the administration's judgment about what was "appropriate" or "inappropriate" for display in a well-travelled campus corridor.[51]

Close may have been biased by another factor: the paintings hung in a corridor through which many campus visitors could not help but pass—

---

45. *DiBona*, 269 Cal Rptr at 882.
46. Id at 889.
47. Id.
48. 303 F Supp 1109.
49. Id at 1120.
50. *Close*, 424 F2d at 990.
51. Id.

among them impressionable school children. To the court, that factor may have been the strongest basis for invoking a higher canon of taste: "Where there was, in effect, a captive audience, [the university administration] had a right to afford protection against 'assault upon individual privacy' . . . short of legal obscenity."[52]

Thus, a public art display may set in motion a conflict between two sets of interests, demanding an accommodation not needed in the film and play cases. Art exhibits in highly visible spaces cannot so easily be avoided or bypassed by potentially surprised or offended viewers; that fact alone makes more complex the artist's claim to the right to display his work, whatever might be said of the antecedent interest in creating the work, or even (as in the case of the play) presenting the art to a class of his own for their comments or evaluation.

The other gallery case, *Piarowski v. Chicago Community College*,[53] reaches, if with somewhat greater care, a consistent conclusion. An Illinois junior college art instructor was ordered by the administration to relocate three stained glass windows he had created for public display as part of an annual faculty exhibit. When the artist went to court, a decade and a half after *Close*, he found a more sensitive view of artistic expression, but fared no better in the end.

The court assumed, but saw no need to decide, that artistic expression enjoyed both first amendment protection and the full benefit of academic freedom.[54] Two elements in the case, however, enabled the court to decide that no violation of the faculty member's first amendment rights had occurred when the adminstration ordered relocation of the windows. First, the college had properly cited a deep concern for the effects such an exhibit might have on its ability to recruit students.[55] Second, the display was prominently visible: "the offending windows could be seen by people not actually in the gallery."[56] These factors helped to justify imposing canons of taste higher than the legal test of obscenity, thereby allowing the windows' relocation.

The critical question raised by the gallery cases is whether it is the *medium* or the *setting* that is constitutionally dispositive. Despite the uncertain status given the creative arts in both cases, the critical factor seems to be the *location*

---

52. Id. Compare *Applegate v Dumke*, 25 Cal App 3d 304, 101 Cal Rptr 645 (1972), a factually somewhat similar case that did not address the constitutional issue because of an apparent waiver of the artist's claims against a state university ban on the display of his works.

53. 759 F2d at 628.

54. Id at 629.

55. The court described the exhibit as follows:

One depicts the naked rump of a brown woman, and sticking out from (or into) it a white cylinder that resembles a finger but on careful inspection is seen to be a jet of gas. Another window shows a brown woman from the back, standing, naked except for stockings, and apparently masturbating. In the third window another brown woman, also naked except for stockings and also seen from the rear, is crouching in posture of veneration before a robed white male whose most prominent feature is a grotesquely outsized phallus (erect penis) that the woman is embracing.

Id.

56. Id at 630.

of the exhibit—evoking the court's concern in one case for possible assault on a captive audience including school children, and in the other a concern that visible and offensive art works pre-empted prime campus gallery space for the display of material of less than universal appeal.

Such tensions are not confined to the courts or to constitutional judgments. They must also play a part in defining the extent and nature of academic freedom for the creative arts. The final report of last spring's Conference on Academic Freedom and Artistic Expression, after a resounding endorsement of maximum freedom for the creative process, addressed just the issue with which we have been dealing.[57] The report closed by striking a somewhat different balance than the courts:

> When academic institutions offer exhibitions or performances to the public, they should ensure that the rights of the presenters and the audience are not impaired by a "heckler's veto" from those who may be offended by the presentation. Academic institutions should ensure that those who choose to view or attend may do so without interference. Mere presentation in a public place does not create a "captive audience." Institutions may reasonably designate specific places as generally available or unavailable for exhibits or performances.[58]

How might such a view have altered the outcome of the Massachusetts and Illinois gallery cases? The report suggests, unlike the courts, that offense taken at a particular work, or fear that someone may take offense, would not justify removing the work once in place. But the report also recognizes that a generalized concern that student or faculty exhibits *might* contain controversial works would presumably justify a general policy that consigns them to a less prominent site.[59]

Finally, the conference report argues that presentation in a public place does not, by itself, create a captive audience.[60] It seems, though, to leave open the possibility that such a condition might occur, and that, if it did, appropriate steps might be taken, consistent with the artist's freedom and the institution's own integrity.[61]

Thus, judgments of constitutional law and ideal precepts of academic freedom diverge on this issue—despite Judge Posner's effort at assimilating the two standards in the course of rejecting the Illinois college instructor's claim in *Piarowski*.[62] The differences are, however, not so much on matters of principle—whether, for example, artistic expression is entitled to full protection—as on such issues as the degree of deference due a college's desire to shield visiting school children or to sustain its capacity to recruit future students.

The latter concerns may indeed generate institutional interests of a rather high order. The courts find them persuasive—superior not to the artist's interest in creating or exhibiting controversial works as such, but rather to the

---

57. The report is reprinted in 76 Academe 13 (July-August 1990).
58. Id.
59. Id.
60. Id.
61. Id.
62. 759 F2d 625.

artist's wish not to have those works removed from the prominent location where the institution originally put them on display. A statement of principles of academic freedom would recognize the institution's dilemma but would insist that it be resolved in a different way—either by demanding that visitors be more tolerant, or by not committing such prominent space to potentially controversial work in the first place.

IV

FREEDOM TO OBTAIN FUNDING

The third area of inquiry, constitutional limits on funding restrictions for the arts, may be the most difficult, and certainly is the most current. It has also elevated the arts to an unaccustomed level of political visibility and controversy. After a year and a half of sparring, the basic status of funding for the National Endowment for the Arts ("NEA")—and the inescapable corollary issue of content restrictions on NEA-funded art works—were resolved in late October in what appears to be a generally satisfactory compromise.[63]

In place of the Helms Amendment,[64] a new grant-evaluation formula appears with two elements. The first is a simple (if ominous) declaration: in the broad provisions that cover grant-making, Congress has now directed the NEA to take into account "general standards of decency and respect for the diverse beliefs and values of the American public."[65] Such language seems to have no independent operative force, and would at most guide panels and agency officers among various desiderata to be applied in the review of proposals. Moreover, a spokesman for the endowment said soon after the congressional compromise that this language on "decency" was "nonbinding."[66]

In its more detailed provisions, the new approach also represents a vast improvement over the Helms Amendment, which during its brief life both constrained and politicized the endowment. Gone from the new reauthorization is the Helms Amendment's restrictive language, which included terms that were imprecise and legally undefined and thus almost certainly unconstitutional.[67] Artists seeking grants under the Helms Amendment were required to swear by oath that they would not transgress lines bounded by such terms as "sadomasochism" and "homoeroticism," and would not create or display works showing "individuals engaged in sex acts."[68] The oath took the form of a certification requirement to the "Request for Advance or Reimbursement." The new section of this form required

---

63. Pub L No 101-512, § 103(b) (1990), amending 20 USC § 954(d).
64. Pub L No 101-121, § 304(a), 103 Stat 741 (1990), amending 20 USC § 954. For a discussion of its provisions, see notes 67-69 and accompanying text.
65. Pub L No 101-512 § 103(b).
66. Christopher Myers, *Arts Backers are Pleased by Congress' 3 Year Reauthorization of NEA without Restrictions*, Chron Higher Educ A19 col 4 (November 7, 1990).
67. See Pub L No 101-121 § 304(a); see also note 71.
68. Id. See HR Conf Rep No 101-264, 101st Cong, 1st Sess 264 (1989). See also Stephen F. Rohde, *Art of the State: Congressional Censorship of the National Endowment for the Arts*, 12 Hastings Comm

recipients to certify to compliance with certain "General Terms and Conditions for Organizations Grant Recipients." Paragraph Two of the Terms and Conditions contained language drawn directly from section 304(a). Therefore, in order for any grant funds to be released, the recipient had to certify in advance that none of the funds would be used "to promote, disseminate, or produce materials which in the judgment of the NEA . . . may be considered obscene."[69]

The change in the locus of decision seems at least as significant an improvement as the terminology. Under the Helms Amendment, the NEA was empowered to determine what was and was not obscene before making grants.[70] In a field where scrupulous adherence to procedure has always been a quid pro quo for substantive restraint, the notion of inviting a grant-making agency to set its own standards on obscenity seemed especially abhorrent. Doubtless that informal process would have been enjoined by the courts had any of the several constitutional challenges to the Helms Amendment come to trial before the reauthorization.[71]

Under the congressional compromise, it is now clear that judgments about obscenity in the arts must be made by the courts. The standards to be applied are those that judges have fashioned over a period of more than three decades.[72] The agency is empowered to seek recovery of a related grant only if a grant recipient is later convicted of an obscenity or child pornography charge. Grant recipients are no longer required to certify under oath that they will adhere to and enforce the statutory ban on any use of NEA funds for purposes the agency "may consider" obscene.[73]

The new 1990 reauthorization approach thus seems a major improvement in both substance and procedure. It removes the most intrusive and demeaning content restriction provisions of the Helms Amendment, and frees a benign agency from the role of policing grant recipients, which is especially important because the NEA must have the confidence of the arts community if it is to carry out the mission given it by Congress a quarter century ago.

The substitute approach is not, however, without potential problems. Reauthorization of the NEA with no content restrictions would have been preferable not only to artists and some members of Congress, but also to a most thoughtful bipartisan presidential commission that filed its report

---

& Ent L J 353, 365 (1990); Note, *Standards for Federal Funding of the Arts: Free Expression and Political Control*, 103 Harv L Rev 1969 (1990).

69. *Bella Lewitzky Dance Foundation v Frohnmayer*, 59 USLW 2436 (CD Cal 1991).

70. Pub L No 101-121, § 304(a).

71. While the Helms Amendment dealt in part with "obscene" material, and to that extent rested on firm and well-defined constitutional ground, the other key terms were not defined in the amendment or elsewhere, and thus would quite surely have been found vague or overbroad or both under well-settled first amendment principles. Thus, not surprisingly, the one case that has come to judgment reached just such a conclusion. See *Bella Lewitzky Dance Foundation*, 59 USLW 2436.

72. See Part II.

73. The NEA announced soon after passage of the reauthorization that it would no longer require grant recipients to sign a pledge of the kind that had been imposed during the previous year. Kim Masters, *NEA Drops Obscenity Pledge; Arts Agency Decision Follows Hill Action*, Washington Post C1 col 1 (October 30, 1990).

shortly before Congress acted on the NEA's future.[74] In its key section, the commission recommended "against legislative changes to impose specific restrictions on the content of works of art supported by the Endowment."[75] The report continued: "Content restrictions may raise serious constitutional issues, would be inherently ambiguous and would almost certainly involve the Endowment and the Department of Justice in costly and unproductive lawsuits."[76]

Some may argue that the new congressional approach does not even involve content restrictions, but simply the addition of a sanction for the violation of existing and constitutionally valid obscenity laws. Yet the effects of the new approach for the sensitive and conscientious artist may also be quite different from the effect that would have followed from reauthorization lacking such language and collateral sanctions.

In four specific ways, the reauthorization may still deter or make anxious the scrupulous creative person who seeks NEA support. The first and perhaps most obvious effect flows from the prominent reference to "decency."[77] Despite the endowment's assurance that such language is nonbinding, and despite the absence of any enforcement provision or penalty, some members of the arts community find it not only offensive but ominous as well. The editor of the *Kenyon Review*, for example, calls the "decency" phrase "dangerously vague" and "incredibly ambiguous."[78] She adds: "Although you don't have to sign anything, it once again leaves open a broad area that was never in question in the past."[79] Surely a conscientious artist might be uneasy both about the contours of "decency" and about their possible application to his or her creative works. Whether such anxiety attains constitutional stature remains, of course, a difficult question.

A second risk is the potential chilling effect created by the new approach to grant eligibility. While the judgment about what is obscene now rests with the courts, the sensitive and conscientious artist might well be fearful about the new collateral sanction the reauthorization creates. Such fears would be heightened by the state of the law reviewed earlier, and the uncertain basis of

---

74. Press release accompanying Independent Commission's Report to Congress on the National Endowment for the Arts (September 11, 1990) (on file with author); see also Kim Masters, *Don't Restrict NEA, Panel Tells Congress; Report Urges Exclusion of Anti-Obscenity Language*, Washington Post B1 col 1 (September 12, 1990).

75. Independent Commission Report to Congress at 2 (cited in note 74).

76. Id at 89.

77. Pub L No 101-512 § 103(b).

78. See Myers, Chron Higher Educ at A23 col 2 (cited in note 66). In March 1991, a group of performing artists and an artists' organization filed suit in federal court, with the support of the American Civil Liberties Union, alleging the unconstitutionality of the "general standards of decency" provision in the 1990 reauthorization. The suit argues that such a standard impermissibly restricts freedom of expression of grantees and applicants.

79. Id. The next week the NEA panel that reviews grants in the field of theater and drama asked for clarification of the term "decency" before its December meeting. Kim Masters, *NEA Panel Seeks Decency Ruling*, Washington Post C2 col 1-2 (November 15, 1990). Later, the panel that reviews proposals from artist-run organizations asked for assurance that "decency" will not be used as a criterion in judging grant applications despite the new language. Kim Masters, *What Makes for Decency? Panel Seeks Clear Wording*, Washington Post C4 col 1-3 (November 27, 1990).

artists' expressive and creative freedoms. Until a few months ago, an established artist would probably have assumed that his or her works were immune from obscenity charges, and that, since no such charges had been brought in recent times, an NEA grant was quite secure.

The prosecution of Cincinnati's Contemporary Arts Center over the Mapplethorpe exhibit—despite the outcome—squarely challenges that assumption. However unusual the circumstances, artists can no longer dismiss the possibility of criminal jeopardy. Creative persons are bound to think twice before testing the limits of taste and decorum. The world of art will suffer from any such diminution of creative spirit.

A third danger is that museums and galleries may be less venturesome in seeking or displaying bold and controversial works. The events in Cincinnati again supply an illustration: the Mapplethorpe exhibit, as well as the artist, had received NEA support.[80] Therefore, a gallery might be forced to forfeit an NEA grant if its director were convicted on charges like those filed against Barrie. Under those conditions, greater caution might be predicted on the part of those galleries that can least afford to forfeit government grants precisely because they tend to test the limits of taste by displaying the avant garde. Here too the world of creative art may stand to lose in the chillier climate that follows the compromise.

There is a fourth and final, if somewhat subtler, risk. Those who pressed so hard to make the NEA an administrative censor are not likely to retreat from the field because they lost this battle. In fact, it is quite possible to imagine all NEA grantees now becoming targets of self-appointed guardians of decency and propriety searching for evidence of obscenity in funded works. This is a frightening prospect indeed. It recalls vigilante movements of earlier and unhappy times in our national life, when the demon was sought in politics[81] rather than in art. But the parallel is uncomfortably close, and the potential chilling effect of private activity may be potentially greater even than that of government policy or prosecution.

Such risks and hazards do not, of course, make a constitutional case. They do, however, set the stage for possible challenges to the far less troubling language that replaced the Helms Amendment.[82] Surely such a challenge would not be averted by Senator Helms' own claim that "refusing to subsidize something does not 'ban' it."[83] The body of law dealing with unconstitutional conditions is far too advanced to permit any branch of government to hide

---

80. See Rohde, 12 Hastings Comm & Ent L J at 360 (cited in note 68).

81. John P. Roche, *The Quest for the Dream* 67-72 (Macmillan, 1963) (recounting the Palmer raids and the post-World War I anti-communist movements).

82. Compare favorably *Advocates for Arts v Thompson*, 532 F2d 792, 797 (1st Cir 1976), a case that approaches this issue on its facts, in which the court expressed concern about New Hampshire's denial of a state grant to a literary magazine on the basis of one controversial poem, but declined to intervene on constitutional grounds in the magazine's favor.

83. See Jesse Helms, *Art, the First Amendment and the NEA Controversy: Tax-Paid Obscenity*, 14 Nova L Rev 317, 320 (1990).

behind distinctions between conditioned benefits and direct sanctions.[84] More troublesome is the unavoidable truth that government cannot possibly fund every applicant or subsidize every work of art, and must therefore adopt and apply some neutral selective criteria.

Dean Geoffrey Stone poses the dilemma in this way:

> Although government may not ban offensive art, it does not necessarily follow that it must therefore subsidize such art. Surely, government is under no constitutional obligation to establish the NEA in the first place. Why, then, if it chooses to fund some art, should it be precluded from exercising reasonable judgment about the types of art it will support? For example, although government cannot ban "bad" art, it surely is under no constitutional obligation to fund "bad" art, even if it supports "good" art. Why, then, must government fund art that denigrates religion or promotes unlawful or undesirable conduct, or is inappropriate for children, or deeply offends others? There is a common sense difference between suppression and failing to subsidize, and government must have greater discretion in the latter situation than in the former.[85]

Dean Stone then offers his own compelling reply to a question he knows is not entirely rhetorical:

> Reasonableness is not and cannot be, the constitutional standard for government efforts to restrict speech because the message is unwise, disagreeable, harmful or offensive. To the contrary, if there is a central principle in our first amendment jurisprudence, it is that government ordinarily may not restrict expression for such reasons, for such suppression distorts public debate, mutilates the thought process of the community, violates the equality of status in the field of ideas and elevates the government to the role of platonic censor.[86]

The crucial question remains: if government cannot fund all artists or all works, how must it choose? If it makes choices, it must adopt and apply standards. And if those standards are not simply broad and bland categories—for example, fund only oil paintings but not water colors, support metal sculpture but not plastic, favor portraits over landscapes—then there is inevitable potential for content differentiation. The difficulty is deciding when that differentiation abridges or inhibits freedom of expression in ways the first amendment will not allow.

Three further observations may help identify possible constitutional issues. It is only artists among all government grantees who forfeit benefits if they are convicted of violating obscenity laws;[87] a public employee, a scholarship holder, a public housing tenant—apparently anyone else who receives government support—would be immune. It is true that obscenity is more closely related to the nature of an NEA grantee's work and status than is the case for most other government beneficiaries. But consider then the other dimension of the grid: no other transgression by an NEA grantee would

---

84. See, for example, Lynn A. Baker, *The Prices of Rights: Toward a Positive Theory of Unconstitutional Conditions*, 75 Cornell L Rev 1185 (1990), and the many materials cited there.

85. Address by Geoffrey Stone at Loop Luncheon, 16-17 (October 18, 1990) (transcript on file with author).

86. Id at 19.

87. But compare 18 USC § 1464 (1990), under which licensed broadcast stations may incur collateral sanctions for the broadcasting of obscene (as well as "indecent" or "profane") material on the air. See *FCC v Pacifica Foundation*, 438 US 726 (1978).

cause the loss of the grant. If, for example, an artist is convicted of fraudulent art sales, or of selling drugs in the studio, or of disposing of toxic chemicals improperly, the NEA grant is unaffected. Ironically, it is the law violation most closely related to the artist's creative process—the most expressive of all the grantee's acts—that has been singled out as the basis of possible forfeiture. To focus in this way on artists among all government beneficiaries, and on their expression among all possible law violations, is at least deserving of further constitutional scrutiny.

A second possible concern relates to procedures. It is quite true that the new reauthorization ties the sanction—potential loss of a prior grant—to a court judgment of obscenity based on criteria that have received the Supreme Court's blessing.[88] Yet those obscenity criteria, and the procedures by which they must be enforced to be constitutionally acceptable, are now to be used to impose not one but two quite unrelated penalties on the artist/grantee. The new approach is not unlike revoking a state university student's scholarship after a conviction for speaking on campus and creating a clear and present danger of lawless action, or barring from future government contracts any professional photographer convicted of child pornography. In each case, the primary sanction is imposed by procedures that are presumptively valid; courts upholding those procedures did not, however, realize they were also validating a secondary or collateral use of the primary sanction. Therein lies the problem.

The function here of the secondary sanction is not to allow government to avoid its obligations of due process, but rather to compound the consequences of a single speech-related offense on the basis of procedures designed only to support a single sanction. Courts have always been uneasy about allowing the outcome of one proceeding to trigger automatically a collateral consequence, even where due process was guaranteed in the primary proceeding. Moreover, the potential chilling effect of the secondary sanction may in this instance far exceed that of the primary sanction—if only because the value of a revoked NEA grant (like the student's scholarship or the photographer's access to government jobs) may be far greater than the fine one pays for a single brush with the criminal law. Thus it is fair to ask whether, especially in the area of expression, the procedures that have been validated for obscenity convictions were really intended also to support the punitive superstructure Congress has now imposed.

Finally, one must bear in mind that we are dealing with obscenity, in all its vagaries. When one considers the potential for regional variations in outcomes under the "community standards" formula,[89] one might also ask whether the primary proceeding was intended to sustain such grave collateral consequences as the reauthorization contemplates. An artist creates a work in one city, but that work may eventually find its way before a jury in a much less enlightened community. That jury, applying its standards, may years later

---

88. *Miller v California*, 413 US 15, 33 (1973).
89. Id.

cause the forfeiture of an NEA grant made to the artist in a vastly different environment.

It is far from clear whether any of these concerns alone, or all of them taken together, create doubts of constitutional magnitude. They are, however, worth exploring and bearing in mind as we watch the new NEA legislation take effect. The day may come when such arguments will need to be made. We cannot, after all, assume that every jury will be as reasonable as the one in Cincinnati.

V

CONCLUSION

Artistic freedom plays a potentially major role in shaping and safeguarding academic freedom. While the extent of constitutional protection for artistic expression remains surprisingly spare and imprecise, the case for such protection seems compelling. That protection should encompass the creative and performing arts in measure comparable to protection for the spoken and printed word, and for recognized media such as film. Protection for artistic expression must not be confined to the creation of works of art, but should extend also to the display, exhibition and performance of those works. To the same extent, government funding for the arts should not attempt to restrict an artist's freedom. Though government is under no duty to fund art at all, once it decides to do so, it may not use that funding to deprive the recipient of otherwise protected freedoms of expression. Artists, like speakers and writers, are engaged in an activity that properly claims, and deserves, the fullest measure of constitutional recognition.

ACADEMIC FREEDOM, HATE SPEECH, AND THE IDEA OF A UNIVERSITY

Rodney A. Smolla*

I

Introduction

The nation is in the midst of a fervent national debate over how universities should respond to "hate speech" on campuses.[1] "Hate speech" is the generic term that has come to embrace the use of speech attacks based on race, ethnicity, religion, and sexual orientation or preference.[2] This article analyzes this debate in two stages. The analysis begins by examining the existing state of first amendment jurisprudence regarding hate speech, exploring the doctrines that currently combine to protect such speech, the

---

* Arthur B. Hanson Professor of Law, and Director, Institute of Bill of Rights Law, College of William and Mary, Marshall-Wythe School of Law.

1. The debate has been prominent at virtually every college and university in the country in the last two years. See generally Steve France, *Hate Goes to College*, ABA J 44 (July 1990); Connie Leslie, *Lessons from Bigotry 101: Racism on Campus*, Newsweek 48-49 (September 25, 1989); Anti-Defamation League of B'nai B'rith Civil Rights Division, *Campus Anti-Bias Codes: A New Form of Censorship?* (1989) (policy background report); *Crowd at Homecoming Boos Black Queen*, Chron Higher Educ A2 (November 8, 1989); Cheryl M. Fields, *Colleges Advised to Develop Strong Procedures to Deal With Incidents of Racial Harassment*, Chron Higher Educ A11 (July 20, 1988); Robin Wilson, *Colleges' Anti-Harassment Policies Bring Controversy Over Free-Speech Issues*, Chron Higher Educ A1 (October 4, 1989). It has received abundant attention in editorial pages. See, for example, Nat Hentoff, *Campus Follies: From Free Speech . . . .*, Washington Post A23 (November 4, 1989); George F. Will, *Liberal Censorship*, Washington Post C7 (November 5, 1989); Debra Everson, *On Outlawing Hate Speech*, Guild Notes 9 (November/December 1989); Charles R. Lawrence, III, *The Debates Over Placing Limits on Racist Speech Must Not Ignore the Damage It Does to Its Victims*, Chron Higher Educ B1 (October 25, 1989); James T. Laney, *Why Tolerate Campus Bigots?*, New York Times A35 (April 6, 1990); Paul R. Verkuil, *Free to Speak, but Willing to Listen and Learn*, New York Times A28 (April 25, 1990).

2. The issues latent in this definition, such as whether racial epithets should qualify as "speech" for constitutional purposes, are discussed in the text accompanying notes 37-57. The debate over hate speech has spawned a rich body of scholarly literature. See, for example, Kammy Au, *Freedom from Fear*, 15 Lincoln L Rev 45 (1984); Richard Delgado, *Words That Wound: A Tort Action for Racial Insults, Epithets, and Name-Calling*, 17 Harv CR-CL L Rev 133 (1982); Kent Greenawalt, *Insults and Epithets: Are They Protected Speech?*, 42 Rutgers L Rev 287 (1990); David Kretzmer, *Freedom of Speech and Racism*, 8 Cardozo L Rev 445 (1987); Kenneth Lasson, *Group Libel Versus Free Speech: When Big Brother Should Butt In*, 23 Duquesne L Rev 77 (1984); Charles R. Lawrence, III, *If He Hollers Let Him Go: Regulating Racist Speech on Campus*, 1990 Duke L J 431; Jean C. Love, *Discriminatory Speech and the Tort of Intentional Infliction of Emotional Distress*, 47 Wash & Lee L Rev 123 (1990); Toni M. Massaro, *Equality and Freedom of Expression: The Hate Speech Dilemma*, 32 Wm & Mary L Rev 211 (1991); Mari J. Matsuda, *Public Response to Racist Speech: Considering the Victim's Story*, 87 Mich L Rev 2320 (1989); Robert C. Post, *Racist Speech, Democracy, and the First Amendment*, 32 Wm & Mary L Rev 267 (1991); Dean M. Richardson, *Racism: A Tort of Outrage*, 61 Ore L Rev 267 (1982); Rodney A. Smolla, *Rethinking First Amendment Assumptions about Racist and Sexist Speech*, 47 Wash & Lee L Rev 171 (1990); Nadine Strossen, *Regulating Racist Speech on Campus: A Modest Proposal?*, 1990 Duke L J 484; R. George Wright, *Racist Speech and the First Amendment*, 9 Miss Col L Rev 1 (1988); Note, *A Communitarian Defense of Group Libel Laws*, 101 Harv L Rev 682 (1988).

theoretical principles underlying those doctrines, and the narrow range of recognized exceptions to constitutional protection for speech that might, in some circumstances, permit hate speech to be punished.

The second stage of the analysis examines the relationship of these first amendment doctrines to notions of academic freedom at both state and private universities. Do the free speech rules prevailing in the general marketplace apply with equal force on university campuses? Or are there first amendment principles that either require or permit a different response to hate speech on campus than current first amendment doctrines allow in other contexts?[3]

II

HATE SPEECH AND THE FIRST AMENDMENT

A. Contrasting "Affirmative" and "Negative" First Amendment Jurisprudence

1. *The "Affirmative" Side of Free Speech.* The "affirmative" side of first amendment jurisprudence approaches free speech issues by emphasizing a group of interrelated doctrines that have combined, in modern times, to create a constitutional jurisprudence highly protective of freedom of speech.[4] The affirmative side begins with the mindset that speech is presumptively protected against any restraint or punishment, and regards any encroachment with intense skepticism.

---

3.   One of the principal issues in contemporary academic life is the question of the extent to which concepts of academic freedom have constitutional status. See, for example, *University of Pennsylvania v EEOC*, 110 S Ct 577, 586-87 & n6 (1990); J. Peter Byrne, *Academic Freedom: A "Special Concern of the First Amendment,"* 99 Yale L J 251 (1989); Walter P. Metzger, *Profession and Constitution: Two Definitions of Academic Freedom in America*, 66 Tex L Rev 1265 (1988); David M. Rabban, *A Functional Analysis of "Individual" and "Institutional" Academic Freedom Under the First Amendment*, 53 L & Contemp Probs 227 (Summer 1990); William W. Van Alstyne, *The Specific Theory of Academic Freedom and the General Issue of Civil Liberty*, in Edmund L. Pincoffs, ed, *The Concept of Academic Freedom* 59 (Univ of Texas Press, 1972); Mark G. Yudof, *Three Faces of Academic Freedom*, 32 Loyola L Rev 831 (1987). The issues in this debate are complicated, and their resolution will be influenced by, among other factors, whether the university in question is public or private. See *University of Pennsylvania*, 110 S Ct at 587 n6 (suggesting that attempts by government to control the content of speech on private universities involve a different constitutional balance than regulation on public campuses, where government has interests both as a speaker and as the regulator). This article does not attempt to join issue on this generic question, but rather is limited to the specific legal and policy conflicts posed by hate speech. On a state university campus, regulation of hate speech is constrained directly by the first amendment. Since government is also in some contexts a "speaker" at a state university campus (as when a faculty member is speaking for the university), striking the appropriate first amendment balance is often complex. See notes 112-19 and accompanying text. A private university, of course, is not legally bound by the first amendment. When discussing the rules governing hate speech that a private university sets for itself, therefore, no issues of constitutional law are formally implicated. While not of first amendment dimension, the policy conflicts posed by hate speech regulations at private universities are, however, no different than those at public institutions. This article thus proceeds on the premise that the resolution of those conflicts pressed here are of equal validity for both public and private universities. See note 87 and accompanying text.

4.   For an insightful and accessible illustration of the principle contending schools of first amendment interpretation during the past several decades, see William W. Van Alstyne, *Interpretations of the First Amendment* 21-40 (Duke Univ Press, 1984).

The affirmative first amendment thinker is constantly looking for ways to stretch existing doctrines to embrace wider and wider protection for speech. Affirmative thinkers are unlikely to rest the justification for freedom of speech on any one theory, but instead point to a cluster of rationales for treating freedom of speech as a specially preferred social value.[5] Most importantly, the affirmative side of first amendment jurisprudence emphasizes both the social value of free speech to the collective good and the private value of free speech to the individual.[6]

As a collective value, freedom of speech serves the general social interest in the pursuit of truth through the "marketplace of ideas."[7] Free speech also serves as a check on tyranny,[8] and is the lifeblood of democratic self-governance.[9] These collective theories justify free speech as a means to an end. But free speech is also an end in itself, an end intimately intertwined with human autonomy and dignity.[10] Free speech is thus especially valuable for reasons that have nothing to do with the collective search for truth or the processes of self-government, or for any other conceptualization of the common good.[11] It is a right to speak one's mind defiantly, robustly, and irreverently, just because it is one's mind.[12]

2. *The "Negative" Side of Free Speech.* The "negative" side approaches the first amendment as a problem to be got around whenever it interferes with

---

5. See generally Rodney A. Smolla, *Law of Defamation* § 1.07 (Clark Boardman, 1986); Edward J. Bloustein, *The Origin, Validity, and Interrelationships of the Political Values Served by Freedom of Expression,* 33 Rutgers L Rev 372, 395 (1981).

6. See Thomas Irwin Emerson, *The System of Freedom of Expression* 6-9 (Random House, 1970).

7. In the words of Oliver Wendell Holmes, Jr., "The best test of truth is the power of the thought to get itself accepted in the competition of the market." *Abrams v United States,* 250 US 616, 630 (1919) (Holmes dissenting). The "marketplace of ideas" is perhaps the most powerful metaphor in the free speech tradition. See generally Stanley Ingber, *The Marketplace of Ideas: A Legitimizing Myth,* 1984 Duke L J 1. In 1644, John Milton wrote in his *Areopagitica:* "And though all the winds of doctrine were let loose to play upon the earth, so Truth be in the field, we do injuriously by licensing and prohibiting to misdoubt her strength. Let her and falsehood grapple; who ever knew Truth put to the worse, in a free and open encounter?"

8. See Vincent Blasi, *The Checking Value in First Amendment Theory,* 1977 Am Bar Found Res J 521.

9. Free speech is an indispensable tool of self-governance in a democratic society. The Supreme Court has stated that "[w]hatever differences may exist about interpretations of the First Amendment, there is practically universal agreement that a major purpose of that Amendment was to protect the free discussion of governmental affairs." *Landmark Communications, Inc. v Virginia,* 435 US 829, 838 (1978), quoting *Mills v Alabama,* 384 US 214, 218 (1966). Justice Louis Brandeis wrote that those who fought for America's independence believed that "freedom to think as you will and to speak as you think are means indispensable to the discovery and spread of political truth." *Whitney v California,* 274 US 357, 375 (1927) (Brandeis concurring). See generally Alexander Meiklejohn, *The First Amendment is an Absolute,* 1961 S Ct Rev 245.

10. See Martin H. Redish, *The Value of Free Speech,* 130 U Pa L Rev 591, 601-04 (1982); David A. J. Richards, *Free Speech and Obscenity Law: Toward a Moral Theory of the First Amendment,* 123 U Pa L Rev 45, 62 (1974).

11. For a recent exposition on the value of freedom of speech as an aspect of individual liberty, see C. Edwin Baker, *Human Liberty and Freedom of Speech* (Oxford Univ Press, 1989).

12. Rodney A. Smolla, *Suing the Press: Libel, the Media, and Power* 257 (Oxford Univ Press, 1986). Even when the speaker has no realistic hope that the audience will be persuaded to his or her viewpoint, even when no plausible case can be made that the search for truth will be advanced, freedom to speak without restraint provides the speaker with an inner satisfaction and realization of self-identity essential to individual fulfillment.

198

constructive social policy goals. The negative side begins with the proposition that the first amendment is not an absolute and that many recognized doctrines exist that permit speech to be regulated or punished.[13] When presented with a problem such as hate speech, the negative first amendment thinker says: "Here are social policy values of enormous magnitude—equality, tolerance, and respect for human dignity—values that are, no less than free speech, of constitutional dimension. Let us employ every conceivable exception to protection for free expression that is currently recognized, so that hate speech can be deterred and these laudable values vindicated."

The negative first amendment thinker accepts freedom of speech as an important constitutional value, but, when matters such as hate speech are at issue, tends to look for ways to stretch the loopholes. The negative thinker will tend to punch holes in the many classic rationales that have been advanced to support expansive protection of freedom of speech. The poetic power of the marketplace image, it is pointed out, is tempered by experience.[14] Grounding freedom of speech in individual fulfillment, it is argued, is inappropriate, for then freedom of speech becomes indistinguishable from any other human desire, losing any claim to unique

13. See generally Harry H. Wellington, *On Freedom of Expression*, 88 Yale L J 1105 (1979).

14. When subjected to severe cross-examination, no single justification for freedom of speech is likely to come through perfectly unscathed, and the marketplace rationale is no exception.

The marketplace of ideas is a marketplace, and like all markets, it may experience positive and negative cycles. The marketplace image is grounded in laissez-faire economic theory. Even if we are to accept the apparent lesson of *perestroika* that, on the whole, free economic markets perform more efficiently than controlled economies, almost all governments utilize some controls on markets to correct for excesses and imperfections that can lead to violent economic swings. The theoretical purity of the models in economic textbooks is not matched by the actual performance of markets in the mundane commercial world. Economists concede the necessity of using governmental regulation to trim the freedom of markets at the edges, correcting their deficiencies in the real world of commerce. See generally C. Edwin Baker, *Scope of the First Amendment Freedom of Speech*, 25 UCLA L Rev 964, 974-78 (1978); Ingber, 1984 Duke L J at 4-5 (cited in note 7).

The marketplace of ideas rationale is also ostensibly contradicted by our everyday experience. There are as many shoddy ideas circulating as there are shoddy products. If the marketplace produces truth, the persistence of falsity seems difficult to explain. Is there any reason to be confident that good thoughts drive out bad ones? Nazis and the Ku Klux Klan continue to parade in America, and racial separatism continues as the formal law of South Africa. The belief in racial and ethnic superiority is still in wide currency throughout the world, from ethnic strife in the Soviet republics to the tense racial politics of New York City and Washington, D.C. Institutions and individuals across the globe continue to espouse and practice the dominance and exploitation of women. See generally Wellington, 88 Yale L J at 1130-32 (cited in note 13).

The hope that the marketplace will lead to truth is further eroded by the infiltration of emotional distortions into the realm of "ideas." Irrational appeals to hate and prejudice have, throughout the experience of man, often overwhelmed thoughtful tolerance and understanding, leading to violence and destruction. Even if we were to accept the marketplace of ideas model as valid, therefore, it would remain to be decided what would count as an "idea." Would it necessarily encompass appeals to hate that shortcut the mind and speak from heart to heart, or could it be limited to speech asserting intellectual propositions? See notes 27-28 and accompanying text.

Finally, there is a curiously ironic shortcoming to the marketplace image. We can never *empirically* test the proposition that truth will triumph over error, because that would itself require some objective measure of what ideas are true and what ideas are false—a measurement that the marketplace theory appears to forbid. Benjamin S. DuVal, Jr., *Free Communication of Ideas and the Quest for Truth: Toward a Teleological Approach to First Amendment Adjudication*, 41 Geo Wash L Rev 161, 190-91 (1972).

shelter from interference by the state.[15] Significantly, the negative free speech thinker is likely to single out one narrow rationale for elevating protection of free expression—the significance of freedom of speech to the process of self-governance—thus treating political speech as the only genre of expression meriting heightened protection.[16]

3. *Free Speech Theory in the Supreme Court.* In the last three decades, the affirmative side of free speech thinking has generally triumphed over the negative. The Supreme Court has tended to accept the affirmative argument that freedom of speech is a preferred value supported by multiple rationales, extending generous levels of constitutional protection to a vast range of expression. Despite the marketplace metaphor's frailties, the Court has enthusiastically embraced it.[17] The Court has declined the invitation to limit first amendment protection to political speech. While recognizing in many cases that political speech lies at the core of the first amendment,[18] it has nevertheless insisted that the "guarantees for speech and press are not the preserve of political expression or comment upon public affairs, essential as those are to healthy government."[19] The Court has declared that the free speech and free press guarantees "are not confined to any field of human interest,"[20] and that "it is immaterial whether the beliefs sought to be advanced . . . pertain to political, economic, religious or cultural matters . . . ."[21] Most significantly, the Court has acknowledged that the first amendment "serves not only the needs of the polity but also those of the human spirit—a spirit that demands self-expression."[22]

---

15. The self-fulfillment rationale has an almost unseemly ring of hedonism. Speakers claim protection for the sheer pleasure of speaking. The objection might thus be made that to ground freedom of speech in the self-fulfillment theory is to indulge the individual in a right of self-gratification that legal systems have traditionally not been obliged to respect. An individual may derive pleasure and fulfillment from many activities other than speech, and so the pleasure principle seems insufficient by itself to justify atypical rules for speech. Individuals may also seek pleasure or fulfillment by taking cocaine or having sex with a prostitute, but those two activities have not, traditionally, been deemed outside the legitimate regulation of the state. Many nonspeech activities through which individuals seek pleasure have conventionally been deemed by society as either illicit or illegal or both, even when they involve no immediate victims, on the theory that they may tend to cause harm. If protection of speech is linked to the pursuit of pleasure, then the state should be permitted to regulate speech in the same manner as it regulates other pleasure-seeking activity. See Robert H. Bork, *Neutral Principles and Some First Amendment Problems*, 47 Ind L J 1, 26-28 (1971).

16. See generally Alexander Meiklejohn, *Free Speech and its Relation to Self-Government* 15-16, 24-27 (Harper, 1948); Robert H. Bork, *The Tempting of America: The Political Seduction of the Law* 333 (Free Press, 1990).

17. See, for example, *Milkovich v Lorain Journal Co.*, 110 S Ct 2695, 2705 (1990); *Hustler Magazine, Inc. v Falwell*, 485 US 46, 50-51 (1988); *New York Times Co. v Sullivan*, 376 US 254, 270 (1964).

18. See note 9.

19. *Time, Inc. v Hill*, 385 US 374, 388 (1974).

20. *United Mine Workers v Illinois Bar Ass'n*, 389 US 217, 223 (1967), quoting *Thomas v Collins*, 323 US 516, 531 (1945).

21. *NAACP v Alabama*, 357 US 449, 460 (1958). See also *Abood v Detroit Board of Educ.*, 431 US 209, 223 (1977).

22. *Procunier v Martinez*, 416 US 396, 427 (1974). The Court has thus found unpersuasive the arguments of theorists such as Robert Bork that the self-fulfillment rationale for free speech fails to distinguish speech from any other human desire. See Bork, 47 Ind L J 1 (cited in note 15). Two strong arguments may be asserted against Judge Bork's position. The first is a broad libertarian

B. Hate Speech and the Affirmative Side of the First Amendment

There are a number of modern affirmative first amendment doctrines that interlock to create a large measure of protection for hate speech.

1. *Neutrality.* The neutrality principle embraces a cluster of precepts that form the core of modern first amendment jurisprudence. Mere opposition to an idea is never enough, standing alone, to justify the abridgment of speech.[23] Government may not pick and choose among ideas, but must always be "viewpoint neutral."[24] All ideas are created equal in the eyes of the first amendment—even those ideas that are universally condemned and run

---

attack on the underlying premise that government may control most activities of human life if it can simply point to reasonable grounds for doing so. A libertarian would argue that the presumption should be exactly the opposite: government normally may not intervene in an individual's affairs, and is justified in doing so only to the extent necessary to prevent the individual from harming others. This means that many pleasure-seeking activities are beyond the legitimate jurisdiction of the state altogether, because they harm only the individual who engages in them. The "harm requirement" may not be satisfied merely by the outrage or moral opprobrium that the majority attaches to the activity. Crimes must have victims—victims other than the perpetrator. In a society organized under strict libertarian principles, free speech receives protection far higher than unweighted balancing for the same reasons that many other forms of activity are protected: because government is often unable to point to palpable harm caused by the activity. One need not adopt the complete libertarian argument, however, to defeat the position that self-fulfillment is mere self-gratification, and thus an insufficient basis for special protection for speech. A second, more modest argument treats the self-fulfillment aspect of speech as qualitatively different from other forms of gratification, and therefore critically important even if one is not a card-carrying libertarian. A persuasive case can be made that speech is a form of self-gratification different in kind from most other forms of self-fulfillment, and therefore deserving of special solicitude. We may start by quibbling on terms. To articulate the theory in terms of "pleasure" and "gratification" is to trivialize it. The term "self-fulfillment" connotes much more than hedonistic pleasure and gratification. The words "pleasure" and "gratification" emphasize those aspects of human life that resemble the lives of animals; the term "self-fulfillment" emphasizes those aspects of humanity that distinguish human beings from other species. The fulfillment that comes from speech is bonded to the human capacity to think, imagine, and create. Conscience and consciousness are the sacred precincts of mind and soul. The linkage of speech to thought, to each person's central capacity to reason and wonder, is what places it above other forms of fulfillment, and beyond the routine jurisdiction of the state. See generally Baker, *Human Liberty and Freedom of Speech* (cited in note 11); Redish, 130 U Pa L Rev at 601-04 (cited in note 10); Richards, 123 U Pa L Rev at 62 (cited in note 10).

23. See, for example, *Ward v Rock Against Racism*, 109 S Ct 2746, 2754 (1989) ("The principal inquiry in determining content neutrality . . . is whether the government has adopted a regulation of speech because of disagreement with the message it conveys.").

24. See, for example, *Cornelius v NAACP Legal Defense & Educ. Fund*, 473 US 788, 806 (1985); *Perry Educ. Ass'n v Perry Local Educators' Ass'n*, 460 US 37, 46, 49 n9 (1983). See generally Robert C. Post, *Between Governance and Management: The History and Theory of the Public Forum*, 34 UCLA L Rev 1713, 1824 (1987).

counter to constitutional principle.[25] While the first amendment is not an absolute, the neutrality principle is.[26]

2. *The Emotion Principle.* Constitutional protection for speech is not limited to its cognitive content alone, but extends also to the emotional components of speech.[27] Speech does not forfeit the protection that it would otherwise enjoy merely because it is laced with passion or vulgarity.[28]

---

25. This notion had its most famous articulation in a defamation case, *Gertz v Robert Welch, Inc.*, 418 US 323, 339-40 (1974): "Under the First Amendment there is no such thing as a false idea. However pernicious an opinion may seem, we depend for its correction not on the conscience of judges and juries but on the competition of other ideas." In *Milkovich*, 110 S Ct at 2705, another defamation case, the Supreme Court recently held that "the fair meaning of the *Gertz* passage is to equate the word 'opinion' in the second sentence with the word 'idea' in the first sentence." In *Milkovich*, the Court refused to create a special constitutional doctrine creating "a wholesale defamation exemption for anything that might be labeled 'opinion.'" Id. Instead, the Court read the *Gertz* passage as a restatement of the "marketplace of ideas" concept. Id. See note 7 and accompanying text.

26. "If there is a bedrock principle underlying the First Amendment, it is that the Government may not prohibit the expression of an idea simply because society finds the idea offensive or disagreeable." *Texas v Johnson*, 109 S Ct 2533, 2544 (1989), citing *Hustler*, 485 US at 55-56; *City Council of Los Angeles v Taxpayers for Vincent*, 466 US 789, 804 (1984); *Bolger v Youngs Drug Products Corp.*, 463 US 60, 65, 72 (1983); *Carey v Brown*, 447 US 455, 462-63 (1980); *FCC v Pacifica Foundation*, 438 US 726, 745-46 (1978); *Young v American Mini Theatres, Inc.*, 427 US 50, 63-65, 67-68 (1976); *Buckley v Valeo*, 424 US 1, 16-17 (1976); *Grayned v Rockford*, 408 US 104, 115 (1972); *Police Dept. of Chicago v Mosley*, 408 US 92, 95 (1972); *Bachellar v Maryland*, 397 US 564, 567 (1970); *United States v O'Brien*, 391 US 367, 382 (1968); *Brown v Louisiana*, 383 US 131, 142-43 (1966); *Stromberg v California*, 283 US 359, 368-69 (1931).

27. In *Cohen v California*, 403 US 15 (1971), for example, the Supreme Court held that it was unconstitutional for the State of California to convict the defendant for wearing a jacket plainly bearing the phrase "Fuck the Draft" in a Los Angeles courthouse corridor where women and children were present.

Several points in *Cohen* merit special emphasis. First, the Court unequivocally rejected the notion that a state may seek to prevent the use of vulgarity merely for the purpose of cleansing public discourse and sheltering citizens from offensive language:

How is one to distinguish this from any other offensive word? Surely the State has no right to cleanse public debate to the point where it is grammatically palatable to the most squeamish among us. Yet no readily ascertainable general principle exists for stopping short of that result were we to affirm the judgment below. For, while the particular four-letter word being litigated here is perhaps more distasteful than most others of its genre, it is nevertheless true that one man's vulgarity is another's lyric.

Id at 25.

Second, the Court made it clear that the shock value of Cohen's language did not justify the California law. The Court rejected the assertion that the state could excise "one particular scurrilous epithet from the public discourse, either upon the theory . . . that its use is inherently likely to cause violent reaction or upon a more general assertion that the States, acting as guardians of public morality, may properly remove this offensive word from the public vocabulary." Id at 22-23.

Finally, the Court held that it made no difference that some members of the general public would inadvertently be exposed to Cohen's vulgarity. Id at 22. The *Cohen* decision, it must be remembered, involved the quintessential example of lewd or profane language—indeed, *the* single most offensive word in the American vocabulary. Further, the case arose inside a courthouse, a setting in which the state traditionally has substantially *more* right to regulate speech than it has in the public streets.

28. In *Hustler*, 485 US 46, the Court was faced with a crude parody run by Hustler Magazine depicting Reverend Jerry Falwell as an incestuous drunk. The Court ruled without dissent that the parody was protected under the first amendment. Chief Justice Rehnquist conceded that the Hustler parody was at best a distant cousin of the conventional political cartoon, "and a rather poor relation at that." Id at 55. Rehnquist argued, however, that there was simply no way to draw a principled distinction between the Hustler parody and other satiric efforts. "If it were possible," he stated, "by laying down a principled standard to separate the one from the other, public discourse would

3. *The Symbolism Principle.* First amendment protection is not limited to the use of language, but also includes expressive conduct, such as mass demonstrations or communication through the use of symbols.[29]

4. *The Harm Principle.* While the neutrality principle forbids penalizing speech merely because of opposition to its content, modern first amendment jurisprudence does permit speech to be penalized when it causes harm. The harm principle defines the types of injuries that will qualify as harms sufficient to justify regulation of speech.[30] The harm principle is a natural corollary to

---

probably suffer little or no harm." Id. But the Supreme Court was doubtful, Rehnquist explained, that any reasonably concrete standard could ever be articulated. Amorphous pejoratives such as "outrageous" or "indecent" were too subjective to withstand first amendment requirements. To permit a jury to impose liability for mere "outrageousness" would invite jurors to base liability on the basis of their tastes and prejudices. Id at 55. See generally, Rodney A. Smolla, Jerry Falwell v. Larry Flynt: *The First Amendment on Trial* (St. Martin's Press, 1988); Paul A. LeBel, *Emotional Distress, the First Amendment, and "This Kind of Speech": A Heretical Perspective on* Hustler Magazine v. Falwell, 60 U Colo L Rev 315 (1989); Robert C. Post, *The Constitutional Concept of Public Discourse: Outrageous Opinion, Democratic Deliberation, and* Hustler Magazine v. Falwell, 103 Harv L Rev 601 (1990); Rodney A. Smolla, *Emotional Distress and the First Amendment: An Analysis of* Hustler v. Falwell, 20 Ariz L J 423 (1988).

29. As early as 1931, the Court had recognized that the constitutional protections for speech extended to more than the use of language, encompassing communication through the use of non-language symbols. In *Stromberg v California*, 283 US 359 (1931), the Court struck down a state statute that barred displaying of a red flag " 'as a sign, symbol or emblem of opposition to organized government . . . .' " Id at 361, quoting Cal Penal Code § 403-a (repealed 1933). The Court ruled that the statute was so vague that it threatened "the opportunity for free political discussion." Id at 369.

The Court's most dramatic confrontations with attempts to punish symbolic speech came in the recent round of flag-desecration cases. In *Texas v Johnson*, 109 S Ct 2533 (1989), the Court overturned the conviction of Gregory Lee Johnson, who had burned an American flag as part of a protest during the Republican National Convention in Dallas. Justice William Brennan's opinion for the majority was a ringing celebration of freedom of speech. The Texas statute singled out "only those severe acts of physical abuse of the flag carried out in a way likely to be offensive." Id at 2543, quoting Brief for Petitioner at 44. Because the conviction rested on "the likely communicative impact of [the] expressive conduct," Brennan reasoned that the state was regulating "emotive impact." Id. This was inconsistent with the principle that speech may never be proscribed merely because society finds its intellectual or emotional message disagreeable. Id at 2544.

United States v Eichman, 110 S Ct 2404 (1990), was the sequel to *Johnson* in which the Court struck down the federal Flag Protection Act of 1989, 18 USCA § 700 (West Supp 1990). Justice Brennan's opinion in *Eichman*, rendered only a little more than a month after the cases had been orally argued before the Court, was flat, matter-of-fact, and brief—barely eight pages long. "Although Congress cast the Flag Protection Act in somewhat broader terms than the Texas statute at issue in *Johnson*," Justice Brennan wrote, "the Act still suffers from the same fundamental flaw: it suppresses expression out of concern for its likely communicative impact." Id at 2409. Brennan's opinion repeated, in relatively summary fashion, the analysis in *Johnson*. The government may foster patriotism and national unity by persuasion and example, he maintained, but not by criminalizing symbolic speech. Id at 2409, quoting *Johnson*, 109 S Ct at 2547, quoting *West Virginia Board of Education v Barnette*, 319 U.S. 624, 640 (1943). Brennan's opinion made only an oblique reference to the political controversy swirling around the flag-burning issue, stating, "We are aware that desecration of the flag is deeply offensive to many." Id at 2410. But the same might be said, he pointed out, of virulent ethnic and religious epithets, vulgar repudiations of the draft, and scurrilous caricatures, all of which were protected under the first amendment. Id at 2410, citing *Terminiello v Chicago*, 337 US 1 (1949) (religious and ethnic attacks); *Cohen*, 403 US 15 (vulgar draft protest); *Hustler*, 485 US 46 (vicious caricature).

30. See generally John Stuart Mill, *On Liberty* (1859), reprinted in *On Liberty, Representative Government, The Subjection of Women: Three Essays by John Stuart Mill* 5 (Oxford Univ Press, 1952); Smolla, 47 Wash & Lee L Rev at 175-76 (cited in note 2); T. M. Scanlon, Jr., *Freedom of Expression and Categories of Expression*, 40 U Pitt L Rev 519 (1979).

the neutrality and emotion principles, serving to preserve the integrity of those two doctrines.

The possible harms caused by speech may be divided into three categories: physical harms, relational harms, and reactive harms.

(a) *Physical Harms.* Speech may cause physical harms to persons or property in a variety of ways. Speech may be used to negotiate a contract soliciting a murder, or to commission an arsonist to burn down a building. Speech may be used to whip an angry crowd of protesters into an emotional frenzy, inciting them to storm barricades and throw rocks at police. The physical violence caused by these examples carries out the wishes of the speaker. Speech may also cause violence counter to the speaker's interests, as when those who hear the message are so outraged that they are moved to physical assault against the speaker.

(b) *Relational Harms.* Speech may interfere with relationships of various kinds, including social relationships, commercial transactions, proprietary interests in information, and interests in the confidentiality of communications.

(c) *Reactive Harms.* Speech can cause reactive harms—injuries caused by emotional or intellectual responses to the content of the speech. These reactive harms may be felt by individuals, or they may be harms conceptualized in some collective sense, such as injuries to community values of morality or civility.

This taxonomy of harms is represented in the chart on the following page:

CHART 1

THE HARMS CHART

CATEGORY I: PHYSICAL HARMS

INJURIES TO PERSONS
Examples:
—Solicitation of murder
—Incitement to riot on behalf of the speaker's cause
—Reactive violence against the speaker in response to the message

INJURIES TO PROPERTY
Examples:
—Solicitation of arson
—Incitement to destroy property
—Reactive violence against the property of the speaker in response to the message

CATEGORY II: RELATIONAL HARMS

INJURIES TO SOCIAL RELATIONSHIPS
Examples:
—Libel and slander
—Alienation of affections

INJURIES TO TRANSACTIONS OR BUSINESS RELATIONSHIPS
Examples:
—Fraud and misrepresentation
—False advertising
—Interference with contractual relations
—Interference with prospective economic advantage
—Insider trading

INJURIES TO INFORMATION OWNERSHIP INTERESTS
Examples:
—Copyright, trademark, or patent infringement
—Appropriation of name or likeness for commercial purposes

INJURIES TO INTERESTS IN CONFIDENTIALITY
Examples:
—Disclosure of national security secrets
—Unauthorized revelation of private personal information

CATEGORY III: REACTIVE HARMS

INJURIES TO INDIVIDUAL EMOTIONAL TRANQUILITY
Examples:
—Infliction of emotional distress
—Invasion of privacy caused by placing the individual in a false light in the public eye
—Invasion of privacy involving intrusion upon seclusion
—Invasion of privacy involving publication of embarrassing facts
—Distress caused by intellectual disagreement with the content of the speech

INJURIES TO COMMUNAL SENSIBILITIES
Examples:
—Insults to human dignity, such as racist or sexist speech
—Vulgarity
—Obscenity
—Interference with political or social cohesiveness or harmony arising from collective disagreement with the content of speech

Though the harms resulting from speech are often limited to only one category, the three categories above are not mutually exclusive. The harms may be a blend of more than one of the categories, and any given act of speech may simultaneously result in all three categories of harms. For example, a speaker might utter a slanderous remark to someone in a face-to-face confrontation that leads to fisticuffs between the speaker and his victim. The remark might in turn be heard by others with whom the victim has social or business relationships, thus interfering with those relationships. Finally, the remark might cause the victim and others in the community to experience powerful feelings of disgust and revulsion.[31]

The three categories represent a hierarchy of governmental justifications for regulating speech. Government has the strongest case for regulating speech posing risks of physical harms. Government's justifications for regulating speech posing risks of relational harms are quite strong, though not as forceful as for physical harms.

The harms posed in Category III may *not* be used as justifications for regulation of speech. This rule simply restates the neutrality and emotion principles: neither intellectual nor emotional revulsion to speech is ever enough, standing alone, to justify its abridgment—government must instead demonstrate an invasion of one of the more palpable physical or relational harms listed in Categories I or II.

5. *The Causation Principle.* The integrity of the neutrality, emotion, and harm principles is dependent upon the adoption of a rigorous causation rule that requires a close causal nexus between speech and harm before penalizing speech. The modern "clear and present danger" test is the most famous articulation of the currently prevailing causation rule. In its current form, the test provides that advocacy of force or criminal activity may not be enough unless "such advocacy is directed to inciting or producing imminent lawless action and is likely to incite or produce such action."[32] Without a strict causation test, government will tend to slip surreptitiously into penalizing opinions, and into permitting regulation of speech purely because of the

---

31. Alternatively, any given act of communication might be relatively pure, implicating only one type of harm. For example, a speaker might copy verbatim from someone else's copyrighted work and sell the copies for profit, without permission from the copyright owner. This could interfere with a relational ownership interest, but not pose any risk of physical harm or cause any negative emotional or intellectual reaction in persons exposed to the speech. (The owner of the copyright might, of course, be emotionally upset that someone has pirated his or her work—but that emotional disturbance is not in reaction to the actual message but rather to the theft of his or her intellectual property.)

32. *Brandenburg v Ohio*, 395 US 444, 447 (1969). *Brandenburg* involved a Ku Klux Klan rally conducted on a farm in Hamilton County, Ohio, outside Cincinnati. A local Cincinnati television station reporter had been invited to witness the rally, and he and a cameraman filmed the event, portions of which were later broadcast on the Cincinnati station and a national network. Id at 445. The film footage is filled with vile, incendiary racist bile. Klan members pronounced that "the nigger should be returned to Africa, the Jew returned to Israel," and "if our President, our Congress, our Supreme Court, continues to suppress the white, Caucasian race, it's possible that there might have to be some revengeance [sic] taken." Id at 446-47.

The state of Ohio prosecuted Brandenburg, the leader of the Klan group, under an Ohio criminal syndicalism law, which made it illegal to advocate "the duty, necessity, or propriety of crime, sabotage, violence, or unlawful methods of terrorism as a means of accomplishing industrial or political reform," or to assemble "with any society, group, or assemblage of persons formed to teach or advocate the doctrines of criminal syndicalism." Id at 444-45, quoting Ohio Rev Code Ann

reactive disturbances it causes. Virtually any opinion might, at some indeterminate future time, "cause" physical harm.[33] Similarly, the emotional and intellectual reactions of others to speech might ripen into violent physical reactions at some indeterminate future time. A society will never have robust freedom of speech if any threat of future physical harm is enough to justify speech regulation.

6. *The Precision Principle.* Precision is a pervasive theme of modern first amendment analysis. Even when regulation of speech is otherwise justified (as when a compelling governmental interest is at stake), the regulation will be struck down if it fails to meet both substantive and definitional precision requirements. A substantive principle requires that regulatory mechanisms implicating speech be precisely designed to effectuate the governmental interest at stake.[34] A parallel rule of definitional precision requires that the

---

§ 2923.13 (repealed 1974). Brandenburg was convicted, fined $1,000, and sentenced to one to ten years' imprisonment. Id at 445.

The Court held the Ohio law unconstitutional. Id at 448. No one was present at the Klan rally except the Klan members themselves, the television reporter, and his cameraman. Id at 445-46. Nothing in the record indicated that the orgy of race hate posed any immediate physical threat to anyone, and the statute, either as written or applied in this case, does nothing to distinguish "mere advocacy" from "incitement to imminent lawless action." Id at 448-49. In these circumstances, the Court said, the Klan was guilty only of the "abstract teaching" of the "moral propriety" of racist violence. Id at 448, quoting *Noto v United States*, 367 US 290, 297-98 (1961). "[T]he constitutional guarantees of free speech and free press," according to the Court, "do not permit a State to forbid or proscribe advocacy of the use of force or of law violation except where such advocacy is directed to inciting or producing imminent lawless action and is likely to incite or produce such action." Id at 447.

33. In *Hess v Indiana*, 414 US 105 (1973), the defendant Gregory Hess was convicted of violating Indiana's disorderly conduct statute in an anti-Vietnam War demonstration on the campus of Indiana University. Between 100 and 150 demonstrators had moved onto a public street, blocking traffic. After refusing to obey the sheriff's command to clear the street, the demonstrators were moved to the curbs by the sheriff and his deputies. Id at 106. As the sheriff passed by Hess, Hess said, "We'll take the fucking street later." The sheriff immediately arrested Hess for disorderly conduct, and he was convicted. Id at 107.

The Supreme Court reversed the conviction, holding that Hess could not be convicted merely for having used the word "fuck," since that word standing alone did not satisfy the legal definition of obscenity. Id. Nor could Hess's statement be seen as a direct verbal challenge to fight the sheriff or his deputies—witnesses testified that he was facing the crowd, not the street, when he made the statement and that his words did not appear to be addressed to any particular person or group. Id at 107-08. Turning to the *Brandenburg* standard, the Court held that Hess was not guilty of any incitement to *imminent* lawless action. Id at 108-09. The words "We'll take the fucking street *later*," the Court maintained, could be taken as a counsel for "present moderation" or as advocacy of illegal action "at some indefinite future time," neither of which were enough to constitute a present threat of imminent disorder. Id at 108.

34. This substantive precision principle is a component of both the "strict scrutiny" level of judicial review applicable to content-based regulation of speech and the reduced level of scrutiny applicable to non-content-based regulation. See, for example, *Sable Communications of California, Inc. v FCC*, 109 S Ct 2829, 2836 (1989) (government may only "regulate the content of constitutionally protected speech in order to promote a compelling interest if it chooses the least restrictive means to further the articulated interest"); *O'Brien*, 391 US at 377 (When government regulation is "unrelated to the suppression of free expression," the "incidental restriction on alleged First Amendment freedoms" must be "no greater than is essential to the furtherance of that interest."). See also *Board of Trustees of State University of New York v Fox*, 109 S Ct 3028, 3035 (1989)(requiring a "reasonable" fit between means and ends in commercial speech cases). These substantive first amendment standards are discussed in greater detail in notes 54-58 and accompanying text.

terms used to identify proscribed speech be defined with a meticulous exactitude well beyond that of other routine legislation, so that speakers know in advance what speech is and is not permitted, thereby avoiding the self-censorship caused by uncertainty.[35]

C. Hate Speech and the Negative Side of the First Amendment

Modern first amendment jurisprudence does permit expression to be penalized in a number of circumstances arguably applicable to hate speech.

1. *The Two-Class Theory.*   Back in an older and simpler time in the history of free expression, the Supreme Court appeared to espouse a theory that treated certain types of expression as taboo forms of speech, beneath the dignity of the first amendment.[36] The most celebrated statement of this view appeared in *Chaplinsky v. New Hampshire:*[37]

> There are certain well-defined and narrowly limited classes of speech, the prevention and punishment of which have never been thought to raise any Constitutional problem. These include the lewd and obscene, the profane, the libelous, and the insulting or "fighting" words—those which by their very utterance inflict injury or tend to incite an immediate breach of the peace.[38]

Hate speech is clearly within the *Chaplinsky* litany. In common sense understanding a vulgar racial slur may variously be described as "lewd," "obscene," "profane," "libelous," or "insulting," and thus the very type of expression "the prevention and punishment of which have never been thought to raise any Constitutional problem." And indeed, in 1952, when this two-class theory of the first amendment was still flourishing, the Court upheld a criminal conviction for spreading racist hate speech. In *Beauharnais v. Illinois,*[39] the Court was faced with a criminal libel case involving an Illinois statute that criminalized any publication portraying "depravity, criminality, unchastity, or lack of virtue of a class of citizens, of any race, color, creed or religion" exposing them "to contempt, derision, or obloquy or which is productive of breach of the peace or riots."[40] The defendant Beauharnais was president of a racist Chicago organization, the White Circle League, which had distributed racist leaflets.[41]

---

35. The first amendment thus imposes meticulous tolerance levels on the "engineering" utilized in speech laws. This is reflected in rules such as the "overbreadth" and "vagueness" doctrines. See *Broadrick v Oklahoma*, 413 US 601 (1973); *Gooding v Wilson*, 405 US 518 (1972); *Baggett v Bullitt*, 377 US 360 (1964).

36. See generally Harry Kalven, *A Worthy Tradition: Freedom of Speech in America* 77-106 (Harper & Row, 1988).

37. 315 US 568 (1942).

38. Id at 571-72, citing Zechariah Chafee, *Free Speech in the United States* (Harvard Univ Press, 1941).

39. 343 US 250 (1952).

40. Id at 251, quoting Ill Rev Stat ch 38, § 471 (1949).

41. Id at 252. The leaflets called on the mayor and city council of Chicago "to halt the further encroachment, harassment and invasion of white people, their property, neighborhoods and persons, by the Negro," and exhorted "[o]ne million self respecting white people in Chicago to unite," proclaiming that "[i]f persuasion and the need to prevent the white race from becoming

In his defense to the Illinois criminal prosecution, Beauharnais asked that the jury be instructed that he could not be found guilty unless the leaflets were "likely to produce a clear and present danger of a serious substantive evil that rises far above public inconvenience, annoyance or unrest."[42] The Illinois court refused to use this instruction, and Beauharnais was convicted.[43] The United States Supreme Court affirmed, in an opinion by Justice Felix Frankfurter.[44] If such a two-class theory of the first amendment still survived, hate speech could be punished with impunity. But the theory is no longer viable; modern first amendment principles have passed it by,[45] and *Beauharnais* is no longer good law. The Court no longer accepts the view that speech may be proscribed merely because it is "lewd," "profane," or otherwise vulgar or offensive—the decisions in cases such as *Cohen*[46] and *Hustler*[47] are illustrative—and libelous speech is no longer beyond first amendment protection.[48] Only one small piece of the two-class theory survives: the Court continues to treat "obscene" speech as not within the protection of the first amendment at all.[49]

2. *The Fighting Words Doctrine.* While the methodology of *Chaplinksy* has been repudiated (for all but obscene speech), the so-called "fighting words" doctrine remains alive, as modified by the current rigorous clear and present danger test. Thus a verbal attack directed at a particular individual in a face-to-face confrontation that presents a clear and present danger of a violent

---

mongrelized by the negro will not unite us, then the aggressions . . . rapes, robberies, knives, guns and marijuana of the negro, surely will." Id.

42. Id at 253.

43. *Illinois v Beauharnais*, 408 Ill 512, 97 NE2d 343 (1951).

44. Justice Frankfurter's opinion contained only a short—but interesting—discussion of freedom of speech. It had been argued against the Illinois law that prohibiting libel of a creed or a racial group is "but a step from prohibiting libel of a political party." 343 US at 263. Frankfurter clearly thought, however, that a sharp first amendment distinction existed between restrictions on political speech and restrictions relating to "race, color, creed or religion." Id at 263 n18. These terms, he insisted, had "attained too fixed a meaning to permit political groups to be brought within" their rubric, and for Frankfurter that rubric was apparently outside the protections of the first amendment. Id. "Of course," he noted, "discussion cannot be denied and the right, as well as the duty, of criticism must not be stifled." Id at 264. But for Frankfurter there was nothing "political" about this speech, nor did it rise to the level of "discussion." "If a statute sought to outlaw libels of political parties," he conceded, "quite different problems not now before us would be raised." Id at 263 n18. Frankfurter was confident that "[w]hile this Court sits, it retains and exercises authority to nullify action which encroaches on freedom of utterance under the guise of punishing libel." Id at 263-64 (citation omitted).

45. See *Cohen*, 403 US 15; *Hustler*, 485 US 46.

46. 403 US 15.

47. 485 US 46.

48. In a line of cases emanating from *Sullivan*, 376 US 254, the Court has created significant first amendment protections for libelous speech. See *Philadelphia Newspapers, Inc. v Hepps*, 475 US 767 (1986); *Gertz*, 418 US 323.

49. In *Roth v United States*, 354 US 476, 485 (1957), the Court held that "obscenity is not within the area of constitutionally protected speech or press." The legal definition of obscenity has gone through several mutations since *Roth*, but the basic principle that obscene speech is not constitutionally protected remains. See *Pope v Illinois*, 481 US 497 (1987); *Miller v California*, 413 US 15 (1973).

physical reaction may be penalized.[50] A statute aimed at hate speech that *only* penalizes such "fighting words" confrontations, and that is applied to require a governmental showing of imminent danger in every individual case, would be constitutional.[51] Such a statute or regulation might also be symbolically valuable, for it at least makes *some* statement concerning human dignity and the repugnance of society for hate speech attacks. A mere fighting words statute, however, will reach only a small percentage of hate speech.[52]

3. *Content-Neutral Protection of Persons or Property.* The clear and present danger test permits speech to be penalized when it is on the brink of erupting into violence against persons or property.[53] Once physical injury to persons or property has taken place, criminal and tort rules of general application may be brought to bear upon the wrongdoer, and it is no defense that the persons were injured or the property destroyed in the cause of free expression. There is no first amendment right to commit physical assault or damage another's property. Under the principles established in *United States v. O'Brien*,[54] when the government promulgates a rule for reasons unrelated to the content of

---

50. In *Cohen*, 403 US at 20, the Court "restated" the fighting words doctrine of *Chaplinsky*, superimposing upon it the requirements of a rigorous clear and present danger test. The Court in *Cohen* thus emphasized that in that case no one was present who would have regarded Paul Cohen's speech as a "direct personal insult," nor was there any danger of reactive violence against Cohen. Id.

51. In this sense the "fighting words doctrine" is not a discrete, free-standing doctrine at all, but merely a specific application of the general clear and present danger test.

It should be emphasized that the rigors of the clear and present danger test must be satisfied case by case. There was a time in our first amendment jurisprudence in which it was taken for granted that a legislature could effectively "precertify" certain identified classes of speech as satisfying the clear and present danger test. This was one of the principal themes in *Gitlow v New York*, 268 US 652 (1952), in which the Court approved proscription of utterances which, "by their very nature, involve danger to the public peace and to the security of the State." Id at 669. You can't start a fire without a spark, and the Court was convinced that a "single revolutionary spark may kindle a fire that, smouldering for a time, may burst into a sweeping and destructive conflagration." Id.

The Court in *Gitlow* did not require that foreseeable harm be demonstrated in each individual prosecution. Id at 670. Rather, the legislature could make a generic determination applicable to a broad class of speech, and thereby estop individuals from claiming that their particular speech posed no serious threats. Thus the Court admonished,

> when the legislative body has determined generally, in the constitutional exercise of its discretion, that utterances of a certain kind involve such danger of substantive evil that they may be punished, the question whether any specific utterance coming within the prohibited class is likely, in and of itself, to bring about the substantive evil, is not open to consideration.

Id.

This device of deference to generic legislative determinations has been abandoned in contemporary first amendment doctrine. In *Landmark Communications, Inc. v Virginia*, 435 US 829, 843 (1978), for example, the Court stated flatly that "[d]eference to a legislative finding cannot limit judicial inquiry when First Amendment rights are at stake." And in *Cohen*, 403 US at 20, the Court rejected the view that the state could specify in advance language that is "inherently likely to provoke violent reaction."

52. Smolla, 47 Wash & Lee L Rev 171 (1990) (cited in note 2).

53. See notes 32-33 and accompanying text.

54. 391 US 367 (1968). In *O'Brien*, the Court upheld convictions for burning draft cards to protest the Vietnam War. The protesters argued that burning a draft card was a form of political protest, and that Congress had purposefully intended to censor freedom of speech in amending federal law to prohibit mutilation of the cards. Id at 376. The Supreme Court refused to scratch beneath the surface of Congress' intent and upheld the convictions. Id at 376-77. O'Brien's burning of his draft card, the Court reasoned, involved a mixture of "speech" and "conduct." Id at 376.

expression, and the governmental interests at stake are substantial, the regulation will normally be upheld even though it may have the incidental effect of interfering with speech.

A student who spray-paints a hate message on the side of a university building might thus be prosecuted for damage to the property.[55] If the university were to engage in selective prosecutions, however, punishing those who desecrate university property with hate speech but ignoring desecration

---

Whenever "speech" and "nonspeech" elements are combined in the same activity, the Court held, the government is permitted to regulate the activity if can meet a four-pronged test:

> (1) the governmental regulation must be "within the constitutional power of the Government";
> (2) the regulation must further an "important or substantial governmental interest";
> (3) the governmental interest must be "unrelated to the suppression of free expression"; and
> (4) the "incidental restriction on alleged First Amendment freedoms" must be "no greater than is essential to the furtherance of that interest."

Id at 377 (citation omitted). The Court's application of this test in the O'Brien case itself was disingenuous—the only credible reading of Congress' intent was that it did wish to stifle dissent by banning mutilation of draft cards as a form of protest. But the basic conceptual point of O'Brien was sound and remains an integral part of modern first amendment jurisprudence. When governmental intent is truly "clean," and genuinely unrelated to the suppression of free expression, then a standard of judicial review less stringent than strict scrutiny is warranted for the incidental "spillover" effect that the law has on free speech.

55. The key here is the third prong of the O'Brien test; it is the "gatekeeper," so to speak, governing entrance to the lower standard in O'Brien. This prong is crucial; much of modern first amendment law turns upon how it is interpreted. Under prong three, the governmental interest used to justify the law must be *unrelated to the suppression of free expression.* Id at 384. What does this phrase mean? In fact, this phrase is susceptible to two different interpretations, and the level of protection for free speech in our society is largely bound up in which of those two meanings we choose.

The first possible interpretation of the phrase "unrelated to the suppression of free expression" is that government must have some reason other than a desire to censor speech as the rationale for its regulation. This seems straightforward enough. In the O'Brien case, the reason was the orderly administration of the selective service system. What could be simpler? The difficulty comes from this: all laws restricting freedom of speech are passed because of some "interest unrelated to free expression."

Governments pass laws restricting freedom of speech because they fear physical violence against persons or property, or because they are concerned about maintaining national security, or because they wish to shelter other citizens from attacks on their reputation, or invasion of their privacy, or insults to their human dignity, or because they wish to protect community morals, or promote tolerance, or encourage cohesiveness—governments pass laws restricting freedom of speech for all of these reasons and many more, and in every instance it is possible to characterize the governmental goal as "unrelated to free expression." No law abridging freedom of speech is ever promoted as a law abridging freedom of speech. The preambles to statutes never announce: "Whereas, there is a social interest in the suppression of free expression, be it enacted . . . ." Because legislatures that pass laws restricting speech always have, as their ultimate goal, some perceived social interest other than suppression of speech, there is no law that could not qualify for the lenient treatment of the O'Brien test if the phrase "an interest unrelated to free expression" refers merely to that ultimate goal. Such an interpretation of O'Brien would make defending the government nice work, for it would insure that the tough, clear and present danger and strict scrutiny tests would always be by-passed. We should thus label this first interpretation of the phrase the "heretical version" of O'Brien and be constantly vigilant against its use.

The sound interpretation of the phrase "unrelated to free expression" focuses not upon the ultimate goal of the legislation, but rather upon whether the justifications for the law advanced by the government have nothing to do with the communicative aspects of the conduct being regulated. When the dangers that allegedly flow from the activity have nothing to do with what is *communicated,* but only with what is *done,* the dangers are unrelated to free expression. But when the dangers the government seeks to prevent are dangers that it fears will arise because of what is communicated,

with other messages, this discriminatory application of the facially neutral law, based on the content of the wrongdoer's message, would violate the Constitution.[56]

4. *Discriminatory Conduct.* Just as the first amendment does not immunize physical attacks on persons or property, it does not immunize discriminatory conduct illegal under the equal protection clause, civil rights acts, or labor laws. Hate speech is often used as evidence of illegal discriminatory behavior.[57] As long as it is the underlying discriminatory behavior and not the speech that is being regulated, the first amendment is not offended. Under the analysis in *O'Brien*, the penalty exacted on speech in such cases is incidental to the governmental purpose of regulating the purely nonexpressive component of the conduct.[58]

---

then the regulation is "related to free expression," and should be subjected to the clear and present danger and strict scrutiny tests, and not to the *O'Brien* test.

This crucial distinction can be most easily illustrated by contrasting a "flag-burning" law with a mere "burning" law. A mere burning law—an ordinance that forbids lighting open fires in a public park—is a law passed to vindicate interests genuinely unrelated to free expression. The government might pass such a law because it believes open fires in the park present fire hazards that might cause injury to park land or patrons. The government might also pass such an ordinance as part of a more general environmental policy, concerned with the serious air pollution effects of open fires in an urban environment. Such an antiburning ordinance could have the *incidental* effect of suppressing speech, for it would prevent persons from burning things to express themselves. (The language of the Court in *O'Brien*, it should be noted, spoke in precisely these terms, referring to "the *incidental* restriction on alleged First Amendment freedoms." Id at 377 (emphasis added).) This incidental impact would be purely happenstance, however, for the law was passed to prevent harms that have nothing whatever to do with the communicative aspect of burning a flag, draft card, effigy, or any other symbol, but rather to prevent the harms of burning, period.

When the government bans flag-burning, by contrast, it does so to prevent harms that do arise from the communicative element of the act. Laws against flag-burning are not passed out of concern for pollution of the physical atmosphere but out of concern for pollution of the political atmosphere. The government does not like what burning the flag *means*. While it is true that government may have, as its ultimate goal, an altruistic concern with political cohesiveness, the justifications that it advances for banning flag-burning are based on the supposition that what is communicated by flag-burning will tend to undermine that cohesiveness. This is the correct interpretation of *O'Brien*, and for the most part the Supreme Court has been conscientious in adhering to this interpretation. The Court has emphasized on several occasions, for example, that the test of whether a law serves purposes unrelated to the content of expression is whether it is "*justified* without reference to the content of the regulated speech." *Ward*, 109 S Ct at 2754.

56. The constitutional violation might be conceptualized in two ways. Discriminatory application of an otherwise neutral law on the basis of a suspect class (such as racial identity) or the exercise of a fundamental right (such as free speech) triggers "strict scrutiny" under the equal protection clause and is usually a constitutional violation. *Yick Wo v Hopkins*, 118 US 356, 373-74 (1886). Alternatively, the act of selective prosecution might simply be used as evidence that the ostensibly content-neutral governmental interest is a sham, and the real motivating force is punishment based on the content (and, indeed, viewpoint) of the speech. This showing should disqualify the government from use of the *O'Brien* test, and trigger strict scrutiny under the first amendment. Under the neutrality principle, such viewpoint-based discrimination is virtually a *per se* constitutional violation. See notes 24-26 and accompanying text.

57. A racist remark by a public official, for example, might be used as proof of discriminatory intent in the administration of a governmental program in a suit alleging a violation of the equal protection clause. The racist statement could be the "smoking gun" that the disparate impact of the program was the result of purposeful governmental discrimination. Similarly, racist speech might be used to demonstrate a violation of federal labor laws, see *Sewell Mfg. Co.*, 138 NLRB 12 (1962), or as proof of housing or employment discrimination in violation of civil rights acts.

58. See note 34 and accompanying text.

5. *The Theory of Hate Speech as a Relational Harm.* The harm principle of modern first amendment jurisprudence forbids punishing speech on the ground that the message is intellectually or emotionally repugnant to a vast majority.[59] When the speech interferes with a "relational interest," however, it may be penalized.[60] Thus, a public figure who is ridiculed through a vicious caricature may not recover in tort merely for the emotional distress caused by the attack, but may recover for libel or invasion of privacy.[61]

The difference between recovery for infliction of emotional distress alone and recovery for libel or invasion of privacy goes to the heart of the harm principle. Permitting recovery for unvarnished emotional distress cannot be reconciled with core first amendment principles—no matter how we dress it up, the tort rests at bottom on the individual distress caused by the message of the speech and on the sense of collective community outrage caused by the violation of accepted rules of civility.[62] These are precisely the types of harms that modern first amendment theory disqualifies as justifications for abridging speech.[63] The torts of libel and invasion of privacy, however, carry additional weight; they implicate harms over and above individual psychological disturbance or collective community outrage. Libel interferes with reputation, a concept that the common law long ago reified as an interest existing outside the individual persona, an intangible asset of social or professional life that may be inventoried like any other stock in trade.[64] Similarly, the four commonly accepted forms of invasion of privacy all implicate interests over and above mere infliction of emotional distress.[65] If

---

59. See notes 27-28 and accompanying text.

60. See text accompanying note 31.

61. *Hustler*, 485 US 46.

62. The writings of Professor Robert Post on the relationship of torts such as defamation, invasion of privacy, and infliction of emotional distress to notions of community, offensiveness, and the purposes of the first amendment are exceptionally insightful. See Robert C. Post, *Cultural Heterogeneity and the Law: Pornography, Blasphemy, and the First Amendment*, 76 Cal L Rev 297 (1988); Robert C. Post, *The Social Foundations of Defamation Law: Reputation and the Constitution*, 74 Cal L Rev 691 (1986); Post, 32 Wm & Mary L Rev (forthcoming) (cited in note 2); Post, 103 Harv L Rev 601 (cited in note 28).

63. See notes 27-30 and accompanying text.

64. See Rodney A. Smolla, *Let the Author Beware: The Rejuvenation of the American Law of Libel*, 132 U Pa L Rev 1, 19 (1983).

65. For the classic restatement of the elements of the four commonly recognized forms of invasion of privacy, "false light," "intrusion," "publication of private facts," and "appropriation," see William L. Prosser, *Privacy*, 48 Cal L Rev 383 (1960). The tort of appropriation, or invasion of the "right of publicity," is the member of the privacy family that most clearly protects interests distinct from emotional distress; it consists of exploitation of the plaintiff's name or likeness, usually for commercial gain. See generally Harold R. Gordon, *Right of Property in Name, Likeness, Personality and History*, 55 Nw U L Rev 553 (1960). The essence of false light, a close cousin of defamation, is a falsehood placing the plaintiff in a light that would be highly offensive to a reasonable person. *Restatement (Second) of Torts* § 652 E (The American Law Institute, 1977). It thus implicates a relational interest similar to that of defamation. The tort of intrusion involves an invasion of the plaintiff's private space or solitude—such as eavesdropping on private conversations or peeping through the bedroom window. See Smolla, *Law of Defamation* at § 10.03 (cited in note 5) (collecting cases). Publication of private facts involves publication of true private facts that would be highly offensive to a person of ordinary sensibilities. See *Sidis v F-R Publishing Corp.*, 113 F2d 806 (2d Cir 1940). Both intrusion and publication of private facts implicate "invasions" of interests distinct from mere outrage at a speaker's message; they are forms, so to speak, of "psychic trespass." Indeed, the

this constitutional divide is conceptually sound, where does hate speech fall in the taxonomy of harms? Is it more like libel and invasion of privacy, or more like intentional infliction of emotional distress? The question is close. Looking back at *Beauharnais v. Illinois*,[66] it is clear that Justice Frankfurter thought that hate speech was closely analogous to libel or invasion of privacy—and that the force of the analogy was not dissipated merely because the slur was aimed at an entire racial group.

Frankfurter observed that if a libelous utterance directed at an *individual* may be punished, "we cannot deny to a State power to punish the same utterance directed at a *defined group*, unless we can say that this is a willful and purposeless restriction unrelated to the peace and well-being of the State."[67] Illinois, Frankfurter observed, did not have to look beyond its own borders "or await the tragic experience of the last three decades" (a reference to Nazi Germany) to conclude that purveyors of racial and religious hate "promote strife and tend powerfully to obstruct the manifold adjustments required for free, ordered life in a metropolitan, polyglot community."[68] Recalling events from the 1837 murder of the abolitionist Lovejoy to the 1951 riots in Cicero, Frankfurter concluded that Illinois might well deduce that racial tensions are exacerbated and more likely to flare into violence when racist messages are tolerated.[69]

Frankfurter also argued that Illinois was entitled to conclude that the dignity of the individual might be inextricably intertwined with protection for the reputation of his racial or religious group. It was not for the Supreme Court, he said, to deny that the "Illinois legislature may warrantably believe that a man's job and his educational opportunities and the dignity accorded him may depend as much on the reputation of the racial and religious group to which he willy-nilly belongs, as on his own merits."[70]

Frankfurter's treatment of group libel as an interference with a relational interest is not without appeal,[71] but current first amendment jurisprudence

---

intrusion tort requires no speech at all—though it is often committed as incident to gathering information.

The point here is not that these privacy torts raise no first amendment problems. The tort of publication of private facts raises such serious first amendment difficulties, for example, that its continuing existence is in genuine doubt. See *Florida Star v B.J.F.*, 109 S Ct 2603 (1989). The point, rather, is that if these privacy torts are to have at least a fighting chance of survival under the modern first amendment, they must be understood to protect individuals from interests other than mere outrage at the content of a speaker's message. The outrage may perhaps be part of the cause of action—as in the requirement of offensiveness that pervades privacy theory—but that offensiveness may not stand alone. Rather, it must be incident to the invasion of some other more palpable interest. To the extent that some of what would pass muster under the law of torts as an invasion of privacy will not pass muster under the first amendment, the first amendment lesson is that the privacy torts should have a structural integrity distinct from sheltering the victim from distress caused by the content of speech.

66. 343 US 250.
67. Id at 258 (emphasis added).
68. Id at 258-59.
69. Id at 259.
70. Id at 263.
71. See Post, 74 Cal L Rev 691 (cited in note 62).

would not accept this characterization, at least when the hate speech involves discussion of public issues.[72] To put the doctrinal issues most simply, *Brandenburg v. Ohio* would not have come out differently if Ohio had chosen to prosecute the Klan under a group libel statute rather than its criminal syndicalism law.[73] *Brandenburg* must be understood as overruling *Beauharnais* and eliminating the possibility of treating group libel under the same first amendment standards as individual libel.[74]

6. *The Public Speech/Private Speech Dichotomy*. If there is an Achilles' heel to modern first amendment jurisprudence, it is the dichotomy between speech of "general public interest or concern" and "private" speech. In a number of cases, the Supreme Court has held that first amendment rules highly protective of freedom of speech do not apply with full force—and indeed, may not apply at all—when the speech is of purely private concern.[75] The public speech/private speech dichotomy is still in an early stage of evolution—the

---

72. See the textual discussion accompanying notes 75-80.

73. See notes 32-33 and accompanying text.

74. The Supreme Court's most recent foray into the fact/opinion distinction in libel law further bolsters this assertion. In *Milkovich*, 110 S Ct at 2706, the Court declined to create a special constitutional doctrine immunizing "opinion" from defamation liability. See note 25. In a backhanded way, however, the Court's ruling did immunize all speech that is not *factual* in nature from defamation liability. The Court thus construed its prior decision in *Philadelphia Newspapers*, 106 S Ct 1558, as standing "for the proposition that a statement on matters of public concern must be provable as false before there can be liability under state defamation law, at least in situations like the present, where a media defendant is involved." *Milkovich*, 110 S Ct at 2706. The Court similarly relied on its prior decision in *Hustler*, emphasizing that an action by a public figure was precluded under the first amendment in the absence of statements that could " 'reasonably have been interpreted as stating actual facts about the public figure involved.' " Id at 2705, quoting *Hustler*, 485 US at 50. The Court also endorsed its prior decisions in *Greenbelt Cooperative Publishing Ass'n v Bresler*, 398 US 6 (1970) and *Letter Carriers v Austin*, 418 US 264 (1974), protecting "rhetorical hyperbole." *Milkovich*, 110 S Ct at 2704-05.

In *Milkovich* the Court thus tied first amendment requirements to the traditional common law doctrines defining what type of speech qualifies as "defamatory." Significantly, the common law excluded name-calling, insults, epithets, and verbal abuse from the definition of "defamatory." Smolla, *Law of Defamation* at § 4.03 (cited in note 5).

75. In *Connick v Myers*, 461 US 138 (1983), the Court dealt with the free speech of employees not relating to general discussion on matters of public interest or concern, but on matters of "insubordination" within the hierarchy of the agency. The case involved Harry Connick, the district attorney for Orleans Parish, Louisiana, and Sheila Myers, an assistant district attorney on Connick's staff. A dispute between Connick and Myers arose when Connick tried to transfer Myers to a different section of the criminal court. Myers prepared and distributed to the other assistants in the office a questionnaire concerning office transfer policy, office morale, the need for a grievance committee, their level of confidence in superiors, and whether they felt pressure from their superiors to work in political campaigns. Connick fired Myers, declaring the questionnaire an act of "insubordination." Id at 141.

The Supreme Court upheld the termination. Justice White noted that for "most of this century, the unchallenged dogma was that a public employee had no right to object to conditions placed upon the terms of employment—including those which restricted the exercise of constitutional rights." Id at 143. After acknowledging the Holmes position and the persistence of the right-privilege distinction, however, Justice White explicitly rejected the distinction as a legitimate framework for analysis. Id at 147.

Yet Myers still lost her case. The Court introduced a dichotomy between speech on matters of "public" concern and speech on matters of "private" concern. "When employee expression cannot be fairly considered as relating to any matter of political, social, or other concern to the community,

Court's few invocations of the distinction have done little to define it.[76] It is clear, however, that the phrase "general or public concern" is broad. Nothing in the public speech/private speech distinction, for example, rolls back the Court's expansive first amendment protection for speech on the wide range of cultural and social topics that are unrelated to politics or self-governance.[77] Similarly, speech may qualify as a matter of public interest even though it occurs in settings that are not part of the general arena of public discourse.[78]

The confluence of first amendment doctrines that protect hate speech uttered or published during the course of discussion of issues of public concern, therefore, might not apply at all when the speech bears no plausible connection to such issues. Thus, a campus newspaper running a racist parody directed against a faculty member, or against an entire racial group, would be fully protected, even if the parody were as vulgar and mean-spirited as the caricature in *Hustler Magazine, Inc. v. Falwell.* Issues concerning race are quintessentially matters of public concern. But a gratuitous racial epithet uttered to a passerby in a context devoid of any plausible patina of intellectual content might be a different matter entirely.[79] The brutal inarticulate speech of the heart, uttered outside of any discussion of public issues or affairs, might thus fall outside of the first amendment's protection entirely.[80]

D.   Summary of Permissible Controls on Hate Speech

The exceptions to first amendment protection recognized under the negative side of free speech jurisprudence permit regulation of hate speech in

---

government officials should enjoy wide latitude in managing their offices, without intrusive oversight by the judiciary in the name of the First Amendment." Id at 146.

Similarly, in *Dun and Bradstreet, Inc. v Greenmoss Builders, Inc.*, 472 US 749, 763 (1985), the Court held that its first amendment rules governing the types of damages recoverable in defamation suits did not apply to defamation actions not involving "matters of public concern." (The case arose out of an erroneous and damaging credit report.)

76.   See Rodney A. Smolla, Dun & Bradstreet, Hepps, *and* Liberty Lobby: *A New Analytic Primer on the Future Course of Defamation*, 75 Georgetown L J 1519, 1540-45 (1987).

77.   See notes 19-22 and accompanying text.

78.   For example, in *Rankin v McPherson*, 483 US 378 (1987), the Supreme Court had before it the issue of whether an employee in a Texas county constable's office could be fired for stating, upon hearing the news bulletin that someone had attempted to assassinate President Ronald Reagan, "If they go for him again, I hope they get him." Id at 380. Notwithstanding the employment setting, the Court held that this speech was clearly on an issue of "public concern," and held that the employee could not be fired. Id at 388.

79.   This is

language that requires no more thought than the ability to spell; language that states no fact, offers no opinion, proposes no transaction, attempts no persuasion; language that contains no humorous punch-line, no melodic rhythm, no color or shape or texture that might pass as art or entertainment; language that embodies emotion with no elaborative gloss other than feeble minimum intellectual current necessary to power the use of words.

Smolla, 47 Wash & Lee L Rev at 183 (cited in note 2).

80.   It is significant in this regard that the milestone modern first amendment decisions involving emotionally graphic speech *all* involved speech containing a social message. See *Brandenburg*, 395 US 444 (racist message); *Cohen*, 403 US 15 (anti-war message); *Texas v Johnson*, 109 S Ct 2533 (anti-patriotic message); *Hustler*, 485 US 46 (antireligion, antihypocrisy message). Hate speech is likely to involve a social message—albeit repugnant and offensive. For hate speech to qualify as private speech, it would have to be essentially devoid of any message.

only a small number of closely confined circumstances. Sweeping prohibitions on hate speech, patterned on the group libel notions of *Beauharnais*, are unconstitutional. The only prohibitions likely to be upheld are narrowly drawn restrictions on fighting words that present a clear and present danger of violence,[81] or that punish physical injury to persons or property,[82] or illegal discriminatory conduct,[83] or that involve purely private speech in a context completely removed from discussion of issues of general or public concern.[84]

III

ACADEMIC FREEDOM AND HATE SPEECH ON CAMPUS

A. Introduction: The "Idea of a University"

The first amendment principles canvassed above permit only the most modest controls on hate speech. But should those rules apply with full force on university campuses? If the regime of *Beauharnais v. Illinois* has been effectively overruled in the general marketplace, might not university campuses be treated as special settings, walled off from the general marketplace, in which the principles of *Beauharnais* still reign supreme?

From the perspectives both of first amendment jurisprudence and of notions of academic freedom, resolution of the conflicts posed by hate speech inevitably turns on how society conceives the idea of a university. What is this idea? Randolph Bourne in 1917 spoke fondly of the "old, noble ideal of a community of scholarship."[85] There is an endearing image of the university as set off from the rest of society—not disconnected or irrelevant, but still somehow specially removed, an island of retreat for the life of the mind. The phrase "academic freedom" conjures up this image of insularity. Wrapped in the phrase are the many claims and intuitions that because the university is special—specially important and specially vulnerable—policies and rules binding on the rest of society should not always apply to it. Campuses today are under pressure from many quarters to compromise the noble idea of the university as an island of intellectual inquiry and robust discourse that ought to maintain some degree of separation from the commands of the sovereign, the tantalizing seductions of gigantic financial grants, and the whimsical ebbs and flows of mass politics and prejudice.

But if a university is an island, what kind of island is it? For many, its principal distinguishing characteristic is unfettered expressive freedom. The university is a libertarian island, the one place that embraces, heart and soul,

---

81. See notes 50-51 and accompanying text.
82. See notes 53-56 and accompanying text.
83. See notes 57-58 and accompanying text.
84. Given the relatively primitive state of the "public speech/private speech" dichotomy, the legitimacy of this final "private speech" exception is far from certain. See notes 16-22 and accompanying text.
85. Randolph S. Bourne, *The Idea of a University*, in Carl Resek, ed, *War and the Intellectuals: Essays by Randolph S. Bourne (1915-1919)* 152, 154 (Harper & Row, 1964).

John Stuart Mill's wide-open marketplace. For others, however, Bourne's phrase "a community of scholarship" seems more apt, with emphasis on the word "community." The university is an island of equality, civility, tolerance, and respect for human dignity; a place where the contemplative and rational faculties of man should triumph over blind passion and prejudice.

These two images live side by side on campus. Most faculty, students, and administrators are attracted to both ideas and are discomfited when they conflict.[86]

B. Universities and the Concept of Open Forums

The free speech status of a state college or university is governed by a branch of first amendment jurisprudence known as "public forum law."[87] The Supreme Court has recognized three distinct categories of public forums. The first, the traditional or quintessential public forum, consists of places such as streets or parks that "have immemorially been held in trust for the use of the public and, time out of mind, have been used for purposes of assembly, communicating thoughts between citizens, and discussing public questions."[88] Content-based regulation of speech in a traditional public forum is governed by the strict scrutiny test: the regulation must be necessary to serve a compelling state interest, and must be narrowly drawn to achieve that end.[89] Content-neutral regulation of the time, place, and manner of speech in a traditional public forum is permitted if it serves an "important," "significant," or "substantial" governmental interest, is narrowly tailored to achieve the interest, and leaves open ample alternative channels of communication.[90]

The second category, the designated open public forum, consists of public property opened by the state for indiscriminate use as a place for expressive

---

86. See notes 2-3.

87. In exploring the idea of a university, it is necessary to distinguish between matters of constitutional law and of academic policy. State institutions, bound by the Constitution, do not enjoy unfettered freedom to choose between the libertarian and communitarian models of university life. Their choices are constricted by first amendment public forum law, which in turn controls whether the constitutional principles of the general marketplace will or will not be activated on the campus. For private universities, identical choices exist—but they are choices of policy, not constitutional law. This article examines the constitutional public forum law applicable to state universities. The constitutional law conclusions drawn herein, however, are also intended to apply fully to private universities—even though private universities are not legally bound to accept them. That, admittedly, is itself an enormously fertile ground for debate: should private universities conduct themselves as if they are bound by the first amendment? (The issue, of course, is not unique to the topic of hate speech.) The assumption made in this article is that the noble idea of a university explored here recognizes no distinction between state and private institutions, because it behooves any university that aspires to greatness to organize itself according to principles of freedom of speech that are at least as protective as those of the Constitution. But obviously, it is for private universities to ask themselves whether they feel it is appropriate to truly take the first amendment to heart. Space does not permit a full treatment of this issue in this article.

88. *Hague v CIO*, 307 US 496, 515 (1939).

89. *Carey*, 447 US at 461-62.

90. See, for example, *Perry Education Assn*, 460 US at 46; *United States Postal Serv. v Council of Greenburgh Civic Ass'ns*, 453 US 114, 132 (1981); *Consolidated Edison Co. v Public Serv. Comm'n*, 447 US 530, 535-36 (1980).

activity. If the government intentionally dedicates a piece of public property to the public at large for assembly and speech, then it will be bound by the same standards applicable to a traditional public forum. Content-based regulation of speech in a designated open public forum must thus satisfy the strict scrutiny test.[91] A state is "not required to indefinitely retain the open character of the facility," [92] but as long as it does so, the strict scrutiny test applies.[93]

The third category, the nonpublic forum, consists of publicly owned facilities that have been dedicated to use for either noncommunicative or communicative purposes, but have never been designated for indiscriminate expressive activity by the general public. "[T]he First Amendment does not guarantee access to property simply because it is owned or controlled by the government."[94]

The content-based regulation of speech in a nonpublic forum is not governed by the strict scrutiny test, but by a "reasonable nexus" standard. The government "may reserve the forum for its intended purposes, *communicative or otherwise*, as long as the regulation on speech is reasonable and not an effort to suppress expression merely because public officials oppose the speaker's view."[95] Entire classes of speech thus may be excluded from a nonpublic forum. Those classes may be identified by content, as long as the exclusion is reasonable in light of the purpose of the forum and there is no discrimination among viewpoints within a class. "Control over access to a nonpublic forum can be based on *subject matter* and *speaker identity* so long as the distinctions drawn are reasonable in light of the purpose served by the forum and are viewpoint neutral."[96]

How should a state university campus be classified for first amendment purposes? The soundest view is to treat the campus not as one unified forum, but as subdivided into multiple forums to which differing free speech standards apply. On the grounds of every state university campus, for example, are located traditional public forums, which serve as the functional equivalent in campus life of the Boston Common, the Washington Mall, or the streets and sidewalks in front of the seat of government. Of course, the geography of campuses differs—at some universities, this traditional forum may be the open campus green or plaza, at others it may be the entrance to the student union or the main classroom building. But every state campus, like every city, should be understood to have at least one location

---

91. See, for example, *Cornelius*, 473 US at 802-03; *Perry Education Ass'n*, 460 US at 45-46.

92. *Perry Education Ass'n*, 460 US at 46.

93. Id. The same legal standards for regulating speech thus apply to Category I traditional forums and Category II designated forums. The only difference between the two categories is that the government has no control over the status of a traditional forum (the United States could not take the Washington Mall out of circulation as a traditional public forum) but government may by designation move a public facility in or out of Category II status. *Cornelius*, 473 US at 802-03; *Perry*, 460 US at 46-47.

94. *Greenburgh Civic Ass'ns*, 453 US at 129.

95. *Perry*, 460 US at 46 (emphasis added), citing *Greenburgh Civic Ass'ns*, 453 US at 131 n7.

96. *Cornelius*, 473 US at 806 (emphasis added).

permanently dedicated to wide-open discourse, a first amendment "free fire zone" in which the principles of free speech in the open marketplace apply with undiminished force.[97]

In addition, most state universities should be treated as having turned large parts of their campuses into designated public forums. The Supreme Court's most significant foray into this issue came in its 1981 decision in *Widmar v. Vincent*,[98] involving the University of Missouri at Kansas City. The university's stated policy was to encourage the activities of student organizations, and it officially recognized over 100 student groups.[99] The university regularly provided facilities for the meetings of registered organizations; students paid an activity fee to help defray the costs to the university.[100] From 1973 until 1977, a registered religious group named Cornerstone, an organization of evangelical Christian students from various denominational backgrounds,[101] regularly sought and received permission to conduct its meetings in university facilities.[102] In 1977, however, the university informed the group that it could no longer meet in the university's buildings.[103] The exclusion was based on a regulation, adopted in 1972 by the university, forbidding the use of university facilities "for purposes of religious worship or religious teaching."[104] The university defended its regulation on the grounds that the prohibition was necessary to avoid a violation of the establishment clause of the first amendment.[105] The Supreme Court rejected this defense and held the Missouri restriction unconstitutional.[106] The Court reasoned that permitting a student religious group to use the university's facilities on the same terms as other student groups could not be construed as an implicit endorsement of the religious group's message, and that therefore the establishment clause was not violated by letting the religious group in.[107] The University had designated its facilities as open forums, the Court held, and consequently could not discriminate against religious speech.[108] "The Constitution forbids a State to

---

97. This requirement is analogous to so-called "green space" restrictions common in modern land use and environmental regulation. In order to preserve the environmental quality of life in every area developed for residential or business use, green space regulations require developers to maintain a specified ratio of developed spaces to open, or green, spaces. We might think of the general marketplace of speech as the green spaces of discourse. Governments own a substantial amount of the space on which this discourse occurs—public parks, streets, sidewalks, plazas, stadiums, auditoriums, and so on. It is essential that, in any given community, sufficient open physical space be dedicated to the general marketplace. For unless we think of these spaces as subject to a perpetual public "easement" for free speech, government could dramatically curtail much of the speech most vital to the general marketplace, such as mass protest demonstrations.

98.   454 US 263 (1981).

99.   Id at 265.

100.   Id.

101.   Id at 265 n2.

102.   Id at 265.

103.   Id.

104.   Id.

105.   Id at 270-71.

106.   Id at 267.

107.   Id at 273-74.

108.   Id at 267-70.

enforce certain exclusions from a forum generally open to the public," the Court stated, "even if it was not required to create the forum in the first place."[109]

What does *Widmar* really mean? Does it require universities to permit all forms of hate speech on campus that must be tolerated in the general marketplace? *Widmar* might be understood as standing for the proposition that, by virtue of the large quantity of diverse speech customarily permitted on state campuses, they are in all respects designated open public forums. That view, however, reads more into *Widmar* than it will legitimately bear, since there was never really any contest concerning the open forum status of the particular university facilities at issue in *Widmar*.[110]

The *Widmar* decision does *not* stand for the proposition that a state university is compelled by the first amendment to treat all places at all times as open public forums. As support for this assertion, consider the following problem. Justice White argued in dissent in *Widmar* that the university should be permitted to exclude religious worship and services from its facilities, even if it were required by the first amendment to permit access to other forms of religious speech.[111] Thus the university would have to permit a Catholic student group access to its classrooms for a meeting, but not permit access for the celebration of Mass. A majority of the Court, however, rejected Justice White's argument, refusing to accept any distinction between religious worship and other forms of religious speech in an open forum.

Now imagine that a professor at the University of Missouri wishes to open his history of religion class, which is conducted in the same classroom in which the student religious group regularly meets by instructing the students to bow their heads and join him in reciting the Lord's Prayer. Surely this instruction would violate the establishment clause. The act of a university official leading a captive group of students in a prayer is totally distinct from a group of students meeting voluntarily on their own to pray. The professor could not successfully defend his actions by asserting that the classroom is an open forum under *Widmar* and that, under first amendment principles or principles of academic freedom, he has a right to lead his students in prayer to commence his class. The constitutional calculus changes as the function of

---

109. Id at 267-68.

110. There was no contest in *Widmar* over the open public forum status of the classroom facilities (outside of normal class usage) on the University of Missouri's Kansas City campus. The university did not defend its position on the basis that it had created only a nonpublic forum for these facilities, nor did it attempt to avoid application of the strict scrutiny test. Rather, the university argued that its interest in maintaining strict separation of church and state created a compelling state interest sufficient to satisfy strict scrutiny review. The Supreme Court in *Widmar* therefore accepted as a given that the facilities at issue on the Missouri campus were open public forums, and it constantly emphasized the breadth of those forums. The Court referred to the Missouri campus as "a forum generally open to the public," id at 268, "a public forum," id at 270, a "public forum, open to all forms of discourse," id at 273, an "open forum," id at 274, and "a forum generally open to student groups." Id at 277. The Court noted that "the forum is available to a broad class of nonreligious as well as religious speakers; there are over 100 recognized student groups at UMKC." Id at 274.

111. Id at 282-89 (White dissenting).

the classroom changes.[112] Principles of academic freedom may well give him a large measure of freedom to choose how he will present the history of religion in that classroom, but that freedom does not extend to actually conducting religious worship or services. The very distinction between religious speech and religious worship advanced by Justice White but rejected by a majority of the Court in the context of the university's open forum would be valid and controlling during actual class times.

An analogous process applies to hate speech. There are settings on the campus in which the rule of *Beauharnais*, and not the rule of *Brandenburg*, should apply.[113] When considered against the backdrop of the complexities of academic freedom, this distinction is most vividly demonstrated by examining the power of a university to discipline its own employees, including its administrators and faculty, for hate speech that would normally be protected by the first amendment.[114]

Principles of free speech and academic freedom should certainly be understood to give faculty a large measure of independence in how they present materials in class on matters relating to race, sex, or sexual orientation. Viewpoint discrimination should not be permitted, even when the university regards the view espoused by the professor as repugnant. Thus a professor should have the right to espouse bona fide academic opinions concerning racial characteristics or capabilities, even though most people of good will and good sense on the campus would find the opinions loathsome. It does not follow, however, that the professor would have the freedom to engage in racist, sexist, or homophobic speech attacks during class, even though those attacks might be protected in the open marketplace. The speech at issue in *Beauharnais* and *Brandenburg* was the same mindless racist diatribe. The professor would have a right to engage in that sort of hate speech in the open forums on campus, but not in the classroom, where the rule of *Beauharnais* should instead govern.

---

112. See Rabban, 53 L & Contemp Probs 227 (cited in note 3).

113. An easy illustration involves a state university radio station run by students. Under the Supreme Court's ruling in *FCC v Pacifica Foundation*, 438 US 726, 747-52 (1978), the government is permitted to exclude "indecent" speech from the airwaves, even though that speech would be fully protected in print media. The *Pacifica* ruling clearly supports the FCC's authority to ban racist speech from the airwaves. On the radio, it is the *Beauharnais* first amendment and not the *Brandenburg* version that controls. No state university radio station could successfully claim a first amendment right to be opted out of the rule of *Pacifica* on the theory that universities are open public forums in which *Brandenburg* principles always apply. At least for that pocket of university discourse—the radio waves—the more restrictive notions of *Beauharnais* and *Pacifica* would trump the open forum principles of *Widmar*.

114. Academic freedom has an institutional and an individual component. In institutional terms, it embodies the principle that universities should be kept largely free of interference from outside forces, including the government. Much more complex is the individual component, in which members of the university community stake out claims against interference from the university. A faculty member or student may thus claim an individual academic freedom right to espouse theories of racial superiority that run contrary to institutional university policy. See William W. Van Alstyne, *Academic Freedom and the First Amendment in the Supreme Court of the United States: An Unhurried Historical Review*, 53 L & Contemp Probs 79 (Summer 1990); Rabban, 53 L & Contemp Probs 227 (cited in note 3).

Academic freedom should be understood as making the professor an *intellectual* free agent, but not a *behavioral* free agent. The members of the faculty act as the representatives of the university in the classroom both on matters intellectual and on matters not plausibly related to intellectual positions. The university is under a constitutional obligation to refrain from stigmatizing hate speech and may likewise require the faculty, as its representatives, to refrain from stigmatizing hate speech in the classroom.[115] Just as a university is required to prevent its faculty from leading students in prayer to begin class sessions—even though that prayer would be constitutionally protected in other contexts—so too the university should be understood as at least permitted (and arguably required) to police gratuitous hate speech by faculty in classroom settings. It should be emphasized that this notion that a university has greater power to control hate speech by faculty or administrators in settings such as classrooms is not a mechanical invocation of the right-privilege distinction, which has been thoroughly discredited in modern constitutional law.[116] Under this distinction, which once dominated American constitutional law, government could attach whatever conditions it pleased to the receipt of governmental largess, including the surrender of constitutional rights that the recipient would otherwise enjoy. Thus, a faculty member could be told by the university, "You are free to exercise your freedom of speech to engage in constitutionally protected hate speech to your heart's content, but if you accept a university appointment here, you do so on the condition that you refrain from exercising that right." The faculty member may have a constitutional right to freedom of speech, but no constitutional right to be a faculty member.[117] Though the distinction has been discredited, the underlying "beggars can't be chosers" premise of the distinction has stamina, and it continues to surface—sometimes in disguise—

115. Stigma is at the heart of modern equal protection analysis. In *Brown v Board of Educ.*, 347 US 483, 494 (1954), the Court stated that to separate black children from white children solely because of their race "generates a feeling of inferiority as to their status in the community that may affect their hearts and minds in a way unlikely ever to be undone." As Professor Charles Lawrence explains, *Brown* held that separate was inherently unequal "because of the *message* that segregation conveys—the message that black children are an untouchable caste, unfit to be educated with white children." Lawrence, 1990 Duke L J at 439 (cited in note 2) (emphasis in the original). In *Anderson v Martin*, 375 US 399 (1964), the Court struck down a state law that required designation of the race of candidates on ballots. The Court reasoned that while no one doubts that voters in the privacy of the voting booth may take racial identity into account in casting their votes, the government may not encourage that accounting by placing the race of the candidate on the ballot. Id at 402. The specification of a candidate's race is different in kind from the designation of a candidate as "Republican" or "Democrat." Id at 402-03. To identify candidates by race, the Court held, places "the power of the State behind a racial classification that induces racial prejudice at the polls." Id at 402. Justice Brennan in *Regents of the University of California v Bakke*, 438 US 265 (1978), pronounced as a "cardinal principle" the proposition that "racial classifications that stigmatize—because they are drawn on the presumption that one race is inferior to another or because they put the weight of government behind racial hatred and separatism—are invalid without more." Id at 357-58 (Brennan concurring in part and dissenting in part).

116. See William W. Van Alstyne, *The Demise of the Right-Privilege Distinction in Constitutional Law*, 81 Harv L Rev 1439 (1968).

117. See *McAuliffe v Mayor of New Bedford*, 155 Mass 216, 220, 29 NE 517, 517 (1892) ("The petitioner may have a constitutional right to talk politics, but he has no constitutional right to be a policeman.").

in modern cases.[118] But at least in first amendment cases, the Supreme Court consistently refuses to accept the distinction.[119] Thus, in controlling the speech of faculty or administrators, the university is emphatically not permitted to rely merely on the leverage of employment, but must justify its regulation of speech according to whatever first amendment principles would otherwise apply.

The principle just stated, however, does not mean that the status of employment is constitutionally irrelevant to the first amendment analysis. The particular circumstances of the employment context may supply the government with justifications for regulating speech that would not exist otherwise. Rather than invoking the right-privilege distinction, the government simply would apply general first amendment principles to the specific facts of a case. When a governmental employee speaks in part for the government, the situation implicates a governmental interest in controlling the content of its own speech and ensuring that it is not, for example, racially or sexually abusive;[120] the presence of this interest therefore creates a justified opportunity for regulation.

The hate speech of students on campus is more problematic. If the setting were high school or elementary school, the role of the school as an inculcator of civic values would permit *Beauharnais*-style controls on the hate speech of students.[121] But college students are adults. Does the idea of a university contemplate a role for the institution as an inculcator of what might be called academic values, as opposed to academic freedom? Might not the university say that part of its legitimate mission is to teach students how to contend vigorously within the marketplace of ideas while nevertheless observing

---

118. See Rodney A. Smolla, *The Reemergence of the Right-Privilege Distinction in Constitutional Law: The Price of Protesting Too Much*, 35 Stan L Rev 69 (1982); Rodney A. Smolla, *Preserving the Bill of Rights in the Modern Administrative-Industrial State*, 31 Wm & Mary L Rev 321 (1990).

119. See, for example, *Rutan v Republican Party of Illinois*, 110 S Ct 2729, 2735-36 (1990).

120. See *University of Pennsylvania*, 110 S Ct at 587 n6 ("Where, as was the situation in the academic-freedom cases, government attempts to direct the content of speech at public educational institutions, complicated First Amendment issues are presented because government is simultaneously both speaker and regulator."). That the government is "simultaneously both speaker and regulator" certainly does not mean that the government has carte blanche—for that would be to reintroduce surreptitiously the right-privilege distinction. The notion of simultaneously speaking and regulating, indeed, is easily abused. In *Meese v Keene*, 481 US 465 (1987), for example, the Supreme Court disingenuously applied this distinction, treating the governmental requirement that foreign films be labeled as "propaganda" as a form of government "speech," when in fact it was purely a form of regulation. See Rodney A. Smolla & Stephen A. Smith, *Propaganda, Xenophobia, and the First Amendment*, 67 Or L Rev 253, 280-83 (1988). The Court's market-participant exception to the commerce clause is a useful analogy. States are exempted from normal commerce clause restrictions when they act as market participants because, as mere participants, they do not impede private trade in the national marketplace. See *Reeves, Inc., v Stake*, 447 US 429, 439 (1980). This immunity is stripped, however, when the state exerts influences on the market beyond whatever natural force it commands as a competitor. See *South-Central Timber Development Inc. v Wunnicke*, 467 US 82, 97-98 (1984).

121. See *Hazelwood School Dist. v Kuhlmeier*, 484 US 260, 266-67 (1988); *Bethel School Dist. No. 403 v Fraser*, 478 US 675, 683 (1986).

certain norms of civility?[122] Might not the university claim that part of its mission is to encourage the triumph of the rational and contemplative sides of the intellect over passion and prejudice?[123] The answer to these questions is bound up in yet one final aspect of the idea of a university—namely, how universities teach.

IV

CONCLUSION

Let there be no doubt that hate speech on campus should be fought with all the vigor a university can muster. Hate speech is an abomination, a rape of human dignity. And let there be no inhibition in punishing hate speech in any of the contexts in which speech may be punished under recognized first amendment doctrines—as when it poses a clear and present danger of violence,[124] or when it is intertwined with actual discriminatory conduct.[125]

But outside those narrowly defined first amendment categories, the battle against hate speech will be fought most effectively through persuasive and creative educational leadership rather than through punishment and coercion. The conflict felt by most administrators, faculty, and students of good will on most American campuses is that we hate hate speech as much as we love free speech. The conflict, however, is not irreconcilable. It is most constructively resolved by a staunch commitment to free expression principles, supplemented with an equally vigorous attack on hate speech in all its forms, emphasizing energetic leadership and education on the academic values of tolerance, civility, and respect for human dignity, rather than punitive and coercive measures.[126] In this respect both of the grand ideas of a university are vindicated. The sense of a community of scholars, an island of reason and tolerance, is the pervasive ethos. But that ethos should be advanced with

---

122. Thus the validity of the marketplace of ideas concept might be understood as contingent on a commitment to rational thinking. See Frederick Schauer, *Free Speech: A Philosophical Enquiry* 25-26 (Cambridge Univ Press, 1982).

123. There was a time in which even mainstream free speech jurisprudence seemed to emphasize the intellectual over the emotional. As Justice Frankfurter put it in *Niemotko v Maryland*, 340 US 268 (1951), "A man who is calling names or using the kind of language which would reasonably stir another to violence does not have the same claim to protection as one whose speech is an appeal to reason." Id at 282 (Frankfurter concurring). "Back of the guarantee of free speech," said the Court in 1941, "lay faith in the power of an appeal to reason by all the peaceful means for gaining access to the mind." *Milk Wagon Drivers Union of Chicago, Local 753 v Meadowmoor Dairies, Inc.*, 312 US 287, 293 (1941). This split between the reason and passion has now largely been swept away by the emotion principle in modern first amendment jurisprudence. See notes 27-28 and accompanying text. It still appears, however, in those areas in which general free speech doctrines do not apply. In the obscenity context, for example, the Court has distinguished control of obscene speech from "control of reason and intellect." *Paris Adult Theatre I v Slayton*, 413 US 49, 67 (1973).

124. See notes 50-51 and accompanying text.

125. See notes 57-58 and accompanying text. Hate speech on campus should thus be punished in any of the situations in which such punishment is permitted under the general first amendment rules discussed in Part II of this article. See notes 1-3 and accompanying text.

126. See Robert M. O'Neil, *Colleges Should Seek Educational Alternatives to Rules that Override the Historic Guarantees of Free Speech*, Chron Higher Educ B1 (October 18, 1989); Report of Workshop on Racist and Sexist Speech on College and University Campuses, The Annenberg Washington Program of Northwestern University, April 12, 1990 (copy on file with author).

education, not coercion. It should be the dominant voice of the university within the marketplace of ideas; but it should not preempt that marketplace.

A FUNCTIONAL ANALYSIS OF "INDIVIDUAL" AND "INSTITUTIONAL" ACADEMIC FREEDOM UNDER THE FIRST AMENDMENT

DAVID M. RABBAN[*]

TABLE OF CONTENTS

---

  * Vinson & Elkins Professor of Law, The University of Texas School of Law.
   I began this article at the College of William and Mary, where I spent the 1989-1990 academic year as the Lee Distinguished Visiting Professor. Charles Koch and Rodney Smolla provided valuable criticisms and suggestions on an early draft. Probing comments and questions from my colleagues during and after a faculty colloquium at the University of Texas School of Law helped enormously as I revised this article. I am grateful to David Anderson, J. Peter Byrne, Matthew Finkin, Steven Goode, Douglas Laycock, Sanford Levinson, William Powers, John Robertson, Jordan Steiker, and Mark Yudof for carefully reading and patiently discussing various drafts. I also thank Amy Gutmann and Walter F. Murphy, professors in the Department of Politics at Princeton University, Thomas M. Scanlon, formerly professor in the Department of Philosophy at Princeton and currently professor of philosophy at Harvard University, and Thomas H. Wright, Princeton's general counsel, for reading and commenting on my treatment of the *Schmid* case at Princeton.
   Much of my thinking about academic freedom derives from fifteen years of stimulating discussions with William Van Alstyne, who was president of the American Association of University Professors ("AAUP") when I joined its staff as associate counsel in 1976. It is a special pleasure to contribute to a symposium on academic freedom edited by the person from whom I have learned most about this subject.

228

I

Introduction

Definitions of academic freedom have developed in response to actual historical circumstances. Threats to professors from university trustees loomed behind the seminal professional definition produced in 1915 by a committee of eminent professors for the first annual meeting of the American Association of University Professors ("AAUP"). Threats to universities from the state, arising out of general concerns during the late 1940s and 1950s about the dangers of communism to American society and institutions, prompted the cases that led the Supreme Court to identify academic freedom as a first amendment right.

Both the professional and the constitutional definitions of academic freedom[1] stressed the value of critical inquiry in universities. But each definition understandably focused on the distinctive contemporary threats to this value. Not surprisingly, the AAUP definition, which was eventually accepted by many universities and educational organizations, emphasized the protection of individual professors against lay trustees, whereas the constitutional definition emphasized the protection of the entire university community against state intervention. Neither definition, however, was monolithic. The AAUP recognized the danger to academic inquiry from legislative interference, and Supreme Court opinions treated constitutional academic freedom as an individual right of professors as well as an institutional right of universities.

For many years, "individual" and "institutional" definitions of academic freedom seemed complementary rather than in tension with each other. Significantly, the AAUP's first Supreme Court brief on the subject of academic freedom stressed that university autonomy from the state is a necessary condition for the academic freedom of professors.[2] Yet the dramatic growth of litigation by students and professors against universities, dating roughly from the late 1960s, has highlighted the tension between individual and institutional academic freedom. Increasingly, administrators and trustees have invoked institutional academic freedom not as an additional layer of protection for professors against the state, but as a bar to judicial review of claims against universities by professors alleging institutional violations of individual academic freedom.

---

1. Walter P. Metzger, *Profession and Constitution: Two Definitions of Academic Freedom in America*, 66 Tex L Rev 1265 (1988), is the work that most explicitly identifies and compares the professional and constitutional definitions. I find these two definitions much more compatible than does Professor Metzger. See, for example, text accompanying notes 4-5, 44-46, 50-57, 254-58. See also J. Peter Byrne, *Academic Freedom: A "Special Concern of the First Amendment,"* 99 Yale L J 251 (1989) (following Metzger in contrasting individual emphasis of professional definition with institutional emphasis of constitutional definition); David M. Rabban, *Academic Freedom*, in Leonard Levy, Kenneth L. Karst & Dennis J. Mahoney, eds, 1 *Encyclopedia of the American Constitution* 12 (MacMillan, 1986) (comparing uncertainty of constitutional definition with elaborated professional definition).

2. AAUP's Brief as Amicus Curiae, *Barenblatt v United States*, 360 US 109 (1959).

Unfortunately, the Supreme Court's glorification of academic freedom as a "special concern of the First Amendment"[3] has produced hyperbolic rhetoric but only scant, and often ambiguous, analytic content. The Court has never explained systematically the theory behind its relatively recent incorporation of academic freedom into the first amendment, a problem occasionally acknowledged by the justices themselves. Without such a theory, it is difficult to address the constitutional implications of the tension between the individual and institutional components of academic freedom.

Some commentators have maintained that the courts, especially the Supreme Court, seem to be defining constitutional academic freedom exclusively in institutional terms.[4] Indeed, a major recent analysis comments approvingly on this perceived development.[5] I disagree. Courts may have been presented with more institutional claims than individual claims of academic freedom, but they have also recognized that the first amendment protects individual academic freedom. Although courts have identified both forms of academic freedom, they have not fully addressed, and certainly have not resolved, the tensions between them.

In this article, I summarize and contrast the professional and constitutional treatments of academic freedom, justify distinctive first amendment analysis of academic speech that differs both from the professional definition of academic freedom and from the constitutional free speech of citizens generally, and respond to arguments that courts lack competence to decide academic freedom disputes between professors and universities. In my opinion, academic freedom is more than just a desirable policy promoted by the AAUP and adopted within the academic world. Core first amendment values—such as critical inquiry, the search for knowledge, and toleration of dissent—support constitutionalizing some, but not all, of the speech covered by the professional definition of academic freedom. These first amendment values justify protecting both the professional speech of faculty and the autonomy of universities to make decisions about educational policy. In order to engage in critical inquiry, professors need some degree of independence from their university employers, and universities need some degree of independence from the state. Asserting constitutional protection for professors and universities is not simply a form of special pleading to elevate the job-related concerns of a particular profession or the institutional interests of a particular enterprise. Rather, constitutional academic freedom promotes first amendment values of general concern to all citizens in a democracy.

This functional justification of academic freedom as "a special concern of the First Amendment" is theoretically defensible as applied only to the distinctive roles of professors and universities. Yet first amendment academic freedom can be viewed doctrinally as an aspect of a developing but

---

3. *Keyishian v Board of Regents*, 385 US 589, 603 (1967).
4. See Byrne, 99 Yale L J 251 (cited in note 1); Metzger, 66 Tex L Rev 1265 (cited in note 1).
5. Byrne, 99 Yale L J 251 (cited in note 1).

insufficiently appreciated judicial trend to construe the first amendment in institutional context. Universities are not the only institutions to which special first amendment rules apply. Courts have increasingly observed that the level of first amendment protection varies with the functions of institutions. Newspapers and libraries, for example, are subject to very different first amendment standards than military bases and prisons. Similarly, the Supreme Court has frequently distinguished institutional functions in explaining why more restrictions on speech are appropriate in elementary and secondary schools than in universities. In a meaningful sense, first amendment academic freedom is only an illustration of the general first amendment principle that special rules about speech must be tailored to the distinctive functions of various institutions. First amendment academic freedom is "special," but so are the free speech rules that apply in other institutions with different functions. These other free speech rules may not have been separately named, as the Supreme Court has specifically extolled "academic freedom," but they serve the similar purpose of applying the first amendment in institutional context.

After attempting to justify the Supreme Court's constitutionalization of academic freedom, I address the complicated circumstances in which first amendment academic freedom claims may arise and potentially conflict. Three basic categories stand out: claims of professors against faculty colleagues, administrators, or trustees; claims of professors against the state; and claims of universities against the state. The state action necessary to invoke the first amendment exists in all three categories of claims at public universities. In private universities, by contrast, state action applies only to claims by professors and universities against the state. Claims by professors at private institutions against faculty colleagues, administrators, or trustees cannot raise first amendment issues because no state action exists. Yet a private university can assert institutional academic freedom as a defense to judicial review of faculty claims that the university violated its contractual commitments to academic freedom. The state action requirement, in addition to complicating constitutional analysis, illustrates one major difference between the constitutional definition of academic freedom and the professional one, which applies equally in public and private universities.

Constitutional analysis is further complicated because public universities may invoke the first amendment to assert independence from the states that create them, and simultaneously are themselves state institutions constrained by the first amendment. For example, state universities may be subject to some legislative controls from which private universities are constitutionally protected. Yet the first amendment might also require state universities to allow more diversity of thought than private universities. Although I address these important issues, I focus on competing first amendment academic freedom claims between individual professors and state universities, which provide the context of most current disputes. I analyze claims by professors that university decisions justified on academic grounds in fact violate academic freedom. Some of these claims allege that the justifications are pretexts, while others allege that the stated grounds themselves reflect impermissible intellectual orthodoxies inconsistent with academic freedom. I conclude by considering attempts to extend individual academic freedom beyond teaching and scholarship to speech on university affairs generally and to faculty participation in university governance.

II

THE THEORY OF ACADEMIC FREEDOM IN THE AAUP's 1915 DECLARATION

The AAUP's 1915 Declaration of Principles,[6] the first comprehensive analysis of academic freedom in the United States, remains the foundation for the nonlegal understanding of academic freedom within the academic world. Adapting the German concept of academic freedom to the American context, the 1915 Declaration limited itself to the academic freedom of the professor, while recognizing that student academic freedom had been a major component of the German tradition. The 1915 Declaration identified three elements of academic freedom: "freedom of inquiry and research; freedom of teaching within the university or college; and freedom of extramural utterance and action." The authors explained their inclusion of extramural freedom, which had not been part of the German understanding of faculty academic freedom, by observing that this issue had arisen more frequently than the other two in the five investigations of university controversies already completed by AAUP committees during the year since the association's founding.[7]

The 1915 Declaration defined academic freedom in relation to the functions of professors and universities. It viewed the basic role of professors as sharing the results of their independent and expert scholarly investigations with students and the general public.[8] Academic freedom, it added, serves the fundamental purposes of universities, identified as promoting inquiry and knowledge, providing instruction to students, and, reflecting a key theme of the progressive era, developing experts for public service.[9] Throughout this discussion, the 1915 Declaration stressed the social benefits of scholarly work in universities. Education and knowledge, it reiterated, are essential to a civilized and democratic society.[10] In florid but deeply felt language, the 1915

---

6. AAUP, *Declaration of Principles* (1915), reprinted in Louis Joughin, ed, *Academic Freedom and Tenure*, app A at 157-76 (Univ of Wisconsin Press, 1969) ("1915 Declaration"); see Appendix A, 53 L & Contemp Probs 393 (Summer 1990) ("Appendix A").

7. 1915 Declaration at 157-58; Appendix A at 393 (cited in note 6). Metzger, 66 Tex L Rev at 1275 (cited in note 1), rather than the 1915 Declaration itself, highlights the inclusion of extramural freedom as an addition to the German model. See also Walter P. Metzger, *The German Contribution to the American Theory of Academic Freedom*, in Walter P. Metzger, ed, *The American Concept of Academic Freedom* (Arno Press, 1977).

8. 1915 Declaration at 162; Appendix A at 396 (cited in note 6).

9. 1915 Declaration at 163-64; Appendix A at 397, 398 (cited in note 6).

10. 1915 Declaration at 161, 163, 166-68; Appendix A at 396, 397-99 (cited in note 6).

Declaration emphasized that the university "should be an intellectual experiment station, where new ideas may germinate and where their fruit, though still distasteful to the community as a whole, may be allowed to ripen until finally, perchance, it may become a part of the accepted intellectual food of the nation or of the world." Yet the 1915 Declaration simultaneously cautioned that the university also makes a social contribution by conserving unfashionable but valuable intellectual traditions and by checking both the hasty impulses of popular opinion and the tendency toward conformity in modern democracies.[11]

The 1915 Declaration identified threats to academic freedom as impediments to these functions. It focused primarily on boards of trustees, the acknowledged source of power in universities.[12] Unfortunately, trustees, who should view themselves as holders of a public trust in private as well as in public institutions, too often acted as if they were simply autocratic employers. Many trustees felt free to use the power of dismissal to impose their personal ideological and pedagogical views on professors. Such a conception of the university as the equivalent of "an ordinary business venture," the 1915 Declaration protested, reveals "a radical failure to apprehend the nature of the social function discharged by the professional scholar."[13] Professorial opinions lose their value if any suspicion exists that they are not the product of free scholarly inquiry but are guided by the untrained and self-interested views of others. Professors, like judges, should be regarded as appointees rather than as employees, because both professors and judges must remain independent of their nominal employers in order to perform their professional functions. It is as inappropriate for trustees to dictate conclusions to a professor as it is for the president to dictate legal reasoning to the judges he appoints. Correspondingly, neither trustees nor presidents are responsible for the opinions their appointees express.[14]

Although the 1915 Declaration focused on trustees, it also identified the threat posed by legislatures to academic freedom in state universities. Observing the dependence of state universities on legislative funding, the 1915 Declaration worried that legislators might try to use the state's purse strings to manipulate the academic inquiries of professors, particularly when scholarly views might deviate from strong public opinions or from established government policies. While trustee interference with academic freedom would typically derive from the opposition of businessmen to the more liberal social and economic views of professors,[15] state and public pressure would

---

11. 1915 Declaration at 167-68; Appendix A at 400 (cited in note 6).

12. Metzger, 66 Tex L Rev at 1276-78 (cited in note 1) makes clear that the drafters of the 1915 Declaration decided not to challenge lay legal control of universities. Convinced about the certain failure of any such challenge, they accepted that " 'outside' was ensconsed within." Id at 1277.

13. 1915 Declaration at 161; Appendix A at 396 (cited in note 6).

14. See generally 1915 Declaration at 160-63; Appendix A at 397 (cited in note 6).

15. The 1915 Declaration observed that ecclesiastical interference with philosophy and the natural sciences constituted the main threat to academic freedom in earlier periods of American history. 1915 Declaration at 165-66; Appendix A at 399-400 (cited in note 6).

predictably threaten conservative professors who disagree with a political program of reform. Whatever the ideological source of these pressures on academic freedom, the 1915 Declaration emphasized, the university should be an "inviolable refuge" for independent scholarly investigation.[16]

The committee of professors who drafted the 1915 Declaration made a special point of dissociating academic freedom from broad claims of faculty autonomy. "It is," they maintained, "in no sense the contention of this committee that academic freedom implies that individual teachers should be exempt from all restraints as to the matter or manner of their utterances, either within or without the university."[17] Professors who fail to meet scholarly standards of competence, or who abuse their positions to indoctrinate students, cannot claim the protection of academic freedom and can be disciplined.[18] Yet while lay governing boards are competent to evaluate disputes over morals or neglect of duties, controversies involving the expression of scholarly opinion must be judged, at least initially, by professional peers, who alone have the necessary qualifications. Assigning this responsibility to others inevitably raises the suspicion of a decision based on irrelevant and improper motives.[19]

After substantial internal debate, the drafters of the 1915 Declaration decided that the academic freedom they were extending to extramural utterances should not be limited to subjects within a scholar's professional specialties. Some expressed concern that broad protection for extramural utterances would encourage professors to speak irresponsibly beyond their expertise and would unjustifiably give them more rights to political expression than other employees. The view that ultimately prevailed acknowledged the "obvious" point that professors speaking outside the university "are under a peculiar obligation to avoid hasty or unverified or exaggerated statements, and to refrain from intemperate or sensational modes of expression." But the 1915 Declaration also quoted with approval the conclusion of a Wisconsin state agency that "it is neither possible nor desirable to deprive a college professor of the political rights vouchsafed to every citizen."[20]

In context, this quotation was seriously misleading. Existing law made clear that both public and private employees could be fired by employers for speech the employees were free to make as citizens. In Holmes's famous phrase, "petitioner may have a constitutional right to talk politics, but he has no constitutional right to be a policeman."[21] Holmes could have made the

---

16. 1915 Declaration at 167-68; Appendix A at 400 (cited in note 6).
17. 1915 Declaration at 173; Appendix A at 404 (cited in note 6).
18. See 1915 Declaration at 170, 173; Appendix A at 402, 404 (cited in note 6).
19. 1915 Declaration at 173-74; Appendix A at 404-05 (cited in note 6); see David M. Rabban, *Does Academic Freedom Limit Faculty Autonomy?*, 66 Tex L Rev 1405, 1408-12 (1988) (discussing limits on faculty autonomy in 1915 Declaration's conception of academic freedom).
20. 1915 Declaration at 172; Appendix A at 404 (cited in note 6). The 1915 Declaration left open to future consideration whether professors should take prominent roles in political parties or run for public office. Id.
21. *McAuliffe v Mayor of New Bedford*, 155 Mass 216, 220, 29 NE 517, 518 (1892).

same statement had the petitioner been a university professor. Perhaps for this reason, and because professors actually were being dismissed for extramural speech unrelated to teaching or research, the 1915 Declaration "stretched the cloak of protection over an area in which academics proved to be most exposed."[22]

The 1915 Declaration conceded that some universities were endowed expressly to propagate certain doctrines, citing as examples universities sponsored by religious denominations, a school established by a manufacturer to advocate a protective tariff, and an institution funded to advance socialism. The 1915 Declaration explicitly refused to comment about whether such "proprietary institutions" should exist, though it did observe that they were becoming increasingly rare. Rather, it emphasized that they "should not be permitted to sail under false colors." Proprietary institutions, which are devoted to the inculcation of ideas, must be distinguished from "ordinary institutions of learning," which are committed to critical inquiry. Any university that denies academic freedom to its faculty, the 1915 Declaration insisted, is a proprietary institution that does not perform the functions of a true university and thus does not merit public support.[23]

III

Constitutionalizing Academic Freedom

The term "academic freedom" first attracted constitutional attention during the 1950s, in connection with the more general response by the Supreme Court to government investigations of alleged communist conspiracies.[24] Yet even Supreme Court decisions that mentioned academic

22. Metzger, 66 Tex L Rev at 1276 (cited in note 1). Although Professor Arthur Lovejoy played a crucial role in convincing his collaborators on the 1915 Declaration to take this position, he subsequently defined academic freedom as limited to teaching and research. Arthur O. Lovejoy, *Academic Freedom*, in Edwin R. A. Seligman, ed, 1 *Encyclopedia of the Social Sciences* 384 (MacMillan, 1930). See Metzger, 66 Tex L Rev at 1275 n23, 1276 (cited in note 1). William W. Van Alstyne, *The Specific Theory of Academic Freedom and the General Issue of Civil Liberty*, in Edmund L. Pincoffs, ed, *The Concept of Academic Freedom* 59, 61-63 (University of Texas Press, 1972) ("*The Specific Theory of Academic Freedom*"), criticizes the extension of academic freedom in the 1915 Declaration to include "aprofessional political liberties."

23. 1915 Declaration at 158-60; Appendix A at 394-95 (cited in note 6). In contrast to the usage of the 1915 Declaration, "proprietary" normally refers to institutions that are organized for profit. See *Marjorie Webster Jr. College v Middle States Ass'n of Colleges and Secondary Schools, Inc.*, 432 F2d 650 (DC Cir 1970) (challenge by proprietary junior college to policy limiting accreditation to nonprofit institutions).

24. Prior Supreme Court decisions, without referring to the first amendment or to academic freedom, protected both teachers and educational institutions from state interference. Chief Justice Marshall's famous opinion in the Dartmouth College case was an early example. *Trustees of Dartmouth College v Woodward*, 17 US (4 Wheat) 518, 652 (1819) (relying on impairment of contracts clause of U.S. Constitution to uphold "will of the donors" against "will of the state"). Several decisions in the 1920s relied on the due process clause of the 14th amendment to invalidate state laws regulating education. See, for example, *Farrington v Tokushige*, 273 US 284 (1927) (invalidating state regulation of instruction and curriculum in foreign language schools); *Pierce v Society of Sisters*, 268 US 510 (1925) (invalidating state law compelling public school attendance); *Meyer v Nebraska*, 262 US 390 (1923) (invalidating state law prohibiting instruction in foreign language before eighth grade). Many scholars have emphasized that these decisions constitutionally safeguarded institutional autonomy and pluralism. See, for example, Mark G. Yudof, *When Government Speaks: Politics, Law, and Government*

freedom did not focus on its meaning. The holdings in those cases were based on traditional constitutional doctrines involving political expression,[25] due process,[26] and the privilege against self-incrimination.[27] The few opinions that invoked academic freedom did so more for rhetorical effect than as an aid to constitutional analysis. Some of these opinions, however, identified academic freedom as a distinctive right within the first amendment and applied the concept to both individuals and institutions. For example, in *Sweezy v. New Hampshire*, the Supreme Court decision that initially incorporated academic freedom within the first amendment, the plurality opinion referred to a lecturer's personal "liberties in the areas of academic freedom and political expression" and added that "[t]he essentiality of freedom in the community of American universities is almost self-evident."[28]

The relationship between the theory of academic freedom elaborated in the 1915 Declaration and the new constitutional right of academic freedom under the first amendment remains unclear.[29] Courts have used academic freedom and free speech interchangeably or ambiguously, have attached

---

Expression in America 227-30 (Univ of Cal Press, 1983); Matthew W. Finkin, *On "Institutional" Academic Freedom*, 61 Tex L Rev 817, 830-40 (1983); Stephen R. Goldstein, *The Asserted Constitutional Right of Public School Teachers to Determine What They Teach*, 124 U Pa L Rev 1293, 1305-09 (1976); William W. Van Alstyne, *Academic Freedom and the First Amendment in the Supreme Court of the United States: An Unhurried Historical Review*, 53 L & Contemp Probs 79, 88-93 (Summer 1990); Mark G. Yudof, *Three Faces of Academic Freedom*, 32 Loyola L Rev 831, 852-53 (1987).

25. See, for example, *Barenblatt v United States*, 360 US 109 (1959); *Sweezy v New Hampshire*, 354 US 234 (1957); *Adler v Board of Educ.*, 342 US 485 (1952).

26. See, for example, *Wieman v Updegraff*, 344 US 183 (1952).

27. See, for example, *Slochower v Board of Educ.*, 350 US 551 (1956). The treatment in constitutional law casebooks of the early Supreme Court decisions mentioning academic freedom reinforces the perception that these cases were primarily about other issues. See, for example, Paul Brest & Sanford Levinson, *Processes of Constitutional Decisionmaking* 1102-09 (Little Brown, 2d ed 1983) (treating Barenblatt under heading "Can the state require speech or expression from an unwilling citizen?"); Gerald Gunther, *Constitutional Law* 1406-10 (Foundation Press, 11th ed 1985) (treating *Sweezy* and *Barenblatt* under heading "legislative investigations"), 1364-66 (treating *Wieman* and *Slochower* under heading "government demands for information and affirmation"); William Lockhart, et al, *Constitutional Law* 983-87 (West, 6th ed 1986) (treating *Barenblatt* under heading "government mandated disclosures and freedom of association"); Geoffrey R. Stone, et al, *Constitutional Law* 1316-18 (Little Brown, 1986) (treating *Sweezy* and *Barenblatt* under heading "legislative investigations"), 1288 (treating *Adler* and *Wieman* under heading "subversive advocacy and association").

In his comprehensive treatise, Professor Tribe does not have a separate section on academic freedom. Rather, he discusses academic freedom in a lengthy footnote in a section entitled "distinguishing government's addition of its own voice from government's silencing of others." Laurence Tribe, *American Constitutional Law* 812-13 n32 (Foundation Press, 2d ed 1988).

28. *Sweezy*, 354 US at 250. See Rabban, *Academic Freedom* at 13 (cited in note 1).

Professors interested in academic freedom immediately recognized the importance of *Sweezy*. "To the members of the academic profession," wrote a professor at Dartmouth College who had served as general secretary of the AAUP,

> *Sweezy v New Hampshire* is quite possibly the most significant decision ever rendered by the Supreme Court. Here for the first time in history a majority of the Court indicates its conviction that academic freedom is protected by the First and Fourteenth Amendments of the Constitution against encroachment by either the federal or state governments.

Robert K. Carr, *Academic Freedom, the American Association of University Professors, and the United States Supreme Court*, 45 AAUP Bull 5, 17 (1959).

29. Byrne, 99 Yale L J 251 (cited in note 1), presents the fullest discussion of the relationship between the AAUP definition and the constitutional definition of academic freedom. Metzger, 66 Tex L Rev 1265 (cited in note 1), provides an excellent taxonomy of these two definitions while emphasizing how they differ rather than how they relate. See especially id at 1267.

academic freedom to professors as well as to universities, and have extended it to teachers in public schools and to students generally without considering how its meaning might differ in these various contexts.[30] In my opinion, a convincing justification for constitutional academic freedom requires a thorough comparison of general first amendment theories with nonlegal theories of academic freedom, yielding conclusions about where these various theories do and do not overlap.[31] I do not attempt such an ambitious task here. But some conception of constitutional academic freedom is necessary to analyze the relationship between the individual academic freedom of the professor and the institutional academic freedom of the university, which is the primary concern of this article. I therefore do consider reasons for protecting academic freedom under the first amendment.

Fitting academic freedom within the rubric of the first amendment is in many respects an extremely difficult challenge. The term "academic freedom," in obvious contrast to "freedom of the press," is nowhere mentioned in the text of the first amendment. It is inconceivable that those who debated and ratified the first amendment thought about academic freedom. Indeed, before the Civil War, when most institutions of higher education were denominational colleges, "the problem of academic freedom as we now understand it was hardly posed"[32] even as a nonlegal matter. These colleges were what the subsequent 1915 Declaration labeled "proprietary," concerned with conserving truth rather than with searching for it. They did not allow intellectual freedom, and their faculties typically did not seek it. Notions of academic freedom, to the extent they existed at all, were associated with institutional autonomy from the democratic vulgarity of the broader society. Only with the emergence of the modern research university in the late nineteenth century did a comprehensive theory of academic freedom, expressed most thoroughly in the 1915 Declaration, emerge in the United States. It took an "educational revolution"[33] following the Civil War to produce the commitment to critical inquiry central to the modern rationale for academic freedom,[34] and arguably related to general free speech theories contained within the first amendment. "It may put some of our current difficulties into perspective," wrote the authors of the leading history of American academic freedom just before the Supreme Court gave the term constitutional meaning, "that the academic freedom which is now

---

30. See Metzger, 66 Tex L Rev at 1291-1322 (cited in note 1); Rabban, *Academic Freedom* at 12 (cited in note 1). Professor Metzger offers a particularly thorough analysis of the many contexts in which the Supreme Court has considered academic freedom claims. In my opinion, he provides a more coherent synthesis and rationale for the Court's decisions addressing academic freedom and free speech at schools and universities than the justices themselves intended or than the cases allow.

31. One obvious difference between the professional and constitutional definitions of academic freedom is that the first amendment, through its incorporation in the 14th amendment, applies only to state action. The professional definition of academic freedom, by contrast, has no state action requirement.

32. Richard Hofstadter & Walter P. Metzger, *Preface*, v, to Walter P. Metzger, *Academic Freedom in the Age of the University* (Columbia, 1961) ("*Age of the University*").

33. Id at vi.

34. Id at v-vi; Metzger, *Age of the University* at 42-44 (cited in note 32).

under fire is not an ancient prerogative but an acquisition of relatively recent date."[35]

A constitutional theory of academic freedom, moreover, understandably implies to many a special first amendment right unique to professors and universities. The free speech guaranteed by the first amendment is generally thought to apply equally to all citizens.[36] Indeed, even the specific protection for the press provided in a separate clause of the first amendment has been read as providing no greater rights to publishers and journalists than the free speech clause guarantees other citizens.[37] In these historical and legal circumstances, it would not have been surprising had the Supreme Court refused to recognize a discrete though unenumerated first amendment right of academic freedom. Even those who defend the extension of first amendment protection to academic freedom would have had difficulty criticizing the Court had it declined to do so.

The AAUP itself, based on more pragmatic concerns, was divided about whether to seek constitutional protection for academic freedom. It decided not to submit an amicus brief in *Sweezy*, in part because it reasonably concluded that the Court was unlikely to address the constitutional implications of academic freedom for the first time,[38] but also because it worried about judicial appropriation of a concept the AAUP had largely defined and successfully advocated throughout the academic world. Even a favorable definition of academic freedom under the first amendment would be subject to further judicial interpretation. What the Court gave, many within the AAUP worried, it could also take away. Relatedly, constitutional recognition of academic freedom could prompt many within the university community to abandon any continuing independent effort to define and refine this crucial concept. The constitutional meaning of academic freedom could displace rather than complement the one set forth in the 1915 Declaration and accepted in the institutional regulations of many universities. Principles of academic freedom not incorporated into the first amendment could thereby be abandoned entirely. For these reasons, many within the AAUP feared that academic freedom would be weakened through judicial constitution-alization.[39]

By identifying academic freedom as a first amendment right, the Supreme Court in *Sweezy* rendered moot the AAUP's reservations about whether to argue for this position. Subsequent decisions, including one that denied a professor's first amendment claim,[40] have reinforced the incorporation of

---

35. Hofstadter & Metzger, *Preface* at vi (cited in note 32).

36. See generally Kenneth L. Karst, *Equality as a Central Principle in the First Amendment*, 43 U Chi L Rev 20 (1975).

37. See text accompanying notes 93-97.

38. Dissenting in a previous case, Justice Douglas objected that a New York law would "raise havoc with academic freedom," but he did not suggest that academic freedom had constitutional dimensions. *Adler v Board of Educ.*, 342 US 485, 509 (1952) (Douglas dissenting).

39. Carr, 45 AAUP Bull at 5, 6, 19-20 (cited in note 28).

40. *Barenblatt*, 360 US at 112.

academic freedom into the first amendment, mostly through additional rhetorical flourishes. Yet some language in Supreme Court decisions suggests the reasoning behind this incorporation, often using terms that echo the 1915 Declaration and indicate close parallels between the justification for academic freedom in the 1915 Declaration and basic themes of general first amendment theory.

One paragraph of Chief Justice Warren's plurality opinion in *Sweezy* contains the Court's fullest discussion of academic freedom.

> The essentiality of freedom in the community of American universities is almost self-evident. No one should underestimate the vital role in a democracy that is played by those who guide and train our youth. To impose any strait jacket upon the intellectual leaders in our colleges and universities would imperil the future of our Nation. No field of education is so thoroughly comprehended by man that new discoveries cannot yet be made. Particularly is that true in the social sciences, where few, if any, principles are accepted as absolutes. Scholarship cannot flourish in an atmosphere of suspicion and distrust. Teachers and students must always remain free to inquire, to study and to evaluate, to gain new maturity and understanding; otherwise our civilization will stagnate and die.[41]

This crucial paragraph, though not very helpful in clarifying the relationship between the new constitutional analysis of academic freedom and its traditional meaning within the university community, does seem to identify two distinct social benefits of academic freedom. Critical inquiry within universities is essential to the preservation of a democratic society and, as a somewhat independent matter, promotes discoveries and understanding necessary for civilization. Justice Frankfurter's famous concurring opinion in *Sweezy* reiterated both themes. Frankfurter invoked democratic values by stressing "the dependence of a free society on free universities,"[42] but focused primarily on knowledge and understanding in the full range of academic disciplines as social goods in themselves. Any "government intrusion into the intellectual life of a university," Frankfurter twice warned,[43] would jeopardize these essential functions of professors in universities.

The Court's next significant discussion of academic freedom under the first amendment, a decade later in *Keyishian v. Board of Regents*, quoted the key paragraph from the plurality opinion in *Sweezy* while emphasizing that academic freedom is "a special concern of the First Amendment, which does not tolerate laws that cast a pall of orthodoxy over the classroom." In describing academic freedom as "a transcendent value to all of us and not merely to the teachers concerned," the Court in *Keyishian* observed that the "classroom is peculiarly the 'marketplace of ideas.'" The future of the country, for reasons the Court did not elaborate, "depends upon leaders trained through wide exposure to that robust exchange of ideas which

---

41. *Sweezy*, 354 US at 250.

42. Id at 262. In an earlier concurrence that did not refer specifically to academic freedom, Justice Frankfurter, in an opinion joined by Justice Douglas, referred to teachers as "the priests of our democracy." Frankfurter emphasized "the special task of teachers to foster those habits of open-mindedness and critical inquiry which alone make for responsible citizens." *Wieman v Updegraff*, 344 US 183, 196 (1952) (Frankfurter concurring).

43. *Sweezy*, 354 US at 261, 262.

discovers truth 'out of a multitude of tongues, [rather] than through any kind of authoritative selection.' "[44]

These passages in *Sweezy* and *Keyishian*, though relatively brief and allusive, still remain the Court's fullest discussions of constitutional academic freedom. Like the 1915 Declaration, they emphasized the social importance of critical inquiry in universities in promoting knowledge and serving democratic values. Both the Supreme Court and the 1915 Declaration maintained that the search for truth, in universities as well as in society generally, is never complete and requires free debate about competing ideas that precludes any imposition of ideological orthodoxy. The judicial opinions and the 1915 Declaration even used similar metaphors. The description of the university in the 1915 Declaration as an "intellectual experiment station" closely resembles the description of the classroom in *Keyishian* as a "marketplace of ideas." Indeed, just as the 1915 Declaration stressed that universities should allow "ideas distasteful to the community as a whole" to "germinate" and perhaps ultimately to become generally accepted,[45] Justice Holmes, who created the marketplace metaphor for the first amendment invoked by the Court in *Keyishian*, stressed that society should allow "the expression of opinions that we loathe" because "the best test of truth is the power of the thought to get itself accepted in the competition of the market."[46]

The Court's use of the "marketplace of ideas" metaphor in *Keyishian* also underlined its view, apparent throughout its decisions, that its general free speech jurisprudence—particularly in relation to the search for knowledge and truth and to the key role of free expression in a democracy—applies to the specific context of academic freedom in universities. The Court in *Keyishian* reiterated in its crucial paragraph identifying academic freedom as "a special concern of the First Amendment" that the "vigilant protection of constitutional freedoms is nowhere more vital than in the community of American schools." This language strengthened the Court's identification of academic freedom with general first amendment values while exacerbating ambiguities about the relationship between them.[47]

The early Supreme Court opinions referring to academic freedom left many questions unanswered. The Court never clarified the relationships among the "special" constitutional right of academic freedom it read into the first amendment, the concept of academic freedom expressed in the 1915 Declaration and broadly accepted within American universities, and the general first amendment right of free speech. Despite significant parallels, these three concepts also contained differences. For example, the focus in the 1915 Declaration on the special training and competence of professors, and

---

44. 385 US 589, 603 (1967).
45. 1915 Declaration at 167-68; Appendix A at 400 (cited in note 6).
46. *Abrams v United States*, 250 US 616, 630 (1920) (Holmes dissenting).
47. 385 US at 603, quoting *Shelton v Tucker*, 364 US 479, 487 (1960). Without referring to academic freedom, Justice Frankfurter similarly emphasized in a previous case that teachers bring the safeguards for freedom of speech, inquiry, and thought in the first amendment "vividly into operation." *Wieman*, 344 US at 195 (Frankfurter concurring).

the corresponding importance of peer review to academic freedom, found no echo in Supreme Court opinions. The "marketplace of ideas" metaphor, though in some respects analogous to characterizing the university as an "intellectual experiment station," implies an equality of discourse appropriate in discussions of political ideas by citizens but insensitive to the relevant differences in expertise between professors and students in the classroom.[48] Numerous general principles of first amendment analysis, moreover, might have little or no relevance to the university context, or might even interfere with legitimate educational decisions by universities based on the content of speech.[49]

IV

A Functional Theory of Constitutional Academic Freedom

The Supreme Court's brief discussions of academic freedom, whatever their analytical shortcomings and lingering ambiguities, reveal sufficient parallels between academic freedom and the first amendment generally to justify, even if not to require, the Court's constitutionalization of academic freedom as "a special concern of the First Amendment."[50] Analyzing academic freedom in terms of the distinctive functions of professors and universities, which is the method of the 1915 Declaration, helps explain, as the Supreme Court never has, the sense in which the academic freedom incorporated into the first amendment is not simply synonymous with the free speech clause. This approach, essentially in agreement with Professor Van Alstyne's classic article, *The Specific Theory of Academic Freedom and the General Issue of Civil Liberty*, views the speech of professors on matters within their expertise as subject to both greater and lesser constitutional protection than the general speech of all citizens, including speech by professors that does not relate to professional issues.[51]

As the 1915 Declaration emphasized, the basic function of professors in universities—critical inquiry on subjects within their scholarly expertise and the dissemination of the results of their scholarship through teaching and publication—requires freedom from constraints that threaten the independence essential to performing this function. Such constraints would deny the general public the contribution to knowledge and democracy that academic work provides. These social benefits, which the Supreme Court recognized as fundamental first amendment values in *Sweezy* and *Keyishian* without tying them in detail to the actual functions of professors in

---

48. See Byrne, 99 Yale L J at 296-97 (cited in note 1).

49. See text accompanying notes 110, 124-25 (discussing emphasis by Justice Stevens on limited applicability of content neutrality in university context).

50. *Keyishian*, 385 US at 603.

51. Van Alstyne, *The Specific Theory of Academic Freedom* (cited in note 22). Byrne, 99 Yale L J at 263-65 (cited in note 1), agrees with Professor Van Alstyne's distinction between free speech and academic freedom.

universities, justify academic freedom under the first amendment as well as under the nonlegal analysis of the 1915 Declaration.

The requirement of scholarly independence for the proper performance of academic work entitles the professor to more freedom from employer control than enjoyed by the typical employee. It makes no sense to expect professors to engage in critical inquiry and simultaneously to allow punishment for its exercise.[52] First amendment academic freedom should preclude an administrator or trustee at a public university from forcing a professor to investigate a particular topic or to reach specified conclusions.[53] Conceivably, constitutional academic freedom might even protect professors at both public and private universities from laws that would apply to other citizens.[54] The owner of a movie theater could be punished for showing a film declared obscene by a jury in his community though protected by juries elsewhere, but a professor at the adjacent university might have an academic freedom right to show the same film in an advanced course on the regulation of mass media to make the intellectual point that the definition of obscenity involves close questions on which community standards vary.[55]

On the other hand, a professor speaking within his field of expertise may be disciplined without violating constitutional academic freedom for speech that otherwise would be protected under the free speech clause of the first amendment. "The price of an exceptional vocational freedom to speak the truth as one sees it," Professor Van Alstyne astutely observes, "is the cost of exceptional care in the representation of that 'truth,' a professional standard of care."[56] Grossly inaccurate speech about the Holocaust, for example, could be cause for dismissing a historian for incompetence, but not for taking any adverse action against a professor in the school of engineering or an employee of the municipal utility commission.[57]

---

52. Van Alstyne, *The Specific Theory of Academic Freedom* at 77 (cited in note 22).

53. Id at 75.

54. An attempt to enforce a law provides the state action that invokes the first amendment at private as well as public universities.

55. The AAUP filed an amicus brief in the Supreme Court of Florida challenging a lower court decision that upheld the seizure of the film "Deep Throat" from a professor of mass communications who had presented an optional viewing to students. The professor showed the movie to give students a "common frame of reference for debate, analogous to what a jury or appellate court might face in deliberating upon the obscenity of a particular work." *Roberts v State*, 373 S2d 672, 674 (Fla 1979). The AAUP claimed that even if the film were obscene, and therefore unprotected by the speech clause of the first amendment, the independent first amendment right of academic freedom safeguarded the professor from state action. AAUP's Brief as Amicus Curiae at 20-25, *Roberts v State*, 373 S2d 672 (Fla 1979). The Supreme Court of Florida found that the film was seized in violation of state law, and thus did not reach the constitutional question. 373 S2d at 674. Van Alstyne, *The Specific Theory of Academic Freedom* at 77-78 (cited in note 22), anticipated such a case.

56. Van Alstyne, *The Specific Theory of Academic Freedom* at 76 (cited in note 22).

57. In 1977, a professor of electrical engineering at Northwestern University wrote a book entitled *The Hoax of the Twentieth Century*, asserting that reports of the systematic killing of Jews in Nazi concentration camps were a myth promoted by Zionists to create support for a Jewish state in Palestine. Responding to protests about the university's failure to condemn the professor, its provost stated: "A faculty member's right to have his writing published is not an academic freedom issue. It is a right available to any citizen of the United States under the first amendment of the Constitution. It is a shame when that right is used to insult survivors of concentration camps." Ellen E. Coughlin, *Professor's Book on Holocaust Attacked at Northwestern U.*, Chron Higher Educ 6 (February 7,

Constitutional academic freedom thus may provide professors more protection for professional speech and less protection for unprofessional speech than the free speech clause would afford the same statements by nonacademics. Yet using the professional functions of professors to justify constitutional academic freedom means that their expressions on matters unrelated to professional concerns, though possibly covered by the free speech clause, have no status under this "special" first amendment right. An engineer who writes about the Holocaust or who shows a film declared obscene by a local jury has no different first amendment rights than other citizens, because neither expression by the engineer concerns his professional expertise.

This constitutional analysis deviates from the controversial position of the 1915 Declaration, subsequently reiterated by recent scholars,[58] that the protection of academic freedom should include the extramural speech of professors on subjects outside their academic specialties. Though the drafters of the 1915 Declaration reached this conclusion under the pressure of cases in which universities fired professors for such extramural statements, they apparently relied on a theoretical justification for their pragmatic position. Institutional neutrality, they implied, is the logical counterpart to the faculty independence protected by academic freedom. If faculty cannot be made to answer to the directives of administrators and trustees, then administrators and trustees should not be held responsible for what the faculty says.[59]

This approach, however, has a serious weakness under the logic of the 1915 Declaration itself. The 1915 Declaration repeatedly stressed that academic freedom is justified by the social contributions of expert and independent scholars. When professors do not speak as scholars, therefore, they are not engaging in speech to which academic freedom should apply. The value of institutional neutrality as a distinctive norm stresses that universities should not be held responsible for the aprofessional speech of professors, whether or not such speech is protected by law.[60] Institutional neutrality, however, relates to academic freedom only to the extent that a

---

1977). See Seth S. King, *Professor Stirs Furor by Saying Nazis' Slaying of Jews is a Myth*, New York Times A10 (January 28, 1977) (similar story); Walter Goodman, *Tenets of Tenure*, New York Times A22 (February 23, 1977) (editorial) (asserting that this professor was appropriately protected by tenure because he was not accused "of carrying out his appointed duties invidiously or incompetently").

58. See, for example, John R. Searle, *Two Concepts of Academic Freedom*, in Edmund L. Pincoffs, ed, *The Concept of Academic Freedom* 86-96 (cited in note 22).

59. The norm of institutional neutrality in the 1915 Declaration, though implicit throughout the document, is made explicit by Metzger, 66 Tex L Rev at 1280-81 (cited in note 1).

60. During World War I, President Lowell of Harvard risked the loss of a $10 million bequest by refusing to deprive an openly pro-German professor of his chair. "Either the university assumes full responsibility for permitting its professors to express certain opinions in public," Lowell wrote in his annual report, "or it assumes no responsibility whatever, and leaves them to be dealt with like other citizens by the public authorities according to the laws of the land." Metzger, *The Age of the University* at 228-29 (cited in note 32). Professor Metzger, following the AAUP conception of academic freedom, understandably views Lowell's moral courage as a rare defense of academic freedom during World War I. Id at 228. But I agree with Professor Van Alstyne that in this statement "Lowell was himself making an implicit distinction between alleged abuses of academic freedom (for which Harvard would doubtless admit its responsibility of review of its own faculty) and alleged abuses of

professor's speech, inside or outside the university, concerns a matter of professional expertise.

Whatever one's view about the application of academic freedom by the 1915 Declaration to the aprofessional extramural speech of professors, additional barriers to protecting such speech arise under a constitutional definition of academic freedom. The drafters of the 1915 Declaration did not have to address the free speech rights of other occupations. They could easily have conceded that the neutrality they urged for universities should also apply to other institutions, while adding that this issue was beyond the appropriate concern of the 1915 Declaration, which focused on the role of university professors. Yet the free speech clause of the first amendment, unlike the 1915 Declaration, covers the speech of all citizens. If academic freedom has a special meaning under the first amendment, it must be distinguished from the general free speech clause. The distinctive professional functions of professors provide the basis for applying a special first amendment concept to them. But what is the first amendment justification for treating the aprofessional speech of professors differently from the speech of anyone else?

The only plausible justification is that the line between professional and aprofessional speech may be controversial, and that protection for clearly aprofessional speech is needed to give "breathing room" to the professional speech that is the special subject of academic freedom. Such a drastic prophylactic rule is unnecessary and would be likely to generate more resentment against the "special pleading" of professors than even a narrow and convincing conception of academic freedom inevitably does. A generous definition of professional speech is a feasible and better response to this legitimate concern.

There are legitimate first amendment reasons for protecting the political speech of public employees generally. Indeed, the Supreme Court has done so while rejecting the "right/privilege" distinction popularized by Holmes. But as the Supreme Court has recognized, it is the free speech clause, not the special first amendment right of academic freedom, that provides the constitutional basis for this protection.[61]

V

HINTS OF JUDICIAL RECOGNITION OF A SPECIFIC THEORY OF ACADEMIC FREEDOM

The Supreme Court has not explicitly distinguished the specific theory of academic freedom from the general protection of the first amendment, and often refers interchangeably to academic freedom and the right to political expression. Yet, as a number of recent lower court decisions indicate, the judicial application of a specific theory of academic freedom would require

---

free speech and the general issue of civil liberty." Van Alstyne, *The Specific Theory of Academic Freedom* at 80 (cited in note 22).

61. See Van Alstyne, *The Specific Theory of Academic Freedom* at 68-70, 80-81 (cited in note 22).

only an elaboration, rather than a reversal, of the current undifferentiated approach. For example, cases involving the rejection of Marxist candidates for appointment have observed that universities violate academic freedom by discharging or refusing to hire a professor "because of his or her political, philosophical, or ideological beliefs."[62] Typically, these cases did not attempt to identify whether the Marxist speech related to academic or political issues. The opinions did reflect, however, the conclusion that the professors' Marxist views are protected by the first amendment in both contexts. It would not be difficult for courts to refine this approach by applying the specific theory of academic freedom to Marxist speech by professors on professional matters, and general first amendment principles to Marxist speech by professors on aprofessional, political issues.

Some decisions, moreover, have protected the specifically academic speech of professors. The first case produced by the recent wave of institutional policies on offensive speech focused on their impact in the classroom. For example, a teaching assistant in a course entitled "Comparative Animal Behavior" wanted to include as a topic in his discussion group the hypothesis that biological differences account for the greater ability of men than of women to perform certain mental tasks based on spatial relationships. The teaching assistant argued, and the judge agreed, that some students and teachers would regard this theory as sexist and that its presentation could subject him to prosecution for harassment under applicable university policies. Without referring explicitly to academic freedom, the judge held that the university policies violated the first amendment.[63]

Other cases do cite academic freedom in addressing the first amendment protection for academic speech and seem at least implicitly to recognize a distinction between academic freedom and general free speech under the first amendment. Judge Posner indicated that first amendment academic freedom may give professors more protection than the first amendment provides to members of the general public. He reasoned that professors may express ideas in places on campus that are not public forums and from which members of the general public may therefore be excluded.[64] Another judge identified more directly a distinction between academic freedom and general first amendment rights. He based his finding of a general first amendment violation on the university's failure to renew the appointment of a Marxist professor due to his aprofessional speech and associations: his belief in communism and his membership in the Progressive Labor Party. This conclusion allowed the judge to finesse the university's claim that it acted because the professor inappropriately injected Marxism into the classroom.

---

62. *Ollman v Toll*, 518 F Supp 1196, 1202 (D Md 1981), aff'd, 704 F2d 139 (4th Cir 1983); *Franklin v Atkins*, 409 F Supp 439, 445 (D Colo 1976), aff'd, 562 F2d 1188 (10th Cir 1977). Both opinions borrowed this language from Justice Douglas's dissent in *Board of Regents v Roth*, 408 US 564, 581 (1972).

63. *Doe v University of Michigan*, 721 F Supp 852, 860, 864-67 (ED Mich 1989).

64. *Piarowski v Illinois Community College Dist.*, 759 F2d 625, 629-31 (7th Cir 1985).

The judge assumed, without deciding, that teaching history from a Marxist orientation would be covered under the first amendment's protection of academic freedom, especially given the fact that other professors in the university's history department taught their courses from various competing perspectives.[65]

Another judge implicitly acknowledged the added limitations on professors imposed by a specific theory of academic freedom. A faculty member claimed that the department of political science denied him tenure because he had associated with the Central Intelligence Agency. In a separate opinion, Judge Kaufman criticized the majority for assuming, without deciding, that this association is protected by the first amendment. According to Judge Kaufman, the candidate's behavior in covertly providing to the CIA information he gathered during academic trips abroad cast legitimate doubt on his commitment to the goals and principles of scholarship, threatened the scholarly pursuits of his colleagues, and unjustifiably inhibited departmental collegiality. Judge Kaufman did not address the relationship between the first amendment and academic freedom. Yet his reasoning closely parallels Professor Van Alstyne's more fully elaborated position that the social value of critical inquiry justifying constitutional protection for individual academic freedom may constrain professors in ways that would be left unrestricted by the application of the general first amendment rights of speech and association to other citizens.[66]

These recent judicial opinions identify the importance of academic speech by professors, occasionally distinguish it from speech in other contexts, and recognize that it may be subject to both greater and lesser protection than the first amendment usually provides. They are cause for optimism that courts can develop a coherent and convincing specific conception of constitutional academic freedom under the first amendment that differs from the free speech rights all citizens possess.

VI

Constitutional Academic Freedom As a Specific Instance of the First Amendment in Institutional Context

The distinctive functions of professors and universities provide a convincing justification for the Court's ambiguous incorporation of academic freedom as "a special concern" of the first amendment. Yet special treatment for a particular occupation or institution, even if analytically sound under general first amendment principles, creates understandable skepticism, especially given the accurate perception that citizens have rights to equal protection under the first amendment. The argument for a constitutional right of academic freedom can be substantially strengthened by viewing it not

---

65. *Cooper v Ross*, 472 F Supp 802, 813-14 (ED Ark 1979).
66. *Selzer v Fleisher*, 629 F2d 809, 814-17 (2d Cir 1980) (Kaufman concurring in part and dissenting in part).

primarily as a special right unique to professors, but as a specific application of the broader principle that the institutional context of speech often has first amendment significance. Under this approach, constitutional academic freedom is simply a convenient name to describe special speech rules governed by the functions of professors and universities, just as other special speech rules, which may not have been separately named, are required by the distinctive yet different functions of institutions as varied as prisons, libraries, the military, the civil service, public schools, and the media.

A. *Tinker* and Its Progeny

The role of institutional context in first amendment interpretation, though made clear by many Supreme Court decisions, has not been sufficiently highlighted in first amendment theory.[67] The Court's most explicit recognition of institutional context occurred in *Tinker v. Des Moines Independent Community School District*, a case upholding the right of junior and senior high school students to wear black armbands to protest American involvement in Vietnam. The Court reasoned that the first amendment rights of teachers and students, which they do not "shed . . . at the schoolhouse gate," must be "applied in light of the special characteristics of the school environment."[68] While stressing the legitimate need of school officials to punish speech that interferes with educational functions, the Court did not find any evidence in the record that wearing the armbands would cause such interference. The Court insisted that "a mere desire to avoid the discomfort and unpleasantness that always accompany an unpopular viewpoint" did not constitute a sufficient reason to give students lesser first amendment rights in the school environment than elsewhere.[69]

While some cases, like *Tinker* itself, conclude in a particular factual setting that the "special characteristics" of an institution do not require any modification of general first amendment rights,[70] other cases, frequently citing *Tinker*, have emphasized that first amendment protections vary with institutional context. Decisions make clear, for example, that the functions of

---

67. Robert C. Post, *Between Governance and Management: The History and Theory of the Public Forum*, 34 UCLA L Rev 1713 (1987), is a major exception. Professor Post stresses that the government can regulate speech to achieve the effective functioning of its own institutions. See also C. Edwin Baker, *Press Rights and Government Power to Structure the Press*, 34 U Miami L Rev 819, 824 (1980) (asserting first amendment's press clause can be interpreted "as granting special constitutional protection to a particular institution, the press"); Stanley Ingber, *Rediscovering the Communal Worth of Individual Rights: The First Amendment in Institutional Contexts*, 69 Tex L Rev 1, 101-02 (1990) (arguing communal as well as individual interests should be weighed in evaluating claims that institutional functions require constraints on speech).

68. *Tinker v Des Moines School Dist.*, 393 US 503, 506 (1969).

69. Id at 509. In his dissent, Justice Black disagreed with the majority's characterization of the record. Citing specific incidents, Black claimed that the record contained overwhelming evidence that the armbands "took the students' minds off their classwork and diverted them to thoughts about the highly emotional subject of the Vietnam war." Id at 518.

70. See, for example, *Wood v Georgia*, 370 US 375, 393-94 (1962) (sheriff's job responsibilities in administration of justice do not impose fewer first amendment rights than other citizens to criticize judicial behavior; no evidence suggests sheriff's criticisms interfered with proper performance of his official functions).

the media and libraries require substantial scope for the exercise of free expression, while the functions of the military and prisons justify restrictions on speech citizens otherwise enjoy.

Two cases since *Tinker* illustrate that its focus on "the special characteristics of the school environment" can limit as well as protect the first amendment rights of students. While reiterating that tolerance of divergent views are among the fundamental democratic values schools should inculcate,[71] the Court has held that "pervasive sexual innuendo"[72] in a student speech at a high school assembly could sufficiently "undermine the school's basic educational mission"[73] to justify the student's suspension. This "vulgar and lewd"[74] language occurred during a speech nominating another student for an office in the school's student government. The Court acknowledged that the first amendment would protect the identical speech uttered by an adult during a political campaign, but denied that "the same latitude must be permitted to children in a public school."[75]

In a subsequent case, the Court upheld the decision by a high school principal to censor from a school newspaper stories dealing with pregnancy and divorce. The Court reasoned that the first amendment does not apply to "school-sponsored expressive activities" if the actions by the school authorities "are reasonably related to legitimate pedagogical concerns."[76] Emphasizing that the standards for student speech disseminated under school auspices legitimately "may be higher than those demanded by some newspaper publishers or theatrical producers in the 'real' world,"[77] the Court upheld the principal's conclusion that the student editors had failed to follow sound journalistic practices regarding the treatment of controversial issues and the need to protect personal privacy.[78]

The Court has relied on the special characteristics of several other institutions to limit first amendment rights. In denying protection to antiwar speech at a military base, the Court reasoned that "the different character of the military community and of the military mission requires a different application" of the first amendment. The fundamental military requirements of obedience and discipline, the Court added, "may render permissible within the military that which would be constitutionally impermissible outside it."[79]

---

71. *Bethel School Dist. v Fraser*, 478 US 675, 681 (1986).

72. Id at 683.

73. Id at 685.

74. Id.

75. Id at 682.

76. *Hazelwood School Dist. v Kuhlmeier*, 484 US 260, 273 (1988). The Court distinguished the school-sponsored student expression in *Hazelwood* from the nonsponsored student expression in *Tinker*. Id at 272-73.

77. Id at 272.

78. Id at 276. Dissenting, Justice Brennan asserted that the school "censorship served no legitimate pedagogical purpose." Id at 289.

79. *Parker v Levy*, 417 US 733, 758 (1974). The Court subsequently cited the military interest in troop readiness in rejecting a first amendment challenge to regulations requiring Air Force personnel to receive approval from their commanders before circulating petitions on Air Force bases. *Brown v Glines*, 444 US 348 (1980).

The Court similarly has held that a prison inmate retains first amendment rights only to the extent that they "are not inconsistent with his status as a prisoner or with the legitimate penological objectives of the corrections system."[80] Upholding regulations forbidding press interviews with individual inmates, the Court observed that under prior, less restrictive rules, inmates who were interviewed gained notoriety and influence within the prison and became severe disciplinary problems.[81]

In a context far less generally restrictive than a military base or a prison, the Court also relied on special institutional functions to reject a first amendment attack on prohibitions in the Hatch Act[82] against active participation by civil servants in partisan political activities. The Court agreed with the legislative judgment that these prohibitions are justified by the valid purposes of preventing improper influence and corruption while preserving efficient and effective government services.[83]

On the other hand, a Court plurality has cited the emphasis in *Tinker* on institutional context to provide greater first amendment rights in a school library than in a classroom. A local school board cannot remove books from a school library, the opinion reasoned, because "the special characteristics of the school *library* make that environment especially appropriate for the recognition of the first amendment rights of students."[84] In response to the school board's claimed discretion to inculcate community values, the plurality highlighted "the unique role of the school library." The opinion distinguished "the compulsory environment of the classroom," where absolute discretion by the board in determining curriculum might be justified by its inculcative functions, from "the regime of voluntary inquiry" that characterizes the school library, where inculcation is not appropriate.[85] Without contrasting the distinctive aspects of the classroom and the library, Justice Blackmun observed in his concurrence that "the unique environment of the school" both allows and limits the immunity of school officials from first amendment restraints. The inculcative functions of schools, Blackmun concluded, must be reconciled with commitment to "diversity of thought," which is itself a social value that schools should inculcate, and which is protected by the "first amendment's bar on 'prescriptions of orthodoxy.' "[86]

B. Media Cases

Without citing *Tinker*, the Court has relied on the distinctive functions of the media in extending broad first amendment rights. The Court held that a legislative ban on editorializing by noncommercial educational broadcasting

---

80. *Pell v Procunier*, 417 US 817, 822 (1974).
81. Id at 831-32. *Saxbe v Washington Post Co.*, 417 US 843 (1974), reaches the same conclusion.
82. 5 USC § 7324(a)(2) (1989).
83. *United States Civil Serv. Comm'n v National Ass'n of Letter Carriers*, 413 US 548, 564-67 (1973).
84. *Board of Educ. v Pico*, 457 US 853, 868 (1982) (emphasis in original). Justices Brennan, Marshall, and Stevens formed the plurality.
85. Id at 869.
86. Id at 879.

stations, though enacted with the laudable aim of preventing them from becoming agencies of government propaganda, violated the first amendment. According to the Court, these stations require first amendment protection of "journalistic freedom" in order to serve their function of informing the public.[87]

Numerous judicial decisions, sometimes relying on the first amendment generally and sometimes citing its press clause specifically, have similarly attributed constitutional significance to the special role of newspapers in contributing to the discussion of public affairs.[88] After several concurring and dissenting opinions by other members of the Court supported press efforts to enter prisons,[89] Chief Justice Burger wrote a plurality opinion granting the general public and the press an equal first amendment right of access to a criminal trial.[90] In the previous prison cases, the Court majority had observed with approval that, as a matter of practice, the press has enjoyed significantly more access than members of the general public to prisons and prisoners. These cases, however, rejected claims that the first amendment mandates such a result.[91] In requiring press and public access to a criminal trial, Burger also took judicial notice of separate press rights such as special seating and priority of entry. Going beyond the simple judicial approval of extra access by the press in the prison cases, Burger tied the favorable treatment of the press to first amendment concerns. He made the historical point that public knowledge of criminal trials, which once came from personal observation or word of mouth, is now generally received through print and electronic journalism. This historical transformation, Burger maintained, "validates the media claim of functioning as surrogates for the public." In this important sense, the media make a unique contribution to public understanding of the criminal justice system.[92]

Although Chief Justice Burger clearly viewed special treatment of the press, justified by its institutional function of informing the public, as serving

---

87. *FCC v League of Women Voters of California*, 468 US 364, 397-99, 402 (1984).

88. See, for example, *Minneapolis Star & Tribune Co. v Minnesota Comm'r of Revenue*, 460 US 575 (1983) (emphasizing importance of an explicit guarantee of freedom of the press in Constitution, id at 584; threat of differential taxation of press can operate "effectively as a censor to check critical comment by the press, undercutting the basic assumption of our political system that the press will often serve as an important restraint on government," id at 585); *Miami Herald Publishing Co. v Tornillo*, 418 US 241, 258 (1974) ("First Amendment guarantees of a free press" preclude government regulation of "exercise of editorial control and judgment" regarding "treatment of public issues and public officials"); *Sheppard v Maxwell*, 384 US 333, 350 (1966) (press subjects entire criminal process to "public scrutiny and criticism"); *Mills v Alabama*, 384 US 214 (1966) (emphasizing consensus that major purpose of first amendment is "to protect the free discussion of governmental affairs," id at 218-19; first amendment has "specifically selected the press . . . to play an important role in the discussion of public affairs," id).

89. See, for example, *Houchins v KQED, Inc.*, 438 US 1, 16 (1978) (Stewart concurring); id at 19 (Stevens dissenting); *Saxbe v Washington Post Co.*, 417 US 843, 850 (1974) (Powell dissenting); *Pell*, 417 US at 835 (Powell concurring in part and dissenting in part); id at 836 (Douglas dissenting).

90. *Richmond Newspapers, Inc. v Virginia*, 448 US 555 (1980).

91. *Saxbe*, 417 US at 849-50; *Pell*, 417 US at 831 n8, 834-35.

92. *Richmond Newspapers, Inc.*, 448 US at 572-73, 577 n12. Subsequent cases reiterated this point while expanding press access. See, for example, *Press-Enterprise Co. v Superior Court*, 478 US 1 (1986) (recognizing qualified first amendment right of access to preliminary hearings).

vital first amendment purposes, he took pains not to assert more first amendment rights for the press than for the general public. This paradoxical view is best revealed in opinions that anticipated Burger's approach while advocating special press access to prisons. For example, Justice Powell cited the "constitutionally established role of the news media" as justifying greater access to prisons than is permitted the general public.[93] Powell stressed that it is "hopelessly unrealistic" for most citizens to obtain information about important public issues without the assistance of the press, and referred to the press as "an agent of the public," whose "underlying right" to information requires special rules giving the press favored treatment.[94] Yet Powell agreed with the majority that the first amendment does "not create special privileges for particular groups or individuals," including journalists. According to Powell, "neither any news organization nor reporters as individuals have constitutional rights superior to those enjoyed by ordinary citizens."[95]

In another case, Justice Stewart also accepted the majority's position that the first amendment does not "guarantee the press any basic right of access superior to that of the public generally." Stewart added, however, that he, unlike the majority, did not "view 'equal access' as meaning access that is identical in all respects." Given the dependence of the general public on the press for information, Stewart reasoned that "the concept of equal access must be accorded more flexibility" to allow the press greater access than the general public.[96] Restrictions reasonable for the general public, Stewart claimed, may be unreasonable, and even unconstitutional, as applied to journalists. Stewart supported his position by emphasizing the existence of a separate press clause in the first amendment, which he considered "no constitutional accident, but an acknowledgment of the critical role played by the press in American society."[97]

I find incoherent the view articulated in many of these opinions that the institutional functions of the press recognized by the first amendment should afford journalists special benefits, but that those benefits should not be interpreted as giving the press a more favored position under the first amendment. Justice Stewart's insistence that "equal" access does not mean "identical" access highlights the problems with this view. Clearly uncomfortable about recognizing additional first amendment rights not generally available to the public, many justices apparently consider the underlying public benefits justifying special press rights as negating any claim that these rights reflect greater first amendment protection for journalists.

A more persuasive analysis would require overcoming the Court's squeamishness about granting unique first amendment rights to a particular profession. The Court should frankly acknowledge, as it seemed to suggest in

---

93. *Saxbe*, 417 US at 864 (Powell dissenting).
94. Id at 863-64.
95. Id at 857.
96. *Houchins*, 438 US at 16 (Stewart concurring).
97. Id at 17.

a case prohibiting differential taxation of the press,[98] that special rights for the press do constitute additional protection under the first amendment, and justify that protection by the public benefits it freely acknowledges the press performs. Just as the institutional functions of the military and the corrections system permit restrictions on general first amendment rights, so the institutional functions of the press should mandate greater first amendment protection than other citizens enjoy. Whether restricting or expanding general first amendment rights, the ultimate contribution to the public derived from the effective operation of vital organizations justifies these special rules tailored to different institutional purposes.

C.   Institutional Context and the University

Cases constitutionalizing academic freedom also indicated that the university is an institution in which first amendment rights have special meaning. Chief Justice Warren's pivotal opinion in *Sweezy* emphasized "the essentiality of freedom" in universities and recognized that "[s]cholarship cannot flourish in an atmosphere of suspicion and distrust."[99] The South African statement quoted at length in Justice Frankfurter's concurrence defined a university as "characterized by a spirit of free inquiry," whose "business" is "to provide that atmosphere which is most conducive to speculation, experiment and creation."[100] *Keyishian* added that the university "classroom is peculiarly the 'marketplace of ideas,'" which cannot function under "a pall of orthodoxy."[101]

More recent higher education cases have tied the intervening focus in *Tinker* on the "special characteristics" of an institutional environment to the earlier first amendment protection of academic freedom in *Sweezy* and *Keyishian*. The two major Supreme Court decisions applying the *Tinker* analysis to universities acknowledged that the distinctive institutional mission of the university may justify fewer first amendment rights on campus than citizens otherwise enjoy.[102] In both cases, however, the Court refused to find such a justification and emphasized that in some respects the first amendment has particular vitality in universities.

---

98.   See *Minneapolis Star*, 460 US at 583-84 (referring to inclusion of an "explicit guarantee of freedom of the press" as "substantial evidence that differential taxation of the press would have troubled the Framers of the First Amendment").

Dissenting from the Court's refusal to grant a reporter's privilege against responding to a grand jury subpoena, Justice Douglas more explicitly advocated special rights for the press. He urged an absolute privilege for reporters based on the "preferred position" of the press "in our constitutional scheme." This "preferred position," Douglas stressed, is not designed "to set newsmen apart as a favored class, but to bring fulfillment to the public's right to know." *Branzburg v Hayes*, 408 US 665, 721 (1972) (Douglas dissenting). See Baker, 34 U Miami L Rev at 829 (cited in note 67) (social functions of the press "justify institutional rights beyond those already accorded by the free speech doctrine").

99.   354 US at 250.

100.   Id at 262-63.

101.   385 US at 603.

102.   *Widmar v Vincent*, 454 US 263, 267-68 n5 (1981); *Healy v James*, 408 US 169, 180-81 (1972).

Overturning the refusal of a college president to recognize a campus chapter of Students for a Democratic Society ("SDS"), the Court in *Healy v. James* found no evidence to support the president's conclusion that the chapter posed a significant threat of disruption. The Court acknowledged that the first amendment does not protect organizations that "infringe reasonable campus rules, interrupt classes, or substantially interfere with the opportunity of other students to obtain an education,"[103] and remanded the case for a determination of whether the local SDS chapter would commit itself to following legitimate university regulations.[104] The majority implied what Justice Rehnquist's concurrence made clear: "The government as employer or school administrator may impose upon employees and students reasonable regulations that would be impermissible if imposed by the government upon all citizens."[105] Yet the majority also warned against inferring from its appreciation of the university's need for order any hint that first amendment "protections should apply with less force on college campuses than in the community at large. Quite to the contrary," the Court added, invoking prior decisions incorporating academic freedom within the first amendment, it is particularly important to protect first amendment rights in universities.[106]

In *Widmar v. Vincent*, a subsequent case upholding the right of a student group to meet on campus, the Court emphasized that the special characteristics of a university can permit restrictions on speech that would violate the first amendment if applied in a public forum. The Court stressed that a university's educational mission can justify "reasonable regulations compatible with that mission upon the use of its campus and facilities."[107] Yet the Court invalidated a university's rules prohibiting the use of its facilities by an organization of evangelical Christian students. The university's institutional mission of providing a "*secular* education,"[108] the Court concluded, was not sufficiently "compelling"[109] to allow a content-based exclusion of religious speech inconsistent with both the free exercise and the free speech clauses of the first amendment.

Concurring, Justice Stevens went further and challenged the very application of traditional first amendment concepts to the university setting. He emphasized that universities, in "performing their learning and teaching missions," routinely and appropriately make decisions based on the content of speech, a suspect category in general first amendment jurisprudence. Selecting the professors to appoint and reward, choosing the books to purchase for the library, developing the curriculum, and allocating scarce university resources and facilities among students groups all require evaluation of the content of expressive activities. Legal terms such as

---

103. *Healy*, 408 US at 189.
104. Id at 194.
105. Id at 203 (Rehnquist concurring).
106. Id at 180-81.
107. 454 US 263, 268 n5.
108. Id at 268 (emphasis in original).
109. Id at 276.

"compelling state interest" and "public forum," Stevens complained, not only distract from the need to focus on the distinctive aspects of the university environment, but "may needlessly undermine the academic freedom of public universities."[110]

Even when asserting that the first amendment should apply with particular force in the university, the Court has never suggested that members of the university community may in some contexts have more first amendment protection than the general public. At most, some of the Court's opinions have indicated that restrictions on speech that may be appropriate for younger students would violate the first amendment in the university context. In determining the constitutionality of school regulations, the Court has cited differences in the "emotional maturity" of students,[111] and Chief Justice Rehnquist, while advocating greater discretion for a school board than the majority of his colleagues allowed, conceded that there are fewer inculcative or pedagogical reasons to limit access to ideas in universities.[112] For example, Rehnquist distinguished "the broad ranging inquiry available to university students" from the need for "an orderly exposure to relevant information" at earlier stages of education.[113]

Yet as in the press cases, it makes sense to assert that the functions of a particular profession that benefit the general public can justify greater first amendment protection than other citizens enjoy. Just as "journalistic freedom"[114] enables the media to make their distinctive professional contribution to the public's first amendment right to learn about and criticize government activities, academic freedom enables professors to serve the public's first amendment interests in fostering critical inquiry and knowledge vital to democracy and civilization. The Court cited these public benefits in identifying academic freedom as a special right under the first amendment.[115] However, constitutionalizing academic freedom seems much less like elitist favoritism for a particular profession when it is appropriately viewed as but one example of the general proposition that first amendment principles vary with institutional context.

Special first amendment protection for journalists and professors benefit the public as much as special restrictions on the first amendment rights of

---

110. Id at 277-81. Concurring in *Healy*, Justice Rehnquist stressed that first amendment cases dealing with criminal sanctions are largely inapplicable in cases where the government is the employer or college administrator. First amendment cases, Rehnquist added, "are not fungible goods." 408 US at 203.

111. *Hazelwood*, 484 US at 272. See also id at 271; *Edwards v Aguillar*, 482 US 578, 606-07 (1987) (Powell concurring); *Widmar*, 454 US at 274 n14. The Supreme Court recently has declined to grant a writ of certiorari in a case that relied on the differences between adult college students and minor high school students to deny college administrators "the same broad discretion in controlling their curriculum as school administrators at the elementary and secondary level." *DiBona v Matthews*, 220 Cal App3d 1329, 1346, 269 Cal Rptr 882, 892 (1990), cert denied, 59 USLW 3402 (No 90-598) (US ed, December 3, 1990).

112. *Pico*, 457 US at 909, 914 (Rehnquist dissenting).

113. Id at 914.

114. See note 87 and accompanying text.

115. See notes 41-47 and accompanying text.

prisoners and military personnel. Moreover, as a functional analysis of academic freedom reveals,[116] the same professional responsibilities that justify additional first amendment rights of professors may also allow limitations on their speech that do not apply to others. For example, a professor who plagiarizes a scholarly paper may be disciplined for a gross violation of professional ethics, while a prisoner, who in many respects has fewer first amendment protections than other citizens, could probably not be punished for copying verbatim the clemency petition of a fellow inmate.

Concern about creating additional first amendment rights for particular professions also should be assuaged by the prevalence throughout the law of legal protections based on distinctive job functions, even in expressive contexts not explicitly covered by the first amendment. The speech or debate clause of the Constitution gives legislators an absolute privilege for statements made during legislative debates in order to protect the independence of Congress as a separate branch of government.[117] Absolute common law privileges in defamation cases similarly protect judges, legislators, and executive officers of government in the performance of functions that ultimately benefit the public.[118] Relying on the first amendment to give special protection to the speech of journalists and professors that also benefits the public seems equally justifiable.

In retrospect, it may be unfortunate that the term academic freedom, with its many and evolving connotations within the university community, became constitutionalized. Conceptual confusion inevitably results when the same term has different meanings in constitutional and academic discourse. The difficulties in distinguishing constitutional academic freedom from general free speech principles are exacerbated by the additional problem of untangling constitutional from professional definitions of academic freedom. It might have been wiser for the Court to have developed a separate term, such as "academic speech,"[119] to refer to distinctive first amendment rights in the university context. Academic freedom, however, has acquired constitutional significance. Rather than abandon this usage after more than a generation, it makes more sense to focus on how constitutional academic freedom, which can legitimately be considered an example of applying the first amendment in institutional context, overlaps with and differs from both professional definitions of academic freedom and general free speech doctrines.

---

116. See notes 50-61 and accompanying text.

117. See, for example, *Hutchinson v Proxmire*, 443 US 111 (1979); *United States v Brewster*, 408 US 501 (1972); *United States v Johnson*, 383 US 169 (1966).

118. W. Page Keeton, et al, *Prosser and Keeton on Torts* 815-23 (West, 5th ed 1984). I am grateful to Guy Wellborn for suggesting the relevance of these privileges to analogous first amendment protection based on the speaker's function.

119. See Byrne, 99 Yale L J at 258-61 (cited in note 1) (using "academic speech . . . to encompass both scholarship and teaching").

VII

The Development of Institutional Academic Freedom Under the First Amendment

While constitutionalizing academic freedom in *Sweezy*, Chief Justice Warren's plurality opinion and Justice Frankfurter's concurrence tied the first amendment values of critical inquiry and the search for knowledge to the independence of both professors and universities from state intrusion. Yet a distinctive conception of institutional academic freedom remained only latent throughout the McCarthy-era cases, largely because they involved state actions against individual lecturers and professors as in *Sweezy* and *Keyishian* rather than direct conflicts between individuals and universities. More recently, however, universities have relied on an institutional right of academic freedom to defend themselves both against the state and against students, professors, and members of the general public. These cases have prompted the courts to consider in new contexts the institutional component of academic freedom.[120]

Court opinions did not focus on institutional academic freedom until 1978, when Justice Powell's opinion provided the fifth vote for the majority in *Regents of the University of California v. Bakke*.[121] Powell reiterated that "[a]cademic freedom, though not a specifically enumerated constitutional right, long has been viewed as a special concern of the First Amendment." He maintained that " 'the four essential freedoms' of a university," identified in the South African statement quoted at length in Justice Frankfurter's concurring opinion in *Sweezy*, "constitute academic freedom." A university, according to the statement, must be able "to determine for itself on academic grounds who may teach, what may be taught, how it shall be taught, and who may be admitted to study."[122] The Court quoted this language from *Sweezy* again in *Widmar v. Vincent*,[123] and Justice Stevens, concurring in *Widmar*, referred to "the academic freedom of public universities."[124] Citing *Sweezy* and *Bakke*, Justice Stevens stressed that educational decisions based on the content of speech "should be made by academicians, not by federal judges."[125] Ironically, even while underlining the institutional component of academic freedom, the Court in both *Bakke* and *Widmar* relied on countervailing constitutional values to overrule the universities' decisions.[126]

---

120. The Supreme Court protected the institutional autonomy of universities through other doctrines before it constitutionalized academic freedom in *Sweezy*. See note 24.

121. 438 US 265 (1978).

122. Id at 312, citing *Sweezy*, 354 US at 263, citing *The Open Universities in South Africa* 10-12 (a statement of a conference of senior scholars from the University of Cape Town and the University of Witwatersrand).

123. 454 US at 276.

124. Id at 278 (Stevens concurring).

125. Id at 279. See also id at 279 n2.

126. In *Bakke*, Justice Powell emphasized that the challenged admissions program violated the 14th amendment by focusing "*solely* on ethnic diversity." 438 US at 315. He cited the admissions program at Harvard College as an example that met 14th amendment requirements. Under Harvard's program, "race or ethnic background may be deemed a 'plus' in a particular applicant's

Two important cases, *Princeton University v. Schmid*[127] and *University of Pennsylvania v. Equal Employment Opportunity Commission*,[128] illustrate the range of complicated issues raised by claims of institutional academic freedom. After discussing these cases, I explore the possibility that institutional academic freedom has a different meaning for state universities than for private ones and discuss the relationship between state legislatures and the universities they create.

A. *Princeton University v. Schmid*

A case at Princeton University first attracted substantial attention to the potential tension between the developing judicial recognition of institutional academic freedom and the individual academic freedom of professors that historically had been the primary focus of this concept. Despite the objections of many of its own faculty, Princeton relied on the first amendment to resist any judicial review of its policies regulating access by outsiders to campus facilities. The case arose when Chris Schmid, a member of the United States Labor Party who had no affiliation with the university, distributed and sold on the campus material dealing with the party and the mayoral campaign in nearby Newark. Existing Princeton regulations prohibited any person without a university connection or sponsorship from entering the campus to solicit support or contributions. Schmid was arrested and convicted of trespass. Although the Supreme Court ultimately held that new, more permissive university regulations rendered the original dispute moot,[129] this litigation generated an important debate about the meaning of institutional academic freedom.

In overturning Schmid's conviction, the Supreme Court of New Jersey relied on the free speech provision of the state constitution, which it acknowledged to be "more sweeping in scope than the language of the first amendment."[130] Contrasting the state action requirement of the fourteenth amendment, the court observed that the free speech rights in the New Jersey Constitution are enforceable against private as well as public bodies.[131] The court recognized that the New Jersey Constitution also protects ownership of private property, and viewed its task as balancing Princeton's property rights against Schmid's expressive rights.

In analyzing these competing claims, the court revealed remarkable sensitivity to the institutional context of campus speech. Citing Princeton's own regulations lauding the importance of free inquiry and free speech in

---

file, yet it does not insulate the individual from comparison with all other candidates for the available seats." Id at 317. In *Widmar*, the majority and Justice Stevens agreed that the University's fear of violating the establishment clause was unwarranted and thus could not justify its content-based restriction on the first amendment rights of students denied a meeting place on campus. 454 US at 278; id at 280-81 (Stevens concurring).

127. 455 US 100 (1982).
128. 110 S Ct 577 (1990).
129. 455 US at 103.
130. *State v Schmid*, 84 NJ 535, 557, 423 A2d 615, 626 (1980).
131. Id at 565-66, 423 A2d at 631.

achieving the university's declared purpose of promoting knowledge, the court concluded that Schmid's presence on campus was "entirely consonant with the University's expressed educational mission."[132] The court acknowledged that "needs, implicating academic freedom and development, justify an educational institution in controlling those who seek to enter its domain" and require substantial judicial deference to university "autonomy and self-governance."[133] Yet it reversed Schmid's conviction because Princeton's regulations contained no reasonable standards relating limitations on expressive freedoms to legitimate educational goals.[134]

In its jurisdictional statement to the United States Supreme Court, Princeton complained that its academic freedom protected by the first amendment was violated when the Supreme Court of New Jersey arrogated to itself "the ancient right of a university community to determine how its educational philosophy may best be implemented."[135] According to Princeton, a private university's choice of educational philosophy, however broad, orthodox, or eccentric, is immunized by first amendment academic freedom from interference by the state. Princeton insisted that no governmental body is constitutionally competent to determine whether a private university has acted in accordance with its educational objectives. Princeton conceded that "the university cannot claim its academic freedom as a shield against state rules concerning health, safety and like matters," but immediately added that correspondingly "the state cannot use its police powers to control in any way the intellectual activities of the university."[136]

Princeton's main brief reiterated and elaborated this theme, asserting that first amendment academic freedom provides greater protection to private than to public universities. The educational judgments of public universities, like those of private universities, are protected against interference from other state entities. Public universities, however, are also subject to the constraints on all government action imposed by the prohibitions in the first and fourteenth amendments against the state's adoption of a particular religious or ideological viewpoint. Princeton maintained that private universities, by contrast, are absolutely unconstrained in their choice of educational philosophy.[137] Stressing "the interrelation of expressive and property rights," Princeton made the historical observation that control by universities over their property helped to provide an educational "atmosphere conducive to learning and to the interchange of ideas between faculty and students."[138] That Princeton chose an expansive view of free expression on its campus, the

---

132. Id at 564, 423 A2d at 631.

133. Id at 566-67, 423 A2d at 632.

134. Id at 567, 423 A2d at 632.

135. Jurisdictional Statement of Princeton University at 6, *Princeton University v Schmid*, 455 US 100 (1982) (No 80-1576).

136. Id at 7-8.

137. Princeton University's Brief at 8-9, *Princeton University v Schmid*, 455 US 100 (1982) (No 80-1576).

138. Id at 12.

brief emphasized in attacking the rationale of the Supreme Court of New Jersey, did not give the government more power to review the implementation of educational policies than if the university had decided to inculcate an ideological orthodoxy.[139]

Though the brief did not focus on the academic freedom of faculty, Princeton did mention in one sentence that the first amendment protects the free speech of professors at public universities from state interference. "Academic freedom," it added in a footnote, "is, of course, especially important to those who teach as well as to the institutions at which they teach, be they public or private." Princeton went on to make clear its own commitment "to the freedom of its faculty and students to pursue knowledge in their own way without interference by governmental or other authority."[140]

Princeton's argument to the United States Supreme Court provoked strong objections from many of its own faculty, particularly those with professional interests in constitutional law.[141] Faculty members urged the administration not to prosecute Schmid[142] and asserted that the decision to prosecute, rather than involving purely a matter of administrative discretion, posed a policy issue in which the entire university community should be involved.[143] When these views did not prevail, the faculty focused on its substantive disagreements with the university's position.

Several professors worried that the broad immunity from judicial scrutiny claimed by Princeton would allow any private university unreviewable discretion to restrict the academic freedom of its faculty. Princeton's "distorted" conception of academic freedom, one faculty member argued, posed a far greater threat to intellectual life in universities than either Schmid's activities or the holding of the Supreme Court of New Jersey. Boards of trustees, following Princeton's theory, could simply assert that faculty ideas are "incompatible" with the university's "educational purposes."[144] Private universities, other faculty members feared, could invoke institutional academic freedom to preclude judicial review of administrative decisions to fire a professor doing controversial research, to determine the content of courses, to revise the grades assigned by faculty to students, and to revoke tenure without cause.[145] Professors criticized Princeton for confusing its own institutional autonomy with the faculty's

---

139. Id at 18.

140. Id at 9, n12.

141. Andrew Barry, *Professors Relieved Over Decision*, Daily Princetonian 1 col 3 (January 15, 1982); Letter from Thomas M. Scanlon to William G. Bowen (June 29, 1981); Memorandum from Walter F. Murphy to William G. Bowen (July 8, 1981). Sanford Levinson, an assistant professor in the Department of Politics at Princeton, represented Schmid from his initial arrest through the oral argument in the United States Supreme Court.

142. Barry, Daily Princetonian at 2 col 5 (cited in note 141); Letter from Scanlon to Bowen (cited in note 141).

143. Barry, Daily Princetonian at 2 col 5 (cited in note 141).

144. Letter from Scanlon to Bowen (cited in note 141). Professor Scanlon quoted from Princeton's Jurisdictional Statement at 8 (cited in note 135).

145. Princeton Alumni Weekly 15 (December 1, 1981); Walter F. Murphy, Informal Memorandum re Schmid Case (November 23, 1981) ("Murphy Informal Memorandum").

academic freedom, and asserted that granting the immunity sought by the university would violate the fundamental principle that no person or institution is above the law.[146] One professor warned Princeton's president that the best result Princeton could hope for in the Supreme Court would be a decision holding it up as a "laughing stock . . . for attacking academic freedom in particular and freedom of discussion in general in the name of private property. Making fun of Princeton—with devastating logic—will become an annual game in which students and faculty elsewhere will delight."[147]

The AAUP filed an amicus brief with the Supreme Court that reiterated and expanded in legal language many of these faculty views.[148] It asserted that Princeton's "novel and sweeping claims"[149] combining institutional autonomy and academic freedom, if accepted, would effectively insulate private universities from any government scrutiny. The AAUP emphasized that academic freedom and institutional autonomy are "related but essentially different concepts."[150] Academic freedom, the AAUP insisted, "is a scholar's right to be free of institutional (or governmental) control in professional utterance."[151] Institutional autonomy can be derived from academic freedom in the sense that university autonomy from external control may be necessary to protect its educational functions, including the functions of professors covered by academic freedom. But institutional autonomy also relates to the general control of private property, traditionally protected by the due process clause of the fourteenth amendment, which is no different when the property owner is a university, the corporate owner of a shopping center, or an individual. According to the AAUP, Princeton made a fundamental mistake by failing to distinguish between these two very different forms of institutional autonomy. Only when a university's claims of institutional autonomy relate to its educational functions, the AAUP maintained, is academic freedom at stake.[152]

The AAUP stressed that Princeton's invocation of institutional academic freedom had no connection with its educational mission. Princeton was not trying to protect against an external threat to internal decisions about curriculum or faculty selection, or to the faculty's freedom to teach or do research. Indeed, the Supreme Court of New Jersey indicated an extraordinary willingness to deny state constitutional protection to expressive activity inconsistent in any way with Princeton's professed educational

---

146. Barry, Daily Princetonian at 2 col 4-5 (cited in note 141); Murphy Informal Memorandum (cited in note 145).

147. Memorandum from Murphy to Bowen (cited in note 141).

148. AAUP's Brief as Amicus Curiae, *Princeton University v Schmid*, 455 US 100 (1982) (No 80-1576) ("*AAUP Princeton Brief*"). Indeed, Professor Thomas M. Scanlon, a professor of philosophy at Princeton who had been involved in the internal university debate over the case (see notes 141-44 and accompanying text), signed the AAUP amicus brief as "of counsel." See also letter from Thomas M. Scanlon to Matthew Finkin (July 22, 1981) (letter to main author of AAUP brief following up telephone conversation and commenting on draft brief).

149. *AAUP Princeton Brief* at 1 (cited in note 148).

150. Id at 5.

151. Id at 2-3.

152. Id at 2, 3, 10, 18-19.

goals.[153] Princeton, moreover, never provided the slightest clue as to how the material Schmid distributed and sold could interfere with these goals, prompting the AAUP to wonder whether the state court decision "is actually one regulating the university's 'academic functions' at all."[154] Princeton asserted only that any judicial review of the relationship between institutional policies and educational objectives itself violates the institutional academic freedom protected by the first amendment. The AAUP disagreed, observing that the free exercise of religion, also protected by the first amendment, does not prevent the courts from inquiring into the nature and authenticity of religious belief.[155]

Not surprisingly, the AAUP emphasized the dangers to faculty members it perceived in Princeton's legal position. Princeton's broad claim of institutional academic freedom, the AAUP warned, would effectively preclude judicial review of institutional decisions "even in cases where the rights or interests of the faculty might be adverse to the institution's administration." Faculty complaints of employment discrimination or of university violations of contractual commitments to academic freedom and tenure, the AAUP observed, relate much more closely to institutional educational policies than did Schmid's distribution and sale of political literature. The institutional academic freedom Princeton invoked against Schmid would apply even more strongly against these faculty complaints. A university could bar judicial scrutiny of faculty contracts merely by claiming that it was following its own educational policies.[156]

In its reply brief, Princeton mostly reiterated its previous position; however, it did respond briefly to some of these faculty concerns. Princeton asserted that the academic freedom protected by the first amendment "is freedom from governmental intrusion into the academic process." It acknowledged that administrators in public universities could engage in prohibited state action by interfering with the individual rights of professors and students. Administrators in private universities, by contrast, are not engaged in state action and thus cannot violate individual first amendment rights even if they, like professors acting against each other, could infringe academic freedom "in a non-constitutional sense." Yet private universities as institutions, Princeton insisted, do have a first amendment right to determine their educational policies free from government interference.[157] The AAUP, moreover, "grossly" misunderstood Princeton's legal argument against Schmid by suggesting that it would enable the university to use the first amendment as a defense to faculty assertions of contractual violations. Princeton tersely commented that the state police power would permit the

---

153. Id at 15.
154. Id at 27 n8.
155. Id at 21.
156. Id at 28. The letter from Scanlon to Bowen (cited in note 141) makes many of the points discussed in the previous two paragraphs.
157. Princeton University's Reply Brief at 8 n8, *Princeton University v Schmid*, 455 US 100 (1982) (No 80-1576).

enforcement of faculty contracts,[158] but never responded to the AAUP's concern that asserted violations of contractual academic freedom and tenure would implicate university educational policies, and thus under Princeton's argument preclude judicial review, much more directly than the regulations on outsider access applied against Schmid.

A letter from Princeton's university counsel to a faculty member who had objected at length to the university's position in its jurisdictional statement captures better than any legal papers the administration's reaction to faculty concerns. The letter stressed that the legal arguments of the university in *Schmid* "have nothing to do with the relative powers or rights within an institution between the Trustees and individual faculty members or students," and promised in the university's next brief to avoid any possible implication that Princeton wanted "to diminish the rights of individual faculty members under the concept of academic freedom." Yet the letter also challenged the view that the state is a better ally of faculty academic freedom than the governing boards of private universities. During the McCarthy era, the university counsel claimed, private institutions were substantially more effective than their public counterparts in protecting scholars from state intervention. He added that private boards of trustees, unlike the state, are constrained by different constituencies within the university as well as by a general ethos supporting academic freedom.

The university counsel assured that a Supreme Court victory for Princeton in *Schmid* would not "directly affect to any degree whatsoever the relationships between the trustees of a private institution and its faculty members." He did concede, however, the possibility that "reasoning by analogy another court down the road would apply rules enunciated in this case to the dissident opinions of faculty and students." Yet a more realistic and directly relevant fear, the counsel warned, was that a defeat for Princeton's position would encourage additional state intervention in university educational decisions in ways that might eventually constrain faculty academic freedom. He observed the historical tendency of increased state power "to homogenization of standards, to fear of the odd case, and to sensitivity to political fashions." The counsel advised that professors, instead of relying on the state, including its courts, to protect their academic freedom, should place their confidence in the diversity of autonomous American universities.[159]

B. *University of Pennsylvania v. Equal Employment Opportunity Commission*

By holding that Princeton's new university regulations on access to the campus by outsiders rendered the original dispute moot, the Supreme Court's decision in *Schmid*[160] produced a severe anticlimax, but it did not end debate on the scope of institutional academic freedom. In *University of Pennsylvania v.*

---

158. Id at 8 n9.
159. Letter from Thomas H. Wright to Thomas M. Scanlon (July 7, 1981).
160. 455 US 100.

Equal Employment Opportunity Commission,[161] the University of Pennsylvania and numerous amici relied on a first amendment claim of institutional academic freedom in asking the Supreme Court to recognize a special privilege against disclosure of confidential peer review materials to the Equal Employment Opportunity Commission ("EEOC") in Title VII cases. The rationale for this special privilege, while made in the context of a Title VII case alleging discrimination based on gender and national origin, would apply as well to a claim that a university impermissibly denied appointment or tenure in violation of a faculty member's academic freedom.

Although various federal circuit courts had held in previous Title VII litigation that constitutional academic freedom requires a qualified privilege against disclosure[162] or a test balancing "academic freedom and educational excellence on the one hand and individual rights to fair consideration on the other,"[163] the Third Circuit "expressly declined to limit the EEOC's subpoena authority to accommodate an academic institution's constitutional right to academic freedom."[164] The court acknowledged that such disclosure "would burden the tenure review process and would impact on academic freedom,"[165] but it rejected both a qualified privilege and a balancing test because they would allow universities "to hide evidence of discrimination behind a wall of secrecy."[166]

The University of Pennsylvania complained that the Third Circuit failed to give any consideration to its first amendment interests in institutional academic freedom. A confidential system of peer review, the university insisted, is essential to determining "who may teach," one of the core components of first amendment academic freedom identified by Frankfurter in *Sweezy*.[167] The university readily conceded that the EEOC and individual litigants may in certain circumstances have access to confidential peer review documents in order to further the compelling state interest in eliminating employment discrimination. It objected, however, to the Third Circuit's "automatic disclosure" rule, which gave no weight whatsoever to university interests in academic freedom[168] and required disclosure of confidential material simply upon the filing of a complaint.[169] According to the university, the party seeking such material should have to demonstrate specific reasons for disclosure that outweigh the first amendment interests in confidentiality

---

161. 110 S Ct 577.

162. *EEOC v University of Notre Dame du Lac*, 715 F2d 331, 337 (7th Cir 1983).

163. *Gray v Board of Higher Educ., City of New York*, 692 F2d 901, 907 (2d Cir 1982).

164. *EEOC v University of Pennsylvania*, 850 F2d 969, 975 (3d Cir 1988), aff'd, 110 S Ct 577 (1990). In reaching this conclusion, the Third Circuit relied on its previous holding in *EEOC v Franklin & Marshall College*, 775 F2d 110 (3d Cir 1985).

165. *University of Pennsylvania*, 850 F2d at 974.

166. Id at 975, quoting from *Franklin & Marshall*, 775 F2d at 115.

167. University of Pennsylvania Brief at 10-11, 17, 37, *University of Pennsylvania v EEOC*, 110 S Ct 577 (1990) (No 88-493) ("*University of Pennsylvania Brief*").

168. Id at 12-14.

169. Id at 32, 34.

shared by universities and the professors who participate in peer review.[170] "Institutional academic freedom—the university's right to some degree of autonomy—is a necessary corollary," the university maintained, "of the First Amendment rights of the individual university professor."[171] As at Princeton, a number of faculty members opposed the University's legal position.[172]

The AAUP, while appearing as a nonaligned amicus and specifically disclaiming any position on whether the university should be required to disclose the confidential peer review materials at issue, challenged the Third Circuit's legal standard as constitutionally inadequate.[173] The AAUP had anticipated this issue in *Schmid*, where it cited unrestrained discovery in Title VII litigation as an example of government regulation that, unlike the holding allowing Schmid access to Princeton's campus, could impinge upon a university's academic freedom.[174] Presented with this precise issue in *University of Pennsylvania*, the AAUP characterized the Third Circuit's holding as containing the "startling proposition" that the first amendment protection for academic freedom "in no way limits the subpoena authority of a government agency."[175]

The AAUP saw a precise analogy between EEOC investigations of tenure files and the investigations into the contents of university lectures conducted by legislative committees concerned about communist subversion during the McCarthy era. "The single most consistent and most rigorous application of this Court's academic freedom decisions," the AAUP stressed citing *Sweezy*, "has related directly to investigative claims pressed by government itself."[176] As in the earlier cases, the AAUP urged, the Court should not immunize universities from government scrutiny, but should balance the competing investigative and academic interests. The AAUP also took pains to note that *University of Pennsylvania* did not pose any tension between the academic

---

170. Id at 45-46, 49. The University of Pennsylvania conceded that the university should provide confidential letters on which the tenure decision is based to the EEOC and a statement of reasons for the decision to the complainant or the EEOC. Substantial evidence of discrimination uncovered from nonconfidential information, the university added, can justify access to otherwise confidential peer review materials. Id at 46-47. This approach closely resembles the one advocated in AAUP, *A Preliminary Statement on Judicially Compelled Disclosure in the Nonrenewal of Faculty Appointments*, 67 Academe 27 (February-March 1981) (attached as appendix A to AAUP's Brief as Amicus Curiae, *University of Pennsylvania v EEOC*, 110 S Ct 577 (1990) (No 88-493) ("*AAUP University of Pennsylvania Brief*").

171. *University of Pennsylvania Brief* at 16 (cited in note 167).

172. The Association of Women Faculty and Administrators of the University of Pennsylvania participated in a brief amici curiae in support of the EEOC. In its statement of interest, the association maintained that its members "know from concrete experience—including the denial of tenure to Professor Rosalie Tung, which gave rise to the present proceeding—that the task of eradicating the effects of gender-based discrimination is far more difficult, and the need to retain unimpaired the ability of the Equal Employment Opportunity Commission to carry out its mission far more critical, than is suggested by petitioner [University of Pennsylvania] here." NOW Legal Defense and Education Fund and Rosalie Tung's Brief as Amici Curiae at 29, *University of Pennsylvania v EEOC*, 110 S Ct 577 (1990) (No 88-493).

173. *AAUP University of Pennsylvania Brief* at 3 n6 (cited in note 170).

174. *AAUP Princeton Brief* at 25 (cited in note 148).

175. *AAUP University of Pennsylvania Brief* at 7 (cited in note 170).

176. Id at 5. See also id at 12.

freedom of the university and the academic freedom of the faculty. Without citing the 1915 Declaration, the AAUP stressed that by giving the faculty primary responsibility for the tenure decision, the university was following a traditional and well-justified academic policy that merited first amendment protection.[177]

The government's brief flatly denied that the Third Circuit's holding interfered with academic freedom. While noting that prior Supreme Court decisions had not clarified the definition of constitutional academic freedom, the government assumed that it included the university's choice of professors. Yet the government emphasized that *Sweezy* itself extended this freedom only to decisions made "on academic grounds." University employment decisions based on the kinds of invidious discrimination prohibited by Title VII, the government suggested, are not made "on academic grounds" and thus are not entitled to constitutional protection. Indeed, the government asserted that individual faculty members have a countervailing academic freedom interest in being evaluated on the basis of their professional performance. EEOC investigations of peer review decisions determine only whether these decisions are based on academic considerations or on discriminatory ones, and thereby reinforce rather than undermine the appropriate tradition of judicial deference to university decision-making.[178] The government observed as well that when removing the exemption of universities from Title VII in 1972, Congress rejected arguments that EEOC investigations would violate academic freedom by intruding on the selection and promotion of faculty.[179]

The Supreme Court unanimously rejected the University of Pennsylvania's first amendment claim and essentially accepted the government's position. Cases such as *Sweezy* and *Keyishian*, the Court observed, involved direct governmental restrictions on the content of speech and on the right of the university to determine who may teach. Unlike *Keyishian*, where the government attempted to substitute its employment criteria for those of the university, the EEOC left the University of Pennsylvania free to select and apply its own standards as long as they did not violate the proscriptions against employment discrimination in Title VII. The Court recognized that the "precise contours"[180] of its prior academic freedom decisions remained undefined. Yet it considered itself fortunate in not having to provide

---

177. Id at 10 n9. See also Brief of Princeton University, Brown University, Harvard University, and Yale University as Amici Curiae, *University of Pennsylvania v EEOC*, 110 S Ct 577 (1990) (No 88-493). Many within the AAUP opposed its policy of limiting disclosure of peer review materials and objected to the official position in the AAUP brief. See Memorandum from Mary Gray, Chair of Committee W of AAUP to Carol Stern, et al, Committee on Litigation (May 3, 1989) (conveying unanimous recommendation of AAUP committee on the status of women that AAUP should not file brief based on its existing Preliminary Statement). See also AAUP, *University of Pennsylvania v EEOC and the Status of Peer Review: A Symposium*, 76 Academe 31 (May-June 1990) (various reactions of professors and a college president to Supreme Court decision).

178. Respondent's Brief at 26-29, 26-27 n19, *University of Pennsylvania v EEOC*, 110 S Ct 577 (1990) (No 88-493).

179. Id at 12-13.

180. 110 S Ct at 586.

additional guidance because *University of Pennsylvania* required only the rejection of the *"expanded* right of academic freedom to protect confidential peer review materials from disclosure."[181] According to the Court, the university's concerns about the impact of disclosure on academic freedom were "extremely attenuated," "remote," and "speculative."[182] At the same time, the Court reiterated its continued support of judicial deference to *"legitimate* academic decisionmaking."[183]

VIII

THE CONSTITUTIONAL CONTOURS OF INSTITUTIONAL ACADEMIC FREEDOM

Cases since *Sweezy* have reinforced without significantly elaborating its indication that first amendment academic freedom applies to universities as well as to professors. The " 'four essential freedoms' of a university," identified in the South African statement incorporated into Frankfurter's concurring opinion in *Sweezy*, apparently have achieved doctrinal status through repeated citation in subsequent opinions. These four freedoms—"to determine for itself on academic grounds who may teach, what may be taught, how it shall be taught, and who may be admitted to study"[184]—seem to cover appointment, promotion, tenuring, and termination of faculty, as well as curriculum, pedagogy, and student admissions. By recognizing a university's constitutional academic freedom to select a diverse student body within the limits of the fourteenth amendment, Justice Powell's opinion in *Bakke* reinforced the inclusion of student admissions within institutional academic freedom.[185] Justice Stevens's concurring opinion in *Widmar*, by emphasizing that decisions about faculty hiring and curriculum should be made by academicians rather than federal judges, reiterated two of the three additional components of institutional academic freedom identified in *Sweezy*.[186] And the Court underlined the university's institutional academic freedom to determine who shall teach by distinguishing the infringement of this right in *Keyishian* from the *"expanded"* and "extremely attenuated" concept of institutional academic freedom it unanimously rejected in *University of Pennsylvania*.[187]

A. The Greater Institutional Academic Freedom of Private Universities

These Supreme Court decisions have recognized institutional academic freedom at both public and private universities. The Court has never had to resolve whether constitutional academic freedom has different meanings at

---

181. Id at 587 (emphasis in original).
182. Id at 587-88.
183. Id at 587 (emphasis in original).
184. 354 US at 263.
185. See note 121 and accompanying text.
186. See notes 110, 125 and accompanying text.
187. See notes 180-82 and accompanying text (emphasis in original).

private than at public universities, but it did recognize this issue in *University of Pennsylvania*, its only major decision involving an academic freedom claim by a private university.[188] The Court noted that attempts by government to regulate the selection of faculty or otherwise influence academic speech at private universities would create obvious first amendment problems. Analogous attempts at public universities, the Court added without further explanation, would present complicated first amendment issues because the government would be both the regulator and the speaker.[189]

Earlier Supreme Court decisions, however, do suggest first amendment constraints on the institutional academic freedom of public universities that may not apply to their private counterparts. The Court in *Sweezy* and *Keyishian*, cases that arose at public universities, emphasized the value of critical inquiry in universities to democracy and civilization while justifying first amendment protection of academic freedom. First amendment academic freedom, the Court stressed, requires a "robust exchange of ideas" in universities and precludes a "pall of orthodoxy" or a "straight jacket" on intellectual life. The search for truth in universities must be open to a "multitude" of views and must not be subject to the "authoritarian selection" of "absolutes."[190] Even while acknowledging greater discretion for state inculcation of societal values in the high school setting than in universities, the Court has warned that public schools must be careful not to "eliminate all diversity of thought."[191]

Recent scholarly exploration of the democratic functions of universities supports this first amendment analysis. Professor Amy Gutmann has argued convincingly that universities serve democracy as institutional sanctuaries against repression of unpopular ideas, an analysis that recalls the emphasis in the 1915 Declaration on the university's role as an "inviolable refuge"[192] for scholarly views that challenge prevailing public opinion and government policy. The academic freedom of universities from state intrusion, Gutmann asserts, protects debate about politically relevant ideas from the potential tyranny of democratic majorities or coalitions of minorities. In universities protected by academic freedom, in possible contrast to legislatures or to

---

188. 110 S Ct 577. The Supreme Court's reliance on Princeton's newly passed regulations mooted the important academic freedom issues presented in *Schmid*, 455 US 100. See text accompanying note 129.

189. 110 S Ct at 586-87, n6, citing Yudof, *When Government Speaks* (cited in note 24). The Court's explicit recognition of academic freedom cases at public universities refutes Dean Yudof's earlier prediction that the ascription of first amendment academic freedom to a public university by Justice Powell in *Bakke* would not be followed in subsequent cases. Yudof, 32 Loyola L Rev at 855-56 (cited in note 24). Indeed, Powell's opinion was not a "revisionist view of institutional academic freedom" with "revolutionary" implications. Id at 855. *Sweezy* and *Keyishian*, the initial Supreme Court decisions constitutionalizing academic freedom, arose at public universities, as did later decisions reiterating first amendment academic freedom such as *Widmar* and *Regents of University of Michigan v Ewing*, 474 US 214 (1985).

190. These quotations are from *Sweezy*, 354 US at 250, and *Keyishian*, 385 US at 603. See notes 41-44 and accompanying text.

191. *Pico*, 457 US at 879 (Blackmun concurring). See also *Bethel School Dist.*, 478 US at 681.

192. 1915 Declaration at 167; Appendix A at 400 (cited in note 6).

general political debate, ideas are evaluated on their scholarly merits, not their political popularity.[193] Unpopular ideas kept alive in universities remain available to the broader society.

The democratic functions of universities, however, may have more salience in public institutions, where, as the Supreme Court has observed, the state is the speaker as well as the regulator. Public universities, themselves bound by the first amendment in their relationships with faculty and students, may have less discretion than private universities in selecting educational purposes that arguably deviate from democratic values. The same educational choices that might violate the first amendment obligations of public universities to diversity of thought might be protected by the first amendment academic freedom of private universities against state intrusion. For example, the private "proprietary institutions" identified in the 1915 Declaration, formed to advocate a protective tariff or socialism, might have institutional academic freedom from state attempts to require more diversity of thought, even though the first amendment might preclude the state from establishing such institutions. Similarly, a private university might have academic freedom to declare itself an "ivory tower" committed to the world of ideas uncontaminated by influences from the outside world, and therefore might be permitted to impose absolute restrictions on public access to the campus that might violate the first amendment if adopted by a public university. If Princeton, rather than inviting public use of its campus, had declared itself such an ivory tower, the Supreme Court of New Jersey might have deferred to this choice of educational policy.[194] However, Rutgers, the major state university in New Jersey, might not have similar discretion in choosing an educational policy that precludes public access.

Arguably, this first amendment combination of limiting state interference with the discretion of private universities while constraining their public counterparts itself promotes democratic values. Private universities may choose to establish educational policies that deviate from democratic values in ways forbidden to state institutions. The resulting pluralism within the academic world, however, may provide more tolerance for diverse and

---

193. Amy Gutmann, *Democratic Education* 174, 179 (Princeton, 1987). See also Amy Gutmann, *Is Freedom Academic?: The Relative Autonomy of Universities in a Liberal Democracy* in J. Roland Pennock & John W. Chapman, eds, *Nomos 25: Liberal Democracy* 257, 271 (New York Univ Press, 1983). Professor Byrne makes a similar point to support first amendment academic freedom for universities. Independent and expert critical thought in universities, he maintains, is "crucial for society as a whole because it provides a standard by which to gauge how trivial, debased, and false is much public discussion of affairs." Byrne, 99 Yale L J at 334 (cited in note 1).

194. See *Schmid*, 84 NJ at 564-65, 423 A2d at 631. But see Sanford Levinson, *Princeton v. Free Speech: A Post Mortem* in Craig Kaplan & Ellen Schrecker, eds, *Regulating the Intellectuals* 200 (Praeger, 1983) ("republican form of government" guaranteed by Article IV of U.S. Constitution requires "voting citizens of the United States freedom to interact with their fellow citizens—whether students or outsiders—in conversation about the great issues of the polity"). See also Gutmann, *Nomos 25: Liberal Democracy* at 267-68 (cited in note 193) (though "secluded residential college dedicated to religious indoctrination" has a better argument than Princeton for restricting access to campus by local political candidates, the democratic "right of political communication" may outweigh the "right of religious education").

unpopular views than a rule that would subject all universities to the commitment to diversity of thought that the first amendment imposes on public ones.[195]

Private universities may have purposes unrelated to education that similarly allow them to deviate from first amendment limitations on public universities. A university affiliated with a religious denomination, another example in the 1915 Declaration of a proprietary institution, may make institutional choices for religious rather than educational reasons, and those choices may be protected by the free exercise clause of the first amendment. A Catholic university could require its teachers to adhere to the Church's theological position on artificial contraception,[196] and a fundamentalist

---

195. Dean Yudof emphasizes that the first amendment can foster pluralism by protecting private speech and by limiting government expression. He prefers the first approach because limiting government expression presents "dangers of judicial overreaching" and "remedial quandaries." Yudof, *When Government Speaks* at 200 (cited in note 24). "Any judicial decision protecting the right of *private* individuals, groups, or organizations to speak," he reasons, "strengthens their ability to communicate and increases their potential to counter government messages." Id at 201. Applying this general principle, he maintains that "institutional academic freedom protects the private school from an overreaching government authority," and "tends to diminish the ability of government to suppress competing ideas and ideologies." Yudof, 32 Loyola L Rev at 852-53 (cited in note 24).

Dean Yudof, who finds prior decisions protecting individual academic freedom "difficult to justify," Yudof, *When Government Speaks* at 215 (cited in note 24), would interpret them as part of his general approach to government speech. He suggests that "the focus should be not on the constitutional entitlements of the teacher *per se*, . . . but on the place of the teacher in the system of government expression." Id at 216. He indicates that first amendment protection for individual academic freedom, though unsupported by arguments derived from personal autonomy, Yudof, 32 Loyola L Rev at 838 (cited in note 24), can be justified by the fact that "the autonomy of the classroom teacher contributes to a diminution of the power of government to work its communication will" and thereby introduces "a sort of pluralism into the school environment." Yudof, *When Government Speaks* at 216 (cited in note 24). Yet Dean Yudof resists constitutional protection for the academic freedom of public institutions. Yudof, 32 Loyola L Rev at 855-56 (cited in note 24). See note 189.

Professor Gutmann might impose greater constraints than Dean Yudof on private universities. She rejects the "corporate pluralist" argument, which is "corporatist in ascribing a right to autonomy to private institutions, and pluralist in proclaiming the value of diversity among those institutions." Gutmann, *Nomos 25: Liberal Democracy* at 261-62 (cited in note 193). The need for universities to serve as an "institutional sanctuary for the process of free intellectual inquiry essential to democratic politics," she maintains, applies to both private and public institutions. Id at 263. A democratic state should promote liberal over nonliberal private universities because it depends "upon the free development and dissemination of ideas to which liberal universities are uniquely dedicated as social institutions." Id at 264. Yet Gutmann acknowledges that "a university with explicitly nonliberal religious purposes may need to restrict the academic freedom of its faculty as a means of furthering its purposes." Apparently, Gutmann favors greater discretion for private universities than for public ones, limited by state determinations that private "purposes and policies" are "incompatible with the effective exercise of other basic rights supporting citizenship in a democratic society." Id at 263. See also Levinson, *Princeton v. Free Speech* at 200-02 (cited in note 194) (constitutional guarantee of "republican form of government" limits discretion of private universities).

Dean Yudof, though perhaps favoring more discretion for private universities than Professors Gutmann or Levinson, agrees that the state can impose limits on institutional autonomy. "In each case," he writes, "the compelling nature of the public policy and the limits of tolerance must balance against the specific infringement on institutional autonomy. Not surprisingly, principled results are frequently illusive." Yudof, 32 Loyola L Rev at 853-54 (cited in note 24). See text accompanying notes 201-08 (discussing tensions between state and university interests).

196. See *Curran v Catholic University of America*, No 1562-87 (DC Superior Ct, filed February 28, 1989) (unpublished opinion on file with court) (rejecting claim that university breached professor's contractual right to academic freedom). "On some issues," the court reasoned, "the conflict between the University's commitment to academic freedom and its unwavering fealty to the Holy See

Protestant university could require the exclusive teaching of "creation science" even if this theory has no respectable scholarly or pedagogical basis.[197]

The freedom of association protected by the first amendment and basic property rights provide additional constitutional protections for the institutional choices of private universities.[198] A private university might decide to limit access by outsiders, not for the educational purpose of creating an ivory tower, but simply to keep its property clean.[199] Yet as the AAUP maintained in *Schmid*, a private university cannot appropriately base its claims of autonomy on institutional academic freedom unless they can be justified on educational grounds.[200]

Even when it is legitimately invoked, institutional academic freedom at both private and public universities may compete with and at times succumb to other state interests. For example, the fourteenth amendment imposes barriers to university affirmative action plans,[201] just as government commitments to affirmative action could jeopardize university interests in

---

is direct and unavoidable. On such issues, the University may choose for itself on which side of that conflict it wants to come down, and nothing in its contract with Professor Curran or any other faculty member promises that it will always come down on the side of academic freedom." Id at 34. But see *Academic Freedom and Tenure: The Catholic University of America*, 75 Academe 27, 37 (September-October 1989) (AAUP investigating committee finds that University violated Curran's academic freedom by forcing him to relinquish all teaching of Catholic theology). Compare Charles E. Curran, *Academic Freedom and Catholic Universities*, 66 Tex L Rev 1441 (1988) (arguing for greater academic freedom at Catholic universities than official Church documents and legislation allow) with Douglas Laycock & Susan E. Waelbroeck, *Academic Freedom and the Free Exercise of Religion*, 66 Tex L Rev 1455 (1988) (arguing that free exercise clause precludes courts from determining extent of academic freedom at Catholic universities). See also Michael W. McConnell, *Academic Freedom in Religious Colleges and Universities*, 53 L & Contemp Probs 303 (Summer, 1990).

197. Compare *Edwards v Aguillard*, 482 US 578 (1987) (law forbidding teaching of evolution in public schools unless "creation science" is also taught violates establishment clause of first amendment).

198. Dean Yudof recognizes freedom of association as "an immensely reasonable gloss to place on freedom of expression once one recognizes the desirability of countering the communications power of governments in a democracy." Yudof, *When Government Speaks* at 258 (cited in note 24). See id at 255-58.

199. Compare *NLRB v Babcock & Wilcox Co.*, 351 US 105, 107, 112 (1956) (employer interest in controlling property and preventing litter justify refusal to allow distribution of literature by union organizers in company parking lot) with *Schneider v State*, 308 US 141, 162 (1939) (city ordinance prohibiting distribution of handbills to pedestrians on public streets violates first amendment; legislative purpose of keeping streets clean is "insufficient to justify an ordinance which prohibits a person rightfully on a public street from handing literature to one willing to receive it").

200. See text accompanying notes 152-55. Professor Finkin, the primary author of the AAUP brief in *Schmid*, reiterated this point in a subsequent article. Professor Finkin finds "particularly perverse" the application of the term "academic freedom" to institutional autonomy based on "an excresence of property rights . . . unrelated to the maintainence of conditions of academic freedom within the institution." Finkin, 61 Tex L Rev at 839 (cited in note 24). Byrne, 99 Yale L J at 321-22 (cited in note 1), agrees with Finkin. See also Gutmann, *Nomos 25: Liberal Democracy* at 276 (cited in note 193) ("academic freedom as an institutional right . . . is not so broad as to permit any university to defend itself against those governmental regulations that are compatible with, or instrumental to achieving, a university's self-proclaimed educational purposes").

201. *Bakke*, 438 US 265.

selecting faculty and students.[202] First amendment public forum analysis can limit the discretion of state universities to restrict even for legitimate educational purposes the use of their facilities unless those purposes are "compelling."[203] State constitutions that give individuals a right to speak on private property must be balanced against the interests of universities in determining their own purposes and policies.[204] Threats to national security or public health may justify state restrictions on university research.[205] Genuine religious beliefs may have to give way to competing public interests.[206] It may be that most government regulations, such as accreditation requirements and prohibitions against racial discrimination, rarely interfere with any legitimate interests of universities.[207] But the interests of universities can conflict with those of governments and citizens, and close questions may arise when these conflicting interests are both strong.[208]

B. Does Institutional Academic Freedom Protect State Universities from Other Branches of Government?

In contrast to private universities, state universities may be constrained by both the first amendment and the state that creates and funds them. Despite judicial reiteration that institutional academic freedom encompasses the four essential freedoms of a university identified in *Sweezy*, substantial ambiguity exists regarding the scope of those freedoms. State legislatures often fund community colleges as well as four-year colleges, establish agricultural colleges as well as liberal arts universities, and determine which state universities may offer graduate degrees in various subjects. Insufficient legislative appropriations can lead to the elimination of existing faculty positions,[209] and legislatures can refuse to provide any funding for universities. These legislative decisions clearly limit the freedom of state colleges and universities to determine "who may teach," "what may be

---

202. See Byrne, 99 Yale L J at 282-83 (cited in note 1) (observing legitimate tension between some affirmative action plans that may be "derogations from accepted notions of professional competence for political reasons" and traditional notions of academic freedom).

203. See, for example, *Widmar*, 454 US 263, 269-70, 276-77.

204. See, for example, *Schmid*, 84 NJ at 560, 423 A2d at 628.

205. See Rabban, 66 Tex L Rev at 1419 (cited in note 19).

206. See *Bob Jones University v United States*, 461 US 574, 602-04 (1983) (denial of student admission based on genuine university belief that Bible forbids interracial dating and marriage outweighed by fundamental government interest in eliminating racial discrimination).

207. See, for example, Gutmann, *Democratic Education* at 179-80 (cited in note 193); Finkin, 61 Tex L Rev at 855-56 (cited in note 24); Gutmann, *Nomos 25: Liberal Democracy* at 276 (cited in note 193); Yudof, 32 Loyola L Rev at 853-54 (cited in note 24). But see Dallin H. Oaks, *A Private University Looks at Government Regulation*, 4 J Coll & Univ L 1, 3-4 (1976) (claiming most federal regulation of universities constitutes interference in management of educational functions that violates academic freedom).

208. See Gutmann, *Democratic Education* at 187 (cited in note 193); Gutmann, *Nomos 25: Liberal Democracy* at 266, 282-83 (cited in note 193).

209. See, for example, *Johnson v Board of Regents of University of Wisconsin System*, 377 F Supp 227 (WD Wis 1974), aff'd, 510 F2d 975 (9th Cir 1975); *Levitt v Board of Trustees of Nebraska State Colleges*, 376 F Supp 945 (D Neb 1974).

taught," and "who may be admitted to study," but no one has ever argued that they violate a public university's institutional academic freedom.

In some states, constitutional provisions establish state university systems as a separate branch of government. State courts have interpreted these provisions to preclude legislative attempts to fix the location of academic departments and the percentage of out-of-state students.[210] But in the majority of states, in which no constitutional separation of powers exists to protect the state university, it seems difficult to argue that the first amendment poses a bar to such legislative decisions.[211] Legislative attempts to dictate to private universities the composition of their student bodies or their general educational purposes, by contrast, would surely implicate their institutional academic freedom.

As decisions like *Sweezy* and *Keyishian* make clear, however, first amendment academic freedom imposes some limitations on legislative and administrative regulation of public universities. In *Sweezy*, the New Hampshire legislature violated the first amendment academic freedom of a university lecturer and of the "academic community"[212] by establishing a program of legislative investigations into subversive activities that included inquiries into the contents of a lecture at the University of New Hampshire. In *Keyishian*, a combination of vague statutes and administrative regulations violated first amendment academic freedom by subjecting professors to possible dismissal for teaching the principles of Marxism.[213]

The solicitor general explicitly distinguished *Sweezy* and *Keyishian* during oral argument in *University of Pennsylvania*, stressing that the EEOC's inquiry into the tenure process had "nothing to do with the world of ideas" and did not touch on classroom speech.[214] The Supreme Court's decision echoed this theme, and reinforced *Sweezy* and *Keyishian* by contrasting the legislative restrictions on the content of speech and on the university's selection of professors in those cases with the EEOC's investigation into whether the university had violated federal prohibitions against employment discrimination. The Court made a special point of emphasizing that it would

---

210. *Regents of the University of Michigan v State*, 47 Mich App 23, 208 NW2d 871 (1973) dismissed as moot, 395 Mich 52, 235 NW2d 1 (1975) (unconstitutional for legislature to fix percentage of out-of-state students); *Sterling v Regents of the University of Michigan*, 110 Mich 369, 68 NW 253 (1896) (unconstitutional for legislature to determine location of departments). See Byrne, 99 Yale L J at 327-28 (cited in note 1).

211. Professor Byrne maintains that state constitutional autonomy for universities as a separate branch of government provides a "legal source for constitutional academic freedom." Byrne, 99 Yale L J at 327 (cited in note 1). I find this argument unpersuasive. The fact that a few states have constitutionally provided for university autonomy does not suggest that similar protection should be read into the first amendment. Byrne cites only nine states that have explicitly provided constitutional autonomy for universities, though he adds that in an unidentified number of other states "courts have been willing to interpret often ambiguous constitutional language as imposing limitations on the legislature." Id at 327 n303.

212. *Sweezy*, 354 US at 245.

213. *Keyishian*, 385 US at 600.

214. Official Transcript Proceedings Before the Supreme Court of the United States at 43, *University of Pennsylvania v EEOC* (Nov 7, 1989) (No 88-493) ("*University of Pennsylvania Oral Argument*").

not "retreat" from its longstanding respect for the right of universities to make their own academic decisions.[215]

Some legislative and administrative controls over state universities seem clearly permissible, while others just as clearly violate the institutional academic freedom constitutionalized by the Supreme Court. Unfortunately, prior cases offer scant guidance in determining exactly when state actions violate the constitutional rights of institutions the state itself has created. As the earlier discussion of institutional context indicates,[216] however, some analytical hints have appeared in recent cases involving a variety of state institutions, including universities.

Federal Communications Commission v. League of Women Voters[217] provides the most clues about first amendment constraints on government regulation of its own institutions. The same congressional legislation that created and funded the Corporation for Public Broadcasting forbade editorializing by noncommercial educational broadcasting stations receiving grants from the corporation. Many of these stations are publicly owned and financed.[218] While recognizing that this congressional ban on editorializing was designed to serve the public's interest in receiving balanced coverage,[219] the Court held that it violated "important journalistic freedoms which the first amendment jealously protects."[220]

Because "broadcasters are engaged in a vital and independent form of communicative activity," the Court reasoned, "the first amendment must inform and give shape to the manner in which Congress exercises its regulatory power in this area." The Court concluded that the legitimate public interest in balanced coverage depends largely on "the editorial initiative and judgment of broadcasters who bear the public trust."[221] Alternative regulatory means, the Court observed, could serve the public interest in balanced coverage without jeopardizing "the 'journalistic freedom' of noncommercial broadcasters."[222] This recognition of the first amendment value of "journalistic freedom" parallels the Court's emphasis on the first amendment value of "academic freedom" in *Sweezy* and *Keyishian*.

Significantly, even the dissenters recognized that broadcasters have first amendment rights. They observed that Congress could not condition funding for public stations on the broadcasters' agreement to avoid controversial subjects[223] or to promote particular viewpoints.[224] Justice Stevens stressed in dissent that the ban on editorializing was enacted "to avoid the risk that some

---

215. 110 S Ct at 587.
216. See Part VI.
217. 468 US 364 (1984).
218. Id at 390 n19, 391 n20.
219. Id at 378.
220. Id at 402.
221. Id at 378.
222. Id at 398, citing *Columbia Broadcasting System, Inc. v Democratic National Committee*, 412 US 94, 110 (1973).
223. Id at 407 (Rehnquist dissenting).
224. Id at 414 (Stevens dissenting).

speakers will be rewarded or penalized for saying things that appealed to—or are offensive to—the sovereign."[225]

In distinguishing state-created institutions from public forums,[226] the Court has underlined both the general first amendment prohibition against viewpoint discrimination and the principle that certain institutions have traditional and broadly accepted expressive functions the state must accept when it creates them. Dissenting in *Southeastern Promotions, Limited v. Conrad*,[227] Justice Rehnquist foreshadowed subsequent majority decisions when he criticized the Court for applying public forum doctrine to the production decisions of a community-owned theater. The majority overturned on first amendment procedural grounds the rejection by the theater directors of an application to present the controversial rock musical "Hair," which contained group nudity and simulated sex. Rehnquist conceded in dissent that a municipal theater, unlike a private one, cannot "judge on a content basis alone" which plays to perform.[228] He noted, for example, that a municipal auditorium could not forbid a production of "Hair" based on opposition to the musical's political and social views while allowing performances of "equally graphic productions" whose ideas did not offend.[229] Yet he added that the element of a municipal theater "which is 'theater' ought to be accorded some constitutional recognition along with that element of it which is 'municipal.' "[230] At the very least, the directors of the municipal theater should have some discretion to decide what performances to book. Surely, Rehnquist suggested, a municipal theater should be able to devote an entire season to Shakespeare rather than to accept all bookings in order of application date until no openings are left.[231]

The Court majority's subsequent recognition in *Widmar v. Vincent* that the educational mission of a university distinguishes it "in significant respects from public forums such as streets or parks or even municipal theaters"[232] seems to accept Justice Rehnquist's distinction in *Southeastern Promotions* between public forums and state-created institutions. The *Widmar* majority's reiteration of the "four essential freedoms" quoted by Frankfurter in *Sweezy*[233] also reinforced Rehnquist's indication that the functions of state institutions may require first amendment protection for content-based decisions made within them. Justice Stevens's concurring opinion elaborated by maintaining that the institutional academic freedom of public universities should allow them to make educationally related appointment and curricular

225. Id.
226. See generally Post, 34 UCLA L Rev 1713 (cited in note 67). Professor Post distinguishes between government management of its own institutions for instrumental purposes and its regulation of public forums.
227. 420 US 546 (1975).
228. Id at 573 (Rehnquist dissenting).
229. Id at 572 n2.
230. Id at 573-74.
231. Id at 571-73.
232. 454 US at 268 n5.
233. Id at 276.

decisions based on the content of speech.[234] Lower-court decisions have underlined this approach, recognizing that the expressive functions of state university newspapers and public broadcasting stations justify first amendment protection for their editorial discretion.[235]

The functions of some state institutions might be contested. For example, the differing conclusions of Justices Brennan and Rehnquist in *Pico*[236] derived largely from their disagreement about the functions of a school library. Both justices agreed that the state cannot force its own institutions to suppress ideas based merely on disagreement with their content, but that it can consider the institution's functions in regulating the content of speech. Justice Brennan stressed the "unique role of the school library" in providing "wholly optional" opportunities for "self-education" and "individual enrichment." He distinguished "the regime of voluntary inquiry" in the school library from the "compulsory environment of the classroom."[237] Justice Rehnquist dismissed this characterization of the role of a school library as Brennan's own unsupported "creation." Criticizing Brennan for relying on precedents dealing with public libraries and universities, Rehnquist concluded that Brennan's "reasoning misapprehends the function of libraries in our public school system." In contrast to "university or public libraries, elementary and secondary school libraries are not designed for freewheeling inquiry; they are tailored, as the public school curriculum is tailored, to the teaching of basic skills and ideas." Indeed, the school library is "the one public institution which, by its very nature, is a place for the selective conveyance of ideas."[238]

It is extremely revealing that the dispute between Justices Brennan and Rehnquist over the function of a school library provoked Justice Rehnquist to affirm his understanding of university libraries as places devoted to "freewheeling inquiry." Quite clearly, Rehnquist would not allow a university

---

234. Id at 277-78. See text accompanying notes 110, 124-25 (discussing Stevens's concurrence).

235. See, for example, *Schneider v Indian River Community College Foundation*, 875 F2d 1537, 1541 (11th Cir 1989) (college trustees, as licensees of public radio station, have first amendment right to exercise programming discretion; "the degree of control which can be exercised consistently with the First Amendment depends on the mission of the communicative activity being controlled"); *Estiverne v Louisiana State Bar Ass'n*, 863 F2d 371, 381-82 (5th Cir 1989) (state bar journal not public forum; editors have "editorial discretion" to refuse to publish letter based on the journal's purposes but not on the letter's viewpoint); *Muir v Alabama Educational Television Comm'n*, 688 F2d 1033, 1041, 1044 (5th Cir 1982) (public television station not public forum; "First Amendment does not preclude the government from exercising editorial control over its own medium of expression"); id at 1052 (Rubin concurring) ("state's discretion is confined by the functions it may perform as a broadcast licensee, and the purpose to which it has dedicated its license"); *Joyner v Whiting*, 477 F2d 456, 460 (4th Cir 1973) (college cannot suppress student newspaper "because college officials dislike its editorial content"); *Bazaar v Fortune*, 476 F2d 570, 574 (5th Cir 1973) (state university cannot " 'support a campus newspaper and then try to restrict arbitrarily what it may publish, even if only to require that material be submitted to a faculty board to determine whether it complies with 'responsible freedom of the press' "), citing *ACLU v Radford College*, 315 F Supp 893, 896-97 (WD Va 1970).

236. 437 US 853.

237. Id at 869.

238. Id at 914-15 (Rehnquist dissenting).

or a state legislature to remove from a university library the books he would have allowed the school board to remove from school libraries in *Pico*.

Regulation of lawyers employed by the state similarly illustrates that appropriate restrictions on speech in one kind of state institution may be unconstitutional in others. The solicitor general, whose function is to support government positions before the Supreme Court, should be able to condition continued employment of staff attorneys on their advocacy of legal arguments that conform to government policy. By contrast, a state university, whose function is to promote critical inquiry in the search for knowledge, should not be able to condition continued employment of law professors on their advocacy of legal arguments favored by the dean or the state legislature.[239] Yet legislation requiring the teaching in law school of "practical" courses designed to prepare lawyers for practice in the state may be justified as furthering a valid institutional purpose.

The reasoning of cases such as *Federal Communications Commission*, *Widmar*, and *Pico* also suggests that a state cannot simply announce its departure from traditionally understood institutional functions.[240] A state could not, for example, create a university devoted exclusively to the inculcation of societal values rather than to critical inquiry. *Pico* indicates that the first amendment requires even a secondary school to allow "*some* limits" on its inculcative functions, and that what may be a permissible mix of inculcation and

---

239. I am grateful to David Anderson for suggesting this comparison.

240. Dean Yudof's analysis of the delegation of authority by political branches of government to institutions exercising specialized functions imposes substantial restrictions on government interference in those institutions. His analysis, however, does not preclude the government from restructuring or changing the functions of its own institutions. See Yudof, *When Government Speaks* at 135-38, 240-45 (cited in note 24); Mark G. Yudof, *Library Book Selection and the Public Schools: The Quest for the Archimedean Point*, 59 Ind L J 527, 553-59 (1984).

Dean Yudof observes that elected government officials frequently delegate specialized government functions to state institutions such as schools and universities, hospitals, student newspapers, public television stations, and libraries. Considerations of expertise and efficiency often lie behind delegations to professionals within state agencies. Yudof, *When Government Speaks* at 136, 243 (cited in note 24). These delegations, as Yudof observes with approval, often have the welcome benefits of serving as "a bulwark against the centralized orchestration of a publicly established orthodoxy," Yudof, 59 Ind L J at 553 (cited in this note), and of preventing "political interference" in state institutions. Yudof, *When Government Speaks* at 136 (cited in note 24). Yudof would even recognize de facto delegations when higher government officials have no policy on institutional functions. Yudof, 59 Ind L J at 555 (cited in this note). Ad hoc revocations of prior voluntary delegations for the purpose of censoring particular ideas, Yudof maintains, should be considered first amendment violations. Yudof, *When Government Speaks* at 243 (cited in note 24).

Although Dean Yudof recognizes that delegations of government authority promote first amendment interests in preventing "government established orthodoxy" and "ideological indoctrination," he would not interpret the first amendment to require delegation. Yudof, 59 Ind L J at 554 (cited in this note). He concludes, based on the general theory of delegation, that "government is not locked into existing institutional arrangements, and barring a restructuring effort growing out of an attempt to censor, government agencies are free to undo their delegations." Yudof, *When Government Speaks* at 244 (cited in note 24). For reasons I discuss throughout the text of this section, I disagree with Dean Yudof and consider the first amendment a constraint on state regulation of the expressive functions of its own institutions.

"diversity of thought" in secondary schools may be unconstitutional in colleges and universities, which have different functions.[241]

Although institutional functions may not be as fixed as the functions of traditional public forums, analogies to public forum doctrine are instructive. A state could not simply announce that a park or a street is no longer a public forum. Historic institutional functions may not have the "immemorial" tradition the Court has cited in declaring streets and parks public forums,[242] but some institutional traditions are sufficiently strong and longstanding that they deserve analogous recognition.[243] The rhetoric the Supreme Court devoted to extolling the social value of critical inquiry in universities while constitutionalizing academic freedom in *Sweezy* and *Keyishian* can legitimately be read as judicial notice of valuable university traditions. The Court has recently observed that all public streets "are properly considered traditional public fora," making unnecessary any "particularized inquiry into the precise nature of a specific street."[244] It is similarly appropriate to view all state universities as devoted to critical inquiry. This university tradition may be only a century old,[245] but it is also important to realize that the Supreme Court's recognition in 1939 of the "immemorial" use of streets and parks for communication in effect reversed an 1897 decision approving an observation by Holmes that the legislature could "forbid public speaking in a highway or public park."[246]

Institutional functions may change over time, as the history of American universities illustrates. Indeed, some see in American universities today an increasing tendency toward "politically correct thought"[247] that is the

---

241. 457 US at 879 (Blackmun concurring) (emphasis in original). See also *Muir*, 688 F2d at 1049 (Rubin concurring) ("Those state employees who are charged with operation of the station, whether high or low in the managerial hierarchy, may have some right to free expression, which may be stronger if, for example, they function in an academic environment devoted to freedom of inquiry.").

242. *Hague v CIO*, 307 US 496, 515 (1939).

243. See *Bazaar v Fortune*, 476 F2d 570, 580 (5th Cir 1973) (citing *Sweezy* and *Keyishian* while noting "the historical role of the University in expressing opinions which may well not make favor with the majority of society and in serving in the vanguard in the fight for freedom of expression and opinion").

244. *Frisby v Schultz*, 487 US 474, 481 (1988).

245. See notes 32-35 and accompanying text.

246. In *Hague*, 307 US at 515, the Court asserted that it had "no occasion to determine" whether its previous decision in *Davis v Massachusetts*, 167 US 43 (1897), "was rightly decided." The Court in *Hague* claimed that the ordinance in *Davis* "was not directed solely at the exercise of the right of speech and assembly" in a public park. Yet this attempt to distinguish *Davis* was unconvincing. "For the legislature absolutely or conditionally to forbid public speaking in a highway or public park," the Court concluded in *Davis*, "is no more an infringement of the rights of a member of the public than for the owner of a private house to forbid it in his house." 167 US at 47.

Professor Kalven's important article generating "public forum" analysis recognizes that *Hague* essentially reversed *Davis*. Harry Kalven, Jr., *The Concept of the Public Forum: Cox v Louisiana*, 1965 S Ct Rev 1, 12-13. See also Post, 34 UCLA L Rev at 1723 (cited in note 67) (asserting that the thrust of *Hague* "is not that speech in streets and parks is especially important or unique, but rather that government could not exercise proprietary control over such places").

247. See, for example, Scott Heller, *Colleges Becoming Havens of 'Political Correctness,' Some Scholars Say*, Chron Higher Educ 1 col 3 (November 21, 1990); Carolyn J. Mooney, *Academic Group Fighting the 'Politically Correct Left' Gains Momentum*, Chron Higher Educ 1 col 2 (December 12, 1990); John Searle, *The Storm Over the University*, NY Rev Books 34 (December 6, 1990).

antithesis of critical inquiry. If this perceived trend toward ideological conformity on issues such as faculty appointments and curriculum becomes dominant, the university itself may undermine its traditional function and with it the justification for academic freedom. But until pervasive evidence of such change exists, the Supreme Court's recognition of universities as institutions devoted to critical inquiry should prevail.

Consistent with this analysis of institutional function, the state could create institutions sharing some characteristics with universities but not devoted to critical inquiry. Illustrations could include postsecondary trade schools and legislative research bureaus employing social scientists to provide intellectual justifications for political decisions. But just as the 1915 Declaration argued that "proprietary institutions" designed to inculcate ideas should not be able "to sail under false colors" by calling themselves universities,[248] states should not constitutionally be able to define as universities institutions uncommitted to critical inquiry. Once a state creates an entity described as a university, a library, a newspaper, or a television station, it should be under a first amendment obligation to respect the expressive functions traditionally associated with these institutions.

Unfortunately, a number of potential government actions raise close questions that even this extended analysis cannot answer. For example, the Supreme Court has recognized the "undoubted right" of a state legislature "to prescribe the curriculum for its public schools" as long as these laws do not otherwise violate the first amendment by constituting an establishment of religion or by discriminating against a particular ideological viewpoint.[249] In relying on the establishment clause to overturn a state statute requiring instruction in "creation science," the Court recently made a special point of stating: "We do not imply that a legislature could never require that scientific critiques of prevailing scientific theories be taught."[250] Various acknowledgments that greater freedom of inquiry is appropriate in universities than at earlier stages of education, combined with the university's academic freedom to determine "what may be taught" identified in the repeatedly cited passage from *Sweezy*, could conceivably lead the Court to impose more restrictions on legislative power to determine curriculum in state universities than in public schools.[251] Yet the Court's untroubled acceptance of legislative control over public school curriculum makes the likelihood of such a holding at best uncertain. Would a court, for example, invoke first amendment academic freedom to invalidate Texas statutes requiring every state-supported university to offer a course in government or

---

248. See text accompanying note 23 (discussing 1915 Declaration).

249. *Epperson v Arkansas*, 393 US 97, 106-08, 107 n15 (1969).

250. *Edwards*, 482 US at 593. See also *Pico*, 457 US at 869 (school boards might have "absolute discretion in matters of *curriculum*") (emphasis in original).

251. See *DiBona*, 220 Cal App3d 1329, 269 Cal Rptr 882 (Cal App 1990) (college administrators have less discretion than school administrators to control curriculum).

political science, which must include consideration of the United States and Texas Constitutions, and a course in American or Texas history?[252]

The oral argument in *University of Pennsylvania* highlighted another unresolved challenge to the scope of institutional academic freedom against other branches of government. One justice asked the lawyer arguing on behalf of the University of Pennsylvania to specify who wields the asserted first amendment right to determine who may teach. "I guess somebody has a right to say who may teach," the justice observed, "but does it have to be the faculty?" The justice went on to wonder "what is the principle that . . . members of a faculty have a constitutional right to . . . replicate themselves?" Could the right to hire faculty in a state university, the justice asked, be reserved to a legislative committee or the governor?

The lawyer for the University of Pennsylvania found it difficult to respond. He claimed that it would be a "harder case" to locate this constitutional right in the legislative or the executive branches than in the faculty, but never really stated why. After some fumbling, he ultimately asserted that if, contrary to tradition, decisions about faculty hiring are made "by someone in government, then it is that entity that would enjoy the first amendment freedom." "So the government," the justice interjected, "has a first amendment right. That's phenomenal."[253]

The Court's decision in *University of Pennsylvania* did not address the issues raised by this colloquy, but its very occurrence dramatically underlines the continuing uncertainty about the meaning of institutional academic freedom. I find it striking that the university's lawyer seemed so unprepared for this line of questioning and so readily conceded that a state legislature or governor could assume the power to appoint faculty under the protection of the first amendment. At least a plausible argument could be made that the institutional academic freedom from legislative control over university teaching established in *Sweezy* and *Keyishian* should be interpreted to preclude a state legislature or governor from appointing faculty. The first amendment interest in critical inquiry identified in those decisions is arguably threatened by the potential that political control over faculty appointments may impose a "pall of orthodoxy" over state universities and transform them into propaganda vehicles indistinguishable from government agencies such as the Voice of America.

---

252. Texas Educ Code Ann §§ 51.301, 51.302 (Vernon 1987). Professor Byrne, it seems to me, is vastly overconfident in asserting that attempts by legislatures or administrative agencies "to compel universities to offer students a particular liberal arts curriculum . . . surely would be unconstitutional" as a violation of institutional academic freedom. Byrne, 99 Yale L J at 331 (cited in note 1). Compare Thomas I. Emerson, *The System of Freedom of Expression* 624 (Random House, 1970) ("the government can prescribe the [broad] character of the curriculum for a particular institution, provide what general areas are to be emphasized or omitted, even require the offering of certain courses").

253. *University of Pennsylvania Oral Argument* at 8-10 (cited in note 214). The official transcript does not include references to particular justices. My recollection from attending the oral argument, confirmed by a law clerk who was also present, is that Justice Scalia asked these questions.

The extent to which institutional academic freedom insulates state universities from other branches of government, though presenting numerous complicated and unresolved issues, remains largely hypothetical. In the generation since the McCarthy period, the legislative and executive branches have not intruded directly into the core academic decisions of state universities. The *University of Pennsylvania* decision may not have protected sufficiently the confidentiality of the peer review process from government intrusion. Yet the Court plausibly distinguished between the legislative attempts to monitor the substance of classroom speech in *Sweezy* and *Keyishian* and the EEOC's effort to determine whether the university had engaged in unlawful employment discrimination. The tension between the institutional academic freedom of universities and the individual academic freedom of faculty, by contrast, has arisen in a number of concrete contexts. It is to this difficult problem that I therefore turn.

IX

THE TENSION BETWEEN INDIVIDUAL AND INSTITUTIONAL ACADEMIC FREEDOM

The focus of several recent Supreme Court decisions on institutional academic freedom, beginning with *Bakke* in 1978, has prompted some commentators to conclude that constitutional academic freedom extends only to institutions. According to these commentators, the traditional nonlegal conception of academic freedom as a right of individual faculty members, identified by the 1915 Declaration and widely accepted within the scholarly world, lacks constitutional protection.[254] In my opinion, this conclusion is mistaken. The accurate perception that the Supreme Court has identified institutional academic freedom as a first amendment right does not support the additional conclusion that the Court has rejected a constitutional right of individual professors to academic freedom against trustees, administrators, and faculty peers.

Early cases such as *Sweezy* and *Keyishian* recognized constitutional academic freedom as an individual as well as an institutional right. In holding that government inquiry into the contents of a university lecture "unquestionably was an invasion of petitioner's [the lecturer's] liberties in the areas of academic freedom and political expression," the Court in *Sweezy* recognized both academic freedom and political expression as individual first amendment rights.[255] The appellants in *Keyishian* were faculty members whose continued employment was conditioned on compliance with a state law requiring them to sign a certificate that they were not members of the Communist Party.[256]

---

254. See Byrne, 99 Yale L J at 255, 257, 313 (cited in note 1); Metzger, 66 Tex L Rev at 1267, 1284-85, 1292, 1322 (cited in note 1). According to Professor Metzger, the professional and constitutional definitions of academic freedom are "seriously incompatible and probably ultimately irreconcilable." Id at 1267.

255. 354 US at 250.

256. 385 US at 591-92, 595-96.

In holding this law unconstitutional, the Court warned that the "chilling effect upon the exercise of vital first amendment rights must be guarded against by sensitive tools which clearly inform teachers what is being proscribed."[257] The law, the Court observed, could be interpreted to bar the employment of a teacher who simply informs his class about Marxism.[258] The Court's emphasis on the impact of the law on teachers indicates its focus on individual interests in academic freedom.

No case to date has presented the Court with a direct conflict between institutional and individual claims of first amendment academic freedom. The closest the Court has come to analyzing this issue is a footnote by Justice Stevens in *Regents of University of Michigan v. Ewing*,[259] a case brought by a medical student challenging a faculty decision to dismiss the student on academic grounds. "Academic freedom," Justice Stevens noted, "thrives not only on the independent and uninhibited exchange of ideas among teachers and students, . . . but also, and somewhat inconsistently, on autonomous decisionmaking by the academy itself . . . ."[260] A subsequent majority opinion by Justice Brennan noted with approval the definition of academic freedom by the lower court as "the principle that individual instructors are at liberty to teach that which they deem to be appropriate in the exercise of their professional judgment."[261] In addition, the Court's recent decision in *University of Pennsylvania*, by facilitating discovery against a university in a Title VII case while rejecting an expanded claim of institutional academic freedom in confidential peer review material, recognized the appropriateness of judicial scrutiny of individual faculty claims against the university. Although the Court's holding applied only to EEOC subpoenas, its reasoning could easily be extended to allow discovery of personnel files by an individual professor asserting that a university appointment or promotion decision constituted employment discrimination prohibited by Title VII or retaliation for speech protected by the first amendment.

Various lower court cases, moreover, have directly addressed the tension between institutional and individual academic freedom while adjudicating disputes between individual faculty members and universities. In a decision involving the dismissal of a Marxist professor, a federal district judge frankly admitted that while academic freedom as an unenumerated first amendment right "is well recognized, its parameters are not well defined." The opinion identified "a fundamental tension between the academic freedom of the individual teacher to be free of restraints from the university administration, and the academic freedom of the university to be free of government, including judicial, interference."[262]

---

257. Id at 604.
258. Id at 600.
259. 474 US 214 (1985).
260. Id at 226 n12.
261. *Edwards*, 482 US at 586 n6. Justice Brennan cited this definition to evaluate its use by a state legislature, not to address its constitutional meaning.
262. *Cooper v Ross*, 472 F Supp 802, 813 (ED Ark 1979).

Judge Posner, whose many years as a law professor undoubtedly contributed to his appreciation of this issue, used similar language. He observed that academic freedom, though frequently described "as an aspect of the freedom of speech that is protected against government abridgment by the first amendment," has an "equivocal" meaning. "It is used to denote both the freedom of the academy to pursue its ends without interference from the government . . . and the freedom of the individual teacher (or in some versions—indeed in most cases—the student) to pursue his ends without interference from the academy; and these two freedoms are in conflict, as in this case."[263] Judge Posner assumed without deciding that a university administration could not forbid the chair of the art department from displaying his stained-glass windows anywhere on campus. He acknowledged the administration's concern that the content of these windows would offend potential applicants and thus make it harder to recruit students, particularly black and female students. Judicial interference with the administration's attempt to protect the university's image, he conceded, would "limit the freedom of the academy to manage its affairs as it chooses." But he reasoned that even this legitimate interest could not justify an absolute proscription against displaying the windows, although he did uphold the administration's decision to move them to a less conspicuous place.[264]

Other lower court decisions, without explicitly addressing the tension between individual and institutional academic freedom, reinforce the conclusion that individual professors can have constitutional academic freedom claims against universities. In reviewing cases in which universities denied appointments to Marxist professors, courts have reiterated that "no more direct assault on academic freedom can be imagined than for school authorities to be allowed to discharge a teacher because of his or her political, philosophical, or ideological beliefs, . . . and the same would be true of a decision not to hire."[265] Recent institutional policies outlawing offensive speech[266] and concerns about the danger of university and external attempts to coerce faculty research into areas likely to attract corporate and government funding[267] illustrate additional contexts that may produce individual academic freedom claims against universities.

---

263. *Piarowski*, 759 F2d at 629.

264. Id at 630. See generally id at 629-31.

265. *Franklin v Atkins*, 409 F Supp 439, 445 (D Colo 1976), aff'd, 562 F2d 1188 (10th Cir 1977). See also *Ollman*, 518 F Supp at 1202.

266. See note 63 and accompanying text.

267. See Stuart W. Leslie, *From Backwater to Powerhouse*, Stanford 55 (March 1990) (Stanford University achieved preeminence in electrical engineering by attracting financial support and faculty from military contractors and by directing its research program and curriculum to military priorities); Eliot Marshall, *Harvard Tiptoes into the Market*, 241 Science 1595 (1988) (citing faculty criticism of proposed university funding for commercial development of professor's efficient method of making bacteria express human genes; concern that such projects would divert faculty from pure scholarship prompted new program to assure all funded projects are of "highest intellectual quality").

Professor Eisenberg convincingly warns that the lure of external financial support from industry and the military may tempt faculty members to compromise academic values. Rebecca S. Eisenberg, *Academic Freedom and Academic Values in Sponsored Research*, 66 Tex L Rev 1363 (1988). She directs

A. Are Judges Competent to Review Academic Freedom Claims By Professors Against Universities?

Some scholars who recognize the tension between individual and institutional academic freedom advocate limiting the constitutional definition of academic freedom to the protection of the university against the state. Professor J. Peter Byrne offers the most comprehensive statement of this position.[268] Byrne repeatedly argues that courts are not equipped to enforce traditional claims of academic freedom by professors against university decision-makers.[269] The appropriate role of the judiciary, he maintains, is to exclude public officials from incursions into basic academic affairs, a role that in his view protects individual faculty members as well as universities as institutions.[270] Byrne stresses that judges themselves are public officials who threaten academic freedom within the university. "Judicial views of civil liberty," he argues citing *Schmid*, "may infringe academic principles just as much as executive or legislative views of national security,"[271] the impetus for the landmark academic freedom cases of the McCarthy era. For a court to resolve a faculty member's assertion that the university violated his academic freedom in denying him tenure, Byrne portentously concludes, "would put the department or school into intellectual receivership, with the court determining the appropriate paradigms of thought."[272]

I disagree strenuously with Professor Byrne's view that judicial review of disputes between professors and universities poses an intolerable threat of state interference with academic freedom. Title VII and first amendment cases at universities have demonstrated that judges can respect academic expertise and values while determining whether stated academic grounds are pretexts for illegal or unconstitutional university decisions. However, I generally agree with Byrne that judges should not review good faith debates within universities about the merits of unpopular or unconventional ideas.

Byrne realizes that his conception of constitutional academic freedom is inconsistent with the tradition of academic freedom derived from the 1915

---

legitimate criticism against recent AAUP reports on external funding of faculty research, whose focus on threats to faculty academic freedom from universities seeking external funding neglects potential abuses by professors themselves. Id at 1378-84. See, for example, AAUP, *Academic Freedom and Tenure: Corporate Funding of Academic Research*, 69 Academe 18a (November-December 1983); AAUP, *Government Censorship and Academic Freedom*, 69 Academe 15a (November-December 1983).

Professor Eisenberg and I disagree, however, about whether the traditional American conception of academic freedom constrains faculty disregard of academic values. Compare Eisenberg, id at 1404 (the "traditional American conception of academic freedom, with its emphasis on defending the professional autonomy of individual faculty members against universities," is ill-adapted to the task of protecting academic values in sponsored research within universities") with Rabban, 66 Tex L Rev at 1408 (cited in note 19) ("the traditional conception of academic freedom constrains faculty autonomy to protect academic values") and Rebecca S. Eisenberg, *Defining the Terms of Academic Freedom: A Reply to Professor Rabban*, 66 Tex L Rev 1431, 1434-35 (1988) (Rabban's "confusing and misleading" usage extends academic freedom beyond any meaningful definition).

268. Byrne, 99 Yale L J 251 (cited in note 1). See especially id at 255.
269. Id at 288. See also id at 255, 305, 306.
270. Id at 304. See also id at 255.
271. Id at 307. See also id at 307-08 n222.
272. Id at 306.

Declaration, which focuses on the rights of individual professors, particularly against lay trustees or regents.[273] Perhaps for this reason, he contrasts a prior "dark age of faculty dependence" with the present, "when most universities voluntarily defend the academic freedom of their faculties,"[274] and the state poses the most serious threats to professors and universities. Byrne thus seems to believe that his constitutional theory of academic freedom makes both theoretical and practical sense. Not only are the courts an inappropriate forum for protecting faculty from administrators and trustees, but in the contemporary world the real dangers to academic freedom come from the state.

Byrne also constructs a "limiting principle" on institutional academic freedom that would allow some legal protection for traditional claims of academic freedom by professors against universities. According to Byrne, "constitutional academic freedom ought not to protect institutions resembling universities but which do not pursue genuine liberal studies—that prohibit or consistently discourage professors from following controversial arguments, that recognize no role for faculty in governance, or that seek to indoctrinate rather than educate students." When universities "do not respect the academic freedom of professors (understood as the core of the doctrine developed by the AAUP)," Byrne reasons, they so deviate from the values that justify institutional academic freedom that they should lose their immunity from judicial review. Byrne anticipates that his limiting principle would "lessen fears that institutional freedom will cloak extensive violations of professors' academic freedom by institutions bent on intellectual orthodoxy."[275] Yet this language suggests that as long as administrators and trustees do not "prohibit or consistently discourage" the exercise of individual academic freedom as understood by the AAUP, they retain constitutional academic freedom against judicial review of any periodic but less extensive repression of academic speech.

Legal cases and reports of AAUP investigating committees provide ample evidence that, even if the "dark age of faculty dependence" has ended (at least temporarily), university violations of faculty academic freedom continue to occur. Many of these violations, moreover, take place in universities that ordinarily respect individual academic freedom. These abridgments of academic freedom, like many state infringements of individual civil liberties, are not frequent events, and thus would not fall under Byrne's limiting principle. The broad institutional immunity advocated by Byrne would heighten the danger that administrators and trustees might violate the academic freedom of professors.

Elsewhere, Byrne seemingly departs from his limiting principle and implies that judicial review is proper whenever administrators fail to justify their decisions on academic grounds. Even under this standard, however,

---

273. See, for example, id at 255, 267, 273, 288, 312.
274. Id at 324.
275. Id at 338. See id at 332.

Byrne still insists that judges can evaluate solely whether administrators acted in good faith and not whether the grounds themselves are adequate.[276] This insistence leaves a crucial problem unresolved. Determining whether an academic judgment purportedly made in good faith is actually a pretext for an improper consideration, including one that might violate individual academic freedom, often requires some assessment of the adequacy of the stated academic ground.

Byrne confuses his analysis by referring to university administrators as "lay persons" in some contexts but as "academics" in others. In discussing the historical roots of the AAUP's conception of individual academic freedom, Byrne recognizes that university presidents, whatever the identification they might previously have had with the faculty, had become "institutional executives and educational entrepreneurs," who shared the business values of trustees more than the academic values of professors.[277] Byrne applauds the emphasis in the 1915 Declaration on the relationship between peer review and academic freedom, deeming it "the insulation of the individual professor from lay interference."[278] Byrne here understands that the laity includes administrators as well as trustees, although in discussing threats to the academic freedom of professors he focuses more on trustees than on administrators.[279]

In analyzing judicial review of universities' academic decisions, by contrast, Byrne groups administrators with faculty as academics, while largely ignoring trustees. He refers to "intra-academic" cases,[280] in which faculty members claim violations of their academic freedom by "other academics, usually administrators and department chairs."[281] Byrne may be correct that some administrators are presumptively competent to apply professional criteria in judging academic speech,[282] but this presumption weakens as one moves up the hierarchy of university administration, and it is invalid as to trustees.

Byrne finds it "incoherent to suggest that academic freedom could be furthered by reducing peer review and substituting the enforcement of rules by lay persons such as judges." Such a transformation "ignores both the historical basis of, and the actual structures that protect, faculty rights."[283] I

---

276. See id at 300, 304, 306, 308.
277. Id at 270. See id at 272.
278. Id at 278.
279. Id at 273, 276.
280. Id at 309.
281. Byrne in this context finds it reasonable for the AAUP, but not for the courts, to criticize administrators who reject the professional judgments of faculty committees "because it is that association's business to enhance the sphere of freedom and control over academic administration of its members." This language portrays a self-interested power struggle between faculty and administrators that seems inconsistent with Byrne's repeated approval of peer review as a safeguard of individual academic freedom against inappropriate intrusions by lay administrators and trustees. At most, Byrne is willing to concede that this struggle may produce "workable norms" that should not be enforced in "the coercive domain of law." Id at 308.
282. Id at 310.
283. Id at 286.

emphatically agree. But this passage does not address the propriety of lay persons such as judges enforcing peer review, and thereby protecting individual academic freedom, against other lay persons such as trustees and administrators. The theory that justifies judicial as well as administrative deference to peer review does not support similar judicial deference to trustees and administrators.

In addition, Byrne's examples of the dangers inherent in judicial review of individual academic freedom claims against universities are frequently inapt. He seems to assume, for example, that a constitutional right of individual academic freedom would force courts to overturn administrative sanctions against professors who deviate from prescribed curricular coverage or who receive poor teaching evaluations from students.[284] But no accepted theory of individual academic freedom, and certainly not the one developed by the AAUP, would identify these professors as engaging in speech to which academic freedom should attach. Academic freedom is not the freedom to be a poor teacher or to refuse to include materials on the Civil War in a survey course in American history.

Byrne also assumes erroneously that a constitutional right of individual academic freedom would be violated if a university administrator, shocked that the philosophy department has no expert on Plato and Aristotle, denies tenure to a creative philosopher with an esoteric specialty.[285] Even if the administrator had overruled a unanimous departmental recommendation, the justification behind this decision reflects the kind of legitimate bureaucratic concern over departmental balance that provides grounds for reversing peer judgments under policies the AAUP accepts. Bureaucratic rationales similarly would justify rejections of peer recommendations by administrators based on programmatic or financial grounds, the candidate's professionally unethical conduct, or the failure of peers to apply appropriate professional standards.[286] By contrast, individual academic freedom would be implicated if administrators denied tenure to a candidate because they feared his eclectic interest in unpopular philosophical positions would alienate a potential donor.

The most important response to Byrne is that judges can enforce the academic freedom of individual professors against administrators, trustees, and faculty peers without violating a legitimate conception of institutional academic freedom or abandoning appropriate judicial deference to academic decision-making. The judiciary is more deliberative and less political than

---

284. Id at 301.

285. Id at 308.

286. See AAUP, American Council on Education, and Association of Governing Boards of Universities and Colleges, *1966 Statement on Government of Colleges and Universities*, reprinted in *Academic Freedom and Tenure* at 90 (cited in note 6) ("*Statement on Government*"). See generally Rabban, 66 Tex L Rev at 1411-12 & n29 (cited in note 19). David M. Rabban, *Distinguishing Excluded Managers From Covered Professionals Under the NLRA*, 89 Colum L Rev 1775, 1840-44 (1989), analyzes the legitimate bureaucratic responsibilities of managers in universities and other organizations in which professionals work.

either the legislature or the executive. Indeed, in these respects courts may resemble universities more than other branches of government. Courts are likely to be more sensitive than legislators or members of the executive branch[287] to the need for independent critical inquiry in universities and to their democratic role as sanctuaries for unpopular ideas. These statements are not merely speculative. A model for appropriate judicial review of individual academic freedom cases already exists in numerous decisions addressing claims by professors that universities have violated Title VII prohibitions against employment discrimination or general rights of free speech protected by the first amendment.

B. Appropriate Judicial Review of Academic Decisions

Title VII and first amendment decisions demonstrate that judges, without undue interference in university affairs, can review whether stated academic grounds are pretexts. Whatever their holdings, these decisions emphasize that courts should afford broad deference to professional expertise. Academic decisions are necessarily subjective and beyond the competence of judges. Courts cannot become a "Super-Tenure Review Committee"[288] or "evaluate the substance of the multitude of academic decisions that are made daily by faculty members of public educational institutions."[289] Rather, judges should override "a genuinely academic decision" only if "it is such a substantial departure from accepted academic norms as to demonstrate that the person or committee responsible did not actually exercise professional judgment."[290]

This standard of judicial review, as the courts announcing it have recognized, requires judges to evaluate the substance of the decision so that they can determine whether "a substantial departure from accepted academic norms" took place. In applying this standard, courts stress that decisions by professionals are "presumptively valid"[291] and are subject to "very limited"[292] judicial scrutiny. If a professional decision has "an adequate factual basis for the conclusions reached,"[293] a court should not substitute its judgment on the merits for the views of the relevant professionals. The role of judges is not to review and correct individual mistakes in academic decision-making, but to make sure that the decisions reached by professionals

---

287. See Alexander Bickel, *The Least Dangerous Branch: The Supreme Court at the Bar of Politics* 25-26 (Yale, 2d ed 1962); Henry P. Monaghan, *First Amendment "Due Process,"* 83 Harv L Rev 518, 523-24 (1970). See also AAUP, *Academic Freedom and Tenure: State University of New York at Stonybrook,* 76 Academe 55 (January-February 1990) (AAUP investigating committee concludes that professor, accused of equating Zionism with racism, protected by academic freedom against interference by state governor and others outside the university in internal review of his candidacy for tenure).

288. *Keddie v Pennsylvania State University,* 412 F Supp 1264, 1270 (MD Pa 1976).

289. *Ewing,* 474 US at 226.

290. Id at 225.

291. *Youngberg v Romeo,* 457 US 307, 323 (1982), cited in *Ewing,* 474 US at 225.

292. *Cooper,* 472 F Supp at 810.

293. *Ollman,* 518 F Supp at 1215.

are consistent with constitutional and statutory obligations.[294] Not surprisingly, these stringent standards have prompted courts to reject the overwhelming majority of Title VII and first amendment claims by individual professors against universities.

Several courts, concerned that appropriate judicial deference to academic decision-making "has been pressed beyond all reasonable limits," have warned against a policy of judicial "self-abnegation where colleges are concerned" that amounts to "abdication" of responsibility to enforce laws protecting individual rights.[295] Academic freedom, they stress, does not include the freedom to engage in employment discrimination or to violate the free speech protected by the first amendment.[296] Even courts that do not express this concern look into the factual background of academic decisions to determine whether a stated academic judgment was a pretext.

The Supreme Court has yet to address the merits of an individual claim by a faculty member against peers, the administration, or the trustees, although *University of Pennsylvania* makes clear that the Court is prepared to do so.[297] However, the Court has reviewed faculty professional judgment in a case brought by a dismissed student. While stressing the importance of judicial deference, the Court felt compelled to examine the evidence underlying the faculty judgment before upholding it. The Court pointed out, for example, that the dismissed student had low grades, many incomplete courses, irregular or reduced course loads, and had failed his medical boards.[298]

Lower courts have adopted a similar approach to Title VII and first amendment claims by faculty members against university decision-makers. In reviewing a claim that a university president unconstitutionally relied on a professor's Marxist beliefs to reject him for department chair, one judge emphasized that the president's reasons "must be examined critically and in detail."[299] A thorough analysis of the record convinced the judge that the president's reasons were not only sincere but also supported by sufficient evidence.[300]

---

294. See, for example, *Brown v Trustees of Boston University*, 891 F2d 337, 356 (1st Cir 1989); *Clark v Whiting*, 607 F2d 634, 639 (4th Cir 1979); *Cooper*, 472 F Supp at 810.

295. *Powell v Syracuse University*, 580 F2d 1150, 1153, 1154 (2d Cir 1978), citing *Sweeny v Board of Trustees of Keene State College*, 569 F2d 169, 176, 177 (1st Cir 1978), judgment vacated, 439 US 24 (1978), appeal after remand, 604 F2d 106 (1st Cir 1979).

296. *Powell*, 580 F2d at 1154; *Brown*, 891 F2d at 360.

297. The Supreme Court's recent decision in *University of Pennsylvania*, 110 S Ct 577, by facilitating discovery against a university in a Title VII case, recognizes the appropriateness of judicial review of individual faculty claims. The Court emphasized that Congress explicitly discounted the danger of improper state intrusion into university autonomy when it amended Title VII in 1972 to cover educational institutions, which were exempted under the original 1964 legislation. Id at 582. University decisions based on race, sex, or national origin, the Court observed, do not constitute the "academic grounds" protected by the first amendment right to academic freedom. Id at 587 n7. The Court thus concluded that judges can enforce Title VII on campus while recognizing "the importance of avoiding second-guessing of legitimate academic judgments." Id at 587.

298. *Ewing*, 474 US at 227.

299. *Ollman*, 518 F Supp at 1203.

300. Id at 1215.

Given the understandable concern about the competence of judges to evaluate sensitive and subjective academic decisions requiring professional expertise, it is striking how much of the evidence cited by judges in Title VII and first amendment cases does not fall into this category. Rather, evidence of pretext has frequently involved familiar judicial analysis of motivation based on factors that are not unique to a university environment, such as the timing of a decision and objective quantitative data. One court found that university administrators had violated a professor's first amendment rights based on two key facts: the university had never previously dismissed or failed to renew the contract of a full-time faculty member, and the university administrators refused to reappoint the plaintiff almost immediately after he created a state-wide public controversy by announcing his belief in communism and his membership in the Progressive Labor Party. These facts convinced the court that the faculty member's protected first amendment speech and association, and not weaknesses in his teaching as the administrators asserted, were the primary factors in the decision against reappointment.[301]

Similar examples abound. Testimony that the administration required publication of two books from a female professor who was denied tenure, but only one book from men who had received tenure, helped an appellate court in a Title VII case reach the inference that the administrators' vigorous criticism of her scholarship was a pretext for discrimination.[302] Another judge upheld a finding of discrimination based on uncontroverted evidence that a black administrator failed to renew the contract of a white professor whose formal educational background met or exceeded those of black colleagues who were retained and promoted.[303] On the other hand, a court that complained about too much judicial deference to universities in Title VII cases nevertheless affirmed the termination of a black female professor who had established a prima facie case of discrimination. The court based its holding in part on the fact that the professor lacked formal training in architecture, the field in which she taught.[304]

Although much of the evidence in these cases did not require judicial analysis of sensitive professional judgments, courts have been willing when necessary to evaluate the substance of academic decisions to determine whether stated academic grounds were pretextual. One judge concluded that a candidate for department chair did not have sufficient administrative experience, and reviewed the conflicting testimony of distinguished scholars to determine whether doubts about the candidate's academic qualifications were plausible.[305] In another case, a circuit court evaluated a complex academic judgment—that a woman denied reappointment lacked the ability to

---

301. *Cooper*, 472 F Supp at 811-12.
302. *Brown*, 891 F2d at 347.
303. *Whiting v Jackson State University*, 616 F2d 116, 123-24 (5th Cir 1980).
304. *Powell*, 580 F2d at 1151, 1156.
305. *Ollman*, 518 F Supp at 1217.

generalize from her admitted competence in her specialized research field to broader issues in her discipline—to determine whether this criterion was applied fairly not just to her, but also to men who were reappointed in the same department.[306]

Courts have cited "obviously weak or implausible"[307] and "ambiguous and poorly substantiated"[308] statements of reasons for personnel decisions as relevant to determining whether stated academic judgments were pretextual. Significantly, even in so doing, one court reiterated that the merits of academic decisions are within university discretion and involve subtle issues that may be difficult to articulate. Universities, the court added, need not ordinarily document or explain their tenure decisions. Yet in analyzing a claim that a university had violated a faculty member's first amendment rights, "the paucity of supporting evidence implies that the reasons given by the University were hastily prepared makeweight reasons which do not fully reflect its true motivation."[309] The unanimous recommendations of faculty committees have also prompted courts, consistent with the theory of peer review, to be skeptical of the administration's stated academic grounds for reversing them.[310]

C. Judicial Review of Internal Debates Over Professional Quality

I have attempted thus far to demonstrate that individual academic freedom is a meaningful concept under the first amendment. Courts have recognized its existence in tension with institutional academic freedom, and judicial techniques for reviewing faculty claims against university decision-makers in Title VII and general first amendment cases can be applied as well to individual claims of academic freedom without undermining critical inquiry. Yet some professors do not allege that stated academic reasons are pretexts, but that those reasons themselves violate academic freedom by relying on intellectual orthodoxies. The university decision-makers may respond that the candidate is not simply unorthodox, but professionally incompetent or undistinguished. Should judges resolve disputes within the university about whether unpopular or unconventional ideas reflect professional merit?

Many of these internal academic debates raise issues that could be brought under conventional Title VII and first amendment theories. Departments of linguistics, English, and economics might tell disappointed candidates for appointment or tenure that studies of black dialects, feminist literary theory, and Marxist economic analysis simply are not useful modes of professional inquiry. Are these reasons evidence of racial, sexual, or political discrimination? Without raising broader issues of discrimination,

---

306. *Smith v University of North Carolina*, 632 F2d 316, 342-44 (4th Cir 1980).
307. *Brown*, 891 F2d at 346, citing *Kumar v Board of Trustees, University of Massachusetts*, 774 F2d 1, 12 (1st Cir 1985) (Campbell concurring).
308. *Cooper*, 472 F Supp at 812.
309. Id.
310. *Brown*, 891 F2d at 347-48; *Kunda v Muhlenberg College*, 621 F2d 532, 548 (3d Cir 1980).

departments may consider quantitative analysis in history or cataclysmic theories of biological change as professionally uninteresting. Do these evaluations impose an ideological orthodoxy that violates the academic freedom of professors denied appointment or tenure because they hold such views?[311]

Recent controversies over the value of "critical legal studies" in law schools prompted the AAUP to address these issues. Though the AAUP admonished departments to base decisions on the professional competence and integrity of candidates rather than on disciplinary orthodoxies, it did not address the extent to which standards of competence within disciplines themselves reflect conventional wisdom. The AAUP concluded that departments do not abridge individual academic freedom as long as they make academic judgments in good faith, a permissive though largely undefined standard. Evidence of bad faith, the AAUP suggested, might include consideration of the possible consequences of a candidate's academic views or penalizing a candidate's "nihilism" about her discipline.[312]

Unfortunately, too many academics find no merit in disciplinary approaches that differ from their own. This position, though narrow and arrogant, may be held in good faith. Indeed, professors who are most obnoxiously confident in the superiority of their own views are also most likely to be acting in good faith.

It is often impossible, moreover, to separate ideological from disciplinary objections to academic work. Does a liberal law professor oppose critical legal studies or the Chicago school of economics because he has political objections to radical and conservative positions, or because he finds little merit in their intellectual approaches to legal issues? Does a radical law professor favor critical and feminist legal theory over traditional doctrinal analysis for intellectual or political reasons? Perhaps in an extremely rare case, a court reasonably could conclude that a claimed disagreement over merit constitutes unjustifiable disciplinary orthodoxy. For example, the explanation by a mediocre university that a prolific and nationally recognized scholar with unorthodox views does not meet its academic standards could legitimately be rejected by a court. But in most cases, where such enormous disparities could not be proved, I favor judicial deference to departmental decisions as long as stated disciplinary judgments are plausible and are not pretexts.

---

311. See Judith Jarvis Thomson, *Ideology and Faculty Competence*, 53 L & Contemp Probs 155 (Summer 1990).

312. AAUP, *Some Observations on Ideology, Competence, and Faculty Selection*, 72 Academe 1a (January-February 1986). An essay by Paul D. Carrington, *Of Law and the River*, 34 J Legal Educ 222 (1984), which contained the statement that "the nihilist who must profess that legal principle does not matter has an ethical duty to depart the law school," id at 227, led to this AAUP document. Correspondence provoked by Carrington's article is collected in "*Of Law and the River," and of Nihilism and Academic Freedom*, 34 J Legal Educ 1 (1985). Rabban, 66 Tex L Rev at 1424-27 (cited in note 19), discusses the tension between the academic freedom of the candidate and the academic freedom of peer review committees in the context of disagreements about the value of a candidate's approach to a discipline.

In my opinion, critical inquiry is assisted by the inclusion of opposing intellectual perspectives within the same institution, and professors should try hard to find merit in disciplinary approaches they oppose. I object, however, to constitutionalizing my own view about appropriate intellectual balance. I agree with Professor Byrne that courts should not adopt a theory of individual academic freedom that protects "all arguably respectable points of view,"[313] and impose on universities unwanted professors opposed by the existing faculty in good faith on academic grounds. As Justice Stevens has effectively pointed out, the academic judgments of universities, including the decisions to "hire professors on the basis of their academic philosophies" and to "reward scholars for what they have written," should not be judged by the same "compelling state interest" standard that applies generally to state regulation of the content of speech.[314]

Byrne essentially incorporates a good faith standard similar to the AAUP's into his analysis of constitutional academic freedom, and extends it to academic decisions by administrators as well as by faculty committees.[315] Byrne never explicitly addresses administrative or trustee reversals of academic judgments by faculty committees. Yet his general reluctance to allow judicial review of internal university disputes over academic issues suggests that he would also favor judicial abstention in this context, despite his recognition that the system of peer review protects the academic freedom of professors from interference by administrators and trustees.

Policies broadly adopted within the academic world, by contrast, suggest that administrators and trustees are not entitled to the same deference regarding academic issues as are faculty peers. The 1966 Statement on Government of Colleges and Universities, endorsed by the AAUP, the American Council on Education, and the Association of Governing Boards of Universities and Colleges, identifies the appropriate roles of different constituencies in the shared system of university governance. Reflecting the relationship between peer review and academic freedom, the 1966 Statement asserts that in matters of faculty status, the governing board and the administration "should concur with the faculty judgment except in rare instances and for compelling reasons which should be stated in detail."[316] The Statement does not elaborate what these compelling reasons are, but the 1915 Declaration and essays on academic freedom by AAUP leaders indicate that they include the failure of peer review bodies to follow professional standards.[317] As one AAUP president observed, sometimes university administrators and trustees have protected the academic freedom of individual professors from faculty colleagues.[318] Presumably, the

---

313. Byrne, 99 Yale L J at 306 (cited in note 1).
314. *Widmar*, 454 US at 277-78 (Stevens concurring).
315. Byrne, 99 Yale L J at 306-08 (cited in note 1).
316. *Statement on Government* at 99 (cited in note 286).
317. 1915 Declaration at 169-70; Appendix A at 402 (cited in note 6).
318. Fritz Machlup, *On Some Misconceptions Concerning Academic Freedom*, reprinted in *Academic Freedom and Tenure* at 177, 182-83 (cited in note 6).

departmental bad faith recently identified by the AAUP[319] would constitute failure to follow professional standards, as would evidence that faculty peers voted for candidates based on friendship or politics, rather than on their academic merits, an accusation increasingly levelled against academic leftists.[320] A number of professors, for example, have recently claimed that they were denied reappointment or tenure because they did not follow a radical party line on issues involving the Third World or were too "Eurocentric."[321]

This analysis suggests judicial deference to administrators who present plausible evidence that faculty committees have deviated from professional standards. But what if no such compelling reasons exist to overturn the academic judgments of faculty bodies? What if administrators or trustees simply disagree with peer assessments of a candidate's academic qualifications? Should courts intervene in the name of academic freedom and protect the proper operation of peer review, particularly when universities themselves adopt the structure of shared governance endorsed by the 1966 Statement?

Judicial enforcement of faculty academic judgments reversed by administrators or trustees without compelling reasons would support the peer review process that contributes to academic freedom. In order to determine whether administrators or trustees have produced sufficient evidence for reversing peer evaluations, judges might have to assess the substance of an academic decision. But judges already perform this task competently, though hesitantly, in determining whether stated academic evaluations are pretexts for reasons that violate Title VII or the first amendment. In addition, courts would not be making entirely independent judgments. They presumably would give greater weight to the more professional decision-maker, defined by the Supreme Court as "a person competent, whether by education, training or experience, to make the particular decision at issue."[322] In *Ewing*, the Court deferred to the professional judgment of the faculty in upholding the student dismissal.[323] With respect to evaluations of professional merit, in contrast to bureaucratic concerns such as finances or abuse of professional discretion, the faculty peers, not the administrators or trustees, meet this definition.

I nevertheless share Byrne's reluctance to allow judges to decide good faith disputes between faculty committees and administrators or trustees about matters of professional quality. Though not as draconian as Byrne maintains, such a judicial role constitutes much more intrusion into academic life than does judicial review of the merits of a decision to determine whether a stated academic reason is a pretext. A constitutionally mandated policy that

---

319. See note 312 and accompanying text (discussing AAUP treatment of departmental bad faith).
320. See Searle, NY Rev Books at 34 (December 6, 1990) (cited in note 247).
321. Heller, Chron Higher Educ at 1 col 3 (cited in note 247).
322. *Youngberg*, 457 US at 323 n30.
323. 474 US at 225-28.

294

faculty committees always prevail over administrators and trustees in good faith disputes over a professor's academic quality seems different in kind from a constitutional requirement that judges must reverse a denial of appointment or tenure upon finding that faculty peers, administrators, or trustees, though claiming that the candidate lacked sufficient qualifications, actually based the decision on ideological objections unrelated to merit or on fear that the candidate's scholarly positions would alienate important legislators and alumni. The 1966 Statement provides an excellent illustration of Byrne's point that not all desirable university policies should be incorporated into a constitutional definition of academic freedom.[324] However, administrative rejections of peer recommendations on matters of faculty status, because they should occur only "in rare instances and for compelling reasons" given faculty expertise in this area, can provide grounds for suspecting that the administrators were not acting in good faith and for examining the stated reasons more closely. Judicial decisions in Title VII and first amendment cases recognize this point by citing, as evidence of pretexts, administrative reversals of unanimous faculty recommendations and weak statements of reasons.[325]

D. The Status of Intramural Speech on University Affairs

Individual professors often claim the protection of academic freedom for intramural speech on university affairs as well as for the views they express in teaching and scholarship. Whether intramural speech by individual professors merits protection under the first amendment is an important topic of current scholarly and judicial debate. I address this issue here to provide a more complete analysis of the tension between individual and institutional academic freedom under the first amendment.

The status of intramural speech by professors has enormous practical significance, for disputes over university policies and personalities have far outnumbered classic academic freedom cases involving the content of teaching or scholarship.[326] The Supreme Court has limited the general first amendment right of intramural speech by public employees to matters of "public concern" and to speech that does not unduly impair efficient and harmonious employment relations.[327] Applying this standard, many lower courts have found that speech by professors on a variety of institutional matters either does not involve public concerns or impairs institutional efficiency or harmony.[328] The limited general first amendment protection for intramural speech, combined with the large number of disputes over this issue

324. Byrne, 99 Yale L J at 308-09 (cited in note 1).
325. See notes 307-10 and accompanying text.
326. Matthew W. Finkin, *Intramural Speech, Academic Freedom, and the First Amendment*, 66 Tex L Rev 1323, 1337-38 (1988); Metzger, 66 Tex L Rev at 1276 (cited in note 1).
327. *Connick v Myers*, 461 US 138 (1983). The Court stressed in *Connick* that it would not "constitutionalize" into a matter of public concern every grievance by a public employee. Id at 154.
328. Finkin, 66 Tex L Rev at 1325-27 (cited in note 326), provides examples.

at American universities, tempts professors to invoke academic freedom as a way to provide constitutional coverage that otherwise would not exist.

Yet as Professor Van Alstyne has effectively demonstrated, the "promiscuous usage" of the term "academic freedom" to cover aprofessional political speech has debased its meaning through overgeneralization and has impeded judicial recognition of a legitimate, distinctive theory of academic freedom as a subset of general first amendment rights.[329] The same danger, it seems to me, applies to disputes over intramural speech. A specific academic freedom right to intramural speech, like other claims relying on academic freedom, must be distinguished from general first amendment principles and justified in reference to the value of critical inquiry that academic freedom promotes. If general first amendment principles governing intramural speech are as inadequate today as the general first amendment principles governing aprofessional political speech were in 1915, the appropriate response is to convince the courts to develop a better first amendment theory covering the intramural speech of all public employees.[330] It would be illogical, and probably counterproductive, to leverage special protection for professors on an extension of the specific theory of academic freedom beyond its legitimate justifications.

Measured by their contribution to critical inquiry, the contents of intramural speech reflect a wide spectrum. Faculty complaints about an institution's parking or medical policies, though they could be connected very indirectly to a professor's teaching and research, are too remote from the value of critical inquiry to justify protection under a specific constitutional theory of academic freedom.[331] Claims by faculty members that the administration or governing board has violated the academic freedom of colleagues seem to fall at the other end of this spectrum. Such claims do not involve the teaching or scholarship of the actual complainants, but do seem sufficiently related to concerns about critical inquiry to merit the coverage of individual academic freedom. Much intramural speech falls between these examples. Claims of administrative abuse of the peer review process and disagreements over curricular and other educational policy issues seem sufficiently linked to critical inquiry to come within the specific theory of academic freedom. Disputes over salary or office space do not.[332] For me, close cases include disputes over student admissions policies and the allocation of financial resources to the library.

The key issue, however, is not how a particular close case should be resolved, but the recognition that some intramural speech on matters beyond an individual's teaching and scholarship should be protected by a first amendment right of academic freedom. Examining whether intramural

---

329. Van Alstyne, *The Specific Theory of Academic Freedom* at 60 (cited in note 22).

330. See Paul Brest, *Protecting Academic Freedom Through the First Amendment: Raising the Unanswered Questions*, 66 Tex L Rev 1359, 1362 (1988).

331. See Mark G. Yudof, *Intramural Musings on Academic Freedom: A Reply to Professor Finkin*, 66 Tex L Rev 1351, 1356 (1988).

332. See id at 1355-56.

speech promotes critical inquiry—the touchstone of academic freedom analysis—may lead to different results than examining whether intramural speech raises issues of public concern, which is the touchstone of general first amendment analysis. For example, a debate within a department over a candidate's qualifications for tenure is less a matter of public concern, but more related to critical inquiry, than accusations that a university president abused office for financial gain. One could argue that the special theory of academic freedom and general first amendment principles converge in the context of intramural speech, because any topic related to critical inquiry is also a matter of public concern. This argument, however, seems to stretch the concept of public concern beyond its plausible limits. Such issues as the decline in educational standards at a state university, on the other hand, may be both matters of public concern and closely related to critical inquiry. Moreover, under the general first amendment analysis of intramural speech, the focus on employee harmony may be less salient in an academic context, where debate is expected and even encouraged, than in other areas of public employment.[333]

Although the courts have not distinguished a specific theory of academic freedom from general first amendment principles regarding intramural speech, the separate opinions of Justices Brennan and Marshall in *Minnesota State Board for Community Colleges v. Knight*, while reaching different conclusions in that case, suggest some appreciation of the relationship between intramural speech and academic freedom. The majority in *Knight* refused to recognize a "constitutional right of faculty to participate in policymaking in academic institutions."[334] "Faculty involvement in academic governance has much to recommend it as a matter of academic policy," the Court concluded, "but it finds no basis in the Constitution."[335]

Justice Brennan dissented based on his interpretation of the first amendment protection for academic freedom. "The first amendment freedom to explore novel or controversial ideas in the classroom is closely linked to the freedom of faculty members to express their views to the administration concerning matters of academic governance."[336] In his opinion, "a direct prohibition of some identified faculty group from submitting their views concerning academic policy questions for consideration by college administrators would plainly violate principles of academic freedom enshrined in the first amendment."[337]

---

333. See, for example, *Johnson v Lincoln University of Com. System of Higher Educ.*, 776 F2d 443, 454 (3d Cir 1985), citing "academic context" in finding first amendment protection for faculty criticism of university president; *Mabey v Reagan*, 537 F2d 1039, 1048 (9th Cir 1976) (less need for harmony in college than in high school); *Landrum v Eastern Kentucky Univ.*, 578 F Supp 241, 246 (ED Ky 1984) ("there must be more room for divergent views in a university situation than in a prosecutor's office").

334. 465 US 271, 287 (1984).

335. Id at 288.

336. Id at 296-97 (Brennan dissenting).

337. Id at 297.

Justice Marshall, by contrast, concurred in the majority's decision, reasoning that courts should be less suspicious of restraints on faculty speech by university administrators than by state legislators. He concluded that universities are most likely to fulfill their social mission when they retain autonomy from external interference. Courts should therefore "defer to the judgment of college administrators—persons we presume to be knowledgeable and to have the best interests of their institutions at heart—in circumstances in which we should not defer to the judgment of government officials who seek to regulate the affairs of the academy."[338]

Yet Justice Marshall maintained that in an appropriate case he would be prepared to include within the first amendment "a measure of freedom on the part of faculty members (as well as students) to present the college administrators their ideas on matters of importance to the mission of the academic community." Such freedom, he added, is essential for universities "to advance the frontiers of knowledge through unfettered inquiry and debate."[339] As Justice Marshall's concurrence suggests, one could agree with the majority that the first amendment does not require faculty participation in university governance, yet still maintain that the individual right of academic freedom under the first amendment protects faculty speech on matters of educational policy related to the value of critical inquiry. Indeed, the majority opinion, without referring explicitly to academic freedom, emphasized the district court finding that all faculty retained their associational and free speech rights to communicate with administrators about matters of educational policy.[340]

E. Should Procedural and Structural Protections for Faculty Academic Freedom be Included Within the First Amendment?

The AAUP and academic commentators often emphasize the importance of various procedural and structural protections for academic freedom, such as peer review, tenure, and faculty participation in university governance. The Supreme Court has recognized in various nonacademic contexts that procedural standards are necessary to protect substantive free speech rights and has interpreted the first amendment to incorporate certain procedural guarantees. Professor Henry Monaghan has felicitously labelled this development "first amendment 'due process.'"[341] Notice, access to information, and rights to appeal during the tenure process are examples of procedural claims related to academic freedom. One could also argue that certain structural arrangements, such as peer review and faculty participation in university governance, similarly are necessary to protect first amendment rights of individuals and institutions. Professor Byrne, for example, maintains that "the structural mechanisms within the university that give precedence to

338. Id at 294-95 (Marshall concurring).
339. Id at 293.
340. Id at 277-78 n4, 288.
341. Monaghan, 83 Harv L Rev 518 (cited in note 287).

peer judgment . . . determine the content of academic freedom."[342] "Academic freedom," he adds, "has no meaning without peer review."[343] Yet, as *Knight* illustrates, the Supreme Court has rejected extending first amendment academic freedom this far.

The Supreme Court's initial and most significant refusal to incorporate faculty procedural interests within the first amendment occurred in a pair of 1972 decisions addressing the rights of nontenured faculty members denied reappointment at state universities: *Board of Regents v. Roth*[344] and *Perry v. Sindermann*.[345] The AAUP filed briefs in both of these cases, arguing that some procedural safeguards for nontenured faculty members are necessary to protect their academic freedom. The relationship between procedural and substantive rights, the AAUP emphasized, "is most significant in higher education, where the Court's special concern for academic freedom is at stake. It would be anomalous to hold that while all faculty members enjoy academic freedom in the classroom and outside, only tenured faculty are effectively able to vindicate or exercise that freedom."[346]

The Supreme Court rejected the AAUP's position. The Court acknowledged previous holdings requiring the opportunity for a fair hearing before state actions that "would directly impinge upon interests in free speech or free press." Examples included the seizure of allegedly obscene books and an injunction against public rallies. Yet the Court denied that the nonrenewal of a faculty member constituted an analogous context. "Whatever may be a teacher's rights of free speech," the Court reasoned, "the interest in holding a teaching job at a state university, *simpliciter*, is not itself a free speech interest."[347]

Just as the AAUP sought to encompass within first amendment academic freedom some procedural protections for nontenured faculty members in *Roth* and *Perry*, it attempted in *University of Pennsylvania* to attach first amendment weight to the institution's peer review process.[348] Once again, the Supreme Court was not convinced. Indeed, the Court sardonically and gratuitously deprecated the value of peer review. After observing that

---

342. Byrne, 99 Yale L J at 267 (cited in note 1).

343. Id at 319. See generally id at 267, 310-11, 318-20.

344. 408 US 564.

345. 408 US 593.

346. AAUP's Brief as Amicus Curiae at 28, *Perry v Sindermann*, 408 US 593 (1972) (No 70-36). See also id at 11, 22-23, 26-28; AAUP's Brief as Amicus Curiae at 7-9, 14, *Board of Regents v Roth*, 408 US 564 (1972) (No 71-162). The AAUP briefs in these cases did not attempt to specify the procedures necessary to protect the substantive right of academic freedom or to clarify the relationship between academic freedom and the first amendment. But see William W. Van Alstyne, *The Constitutional Rights of Teachers and Professors*, 1970 Duke L J 841, 860-61 (the "first amendment itself implicitly affords the right to a pretermination hearing or at least to some right of efficacious intramural or administrative review sufficient to assure the timely protection of freedom of speech").

347. *Roth*, 408 US at 575 n14. Dissenting, Justice Douglas seemed essentially to agree with the AUAP approach. He quoted the district court statement that "[s]ubstantive constitutional protection for a university professor against non-retention in violation of his First Amendment rights or arbitrary non-retention is useless without procedural safeguards." Yet Douglas referred to these procedural safeguards as due process "apart from the First Amendment." Id at 585.

348. *AAUP University of Pennsylvania Brief* at 10 n9 (cited in note 170).

taxation or other government regulation of universities, without violating the first amendment, might deprive them of money they could otherwise use to attract professors, the Court added: "We doubt that the peer review process is any more essential in effectuating the right to determine 'who may teach' than is the availability of money."[349] This dictum might be only a sign of judicial frustration with an "extremely attenuated" university claim based on dubious assumptions about the need for confidentiality in tenure evaluations. It does, however, reinforce the Court's reluctance in *Roth* and *Perry* to extend constitutional academic freedom to procedural protections for this substantive right. The Court's rejection in *Knight* of Justice Brennan's position that first amendment academic freedom includes faculty participation in university governance provides additional evidence of this reluctance to safeguard more than the substance of academic speech.[350]

In my opinion, the inclusion of procedural and structural protections within constitutional academic freedom is defensible but not necessary. The "first amendment 'due process' " recognized in other contexts can plausibly be extended to academic freedom. The right to a faculty position may not itself be a free speech interest. But critical inquiry about professional issues, the key function of professors, depends, as do other substantive free speech rights, on procedural and structural safeguards. If universities can summarily dismiss controversial faculty members, for example, the social benefits of critical inquiry safeguarded by the individual academic freedom of professors may too easily be impaired.

On the other hand, the Supreme Court's apparent limitation of individual academic freedom under the first amendment to a substantive right against the university and the state has several significant advantages. Most importantly, confining the scope of constitutional academic freedom can increase its power within its remaining sphere. It may make more conceptual sense to apply constitutional academic freedom to procedural and structural safeguards than to aprofessional political speech or to intramural speech unrelated to educational concerns. But in all three situations, denying the protection of constitutional academic freedom may provide more popular and judicial support for enforcement of its substantive core. In addition, understandable concerns about judicial intrusions into university life, as in the debate over professional quality,[351] are assuaged by letting university constituencies themselves work out these procedural and structural issues.[352] The substantive individual right of academic freedom, as the Supreme Court

---

349. *University of Pennsylvania*, 110 S Ct at 588.

350. The AAUP brief in *Knight* was silent on this constitutional issue, though it emphasized as a matter of policy that faculty participation in governance assists the search for truth, a familiar rationale for academic freedom. AAUP's Brief as Amicus Curiae at 2, 4, 11, *Minnesota State Board for Community Colleges v Knight*, 465 US 271 (1984).

351. See notes 312-25 and accompanying text.

352. "It is easier for faculty members to fight their board of trustees or administration," Professor Gutmann concludes, "than for them to wrest policy-making authority from their state legislature or the U.S. Supreme Court." Gutmann, *Nomos 25: Liberal Democracy* at 280-81 (cited in note 193).

emphasized in *Roth* and *Perry*, can still be vindicated in court, even if the absence of constitutionally required additional safeguards within the university makes it harder to do so.

X

CONCLUSION

Although the meaning of constitutional academic freedom remains ambiguous, the Supreme Court has clearly recognized it as an unenumerated first amendment right with both individual and institutional components that can be in tension with each other. Individual and institutional academic freedom provide protection for professors and universities against the state. But when a professor asks a court to adjudicate a claim that a university violated his constitutional or contractual academic freedom, the university may respond that judicial resolution of the professor's claim would constitute state intervention in university affairs and thereby infringe the university's own academic freedom.

It makes sense to derive institutional academic freedom from the same value of independent critical inquiry that underlies individual academic freedom,[353] but it perverts the first amendment and the concept of a bill of rights to subordinate individual academic freedom to broad institutional autonomy from judicial review. I have attempted in this article to suggest clarifications in the constitutional meaning of academic freedom that would enable courts to respect both individual and institutional interests. Individual academic freedom should cover expression within a professor's scholarly expertise and intramural speech on matters of educational policy. Institutional academic freedom should similarly relate to the educational functions of universities, such as the "four essential freedoms" identified by Justice Frankfurter in *Sweezy*: selection of teachers, students, curriculum, and pedagogy. Independent constitutional rights, such as the free exercise clause and freedom of association, may protect the autonomy of private universities, just as the free speech clause may protect the aprofessional political expressions of faculty. But these additional constitutional rights, because they do not address the distinctive functions of professors and universities, should not fall under the rubric of academic freedom.

Courts are competent to review, without infringing the academic freedom of a university, a professor's claim that a stated academic ground was a pretext for a university decision that violated his academic freedom. Concern about judicial competence and respect for institutional academic freedom, however, should preclude courts from intervening in internal debates between faculty and administrators over the definition of professional quality. Although peer review, procedural safeguards in tenure decisions, and faculty participation in university governance may all promote individual academic freedom, courts should also be reluctant to impose them on universities as first amendment

---

353. See Gutmann, *Democratic Education* at 177 (cited in note 193).

requirements, particularly because doing so might weaken academic freedom at its substantive core. Constitutional academic freedom, despite tensions between its individual and institutional components, can protect universities without sacrificing professors.*

---

* The Supreme Court decided *Rust v Sullivan*, 59 USLW 4451 (US May 21, 1991) while this article was in final page proofs. One passage in Chief Justice Rehnquist's majority opinion directly supports my assertion that the traditional functions of public universities require first amendment protection from government attempts to restrict academic speech. See notes 242-46 and accompanying text; see generally Part VIIIB. See also Van Alstyne, 53 L & Contemp Probs at 109-10 (cited in note 24). After upholding against first amendment challenges government restrictions on discussion about abortion in health care organizations that receive Title X funds, Rehnquist added:

This is not to suggest that funding by the Government, even when coupled with the freedom of the fund recipients to speak outside the scope of the Government-funded project, is invariably sufficient to justify government control over the content of expression. For example, this Court has recognized that the existence of a Government "subsidy," in the form of Government-owned property, does not justify the restriction of speech in areas that have "been traditionally open to the public for expressive activity," *United States v. Kokinda*, 110 S. Ct. 3115, 3119 (1990); *Hague v. CIO*, 307 U.S. 496, 515 (1989) (opinion of Roberts, J.), or have been "expressly dedicated to speech activity." *Kokinda, supra*, 110 S. Ct. at 3119; *Perry Education Assn. v. Perry Local Educators' Assn.*, 460 U.S. 37, 45 (1988). Similarly, we have recognized that the university is a traditional sphere of free expression so fundamental to the functioning of our society that the Government's ability to control speech within that sphere by means of conditions attached to the expenditure of Government funds is restricted by the vagueness and overbreadth doctrines of the First Amendment, *Keyishian v. Board of Regents*, 385 U.S. 589, 603, 605-606 (1967).

59 USLW at 4458.

ACADEMIC FREEDOM IN RELIGIOUS COLLEGES AND UNIVERSITIES

MICHAEL W. McCONNELL*

I

INTRODUCTION

Standard principles of academic freedom forbid most interference with the right of faculty members to write, teach, or speak within the limits of their professional discipline in accordance with their own opinions, no matter how pernicious or erroneous those opinions appear to others to be.[1] It is widely assumed that extension of these principles to religious colleges and universities would advance the cause of scholarly inquiry. This would prevent religious institutions from maintaining any vestige of creedal orthodoxy through the hiring, firing, rewarding, or disciplining of faculty. The long-standing position of the American Association of University Professors ("AAUP") and the Association of American Colleges ("AAC") is that religious schools are entitled to depart from these principles so long as they clearly announce their intention to do so in advance. However, this position is now widely regarded as an unprincipled and undesirable exception and may well be abandoned.

The thesis of this article is that the underlying purposes of academic freedom would not be advanced by its indiscriminate extension to religious colleges and universities and that, insofar as state action is involved in enforcing the norms of academic freedom, such extension would be unconstitutional. The effect of forcing religious schools to disregard religion in the hiring, tenuring, and disciplining of faculty would be to destroy the distinctive character of these intellectual communities. If we assume that sectarian ideas and approaches to knowledge are worth preserving (if only as a challenge to predominant secular ideology), it is a mistake to destroy the very institutions responsible for developing, preserving, and presenting those ideas.

Academic freedom, as understood in the modern secular university, is predicated on the view that knowledge is advanced only through the

Copyright © 1990 by Law and Contemporary Problems

* Professor of Law, University of Chicago Law School.

The author wishes to express appreciation to Albert Alschuler, Akhil Amar, David Currie, Charles Fried, Douglas Laycock, William Marshall, Michael Stokes Paulsen, Robert Post, and Oliver S. Thomas for helpful comments on an earlier draft, and to the James H. Douglas Jr. Fund and the Kirkland & Ellis Professorship for financial support during the preparation of this article.

1. Of course, disciplinary norms are themselves contested, as current disputes over the evaluation of feminist, racial minority, and critical legal studies scholarship indicate. For the effect of professional norms on religion, see notes 34-37 and accompanying text.

unfettered exercise of individual human reason in a posture of analytical skepticism and criticism. In some religious traditions, however, reason is understood to require reference to authority, community, and faith, and not just to individualized and rationalistic processes of thought. If religious ideas and approaches have anything positive to contribute to the sum of human knowledge, we should recognize that secular methodology cannot be universalized. To impose the secular norm of academic freedom on unwilling religious colleges and universities would increase the homogeneity—and decrease the vitality—of American intellectual life.

Moreover, imposition of the secular norm of academic freedom would pose a serious threat to the ability of nonmainstream religions to maintain their identity and proclaim their vision in secular America. Even if the accommodation of religious approaches to knowledge were not valuable to the advancement of knowledge itself, a modification of academic freedom principles would nonetheless be justified because of its importance to religious freedom.

Before entering the argument, I wish to offer two qualifications. First, it is not my position that in all cultures under all circumstances the extension of secular norms of academic freedom to religious institutions would be unwise. My position is that it would be unwise in modern America, where religion is highly pluralistic, academia is overwhelmingly secular, and the number of institutions of higher learning is sufficiently large to permit genuine diversity. Where the church is established by the state, the religious world is monolithic, the number of institutions is small, or the secular world is vulnerable, my assessment would likely be different. Second, it is not my position that religious colleges and universities *should* reject or modify academic freedom principles. Some religious groups will conclude that secular methodologies are appropriate to the development of religious knowledge within their traditions, and some will be sufficiently aligned with majoritarian culture that they will not feel the need to maintain a separate intellectual identity. My point is that religious bodies should be free to decide this question for themselves, on religious or other grounds, free from pressure from organized academia or the government.[2] It is sufficient for these purposes to show that a departure from secular academic freedom norms might reasonably be seen as promoting the advancement of knowledge within some religious traditions. It is not for the rest of us to attempt to determine which ones they are.

---

2. During the past year, a number of religiously affiliated colleges and universities changed their relationships with their respective religious denominations, some in the direction of greater, and some of lesser, denominational control. For examples of the former, see note 16. For an example of the latter, see *Conversation with the President: "We Will Remain a Texas Baptist Institution,"* 52 The Baylor Line 8-9, 47 (November 1990) (interview with the President of Baylor University discussing the university trustees' decision to amend the university charter to gain autonomy from the Baptist General Convention of Texas and thereby avert what they saw as an impending "fundamentalist" takeover). Nothing in my argument here should be interpreted as endorsing or disapproving such developments, in either direction.

I will proceed in three stages. The first section will review the authoritative definition of secular academic freedom as espoused by the AAUP and the AAC and the history of its application to religious institutions. The second section will present reasons why that understanding of academic freedom should not be imposed on unwilling religious colleges and universities. The third section will discuss three issues of particular concern: academic freedom in seminaries and theological schools, behavioral restrictions on faculty in religious colleges and universities, and application of laws against discrimination on the basis of religion.

II

THE EVOLVING STATUS OF SECULAR ACADEMIC FREEDOM AS APPLIED TO RELIGIOUS INSTITUTIONS

A. The Two Faces of Academic Freedom

The term "academic freedom" is used to express two different concepts, which are sometimes in harmony and sometimes in discord. The term refers both to the freedom of the individual scholar to teach and research without interference (except for the requirement of adherence to professional norms, which is judged by fellow scholars in the discipline) and to the freedom of the academic institution from outside control. Academic freedom thus has two faces: one individual, the other institutional. Outside interference with a scholar's work (as, for example, by legislators during the McCarthy period) violates both principles: it takes away the scholar's freedom of research or teaching, and it also takes away the institution's exclusive authority to govern academic matters within its walls. In such a case, the two aspects of academic freedom are in harmony. Internal interference with a scholar's work (by faculty peers, departments, or administration), however, can generate conflict between the two faces of academic freedom. If the scholar calls upon the assistance of extramural authorities (as, for example, by filing a lawsuit challenging a denial of tenure), the institution's own autonomy may be threatened.[3]

For obvious reasons, the AAUP has tended to emphasize individual academic freedom in its pronouncements. The Supreme Court, however, has tended to emphasize institutional academic freedom. In its most famous formulation, first offered by Justice Felix Frankfurter, who as a Harvard professor had been involved in several important academic freedom controversies,[4] academic freedom encompasses "the four essential freedoms of a university—to determine for itself on academic grounds who may teach,

---

3. For discussions of the conflict between the two faces of academic freedom, see David M. Rabban, *Does Academic Freedom Limit Faculty Autonomy?*, 66 Tex L Rev 1405 (1988); J. Peter Byrne, *Academic Freedom: A "Special Concern of the First Amendment"*, 99 Yale L J 251 (1989); Matthew W. Finkin, *On "Institutional" Academic Freedom*, 61 Tex L Rev 817 (1983); David M. Rabban, *A Functional Analysis of "Individual" and "Institutional" Academic Freedom Under the First Amendment*, 53 L & Contemp Probs 227 (Summer 1990).

4. See Finkin, 61 Tex L Rev at 846 n118, 847 n121 (cited in note 3).

what may be taught, how it shall be taught, and who may be admitted to study."[5]

The controversy with regard to religious colleges and universities presents the conflict between individual and institutional academic freedom at its most extreme. The question is whether a religious institution should have the authority to ensure that its faculty (particularly in theological disciplines) teach and research within the parameters of the religious tradition. In this context, the scholar may invoke the individual face of academic freedom, while the college may invoke the institutional face to defend its desire to determine for itself who may teach, what may be taught, and how it shall be taught.

For the most part, references to "academic freedom" in this article are to individual academic freedom, though for reasons that will become apparent I believe that institutional academic freedom should be the dominant conception within religious institutions.

B. The Position of the AAUP

Through the middle of the 19th century, an essentially religious, or dogmatic, understanding of truth pervaded higher education in America, especially at such elite institutions as Harvard, Yale, Amherst, and Princeton. Colleges existed to impart knowledge; the test of knowledge was its conformity to the revealed truths of scripture, religious traditions, and authorities; the advancement of knowledge therefore required that the work of teachers and scholars be tested against the truths of religion. The modern university was born in a conscious attempt to free scholarly investigation from the strictures of this single, constrained understanding of the advancement of knowledge. Academic freedom became the central operating tenet of the modern secular university. Under this modern view, colleges and universities exist to advance the frontiers of knowledge; the test of knowledge is its ability to withstand the rigors of debate and disputation; the advancement of knowledge requires that the work of teachers and scholars be free from all constraints other than those of the academic discipline.

It was not long before the modern secular university came to dominate American higher education, and this secular, noninstitutional understanding of academic freedom became part of the higher law of American higher education. This understanding assumed its canonical form in the 1940 Statement of Principles on Academic Freedom and Tenure, jointly issued by the AAUP and the AAC.[6] While the 1940 Statement technically has no legal force in its own right (though its extralegal authority is considerable), it has been adopted by most accrediting agencies, whose determinations *do* have

---

5. *Sweezy v New Hampshire*, 354 US 234, 263 (1957). The formulation came from a conference of scholars from the Universities of Cape Town and Witwatersrand.

6. Reprinted in AAUP, *Policy Documents and Reports* 3 (AAUP, 1990), and in 76 Academe 37 (May-June 1990) ("1940 Statement"); see Appendix B, 53 L & Contemp Probs 407 (Summer 1990).

legal effect.[7] For example, the two agencies that are responsible for accreditation of law schools—the American Bar Association ("ABA") and the Association of American Law Schools ("AALS")—both use the 1940 Statement as their standard for academic freedom.[8]

As set forth in the 1940 Statement, academic freedom has three aspects: (1) the teachers' "full freedom in research and in the publication of the results"; (2) their "freedom in the classroom in discussing their subject"; and (3) their freedom "from institutional censorship and discipline" when they "speak or write as citizens." These few words have given rise to an elaborate "common law" of academic freedom through the written opinions of the AAUP's Committee A on Academic Freedom and Tenure, which investigates and issues reports on alleged violations. The 1940 Statement contains no acknowledgement of the institutional dimension of academic freedom.

The 1940 Statement, however, did not require religious institutions to adopt this particular conception of academic freedom. Recognizing that the older tradition of the pursuit of knowledge through fealty to religious authority was still common, the 1940 Statement said that "[l]imitations of academic freedom because of religious or other aims of the institution should be clearly stated in writing at the time of the appointment."[9] This statement was ambiguous, presumably deliberately so. It did not explicitly authorize or condone limitations on academic freedom; but it assumed they would exist and regulated them through the requirement of open disclosure. In practice, the limitations clause was taken to mean that religious colleges and universities were free to adopt their own principles of academic freedom

---

7. A significant exception is the accreditation standards of the American Association of Theological Schools ("AATS"), which do not follow the 1940 Statement. See AATS, *Bulletin* 9, 11, Pt 3 (1972) (Standards for Accrediting); id at 3-8, Pt 5 (Academic Freedom and Tenure).

8. ABA Standard 405(d) provides: "The law school shall have an established and announced policy with respect to academic freedom and tenure of which Annex I herein is an example but is not obligatory." ABA, *Standards for Approval of Law Schools*, § 405(d) (1987). Annex I, in turn, follows the text of the 1940 Statement, including the limitations clause. Id at Annex I.

Bylaw 6-8(d) of the AALS provides: "A faculty member shall have academic freedom and tenure in accordance with the principles of the American Association of University Professors." AALS, *Association Handbook* 24 (1990) (Bylaws of the Association of American Law Schools, Inc.). It is noteworthy that this refers to the "principles" of the AAUP and not to the 1940 Statement as such, apparently indicating that the AALS standards on academic freedom are set by the AAUP and will change as the AAUP's "principles" change. The Regulations of the AALS Executive Committee clarify the bylaw as follows:

Those principles are defined by the American Association of University Professors' 1940 Statement on Academic Freedom and Tenure and the Interpretive Comments adopted in 1970. Specifically, the Association of American Law Schools adopts the position of the 1970 Interpretive Comments that: "most church-related institutions no longer need or desire the departure from the principles of academic freedom implied in the 1940 Statement, and we do not now endorse such a departure."

Id at 38 (Association of American Law Schools Executive Committee Regulations, Regulation 6.16). For a discussion of the 1970 Interpretive Comments, see notes 13-16 and accompanying text.

9. AAUP, *Policy Documents* at 3, 76 Academe at 37, Appendix B at 407 (cited in note 6). Although the words of the limitation apply to all aspects of academic freedom, the limitations clause appears only in the paragraph of the 1940 Statement pertaining to academic freedom in the classroom.

without interference or censure by the academic community, so long as those principles were clearly announced in advance.

For example, in a leading case in 1965 involving Gonzaga University, a Jesuit institution, Committee A opined that "satisfactory conditions of academic freedom and tenure now prevail at Gonzaga University,"[10] even though the university required each faculty member to "be careful not to introduce into his teaching controversial matter which . . . is contrary to the specified aims of the institution"[11] and reserved the right to dismiss nontenured faculty for "inculcation of viewpoints which contradict explicit principles of Catholic faith and morals."[12]

Thus secular and religious universities could coexist, each operating within its own understanding of the principles needed for the advancement of knowledge. Many religiously affiliated schools freely adopted the academic freedom norms of the secular universities. A very small number maintained the older dogmatic approach within the entire institution, requiring faculty and sometimes students to abide by religious codes of conduct and faith. A larger number adopted various compromises with the secular position, embracing academic freedom in its essentials but taking certain steps to preserve the religious identity of the school. Many of these institutions confined religious constraints to those disciplines, such as theology, where religious norms were most directly relevant. The organized academic community did not attempt to interfere with these choices under the 1940 Statement, so long as they were clearly stated in writing.

After World War II, the secular vision of knowledge gained in power, and many religious colleges and universities came to accept the rationalist methodology that underlies the prevailing modern understanding of academic freedom. Opposition to any limitation on the scope of secular academic freedom mounted within academic institutions. The coexistence of different approaches to academic inquiry came to be seen as anachronistic and intolerable. In 1970, a committee of the AAUP issued an "Interpretive Comment" to the 1940 Statement, stating that "[m]ost church-related institutions no longer need or desire the departure from the principle of academic freedom implied in the 1940 Statement, and we do not now endorse such a departure.[13]

This Interpretive Comment was of uncertain authority. How could a mere committee alter the terms of a fundamental charter that had been unanimously endorsed by 120 educational and disciplinary organizations?[14]

---

10. *Academic Freedom and Tenure: Gonzaga University*, 51 AAUP Bull 8, 17 (Spring 1965).

11. Id at 17.

12. Id at 19. While "commending" the University for its revised statement of policy and making no objection to the policies quoted in the text, Committee A criticized the procedural aspects of the Gonzaga policy in some detail. Id at 17-20.

13. AAUP, *Policy Documents* at 5 (cited in note 6).

14. See The *"Limitations" Clause in the 1940 Statement of Principles*, 74 Academe 52, 56 (September-October 1988). Moreover, it should be noted that the Interpretive Comment was not adopted by the AAC.

More importantly, it seemed to link the status of the exception for religious institutions to the current demands of "most" of such institutions, rather than to a principled determination of whether any such institutions *should* have the option to depart from the prevailing understandings of academic freedom.[15] Developments since 1970, especially within the Roman Catholic Church and some evangelical denominations, cast doubt on the empirical basis for this Interpretive Comment.[16] It is evident today that a significant (though of course numerically small) number of church-related institutions do in fact need or desire to depart from the vision of secular academic freedom embodied in the 1940 Statement. Accordingly, the AAUP has been forced to confront the normative question more directly.

In 1988, a subcommittee of the AAUP's Committee A on Academic Freedom and Tenure issued a report recommending that the limitation in the 1940 Statement be interpreted as disapproving any departure from the Statement's position on academic freedom. The subcommittee stated that the "necessary consequence" of the decision by religious institutions to invoke the exception in the 1940 Statement is that they forfeit "the moral right to proclaim themselves as authentic seats of higher learning."[17] According to the subcommittee, "[a]n institution has no 'right' under the 1940 Statement simultaneously to invoke the Limitations Clause and to claim that it is an institution of learning to be classed with institutions that impose no such restriction."[18]

---

15. See id at 53 (observing that the Interpretive Comment "becomes exceedingly fragile, subject, as it logically would seem to be, to shifts in the felt needs of the institutions affected by it").

16. Pope John Paul II recently announced that "all Catholic teachers are to be faithful to, and all other teachers are to respect, Catholic doctrine and morals in their research and teachings," and that all church-run colleges and universities must include as part of their identity "a recognition of and adherence to the teaching authority of the church in matters of faith and morals." 4 *National and International Religion Report* 6-7, 21 (October 8, 1990). New trustees installed by the Southern Baptist Convention at church-run seminaries have introduced more stringent creedal requirements for seminary teaching. See id at 6 (describing new requirements at Southern Baptist Seminary in Louisville, KY). See also *Academic Freedom and Tenure: Concordia Theological Seminary (Indiana)*, 75 Academe 57 (May-June 1989) (describing new requirements at seminary run by the Evangelical Lutheran Church, Missouri Synod).

17. *The "Limitations" Clause*, 74 Academe at 55 (cited in note 14).

18. Id. The subcommittee characterized this as a "return to the original basis of the 1940 Statement's limitation clause." Id at 56. This claim is difficult to credit. Under the subcommittee's interpretation, the "limitation" in the 1940 Statement imposes an obligation on schools that depart from its academic freedom rules (the obligation to announce the departure in advance), without giving such schools any benefit or indulgence in return. Besides being inherently implausible (if institutions that depart from academic freedom as defined in the 1940 Statement are not truly colleges or universities, how do the AAUP and the AAC gain jurisdiction over them to require that they publish their policies in advance?), the subcommittee's interpretation is contradicted by the history of the 1940 Statement. As the subcommittee noted, id at 52, the AAC's chief negotiator of the 1940 Statement believed that it was in substance the same as the 1925 Conference Statement to which the AAUP was a party. This Conference Statement read:

> A university or college may not impose any limitation upon the teacher's freedom in the exposition of his own subject in the classroom or in addresses and publications outside the college, except in so far as the necessity of adopting instruction to the needs of immature students, or in the case of institutions of a denominational or partisan character, specific stipulations in advance, fully understood and accepted by both parties, limit the scope and character of instruction.

Significantly, the subcommittee refused to countenance any distinction between secular disciplines and theological disciplines, even including programs of professional instruction for clergy. "[I]f theology is an academic discipline," the subcommittee opined, "it must be treated as any other discipline. Higher education is not catechesis, and this is no less true for professional clerical education than for any other professional calling."[19] Moreover, the subcommittee concluded that what it called a "free university" may not include within itself a component, such as a seminary, that "requires creedal orthodoxy as a consequence of its singular religious mission." Not only is such a seminary deprived of its status as an "authentic seat of higher learning," but the university of which it is a part shares in the opprobrium. Inclusion of such a component, according to the subcommittee, would be "wrong" because of its effect on the scholars in the seminary itself, on their colleagues in other disciplines—whose academic freedom would not be "secure"—and on the institution as a whole, which would "labor under a cloud of suspicion that the teachings and writings of its faculty may not be truly free."[20]

After publishing the subcommittee report for comment, the full Committee A adopted the following, somewhat ambiguous, restatement of its position:

> Committee A considered the report of the subcommittee on "The 'Limitations' Clause in the 1940 Statement of Principles" and the published and unpublished commentary on it. The committee declined to accept the subcommittee's invitation to hold that the invocation of the clause exempts an institution from the universe of higher education, in part due to the belief that it is not appropriate for the Association to decide what is and what is not an authentic institution in higher education. The committee did conclude, however, that invocation of the clause does not relieve an institution of its obligation to afford academic freedom as called for in the 1940 Statement.[21]

Unfortunately, not even the members of Committee A know what this statement means. The chair of the committee has written that he thought that the restatement "would have put the issue to rest, that in Committee A's

---

Id, reprinted in 18 AAUP Bull 329 (1932). The language of the 1925 Conference Statement obviously created an *exception* for denominational schools. If the 1940 Statement was in substance the same, then its limitation should be read in the same way. Moreover, this was the consistent interpretation by AAUP committees until 1988. See *Report of the Special Committee on Academic Freedom in Church-Related Colleges and Universities*, 53 AAUP Bull 369, 370 (Winter 1967) (characterizing the limitations clause as "accommodat[ing] the church-related institutions"); see also *Gonzaga University*, 51 AAUP Bull at 27 (cited in note 10). The 1970 "de-endorsement" is further confirmation that the limitations clause was understood to serve the "need or desire" of the religious institution and not simply to impose an unrequited burden.

The 1988 subcommittee frankly acknowledged that one "decided advantage" of its strategy of reinterpreting the limitations clause of the 1940 Statement rather than "de-endorsing" it, as had been done by the committee in 1970, is that this would avoid the "parliamentary quandary" of how to amend "a jointly drafted document that is now endorsed by over 120 educational and disciplinary organizations." *The "Limitations" Clause*, 74 Academe at 56 (cited in note 14). This appears to be an open confession of an attempt to avoid the parliamentary processes of the AAUP and the AAC through creative interpretation. Independent of its merits, so disingenuous a recommendation should be resoundingly rejected.

19. *The "Limitations" Clause*, 74 Academe at 55 (cited in note 14).

20. Id at 55-56.

21. *Report of Committee A 1988-89*, 75 Academe 49, 54 (September-October 1989).

judgment a church-related institution must afford the same academic freedom that all other accredited degree-granting institutions must observe."[22] He went on to note that "[a]t our June meeting, however, I was badly disabused of this simplistic, or perhaps simpleminded notion," finding that a "majority of the committee now consider the last sentence to be no more than a truism that begs the question of what obligation a church-related institution has to afford academic freedom." He concluded that "[t]hat question will apparently continue to vex us."[23]

Undoubtedly that question will continue to vex church-related institutions as well. They will continue to operate in the dark about what obligations the AAUP considers them to bear and when to expect a judgment of censure for their practices. Three of the cases discussed in the same report resulted in formal censure of church-related institutions, in one case a distinguished university, for actions designed to ensure that doctrinal instruction in their seminaries or theology schools was in accordance with the institution's doctrine.[24] The full reports in those cases suggest that Committee A has repudiated the limitations clause of the 1940 Statement de facto, even if it continues to wallow in standardless ambiguity de jure. One would think that the affected institutions are as entitled to a clear statement of the rules said to govern their conduct as the AAUP's 1940 Statement insists their faculty must receive.

III

WHY PROTECT THE INSTITUTIONAL ACADEMIC FREEDOM OF RELIGIOUS INSTITUTIONS?

Even while adhering to the limitations clause accommodating religious colleges and universities, organized academia never articulated any principled justification for doing so. An AAC report in 1922 characterized limitations on teachers' freedoms as "concessions to weakness,"[25] perhaps owing to the fact that "such a large percentage of institutions were then under denominational control."[26] If the latter is the explanation, this implies that the current move to eliminate the accommodation is attributable to the fact that affected institutions are now so badly outnumbered. But the small number of exceptional institutions remaining argues for, not against, their accommodation. When the vast majority of academic institutions are

22. Id.

23. Id.

24. See id at 49-50 (Southeastern Baptist Theological Seminary (North Carolina)); id at 51-52 (Concordia Theological Seminary (Indiana)); id at 54 (Catholic University of America, Washington, D.C.). Although mentioned in the 1988-89 Report, the formal resolution of censure against Catholic University occurred the following year.

25. The 1922 AAC Committee proposed certain "temporary conventions," which were precursors of the 1940 Statement. See The "Limitations" Clause, 74 Academe at 52 (cited in note 14), referring to Report of the Association of American Colleges Commission on Academic Freedom and Academic Tenure, 8 AAUP Bull 543 (1922).

26. The "Limitations" Clause, 74 Academe at 53 (cited in note 14).

committed to the view of knowledge reflected in the principle of secular academic freedom, there is little to be gained and much to be lost from quelling the few dissenting institutional voices. As *religious* institutions, such schools are more valuable as exemplars of an alternative understanding of knowledge than they could ever be as (in many cases, unexceptional) secular colleges.

As an alternative rationale for the religious accommodation, the 1988 subcommittee mentioned (without repudiating or endorsing) the argument that "many of these institutions usefully function as 'decompression chambers' that ease the passage into the larger world for the religiously provincial."[27] The condescension—indeed bigotry—of this suggestion seems to have passed unnoticed.

The AAUP's experts on academic freedom have confessed themselves unable to "discern a principled reason" why religious colleges and universities should not be required to conform to the same standards of academic freedom appropriate to secular institutions.[28] I would suggest three reasons: (1) religiously distinctive colleges and universities make important contributions to the intellectual life of their faculty, their students, and the nation, and secular academic freedom in its unmodified form would lead quickly to the extinction of these institutions; (2) the insistence on a single model of truth-seeking is inconsistent with the antidogmatic principles on which the case for academic freedom rests; and (3) even if the extension of secular academic freedom to religious institutions were desirable on intellectual grounds, it would subvert the ability of religious communities to maintain and transmit their beliefs, and thus undermine religious freedom.

A. The Value of Religious Colleges and Universities

Few observers would doubt that religious scholars and institutions have made significant contributions to the ethical, cultural, and intellectual life of our nation. Religious notions of the pursuit of knowledge might well be intolerable for a modern scientific, pluralistic nation if universally imposed; but, as adopted voluntarily by a limited number of institutions, they enrich our intellectual life by contributing to the diversity of thought and preserving important alternatives to post-Enlightenment secular orthodoxy. Their very distinctiveness makes them better able to resist the popular currents of majoritarian culture and thus to preserve the seeds of dissent and alternative understandings that may later be welcomed by the wider society.

But though few openly challenge the worth of religious colleges and universities, many are indifferent or even hostile to the practices that may be necessary for their preservation.[29] Principal among these practices is a

---

27. Id, citing David Riesman, *On Higher Education* 172-75 (Jossey-Bass, 1980).
28. Id.
29. In a recent article, for example, a professor of religious studies concluded a call for extending secular academic freedom to religious institutions with the remarkable assertion that "[a]ll closed systems threaten the critical mind and the open society, especially those systems of thought

vigilance to preserve a distinctive character in the face of the pervasively secular academic culture. One of the primary tenets of secular academic freedom is that scholars must be appointed and retained without regard to their creedal or philosophical commitments, other than to the established norms of their professional disciplines. At best, the effect of this application of academic freedom is to randomize every faculty with respect to creed and philosophy. This increases diversity within each faculty, but it eliminates diversity among faculties. Every faculty will tend to resemble every other faculty, subject only to statistical deviations from the mean. Under such a system, religiously distinctive institutions necessarily will cease to exist. The faculty manage the institution; if they are hired and retained without regard to their religious commitments, only a small minority will hold to the tenets of the institution, and the institution will inevitably lose its essential character.[30]

Extension of the secular understanding of academic freedom would effectively expel religiously distinctive colleges from American intellectual life, either putting them out of business or, which is much the same thing, forcing them to adopt the intellectual mores of secular academia. The desirability of that extension must be judged according to the desirability of that consequence.

B. Consistency with the Purposes of Academic Freedom

As a normative principle, academic freedom is justified primarily in terms of its necessity for the advancement of "learning and scholarship."[31] Scholars are not accorded this extraordinary degree of autonomy as a privilege, but because we understand the clash of competitive ideas to be the method by which truth is best discovered. But this idea, too, must be subject to testing and falsification. It contradicts the premises of academic freedom to state that one idea—the idea of academic freedom—must be given a privileged status and imposed universally by coercive means.

The older religious, or dogmatic, tradition also had its theory of knowledge. It held to certain propositions: (1) truth is unchanging and exists prior to and independent of the process of discovery; (2) truth is only partially discernible through human efforts; indeed, the products of human effort,

---

and life that enjoin religious obligations and enjoy religious legitimations." Lonnie D. Kliever, *Academic Freedom and Church-Affiliated Universities*, 66 Tex L Rev 1477, 1480 (1988). If any system of thought that seeks to enforce norms it considers authoritative is a threat to the critical mind and the open society, then the free exercise of religion, far from being the hallmark of a free society, is its nemesis.

30. A similar argument can be made for other distinctive colleges, such as single-sex colleges, and may well have merit in those contexts as well. But our society is morally and perhaps constitutionally committed to eradication of differences based on gender (and other distinctions of an invidious character). It is not committed to eradication of differences based on religion; to the contrary, it is committed to preservation of pluralism and diversity in matters of religion. Religiously distinctive institutions thus stand on a different footing.

31. See Byrne, 99 Yale L J at 275-78 (cited in note 3). "The First Amendment protects the central intellectual efforts of the modern university. These efforts include teaching, scholarship, and experimentation, all of which contribute unique cultural and intellectual values to a free society." Id at 258.

being a manifestation of a fallen nature, should always be tested against divine authority; (3) truth is imparted to humanity, at least in part, through divine agency, whether this is the Holy Bible, the tradition and teaching authority of the church, or the unaided inner light of conscience; (4) departures from established understandings are as likely to result in error as in advancement of truth; and (5) the consequences of the spread of error are serious and eternal. It is easy to see why an adherent to these propositions would be unwilling to accept secular academic freedom, which assumes that truth is always in the process of discovery through human reason, and that error must be tolerated (perhaps even welcomed) as necessary to the discovery of truth.

It would be a mistake to dismiss the religious understanding as mere obscurantism. Its presuppositions regarding the pursuit of knowledge differ substantially from those most of us in modern academia share, but they have an integrity and a coherence. Whether they are right or wrong is not susceptible to proof; this is ultimately a proposition of faith. But the same must be said of the scientific method that underlies academic freedom. Neither religious nor rationalist methodology can be "proven" from an objective standpoint. Both systems of thought claim to be self-validating, in that practitioners of both believe that their results are so compelling that one who engages in them will be compelled to assent to their validity.[32]

For a limited number of institutions to adhere to the older norm is therefore not antithetical to but rather consistent with the purposes behind the institution of academic freedom. It will increase diversity in the culture as a whole and enable the competition of ideas to continue. As Douglas Laycock and Susan Waelbroeck observed in a recent article, "from a societal perspective, pluralism and the search for truth may be more helped than hindered by distinctive institutions forcefully representing each of the country's many religious traditions."[33] It is important that a principle born of opposition to dogmatism not itself become dogmatic and authoritarian.

Moreover, extension of secular principles of academic freedom could be particularly self-defeating under current circumstances in academia. As noted above, the freedom of the individual scholar under standard principles of academic freedom is limited by the professional norms of the scholar's discipline. A Ptolemaist in an astronomy department would not last long. Recent disputes over the evaluation of the work of scholars writing from the perspectives of racial minorities or of feminism have highlighted the

---

32. A Catholic philosopher put the point in this way:

> The truth of faith makes an incontrovertible demand upon the intellect of the believer, a demand no more open to denial than that made by facts of experience or evident logical truths. The unbeliever is unaware of this demand, not because of any greater freedom on his part, but rather because of incapacity—as the blind man is unaware of the demand that visible evidence makes upon the minds of those who can see.

Germain Gabriel Grisez, *Academic Freedom and Catholic Faith*, NCEA Bull 15, 17 (November 1967).

33. Douglas Laycock & Susan E. Waelbroeck, *Academic Freedom and the Free Exercise of Religion*, 66 Tex L Rev 1455, 1458 (1988).

subjectivity of these professional norms, which many now see as mere screens for the dominant ideology.[34]

Whatever the merits of the argument in those contexts, it can scarcely be doubted that religious perspectives are systematically suppressed and silenced in the modern academy under the banner of "objective" professional or disciplinary norms. There are courses in Feminist Jurisprudence at most major secular law schools; I am not aware of any such course in Christian (or other religious) Jurisprudence.[35] Would such a course be approved? If approved by the authorities, how would it be greeted by the students? If offered, would the professor feel free to "proselytize" for his or her position, in the way the professor of a course in Feminist Jurisprudence would feel free to "proselytize"? I suspect that any hint of a religious approach to the subject matter would be deemed academically inappropriate.[36] Is there any major intellectual or ideological perspective so "invisible" in the modern academy as the religious? Given the antireligious[37] character of modern academic culture, serious religious scholarship would be in danger of extinction if it were not for particular institutions in which it is valued and protected. It is no coincidence that the rise in religious particularism has occurred most prominently in institutions connected with perspectives (evangelical and fundamentalist Protestantism, conservative Catholicism) that consider themselves most ruthlessly suppressed in the secular academy.

C. Religiously Distinctive Institutions of Higher Education Are Necessary for Religious Freedom

Even if the survival of religiously distinctive colleges and universities could not be defended on academic grounds, our society's commitment to freedom of religion would demand some accommodation of the need of religious colleges and universities to modify the secular principles of academic

---

34.   See, for example, Richard Delgado, *The Imperial Scholar: Reflections on a Review of Civil Rights Literature,* 132 U Pa L Rev 561 (1984); Lucinda M. Finley, *Breaking Women's Silence in Law: The Dilemma of the Gendered Nature of Legal Reasoning,* 64 Notre Dame L Rev 886 (1989). Consider also the dispute over whether critical legal studies should be considered a legitimate mode of discourse in academic law. See Paul D. Carrington, *"Of Law and the River,"* 34 J Legal Educ 222 (1984); Symposium, *"Of Law and the River," and of Nihilism and Academic Freedom,* 35 J Legal Educ 1 (1985); see also Judith Jarvis Thomson, *Ideology and Faculty Selection,* 53 L & Contemp Probs 155 (Summer 1990).

35.   That theology speaks usefully to jurisprudence can be seen through such works as Peter Kaufman, *Redeeming Politics* (Princeton Univ Press, 1990); Arthur J. Jacobson, *The Idolatry of Rules: Writing Law According to Moses, With Reference to Other Jurisprudences,* 11 Cardozo L Rev 1079 (July-August 1990); Elizabeth Mensch & Alan Freeman, *The Politics of Virtue: Animals, Theology, and Abortion,* 25 Ga L Rev (forthcoming in 1991)—to mention just three recent works on different subjects from disparate theological perspectives.

36.   A tenured professor at the University of Alabama, for example, was recently instructed to refrain from making occasional references in the classroom to his religious views, clearly labelled as personal opinion, or from offering an optional after-class session on the Christian implications of the subject matter. The University explicitly permits the expression of personal opinions and the holdings of after-class meetings with students if discussions are not from a religious perspective. Challenged on free speech, free exercise, and academic freedom grounds, this directive was upheld by the Eleventh Circuit. *Bishop v Aronov,* No 90-7239, 1991 WL 23706 (March 15, 1991).

37.   By "antireligious," I do not mean that most modern academics oppose the private practice of religion. What they oppose is the application of religious thought to "real" subjects.

freedom. These institutions are an important means by which religious faiths can preserve and transmit their teachings from one generation to the next, particularly for nonmainstream religions whose differences from the predominant academic culture are so substantial that they risk annihilation if they cannot retain a degree of separation. The right to develop and pass on religious teachings is at the very heart of the first amendment, and there should be no doubt that these concerns override whatever exiguous benefit to society might be achieved by forcing religiously distinctive institutions to conform to secular academic freedom.[38]

Constitutional principles serve as a legal limit only on actors who exercise governmental power, such as accrediting agencies,[39] regulatory bodies, and courts. Others have made the case that the first amendment protects religious institutions, especially their theology schools and seminaries, from regulation designed to enforce secular academic freedom, and I will not repeat their arguments.[40] One point must be addressed, however: the impact of *Employment Division v. Smith*,[41] the recent decision that held that the free exercise clause does not require exemptions from neutral laws of general applicability.[42] Upon cursory examination, the Court's opinion might be thought to allow enforcement of uniform academic freedom principles against religious institutions. However, the *Smith* opinion recognized a number of exceptions to its rule of facial neutrality, three of which are relevant to this context: (1) "hybrid" claims, in which free exercise is combined with other constitutional claims, including the freedoms of speech and association, (2) the right of parents to control the education of their children, and (3) the right of religious institutions to control their internal governance in cases such as property disputes.[43] Any or all of these exceptions should apply here, and should prevent state actors from interfering with the ability of religious institutions to require doctrinal fidelity of their faculties.

Beyond the legal limits of the Constitution, however, private actors such as the AAUP *should* uphold the free exercise rights of religious institutions and

---

38. If religion is viewed primarily as an ideological commitment, it would follow that other ideological positions are similarly entitled to establish colleges and universities with specific creedal limitations. But religions are more than an ideological commitment. They are also communities of believers with mutual ties of loyalty and common purpose. Religious colleges and universities do more than transmit creeds; they also raise up leaders and members in the tradition and communion of the faith. As such, the function of religious institutions may resemble that of traditional black colleges more closely than that of an ideological academy. This additional function of religious institutions probably accounts for the fact that religiously distinctive colleges and universities have met with a degree of acceptance that would not have been accorded to ideological institutions.

39. Accrediting agencies are generally private organizations, but for these purposes they wield state power. For example, in most states only a graduate of an accredited law school can stand for the bar examination, and thus obtain a license to practice law.

40. See Laycock & Waelbroeck, 66 Tex L Rev 1455 (cited in note 33); April Kestell Cassou & Robert F. Curran, *Secular Orthodoxy and Sacred Freedoms: Accreditation of Church-Related Law Schools*, 11 J Coll & Univ L 293 (1984).

41. *Employment Div., Dep't of Human Res. of Oregon v Smith*, 110 S Ct 1595 (1990).

42. For a critique of the case, see Michael W. McConnell, *Free Exercise Revisionism and the* Smith *Decision*, 57 U Chi L Rev 1109 (1990).

43. 110 S Ct at 1601-02.

need not be limited to the narrow conception of these rights expressed in *Smith*. The AAUP purports to speak in the name of the academy, and not as a mere partisan for a particular faction or point of view. Its pronouncements regarding academic freedom carry weight among academics and the public in large part because it is seen as objective. Such an association has a moral responsibility to respect the rights of religious bodies, even if those bodies entertain an understanding of knowledge contrary to that of the majority of the AAUP.

Even so, the pronouncements of the AAUP would be of no concern if they confined themselves to assuring that prospective faculty appointees and possibly others are not misled into assuming that a religious school complies with the usual secular norms of academic freedom—what might be called a "truth in advertising" function. In 1939, on the eve of promulgation of the 1940 Statement, Committee A reported:

> [T]his Association would not deny to a group which desires to do so the right to support an institution for propagating its views. It merely insists that such an institution ought not to be represented to the public as a college or university for the promotion of the liberal arts and sciences, in which scholars and teachers are free to seek and impart truth in all of its aspects.[44]

If truth in advertising were the purpose of Committee A's activities, there would be no reason to object to its standards. Religious colleges and universities should not be shy to admit that their understanding of academic freedom differs from that of the AAUP, and a clear declaration to that effect should serve to prevent misunderstanding. Margarine is not the same thing as butter, and margarine producers can have no legitimate objection to a requirement that they designate their product as such.

The actions and statements of Committee A demonstrate, however, that its purpose goes far beyond mere truth in advertising. When issuing a report, the committee does not state that "Institution X abides by standards of academic freedom different from those required of secular institutions." Rather, it "censures" the institution for violating academic freedom. The 1988 subcommittee proposal would purport to drum offending institutions out of the universe of "authentic seat[s] of higher learning"—a position the full committee recognized as presumptuous, but which continues to animate its decisions.[45] There can be no doubt that the purpose of the enterprise is to

---

44. *Report of Committee A for 1939*, 26 AAUP Bull 45 (1940) (excerpted in *The "Limitations" Clause*, 74 Academe at 54 (cited in note 14)). Note the unfair twist on the word "truth" in this statement. A religious college *does* believe that its "teachers are free to seek and impart truth in all its aspects." What they object to is the teaching of error. To ask a religious institution to advertise itself in this way is to ask it to affirm that what it deems error is *in fact* "truth." It would be more in keeping with the methodological assumptions of secular academic freedom to affirm that "teachers are free to seek and impart *what they consider to be* truth in all of its aspects."

45. For example, Committee A stated that it "questions" whether "[Concordia Theological Seminary] can be said to function as truly an institution of higher learning." *Concordia Theological Seminary*, 75 Academe at 65 (cited in note 16). It is difficult to reconcile this with Committee A's statement in the 1988-89 Report "that it is not appropriate for the Association to decide what is and what is not an authentic institution in higher education." *Committee A Report*, 75 Academe at 54 (cited in note 21).

pressure the offending institutions to conform to the AAUP's position or, in the alternative, to ostracize them. Margarine must not only be clearly labelled; it must also be driven from the market. This is inconsistent with a commitment to religious freedom, which the AAUP ought to value even though it is not legally obliged to do so.

IV

SPECIFIC APPLICATIONS TO THEOLOGY SCHOOLS, MORALS REGULATION, AND DISCRIMINATION ON THE BASIS OF RELIGION

While the rights of religious colleges and universities should not be limited to these contexts, a large majority of academic freedom disputes arise in connection with doctrinal limitations on faculty teaching in theological disciplines, behavioral restrictions in conformity with the moral tenets of the religious tradition, and enforcement of antidiscrimination laws.

A. Theology Schools

Application of secular norms of academic freedom to seminaries and schools of theology is particularly inappropriate. Yet this has long been the goal of a segment within organized academia. The AAUP's influential 1915 Declaration of Principles stated:

> Finally, in the spiritual life, and in the interpretation of the general meaning and ends of human existence and its relation to the universe, we are still far from a comprehension of the final truths, and from a universal agreement among all sincere and earnest men. In all of these domains of knowledge, the first condition of progress is complete and unlimited freedom to pursue inquiry and publish its results. Such freedom is the breath in the nostrils of all scientific activity.[46]

Anyone with a passing familiarity with religious history will recognize the narrowness and sectarianism of this declaration. It is a statement that virtually no orthodox Christian of any denomination could accept.[47] Its very choice of words suggests a hostility toward revealed religion. The assertion that "[s]uch freedom is the breath in the nostrils of all scientific activity" takes its image from *Genesis* 2:7, which states that God "breathed into [Adam's] nostrils the breath of life." The 1915 Declaration thus suggests metaphorically that, in the modern academy, academic freedom has taken the place formerly

---

46. AAUP, *General Declaration of Principles*, reprinted in Richard Hofstadter & Wilson Smith eds, *American Higher Education: A Documentary History* 860, 867 (U Chicago Press, 1961); see Appendix A, 53 L & Contemp Probs 393, 398 (Summer 1990).

47. Even those Christian theologians who place a high value on academic freedom would surely insist that the "first condition of progress" is an openness to the leading of the Holy Spirit. The noted Protestant theologian Karl Barth, for example, insisted that "reason, if left entirely without grace, is incurably sick and incapable of any serious theological activity" and can produce statements of truth "[o]nly when it has been illumined, or at least provisionally shone upon by faith." Peter Fraenkel, trans, *Natural Theology: Comprising "Nature and Grace" by Professor Dr. Emil Brunner and the Reply "No!" by Dr. Karl Barth* (1946), quoted in Mensch & Freeman, 25 Ga L Rev (forthcoming 1991) (cited in note 35). This, according to Barth, is one of the points Catholicism and Protestantism have in common.

occupied by God. For the dominant forces of secular academia to attempt to impose dogmas of this sort even in the spiritual realm was an ironic reversal of roles; only a few generations earlier, the dominant forces of religious academia had successfully imposed the opposite dogmas on the sciences.

The assumption that theology should be conducted according to the epistemological principles of science is ill-considered. Unlike the scientific disciplines, in which individual inquiry is the chosen path to discovery and truth is understood to be independent of the ideas and beliefs of others, the theological disciplines are communitarian by their very nature. Catholic theology is not the same as Islamic theology. An atheist, however brilliant, is likely to be a deficient theologian and poor mentor for aspiring clergy. The theologian is engaged in working out the ramifications of common beliefs that unite large numbers of people, and the present with the past. The advancement of knowledge within a theological tradition occurs principally through thought and discussion based on shared principles.[48] While comparative religion (like comparative law) is a valuable supplementary perspective, it makes no more sense for the Catholic theologian to be allowed to expound non-Catholic doctrine in the name of the Church than it would for an American torts professor to teach Chinese tort law as if it were American law.

Doctrinal limitations are therefore necessary to the theological disciplines in a way that they are not for the scientific disciplines.[49] It is nothing short of destructive for the organized forces of academia to attempt to coerce seminaries and schools of theology into ceasing to enforce their doctrinal boundaries or adopting the scientific method for the pursuit of spiritual understanding.

In recent years, Committee A has articulated greater awareness of the inherent conflict between the purposes of theological education and the methods of academic freedom. In a recent report, the committee quoted a statement on academic freedom by the Association of Theological Schools ("ATS") that theological schools may require "confessional adherence" but at the same time must "practice the highest ideals of academic freedom." The

---

48. Even in secular disciplines, it is questionable that the pursuit of knowledge is best advanced through randomizing faculties as to point of view. It is no secret that some departments have a disproportionate concentration of faculty from a particular school of thought within the discipline. This presumably is evidence of a departure, conscious or unconscious, from the pure theory of academic freedom; but it is probably a good thing, at least when different institutions "specialize" in different schools of thought, thus preserving an overall diversity within academia. This specialization enables scholars with similar presuppositions to advance the boundaries of knowledge within their school of thought rather than to divert their energies into disputations over issues so fundamental that they are unlikely to result in a change of position.

49. Father Charles Curran, who was dismissed from his position as a professor of Catholic theology at Catholic University, is one of the foremost proponents of increasing the degree of individual academic freedom in theology schools. Yet even he concedes that "a Catholic theologian [must] theologize within the sources and parameters of the Catholic faith" and that a Catholic theologian "who does not believe in Jesus or does not accept a role for the pope in the Church" could be dismissed for incompetence. Charles E. Curran, *Academic Freedom and Catholic Universities*, 66 Tex L Rev 1441, 1453-54 (1988).

committee observed that "one may question whether an institution can do both at the same time."[50] Notwithstanding this recognition of the contradiction, the committee continues to engage in the intrusive process of attempting, as secular outsiders, to determine what degree of doctrinal fidelity is necessary within the seminary or theological faculty—in the committee's words, "how far an institution may go in announcing and implementing limitations on academic freedom without effectively negating any meaningful presence of academic freedom at that institution."[51]

Thus, the attempted resolution of the contradiction seems to be to steer a middle course: to allow theological schools to maintain some degree of creedal orthodoxy, but to require them to permit a considerable degree of freedom within those constraints. As stated by the ATS, "[s]o long as the teacher remains within the accepted constitutional and confessional basis of his school, he should be free to teach, carry on research, and to publish, subject to his adequate performance of his academic duties as agreed upon with the school."[52]

While this may well be an appropriate statement of academic freedom within a religious institution for intramural purposes, there are two serious problems with any attempt by secular outsiders to enforce it. First, the degree of doctrinal freedom consistent with religious orthodoxy varies markedly from one religious tradition to another and is often a matter of internal controversy. The determination of how much latitude should exist cannot be made on a doctrinally neutral basis. Rigid adherence to particular beliefs is the defining characteristic of some religious traditions, while theological flexibility and latitudinarianism are the hallmarks of others. To insist on the maximum degree of academic freedom possible within the tradition is to press systematically in the direction of latitudinarianism.

For example, in the past decade the Southern Baptist Convention has been convulsed by an intense doctrinal battle between the so-called "fundamentalists" and the so-called "moderates." One of the key defining issues in the controversy is the degree of doctrinal flexibility permitted in the reading of the Holy Bible, and among the key positions of influence within the denomination are its seminaries. When the AAUP investigated alleged academic freedom violations at fundamentalist-controlled Southeastern Baptist Theological Seminary in Wake Forest, North Carolina, it was put in the position of adjudicating the merits of these doctrinal positions—though the committee apparently did not recognize this. Is a strict view of Biblical inerrancy necessary in order to remain "within the accepted constitutional and confessional basis" of the Baptist faith? Or is a more "moderate" hermeneutic theologically acceptable? The permissible degree of departure from secular academic freedom depends upon the answer to these questions. While the report of the committee censuring the Southeastern Baptist

---

50. *Concordia Theological Seminary*, 75 Academe at 64 (cited in note 16).
51. Id at 63.
52. Id at 64.

Seminary for its "academic freedom violations" may have been a victory for those who share the "moderate viewpoint" in the doctrinal battle, why should anyone believe that a committee of the AAUP is competent to decide such questions? In such a case, the interpretation of academic freedom is not, and cannot be, anything other than a doctrinal and ecclesiological judgment.

Second, even if the standard were not itself loaded in favor of more latitudinarian doctrinal positions, investigations by secular outsiders are likely, consciously or unconsciously, to result in doctrinal judgments. One assumes that Committee A investigations are the fairest and most scrupulously neutral one could reasonably hope for, but their reports on alleged academic freedom violations in religious settings are highly insensitive to the need for outsiders to refrain from taking sides in intradenominational religious disputes[53] or from second-guessing the judgments of religious authorities regarding religious matters.[54]

In an analogous context, the Supreme Court insists that civil courts must not apply their own criteria to the resolution of intrachurch property disputes, even when the defeated faction was treated unfairly, because of the danger that such decisions would touch upon disputed doctrinal issues. Instead, the courts must apply neutral principles of property law to the formal legal documents of the church, or defer to the church authorities.[55] The AAUP would be wise to adopt a similar policy. Its attempt to strike a middle ground between complete imposition of secular academic freedom and complete recognition of institutional autonomy embroils the organization in doctrinal disputes in which it has no competence. At least in the context of seminaries and theological schools, the AAUP should formally abandon any attempt to second-guess the regulation of doctrinal purity and academic freedom.

---

53. For example, Committee A's report on Southeastern Baptist Theological Seminary (North Carolina) reported the "sense of grievance and persecution" felt by "[s]tudents" at the school (not some students, but "students"), and equated "student" opinion with the views of "the moderate Southern Baptist Alliance." *Academic Freedom and Tenure: Southeastern Baptist Theological Seminary (North Carolina)*, 75 Academe 35, 44 (May-June 1989). Yet the report mentions the existence of another student organization evidently aligned with the administration, only to criticize members of this organization for their alleged "rude and sententious questioning and confrontation in classes." Id. Why does one faction receive the mantle of speaking for "students"? Is it because one is more numerous? Is it because one is more polite? Is it because one takes a position in the dispute that AAUP committee members find more congenial?

54. For example, after its investigation of the Catholic University of Puerto Rico, Committee A reported that the university's statutes had been revised in 1981 "to reflect the views of the Conference of Bishops of Puerto Rico on the norms of morality that should guide the conduct of Catholics," including civil divorce and remarriage, but that the new interpretation would not be applied retroactively to canonically invalid marriages performed before the statement. *Academic Freedom and Tenure: The Catholic University of Puerto Rico*, 73 Academe 33, 36 (May-June 1987). The AAUP committee commented: "Prearranged sin, it seems, is preferable to impulsive iniquity." Id. The AAUP committee may have jurisdiction to opine that a university's disciplinary regulations are unjustified, but it has no competence to evaluate the validity of Catholic moral teachings. That it would make sarcastic remarks about them says much about the nature of the process.

55. See *Jones v Wolf*, 443 US 595, 603 (1979); *Serbian Eastern Orthodox Diocese v Milivojevich*, 426 US 696 (1976); *Presbyterian Church v Mary Elizabeth Blue Hull Presbyterian Church*, 393 US 440 (1969); *Kedroff v St Nicholas Cathedral*, 344 US 94 (1953).

B. Behavioral Regulation

Some religious colleges and universities require their faculty and students to adhere to certain standards of conduct, such as not drinking or smoking, or not (for some Catholic institutions) remarrying following a divorce.[56] The theory behind these regulations is that the institution is attempting to communicate a particular way of life to its students and that violation by the faculty of those precepts would undermine the moral teaching. Behavioral regulation can be no less important than doctrinal standards to a religious institution, for actions often speak louder than words.

A particularly egregious example of interference with the rightful authority of a religious institution occurred recently in the Louisiana state courts. In *Babcock v. New Orleans Baptist Theological Seminary*,[57] the court ordered a seminary to grant a Master of Divinity degree in marriage and family counseling to a student despite a determination by the institution that he was "unfit for spiritual, moral, mental, or other reasons" stemming from alleged physical abuse of his wife.[58] The court held that the student's conduct did not "touch upon theological or ecclesiastical matters" and that the seminary, an arm of the Southern Baptist Convention, does not "have any power to determine a student's fitness for ministry."[59] Such a judgment mocks the first amendment's insistence that civil authorities not meddle with religious decisions and leave determinations regarding the spiritual qualifications of clergy to the religious bodies themselves.

Moreover, the countervailing concerns for academic freedom are far less powerful in cases of behavioral regulation than in cases involving creedal limitations. Restrictions on behavior are not restrictions on thought; indeed, the connection to academic freedom is rather attenuated. To tell a professor he may not smoke does not limit the professor's freedom to teach, research, or write in accordance with his scholarly judgment.[60] Presumably, the only reasons moral regulation is deemed to raise an academic freedom problem are that it has an indirect effect on the pool of faculty (to restrict the faculty to nondrinkers, for example, might tend to produce a faculty with certain attitudes of mind) and that it creates opportunities for hiding improper disciplinary actions. Tenure systems are easier to police if the grounds for dismissal are few and extreme. These reasons may be sufficient to treat moral regulation as an academic freedom problem in the usual case, but they are not sufficient to overcome the institution's interest in communicating through deed as well as word. The AAUP should formally declare that it will no longer interfere with behavioral regulation within religious institutions, where the

---

56. See, for example, *Catholic University of Puerto Rico*, 73 Academe 33 (cited in note 54). The case involved the dismissal of a Catholic faculty member for a canonically invalid marriage.

57. 554 S2d 90 (La App 1989), cert denied, 111 S Ct 214 (1990) (Justice Blackmun dissented from the Court's denial of certiorari).

58. 554 S2d at 96.

59. Id at 97.

60. Sanford H. Kadish, *Church-Related Law Schools: Academic Values and Deference to Religion*, 32 J Legal Educ 161, 169 (1982).

regulation leaves the faculty freedom to teach, research, and publish without interference.

C. Antidiscrimination Claims

Sometimes the objection to creedal limitations on faculty or students is described in terms of discrimination rather than academic freedom. The problem, it is said, is that faculty or students are being discriminated against based on their religion.[61]

In the context of federal employment discrimination laws, Congress passed legislation exempting religious institutions from any prohibition on discriminating in favor of members of their own denomination,[62] and the Supreme Court unanimously upheld the law.[63] Justice Brennan explained that religious organizations must be "able to condition employment in certain activities on subscription to particular religious tenets" because "we deem it vital that, if certain activities constitute part of a religious community's practice, then a religious organization should be able to require that only members of its community perform those activities."[64]

A similar principle should be applied to claims of discrimination in admissions or other academic decision-making. If the need for religious discrimination is legitimate in the case of janitors in a church-owned gymnasium, as the Court held, it is even more legitimate in the case of those appointed to teach in institutions responsible for education within the tradition of the faith. For the same reasons that secular academic freedom norms should be accommodated to the needs of religious institutions, accommodations should be made to the prohibition of discrimination on the basis of religion.

V

CONCLUSION

Academic freedom is central to the conception and function of a secular university, where the clash of ideas and the process of unfettered investigation lie at the heart of teaching and research. But that does not mean that the same norms of academic freedom must or should be applied indiscriminately to institutions with a different conception and function. Secular academic freedom could be as destructive of religious education, in some traditions at least, as the earlier dogmatic approach to knowledge would be of secular

---

61. Discrimination on the basis of gender (or, much more rarely, race) can also give rise to free exercise problems in religious institutions. These problems are not related to academic freedom and are beyond the scope of this article. For analyses of the problem, see Bruce N. Bagni, *Discrimination in the Name of the Lord: A Critical Evaluation of Discrimination by Religious Organizations*, 79 Colum L Rev 1514 (1979); Douglas Laycock, *Tax Exemptions for Racially Discriminatory Schools*, 60 Tex L Rev 259 (1982); Ira C. Lupu, *Free Exercise Exemption and Religious Institutions: The Case of Employment Discrimination*, 67 BU L Rev 391 (1987).

62. Civil Rights Act of 1964, 42 USC § 2000e-1 (1988).

63. *Corporation of Presiding Bishop v Amos*, 483 US 327 (1987).

64. Id at 342-43 (concurring opinion).

research universities. Most observers readily concede the value of religiously distinctive institutions, especially in the theological disciplines, within a pluralistic system of American higher education. But many, including the dominant forces within organized academia, are unwilling to accept that the preservation of these distinctive institutions requires some accommodation of the principle of secular academic freedom, and that the degree of accommodation depends crucially on the doctrinal position of the individual institution. The result has been a series of unhappy incursions into the religious field that have left both defenders of religious autonomy and advocates of secular academic freedom dissatisfied with the determinations.

It would be far better for the secular academic world to return to the letter of the 1940 Statement, which allowed religious institutions to determine for themselves what "limitations" on secular academic freedom are necessary to maintain their own sense of mission, subject only to the requirement that these be stated clearly in advance.[65] If it did so, secular and religious higher education would again be able to coexist in fruitful exchange, without intrusion or interference.

---

65. Even the requirement of advance notice should not be interpreted to preclude a religious institution from making good faith changes in its internal rules of religious governance, but only to require the institution to reveal its rules to faculty and prospective faculty. Religious freedom includes the right to change belief as well as to stick by it. As long ago as 1929, the Supreme Court held that it would be unconstitutional for civil authorities to interfere in the decisions of church tribunals on ecclesiastical affairs, even when changes in doctrine affected private rights. *Gonzalez v Roman Catholic Archbishop of Manila*, 280 US 1 (1929).

ACADEMIC TENURE AND ACADEMIC FREEDOM

RALPH S. BROWN* AND JORDAN E. KURLAND**

I

INTRODUCTION

Anyone with enough interest in academic tenure to glance at this article knows what tenure is.

Are you sure? Here are two rather varying definitions. The first, by a former president of Yale University, Kingman Brewster, is from the best brief statement about tenure in a research university: "The practical fact in most places, and the unexceptional rule at Yale, is that tenure is for all normal purposes a guarantee of appointment until retirement age."[1] The second, by Duke law professor William W. Van Alstyne, is found in the best general defense of tenure: "Tenure, accurately and unequivocally defined, lays no claim whatever to a guarantee of lifetime employment. Rather, tenure provides only that no person continuously retained as a full-time faculty member beyond a specified lengthy period of probationary service may thereafter be dismissed *without adequate cause*."[2]

Both definitions are close to the truth: President Brewster's as a realistic observation, Professor Van Alstyne's as a cautious scholar's synthesis. We will have more to say about their apparent differences. The conventions and legal status that both address affect all but a very few of the nation's accredited universities and four-year colleges.[3] This article will say little or nothing

* Simeon E. Baldwin Professor Emeritus, Yale Law School.

** Associate General Secretary, American Association of University Professors.

When this article was prepared, Brown was serving as interim general counsel of AAUP. It is accordingly important to declare that neither author is speaking for the AAUP, although, as will appear, both draw heavily from AAUP policies and practices, and from their own long experience in the AAUP. Brown is the primary author of Parts I-VI, Kurland of Part VII. However, they share responsibility for the total effort.

1. Kingman Brewster, Jr., *On Tenure*, 58 AAUP Bull 381 (1972) (excerpted from his 1971-72 Report as President of Yale University).

2. William W. Van Alstyne, *Tenure: A Summary, Explanation, and "Defense,"* 57 AAUP Bull 328 (1971) (emphasis in original). Further, Van Alstyne writes,

> [i]t is but a limited statement that each faculty member possessing it, receiving it only after a stipulated period of probationary service, is thought worthy of a rebuttable presumption of professional excellence in continuing service to the institution. Thereafter, when termination of his services is sought for any reason inconsistent with that presumption, it requires only that the burden of justification be fairly discharged under conditions of academic due process by those with whom it properly rests.

Id at 329.

3. Colleges with no tenure system are at some risk of winding up on the AAUP's list of Censured Administrations (reprinted regularly in AAUP's *Academe*). A recent instance is Alvernia

about two-year community colleges. While two-year institutions account for almost 40 percent of post-secondary enrollments,[4] their practices range from a tenure system following the higher education model, to the public school model of granting tenure routinely after the teacher has served for two or three years without running into difficulties, to no tenure system at all.[5]

The conventions and entitlements of tenure have existed for generations. Walter Metzger, in a comprehensive historical essay on academic tenure, describes the judicial mode of controlling dismissals demonstrated by university tribunals affording due process.[6] Metzger ascribes the recognition of the judicial mode to the famous 1915 "philosophical birth cry"[7] of the American Association of University Professors ("AAUP"), the Declaration of Principles of its Committee on Academic Freedom and Academic Tenure. That Declaration, in its "Practical Proposals," declared firmly that

> [i]n every institution there should be an unequivocal understanding as to the term of each appointment; and the tenure of professorships and associate professorships, and of all positions above the grade of instructor after ten years of service, should be permanent (subject to the provisions hereinafter given for removal upon charges).[8]

The next major milestone in the development of tenure was the 1940 Statement of Principles on Academic Freedom and Tenure.[9] While the 1915 Declaration was the work of a committee of professors, the 1940 Statement was a joint production of professors and university and college presidents.[10] Endorsed by the Association of American Colleges ("AAC") (and over the ensuing fifty years by more than 140 professional organizations),[11] the 1940 Statement proclaimed that

> [t]enure is a means to certain ends; specifically: (1) Freedom of teaching and research and of extramural activities and (2) a sufficient degree of economic security to make the profession attractive to men and women of ability. Freedom and economic security, hence, tenure, are indispensable to the success of an institution in fulfilling its obligations to its students and to society.[12]

College (Pennsylvania), the subject of a report in 76 Academe 67 (January-February 1990), and censured in June 1990.

    4.   U.S. Bureau of the Census, Statistical Abstract of the U.S. 153 (110th ed 1990).

    5.   In 1987, 62% of public two-year colleges had a tenure system, compared to 99% of four-year public institutions, according to a 1988 U.S. Department of Education survey reported in Carolyn J. Mooney, *New U.S. Survey Assembles a Statistical Portrait of the American Professoriate*, Chron Higher Educ A15, A19 (February 7, 1990).

    6.   Walter P. Metzger, *Academic Tenure in America: A Historical Essay*, in Commission on Academic Tenure in Higher Education, *Faculty Tenure* 93 (Jossey-Bass, 1973) ("*Academic Tenure*"). The pioneering work on tenure practices and law is Clark Byse & Louis Joughin, *Tenure in American Higher Education: Plans, Practices, and the Law* (Cornell Univ Press, 1959).

    7.   Metzger, *Academic Tenure* at 148 (cited in note 6).

    8.   *General Report of the Committee on Academic Freedom and Academic Tenure*, 1 AAUP Bull 17, 40-41 (1915) ("1915 Declaration"); see Appendix A, 53 L & Contemp Probs 393, 405-06 (Summer 1990).

    9.   *1940 Statement of Principles on Academic Freedom and Tenure* ("1940 Statement"), in *Policy Documents and Reports* 3 (AAUP, 1984) ("*1984 AAUP Red Book*"); see Appendix B, 53 L & Contemp Probs 407 (Summer 1990).

    10.   See Walter P. Metzger, *The 1940 Statement of Principles on Academic Freedom and Tenure*, 53 L & Contemp Probs 3 (Summer 1990).

    11.   There was an intermediate "Conference Report" of 1925, not germane to this survey. For the most recent list of endorsers of the 1940 Statement, see AAUP, *Policy Documents and Reports* 3 (AAUP, 1990) ("*1990 AAUP Redbook*").

    12.   1940 Statement at 3; Appendix B at 407 (cited in note 9).

Here one finds a second emphasis—on economic security—and, further on in the Statement, a refinement of procedural protections, along with a shortening of the allowable probationary period to seven years.

The 1940 Statement marks the maturity of the linkage of academic tenure to academic freedom. The Statement—incorporated, often verbatim, in the policies of hundreds of colleges and universities—is the yardstick for measuring adherence to proper standards of academic freedom and tenure.[13] Although many would limit academic freedom, some very seriously, hardly anyone nowadays attacks it head on. But academic tenure is *always* under attack. Usually we hear only grumbling and rumbling, as of distant artillery. But occasionally there is a prolonged fire-fight. The last such episode flared up in the early 1970s, when the long postwar expansion of higher education slowed. Jobs became scarce. Many institutions that had been lavish in conferring tenure proclaimed themselves "overtenured."[14] Much of the disputation upon which this paper relies comes from that decade.[15] Now, in 1990, the pendulum may have swung. Those hired to teach the baby-boomers are approaching retirement. We are told that there will be more jobs.[16] Yet dissatisfaction still surfaces.[17] It is noteworthy that proponents of tenure are perennially on the defensive; recall the title of Van Alstyne's article, *Tenure: A Summary, Explanation, and "Defense."*[18] The attacks tend to be hit-and-run;[19] the defensive statements are more sustained.[20]

13. "Probably because it was formulated by both administrators and professors, all of the secondary authorities seem to agree that it is the 'most widely-accepted academic definition of tenure'." *Krotkoff v Goucher College*, 585 F2d 675, 679 (4th Cir 1978) (citations omitted). See generally Note, *The Role of Academic Freedom in Defining the Faculty Employment Contract*, 31 Case W Res L Rev 608 (1981) (authored by Richard H. Miller); Ralph S. Brown & Matthew W. Finkin, *The Usefulness of AAUP Policy Statements*, 59 Educ Record 30 (1978).

14. See Fred M. Hechinger, *Job Crunch Spurs Debate on Tenure*, New York Times § 3 at 5 col 4 (January 16, 1979). After noting the "huge expansion" of the 1950s and 1960s, and the attendant "crippling shortage of teachers," Hechinger writes that "[f]aculty members were hired . . . with a diminishing concern for their true, lasting capacities. Often, they were given tenure after less than complete scrutiny. Such profligate uses of tenure did much to bring it into disrepute." Id.

15. See also Malcolm G. Scully, *Attacks on Tenure Mount; Limitations are Proposed in 5 States*, Chron Higher Educ 1 (March 22, 1971) ("*Attacks on Tenure Mount*").

16. See William G. Bowen & Julie Ann Sosa, *Prospects for Faculty in the Arts and Sciences: A Study of Factors Affecting Demand and Supply, 1987-2012* 134-35, 142-43 (Princeton Univ Press, 1989). Carolyn J. Mooney, *Uncertainty is Rampant as Colleges Begin to Brace for Faculty Shortages Expected to Begin in 1990s*, Chron Higher Educ A14 (January 25, 1989).

17. See, for example, Page Smith, *Killing the Spirit: Higher Education in America* 114-22 (Viking Press, 1990) ("*Killing the Spirit*").

18. See note 2.

19. A recent instance is a short editorial piece, *The Tenure Temptation: Don't Give Professors Lifetime Jobs*, 302 The Economist 15 (February 28, 1987).

20. In the last 20 years, there has been an impressive array of statements that, on balance, support academic tenure. A varied collection of essays—some critical—is Bardwell L. Smith & Associates, eds, *The Tenure Debate* (Jossey-Bass, 1973). In the same year appeared *Faculty Tenure* (cited in note 6), the report of an independent Commission on Academic Tenure in Higher Education sponsored by the AAC and the AAUP, and funded by the Ford Foundation. Two university committees produced substantial reports that, even though they reflect the acute tensions of their times, have continuing interest: *University of Utah Commission to Study Tenure*, 57 AAUP Bull 421 (1971); *Academic Tenure at Harvard University*, 58 AAUP Bull 62 (1972). See also Fritz Machlup, *In Defense of Academic Tenure*, 50 AAUP Bull 112, 118 (1964). A recent temperate appraisal is Henry

Although this paper will accentuate the affirmative, it too will unavoidably take a counter-attacking posture. Part II will address briefly the heart of the matter: does academic tenure reinforce academic freedom? Of course it does. We will then consider in Part III the asserted costs of tenure and the reasons behind the chronic criticism. Part IV, accepting the significant economic and social costs of tenure, will describe other substantial advantages of the practice, beyond the direct safeguarding of academic freedom. We will then ask in Part V whether alternative devices would effectively protect academic freedom—devices such as legal defenses, internal safeguards, less-than-career tenure, or tenure reviews—and conclude that they would not. Part VI examines leaks in the dike of conventional tenure: due process deficiencies; the extent to which tenure may be undermined by financial exigency claims or by discontinuing entire programs; and the unease occasioned by the coming demise of mandatory retirement. Part VII turns to the plight of the untenured. What protects *their* academic freedom?

II

ACADEMIC TENURE AS THE PRIMARY DEFENSE OF ACADEMIC FREEDOM

The conferral of tenure makes it very difficult thereafter to dismiss a professor for views expressed in the classroom, in scholarly writing, or in public arenas.[21] As Van Alstyne's definition emphasizes, the university has the burden of demonstrating that the faculty member has said or done things offensive enough to warrant dismissal. But there is more involved than burden of proof. What constitutes adequate cause for dismissal? Some university regulations provide laundry lists of potential offenses, but more are silent on the matter. A fairly standard formulation would resemble the recommendation of the 1973 Commission on Academic Tenure, that " 'adequate cause' in faculty dismissal proceedings should be restricted to (a) demonstrated incompetence or dishonesty in teaching or research, (b) substantial and manifest neglect of duty, and (c) personal conduct which substantially impairs the individual's fulfillment of his institutional responsibilities."[22]

There seems to be little room here for seizing on heterodox or unpopular views as a ground for dismissal or for any lesser sanction. It would be possible to argue in extreme cases that a scholar who published wildly was incompetent; but we know of no such recent actual cases (as distinct from general allegations of incompetence found in hostile criticisms of tenure).

Rosovsky, *The University: An Owner's Manual* 117-87, 189-212 (W. W. Norton, 1990) (*"The University"*).

21. The important study, Howard R. Bowen & Jack H. Schuster, *American Professors: A National Resource Imperiled* 235-44 (Oxford Univ Press, 1986) (*"American Professors"*), in a significant passage supporting tenure, but decrying certain rigidities in "present rules and practices," id at 244, declares that the procedures for ridding the profession of misfits are so arduous and embarrassing that they take on the flavor of a trial for murder, id at 243.

22. Commission on Academic Tenure in Higher Education, *Faculty Tenure* at 75 (cited in note 6).

The word "dishonesty" can, of course, be twisted to fit an accusation that the scholar who advances unpopular beliefs must not honestly believe what he professes. Communists, in the McCarthy era, were so stigmatized.[23] An institution might also attempt to proscribe by regulation certain teaching or writing, and then charge anyone who defied the ban with insubordination.

The only sector of higher education where one can find avowed denials of academic freedom is occupied by religiously controlled institutions that impose limitations they consider essential to the purity of their faith. Such limitations were tolerated by the 1940 Statement. In 1970 a set of interpretations formulated by the AAC and the AAUP asserted, perhaps prematurely, that "[m]ost church-related institutions no longer need or desire the departure from the principle of academic freedom implied in the 1940 *Statement*, and we do not now endorse such a departure."[24] The interpreters did not foresee the recrudescence of Protestant and Moslem fundamentalisms, and the constraints on dissent imposed on Roman Catholic scholars in recent years.[25] These religious limitations on academic freedom are dealt with elsewhere in this symposium[26] and need not be elaborated here.

We return to the central issue of this article: does academic tenure reinforce academic freedom? As we have already asserted, of course it does. Allowing always for the human capacity to evade and distort punitive measures, and for the tendency of any system to become leaky under heavy pressures, a system that makes it difficult to penalize a speaker does indeed underwrite the speaker's freedom.[27]

Before going on to inquire whether tenure performs its intended function at too great a cost, let us offer a rapid look at the academic freedom scene as it appeared early in the century, in contrast to the seeming security that prevails toward the end of 1990. One has only to peruse the still standard work of 1955, *The Development of Academic Freedom in the United States*, by Richard Hofstadter and Walter Metzger,[28] or other histories of higher education, to be reminded that, before 1915, respected university presidents and boards of

---

23. See Sidney Hook, *Should Communists be Permitted to Teach?*, New York Times Magazine 7 (February 27, 1949). For rebuttal, compare Fritz Machlup, *On Some Misconceptions Concerning Academic Freedom*, 41 AAUP Bull 753 (1955).

24. *1990 AAUP Red Book* at 6 (cited in note 11).

25. See *Report: Academic Freedom and Tenure: Southeastern Baptist Theological Seminary (North Carolina)*, 75 Academe 35 (May-June 1989); *Concordia Theological Seminary (Indiana)*, 75 Academe 57 (May-June 1989); *Catholic University of America*, 75 Academe 27 (September-October 1989).

26. Michael W. McConnell, *Academic Freedom in Religious Colleges and Universities*, 53 L & Contemp Probs 303 (Summer 1990).

27. Without suppressing the status of the speaker, it is of course possible to infringe academic freedom by suppressing specific speech. Works of art, either dramatic or visual, are especially vulnerable to this kind of denial of freedom. See Robert M. O'Neil, *Artistic Freedom and Academic Freedom*, 53 L & Contemp Probs 177 (Summer 1990); Paul Strohm, *Academic Freedom and Artistic Expression*, 76 Academe 7 (July-August 1990); Paul Strohm, *Statement on Academic Freedom and Artistic Expression*, 76 Academe 13 (July-August 1990). Such denials, however, ordinarily do not impinge on tenure.

28. Richard Hofstadter & Walter P. Metzger, *The Development of Academic Freedom in the United States* 420-21 (Columbia Univ Press, 1955).

trustees had little hesitation in firing senior professors who took positions on great issues of the day contrary to the conventional wisdom. Indeed, presidents themselves were not immune.[29] Immediately after the seminal 1915 Declaration, our entry into World War I extinguished academic freedom for critics of the war; the AAUP itself joined in condoning dismissals for wartime disloyalty.[30] Tenure, even if nominally recognized, apparently provided little protection.

For an oblique snapshot of the near impregnability that tenure has attained by 1990, we adduce as evidence two fierce books published in that year. Both are sharply critical of the damage that their authors think influential faculty are wreaking on higher education. Both conclude, though they do not accept, that nothing can be done to repress the malignants.

Page Smith, a prolific popular historian who fled academe in 1974, published a wide-ranging polemic, *Killing the Spirit*.[31] Smith believes that higher education has gone so desperately astray from the ideals of the American Enlightenment, which flourished in a golden age at Johns Hopkins University roughly a century ago,[32] that it is now dominated by presentism, excessive specialization, relativism, and giantism.[33] He considers the greatest evils of the system to include the dominance of the Ph.D. and the institution of tenure.[34] Repeatedly he blames tenured faculty for what he considers the current perversions of the humanities,[35] the social sciences,[36] and the curriculum,[37] reserving special disdain for women's studies.[38] In the end, he can only ask, "Can a more humane and sensible system of tenure be worked out? Or should the whole system be abandoned?"[39] The other recent polemic, *Tenured Radicals*, by Roger Kimball,[40] is thinner and shriller than *Killing the Spirit*.[41] It concentrates on the invasion of academic letters by women's studies, black studies, gay studies, deconstruction, poststructuralism, and so on.[42] Kimball dislikes everything he sees. The only reference to tenure is in the title; it is apparently significant to Kimball that the radicals pushing these abominations are tenured. The point for our purposes is that both authors seem to accept that their enemies are immovable. Tenure does

---

29. Id.

30. Id at 504.

31. Smith, *Killing the Spirit* (cited in note 17).

32. Id at 54-55.

33. Id at 294.

34. Id at 108ff.

35. Id at 253ff.

36. Id at 223ff.

37. Id at 140ff.

38. Id at 285ff.

39. Id at 304.

40. Roger Kimball, *Tenured Radicals: How Politics Has Corrupted Our Higher Education* (Harper & Row, 1990) ("*Tenured Radicals*").

41. Smith, *Killing the Spirit* (cited in note 17).

42. Kimball, *Tenured Radicals* at xi-xviii (cited in note 40).

protect academic freedom, even when that freedom is accused of being put to bad purposes.[43]

III

THE COSTS OF TENURE

Quite aside from the possibility that the wrong people may have tenure, the conferral of tenure certainly entails costs—for the institution, for the recipient, and for society. For the institution, the first cost is the long-term financial commitment. If we assume a thirty-five year duration of tenure until a normal retirement age, with annual compensation starting at $40,000 (and sure to increase with time and inflation), the employing institution incurs a commitment that will doubtless reach two million dollars.

The second and more troubling cost (one that will be borne, directly or indirectly, by all the participants) arises from the risk that the tenure decision will turn out to have been unwise. The teacher may not teach well; the scholar may not publish; the university may have acquired a poor citizen. All these shortfalls are expectable, in every possible combination. Note that these risks are present despite the long probationary period. If the full seven year period allowed by the 1940 Statement is taken (or even an extra two or three years in certain prestigious and cautious universities), the candidate will have been thoroughly scrutinized and appraised. Because of the magnitude of the commitment, anxious judgment will have been applied, surely by the administration, even if the candidate's department is careless, or overeager to retain a colleague. There are few counterparts to this long apprenticeship, which, one should remember, commences only when the teacher has completed or almost completed his formal schooling. The medical postdoctoral ordeal of internship and residency can stretch almost as long. The time to make (or not make) partner in a large law firm is also comparable. Contrast the attainment of civil service tenure by a bureaucrat, a police officer, or a teacher. That process will rarely require more than three years.

Thus, the decision-makers will have made every effort to satisfy themselves of a candidate's worth; but their judgments may turn out to have been misjudgments. If so, we will eventually confront the universal cliché—that the university is spotted, or even riddled, with deadwood.

Why this particular metaphor? After all, as Metzger has tartly observed, the university is not a lumber warehouse.[44] One would welcome a lexicographer's search to learn how it started. Without waiting for that enterprise, we must confront the denigration.

Perhaps the prevalence of deadwood is assumed because of the conceded difficulty of removing a tenured professor. It is also difficult to remove a laggard civil servant, and complaints about the efficiency of the government's

---

43. The authors take no position on the validity of the indictments brought by Smith and Kimball. Their works are relevant for us only as testimonies to the strength of tenure.

44. Metzger, *Academic Tenure* at 159 (cited in note 6).

many branches are not unfamiliar. But the contemplation of faculty deadwood seems to arouse special emotions. Is this because the claims for academic tenure, and our concern with protecting academic freedom, are viewed as overblown? After all, how many tenured faculty members face threats to their freedom during their careers? There is no evidence that many of those tenured have more than fleeting brushes with hostile authorities, be they colleagues, administrators, or outsiders who are in positions of power.

The usual rejoinder to this observation is that all must be protected for the sake of the occasional heretic from whose heresies we learn something. Who in academic life is going to make dangerous contributions to learning? There is no way to know in advance. Therefore everyone, the timeserver as well as the prophetic genius, should have the opportunity to qualify for the shelter of tenure. Unsettling genius may bloom late.

All the handwringing over deadwood is itself remarkably devoid of anything resembling data about the extent of the blight. The present writers have been paying attention for thirty years to controversies about the value of tenure; they cannot recall ever seeing anything resembling a statistic. In fact, the only numerical estimate that they can summon is from Dean Rosovsky's genial appraisal of tenure, based chiefly on his long experience at Harvard. He opines that "the label deadwood would apply only to under 2 percent of a major university faculty; that is my totally unscientific conclusion."[45] If that is a plausible guess, how many more could be labelled deadwood at universities and four-year colleges that make less demanding requirements for tenure? Might we guess 5 percent? The issue whether any small number, 2 percent or 5 percent, justifies undoing the tenure system leads to further questions. What is the deadwood index for comparable sectors of the workforce? What sectors are comparable? Do these sectors have de facto tenure, in that, after a certain period of employment, stability is expected and achieved? Is the detriment to society from the existence of unpruned deadwood among civil servants, accountants, bankers, or lawyers (to pick examples almost at random) more or less severe than the harm caused by sloth among tenured academics?[46] Such questions are rarely asked, let alone answered. It would be so difficult to make effective inquiries that their absence is understandable.

Thus far we have established two conclusions. First, tenure does safeguard academic freedom. Second, it does so at a cost, in the occasional case when a tenured scholar becomes deadwood, yet does not function so poorly as to warrant removal. The academic enterprise in that case is not getting its money's worth, especially when deserving candidates are available for the poorly filled position. It is perhaps comforting to think that in the absence of a tenure system, substandard performers would be more easily separated. But there is surely a countervailing costly risk that, without the up-

---

45. Rosovsky, *The University* at 210-11 (cited in note 20).

46. An engaging impressionistic survey of the prevalence of de facto tenure in many walks of life is to be found in John R. Silber, *Tenure in Context*, in Bardwell L. Smith & Associates, eds, *The Tenure Debate* at 34-42 (cited in note 20).

or-out decision that is crucial to conferring or denying tenure, marginal performers would simply be allowed to linger on and on until retirement.

There is yet another cost, which is imposed upon scholars who do become tenured. Tenured stability is conventionally supported as a tradeoff for the lower salaries paid to faculty members, compared to other highly trained professionals. But as Fritz Machlup showed in a pioneering examination of tenure as viewed by an economist, those lower salaries should also be viewed as a cost.[47] Without tenure, the uncertainty of employment would require higher salaries.

IV

OTHER GAINS FROM TENURE THAT OFFSET THE COSTS

Conceding social and economic loss from those who attain tenure and then perform submarginally, are there other offsetting gains from the practice?

We have already mentioned economic security; tenured faculty members accept low wages in return for appointment until retirement. The emphasis on security in the 1940 Statement ("Freedom and economic security, hence tenure, are indispensable . . . .") represents, according to Metzger, a "routinization of job security that might have been picked up from Civil Service situations."[48] One might guess that the experience of the Great Depression, not entirely dispelled, might also have influenced the drafters of 1940. If the AAUP were writing the 1940 Statement in 1990, we doubt that economic security would be given parity with academic freedom as the *raison d'etre* of tenure. Faculty salaries, we suggest, should be equivalent to average earnings in comparable professions. This seems a more worthy goal than keeping academics one step ahead of shabby gentility.

However, long-term employment stability represents an important benefit of tenure, quite aside from the assurance of a salary. The assurance that one can get on with one's work without much interference, that one has status in a company of learned men and women, that one can grow old without fearing the axe of age discrimination (now illegal but surely still wielded)—all these are advantages of tenure. They are what Rosovsky aptly calls "tenure as social contract."[49] The social contract aspects of tenure must also create a favorable climate for academic freedom (except when the contract is broken, and colleagues become enemies). Similarly, the extended duration of a tenured

---

47. Machlup, 50 AAUP Bull at 118 (cited in note 20).

48. Metzger, *Academic Tenure* at 152 (cited in note 6).

49. Rosovsky, *The University* at 183 (cited in note 20). A similar view is well expressed by Bowen and Schuster. They write that tenure

> is conducive to collegiality. A college or university to be maximally effective must be a community to which people belong and which they care about . . . . Such collegiality is not created instantly or spontaneously. It is developed over time through the presence of committed faculties. Tenure is a powerful tool for enlisting that commitment.

Bowen & Schuster, *American Professors* at 236-37 (cited in note 21).

appointment aids academic freedom in that it makes possible commitments to very long-term projects.[50]

Leaving academic freedom considerations aside, McPherson and Winston show in a valuable paper that "[t]he tenure institution has some desirable efficiency properties that are often overlooked."[51] Stable employment, they point out, promotes efficiency by diminishing uncertainty. Academic employment differs from business employment in that the corporation is free to move people around and shift their fields. On the other hand, faculty members are trained to rather intense specialization. Their capacities can be measured only by their professional peers. Once that has been done during the long probationary period, and the tenure decision has been reached, further continuous monitoring is usually unnecessary. Such monitoring takes up very heavy resources in business enterprises. It would be especially costly for academic institutions if attempted by inexpert central administrations. Because of their own tenure, the senior professors who in practice make the tenure decision are not threatened by bringing on able colleagues. This fact helps to maintain quality. Indeed, a cynical-seeming paper by Lorne Carmichael argues that tenure is essential to prevent declines in quality. "Loosely, tenure is necessary because without it incumbents would never be willing to hire people who might turn out to be better than themselves," Carmichael asserts.[52]

Still another variant on the economic arguments describes the university as a principal in a frequent business pattern called "hands-tying." In dealing with promising researchers, the university induces them with tenure. That is, the university ties its hands so that it cannot renege just because a particular appointment does not pan out. If it selects shrewdly, it will, on balance, gain, and able scholars will sign on because of the tenure commitment.[53]

Since much of the opposition to tenure decries its supposed inefficiency (because of the deadwood risk), it is reassuring to have economists, habituated as they are to following through all the implications of a problem, emerging with efficiency rationales for tenure. Of course, none of the arguments we have advanced is amenable to quantification. We have pointed out familiar, indeed obvious, reasons why tenure supports academic freedom. We have conceded that tenure does impose some costs on society, universities, and teachers, while arguing that deadwood costs are unknown and probably exaggerated. We then described benefits of tenure independent of the central theme of academic freedom. The reader must strike her own balance.

---

50. Brewster, 58 AAUP Bull at 382 (cited in note 1).

51. Michael McPherson & Gordon C. Winston, *The Economics of Academic Tenure: A Relational Perspective*, 4 J Econ Behavior & Org 163 (1983).

52. H. Lorne Carmichael, *Incentives in Academics: Why Is There Tenure?*, 96 J Pol Econ 453, 454 (1988).

53. Henry Hansmann & Reinier Kraakman, Hands-Tying in Principal-Agent Relationships: Venture Capital Financing, Publishing Contracts, and Academic Tenure 26 (December 1989) (unpublished manuscript, on file with authors).

V

ALTERNATIVES TO TENURE

Critics propose four possible alternatives to tenure, all of which are advocated as safeguarding academic freedom. The first alternative advanced is that of legal tribunals, affording both procedural and substantive due process; supporters argue these protections would make conventional tenure unnecessary. The second, related to the first, would rely on internal university tribunals. The third and fourth, almost interchangeable in their advantages and disadvantages, are "term tenure"—successive term appointments, of five years or more, until retirement—and "interruptible tenure"—periodic formal review that can lead to a termination of tenure.

A. Reliance on the Law

The disputants who blithely declare that academics do not need tenure because the courts will protect academic freedom are not relying on close analysis of the relevant case law.[54] The first and fourteenth amendments do offer some aid to injured professors; but the scope of protection is hardly sufficient to supplant the safeguards of contractual or statutory tenure.

Although several ringing affirmations of academic freedom have emanated from the Supreme Court, it is still uncertain what that Court would do in a straightforward case in which an untenured professor has been disciplined for the content of classroom utterances or scholarly writing. A first obstacle arises from the proposition that the academic freedom extolled by the Court is that of the institution, not of individual faculty members.[55] The terrain is too extensive to be retravelled here.[56] Consider only Justice Frankfurter's famous dictum in his concurrence to *Sweezy v. New Hampshire*,[57] where he quoted South African academics on "[t]he four essential freedoms *of a university*—to determine *for itself* on academic grounds who may teach, what may be taught, how it shall be taught, and who may be admitted to study."[58]

---

54. See James O'Toole, *Tenure: A Conscientious Objection*, Change 24, 29 (June-July 1978). This article is a relatively sustained denunciation and renunciation (by its author) of tenure. It was responded to by William W. Van Alstyne, *Tenure: A Conscientious Objective*, 10 Change 44 (October 1978); compare the remark of an unnamed "official of an educational institution" in Malcolm G. Scully, *Attacks on Tenure Mount* at 15 (cited in note 15): "As I see it, academic freedom is just another phrase for constitutional rights, properly understood."

55. This thesis is well developed in J. Peter Byrne, *Academic Freedom: A "Special Concern of the First Amendment*," 99 Yale L J 251 (1989). Compare Walter P. Metzger, *Profession and Constitution: Two Definitions of Academic Freedom in America*, 66 Tex L Rev 1265 (1988) (similar approach); Matthew W. Finkin, *On "Institutional" Academic Freedom*, 61 Tex L Rev 817 (1983); William W. Van Alstyne, *The Specific Theory of Academic Freedom and the General Issue of Civil Liberties*, 404 Annals Am Acad Pol Soc Sci 140 (November 1972).

56. See David M. Rabban, *A Functional Analysis of "Individual" and "Institutional" Academic Freedom Under the First Amendment*, 53 L & Contemp Probs 227 (Summer 1990); William W. Van Alstyne, *Academic Freedom and the First Amendment in the Supreme Court of The United States: An Unhurried Review*, 53 L & Contemp Probs 79 (Summer 1990).

57. 354 US 236, 263 (1957).

58. Id (emphasis added).

Other pronouncements by members of the Court similarly deal with *institutional* freedom rather than that of individuals.[59]

Two lower-court decisions do bring the first amendment into the classroom. One, *Cooper v. Ross*,[60] is quite remarkable. Judge Heaney of the Eighth Circuit, sitting as a district judge, found that the plaintiff had been denied reappointment at the University of Arkansas at Little Rock because he had made known in his classes and elsewhere that he was a communist, a member of the Progressive Labor party. These disclosures had inflamed many members of the legislature. Apparently without any difficulty, Judge Heaney wrote,

> [i]n summary, the Court concludes that Cooper's membership in the PLP and his public acknowledgement of his beliefs, both inside and outside the University classroom, were protected conduct under the First and Fourteenth Amendments. The Court finds that this protected activity was a substantial or motivating factor in the University's decision not to reappoint Cooper.[61]

Another decision encouraging the view that courts will protect the academic freedom of the untenured is *Dube v. State University of New York*.[62] In this recent case, the Second Circuit held that Professor Ernest Dube was entitled to a trial on his allegations that the State University of New York denied him tenure in retaliation against what some perceived to be his suggestions (made in a seminar) that there are racist strains in Zionism. Dube's alleged heresies aroused the ire of many Jewish persons and groups, with Governor Mario Cuomo joining in a sharp expression of concern.[63] The court agreed that Dube's first amendment rights might have been impaired.[64] This case was complicated by issues of qualified immunity of state officials, who by virtue of the eleventh amendment enjoy considerable protection against suit. These issues led the other two members of the panel to write separate concurring opinions,[65] but were apparently not even raised in *Cooper*.

---

59. Consider especially the slighting reference by Justice Blackmun (writing for a unanimous Court) to "the so-called academic freedom cases." *University of Pennsylvania v EEOC*, 110 S Ct 577, 586 (1990). This case denied any academic freedom privilege for the University to protect peer review materials from disclosure to the Equal Employment Opportunity Commission on behalf of a plaintiff claiming race and sex discrimination. However, the Court went on to say, "Fortunately, we need not define today the precise contours of any academic freedom right against government attempts to influence the content of academic speech . . ." . Id. A footnote went farther:

> Obvious First Amendment problems would arise where government attempts to direct the content of speech at private universities. Such content-based regulation of private speech traditionally has carried with it a heavy burden of justification. Where, as was the situation in the academic-freedom cases, government attempts to direct the content of speech at public educational institutions, complicated First Amendment issues are presented because government is simultaneously both speaker and regulator.

Id at 587 n10 (citations omitted).

60. 472 F Supp 802 (ED Ark 1979).
61. Id at 814.
62. 900 F2d 587 (2d Cir 1990).
63. Id at 590.
64. Id at 597.
65. Id at 600 (Miner concurring; Mahoney generally concurring).

It would take this article far afield if it did any more than to note their existence.[66]

Thus, we find some support for faculty members in these two instances of alleged or actual invasions of academic freedom in the classroom. Similarly, university professors have fared well when subjected to discipline for critical statements directed at colleagues or administrators.[67]

The constitutional standards that apply here come from a quartet of Supreme Court decisions that focus not on the academy, but on general standards of critical speech by public employees. In two of the four cases, teachers were plaintiffs. The wellspring of this little fountain of constitutional law is *Pickering v. Board of Education*,[68] which held, with respect to a high school teacher who wrote a letter to the local newspaper criticizing the handling of a bond issue for new schools, that the Board of Education could not fire him unless his critical statements were knowingly or recklessly false, which the Court said they were not.[69] The Court did, however, recognize an "interest of the State, as an employer, in promoting the efficiency of the public services it performs through its employees."[70] A balance had to be struck. That balance was tilted somewhat against the employee fifteen years later in *Connick v. Myers*,[71] where an assistant district attorney was fired for distributing a slanted "questionnaire" to her colleagues. The Court found that "Myers' questionnaire touched upon matters of public concern in only a most limited sense."[72] It could be "most accurately characterized as an employee grievance concerning internal office policy."[73] The balance tilted again toward the employee in the bizarre case of *Rankin v. McPherson*.[74] *Rankin* concerned an incautious remark by a clerk in a county constable's office, following the 1981 attempt to assassinate President Reagan: "If they go for him again, I hope they get him."[75] The Court held this statement not to warrant her dismissal.[76] (Both *Connick* and *McPherson* were 5-4 decisions.)

The fourth player in the quartet of Supreme Court decisions is *Mt. Healthy City School District Board of Education v. Doyle*.[77] In that case, the Court held that

---

66. Summarily, the officials would have qualified immunity from damages if their conduct did not violate "clearly established statutory or constitutional rights of which a reasonable person would have known." Id at 596, quoting *Harlow v Fitzgerald*, 457 US 800, 818 (1982). But, Judge Meskill wrote, the conduct alleged, if established at trial, would violate "long-standing and clearly established First Amendment law." Id at 597. Dube, however, showed no 14th amendment due process violations, because *Board of Regents v Roth*, 408 US 564 (1972), controlled. 900 F2d at 599.

67. See notes 82-88 and accompanying text.

68. 391 US 563 (1968).

69. Id at 574. The *Pickering* court borrowed the "knowingly or recklessly false" yardstick as a limit for protection of plaintiff's speech from *New York Times v Sullivan*, 376 US 254 (1964) (the famous case narrowing libel recovery by public officials).

70. 391 US at 568.

71. 461 US 138 (1983).

72. Id at 154.

73. Id.

74. 483 US 378 (1987).

75. Id at 380.

76. Id at 383.

77. 429 US 274 (1977).

a school teacher who instigated over-the-air critical comments about the school's principal could claim *Pickering* protection when he was not reappointed.[78] The teacher would have the burden of showing that protected speech was a "motivating" or "substantial" factor in the board's adverse decision.[79] But then, the Court held unanimously, the board need only show by a preponderance of the evidence that it had other adequate grounds for a dismissal.[80] On remand, the district court so found, and this outcome was affirmed.[81] *Mt. Healthy's* reach is not confined to cases arising from critical statements. Rather, *Mt. Healthy's* standard will surely be involved if the Dube case goes to trial, because the announced ground for the denial of tenure was Dube's very modest scholarly production.

The balancing act called for by *Pickering, Connick,* and *Rankin* has been applied to the advantage of both tenured and nontenured professors. In *Kurtz v. Vickrey*,[82] a tenured associate professor, whose carping clearly overtried the patience of the defendant president, escaped summary judgment against him because the reviewing court found some of his criticisms sufficiently related to matters of public concern.[83] The issue here was not dismissal; instead, it was Kurtz's demand for promotion to the rank of professor.[84] At trial, Kurtz would still face the *Mt. Healthy* standard and the university's claim that his scholarly activity was deficient.[85]

Even more remarkable was the application of *Pickering* in *Johnson v. Lincoln University*[86] to reverse a summary judgment and gain a judicial hearing for a tenured faculty member who was dismissed on a variety of charges, some of which the court found to stem from his criticisms on matters of public concern.[87] The court found no want of due process in the internal removal. It went straight to the first amendment challenges.[88]

Absent an unfavorable disposition in the Supreme Court that derails the momentum in the courts of appeal, it appears that direct resort to the first amendment in support of claims of denials of academic freedom[89] has a brightening future. *Mt. Healthy*, however, always casts an overhanging shadow, for it practically invites censorious administrations to dredge up

---

78. Id at 284.
79. Id at 287.
80. Id.
81. *Doyle v Mt. Healthy City School District*, 670 F2d 59, 61 (6th Cir 1982), aff'g decision of US Dist Ct (SD Ohio) after remand (unpubl opinion).
82. 855 F2d 723 (11th Cir 1988).
83. Id at 733-34.
84. Id at 725.
85. Id at 734.
86. 776 F2d 443 (3d Cir 1985).
87. Id at 451-53.
88. Id at 449-50, 455. This was part of deep troubles at Lincoln that had supposedly been resolved by a consent decree. Id at 448. See *Trotman v Board of Trustees of Lincoln University*, 635 F2d 216 (3d Cir 1980). See also *D'Andrea v Adams*, 626 F2d 469 (5th Cir 1980) (another successful invocation of *Pickering* by a tenured faculty member).
89. The almost invariable jurisdictional basis for actions against state officials in any of the cases discussed here is by way of the Civil Rights Act of 1871, 42 USC § 1983; 28 USC §§ 1343(3), (4) (1979).

other deficiencies of a professor facing discipline, so as to be able to say, "We would have fired her anyway." Indeed, a capable administrator, even though bothered beyond endurance by a troublemaker, as in *Kurtz*, or buffeted by outside powers, will try to avoid offering up the victim's head on a first amendment platter. Such an administrator does not need the nudge of *Mt. Healthy* to search for adequate independent grounds that will support adverse action.

Now tenure does make a difference. The untenured faculty member, who needs a hearing in order to challenge the adequacy of asserted grounds for termination, will find that the Constitution does not entitle her to a hearing. For that matter, she has no legal right to know why she is being fired. This state of affairs is the result of the well-known 1972 decision of the Supreme Court in *Board of Regents of State Colleges v. Roth*.[90] In *Roth*, Justice Stewart pointed out that, to claim due process under the fourteenth amendment, Roth had to have either a property interest or a liberty interest.[91] As a term appointee whose term had expired, he had neither.[92] The university need say nothing; Roth's contract was at an end.[93] *Roth* is usually bracketed with *Perry v. Sindermann*,[94] decided along with *Roth*, and pointedly connected for our purpose. Sindermann claimed he had been let go because of his lawful political activities. His college had no formal tenure system; but the Court, by an indulgent interpretation of a pompously phrased but ambivalent college statement on job security that could equally have been taken to negate tenure, concluded that Sindermann must be given an opportunity to show that he had acquired tenure in his ten years of teaching (albeit at three different institutions) through an "unwritten 'common law'."[95]

Both cases make it clear that the property or liberty entitlements that would activate fourteenth amendment due process must ordinarily come from outside the Constitution—from common law, contract, or statute.[96] This proposition remains unchallenged. While the professor has the burden of proving that he has tenure or its equivalent, once he has it, the core legal meaning of tenure comes to bear: the burden of proof is then on the institution to establish valid grounds for discipline. In any case, therefore,

---

90. 408 US 564 (1972).
91. Id at 570-71.
92. Id at 578.
93. Id.
94. 408 US 593 (1972).
95. 408 US at 602-03. Sindermann ultimately accepted a substantial settlement. The policy statement read as follows:

> *Teacher Tenure*: Odessa College has no tenure system. The Administration of the College wishes the faculty member to feel that he has permanent tenure as long as his teaching services are satisfactory and as long as he displays a cooperative attitude toward his co-workers and his superiors, and as long as he is happy in his work.

Id at 600.
96. 408 US at 577. Commentary on *Roth* and *Sindermann* is extensive. See, for example, Peter N. Simon, *Liberty and Property in the Supreme Court: A Defense of* Roth *and* Perry, 71 Cal L Rev 146 (1983); William W. Van Alstyne, *Cracks in "The New Property": Adjudicative Due Process in the Administrative State*, 62 Cornell L Rev 445 (1977).

where the academic freedom elements are masked, ambiguous, or indirect, tenure matters a great deal.

One can also boldly imagine a transformation of our legal system so that it would offer comprehensive relief for persons deprived of their academic freedom, relief free of such roadblocks as the necessity to show state action in order to gain shelter under the Constitution. The state action requirement effectively leaves unprotected teachers at private institutions, who still represent one-fourth of the total scene.[97]

Such a transformation is not entirely imaginary. In the United Kingdom, when a 1988 Act of Parliament set about to abolish tenure for the future, outcries in defense of academic freedom were raised, especially in the House of Lords. This far-reaching legislation included a stirring declaration that directed the five university commissioners who would henceforth rule the academic roost to "ensure that academic staff have freedom within the law to question and test received wisdom, and to put forward new ideas and controversial or unpopular opinions, without placing themselves in jeopardy of losing their jobs or privileges that they may have at their institutions."[98]

Government ministers opposing this soothing generality argued that it would not be "justiciable."[99] It is not beyond the capacity of the British courts either to make the new charter toothsome or to render it toothless. Such transatlantic surmise would be premature. In any case, for our Congress and legislatures, a measure of this sort is at present beyond imagining. Consequently, unless it is buttressed by tenure, the realm of law outside the university provides an imperfect protection for academic freedom.[100]

B. Internal Tribunals

We next ask whether internal tribunals, *if* they afforded a full panoply of due process guarantees, would or could provide justice for aggrieved professors, without any system of tenure as we now know it. That such tribunals might suffice has been suggested both by Dean Henry Rosovsky of Harvard, a friend of tenure, and by President John Silber of Boston University, assuredly not a friend of tenure.[101] Neither they, nor any other commentator we are aware of, has fleshed out this suggestion, which bristles with both possibilities and problems.

---

97. Although there is no reason why state courts cannot serve the private sector by recognizing academic freedom rights in *state* constitutions. These problems are succinctly addressed in Byrne, 99 Yale L J at 299, 327 (cited in note 55).

98. Education Reform Act, Ch 40, § 202(2)(a) (1988).

99. See Ekkehard Kopp, *Higher Education (Not Yet Post-Thatcher) in the United Kingdom*, 74 Academe 67, 69 (September-October 1988). Attempts to end tenure in Australia and New Zealand have been rebuffed. In Australia, there is currently a fitful move to enact an academic freedom statute (conversations with Ann H. Franke, Esq., scholar in residence 1990-91 at Bond University, the first private university in Australia).

100. We have perhaps failed to emphasize the uncertainties, and the attendant stress, expense, and delay, that are built into the trial and appellate process.

101. Rosovsky's suggestion is at the end of a footnote to his supportive discussion of tenure. Rosovsky, *The University* at 181 n7 (cited in note 20). Silber's comes from a journalist's survey. Scully, *Attacks on Tenure Mount* at 1, 4 (cited in note 15).

First, what would be the structure of academic appointments? Would they be for one-year terms only? State law nominally compels annual contracts at many public institutions, but such institutions have the backup of tenure and often of de facto multiyear term appointments for probationers.

Try another no-tenure scenario. Assume that all appointments were indefinite in duration, and went on year-to-year unless terminated. Could they be terminated at the employer's will, except when the teacher prevailed on a claim of infringement of academic freedom (or, though it is not our topic, of unlawful discrimination)? Employment at will is no longer tolerable in large sectors of the labor market; we doubt that most players in the academic marketplace would accept a regime that gave no job security except for a one-year period. That regime is what teachers off the tenure track endure now, to scarcely anyone's satisfaction.

In a due process, no-tenure world, the missing element is not procedural due process but the substance on which it would act in a disputed dismissal. If something resembling adequate cause is the basis for termination, we quickly arrive at the critical question: does the employer have the burden of establishing adequate cause, whatever its content, or must the imperilled teacher establish its absence? If the former, we are back to the key element of a tenure status! And, what is probably not desired by those who want to substitute internal due process for tenure, the burden on the administration to demonstrate cause would also protect those who are now considered probationers, unless we re-created that lower status as well.

If a threatened teacher has the burden of proving that her performance met prevailing standards, would the injection of an academic freedom issue then shift the burden again as to that issue? Could the teacher simply assert a violation, or would she first have to establish a prima facie case? That is what AAUP standards now require a nontenured faculty member to do if she is not reappointed and alleges that the decision was based on considerations that violate her academic freedom.[102]

There simply is no direct experience, and too little comparable experience, to reach any comfortable prediction about the adequacy of a due-process-only regime. Evergreen State College and Hampshire College, two small progressive colleges, have experimented with a system of no tenure, coupled with intricate due process protections in academic freedom cases. These colleges have not, so far as we know, had occasion to process a case all the way through their complicated procedures.

Richard Chait and Andrew Ford, who paid close attention to Evergreen and Hampshire in their 1982 study, asserted that "the fact remains that

---

102. Although Regulation 10 of the AAUP Recommended Institutional Regulations on Academic Freedom and Tenure does not so specify, it is presumably the hearing committee that decides whether a prima facie case has been made. AAUP, *Recommended Institutional Regulations*, in *1990 AAUP Red Book* at 21, 28 (cited in note 11) ("RIR"). Once that crevasse is bridged, the administration must then "come forward with evidence in support of [its] decision." Id. But the burden of proof still "rest[s] upon the faculty member." Id.

academic freedom can survive apart from tenure and together with term contracts."[103] No doubt it can survive, with high-minded people in charge, but *will* it survive when exposed to less tender mercies? The central difficulty lies in the expectable failure of academic freedom issues to present themselves with their prima facie dress already properly adjusted. The real world is filled rather with ambiguity, rationalization, and subterfuge. Ambiguity: was the nonrentention of Professor X, who believes that the Holocaust never happened, really a case of academic freedom at all? Rationalization: his bizarre views aside, Professor X is in fact not a good teacher. Subterfuge: Professor X's views are causing alumni to stop contributing, but we don't have to say so; we can devise another reason for nonretention.

This large gray area is what causes the writers to want to know more about the context of employment security in which an internal due process model would operate, if such a system's guarantees were confined to academic freedom cases.

C.   "Term Tenure" and "Interruptible Tenure"

The third and fourth alternatives to tenure are schemes for what may be called "term tenure" or "interruptible tenure." By "term tenure," we mean the substitution of a series of fairly long term appointments—say five or seven years—with no assurance of continuation; "tenure" is here misapplied, because one would have the protections of tenure only during a given term. Term tenure surely takes its place among the oxymora that confuse thought. Tenure means indefinite employment terminable only for cause (or for certain specified constraints such as financial exigency). Term tenure is *not* tenure, and does little to protect academic freedom. Moreover, reappointment decision-making under term tenure is burdensome, a failing shared by interruptible tenure.

By "interruptible" tenure we mean a system that purports to confer tenure, and then, at intervals of five or possibly ten years, conducts a periodic review of the tenured professor's performance. If the outcome of this review is unsatisfactory, it can result in dismissal. Periodic reviews of varying intensity are a frequently prescribed nostrum for the deficiencies of the professoriate.[104] Most such proposals are put forward as tools for faculty development. If they are routinely required, they generate a great deal of paperwork and take up a great deal of time and energy for the colleagues, chairs, deans, and provosts who must do the reviewing.[105] The benefits are uncertain enough that the idea has not widely taken hold.

---

103.   Richard P. Chait & Andrew T. Ford, *Beyond Traditional Tenure* 58 (Jossey-Bass, 1982).

104.   For example, Martin Bronfenbrenner, *Toward Compromise on Tenure*, 5 Atlantic Econ J 22 (March 1977); Ernst Mayr, *Tenure: A Sacred Cow?*, 199 Science 1293 (March 1978).

105.   Committee A has reported that:

The University of Colorado initiated a systematic program of post-tenure review [in 1983], and a thorough study of the fruits of that program—apparently the first such study—was undertaken and published in 1989. The study, prepared by Associate Vice President for

By way of contrast, in the Wingspread Conference on Evaluation of Tenured Faculty in 1983, the participants (who included the present writers and a substantial number of senior university officers) delineated with approval the manifold formal and informal evaluations that take place all the time.[106] Going far beyond these models are suggestions that performance reviews may lead to termination. The 1983 Conference consensus statement deprecated the use of either systematic or informal evaluations as a ground for dismissal: "Where grounds for dismissal are believed to exist, informal resolutions of the problem should be pursued first. If these fail, then existing due process procedures can be employed."[107]

In the keynote address for that conference, Harold Shapiro, then president of the University of Michigan and later of Princeton, offered a concise and eloquent appraisal of tenure. While cautiously endorsing "periodic evaluation of tenured faculty [as] simply good personnel policy,"[108] he warns that

> we should disconnect such ongoing periodic evaluations from the question of tenure itself. Any attempt to link the issue of tenure and periodic evaluation of tenured faculty, no matter how well-meaning, is, in my judgment, unlikely to strengthen our institutions . . . . To the extent that the present tenure system serves society well, it does so independent of periodic evaluation. To the extent that the present system does not serve society well, a system of periodic posttenure evaluation linked to tenure itself will not rectify the situation.[109]

We will conclude this survey of alternatives to tenure with the "confession" of the authors of *Beyond Traditional Tenure*, the most extensive survey of the subject (although it does not include judicial protections). Chait and Ford wrote:

> When we first decided to examine alternatives to traditional tenure policies, we assumed, at least tacitly, that we would discover one or several alternatives superior to tenure. We had heard too many criticisms of tenure and read too many indictments to believe that there were not more attractive alternatives. We would discover, analyze, and report these options; as a result, some colleges would abandon tenure. In turn, we would win a niche in academe as dragon slayers.
>
> We were mistaken. The more we examined the alternatives, the less we were persuaded that any were markedly superior to tenure or irresistibly attractive. Instead, we reached essentially the same conclusion as the Keast Commission: effectively administered by a campus community, academic tenure can be an effective policy.[110]

Academic Affairs Marianne Wesson and Director of Policy and Planning Sandra Johnson, supports the conclusion that the benefits to be gained from such review are modest or speculative while the costs, principally consumption of time, are substantial and demonstrable.

Report of Committee A, 76 Academe 32, 38 (September-October 1990).

106. *Statement of the Wingspread Conference on Evaluation of Tenured Faculty*, 69 Academe 14a (November-December 1983).

107. Id.

108. Harry Shapiro, *The Privilege and the Responsibility: Some Reflections on the Nature, Function, and Future of Academic Tenure*, in *Report on Periodic Evaluation of Tenured Faculty: A Discussion at Wingspread: August 24-26, 1983*, 69 Academe 1a, 3a, 7a (November-December 1983).

109. Id.

110. Chait & Ford, *Beyond Traditional Tenure* at 143 (cited in note 103).

VI

LEAKS IN THE DIKE: WEAKNESSES IN THE SAFEGUARD OF TENURE

Before turning to the problems of the untenured, we conclude this segment of our examination of tenure and academic freedom by looking at four characteristics of the system that may weaken it. These characteristics are, first, the adequacy of due process for professors threatened with dismissal; second, the possible abuse of financial exigency as a ground for termination; third, the risk that program changes will be used as a ground for termination; and, fourth, the concern that the end of mandatory retirement will somehow make tenure insupportable.

The suggestion that it might be too easy to fire a tenured professor would surely provoke nothing but derision among most administrators. Just the opposite view is imbedded in the conventional wisdom of academe. But firing a tenured professor is possible; it happens several times each year.[111] It is meant to be difficult; otherwise the high threshold of adequate cause, and the allocation of the burden of proof to those who bring charges, would not have been called into being.

There is no way of knowing how many tenured faculty members, faced with implicit or explicit threats of dismissal for cause, simply go away quietly. As in the outside world, they take early retirement; they leave "to pursue other interests"; they are handed on to a less demanding institution. There are also stratagems of varying legitimacy. Departure may be purchaseable; poor working conditions, such as unwanted teaching assignments or cramped research space, can be pushed from the unpleasant to the intolerable. Ostracism by one's colleagues is not unheard of.

The disputed cases that attract attention, either through the press, through condemnation by means of an AAUP censure, or through a professor's resort to the courts, seem to fall loosely into three categories. In the first category are genuine invasions of freedom to teach or publish. These, we believe, would usually be exposed and repudiated by a fair hearing. They come most often to the AAUP's attention from institutions that neither recognize tenure nor afford fair procedures.[112] The second category involves situations where there is a genuine difference of opinion whether the conduct charged deserves dismissal. Presumably, the professors who went to the

---

111. For an instructive example of a hard-fought case in which the former chair of the Department of Afro-American and African Studies was dismissed on wide-ranging charges of incompetent performance, see *King v University of Minnesota*, 774 F2d 224 (8th Cir 1985). See also *Mueller v Regents of the University of Minnesota*, 855 F2d 555, 558 (8th Cir 1988) (dismissal for alleged "misuse of the university personnel, name and resources"). Contrast with *Mueller, San Filippo v Bongiovanni*, 743 F Supp 327, 328 (D NJ 1990), in which the judge lamented that "[i]t is a disgrace that Rutgers, the State University of New Jersey, cannot terminate a faculty member when he or she has committed ethical violations of a high order because, for whatever reason, Rutgers has not seen fit to adopt regulations which would permit it to do so."

112. See, for example, the AAUP's case report, *Academic Freedom and Tenure: Northern State College (South Dakota)*, 54 AAUP Bull 306 (1968), and its supplementary report on the University of Northern Colorado, *University of Northern Colorado: A Supplementary Report on a Censured Administration*, 71 Academe 2a (November-December 1985).

courts of appeal to challenge their dismissals for homosexual relations with students did not think themselves guilty of grave misconduct.[113] At another extreme, church-related institutions that dismiss dissidents do not believe that they are improperly limiting academic freedom (or in some cases simply do not claim to provide academic freedom).[114] The third category of challenges to the system comes from troublemakers. They may be voices crying in the wilderness; they may be intolerable boors.[115] Simple incapacity to perform effectively rarely surfaces.

The dedication to judgment by one's peers, that is by one's colleagues, on which the AAUP is insistent, may pose a special problem that is rather likely to crop up in the third category: that of the obnoxious colleague. A tribunal of peers might be expected to stand up against the administration; but suppose the demand for removal came from other peers? The AAUP Recommended Institutional Regulations on Academic Freedom and Tenure, first promulgated in 1957 and frequently revised, assign a primary role to a faculty hearing committee, while recognizing the ultimate authority of the governing board. The only provision they make for impaired objectivity is to prescribe that "members deeming themselves disqualified for bias or interest will remove themselves from the case, either at the request of a party or on their own initiative. Each party will have a maximum of two challenges without stated cause."[116] The Recommended Institutional Regulations do not deal with the possibility that a case may so deeply divide a faculty (especially in a small institution) that an open-minded committee cannot be found. In a few instances where such an impasse existed, assistance was solicited from colleagues in neighboring institutions. The governing board should be in a position to review a claim of pervasive bias—unless the board also is steeped in the imbroglio.[117]

Tenured professors faced with dismissal generally receive due process nowadays.[118] To be sure, if the system is put under severe stress by a war or a

---

113.   See *Korf v Ball State University*, 726 F2d 1222 (7th Cir 1984); *Corstvet v Boger*, 757 F2d 223 (10th Cir 1985).

114.   See notes 25-26.

115.   See *Huang v Board of Governors of the University of North Carolina*, 902 F2d 1134 (4th Cir 1990) (involuntary transfer out of department, on unanimous recommendation of 23 colleagues, upheld).

116.   RIR § 5(c), at 26 (cited in note 102).

117.   Another way out is to submit the case to arbitration, as would be commonplace under collective bargaining. There are unresolved tensions within the AAUP over the appropriate spheres of peer adjudication and outside arbitration. See 76 Academe 37 (cited in note 105).

118.   One shortcoming may be in the handling of sexual harassment cases. A paper presented at the 1990 AAUP Annual Meeting, characterized as a "vulnerable" area of tenure protection,

> [t]he quiet, quick way that tenured professors facing sexual harassment charges are being pressured to resign without formal review or due process. Frequently such cases are handled by the affirmative action officer and never receive formal review through faculty governance procedures. If guilty, the professor is allowed to leave without exposure, perhaps to repeat such conduct elsewhere, and without any redress to injured parties. If not guilty, the costs of fighting such charges—financially, professionally, and personally—may be too high to pay. AAUP officials report that sexual harassment is now the most frequent cause of stripping tenure. The absence of due process in these cases should alarm all faculty.

Linda Ray Pratt, *Changes in the Tenure System: A Twenty Year Overview*, 10 Footnotes 4 (Fall 1990).

demagogue, fissures will develop; moreover, due process is costly for both sides. However, an administration faced with an obdurate miscreant will prevail if it will bear the costs; and the dismissal will be upheld in the courts.

Does financial exigency lead to a leak in the dike? The recognized legitimacy of letting go even tenured faculty if finances are sufficiently desperate surely impairs the security of tenure. Whether such dismissals have any adverse implications for academic freedom is a function of fairness in administering the layoffs. The AAUP's policies on financial exigency, as usual, trust in heavy faculty participation in the process.

In the decision to declare a condition of exigency and, closer to the concerns of this paper, in the identification of those who must go, the Recommended Institutional Regulations give a faculty member marked for termination "the right to a full hearing before a faculty committee."[119] In that hearing, a faculty member can raise, along with other considerations, "[w]hether the criteria are being properly applied in the individual case."[120] This would appear to provide an appropriate forum in which to claim that academic freedom violations lay behind that individual's release.

There have been a substantial number of financial exigency episodes in the last twenty years, and there will doubtless be more. Where controversies have gone to litigation, the predominant issue has been whether the declaration of financial exigency was, in the words of the 1940 Statement, "demonstrably *bona fide*."[121] The AAUP is exceedingly cautious in recognizing financial exigency; nothing less than "an imminent financial crisis which threatens the survival of the institution as a whole and which cannot be alleviated by less drastic means"[122] will justify terminations of tenured faculty, or of others during a stated term. The courts have been more indulgent in accepting institutional claims of exigency.[123] Thus, defining exigency is where the action has been.

In a few cases, faculty members marked for dismissal have complained that they were selected for improper reasons. In one such case, a North Dakota jury awarded damages to a dismissed faculty member, apparently persuaded that his "squabbles with the administration" led to his nonrenewal, rather than financial exigency, which was very likely genuine.[124] Other cases have made it fairly clear that a faculty member is entitled to a hearing when asserting that his or her layoff was based on improper reasons—although the

---

119. RIR § 4(c)(2), at 24 (cited in note 102).

120. Id.

121. 1940 Statement at 4; Appendix B at 409 (cited in note 9).

122. RIR § 4(c)(1), at 23 (cited in note 102).

123. See generally Robert C. Ludolph, *Termination of Faculty Tenure Rights Due to Financial Exigency and Program Discontinuance*, 63 U Det L Rev 609, 610 n1 (1986), citing other extensive "recent commentary". See also Ralph S. Brown, *Financial Exigency*, 62 AAUP Bull 5 (Spring 1976); David Fellman, *The Association's Evolving Policy on Financial Exigency*, 70 Academe 14 (May-June 1984).

124. *Vallejo v Jamestown College*, 294 NW2d 753 (ND 1976) (separation was through nonrenewal of annual contract; nothing was said about tenure).

hearing need not have all the refinements of a full-blown dismissal proceeding.[125]

Discontinuing a department or a program of instruction is another accepted ground for terminating tenured appointments—accepted by the AAUP, that is, under strict guidelines. These guidelines insist that the action be based "essentially upon educational considerations" and that "every effort" be made to relocate such displaced persons within the institution. Again, a full hearing is called for,[126] one function of which must be to guard against the intrusion of improper considerations. Discontinuing an entire program would seem to appear neutral in application. But the department or program may be a small one, and all of its tenured members may be *non grata*. The leading case defining what a "program" is arose from the dismissal of only one tenured faculty member.[127] Financial exigency had also been stipulated. Judge Skelly Wright, in an opinion that paid considerate attention to AAUP norms, recognized that "[f]inancial exigency can become too easy an excuse for dismissing a teacher who is merely unpopular or controversial or misunderstood . . . without according him his important procedural rights."[128]

The most potent recent threat to the integrity of tenure arises from the prospective end of mandatory retirement for tenured professors. When retirement for age was generally abolished in 1986,[129] an exception was made for "any employee who has attained 70 years of age, and who is serving under a contract of unlimited tenure."[130] This exception is due to expire on December 31, 1993.[131] On that date, unless the exception is extended, which seems unlikely, tenured faculty will be treated like everyone else, and may not be required to retire on account of age. Of course, faculty members could still under the law be discharged or disciplined "for good cause."[132]

Impending expiration of the age discrimination exception for professors led to rather hasty (and usually private) predictions by senior administrators, like one reported to this writer, that "tenure as we know it cannot survive the ending of retirement for age." Why should this be so? Because, it was believed, faculty members would linger on until death or physical disability

---

125. RIR § 4(c)(2), at 24 (cited in note 102). The cases include *Mabey v Reagan*, 537 F2d 1036 (9th Cir 1976); *Bignall v North Idaho College*, 538 F2d 243 (9th Cir 1976); see Ludolph, 63 U Det L Rev at 620-26 (cited in note 123).

A significant recent case is *Johnston-Taylor v Gannon*, 907 F2d 1577 (6th Cir 1990). Two professors selected for dismissal in an alleged financial exigency complained that the procedures of a collective bargaining agreement were inadequate. One had tenure; one was on a "continuing appointment," which the court treated as equivalent to tenure, so that both could invoke constitutional due process under *Perry*, 408 US 593, and were entitled to a proper hearing.

126. RIR § 4(d), at 24-25 (cited in note 102).

127. *Browzin v Catholic University of America*, 527 F2d 843 (DC Cir 1975).

128. Id at 847.

129. Age Discrimination in Employment Act Amendments of 1986, Pub L No 99-592, 100 Stat 3342; 29 USC § 621 (1988).

130. 29 USC § 631(d) (from 1989 amendment) (1988, Supp 1990).

131. Pub L No 99-592 §§ 2(c), 6(b).

132. 29 USC § 623(f)(3).

forced them out, thus lowering the quality of teaching and frustrating the prospects of recruitment and promotion for younger scholars.[133]

Such concerns were given temperate consideration by Oscar Ruebhausen, the distinguished lawyer who chaired the Commission on College Retirement that produced a very useful report in 1986.[134] Ruebhausen (independently of the commission) pointed out correctly that retirement upon reaching a certain age had long been the expectation—rarely challenged—in higher education. Believing that universities should have some flexibility in dealing with aged faculty, he proposed that professors, on accepting tenure, should also accept a long-term contract, possibly lasting thirty-five years. On its expiration, tenure would end, and any longer retention would be the subject of new contracts.[135] The feasibility and legality of Ruebausen's proposals were rebutted by Professor Finkin.[136] We are not aware of any initiative to implement them. We have outlined them as an example of a cautious reaction to sometimes incautious alarms.

No one will be able to assert with assurance, until some time after 1993, whether the alarms have been well founded. Two substantial studies attempt to explore the future. One, mandated by Congress,[137] is being carried out by the National Academy of Sciences, and is still in process. The other, financed by foundations, was performed at Princeton University under the direction of Professor Albert Rees. It is awaiting publication.[138]

Rees' study, which focused on the arts and sciences faculties of doctoral degree-granting institutions and selective liberal arts colleges, states as its principal conclusion that "statements of alarm and concern have surprisingly little basis in fact, and are considerably overblown."[139] The project did not have to rely on predictions. In several states, mandatory retirement, especially in public institutions, has been "uncapped" for several years. The Project found "no significant differences in mean retirement age between capped and uncapped public universities or capped and uncapped liberal arts colleges."[140] We do not think it appropriate to divulge more fully the findings of a study that, as we write, is still unpublished. But we think that it will dispel

---

133. See generally Martin L. Levine, *Age Discrimination and the Mandatory Retirement Controversy* (Johns Hopkins Univ Press, 1988); Karen Holden & W. Lee Hansen, eds, *The End of Mandatory Retirement: Effects on Higher Education* (Jossey-Bass, 1989); Report, *Ending Mandatory Retirement in Higher Education*, 76 Academe 52 (January-February 1990).

134. Commission on College Retirement, *A Pension Program for College and University Personnel*, in Oscar M. Ruebhausen, ed, *Pension and Retirement Policies in Colleges and Universities; An Analysis and Recommendations* (Jossey-Bass, 1990).

135. Oscar M. Ruebhausen, *The Age Discrimination in Employment Act Amendments of 1986: Implications for Tenure and Retirement*, 14 J Col & Univ L 561 (1988).

136. Matthew W. Finkin, *Tenure After an Uncapped ADEA: A Different View*, 15 J Col & Univ L 43 (1988).

137. 29 USC § 622(a).

138. Albert Rees & Sharon P. Smith, *Faculty Retirement in the Arts and Sciences* (Princeton Univ Press, forthcoming 1991).

139. Id at ch 6 (conclusions).

140. Id.

any notion that the end of mandatory retirement will place tenure under substantial stress.

In sum, there are no major leaks in the dike. Tenure, always under attack, seems to be generally secure.

VII

ACADEMIC FREEDOM FOR ACADEMICS WHO DO NOT HAVE TENURE

If, as this article has reaffirmed, academic tenure serves substantially to protect academic freedom, we still must consider, albeit briefly, what protects the academic freedom of the significant minority of teachers and researchers who have not yet attained tenure or who have been kept outside the tenure system.

The 1940 Statement asserts that "during the probationary period a teacher should have the academic freedom that all other members of the faculty have,"[141] and the AAUP asserts in its Recommended Institutional Regulations that "[a]ll members of the faculty, whether tenured or not, are entitled to academic freedom."[142] Merely setting forth these assertions does not, however, ensure academic freedom for faculty members who are subject to nonreappointment at an administration's pleasure, and one can fairly wonder whether, if tenure is vital for academic freedom, it is only the tenured whose academic freedom is truly protected.[143]

Our experience shows that there is some truth, as well as considerable paternalism, in the statement that the best protection for the academic freedom of the nontenured is a strong tenured faculty. Administrators with a strong devotion to academic freedom have on occasion provided this protection too—sometimes, as AAUP's Alexander Meiklejohn Awards have testified, with commendable courage.[144] The hope of protection from above, however, is no substitute for specific procedural safeguards. The need for the latter became manifest during the McCarthy era, when the number of tenured professors dismissed in disregard of principles of academic freedom was relatively small compared with the hundreds of politically suspect faculty members serving on term appointments that were not renewed. These faculty members were afforded no opportunity to contest the action.[145] The AAUP responded to this situation in its 1956 report on Academic Freedom and Tenure in the Quest for National Security, calling for a faculty review procedure in a case of nonreappointment on grounds that allegedly violate academic freedom, with a full adjudicative hearing to occur upon

---

141.   1940 Statement at 4, Appendix B at 408 (cited in note 9).

142.   RIR § 9(a), at 28 (cited in note 102).

143.   See Van Alstyne, 57 AAUP Bull at 331-33 (cited in note 2).

144.   The Alexander Meiklejohn Award is presented to an American college or university administrator or trustee in recognition of an outstanding contribution to academic freedom. See, for example, *The Seventeenth Alexander Meiklejohn Award*, 74 Academe 42 (September-October 1988).

145.   Lionel S. Lewis, *Cold War on Campus: A Study of the Politics of Organizational Control* 29-47 (Transaction Books, 1988).

establishment of a prima facie case.[146] This recommended procedural safeguard for nontenured faculty was adopted by a wide segment of the academic community within a few years. So, in the next decade, was the AAUP's 1964 Standards for Notice of Nonreappointment, calling for notice by March 1 in the first year of appointment, by December 15 in the second year, and twelve months in advance thereafter. The deadlines for notice provided affected faculty members with time to relocate, or to seek reconsideration of a negative decision before their existing appointments expired; along with other procedural developments discussed in Parts VII A-C, they also contributed to a more orderly and equitable system of evaluation.

A. Obtaining Reasons for a Nonreappointment Decision and Opportunity for Review of the Decision

The probationary faculty member who refused to testify before a congressional committee about his political associations, and who the next day was notified by his dean that he was not being reappointed, had a pretty good idea of the reason for the decision. More often than not, however, notice of nonreappointment unaccompanied by any explanation left the faculty member unclear why the notice was issued. A person in this plight was ill informed to determine whether and on what grounds to seek review of the decision. A quarter of a century ago, relatively few institutions, and very few prestigious universities and liberal arts colleges, had policies calling for the issuance of reasons for nonreappointment. In 1964 the AAUP itself published an advisory letter from its staff that cautioned against providing reasons. The letter offered arguments that in retrospect seem embarrassingly overprotective of those who make the decision (because they need "the utmost latitude in determining who will be retained") and embarrassingly paternalistic toward the junior faculty member who is left in the dark (in order to spare upsetting the poor candidate by revealing reasons "that are either very difficult to discuss frankly or which the faculty member cannot appreciate").[147]

Increasing demand for openness in the decision-making process, and for grievance procedures that would afford opportunity for review of allegedly arbitrary and unfair decisions, led AAUP's Committee A into a two-year examination that resulted in the Association's 1971 Statement on Procedural Standards in the Renewal or Nonrenewal of Faculty Appointments.[148] The new procedural standards, after explaining the arguments for and against providing reasons for nonreappointment, came down clearly in favor of providing reasons when the faculty member so requests. Upon such request, the standards called for an oral explanation of the decision against reappointment and then, upon further request, for a written statement of the reasons. The standard extended the right of review to an allegation of

---

146. *Academic Freedom and Tenure in the Quest for National Security*, 42 AAUP Bull 61 (1956).
147. *Letter Number Thirteen*, 50 AAUP Bull 85 (1964).
148. *1990 AAUP Red Book* at 15 (cited in note 11).

inadequate consideration in the decision-making process, rather than limiting appeals to decisions allegedly based on impermissible factors, and thus violative of academic freedom. The procedures thereby afforded access to a faculty grievance committee which, if it found merit in the allegation, could remand the matter to the decision-making body for its further consideration.

The 1971 procedural standards had just been published when the case of *Board of Regents of State Colleges v. Roth* came before the Supreme Court.[149] The AAUP, in a brief amicus curiae, supported the contention of Professor Roth, a nontenured faculty member in the Wisconsin State University system who was challenging nonreappointment, that he was entitled under the fourteenth amendment to due process. The AAUP's brief, citing the procedural standards extensively, argued for "minimal due process, as exemplified by a statement of reasons and a limited hearing."[150] As we have observed earlier,[151] the Court, holding that Roth had not been deprived of liberty or property, rejected his constitutional claim. It noted, however, that its analysis of Roth's rights under the Constitution did not speak to whether it is "appropriate or wise in public colleges and universities" to afford "opportunity for a hearing or a statement of reasons for nonretention," citing AAUP's procedural standards to illustrate what might be afforded.[152]

Even though, after *Roth*, reasons and opportunity for review are not constitutionally required, and though many university attorneys argue that it is safer to give no reasons than to give and then have to defend them, policies calling for reasons and review have become quite common. What was the exception twenty-five years ago now seems to be pretty much the rule.[153]

B. Access to Faculty Personnel Records in Contesting Nonreappointment

Access to personnel records is an important remaining issue, and not only in the sense that is has not yet been discussed in this paper. Key elements of this issue that bear on procedural safeguards for nontenured faculty members remain to be resolved in the academic community. Colleges and universities traditionally have been left largely to themselves, with practices varying widely, in determining which records are closed and which are open, both to the subject faculty member and to others. The issue became one of sharp concern over the past decade, in the context of judicially compelled disclosure

---

149.   408 US 564 (1972).

150.   AAUP's Brief as Amicus Curiae, *Board of Regents of State Colleges v Roth* 10-14 (No 71-162) (January 1972).

151.   See notes 90-93 and accompanying text.

152.   408 US at 578-79. See also William W. Van Alstyne, *The Supreme Court Speaks to the Untenured*, 58 AAUP Bull 267-70 (1972).

153.   An additional salutary development in procedures for review available to nontenured faculty members involves protections against improper discrimination. AAUP's Recommended Institutional Regulations and its procedural standards as now revised, have come to specify a complaint of discrimination in nonreapointment, as well as a complaint of violation of academic freedom, as potentially involving impermissible actions that warrant adjudication through a full hearing of record if a prima facie case is established. Moreover, statistical evidence of improper discrimination can be used in establishing the case. RIR at 28 (cited in note 102).

in the processing of discrimination complaints.[154] Markedly different conclusions of law from different federal appellate courts were resolved earlier in 1990 when the Supreme Court handed down its decision in *University of Pennsylvania v. EEOC,* unequivocally rejecting any claim of privilege from disclosure.[155] Henceforth, we can presume, a faculty plaintiff who is litigating under federal antidiscrimination law will have access to all documentation in her or his files, and in others' files as well, that arguably relates to the plaintiff's complaint.

Thus, the law is clear regarding judicial or administrative proceedings pursuant to discrimination complaints; but what of internal appeals of decisions to deny reappointment? An AAUP subcommittee has concluded, with respect to complaints involving a claim of violation of academic freedom or of antidiscrimination policy, that the faculty review committee should be granted access to relevant documentation in the files of the complainant and of others, and should have the discretion to share it with the complainant under certain circumstances. Whether and how these circumstances should be specified is still being discussed, as is whether committees should have access to relevant documentation in all cases in which a nonreappointment decision is alleged to be unfair or irregular, or only those in which the faculty member alleges violation of academic freedom or discrimination. Beyond access to documentation, there is the question whether the faculty complainant, at least when discrimination is alleged, should have the same right of access (without depending on the faculty committee's discretion) that a plaintiff now has in a judicial proceeding. This issue sharply divided the AAUP's subcommittee in its initial report. These are but some of the questions relating to access to personnel records that await resolution.

C. Delaying the Granting of Tenure by Lengthening the Probationary Period

As emphasized earlier, the seven-year maximum set by the 1940 Statement allows a probationary period that is quite long when measured against apprenticeship periods common in other skilled professions and occupations. Pressures to allow an even longer probation abound, however. These pressures come from both faculty and administration (albeit usually for different reasons) in the form of proposed changes in general policy and proposed exceptions in individual cases. They come in a fairly steady stream to the AAUP, especially when it is seen that AAUP-recommended standards do not permit a particular lengthening that is sought. The AAUP's blessing on a breach of its rules is solicited; the AAUP is then often cast as the villain for not endorsing an arrangement the parties immediately involved consider the best way to solve a problem.

---

154. For AAUP's position when the issue initially surfaced, see *A Preliminary Statement on Judicially Compelled Disclosure in the Nonrenewal of Faculty Appointments,* 67 AAUP Bull 27, 28 (1981).

155. 110 S Ct 577 (1990).

One device for lengthening the probationary period is to decline to grant credit toward tenure for previous service at another institution; despite the 1940 Statement's requirement that at least three years of such service should be credited. From the outset, some major universities, otherwise models in terms of their general adherence to the 1940 Statement and its derivative principles and standards, have simply declined to give probationary credit for previous service elsewhere. As pressures to extend probationary time grew, with numerous additional colleges and universities either refusing to continue crediting previous service or calling upon the AAUP to reconsider the requirement, the AAUP in 1978 adopted an interpretive statement.[156] This statement acknowledges that it may be in the best interests of all parties to determine *at the time of initial appointment* whether credit for prior service can be waived, requiring a full seven-year probationary period at the current institution. If certain conditions (including faculty approval of the policy) prevail, the statement declares, the AAUP will not consider an agreement to waive credit to be "a violation of principles of academic freedom and tenure warranting an expression of Association concern."[157]

A second device for allowing more probationary time has been to place new faculty members who have not completed the terminal degree in a kind of preprobationary status, with the probationary years commencing only after the degree is obtained. This practice is also unacceptable under the 1940 Statement, which applies the probationary period to all full-time faculty members regardless of academic rank and credentials. Some institutions place a cap (usually two years) on the amount of full-time pre-Ph.D. service that will be permitted, but others permit such service to go on and on; the AAUP has reported on cases in which probationary time *began to be* counted only after the faculty member's years of service had already exceeded the seven years of probation that the 1940 Statement permits.[158] Interest in allowing an extension of the probationary period for parents of young children has gathered momentum in recent years and has been the subject of considerable debate. Some major research universities have adopted policies to that effect; others have rejected them. Most such policies that have been considered would permit only one or two one-year extensions.

Pleas for extensions of probation to meet special needs in particular academic fields have been too numerous and diverse to be listed here. One prominent example is the person recruited to a medical school faculty to perform simultaneously as researcher, teacher, and clinician. Meeting the requirements for tenure within seven years in any one of these capacities is difficult enough, so the persuasive argument for more probationary time goes, but meeting them in all three capacities is well nigh impossible.

---

156. AAUP, *On Crediting Prior Service Elsewhere as Part of the Probationary Period*, in *1990 AAUP Red Book* at 69 (cited in note 11).

157. Id at 70.

158. See *Pennsylvania State University: A Report on Two Cases of Excessive Probation*, 72 Academe 15a-19a (May-June 1986).

If a university yields to the urging of its medical school and grants an extension, it is likely to confront similar demands from, for example, its business school, its school of social work, and its computer science department. If extensions are granted to persons rearing children, it becomes more difficult to refuse them to those who need to complete their doctoral degrees or who are saddled with prior service elsewhere. The increase in what one needs to do to prove oneself has indeed been explosive in some academic fields, for there is always more to learn and to do. Extensions of the stated maximum probationary period, if permitted for less than highly extraordinary reasons, will tend to be granted with increasing frequency and casualness. The resulting general erosion of the fixed probationary period would undermine the system of academic tenure and weaken the safeguards it provides for academic freedom.

D. Avoiding the Granting of Tenure by Keeping Faculty Members Out of the Tenure System

The procedural safeguards developed and broadly accepted by the academic community over the past fifty years, recounted in Parts VII A-C, have done a good deal to buttress the 1940 Statement's assertion that probationary faculty should have the same academic freedom as their tenured colleagues. Most regrettably, however, increasing numbers of faculty members are being excluded from the system of tenure and probation. Neither tenured nor probationary, they serve with scant protection for their academic freedom.

Under the AAUP's recommended standards, all full-time faculty appointments are either probationary or with continuous tenure; exceptions are limited to "special appointments clearly limited to a brief association with the institution, and reappointments of retired faculty members on special conditions."[159] Many colleges and universities have treated teachers in clinical programs or of elementary or remedial courses as holders of "special appointments" outside the system of probation and tenure, even though the courses may carry academic credit. The teacher's association with the institution may be of brief duration, but it may just as likely continue indefinitely through successive one-year (or even one-semester) appointments renewable at the administration's pleasure. Often these appointments are designated "temporary," although a faculty member may have served under them for ten or twenty or more years. "Temporary" in such cases does not mean what it is supposed to mean in the English language; it is twisted to mean that the regular rules (such as standards for notice, obtaining reasons for nonretention, and access to grievance procedures) do not apply.[160]

---

159. RIR § 1(b) at 21 (cited in note 102).

160. Equally offensive to the English language and to concepts of fairness is the placement of a faculty member on an appointment designated as "part-time," and paying dismally low per-course wages, with teaching assignments that meet or even exceed what for more fortunate colleagues is a full-time load. On the use and abuse of part-time appointments, see *The Status of Part-Time Faculty*, in *1990 AAUP Red Book* at 52 (cited in note 11).

Placing faculty members in this kind of inferior status because their responsibilities are deemed insufficiently lofty to let them into the tenure system is bad enough. Worse, as an abuse of principles of academic freedom and tenure, is the placement on these nontenure-track appointments of faculty members whose academic responsibilities are indistinguishable from those of their probationary and tenured colleagues. Managerial concerns for flexibility and economy lie behind these abuses but do not justify them. The devices are academically unsound and plainly unfair.[161] Until the managers of higher education bring into the tenure system the large numbers of our colleagues who are being improperly kept out of it, academic freedom for them will be poorly protected and for all will be less than secure.

VIII

CONCLUSION

Tenure, like any other large, occasionally inefficient system, will probably remain under attack for years to come. Anecdotal evidence of inferior scholars and teachers shielded by tenure makes a powerful hostile argument, though not a valid one. The economic and social costs of the tenure system are, we believe, outweighed by the fact that tenure is vital to academic freedom. No other proposed alternative (such as legal defenses, internal safeguards, less-than-career tenure, or tenure review) can provide adequate protection to the academic community. A greater danger to the tenure system than outright abrogation is continued circumvention. Deficiencies in the due process accorded fired professors, dubious financial exigency claims by colleges and universities, the discontinuation of entire programs, and, especially, runaway expansion of nontenure-track positions threaten not to tear down the tenure system, but to weaken it severely.

---

161. For a report on the range of problems arising from these practices (and their prevalence), see *On Full-Time Non Tenure-Track Appointments*, in *1990 AAUP Red Book* at 40 (cited in note 11).

"A HIGHER ORDER OF LIBERTY IN THE WORKPLACE": ACADEMIC FREEDOM AND TENURE IN THE VORTEX OF EMPLOYMENT PRACTICES AND LAW

MATTHEW W. FINKIN[*]

I

INTRODUCTION

In 1915, the American Association of University Professors ("AAUP") issued a manifesto proclaiming the need for academic freedom and tenure for professors. Critics challenged these demands in part because they claimed for professors liberties and job security not vouchsafed to other employees. A committee of the Association of American Colleges ("AAC"), then the leading organization of liberal arts institutions, replied to the 1915 Declaration by invoking the principle of subordination embedded in the employment relationship:

> It has been said that the man, to be efficient, must always come before the official. Not only is this not true in academic life, but it is not true in any form of organized activity. Official relationships form the circle within which individual initiative must find room for play, and sufficient academic freedom would seem to be granted when there is no interference *within the circle first prescribed* of research, thought and utterance.[1]

The AAC left no doubt that the power so to prescribe did not lie with the faculty.[2] When a college president was urged some years later to provide a hearing before he dismissed a professor, he replied, "When you want to fire a cook, you don't go out and get a committee of the neighbors to tell you what to do, do you?"[3]

The 1940 Statement of Principles on Academic Freedom and Tenure, jointly formulated with the AAC, codified the profession's claims and has since achieved nearly universal institutional acceptance; however, the claim

---

    * Professor of Law, University of Illinois.

    1. Report of the Committee of the Association of American Colleges reprinted in *The Reference Shelf: Academic Freedom* 83, 83-84 (H.W. Wilson, 1925) (emphasis added). This was prefaced with the observation that: "[W]hen a new member is added to an academic staff, he, by virtue of the acceptance of the position, is under an obligation to recognize that the freedom of the institution must be placed before the freedom of the individual." Id at 83.

    2. Id at 85 ("No way has yet been found to play the 'cello or the harp and at the same time to direct the orchestra.").

    3. Arthur O. Lovejoy, *Academic Freedom and Tenure: Rollins College Report*, 19 AAUP Bull 416, 422 (1933).

that these demands are extraordinary has continued unabated. Tenure—"this peculiar right we claim"—has been attacked persistently on that very ground.[4] And academic freedom in the broad sense espoused in the 1940 Statement, that is, as reaching not only teaching and publication but also extramural political utterance and intramural speech in matters of institutional policy and action, has been similarly challenged. As one critic put it, "Why would anyone have ever supposed that professors should have more liberty in the workplace than anyone else?"[5] Another wrote,

> I do not think that academic freedom is simply another articulation of the goals of the labor reform movement. If it is, [house] painters ought to have the same range of protections. . . . The question is why academics, with respect to matters not directly related to teaching and scholarship, have a higher order of liberty in the workplace than others.[6]

What follows is an assessment of this argument from the perspective of the history of employment practices and law. As will appear directly, most of what may have appeared exceptional at the time of the 1940 Statement is no longer exceptional today, as employer policies and employment law have extended to employees in other fields much of the job protection and workplace liberty the 1940 Statement accorded to professors. Interestingly, the academic profession's demand for tenure and its broadly conceived scope of workplace liberty may have anticipated the development of security and freedom within the employment relationship in general.

II

ACADEMIC TENURE AND "TENURE-LIKE" EMPLOYER POLICIES

At the time of the 1915 Declaration, it was not generally assumed that the employment relationship would be of long duration. Federal civil servants had secured in 1897 the right not to be dismissed "except for just cause and upon written charges . . . of which the accused shall have full notice and an opportunity to make defense."[7] But the federal sector, and public employment more generally, represented a relatively small component of the labor market.[8] Industrial employees were commonly assumed to be in a

---

4. For example, Carol Stern writes: "Our [professorial] claims of privilege and separateness do not always serve us well. During the two years of my [AAUP] presidency, I have frequently been chided by politicians and challenged by the press to defend this peculiar right we claim—the right to tenure." Carol Simpson Stern, *Time Past and Time Future: A 75th Anniversary Address*, 76 Academe 47 (1990). For the flavor of the ongoing contention surrounding tenure, see Henry Rosovsky, *The University: An Owner's Manual* (W.W. Norton, 1990); Richard P. Chait & Andrew T. Ford, *Beyond Traditional Tenure* (Jossey-Bass, 1982); Bardwell L. Smith, et al, *The Tenure Debate* (Jossey-Bass, 1973); Commission on Tenure in Higher Education, *Faculty Tenure: A Report and Recommendations* (Jossey-Bass, 1973).

5. Robert F. Ladenson, *Is Academic Freedom Necessary?*, 5 L & Phil 54, 68 (1986).

6. Mark Yudof, *Intramural Musings on Academic Freedom: A Reply to Professor Finkin*, 66 Tex L Rev 1351, 1355 (1988).

7. Presidential Executive Order No 101 (July 27, 1897). See generally Paul P. Van Riper, *History of the United States Civil Service* 144 (Row, Peterson, 1958).

8. Federal, state, and local governmental employees constituted about 1.8 million in a workforce of 23 million in 1915, that is, about 8%. This number has grown until it represented

continuous spot market for labor, in which they had to compete for their jobs virtually day by day with the unemployed waiting at the gate. There were few employer policies or benefits to encourage or reward long service; the handful of firms that had adopted profit sharing systems before 1900 had abandoned them by 1916; in 1929, only 17 percent of the firms reporting in one survey had a plan for internal promotion.[9] One consequence was a yearly rate of employee turnover that would be considered horrendous by contemporary standards: 100 percent in Armour meat-packing in 1914, 370 percent at Ford in 1913.[10] Another result was a kind of footloose independence, or a willingness (and ability) on the part of employees to quit.

Absent express agreement upon a fixed duration of employment, or terms such as an annual salary for middle-class white-collar employees that would imply such duration,[11] the relationship was assumed to be one of employment at will: the employee was free to quit at any time, and the employer was equally free to discharge at any time and for any reason. The idea of "permanent" employment was considered so unusual, so unlikely, as to require consideration additional to the performance of service to render the promise contractually binding;[12] and often the judicial understanding of "permanence" misidentified a commitment not to dismiss without just cause as one of lifetime employment, akin to a sinecure granted in return for a release of employer liability for an on-the-job injury.[13]

After World War II, the emergence of organized labor helped refashion these fundamental assumptions governing the employment relationship. Organized labor's consolidation in the mass production industries guaranteed that incumbent workers would not compete day by day for their jobs with the labor force at large. Workers would be retained by commitments to job security, a wide array of company benefits, and internal lines of progression and promotion. Nonunion firms, in order to remain nonunion, emulated the pattern in unionized industry. In 1929, 2 percent of industrial firms had pension plans; in 1957, 73 percent of industrial firms with more than 250 employees provided them.[14] In 1929, 34 percent of those firms had personnel departments; in 1963, 81 percent did.[15]

> Nowhere is the shift from the unstable, market-oriented employment system to the system of internal labor markets—and to the assumption of stability—better illustrated than in the dissemination of employee policy handbooks and manuals. In the

---

about 18% of the 1970 workforce. United States Department of Commerce, *Historical Statistics of the United States* 137 (1975).

9. Archibald Cox, et al, *Labor Law* 514 (Foundation, 1991).

10. Id.

11. Sanford M. Jacoby, *The Duration of Indefinite Employment Contracts in the United States and England: A Historical Analysis*, 5 Comp Labor Law 85 (Winter 1982).

12. See generally Annotation, *Comment Note—Validity and Duration of Contract Purporting to be for Permanent Employment*, 60 ALR 3d 226 (1974).

13. 1 Howard Specter & Matthew W. Finkin, *Individual Employment Law and Litigation* § 2.09 (Michie, 1989) ("Specter & Finkin").

14. Matthew W. Finkin, *The Bureaucratization of Work: Employer Policies and Contract Law*, 1986 Wis L Rev 733, 741.

15. Id.

nineteenth century the employer's work rules, if not brutish, were short; as much information as the employee needed to know was ordinarily conveyed by the foreman. As late as 1935, only 13% of industrial firms had adopted employee rulebooks. The bureaucratization of work, however, enmeshes the worker in a "web of rules" and it requires that the rules be known. By 1948, 30% of industrial firms had adopted employee handbooks. A 1979 survey of 6,000 companies revealed that employee handbooks were distributed by approximately 75% of the companies responding. Notably, the employer's personnel policies were included in 85% of the handbooks given to production workers, and in 90% of those given to office, clerical, and lower level exempt employees.[16]

Many of these policies contain rules providing for progressive discipline, fair evaluation, and just cause to discharge—rules, that is, that replicate in form the protections afforded by collective bargaining agreements, in part to maintain a stable complement of satisfied and therefore productive employees, and in part to avoid unionization. One consequence is the widespread expectation—and reality—of job security in a great many nonunionized jobs.[17] Thus, the basic concept that after a period of probation the employee will not be dismissed except for just cause is, as a practical matter, no longer peculiar to the academic profession. It has become the norm for classified civil servants, for employees under collective bargaining agreements, and for a great many nonunionized employees as well.

Nor is tenure, as a legally enforceable obligation, exceptional. When Clark Byse considered the legal status of academic tenure a generation ago, it was not entirely clear that tenure would be legally enforceable. He identified four unresolved and potentially problematic questions: (1) whether institutional rules governing tenure and dismissal, in the absence of express incorporation into a contract of employment, would be understood to supply those terms; (2) whether the doctrine of mutuality of obligation would render tenure legally illusory; (3) whether an institutional disclaimer of contractual status for its rules would be given legal effect; and (4) whether a provision reserving to the governing board final power to decide if cause to dismiss were shown would preclude judicial review.[18] A further question is what constitutes just cause for dismissal, and how it should be determined. As discussed in Parts IIA-E, all these questions have been more recently addressed by the courts. And, in answering them, the courts have developed a useful dialogue between the law of academic tenure and the law of individual (nonunionized) employment security. This dialogue demonstrates that tenure is not the only form of employment security that is legally enforceable.

A. The Role of Institutional Policies and Practices

In what has become the leading decision regarding faculty employment in higher education, *Greene v. Howard University*,[19] Judge Carl McGowan observed

---

16. Id at 742-43.

17. Robert E. Hall, *The Importance of Lifetime Jobs in the U.S. Economy*, 72 Am Econ Rev 716 (1982).

18. Clark Byse & Louis Joughin, *Tenure in American Higher Education* (Cornell Univ Press, 1959) ("Byse & Joughin").

19. 412 F2d 1128 (DC Cir 1969).

that faculty employment contracts "comprehend as essential parts of themselves the hiring policies and practices of the University as embodied in its employment regulations and customs."[20] All the terms and conditions of professorial employment cannot be spelled out in the letter or notice of appointment—or even, for those institutions that use them, in a document expressly captioned as a "contract" of employment. The rules by which institutions govern themselves, including institutional commitments to academic freedom and tenure, as well as the procedures for according and terminating tenure, customarily are contained in a compendium of institutional policy statements, usually captioned as a Faculty Handbook or the like. The courts have treated these policies and procedures as contractual commitments, virtually without discussion.[21] There is nothing exceptional in this. In the late 19th and early 20th centuries, employees were held to be bound by the employer's posted rules providing for forfeitures, fines, or other terms and conditions of employment.[22] However, the contemporary contractual status of employee manuals and handbooks issued by industrial employers has been strongly contested.[23] A majority of jurisdictions have rightly recognized these policy manuals as stating contractual terms, though they have divided upon whether promulgation alone is sufficient—as in higher education—or whether express employee reliance must be shown. The decisions in the minority of jurisdictions rejecting contractual status have variously accepted one or another of the arguments that concerned Byse, and are discussed further here, as potentially vitiating the legal enforceability of academic tenure; these decisions are not legally defensible.

B. Mutuality of Obligation

A tenured professor is free to quit merely upon submission of a timely resignation. The institution, however, if it wishes to discharge a tenured professor, customarily must proceed through a trial-like hearing before a faculty hearing committee. The respective obligations are therefore unequal, and there is some authority in the law of employment—even relatively modern authority—for the proposition that, where the reciprocal obligations of employer and employee are not equal, the contract is unenforceable for

---

20. Id at 1135.

21. In addition to the cases cited elsewhere in this piece, see *Rose v Elmhurst College*, 62 Ill App 3d 824, 379 NE2d 791 (1978); *Mendez v Trustees of Boston University*, 362 Mass 353, 285 NE2d 446 (1972); *Griffin v Board of Trustees of St. Mary's College*, 258 Md 276, 265 A2d 757 (1970); *Bruno v Detroit Inst. of Technology*, 36 Mich App 61, 193 NW2d 322 (1971). Compare *Holland v Kennedy*, 548 S2d 982, 986 (Miss 1989) (applying industrial case law to Belhaven College's faculty manual and concluding that the plaintiff administrator may introduce "evidence of past employment practices of the college, oral representations made to him by agents of his employer as well as the policy handbook to support his claim that his employment was for a definite term").

22. H. G. Wood, *A Treatise on the Law of Master and Servant* § 94 (Bancroft-Whitney, 2d ed 1886). The employee would not be bound in the absence of knowledge of the rule. *Collins v New England Iron Co.*, 115 Mass 23 (1874); *Bradley v Salmon Falls Mfg. Co.*, 30 NH 487 (1855); *Hamilton v Love*, 152 Ind 641, 53 NE 181 (1899).

23. Specter & Finkin at §§ 1.28-1.72 (cited in note 13).

want of "mutuality of obligation."[24] The doctrine, as so framed, makes no sense; so long as the employer and employee are both bound by the employer's rules, it should be irrelevant that there is no precise equality of obligation. At least one court has rejected the claim that academic tenure is unenforceable on this ground.[25] The weight of modern authority in employment law has declined to hold employer policies assuring job security unenforceable based on lack of mutual obligation,[26] in one case relying expressly on an analogy to tenure.[27]

C. Disclaimer

An employer may wish to secure the benefit of rules assuring fair treatment of employees while simultaneously seeking to avoid having to subject itself to litigation about its adherence to them. In *Greene v.Howard University*, the court confronted such a disclaimer contained in rules providing for timely notice of nonrenewal of appointment. Judge McGowan noted the university's argument that "what it gave with one hand it took away simultaneously with the other."[28] This it could not do:

> Contracts are written, and are to be read, by reference to the norms of conduct and expectations founded upon them. This is especially true of contracts in and among a community of scholars, which is what a university is. The readings of the market place are not invariably apt in this non-commercial context.[29]

The first sentence has it exactly right. Indeed, an entire body of law has developed, consistent with the general law of custom and usage, founded on the proposition that the "norms and expectations" of the academic profession give meaning to institutional rules.[30] But Judge McGowan's latter two sentences give pause to the extent they suggest that the court's refusal to give effect to the disclaimer was for a reason particular to the academic setting. If *Greene* is good law—as it is—in the face of decisions that would give effect to disclaimers in employee handbooks, the case would be an instance of professorial exceptionalism. One cannot find a principled basis for

---

24. See, for example, *Buian v J.L. Jacobs & Co.*, 428 F2d 531, 533 (7th Cir 1970); *Shaw v S.S. Kresge Co.*, 167 Ind App 1, 328 NE2d 775 (1975); *Koch v Illinois Power Co.*, 175 Ill App 3d 248, 529 NE2d 281 (1988).

25. *Collins v Parsons College*, 203 NW2d 594 (Iowa 1973).

26. Specter & Finkin § 1.06 (cited in note 13).

27. The federal district court reasoned:

Although this idea is not easily understood in the context of industrial employment, it is similar to the concept of tenure in the academic community. When a college grants a professor tenure, it is giving away its right to terminate the professor at will. The college usually retains the power to discharge the professor for specified causes. But so long as the professor faithfully performs his duties he usually has job security. Even though the professor is free to leave and his term of employment is indefinite, tenure rights are generally viewed as enforceable contract rights.

Barger v General Elec. Co., 599 F Supp 1156, 1161 n6 (WD Va 1984).

28. *Greene v Howard University*, 412 F2d 1128, 1134 (DC Cir 1969).

29. Id at 1135.

30. Id at 1133-34 n7. See also *Browzin v Catholic University*, 527 F2d 843 (DC Cir 1975); *Krotkoff v Goucher College*, 585 F2d 675 (4th Cir 1978); *Drans v Providence College*, 383 A2d 1033 (RI 1978); *Jimenez v Almodovar*, 650 F2d 363 (1st Cir 1981); *McConnell v Howard University*, 818 F2d 58 (DC Cir 1987).

distinguishing a professor from a painter in terms of an employer's ability to declare its internal rules unenforceable against itself. However, there is abundant precedent in the law of individual employment that denies an employer the power to declare its obligations an illusion.[31] *Greene* stands for the proposition that an employer cannot take away with one hand what it gave with the other; and if that is so, it ought to be applicable in both professorial and nonprofessorial settings.[32]

D. Finality and Preclusion of Judicial Review

A university's rules may reserve "final" decisional authority in dismissal cases to the institution's governing board. As Byse noted, it could be argued that such a reservation would work a preclusion of judicial review, akin to a participant's submission to a contest in which "the decision of the judges will be final." Such an approach, however, would produce the same result as a disclaimer; it would render the university's trustees, the final authority for the employer, judges in their own cause.[33] There is authority in employment law

---

31. Thus an employer may not enter upon a contract of fixed duration while reserving to itself the power to terminate earlier for no reason. See, for example, *Carter v Bradlee*, 245 AD 49, 280 NYS2d 368, aff'd 269 NY 664, 200 NE 48 (1936) (followed in *Rotherberg v Lincoln Farm Camp, Inc.*, 755 F2d 1017 (2d Cir 1985)). See also *Yazujian v J. Rich Steers, Inc.*, 195 Misc 694, 89 NYS2d 551 (Sup Ct 1949); *Dallas Hotel v Lackey*, 203 SW2d 557 (Tex Civ App 1947); *King v Control Systematologists, Inc.*, 479 S2d 955 (La App 1985). An employer's reservation of "sole discretion" to pay a commission may not defeat an obligation to pay. See, for example, *Allen D. Shadron, Inc. v Cole*, 101 Ariz 122, 416 P2d 555, aff'd 101 Ariz 341, 419 P2d 520 (1966); *Spencer v General Elec. Co.*, 243 F2d 934 (8th Cir 1957); *Tymrshare, Inc. v Covell*, 727 F2d 1145 (DC Cir 1984). Similarly, an employer may not obligate itself to pay a bonus while disclaiming a legal obligation to pay. See, for example, *Wellington v Con P. Curran Printing Co.*, 216 Mo App 358, 268 SW2d 396 (1925); *George A. Fuller Co. v Brown*, 15 F2d 672 (4th Cir 1926); *Molbey v Hunter Hosiery, Inc.*, 102 NH 422, 158 A2d 288 (1960); *Ellis v Emhart Manuf. Co.*, 150 Conn 501, 191 A2d 546 (1963); *Patterson v Brooks*, 285 Ala 349, 232 S2d 598 (1970); *Oiler v Dayton Reliable Tool & Mfg. Co.*, 42 Ohio App 2d 26, 326 NE2d 691 (1974); *Cinelli v American Home Products Corp.*, 785 F2d 264 (10th Cir 1986); *Goudie v HNG Oil Co.*, 711 SW2d 716 (Tex App 1986). Nor may an employer promise benefits while disclaiming a legal obligation to pay, see, for example, *Tilbert v Eagle Lock Co.*, 116 Conn 357, 165 A 205 (1933); *Mabley & Carew Co. v Borden*, 129 Ohio St 375, 195 NE 697 (1935); *Psutka v Michigan Alkali Co.*, 274 Mich 318, 264 NW2d 385 (1936); *Schofield v Zion's Co-op Merchantile Institution*, 85 Utah 281, 39 P2d 342 (1934).

32. *Jones v Central Peninsula General Hospital*, 779 P2d 783, 789 (Alaska 1989).

33. As Byse cautioned:

Not many trustees can be expected to take a completely independent and objective position if dismissal proceedings are instituted by the president, for it must be remembered that the president was appointed by the trustees and in a very real sense is their representative. If the president, perhaps after consultation with the chairman or executive committee of the governing board, alleges that the acts committed by the teacher disqualify him from continuing as a member of the faculty, it would not be surprising if most trustees were to conclude that the president correctly interpreted the termination criteria. If in turn the reviewing court must defer to the governing board's interpretation of termination criteria, the tenure principle could be seriously undermined by a parochial or prejudiced president.

Byse & Joughin at 109 (cited in note 18) (footnotes omitted).

disallowing the preclusive effect of such provisions;[34] and, more recently, preclusion has been rejected in higher education.[35]

E.   Cause to Discharge and Deference to Employer Judgment

Where, by individual contract, the employer has bound itself for a term of employment, and so by law cannot dismiss except for good cause, adjudication is necessary in contested cases to determine what conduct the employee engaged in and whether the conduct justified discharge. This would seem to be so whether or not the just cause obligation was contained in the individual contract or in a statement of employer policy. But this area is not altogether free of confusion.

Where tenure is held in a public institution by virtue of state law or of institutional policy authorized by law, some jurisdictions have held that a decision of the trustees to dismiss, challenged as a matter of state administrative law, is to be reviewed judicially only under a standard of "loose rationality."[36] In fact, even in a recent dismissal case in a private university, where the faculty hearing committee found no cause to discharge a professor of twenty years' service on grounds of alleged incompetence, the trustees dismissed nevertheless, and the appellate court seems to have assumed that the dismissal, challenged as a breach of the individual's tenure contract, would be reviewed as if it were subject to the same loose rationality standard.[37]

Moreover, some courts have taken an analogous approach where an industrial employer's commitment to job security arises under the employer's rules rather than under a contract of express duration. In Oregon and Washington, the test is whether the employer had a good faith belief that the facts relied upon justified the discharge; there is no independent fact-finding.[38] These courts have reasoned that because the rules are self-limiting, and are unilaterally adopted by employers, the meaning intended by the employer, "the drafter," is controlling: "[T]here is no reason to infer that the employer intended to surrender its power to determine whether facts constituting cause for termination exist."[39] California allows a role for the

---

34. The Michigan Supreme Court observed regarding the dismissal of a steamboat captain that, in the absence of a finality clause, "We think there is neither reason nor law for making employers, in such cases, final judges in their own behalf of the propriety of dismissing their employees during their term of employment. They cannot avoid the responsibility which attaches to dismissals without actual cause." *Jones v Graham & Morton Transp. Co.*, 51 Mich 539, 541 (1883). For the treatment of expressed finality clauses, see *In the Matter of Arbitration between Cross & Brown Co.*, 4 AD2d 501, 167 NYS2d 573 (1957); *Burger v Jan Garment Co.*, 52 Luz L Reg 33 (Pa Com Pleas 1962).

35. *Manes v Dallas Baptist College*, 638 SW2d 143 (Tex App 1982) *McConnell*, 818 F2d 58.

36. *Harris v Board of Trustees of State Colleges*, 405 Mass 515, 542 NE2d 261, 268 (1989). Chief Judge Liacos was evidently troubled by the standard. Id at 267-68.

37. *Olivier v Xavier University*, 553 S2d 1004 (La App 1989), cert denied, 556 S2d 1279 (La 1990).

38. *Simpson v Western Graphics Corp.*, 293 Or 96, 643 P2d 1276 (1982); *Baldwin v Sisters of Providence In Washington, Inc.*, 112 Wash 2d 127, 769 P2d 298 (1989).

39. *Baldwin*, 112 Wash 2d at 138, 769 P2d at 304, quoting *Simpson*, 293 Or at 100, 643 P2d at 1278. This reasoning neglects even to mention the common maxim that contractual ambiguities are to be resolved against the interests of the drafting party.

finder of fact, but has stressed that the employer must be allowed to set its own standards of performance, and that the question for the jury—once the facts have been found—is to determine whether a discharge for the reasons found is within the bounds of discretion accorded to the employer.[40]

The issue of the appropriate standard of review was squarely presented in *McConnell v. Howard University*.[41] McConnell, a tenured professor of mathematics, refused to continue teaching a class in which an obstreperous student had enrolled unless the student apologized (for calling him a racist) or the administration either removed her from the class or took some other remedial action. Instead, the administration sought to dismiss Professor McConnell for neglect of duty. The faculty hearing committee found no basis for dismissal; nevertheless, the trustees discharged. The professor sued for breach of contract, and the university administration argued that the trustees' decision should be given deference, either by analogy to the scope of review in the public sector or because of the "special nature" of the university. The District of Columbia circuit, in an opinion written by Judge Harry Edwards, rejected the administration's argument and rather bluntly.

> If we were to adopt a view limiting judicial review over the substance of the Board of Trustees' decision, we would be allowing one of the parties to the contract to determine whether the contract had been breached. This would make a sham of the parties' contractual tenure arrangement.
> On remand, the trial court must consider *de novo* the appellant's breach of contract claims; no special deference is due the Board of Trustees once the case is properly before the court for resolution of the contract dispute.[42]

As in any other contract case, there must be a "*de novo* determination of the facts and of the application of the facts to the terms of the contract."[43] *McConnell* represents the better view.[44]

Turning to the question of what constitutes cause to dismiss, it was not contested that Professor McConnell refused to perform an assigned duty; to the district court, that put an end to the matter.[45] But the court of appeals held that that question "must be construed in keeping with general usage and custom at the University and within the academic community,"[46] noting cases that have relied upon AAUP standards as evidencing the custom and usage of the academic community. The court noted that the faculty hearing committee's findings suggested that Professor McConnell's actions did not constitute neglect of professional responsibility under all the circumstances in the case, and that his action might be justifiable in light of the administration's

---

40. *Pugh v See's Candies, Inc.*, 203 Cal App 3d 743, 250 Cal Rptr 195 (1988); *Wilkerson v Wells Fargo Bank*, 212 Cal App 3d 1217, 261 Cal Rptr 185 (1989).

41. 818 F2d 58 (DC Cir 1987), rev'g 621 F Supp 327 (DC 1985).

42. 818 F2d at 68.

43. Id at 70 n14.

44. See, for example, *Danzer v Professional Insurers, Inc.*, 101 NM 178, 679 P2d 1276 (1984); *Davis v Tucson Ariz. Boys Choir Soc'y*, 137 Ariz App 228, 669 P2d 1005 (1983) (rejecting employer good faith as a defense). See generally Specter & Finkin at § 4.13 (cited in note 13).

45. 621 F Supp 327, 331 (DC 1985).

46. 818 F2d at 64.

abnegation of a responsibility it arguably had to the professor vis-a-vis the student.

The court's approach does not establish a different set of rules for professors than for other employees. The law regarding the determination of sufficient cause to discharge has always rested upon the nature of the particular employment. A factory superintendent's refusal to obey an order of the corporation's board of directors to present himself before them might not supply a basis for discharge, grounded in the common law duty of obedience, because a court should consider not only "the reasonableness and importance of the order when given," but also "the degree of discretion entrusted to the employee or required by the nature of [the] work."[47] "An employee's lack of wit or charm," one court more recently opined, "is more tolerable in the accounting or shipping department than in the sales or personnel department."[48] And it is black letter law that relevant customs and usages inform the meaning of contract terms.

In sum, the principle of tenure, that is, of a right not to be dismissed except for just cause, as a mutually engendered expectation and as an enforceable obligation, is not peculiar to the academic world. What remains unique to academic tenure, and defensible in terms of the special relationship of tenure to academic freedom, are the requirement of a hearing by one's academic peers before the dismissal may occur, and the limitation the tenure obligation independently imposes upon the institution's ability to reallocate resources. These are important but subsidiary features of the principal obligation; the obligation itself may no longer be criticized on any ground of special pleading.

III

ACADEMIC FREEDOM AND WORKPLACE LIBERTY

The 1940 Statement recognized academic freedom as extending to professors simultaneously as ". . . citizen[s], . . . member[s] of a learned profession, and . . . officer[s] of an educational institution."[49] Thus, it accorded the freedom of utterance due a citizen in the larger body politic; the

---

47. *Crabtree v Bay State Felt Co.*, 227 Mass 68, 116 NE 535 (1917). When a foreman was discharged for absenting himself for a day on pressing personal business over the objection of his employer, the Supreme Court of Michigan held it to be a jury question whether such disobedience constituted cause to dismiss, observing:

> In such employments as involve a higher order of services, and some degree of discretion and judgment, it would in our opinion be unauthorized and unreasonable to regard skilled mechanics or other employees, as subject to the whim and caprice of their employers or as deprived of all right of action to such a degree as to be liable to lose their places upon every omission to obey orders, involving no serious consequences.

Shaver v Ingham, 58 Mich 649, 654, 26 NW 162, 165 (1886).

48. *Sherriff v Revell, Inc.*, 162 Cal App 3d 297, 211 Cal Rptr 465, 471 (1985). See generally Specter & Finkin at § 4.13 (cited in note 13).

49. *1940 Statement of Principles on Academic Freedom and Tenure* ("1940 Statement"), in *Policy Documents and Reports* 3, 4 (AAUP, 1990) ("*1990 AAUP Redbook*"); see Appendix B, 53 L & Contemp Probs 407 (Summer 1990). As Henry Wriston, President of Brown University and the AAC's chief negotiator, put it in presenting the document to the AAC, "The new statement . . . recognizes the tri-

freedom due a member of a discipline to teach, research, and publish; and the freedom of speech on any matter of intramural concern due an "officer," or, as Henry Rosovsky has more recently put it, a "shareholder"[50] of the institution.

A. Political Speech

The extension of academic freedom to political utterance has been powerfully criticized by Professor William Van Alstyne.[51] One cannot, he argues, abstract a liberty for utterance unrelated to vocation from a doctrine grounded in the need to protect vocational utterance. From this perspective, the negotiators of the 1940 Statement, acting out of a laudable impulse and at a time when the political expression of public employees was not constitutionally protected, nevertheless sought the wrong shelter. Effectively, they separated out a special claim for academics from what should have been a general claim of civil liberty. Moreover, to categorize professorial political utterance as an aspect of academic freedom is, Van Alstyne argues, necessarily to hold it to a professional standard of care—as the 1940 Statement seems rather straightforwardly to do[52]—that results in academics having potentially less protection for their political speech than other employees. The 1940 Statement's special claim of protection is no longer necessary, even as a prudential factor, inasmuch as the Supreme Court has extended the protection of the first amendment to the political utterances of public employees in *Pickering v. Board of Education*.[53]

The force of Van Alstyne's argument is illustrated, if unintentionally, in John Silber defense of action he had taken while a dean at the University of Texas to deny the reappointment of a young professor of philosophy. The young academic had given a political speech on the steps of the state capitol before a crowd containing a large number of students, and had, in Silber's terms, "willingly and knowingly told a lie in order to make a rhetorical point"[54] by asserting the existence of concentration camps in the state. This, to Silber, was "a clear case of poisoning the well in the marketplace of ideas, and a gross betrayal of academic freedom through gross academic

---

partite relationship . . . ." Henry M. Wriston, *Academic Freedom and Tenure*, reprinted in 25 AAUP Bull 333 (1939).

50. Rosovsky, *The University* at 165 (cited in note 4).

51. See William Van Alstyne, *The Specific Theory of Academic Freedom and the General Issue of Civil Liberty*, in Edmund L. Pincoffs, ed, *The Concept of Academic Freedom* 59 (Univ of Texas Press, 1975) ("*Specific Theory*").

52. The 1940 Statement provides in pertinent part that when the academic speaks as a citizen his special position in the community imposes special obligations. As a man of learning and an educational officer, he should remember that the public may judge his profession and his institution by his utterances. Hence he should at all times be accurate, should exercise appropriate restraint, should show respect for the opinions of others, and should make every effort to indicate that he is not an institutional spokesman.
1940 Statement at 4; Appendix B at 407-08 (cited in note 49).

53. 391 US 563 (1968).

54. John Silber, *Poisoning the Wells of Academe*, 43 Encounter 30, 37 (1974).

irresponsibility."[55] On those grounds, Dean Silber decided not to reappoint the instructor. "[T]he academic," Silber argued, "neither needs nor deserves greater protection for his political freedom than that afforded the ordinary citizen. There is (and in my opinion, should be) a price for glory."[56]

But the philosophy professor was not accorded the same protection by Dean Silber that the law accords to other public employees. *Pickering* supplies a two-part test for public employee speech. First, the speech must itself be upon a matter of public concern to the larger body politic. Second, the speech must be weighed in a balance against the employer's need to maintain the discipline of the workforce and to ensure harmony with superiors and among coworkers.

The young academic's speech was on a matter of public concern and did not bring him into conflict with his immediate superiors or coworkers; indeed, his departmental colleagues voted to recommend his renewal, a recommendation Dean Silber rejected. Had a house painter employed by the university been dismissed for making the same political harangue, the university could not have defended itself against first amendment attack. Dean Silber extended the claim of *academic* freedom to the young instructor's political speech, and then took that extension to impose a standard of care as to the accuracy of his statements; the extension would grant the instructor *less* political freedom than the hypothetical house painter.

It is far from clear, however, that the young philosopher had fallen afoul of the profession's norm for political expression. Before *Pickering*, the AAUP's Committee A on Academic Freedom and Tenure reconsidered the appropriate standard of institutional sanction for political speech under the 1940 Statement and concluded:

> The controlling principle is that a faculty member's expression of opinion as a citizen cannot constitute grounds for dismissal unless it clearly demonstrates the faculty member's unfitness for his position. Extramural utterances rarely bear upon the faculty member's fitness for his position. Moreover, a final decision should take into account the faculty member's entire record as a teacher and scholar.[57]

And the *Pickering* court was at pains later to observe:

> What we do have before us is a case in which a teacher has made erroneous public statements upon issues then currently the subject of public attention, which are critical of his ultimate employer but which are neither shown nor can be presumed to have in any way either impeded the teacher's proper performance of his daily duties in the classroom or to have interfered with the regular operation of the schools generally.[58]

---

55. Id.

56. Id at 39.

57. Committee A, *Statement on Extramural Utterances*, in *1990 AAUP Redbook* at 58 (cited in note 49).

58. 391 US at 572-73 (footnote omitted). It went on to illustrate and emphasize the point in a note:

> [T]his case does not present a situation in which a teacher's public statements are so without foundation as to call into question his fitness to perform his duties in the classroom. *In such a case, of course, the statements would merely be evidence of the teacher's general competence, or lack thereof, and not an independent basis for dismissal.*

Id at 573 n5 (emphasis added).

The constitutional standard embraced in the emphasized portion of the opinion[59] seems congruent with the gloss placed on the 1940 Statement by the AAUP. Consequently, a singular incident of knowing misrepresentation as part of a patently radical political harangue would not be expected to provide cause to inquire into the young instructor's professional fitness, Dean Silber's decision to the contrary notwithstanding. At a minimum, the seemingly perverse reversal of protections Van Alstyne contemplated would appear to be obviated by the Court's conflation of the professional and constitutional tests; this is not to say that the test itself is without difficulty.[60]

More important, the professional standard may at one point be more protective than the first amendment as currently construed. The Court has stressed that the impairment of workplace discipline and the creation of "disharmony" with coworkers[61] are factors to be weighed in the balance, and at least theoretically, may deprive the utterance of constitutional protection. The constitutional question whether a sufficient level of disharmony would justify the dismissal of an employee even for speaking dispassionately and accurately to issues of public concern remains unresolved.[62] But the profession has understood that sharp, even violent, disagreement with the content of the utterance cannot supply grounds for discharge if the expression is otherwise consistent with the exercise of academic freedom. A professor's outspokenness in defense (or criticism) of efforts to legalize homosexual relations; to equate Zionism with racism; to urge the transportation of the Palestinian population; to suppress (or secure) the availability of abortion or pornography; to assert the genetically transmitted intellectual inferiority (or superiority) of a particular race; and the like— expression, in other words, that fires deep contemporary passions, is not

---

59. See note 58.

60. Professor Van Alstyne has been critical of the test. William Van Alstyne, *The Constitutional Rights of Teachers and Professors*, 1970 Duke L J 841, 854.

61. *Pickering*, 391 US at 570-73; *Connick v Myers*, 461 US 138, 152-53 (1983); *Rankin v McPherson*, 483 US 378, 388 (1987).

62. In *National Gay Task Force v Board of Education*, 729 F2d 1270 (10th Cir 1984) aff'd, 470 US 903 (1985), the Tenth Circuit struck down on overbreadth grounds portions of a statute that provided for the refusal to hire high school teachers who "advocate" homosexual activity in a manner such that prospective co-workers may become aware of it. On appeal, the Board of Education argued that a limitation, which required that the advocacy have an "adverse effect" on coworkers, saved the statute: "When [the advocacy] comes to the attention of other teachers or co-workers, it is likely to produce sufficient controversy, suspicion, and mistrust so as to threaten employee discipline, co-worker harmony, and that personal loyalty and confidence requisite to particularly close employee relationships." Appellant's Brief at 36, quoted in AAUP's Brief as Amicus Curiae at 12, 470 US 903 (No 83-2030). The AAUP took sharp issue with the argument:

> An advocate upon any controversial subject could be disqualified not because the speech fell afoul of any test of lawlessness, not because it reflected any want of scholarship, and not because it lacked in moderation or restraint in any way, but because one's prospective colleagues or superiors found the advocate's position upon a general question of public policy too "controversial" and so "disharmonious." But to make appointment contingent upon the degree of approval of one's social, economic, or political views by one's co-workers or superiors is to eviscerate the First Amendment.

Id at 13-14. Ominously, the Tenth Circuit's decision was affirmed by an equally divided Court. 470 US 903.

subject to sanction based upon the depth and intensity of collegial sentiment contrary to the ideas expressed.

From an historical perspective, the demand for freedom of political expression and activity in the employment relationship, as an aspect not only of citizenship but of status, is not unprecedented. In the early days of the Republic, employer efforts to control the political behavior of employees were strenuously and sometimes violently resisted as a threat to democracy and an affront to artisanal independence, in appeals straightforwardly to the solidarity of the "mechanical class."[63]

Most states now forbid by legislation employer attempts to control employees' political activity, and some insulate political speech and association generally from employer reprisal.[64] In addition, the emerging tort of discharge for reasons violating public policy[65] has been extended to encompass the dismissal of a manager for refusal to support his employer's lobbying effort on behalf of a bill favorable to the company;[66] the dismissal of an employee for protesting the unauthorized use of his name in the company's lobbying effort;[67] and the discharge of a bank executive for the content of testimony he gave a committee of the United States Senate.[68] In other words, the law of employment may be edging toward a general public policy forbidding employers from interfering in employee political speech and activity. If this is so, and putting the question of standards aside, it would not appear that professors have claimed a higher order of workplace liberty than that claimed by others.

B. Speech on Workplace Issues

The profession has subsumed as an aspect of academic freedom intramural speech on any matter of academic interest—that is, speech made as a "shareholder" in the institution. That formulation has been challenged by

---

63. In 1798, the "mechanics" of Baltimore protested vehemently about a Federalist employer who would hire no men opposed to his candidate. They published a statement in the press: "The statement claimed that 'unwarrantable and degrading means' had been used to manipulate the mechanics' vote, that these 'base designs' must be frustrated, and that the mechanics 'have and will maintain an opinion of our own.' " Charles G. Steffen, *The Mechanics of Baltimore: Workers and Politics in the Age of Revolution 1763-1812*, 162 (Univ of Illinois Press, 1984). Howard Rock recounts a series of such incidents—and protests—in New York City around the turn of the century, including a broadside of 1808: "*Fellow citizens* — LET us support our independence! If we are Mechanics, Labourers and Artizans — Why should we surrender our opinions and our rights to the arbitrary mandate of a Tory Employer, and that employer, perhaps a foreign emissary!" Howard Rock, *Artisans of the New Republic: The Tradesmen of New York City in the Age of Jefferson* 54 (New York Univ Press, 1979) ("*Artisans*"). Similar employer action was later to occur, especially in the presidential election of 1896. See Walter Licht, *Working for the Railroad: The Organization of Work in the Nineteenth Century* 230-31 (Princeton Univ Press, 1983); Lawrence Goodwyn, *The Populist Moment* 286 (Oxford Univ Press, 1978).

64. Specter & Finkin at § 10.25 (cited in note 13).

65. Id at §§ 10.33-10.48.

66. *Novosel v Nationwide Ins. Co.*, 721 F2d 894 (3d Cir 1983) (applying Pennsylvania law).

67. *Chavez v Manville Products Corp.*, 108 NM 643, 777 P2d 371 (1989).

68. *Bishop v Federal Intermediate Credit Bank of Wichita*, 908 F2d 658 (10th Cir 1990) (applying Oklahoma law).

Dean Mark Yudof.[69] Unlike Van Alstyne's treatment of professorial political speech, which he would shelter under a more generous rubric of civil liberty, and which he would extend to private institutions under that head,[70] Yudof's criticism is not solely a matter of the derivation of the claim. Even had the profession claimed academic freedom only for disciplinary discourse, and coupled it, following the line of Van Alstyne's argument, with an assertion of academic civil liberty for nondisciplinary discourse, Yudof's question—why academics should have workplace liberties higher than those conceded to others—would seem to persist.

The question assumes that other occupations have failed to propound, and secure, any analogous freedom. A fuller examination of that question is called for, and for that an historical perspective is essential.

In the pre-industrial, artisanal world of the early Republic, the implied obligations of obedience and respectfulness owed by servant to master were, at least for the highly skilled, irrelevant. Journeymen worked under little supervision; and, for some, any supervision was not to be endured. Paid by the piece, artisans often came and went as they pleased.[71] Drinking on the job was asserted not only as a matter of custom, but as of right.[72] Independence from authority was insisted upon. "If a master said a word that wasn't deserved," Andrew Mayhew was told by a hatmaker in 1850, "a journeyman would put on his coat and walk out."[73] If a word could capture the spirit of these craftsmen, it would be "manliness." As David Montgomery explains:

> Few words enjoyed more popularity in the nineteenth century than this honorific, with all its connotations of dignity, respectability, defiant egalitarianism, and patriarchal male supremacy. The worker who merited it refused to cower before the foreman's glares—in fact, often would not work at all when a boss was watching.[74]

By the time of the 1915 Declaration, however, much had changed. The small artisanal workshop had been replaced by the factory. Many of the traditional crafts had become totally deskilled; the craftsmen were replaced by

---

69. *Musings* at 1355 (cited in note 6). Interestingly, action taken not as a metaphorical but as an actual shareholder of an employing corporation has been held in several jurisdictions to be insulated from employer reprisal. Specter & Finkin at § 10.44 (cited in note 13).

70. *Specific Theory* at 81 (cited in note 51).

71. See generally Daniel T. Rodgers, *The Work Ethic in Industrial America* 1850-1920 (Univ of Chicago Press, 1974); Stephen J. Ross, *Workers on the Edge: Work, Leisure, and Politics in Industrializing Cincinnati*, 1788-1890 (Columbia Univ Press, 1985); Jonathan Prude, *The Coming of Industrial Order: Town and Factory Life in Rural Massachusetts*, 1810-1860 (Cambridge Univ Press, 1983); David Montgomery, *The Fall of the House of Labor* (Cambridge Univ Press, 1987).

72. See, for example, Rock, *Artisans* at 53 (cited in note 63); David Bensman, *The Practice of Solidarity: American Hat Finishers in the Nineteenth Century* 53 (Univ of Illinois Press, 1985) ("*The Practice of Solidarity*").

73. Bensman, *The Practice of Solidarity* at 53 (cited in note 72). The spirit was captured in Robert Rollins' song, "The Jovial Hatter":
   We unto no bosses humble
   When our trade begins to flag
   When they begin to growl and grumble
   We resent and give the bag [quit]
Id.

74. David Montgomery, *Workers' Control in America: Studies in the History of Work, Technology, and Labor Struggles* 13 (Cambridge Univ Press, 1979).

semiskilled machine operators, who were subject to industrial demands of punctuality and discipline, enforced by fines, forfeitures, harsh words, and summary dismissal. In some employments, the regulation of even private life could be far-reaching.[75]

At the same time, however, the academic profession was emerging from the era of the "Old-Time College"[76]—where professing was a brief interlude for the young bent upon a clerical career, or for the old in a case of downward mobility, and where institutions were more concerned with doctrinal fidelity and social acceptability than the advancement and testing of truth—to the "Age of the University,"[77] collectively to demand its freedom in 1915. While, in other words, artisans were becoming workers,[78] and, in the process, losing their traditional independence, college and university teachers were developing into a profession seeking to establish theirs. Thus Yudof is partially correct: the claims of freedom of speech on intramural policy and action codified in 1940 may appear remarkable when measured by the practices of much unskilled and semiskilled factory labor of the time. But the claim was modest measured by the practices of artisanal employment in the early to mid-nineteenth century.

Nor is the profession's demand unique even in terms of law. To be sure, speech in the public sector in connection with workplace disputes that do not implicate any matter of "political, social, or other concern" to the larger community is not constitutionally protected. But under the National Labor Relations Act ("NLRA"), enacted only a few years before the 1940 Statement was adopted, speech connected to workplace issues and disputes having no larger political content at all were insulated against employer reprisal as a

---

75. Many of these intrusions were part of company welfare plans, intended to "uplift" their working forces, and were often received less than enthusiastically by the intended beneficiaries. The "service secretary" of a Maine manufacturing firm recalled the occasion when "thirty angry girls descended on her office and declared that they were just as clean as she was and that they would not submit to physical examinations or take off their shoes and stockings for anyone." Stuart D. Brandes, *American Welfare Capitalism*, 1880-1940, 139 (Columbia Univ Press, 1970).

76. Richard Hofstadter & Walter P. Metzger, *The Development of Academic Freedom in the United States* 209 (Columbia Univ Press, 1955).

77. Id at 275.

78. Bruce Lurie, *Artisans into Workers: Labor in Nineteenth Century America* (Noonday Press, 1989). The change was graphic. An American woodcut of 1836, reproduced in Howard B. Rock, *The New York City Artisan 1789-1825* at 116 (State Univ of New York Press, 1989), depicts a turner's shop. In the background, a boy—presumably an apprentice, perhaps the master's son—turns a wheel that supplies power to the belting. In the left middle ground, a worker with an awl is cutting wood blanks; and in the right foreground, another is turning the wood on the hand-powered lathe. The men are virtually identical; both are wearing long-sleeved shirts, vests, aprons, and the high stiff hats of the period. It is impossible to tell which is master and which is journeyman; or, perhaps, both are journeymen, working quite independently. An oil painting of 1902 by Iwan Wladimiroff entitled "*Werkstückkontrolle*" (roughly, "quality control") shows a contemporary workplace. In the background a boy is holding a small piece of apparatus. In the foreground are two men. One, bearded, slightly gaunt, of middle age, dressed in work clothes, applies himself to a piece of equipment on a workbench attached to mechanically powered belting. Next to him stands another, observing every detail of the work, dressed in grey trousers, a frock coat, vest·with gold chain, a stiff collar and cravat; he is expressionless, hands in his pockets, smoking a cigar. At a glance one sees immediately who is the worker and who is the boss. The painting is reproduced in *Industrie Im Bild* 19 (Westfälisches Landesmuseum für Kunst und Kulturgeschichte, Münster, 1990).

matter of industrial liberty.[79] Analogous legislation has been adopted by a number of states providing parallel protection for public employees.[80]

The theory of industrial democracy underpinning the NLRA drew a close connection between the employee's liberty in the workplace, including freedom of expression on workplace issues, and the maintenance of a political democracy. Rather than compartmentalize the industrial employee into a worker, who must obey unquestioningly, and a citizen, who is free to question, the reformers of the period thought the employee's habituation in the one sphere might have consequences in the other.[81] Thus, one could well argue that the 1940 Statement assured for professors the protection of speech on internal issues, as a matter of the academic freedom of institutional citizens, that external law guaranteed to other work groups as a matter of industrial democracy.

C. Disciplinary Discourse and Professional Autonomy

Dean Yudof concedes the claim of academic freedom in the unique function of institutions of *higher* education to test, advance, and disseminate knowledge when that claim is grounded not in personal autonomy but in social utility.[82] But he has distinguished and resisted the claim when based upon a theory of professional autonomy:

> The problem is that the equation of academic freedom with a broad conception of professionalism releases academic freedom from its conceptual moorings. The engineer at NASA, the physician at a public hospital, and the accountant in the state budget office have equally plausible claims to such a distended version of academic freedom, though they are not working in the academy.[83]

On such a theory of vocational freedom, he argues, professors are no different from other employees, such as house painters. They too may lay claim to

---

79. 29 USC §§ 151 et seq (1988). See, for example, *NLRB v Coca-Cola Co. Foods Div.*, 670 F2d 84 (7th Cir 1982).

80. See *Developments in the Law—Public Employment*, 97 Harv L Rev 1611, 1678-80 (1984).

81. The view was shared by Louis Brandeis: "Can this contradiction—our grand political liberty and this industrial slavery—long coexist? Either political liberty will be extinguished or industrial liberty must be restored." Louis D. Brandeis, *The Curse of Bigness* 39 (Kinnifat Press, 1934). By the reformer and department store tycoon, A. Lincoln Filene:

> And it is still harder to see how we can much longer send Jones the worker in steel or shoes or sealing-wax to the exercise of his rights as an American, and if an industrial order in which he is habituated to an autocratic control that was old before his country was born.

A. Lincoln Filene, *A Merchant's Horizon* 47 (Houghton-Mifflin, 1924). By the industrialist, John D. Rockefeller: "Surely it is not consistent for us as Americans to demand democracy in government and practice autocracy in industry." John D. Rockefeller, Jr. *The Personal Relation in Industry* 86 (Boni & Liveright, 1923). By attorney Donald Richberg, who participated in drafting both the Railway Labor Act, 45 USC § 151 et seq (1926), and the Norris-LaGuardia Act, 29 USC §§ 101-115 (1932), "To put it bluntly, an economic autocracy and a democratic government cannot support each other long. There will be an eventual choice between the ideals of mastery and service." Donald R. Richberg, *The Rainbow* 47 (Doubleday, 1936). And by Senator Robert F. Wagner: "Let men become the servile pawns of their masters in the factories of the land and there will be destroyed the bone and sinew of resistance to political dictatorship." Quoted in R. W. Fleming, *The Significance of the Wagner Act*, in Milton Derber & Edwin Young, eds, *Labor and the New Deal* 121, 135 (Da Capo Press, 1972).

82. Mark G. Yudof, *Three Faces of Academic Freedom*, 32 Loyola L Rev 831, 834-35 (1987).

83. Yudof, 66 Tex L Rev at 1354-55 (cited in note 6).

professional autonomy based upon their mastery of the craft—so to require, for example, " 'brush work' over rollers"[84] as part of their freedom on the job.

The distinction is important to the extent that it is grounded in the first amendment, as Yudof's implications illustrate;[85] but that would assume the profession's claim of autonomy was anchored in—or seeking to be anchored in—the constitution, the source of the arguably indistinguishable claims of other publicly employed professionals, and of painters. However, such was not the case.

The 1940 Statement, a pact between representatives of institutions and the professoriate,[86] is normative. It speaks to how institutions of higher education, public and private, ought to behave. The 1940 Statement claimed no support in the first amendment, or in external law. Indeed, given the state of constitutional law in 1940, it would have been difficult to fashion any such constitutional theory at the time.[87] That kind of theorizing came later, following Supreme Court decisions that seemed to begin to join academic freedom with the first amendment,[88] a jointure that has, at best, been imperfectly realized.[89]

Moreover, Dean Yudof seems to assume that other vocations have failed to propound (and secure) analogous workplace freedom. But, as noted earlier, before artisanal manufacture was eroded by technology and the extensive division of labor, workers often did control a good deal of the job. As a leader of the painters' union in New York City lamented in 1926:

> The painter has drifted, under the pressure of new building methods, from the highly skilled craftsmanship of the past to a semi-skilled laborer. When painting was a real craft, the men served apprenticeship, attended schools of drawing and design, learned the nature of the pigments which are used in paints, studied the idea of the relation of color to paints and of color harmony. They had to know the nature of the different woods and the reaction of the various chemicals—for dyeing, finishing, etc.

---

84. Id at 1351.

85. This is made explicit in his earlier piece:

Is there a constitutional right to embrace an assertedly superior educational philosophy or are we left only with recent yuppie theories of free speech, the assertion that expression promotes self-realization? If so, why do not engineers at NASA have the constitutional right to engineer rockets in the most efficient, productive and self-realizing manner—even if their managers and the Congress disagree with them? To be sure, professors speak and write for a living and engineers conceptualize problems and design solutions (a form of communication) but why should that matter? So too, hot tubs, home ownership, and football games, sometimes, may also promote self-realization; but constitutional entitlements to those aspects of the good life have yet to be established.

Yudof, 32 Loyola L Rev at 840 (cited in note 82) (footnotes omitted).

86. See Walter P. Metzger, *The 1940 Statement of Principles on Academic Freedom and Tenure*, 53 L & Contemp Probs 3 (Summer 1990).

87. See Note, *Academic Freedom and the Law*, 46 Yale L J 670 (1937).

88. William P. Murphy, *Academic Freedom—An Emerging Constitutional Right*, 28 L & Contemp Probs 447, 453-57 (Summer 1963), Thomas I. Emerson & David Haber, *Academic Freedom of the Faculty Member is a Citizen*, 28 L & Contemp Probs 525 (Summer 1963).

89. See Walter P. Metzger, *Profession and Constitution: Two Definitions of Academic Freedom*, 66 Tex L Rev 1265 (1988); William W. Van Alstyne, *Academic Freedom and the First Amendment in the Supreme Court of the United States: An Unhurried Historical Review*, 53 L & Contemp Probs 79 (Summer 1990).

> It is entirely different today. The painting business is a highly commercialized industry. Buildings comprising hundreds of rooms must be completed in 5% of the time it took fifteen or twenty years ago. To meet that condition, the chemist has been brought into play. Employed by the paint manufacturer, he solves all the problems of the contractor concerning the application of paint. The painter's job is not to reason why; his is but the task of doing what the chemist and the contractor find it necessary to do.[90]

Even at the time the 1940 Statement was promulgated, organized house painters had unilaterally adopted work rules that, among other things, *did* limit the use of rollers in preference for brush work,[91] as well as regulate the width of the brush to be used (not more than four-and a half inches),[92] and, later, limit the number of rooms per week painters would paint.[93]

Were the academic profession's appeal grounded in the authority of the constitutional, statutory, or common law, the profession would have had to explain why workplace liberties ought be conceded to academics that the law did not accord to others. But in speaking to its own institutions, the profession labored under no such obligation.[94] Organized painters demanded and exercised important unilateral controls over the manner in which their jobs would be performed, even the amount of work they would do. Organized printers had the right to determine if there was cause to dismiss a fellow printer, to control their supervision (even to the point of

---

90. Quoted in William Haber, *Industrial Relations in the Building Industry* 42 (Harvard Univ Press, 1930).

91. The painters' locals have adopted somewhat similar policies toward the use of the roller as toward the spray gun, although the restrictions were much less severe in some localities.

. . .

The reasons for union opposition to the roller were more nebulous than in the case of the spray gun. There was much resentment expressed against it as a "housewife's toy," or "gadget," involving little skill, and hence unworthy of attention or use by a skilled journeyman. Many union spokesmen also claimed it did a job of inferior quality for which the union did not wish to accept responsibility.

William Haber & Harold M. Levinson, *Labor Relations and Productivity in the Building Trades* 125-26 (Univ of Michigan, 1956).

92. The reasons given for limiting the brush width on oil paint were two. First, oil paint is relatively heavy, so that it imposes a fatiguing "drag" on the arm and wrist when it is applied. Second, the painter must maintain a "wet edge," that is, he must apply the paint continuously so that the edge of the paint does not become too dry before the next stroke is applied; otherwise, a poor quality finish is the result. Contractors generally agreed, therefore, that a painter cannot steadily maintain a good quality and quantity of work over a period of time unless the width of the brush is not too great; the continued use of a too wide brush would impose a strain, cause excessive fatigue, and result in a poorer quality finish. In the case of water paint, a wider brush was both feasible and permitted.

Id at 164-65.

93. The latter was declared an unfair labor practice on the odd theory that the union had not first bargained before it, rather than the employer, unilaterally changed terms of employment. *New York Dist. Council No 9, Int'l Brotherhood of Painters & Allied Trades v NLRB*, 453 F2d 783 (2d Cir 1971).

94. Had the profession asserted that institutional observance of its standards was a legal obligation imposed from without, such, for example, that an institution's violation of academic freedom were to be a tort, Thomas A. Cowan, *Interference with Academic Freedom: The Pre-Natal History of a Tort*, 4 Wayne L Rev 205 (1958), it would have to explain why faculty speech on workplace disputes was protected while painters' speech was not. But the profession never has so asserted. It has argued, and with considerable success, that institutional acceptance of the 1940 Statement's conception of academic freedom becomes an express or implied obligation to the faculty. Note, *The Role of Academic Freedom in Defining the Faculty Employment Contract*, 31 Case W Res L Rev 608 (1981) (authored by Richard H. Miller).

excluding management from the pressroom when the presses were running), and to designate a substitute if they decided to take the day off.[95] Organized symphonic musicians have more recently secured final authority in disputed cases of seating and tenure.[96] None of them was obliged, in order to sustain their claims, to explain why professors could not routinely escape teaching as a matter of right merely by designating substitutes, could not collectively dictate the number of classes they would teach, and had nowhere achieved final authority in cases of dismissal. Nor would we expect professors to lay claim to these rights because painters, printers, and pianists had them. "Questions," William Gerhardie observed, "no less than answers, can be demonstrably wrong."[97] And the question—why academics should have a "higher order of liberty in the workplace" than others—is wrong, not only because other employees do have such liberties, but because the comparison is irrelevant.

Of the freedoms the 1940 Statement vouchsafed, the freedom of teaching, research, and publication remains the least controversial, perhaps for the

---

95. [International Typographical Union] laws which determine conditions of employment, maximum length of work week or work day, priority, closed shop, use of reproduced material, control over all composing room work, and other work conditions, are nonnegotiable in local contracts. All union employers must accept all provisions of the ITU law. Any dispute about an interpretation of such laws between an employer and his employees can be appealed only within the political structure of the union. For example, if an employer wishes to discharge a man with priority standing and the local union objects, the employer can appeal the decision of the local union to the international Executive Council of the ITU and to its annual convention if the issue in dispute involves a point of union law. The ITU's position regarding union law is that workers have a right to set the conditions under which they will work, and employers must accept these conditions or face sanctions. These rigid provisions have led to many disputes with newspaper publishers and other printing employers, but in general the ITU has been able to enforce union law.

The nature of the job control exercised by the ITU has meant that to a considerable extent the workers run the composing room. The employers' main rights concern the way in which work shall be done. The job, however, belongs to the man rather than to the foreman or the shop. So strong is the workers' proprietary right to their jobs that a printer with a regular situation designates the substitute who shall take his place if he decides to take a day off or is obliged to take one off because of the need to cancel overtime. This rule that a man may designate his temporary replacement has been in existence since the turn of the century.

Seymour Martin Lipset, Martin A. Trow & James S. Coleman, *Union Democracy: The Internal Politics of the International Typographical Union* 24 (The Free Press, 1956).

96. This concession to professional musicians was adverted to in arguing that college and university faculty members should not be held to be managerial employees under the National Labor Relations Act:

Master Agreement of the Milwaukee Symphony Orch. 1974-1977 § 10.5 (tenured musician may have Music Director's dismissal order reviewed by a player committee whose decision is final and binding), Master Agreement of the Buffalo Philharmonic 1976-1977 Art. IX(d) (Auditioning Committee's Control of Reseating and Non-Renewal), Master Agreement of the National Symphony 1973 § 6.05 (Player's Committee review of dismissal and demotion based upon musical deficiency).

AAUP's Brief as Amicus Curiae at 21-22 n12, *NLRB v Yeshiva University*, 582 F2d 686 (2d Cir 1978) (No 77-4182), aff'd 444 US 672 (1980).

97. William Gerhardie, *God's Fifth Column* 67 (Simon and Schuster, 1981). Compare Aileen S. Kraditor, *The Radical Persuasion, 1890-1917: Aspects of the Intellectual History and the Historiography of Three American Radical Organizations* (Louisiana State Univ Press, 1981) (arguing that Werner Sombart's famous question—Why Is There No Socialism in the United States?—is wrong).

simple reason that it is contradictory to demand that professors test, explore, and disseminate knowledge, and then to punish them for doing precisely what they were asked to do.[98] Interestingly, even in industrial employment, an employee discharged for doing what was expressly authorized has been afforded a remedy.[99] And the law of contract has long recognized that the relationship may cede large areas of liberty to an employee, even if the exercise of that liberty is in derogation of the implied obligations of servant to master, of obedience and respectfulness.[100]

IV

CONCLUSION

The critics of the profession's expansive notion of academic freedom proceed from the idea of a core disciplinary claim, deriving from the special function of institutions of higher education. They see the profession's extension of the claim beyond the core, to reach speech as citizen, in Van Alstyne's case, or speech as employee, in Yudof's, as unjustifiable; the illegitimacy is emphasized by comparison with the liberties of nonacademics, who have potentially greater liberty of political utterance in Van Alstyne's analysis, and lesser liberty of intramural utterance in Yudof's. Even a writer as sympathetic to the profession as David Rabban would shelter "aprofessional" speech only "to give 'breathing room' to the professional speech that is the special subject of academic freedom."[101] "[L]ines," says Yudof, "must be drawn."[102]

The process of drawing lines, however, is not without difficulty. If a professor draws upon the discipline in taking a political position, by what standard is the utterance to be measured? Must a professor of chemistry addressing a political audience in the matter of acid rain observe a more exacting standard of accuracy than a professor of French? When is a speech by a philosopher ever aprofessional? And to make some, but not all, speech on matters of intramural concern an exercise of academic freedom because of its connectedness to core faculty concerns such as curriculum and hiring, as

---

98. Van Alstyne, *Specific Theory* at 77 (cited in note 51).

99. *Crowell v Transamerica Delaval, Inc.*, 206 NJ Super 298, 502 A2d 573 (1984); *Wandry v Bull's Eye Credit Union*, 129 Wis 2d 37, 384 NW2d 325 (1986) (both based on public policy); *Hammond v Heritage Commun., Inc.*, 756 SW2d 152 (Ky App 1988) (based on contract); *Paul v Lankenau Hosp.*, 375 Pa 1, 543 A2d 1148 (1988) (based on promissory estoppel).

100. An actress, for example, was held privileged to offer criticism for the betterment of the performance:

> Was respondent compelled by the contract to go through her scenes as a mere puppet responding to the director's pull of the strings, regardless of whether or not he pulled the right or the wrong string, or was she called upon by the language and spirit of the contract to give an artistic interpretation of her scenes, using her intelligence, experience, artistry, and personality to the ultimate end of securing a production of dramatic merit? We believe that the latter is the correct interpretation.

Goudal v Cecil B. DeMille Pictures Corp., 118 Cal App 407, 410, 5 P2d 432, 433 (1931).

101. David M. Rabban, *A Functional Analysis of "Individual" and "Institutional" Academic Freedom Under the First Amendment*, 53 L & Contemp Probs 227 (Summer 1990).

102. Yudof, 66 Tex L Rev at 1355 (cited in note 6).

Dean Yudof concedes,[103] is to place the professor in the position of having to guess where his or her utterance might lie on a spectrum from the purely professional to the purely aprofessional. A complaint to an accrediting association? A protest of unfair treatment of a colleague? An expression of lack of confidence in the administration?

More important, the architects of the American idea of academic freedom declined the invitation to engage in line drawing, not only as a potential trap for the unwary, but as an activity at odds with the theory of the profession they propounded. They, like the Progressive reformers' connection of political with industrial democracy, saw the professor as an uncompartmentalized whole, in consequence of which no hierarchical significance was attached to the category of utterance, no core identified from which some, but not other, emanations could be derived.

One does find in their theory a concern for the profession's dignity and self-respect.[104] But these did not derive from an anachronistic "yuppie theory of free speech";[105] the claim was not premised upon any notion of "self-realization."[106] It was an assertion of the total condition of freedom under which the profession best performed and, importantly, of the kinds of persons it is most desirable to attract.[107] If there is an historical antecedent, it may be the pre-industrial artisanal ideal. The mechanic of the new Republic asserted simultaneously an independence of craftsmanship that brooked no supervision,[108] a vigorous defense of workplace rights—of artisanal dignity

---

103. Id.

104. Matthew W. Finkin, *Intramural Speech, Academic Freedom, and the First Amendment*, 66 Tex L Rev 1323, 1342-43 (1988).

105. Yudof, 32 Loyola L Rev at 840 (cited in note 82).

106. Yudof, 66 Tex L Rev at 1356 (cited in note 6).

107. As the 1915 Declaration put it:

The . . . conception of a university as an ordinary business venture, and of academic teaching as a purely private employment, manifests also a radical failure to apprehend the nature of the social function discharged by the professional scholar. . . . [I]t is to the public interest that the professorial office should be one both of dignity and of independence.

If education is the corner stone of the structure of society and if progress in scientific knowledge is essential to civilization, few things can be more important than to enhance the dignity of the scholar's profession, with a view to attracting into its ranks men of the highest ability, of sound learning, and of strong and independent character.

Richard Hofstadler & Wilson Smith, eds, 2 *American Higher Education: A Documentary History* 860, 864 (Univ of Chicago Press, 1961); see Appendix A, 53 L & Contemp Probs 393, 396 (Summer 1990). As Arthur O. Lovejoy was later to opine concerning a college president's demand that faculty members who disagreed with him should leave:

The position and utterances of President Holt . . . were, in the Committee's opinion, a manifest infringement of academic freedom, though the issue over which it took place was an educational rather than a theological, political, or economic one. . . . No teacher having a high degree of professional self-respect is, the Committee believes, likely to accept service in an institution in which freedom of individual opinion, and the exercise of professional responsibility, on educational matters is denied in the degree in which it was denied by President Holt on this occasion.

Lovejoy, 19 AAUP Bull at 421-22 (cited in note 3).

108. Marc Linder has explained the law of respondeat superior at the time of the 1915 Declaration: "Where the worker possessed a skill the employer did not possess and could not integrate into its business, courts held the workers to be pursuing an independent . . . calling." Marc Linder, *Towards Universal Worker Coverage Under the National Labor Relations Act: Making Room for*

and self-respect—and a robust liberty of political association and expression. It was this very combination of attributes that was taken by the mechanical class to distinguish it, as "free labor," from apprenticeship, domestic service, indentured servitude, and slavery. Rather than claiming a novel "higher order of workplace liberty" for professors, the 1940 Statement resonates against an older ideal, one to which the nation may be returning in some aspects of the unfolding law of employment.

Uncontrolled Employees, Dependent Contractors, and Employee-Like Persons, 66 U Det L Rev 555, 570 (1989). See also Marc Linder, *The Employment Relationship in Anglo-American Law: A Historical Perspective* 142-143 (Greenwood Press, 1989). In other words, despite the obvious fact of an employment relationship, for the purpose of vicarious liability the employee was not legally to be thought of in those terms because of the employer's inability to control the employee's work. Judge Cardozo applied that body of law to case of alleged professorial negligence in the conduct of a laboratory experiment:

> The governing body of a university makes no attempt to control its professors and instructors as if they were its servants. By practice and tradition, the members of the faculty are masters, and not servants, in the conduct of the classroom. They have the independence appropriate to a company of scholars.

Hamburger v Cornell University, 240 NY 328, 336, 148 NE 539, 541 (1925).

ACADEMIC FREEDOM: A BIBLIOGRAPHY

JANET SINDER*

Academic freedom is a subject with many facets: academic freedom of public and private school teachers, of university professors, of universities themselves, and of students. In this bibliography, I have concentrated on articles about academic freedom at a post-secondary level. There are some articles concerning the academic freedom of universities, but most deal with professors. Because this issue celebrates the fiftieth anniversary of the 1940 Statement of Principles on Academic Freedom and Tenure, I have examined publications only from 1940 to the present. The books included are those that focus mainly on academic freedom, rather than those with only a small section on that topic. The articles deal with the legal aspects of academic freedom, and almost all are from legal periodicals.[1] All materials are in English and concern academic freedom issues in the United States.

Within the criteria stated above, I have tried to be comprehensive in my search for materials. I have searched both through the legal journal indexes and through the footnotes of the articles themselves. Omitted entirely are articles about specific challenges to academic freedom reported on in the journal of the American Association of University Professors, at different times called *Academe* and the *AAUP Bulletin*. The association has devoted much space to particular academic freedom cases, and anyone interested in these reports need only look at individual issues of the journal.

American Association of University Professors. *Policy Documents & Reports*. Washington, D.C.: The Association, 1990.

Annarelli, James John. *Academic Freedom and Catholic Higher Education*. New York: Greenwood Press, 1987.

Baade, Hans W. and Robinson O. Everett, eds. *Academic Freedom: The Scholar's Place in Modern Society*. Dobbs Ferry, N.Y.: Oceana Pubs., 1964. Reprint of *Law and Contemporary Problems* 28 (1963): 429-671.

Bard, Robert L. "Protecting the Academic Community Against Internal Assault." *Connecticut Law Review* 3 (1971): 433-65.

Brest, Paul. "Protecting Academic Freedom Through the First Amendment: Raising the Unanswered Questions." *Texas Law Review* 66 (1988): 1359-62.

---

* Senior Reference Librarian and Senior Instructor in Legal Research, Duke University School of Law.

1. Individual articles from this issue of *Law and Contemporary Problems* are listed below by author's name.

Brown, Ralph S. and Jordan E. Kurland. "Academic Tenure and Academic Freedom." *Law and Contemporary Problems* 53 (Summer 1990): 325-55.

Brown, Ronald C. "Tenure Rights in Contractual and Constitutional Context." *Journal of Law and Education* 6 (1977): 279-318.

Bunting, David Edison. *Liberty and Learning: The Activities of the American Civil Liberties Union in Behalf of Freedom of Education*. Washington, D.C.: American Council on Public Affairs, 1942.

Burke, William T. III and Frank J. Cavaliere. "*E.E.O.C. v. Franklin and Marshall College*: Confidential Promotion and Tenure Materials Subject to Civil Rights Investigation and Enforcement." *Saint Louis University Public Law Review* 7 (1988): 423-31.

Byrne, J. Peter. "Academic Freedom: A 'Special Concern of the First Amendment.'" *Yale Law Journal* 99 (1989): 251-340.

Byse, Clark. "Academic Freedom, Tenure, and the Law: A Comment on *Worzella v. Board of Regents*." *Harvard Law Review* 73 (1959): 304-22.

――――. "Teachers and the Fifth Amendment." *University of Pennsylvania Law Review* 102 (1954): 871-83.

Carr, Robert K. "Academic Freedom, the American Association of University Professors, and the United States Supreme Court." *AAUP Bulletin* 45 (1959): 5-24.

Carrington, Paul D. "Freedom and Community in the Academy." *Texas Law Review* 66 (1988): 1577-89.

Cassou, April Kestell and Robert F. Curran, S.J. "Secular Orthodoxy and Sacred Freedoms: Accreditation of Church-Related Law Schools." *Journal of College and University Law* 11 (1984): 293-344.

Chafee, Zechariah, Jr. *The Blessings of Liberty*. Philadelphia and New York: J.B. Lippincott, 1956.

Comment. "Academic Freedom and the Law." *Yale Law Journal* 46 (1937): 670-86.

Comment. "Academic Freedom—Its Constitutional Content." *University of Colorado Law Review* 40 (1968): 600-616 (authored by Richard P. Tisdel).

Comment. "An Academic Freedom Privilege in the Peer Review Context: *In re Dinnan* and *Gray v. Board of Higher Education*." *Rutgers Law Review* 36 (1983): 286-345 (authored by Jerry P. Sattin).

Comment. "Colleges and Universities—Constitutional Law: Professor's Assignment of Grade to Students is Symbolic Communication Protected by the First Amendment." *North Dakota Law Review* 66 (1990): 297-308 (authored by Rosanna Malouf Peterson).

Comment. "Drawing the Line on Academic Freedom: Rejecting an Academic Peer-Review Privilege for Tenure Committee Deliberations."

Washington University Law Quarterly 64 (1986): 1271-78 (authored by Jason A. Parson).

Comment. "*Kahn v. Superior Court of the County of Santa Clara*: The Right to Privacy and the Academic Freedom Privilege with Respect to Confidential Peer Review Materials." *Journal of College and University Law* 15 (1988): 73-85 (authored by Maureen P. Cunningham, Todd A. Leeson and James R. Stadler).

Comment. "*Parate v. Isibor*: Resolving the Conflict Between the Academic Freedom of the University and the Academic Freedom of University Professors." *Journal of College and University Law* 16 (1990): 713-30 (authored by David M. Dumas, Caroline McIntyre and Katherine L. Zelenock).

Comment. "Personality Control and Academic Freedom—*Rampey v. Allen*." *Utah Law Review* (1975): 234-45 (authored by Katherine W. Adams).

Comment. "Testing the Limits of Academic Freedom." *University of Pennsylvania Law Review* 130 (1982): 712-43.

Committee of the University of Miami Chapter of the AAUP. "Academic Freedom: Tenure is Not Enough." *AAUP Bulletin* 53 (1967): 202-9.

Communism and Academic Freedom: The Record of the Tenure Cases at the University of Washington. Seattle: University of Washington Press, 1949.

Cowan, Thomas A. "Interference with Academic Freedom: The Pre-Natal History of a Tort." *Wayne Law Review* 4 (1958): 205-27.

Curran, Charles E. "Academic Freedom and Catholic Universities." *Texas Law Review* 66 (1988): 1441-54.

———. "Academic Freedom: The Catholic University and Catholic Theology." *Academe: Bulletin of the American Association of University Professors* 66 (1980): 126-35.

Cushman, Robert E. *Academic Freedom and Responsibility*. Ithaca, N.Y.: Cornell University Press, 1952.

Davis, Frederick. "Enforcing Academic Tenure: Reflections and Suggestions." *Wisconsin Law Review* (1961): 200-220.

Davis, Michael. "Academic Freedom, Impartiality, and Faculty Governance." *Law and Philosophy* 5 (1986): 263-76.

Days, Drew S. III, " 'Enemies or Allies?': Widening the Scope of Conflict." *Texas Law Review* 66 (1988): 1621-28.

"Developments in the Law—Academic Freedom." *Harvard Law Review* 81 (1968): 1045-1159.

Dimensions of Academic Freedom. Urbana, Ill.: University of Illinois Press, 1969.

Dodds, Harold W. "Academic Freedom and the Academic President." *Law and Contemporary Problems* 28 (1963): 602-6.

384

Eagle, Joan M. "First Amendment Protection for Teachers Who Criticize Academic Policy: Biting the Hand That Feeds You." *Chicago-Kent Law Review* 60 (1984): 229-59.

Earle, Valerie, ed. *On Academic Freedom*. Washington, D.C.: American Enterprise Institute, 1971.

Eisenberg, Rebecca S. "Academic Freedom and Academic Values in Sponsored Research." *Texas Law Review* 66 (1988): 1363-1404.

———. "Defining the Terms of Academic Freedom: A Reply to Professor Rabban." *Texas Law Review* 66 (1988): 1431-39.

Emerson, Thomas I. and David Haber. "Academic Freedom of the Faculty Member as Citizen." *Law and Contemporary Problems* 28 (1963): 525-72.

Fellman, David. "Academic Freedom in American Law." *Wisconsin Law Review* (1961): 3-46.

Finkelhor, Marion K. & Craig T. Stockdale. "The Professor and the Fifth Amendment." *University of Pittsburgh Law Review* 16 (1955): 344-59.

Finkin, Matthew W. " 'A Higher Order of Liberty in the Workplace': Academic Freedom and Tenure in the Vortex of Employment Practices and Law." *Law and Contemporary Problems* 53 (Summer 1990): 357-79.

———. "Intramural Speech, Academic Freedom and the First Amendment." *Texas Law Review* 66 (1988): 1323-49.

———. "On 'Institutional' Academic Freedom." *Texas Law Review* 61 (1983): 817-57.

———. "Regulation By Agreement: The Case of Private Higher Education." *Iowa Law Review* 65 (1980): 1119-1200.

———. "Toward a Law of Academic Status." *Buffalo Law Review* 22 (1973): 575-602.

Finman, Ted. "Critical Legal Studies, Professionalism, and Academic Freedom: Exploring the Tributaries of Carrington's River." *Journal of Legal Education* 35 (1985): 180-207.

Fract, Arthur N. "Non-Tenure Teachers and the Constitution." *University of Kansas Law Review* 18 (1969): 27-54.

Fuchs, Ralph F. "Academic Freedom—Its Basic Philosophy, Function and History." *Law and Contemporary Problems* 28 (1963): 431-46. Reprinted in *Academic Freedom and Tenure*, edited by Louis Joughin, 242-63. Madison: University of Wisconsin Press, 1969.

Gardner, David P. *The California Oath Controversy*. Berkeley and Los Angeles: University of California Press, 1967.

Gee, Thomas Gibbs. " 'Enemies or Allies?': In Defense of Judges." *Texas Law Review* 66 (1988): 1617-19.

Getman, Julius G. and Jacqueline W. Mintz. "Foreword: Academic Freedom in a Changing Society." *Texas Law Review* 66 (1988): 1247-64.

Gray, Mary. "Academic Freedom and Nondiscrimination: Enemies or Allies?" *Texas Law Review* 66 (1988): 1591-1615.

Gregory, John DeWitt. "Secrecy in University and College Tenure Deliberations: Placing Appropriate Limits on Academic Freedom." *U.C. Davis Law Review* 16 (1983): 1023-46.

Gutmann, Amy. *Democratic Education*. Princeton, N.J.: Princeton University Press, 1987.

van den Haag, Ernest. "Academic Freedom in the United States." *Law and Contemporary Problems* 28 (1963): 515-24.

Haddon, Phoebe A. "Academic Freedom and Governance: A Call for Increased Dialogue and Diversity." *Texas Law Review* 66 (1988): 1561-75.

Hamilton, Walton H. "Trial by Ordeal, New Style." *Yale Law Journal* 50 (1941): 778-86.

Haskell, Thomas and Sanford Levinson. "Academic Freedom and Expert Witnessing: Historians and the *Sears* Case." *Texas Law Review* 66 (1988): 1629-59.

Hendrick, Rhoda. "Report on Academic Freedom: Address." *Lawyers Guild Review* 13 (Winter 1953): 30-33.

Hodges, Debra K. "Postsecondary Faculty Members' Rights of Free Speech." *Journal of College and University Law* 9 (1982-83): 85-99.

Hofstadter, Richard and Walter P. Metzger. *The Development of Academic Freedom in the United States*. New York: Columbia University Press, 1955.

Hook, Sidney. *Academic Freedom and Academic Anarchy*. New York: Cowles Book Co., 1970.

_____. *Heresy Yes, Conspiracy No*. New York: John Day Co., 1953.

Hoornstra, Charles D. and Michael A. Liethen. "Academic Freedom and Civil Discovery." *Journal of College and University Law* 10 (1983): 113-28.

Hunt, John F. and Terrence R. Connelly. *The Responsibility of Dissent: The Church and Academic Freedom*. New York: Sheed and Ward, 1969.

Hunter, Howard O. "Federal Antibias Legislation and Academic Freedom: Some Problems with Enforcement Procedures." *Emory Law Journal* 27 (1978): 609-71.

Hutchins, Robert Maynard. "What Price Freedom?" *AAUP Bulletin* 35 (1949): 211-15.

Irons, Peter H. " 'Fighting Fair': Zechariah Chafee, Jr., the Department of Justice, and the 'Trial at the Harvard Club'." *Harvard Law Review* 94 (1981): 1205-36.

Jones, Howard Mumford. "The American Concept of Academic Freedom." *AAUP Bulletin* 46 (1960): 66-72. Reprinted in *Academic Freedom and Tenure*, edited by Louis Joughin, 224-41. Madison: University of Wisconsin Press, 1969.

Joughin, Louis. "Academic Due Process." *Law and Contemporary Problems* 28 (1963): 573-601. Reprinted in *Academic Freedom and Tenure*, edited by Louis Joughin, 264-305. Madison: University of Wisconsin Press, 1969.

Joughin, Louis, ed. *Academic Freedom and Tenure: A Handbook of the American Association of University Professors*. Madison, Wis.: University of Wisconsin Press, 1969.

Kadish, Sanford H. "Church-Related Law Schools: Academic Values and Deference to Religion." *Journal of Legal Education* 32 (1982): 161-71.

Kaplan, Craig and Ellen Schrecker, eds. *Regulating the Intellectuals: Perspectives on Academic Freedom in the 1980s*. New York: Praeger, 1983.

Kaplan, David A. and Brian M. Cogan. "The Case Against Recognition of a General Academic Privilege." *University of Detroit Journal of Urban Law* 60 (1983): 205-39.

Katz, Katheryn. "The First Amendment's Protection of Expressive Activity in the University Classroom: A Constitutional Myth." *U.C. Davis Law Review* 16 (1983): 857-932.

Kennedy, Walter B. "The Bertrand Russell Case Again: Portrait of a Realist, New Style." *Fordham Law Review* 10 (1941): 196-205.

Kessler-Harris, Alice. "Academic Freedom and Expert Witnessing: A Response to Haskell and Levinson." *Texas Law Review* 66 (1988): 429-40.

Kidd, Charles V. "The Implications of Research Funds for Academic Freedom." *Law and Contemporary Problems* 28 (1963): 613-24.

Kirk, Russell. *Academic Freedom: An Essay in Definition*. Westport, Conn.: Greenwood Press, 1955.

——. "Massive Subsidies and Academic Freedom." *Law and Contemporary Problems* 28 (1963): 607-12.

——. "Shelton College and State Licensing of Religious Schools: An Educator's View of the Interface Between the Establishment and Free Exercise Clauses." *Law and Contemporary Problems* 44 (Spring 1981): 169-84.

Kirkland, Edward C. "Academic Freedom and the Community." In *Freedom and the University: The Responsibility of the University for the Maintenance of Freedom in the American Way of Life*, edited by Edgar N. Johnson, *et al.*, 115-29. Ithaca, N.Y.: Cornell University Press, 1950.

Kliever, Lonnie D. "Academic Freedom and Church-Affiliated Universities." *Texas Law Review* 66 (1988): 1477-80.

————. "Religion and Academic Freedom: Issues of Faith and Reason." *Academe: Bulletin of the Amercian Association of University Professors* 74 (Jan.-Feb. 1988): 8-11.

Kutner, Luis. "The Freedom of Academic Freedom: A Legal Dilemma." *Chicago-Kent Law Review* 48 (1971): 168-89.

Lacovara, Philip A. "How Far Can the Federal Camel Slip Under the Academic Tent?" *Journal of College and University Law* 4 (1977): 223-40.

Ladenson, Robert F. "Is Academic Freedom Necessary?" *Law and Philosophy* 5 (1986): 59-87.

Laycock, Douglas and Susan E. Waelbroeck, "Academic Freedom and the Free Exercise of Religion." *Texas Law Review* 66 (1988): 1455-75.

Leleiko, Steven H. "The Opportunity to Be Different and Equal—An Analysis of the Interrelationship Between Tenure, Academic Freedom and the Teaching of Professional Responsibility in Orthodox and Clinical Legal Education." *Notre Dame Lawyer* 55 (1980): 485-512.

Machlup, Fritz. "In Defense of Academic Tenure." *AAUP Bulletin* 50 (1964): 112-24. Reprinted in *Academic Freedom and Tenure*, edited by Louis Joughin, 306-38. Madison: University of Wisconsin Press, 1969.

————. "On Some Misconceptions Concerning Academic Freedom." *AAUP Bulletin* 41 (1955): 753-84. Reprinted in *Academic Freedom and Tenure*, edited by Louis Joughin, 177-209. Madison: University of Wisconsin Press, 1969.

MacIver, Robert M. *Academic Freedom in Our Time*. New York: Columbia University Press, 1955.

Malin, Martin H. and Robert Ladenson. "University Faculty Member's Right to Dissent: Toward a Unified Theory of Contractual and Constitutional Protection." *U.C. Davis Law Review* 16 (1983): 933-73.

Manier, Edward and John W. Houck, eds. *Academic Freedom and the Catholic University*. Notre Dame, Ind.: Fides Publishers, 1967.

Mark, Max. "The Meanings of Academic Freedom." *AAUP Bulletin* 43 (1957): 498-506.

Martin, Peter W., *et al.* " 'Of Law and the River,' and of Nihilism and Academic Freedom." *Journal of Legal Education* 35 (1985): 1-26.

Matheson, Alan A. "Judicial Enforcement of Academic Tenure: An Examination." *Washington Law Review* 50 (1975): 597-622.

May, William W. "Academic Freedom in Church-Related Institutions." *Academe: Bulletin of the American Association of University Professors* 74 (July-Aug. 1988): 23-28.

McConnell, Michael W. "Academic Freedom in Religious Colleges and Universities." *Law and Contemporary Problems* 53 (Summer 1990): 303-24.

388

Mertz, Elizabeth. "The Burden of Proof and Academic Freedom: Protection for Institution or Individual?" *Northwestern University Law Review* 82 (1988): 492-539.

Metzger, Walter P. "The 1940 Statement of Principles on Academic Freedom and Tenure." *Law and Contemporary Problems* 53 (Summer 1990): 3-77.

_____. "Profession and Constitution: Two Definitions of Academic Freedom in America." *Texas Law Review* 66 (1988): 1265-1322.

Metzger, Walter P., ed. *The American Concept of Academic Freedom in Formation: A Collection of Essays and Reports*. New York: Arno Press, 1977.

_____. *The Constitutional Status of Academic Freedom*. New York: Arno Press, 1977.

Miller, Richard H. "The Role of Academic Freedom in Defining the Faculty Employment Contract." *Case Western Reserve Law Review* 31 (1981): 608-55.

Mobilia, Marcia Anne. "The Academic Freedom Privilege: A Sword or a Shield?" *Vermont Law Review* 9 (1984): 43-67.

Monypenny, Phillip. "Toward a Standard for Student Academic Freedom." *Law and Contemporary Problems* 28 (1963): 625-35.

Morris, Arval A. "Academic Freedom and Loyalty Oaths." *Law and Contemporary Problems* 28 (1963): 487-514.

Moskowitz, Ivor R. and Richard E. Casagrande. "Teachers and the First Amendment: Academic Freedom and Exhaustion of Administrative Remedies under 42 U.S.C. Section 1983." *Albany Law Review* 39 (1975): 661-705.

Murphy, William P. "Academic Freedom—An Emerging Constitutional Right." *Law and Contemporary Problems* 28 (1963): 447-86.

Note. "Academic Freedom and Federal Regulation of University Hiring." *Harvard Law Review* 92 (1979): 879-97.

Note. "Academic Freedom and the University Title VII Suit after *University of Pennsylvania v. EEOC* and *Brown v. Trustees of Boston University*." *Vanderbilt Law Review* 43 (1990): 1571-1606 (authored by Clisby Louise Hall Barrow).

Note. "Academic Freedom for Public Universities after *Widmar v. Vincent*." *University of Bridgeport Law Review* 4 (1983): 335-58 (authored by Melanie B. Abbott).

Note. "Academic Freedom: How Does Florida Stand?" *University of Florida Law Review* 17 (1965): 564-85 (authored by Jere E. Lober).

Note. "Academic Freedom Privilege: An Excessive Solution to the Problem of Protecting Confidentiality." *University of Cincinnati Law Review* 51 (1982): 326-52 (authored by Carol A. Remler).

Note. "Academic Freedom vs. Title VII: Will Equal Opportunity Be Denied on Campus?" *Ohio State Law Journal* 42 (1981): 989-1004 (authored by John J. Byrnes).

Note. "Balancing Academic Freedom and Civil Rights: Toward an Appropriate Privilege for the Votes of Academic Peer Review Committees." *Iowa Law Review* 68 (1983): 585-600 (authored by Julia A. Wentz).

Note. "The Bertrand Russell Case: The History of a Litigation." *Harvard Law Review* 53 (1940): 1192-97.

Note. "The Bertrand Russell Litigation." *University of Chicago Law Review* 8 (1941): 316-25.

Note. "The Challenge to Antidiscrimination Enforcement on Campus: Consideration of an Academic Freedom Privilege." *St. John's Law Review* 57 (1983): 546-71 (authored by Joanne F. Catanese).

Note. "Civil Rights—Academic Freedom, Secrecy and Subjectivity as Obstacles to Proving a Title VII Sex Discrimination Suit in Academia." *North Carolina Law Review* 60 (1982): 438-50 (authored by R. Joyce Burriss Garrett).

Note. "Constitutional Law—Civil Rights—Refusal to Renew Employment Contract of Professor in Absence of Tenure or Employment Contract." *Wayne Law Review* 16 (1969): 252-59 (authored by Gilbert D. Butson).

Note. "Constitutional Law—Restriction of the First Amendment in an Academic Environment." *Kansas Law Review* 22 (1974): 597-605 (authored by Mary L. Barrier).

Note. "The Double-Edged Sword of Academic Freedom: Cutting the Scales of Justice in Title VII Litigation." *Washington University Law Quarterly* 65 (1987): 445-70 (authored by William A. Kohlburn).

Note. "Economically Necessitated Faculty Dismissals as a Limitation on Academic Freedom." *Denver Law Journal* 52 (1975): 911-37 (authored by Charles P. Leder).

Note. "Evidence—Privileges—A Privilege Based on Academic Freedom Does Not Insulate a University from Disclosing Confidential Employment Information." *Mississippi Law Journal* 52 (1982): 493-508 (authored by Sally A. Atkinson).

Note. "*Papish v. University of Missouri*: First Amendment Due Process and the University." *UMKC Law Review* 42 (1974): 390-95 (authored by Eric Tanner).

Note. "Preventing Unnecessary Intrusions on University Autonomy: A Proposed Academic Freedom Privilege." *California Law Review* 69 (1981): 1538-68 (authored by Charles F. Stevens).

Note. "The Role of Academic Freedom in Defining the Faculty Employment Contract." *Case Western Reserve Law Review* 31 (1981): 608-55 (authored by Richard H. Miller).

Note. "The Second Circuit Strikes a Balance Between Academic Freedom and Individual Employment Rights." *Brooklyn Law Review* 50 (1984): 627-55 (authored by Betsey Nathan).

Note. "Title VII and Academic Freedom: The Authority of the EEOC to Investigate College Faculty Tenure Decisions." *Boston College Law Review* 28 (1987): 559-94 (authored by Ieuan G. Mahony).

Note. "*University of Pennsylvania v. EEOC* and *Dixon v. Rutgers*: Two Supreme Courts Speak on the Academic Freedom Privilege." *Rutgers Law Review* 42 (1990): 1089-1131 (authored by David McMillin).

O'Neil, Robert M. "The AAUP at 75: Three Academic Freedom Challenges." *Academe: Bulletin of the American Association of University Professors* 77 (Jan.-Feb. 1991): 32-33.

——. "Academic Freedom and the Constitution." *Journal of College and University Law* 11 (1984): 275-92.

——. "Artistic Freedom and Academic Freedom." *Law and Contemporary Problems* 53 (Summer 1990): 177-93.

——. "Scientific Research and the First Amendment: An Academic Privilege." *U.C. Davis Law Review* 16 (1983): 837-55.

Pettigrew, Harry W. " 'Constitutional Tenure': Toward a Realization of Academic Freedom." *Case Western Reserve Law Review* 22 (1971): 475-514.

Pincoffs, Edmund L., ed. *The Concept of Academic Freedom*. Austin: University of Texas Press, 1975.

Poulos, John W. "Foreword (The Academy in the Courts: A Symposium on Academic Freedom)." *U.C. Davis Law Review* 16 (1983): 831-35.

——. "Does Academic Freedom Limit Faculty Autonomy?" *Texas Law Review* 66 (1988): 1405-30.

Rabban, David M. "A Functional Analysis of 'Individual' and 'Institutional' Academic Freedom Under the First Amendment." *Law and Contemporary Problems* 53 (Summer 1990): 227-301.

Ramirez, M. Christina, "The Balance of Interests Between National Security Controls and First Amendment Interest in Academic Freedom." *Journal of College and University Law* 13 (1986): 179-227.

"Report of the Committee on Freedom of Expression at Yale." *Human Rights* 4 (1975): 357-90.

Recent Development. "Church Licensed Professors: The Curran Controversy." *Journal of College and University Law* 13 (1987): 375-95 (authored by Judith L. Andrews, Phuong-Lien Dang and Timothy M. McLean).

Recent Development. "A Qualified Academic Freedom Privilege in Employment Litigation: Protecting Higher Education or Shielding Discrimination?" *Vanderbilt Law Review* 40 (1987): 1397-1432 (authored by Jayna Jacobson Partain).

Roche, George. "The Still-Open Issue." *Detroit College of Law Review* 4 (1988): 929-35.

Rose, Arnold M. *Libel and Academic Freedom*. Minneapolis: University of Minnesota Press, 1968.

Sanders, Jane. *Cold War on the Campus: Academic Freedom at the University of Washington, 1946-64*. Seattle: University of Washington Press, 1979.

Scanlan, John A. "Aliens in the Marketplace of Ideas: The Government, the Academy and the McCarran-Walter Act." *Texas Law Review* 66 (1988): 1481-1546.

Schneider, Elizabeth M. "Political Interference in Law School Clinical Programs: Reflections on Outside Interference and Academic Freedom." *Journal of College and University Law* 11 (1984): 179-213.

Schrecker, Ellen W. *No Ivory Tower: McCarthyism and the Universities*. New York; Oxford: Oxford University Press, 1986.

Sherman, Edward F. "The Immigration Laws and the 'Right to Hear' Protected by Academic Freedom." *Texas Law Review* 66 (1988): 1547-59.

Shulman, Carol H. "Employment of Nontenured Faculty: Some Implications of *Roth* and *Sindermann*." *Denver Law Journal* 51 (1974): 215-33.

Smith, T.V. "Academic Freedom Revisited." In *Vision and Action: Essays in Honor of Horace M. Kallen on His 70th Birthday*, edited by Sidney Ratner, 3-26. New Brunswick, N.J.: Rutgers University Press, 1953.

Smolla, Rodney A. "Academic Freedom, Hate Speech, and the Idea of a University." *Law and Contemporary Problems* 53 (Summer 1990): 195-225.

Stewart, George R. *The Year of the Oath: The Fight for Academic Freedom at the University of California*. Garden City, N.Y.: Doubleday, 1950. Reprint. New York: Da Capo Press, 1971.

Sutherland, Arthur E. "The American Teacher's Freedom and Responsibility." *Journal of the Society of Public Teachers of Law* 3 (1956): 220-32.

Tepker, Jr., Harry F. "Title VII, Equal Employment Opportunity, and Academic Autonomy: Toward a Principled Deference." *U.C. Davis Law Review* 16 (1983): 1047-88.

Thomson, Judith Jarvis. "Ideology and Faculty Selection." *Law and Contemporary Problems* 53 (Summer 1990): 155-76.

392

Van Alstyne, William W. "Academic Freedom and the First Amendment in the Supreme Court of the United States: An Unhurried Historical Review." *Law and Contemporary Problems* 53 (Summer 1990):79-154.

———. "The Constitutional Rights of Teachers and Professors." *Duke Law Journal* (1970): 841-79.

———. "Political Speakers at State Universities: Some Constitutional Considerations." *University of Pennsylvania Law Review* 11 (1963): 328-42.

———. "The Specific Theory of Academic Freedom and the General Issue of Civil Liberties." *Annals of the American Academy of Political and Social Science* 404 (1972): 140-56. Reprinted in *The Concept of Academic Freedom*, edited by Edmund L. Pincoffs, 59-85. Austin: University of Texas Press, 1975.

———. "Student Academic Freedom and the Rule-Making Powers of Public Universities: Some Constitutional Considerations." *Law in Transition Quarterly* 2 (1965): 1-34.

Vickory, Frank A. "The Impact of Open-Meetings Legislation on Academic Freedom and the Business of Higher Education." *American Business Law Journal* 24 (1986): 427-48.

Walter, Paul H. L. "Academic Freedom—Seventy Years Later." *Academe: Bulletin of the American Association of University Professors* 72 (Sept.-Oct. 1986): 1a-5a.

Weston, Michael C. " 'Outside' Activities of Faculty Members." *Journal of College and University Law* 7 (1980-81): 68-77.

White, William R., Jr. "The Bertrand Russell Case Again: Professor Hamilton's Law." *Fordham Law Review* 10 (1941): 205-16.

York, Kenneth H. "Legal Nature of Academic Freedom." *The Brief* 48 (1953): 246-56.

Yudof, Mark G. "Intramural Musings on Academic Freedom: A Reply to Professor Finkin." *Texas Law Review* 66 (1988): 1351-57.

———. "Three Faces of Academic Freedom." *Loyola Law Review* 32 (1987): 831-58.

APPENDIX A
GENERAL REPORT OF THE COMMITTEE ON ACADEMIC FREEDOM AND ACADEMIC TENURE (1915)*

I

GENERAL DECLARATION OF PRINCIPLES

The term "academic freedom" has traditionally had two applications—to the freedom of the teacher and to that of the student, *Lehrfreiheit* and *Lernfreiheit*. It need scarcely be pointed out that the freedom which is the subject of this report is that of the teacher. Academic freedom in this sense comprises three elements: freedom of inquiry and research; freedom of teaching within the university or college; and freedom of extra-mural utterance and action. The first of these is almost everywhere so safeguarded that the dangers of its infringement are slight. It may therefore be disregarded in this report. The second and third phases of academic freedom are closely related, and are often not distinguished. The third, however, has an importance of its own, since of late it has perhaps more frequently been the occasion of difficulties and controversies than has the question of freedom of intra-academic teaching. All five of the cases which have recently been investigated by committees of this Association have involved, at least as one factor, the right of university teachers to express their opinions freely outside the university or to engage in political activities in their capacity as citizens. The general principles which have to do with freedom of teaching in both these senses seem to the committee to be in great part, though not wholly, the same. In this report, therefore, we shall consider the matter primarily with reference to freedom of teaching within the university, and shall assume that what is said thereon is also applicable to the freedom of speech of university teachers outside their institutions, subject to certain qualifications and supplementary considerations which will be pointed out in the course of the report.

An adequate discussion of academic freedom must necessarily consider three matters: (1) the scope and basis of the power exercised by those bodies having ultimate legal authority in academic affairs; (2) the nature of the academic calling; (3) the function of the academic institution or university.

* Reprinted, with permission of the American Association of University Professors, from 1 AAUP Bull 17 (1915).

1. Basis of Academic Authority

American institutions of learning are usually controlled by boards of trustees as the ultimate repositories of power. Upon them finally it devolves to determine the measure of academic freedom which is to be realized in the several institutions. It therefore becomes necessary to inquire into the nature of the trust reposed in these boards, and to ascertain to whom the trustees are to be considered accountable.

The simplest case is that of a proprietary school or college designed for the propagation of specific doctrines prescribed by those who have furnished its endowment. It is evident that in such cases the trustees are bound by the deed of gift, and, whatever be their own views, are obligated to carry out the terms of the trust. If a church or religious denomination establishes a college to be governed by a board of trustees, with the express understanding that the college will be used as an instrument of propaganda in the interests of the religious faith professed by the church or denomination creating it, the trustees have a right to demand that everything be subordinated to that end. If, again, as has happened in this country, a wealthy manufacturer establishes a special school in a University in order to teach, among other things, the advantages of a protective tariff, or if, as is also the case, an institution has been endowed for the purpose of propagating the doctrines of socialism, the situation is analogous. All of these are essentially proprietary institutions, in the moral sense. They do not, at least as regards one particular subject, accept the principles of freedom of inquiry, of opinion, and of teaching; and their purpose is not to advance knowledge by the unrestricted research and unfettered discussion of impartial investigators, but rather to subsidize the promotion of opinions held by the persons, usually not of the scholar's calling, who provide the funds for their maintenance. Concerning the desirability of the existence of such institutions, the committee does not desire to express any opinion. But it is manifestly important that they should not be permitted to sail under false colors. Genuine boldness and thoroughness of inquiry, and freedom of speech, are scarcely reconcilable with the prescribed inculcation of a particular opinion upon a controverted question.

Such institutions are rare, however, and are becoming ever more rare. We still have, indeed, colleges under denominational auspices; but very few of them impose upon their trustees responsibility for the spread of specific doctrines. They are more and more coming to occupy, with respect to the freedom enjoyed by the members of their teaching bodies, the position of untrammeled institutions of learning, and are differentiated only by the natural influence of their respective historic antecedents and traditions.

Leaving aside, then, the small number of institutions of the proprietary type, what is the nature of the trust reposed in the governing boards of the ordinary institutions of learning? Can colleges and universities that are not strictly bound by their founders to a propagandist duty ever be included in the class of institutions that we have just described as being in a moral sense proprietary? The answer is clear. If the former class of institutions constitute a private or proprietary trust, the latter constitute a public trust. The trustees are trustees for the public. In the case of our state universities this is self-evident. In the case of most of our privately endowed institutions, the situation is really not different. They cannot be permitted to assume the proprietary attitude and privilege, if they are appealing to the general public for support. Trustees of such universities or colleges have no moral right to bind the reason or the conscience of any professor. All claim to such right is waived by the appeal to the general public for contributions and for moral support in the maintenance, not of a propaganda, but of a non-partisan institution of learning. It follows that any university which lays restrictions upon the intellectual freedom of its professors proclaims itself a proprietary institution, and should be so described whenever it makes a general appeal for funds; and the public should be advised that the institution has no claim whatever to general support or regard.

This elementary distinction between a private and a public trust is not yet so universally accepted as it should be in our American institutions. While in many universities and colleges the situation has come to be entirely satisfactory, there are others in which the relation of trustees to professors is apparently still conceived to be analogous to that of a private employer to his employees; in which, therefore, trustees are not regarded as debarred by any moral restrictions, beyond their own sense of expediency, from imposing their personal opinions upon the teaching of the institution, or even from employing the power of dismissal to gratify their private antipathies or resentments. An eminent university president thus described the situation not many years since:

> In the institutions of higher education the board of trustees is the body on whose discretion, good feeling, and experience the securing of academic freedom now depends. There are boards which leave nothing to be desired in these respects; but there are also numerous bodies that have everything to learn with regard to academic freedom. These barbarous boards exercise an arbitrary power of dismissal. They exclude from the teachings of the university unpopular or dangerous subjects. In some states they even treat professors' positions as common political spoils; and all too frequently, both in state and endowed institutions, they fail to treat the members of the teaching staff with that high consideration to which their functions entitle them.[1]

It is, then, a prerequisite to a realization of the proper measure of academic freedom in American institutions of learning, that all boards of trustees should understand—as many already do—the full implications of the distinction between private proprietorship and a public trust.

---

1. From "Academic Freedom," an address delivered before the New York Chapter of the Phi Beta Kappa Society at Cornell University, May 29, 1907, by Charles William Eliot, LL.D., President of Harvard University.

2.   The Nature of the Academic Calling

The above-mentioned conception of a university as an ordinary business venture, and of academic teaching as a purely private employment, manifests also a radical failure to apprehend the nature of the social function discharged by the professional scholar. While we should be reluctant to believe that any large number of educated persons suffer from such a misapprehension, it seems desirable at this time to restate clearly the chief reasons, lying in the nature of the university teaching profession, why it is to the public interest that the professorial office should be one both of dignity and of independence.

If education is the corner stone of the structure of society and if progress in scientific knowledge is essential to civilization, few things can be more important than to enhance the dignity of the scholar's profession, with a view to attracting into its ranks men of the highest ability, of sound learning, and of strong and independent character. This is the more essential because the pecuniary emoluments of the profession are not, and doubtless never will be, equal to those open to the more successful members of other professions. It is not, in our opinion, desirable that men should be drawn into this profession by the magnitude of the economic rewards which it offers; but it is for this reason the more needful that men of high gift and character should be drawn into it by the assurance of an honorable and secure position, and of freedom to perform honestly and according to their own consciences the distinctive and important function which the nature of the profession lays upon them.

That function is to deal at first hand, after prolonged and specialized technical training, with the sources of knowledge; and to impart the results of their own and of their fellow-specialists' investigations and reflection, both to students and to the general public, without fear or favor. The proper discharge of this function requires (among other things) that the university teacher shall be exempt from any pecuniary motive or inducement to hold, or to express, any conclusion which is not the genuine and uncolored product of his own study or that of fellow-specialists. Indeed, the proper fulfillment of the work of the professorate requires that our universities shall be so free that no fair-minded person shall find any excuse for even a suspicion that the utterances of university teachers are shaped or restricted by the judgment, not of professional scholars, but of inexpert and possibly not wholly disinterested persons outside of their ranks. The lay public is under no compulsion to accept or to act upon the opinions of the scientific experts whom, through the universities, it employs. But it is highly needful, in the interest of society at large, that what purport to be the conclusions of men trained for, and dedicated to, the quest for truth, shall in fact be the conclusions of such men, and not echoes of the opinions of the lay public, or of the individuals who endow or manage universities. To the degree that professional scholars, in the formation and promulgation of their opinions, are, or by the character of their tenure appear to be, subject to any motive other than their own scientific conscience and a desire for the respect of their fellow-experts, to that degree the university teaching profession is corrupted; its proper influence upon public opinion is diminished and vitiated; and society at large fails to get from its scholars, in an unadulterated form, the peculiar and necessary service which it is the office of the professional scholar to furnish.

These considerations make still more clear the nature of the relationship between university trustees and members of university faculties. The latter are the appointees, but not in any proper sense the employees, of the former. For, once appointed, the scholar has professional functions to perform in which the appointing authorities have neither competency nor moral right to intervene. The responsibility of the university teacher is primarily to the public itself, and to the judgment of his own profession; and while, with respect to certain external conditions of his vocation, he accepts a responsibility to the authorities of the institution in which he serves, in the essentials of his professional activity his duty is to the wider public to which the institution itself is morally amenable. So far as the university teacher's independence of thought and utterance is concerned—though not in other regards—the relationship of professor to trustees may be compared to that between judges of the Federal courts and the Executive who appoints them. University teachers should be understood to be, with respect to the conclusions reached and expressed by them, no more subject to the control of the trustees, than are judges subject to the control of the President, with respect to their decisions; while of course, for the same reason, trustees are no more to be held responsible for, or to be presumed to agree with, the opinions or utterances of professors, than the President can be assumed to approve of all the legal reasonings of the courts. A university is a great and indispensable organ of the higher life of a civilized community, in the work of which the trustees hold an essential and highly honorable place, but in which the faculties hold an independent place, with quite equal responsibilities—and in relation to purely scientific and educational questions, the primary responsibility. Misconception or obscurity in this matter has undoubtedly been a source of occasional difficulty in the past, and even in several instances during the current year, however much, in the main, a long tradition of kindly and courteous intercourse between trustees and members of university faculties has kept the question in the background.

3. The Function of the Academic Institution

The importance of academic freedom is most clearly perceived in the light of the purposes for which universities exist. These are three in number:

  A. To promote inquiry and advance the sum of human knowledge.
  B. To provide general instruction to the students.
  C. To develop experts for various branches of the public service.

Let us consider each of these. In the earlier stages of a nation's intellectual development, the chief concern of educational institutions is to train the growing generation and to diffuse the already accepted knowledge. It is only slowly that there comes to be provided in the highest institutions of learning the opportunity for the gradual wresting from nature of her intimate secrets. The modern university is becoming more and more the home of scientific research. There are three fields of human inquiry in which the race is only at the beginning: natural science, social science, and philosophy and religion, dealing with the relations of man to outer nature, to his fellow men, and to the ultimate realities and values. In natural science all that we have learned but serves to make us realize more deeply how much more remains to be discovered. In social science in its largest sense, which is concerned with the relations of men in society and with the conditions of social order and well-being, we have learned only an adumbration of the laws which govern these vastly complex phenomena. Finally, in the spirit life, and in the interpretation of the general meaning and ends of human existence and its relation to the universe, we are still far from a comprehension of the final truths, and from a universal agreement among all sincere and earnest men. In all of these domains of knowledge, the first condition of progress is complete and unlimited freedom to pursue inquiry and publish its results. Such freedom is the breath in the nostrils of all scientific activity.

The second function—which for a long time was the only function—of the American college or university is to provide instruction for students. It is scarcely open to question that freedom of utterance is as important to the teacher as it is to the investigator. No man can be a successful teacher unless he enjoys the respect of his students, and their confidence in his intellectual integrity. It is clear, however, that this confidence will be impaired if there is suspicion on the part of the student that the teacher is not expressing himself fully or frankly, or that college and university teachers in general are a repressed and intimidated class who dare not speak with that candor and courage which youth always demands in those whom it is to esteem. The average student is a discerning observer, who soon takes the measure of his instructor. It is not only the character of the instruction but also the character of the instructor that counts; and if the student has reason to believe that the instructor is not true to himself, the virtue of the instruction as an educative force is incalculably diminished. There must be in the mind of the teacher no mental reservation. He must give the student the best of what he has and what he is.

The third function of the modern university is to develop experts for the use of the community. If there is one thing that distinguishes the more recent developments of democracy, it is the recognition by legislators of the inherent complexities of economic, social, and political life, and the difficulty of solving problems of technical adjustment without technical knowledge. The recognition of this fact has led to a continually greater demand for the aid of experts in these subjects, to advise both legislators and administrators. The training of such experts has, accordingly, in recent years, become an important part of the work of the universities; and in almost every one of our higher institutions of learning the professors of the economic, social, and political sciences have been drafted to an increasing extent into more or less unofficial participation in the public service. It is obvious that here again the scholar must be absolutely free not only to pursue his investigations but to declare the results of his researches, no matter where they may lead him or to what extent they may come into conflict with accepted opinion. To be of use to the legislator or the administrator, he must enjoy their complete confidence in the disinterestedness of his conclusions.

It is clear, then, that the university cannot perform its threefold function without accepting and enforcing to the fullest extent the principle of academic freedom. The responsibility of the university as a whole is to the community at large, and any restriction upon the freedom of the instructor is bound to react injuriously upon the efficiency and the *morale* of the institution, and therefore ultimately upon the interests of the community.

———

The attempted infringements of academic freedom at present are probably not only of less frequency than, but of a different character from, those to be found in former times. In the early period of university development in America the chief menace to academic freedom was ecclesiastical, and the disciplines chiefly affected were philosophy and the natural sciences. In more recent times the danger zone has been shifted to the political and social sciences—though we still have sporadic examples of the former class of cases in some of our smaller institutions. But it is precisely in these provinces of knowledge in which academic freedom is now most likely to be threatened, that the need for it is at the same time most evident. No person of intelligence believes that all of our political problems have been solved, or that the final stage of social evolution has been reached. Grave issues in the adjustment of men's social and economic relations are certain to call for settlement in the years that are to come; and for the right settlement of them mankind will need all the wisdom, all the good will, all the soberness of mind, and all the knowledge drawn from experience, that it can command. Towards this settlement the university has potentially its own very great contribution to make; for if the adjustment reached is to be a wise one, it must take due account of economic science, and be guided by that breadth of historic vision which it should be one of the functions of a university to cultivate. But if the universities are to render any such service towards the right solution of the social problems of the future, it is the first essential that the scholars who carry on the work of universities shall not be in a position of dependence upon the favor of any social class or group, that the disinterestedness and impartiality of their inquiries and their conclusions shall be, so far as is humanly possible, beyond the reach of suspicion.

The special dangers to freedom of teaching in the domain of the social sciences are evidently two. The one which is the more likely to affect the privately endowed colleges and universities is the danger of restrictions upon the expression of opinions which point towards extensive social innovations, or call in question the moral legitimacy or social expediency of economic conditions or commercial practices in which large vested interests are involved. In the political, social, and economic field almost every question, no matter how large and general it at first appears, is more or less affected with private or class interests; and, as the governing body of a university is naturally made up of men who through their standing and ability are personally interested in great private enterprises, the points of possible conflict are numberless. When to this is added the consideration that benefactors, as well as most of the parents who send their children to privately endowed institutions, themselves belong to the more prosperous and therefore usually to the more conservative classes, it is apparent that, so long as effectual safeguards for academic freedom are not established, there is a real danger that pressure from vested interests may, sometimes deliberately and sometimes unconsciously, sometimes openly and sometimes subtly and in obscure ways, be brought to bear upon academic authorities.

On the other hand, in our state universities the danger may be the reverse. Where the university is dependent for funds upon legislative favor, it has sometimes happened that the conduct of the institution has been affected by political considerations; and where there is a definite governmental policy or a strong public feeling on economic, social, or political questions, the menace to academic freedom may consist in the repression of opinions that in the particular political situation are deemed ultra-conservative rather than ultra-radical. The essential point, however, is not so much that the opinion is of one or another shade, as that it differs from the views entertained by the authorities. The question resolves itself into one of departure from accepted standards; whether the departure is in the one direction or the other is immaterial.

This brings us to the most serious difficulty of this problem; namely, the dangers connected with the existence in a democracy of an overwhelming and concentrated public opinion. The tendency of modern democracy is for men to think alike, to feel alike, and to speak alike. Any departure from the conventional standards is apt to be regarded with suspicion. Public opinion is at once the chief safeguard of a democracy, and the chief menace to the real liberty of the individual. It almost seems as if the danger of despotism cannot be wholly averted under any form of government. In a political autocracy there is no effective public opinion, and all are subject to the tyranny of the ruler; in a democracy there is political freedom, but there is likely to be a tyranny of public opinion.

An inviolable refuge from such tyranny should be found in the university. It should be an intellectual experiment station, where new ideas may germinate and where their fruit, though still distasteful to the community as a whole, may be allowed to ripen until finally, perchance, it may become a part of the accepted intellectual food of the nation or of the world. Not less is it a distinctive duty of the university to be the conservator of all genuine elements of value in the past thought and life of mankind which are not in the fashion of the moment. Though it need not be the "home of beaten causes," the university is, indeed, likely always to exercise a certain form of conservative influence. For by its nature it is committed to the principle that knowledge should precede action, to the caution (by no means synonymous with intellectual timidity) which is an essential part of the scientific method, to a sense of the complexity of social problems, to the practice of taking long views into the future, and to a reasonable regard for the teachings of experience. One of its most characteristic functions in a democratic society is to help make public opinion more self-critical and more circumspect, to check the more hasty and unconsidered impulses of popular feeling, to train the democracy to the habit of looking before and after. It is precisely this function of the university which is most injured by any restriction upon academic freedom; and it is precisely those who most value this aspect of the university's work who should most earnestly protest against any such restriction. For the public may respect, and be influenced by, the counsels of prudence and of moderation which are given by men of science, if it believes those counsels to be the disinterested expression of the scientific temper and of unbiased inquiry. It is little likely to respect or heed them if it has reason to believe that they are the expression of the interests, or the timidities, of the limited portion of the community which is in a position to endow institutions of learning, or is most likely to be represented upon their boards of trustees. And a plausible reason for this belief is given the public so long as our universities are not organized in such a way as to make impossible any exercise of pressure upon professorial opinions and utterances by governing boards of laymen.

Since there are no rights without corresponding duties, the considerations heretofore set down with respect to the freedom of the academic teacher entail certain correlative obligations. The claim to freedom of teaching is made in the interest of the integrity and of the progress of scientific inquiry; it, is, therefore, only those who carry on their work in the temper of the scientific inquirer who may justly assert this claim. The liberty of the scholar within the university to set forth his conclusions, be they what they may, is conditioned by their being conclusions gained by a scholar's method and held in a scholar's spirit; that is to say, they must be the fruits of competent and patient and sincere inquiry, and they should be set forth with dignity, courtesy, and temperateness of language. The university teacher, in giving instruction upon controversial matters, while he is under no obligation to hide his own opinion under a mountain of equivocal verbiage, should, if he is fit for his position, be a person of a fair and judicial mind; he should, in dealing with such subjects, set forth justly, without suppression or innuendo, the divergent opinions of other investigators; he should cause his students to become familiar with the best published expressions of the great historic types of doctrine upon the questions at issue; and he should, above all, remember that his business is not to provide his students with ready-made conclusions, but to train them to think for themselves, and to provide them access to those materials which they need if they are to think intelligently.

It is, however, for reasons which have already been made evident, inadmissible that the power of determining when departures from the requirements of the scientific spirit and method have occurred, should be vested in bodies not composed of members of the academic profession. Such bodies necessarily lack full competency to judge of those requirements; their intervention can never be exempt from the suspicion that it is dictated by other motives than zeal for the integrity of science; and it is, in any case, unsuitable to the dignity of a great profession that the initial responsibility for the maintenance of its professional standards should not be in the hands of its own members. It follows that university teachers must be prepared to assume this responsibility for themselves. They have hitherto seldom had the opportunity, or perhaps the disposition, to do so. The obligation will doubtless, therefore, seem to many an unwelcome and burdensome one; and for its proper discharge members of the profession will perhaps need to acquire, in a greater measure than they at present possess it, the capacity for impersonal judgment in such cases, and for judicial severity when the occasion requires it. But the responsibility cannot, in this committee's opinion, be rightfully evaded. If this profession should prove itself unwilling to purge its ranks of the incompetent and the unworthy, or to prevent the freedom which it claims in the name of science from being used as a shelter for inefficiency, for superficiality, or for uncritical and intemperate partisanship, it is certain that the task will be performed by others—by others who lack certain essential qualifications for performing it, and whose action is sure to breed suspicions and recurrent controversies deeply injurious to the internal order and the public standing of universities. Your committee has, therefore, in the appended "Practical Proposals" attempted to suggest means by which judicial action by representatives of the profession, with respect to the matters here referred to, may be secured.

There is one case in which the academic teacher is under an obligation to observe certain special restraints—namely, the instruction of immature students. In many of our American colleges, and especially in the first two years of the course, the student's character is not yet fully formed, his mind is still relatively immature. In these circumstances it may reasonably be expected that the instructor will present scientific truth with discretion, that he will introduce the student to new conceptions gradually, with some consideration for the student's preconceptions and traditions, and with due regard to character-building. The teacher ought also to be especially on his guard against taking unfair advantage of the student's immaturity by indoctrinating him with the teacher's own opinions before the student has had an opportunity fairly to examine other opinions upon the matters in question, and before he has sufficient knowledge and ripeness of judgment to be entitled to form any definitive opinion of his own. It is not the least service which a college or university may render to those under its instruction, to habituate them to looking not only patiently but methodically on both sides, before adopting any conclusion upon controverted issues. By these suggestions, however, it need scarcely be said that the committee does not intend to imply that it is not the duty of an academic instructor to give to any students old enough to be in college a genuine intellectual awakening and to arouse in them a keen desire to reach personally verified conclusions upon all questions of general concernment to mankind, or of special significance for their own time. There is much truth in some remarks recently made in this connection by a college president:

> Certain professors have been refused reëlection lately, apparently because they set their students to thinking in ways objectionable to the trustees. It would be well if more teachers were dismissed because they fail to stimulate thinking of any kind. We can afford to forgive a college professor what we regard as the occasional error of his doctrine, especially as we may be wrong, provided he is a contagious center of intellectual enthusiasm. It is better for students to think about heresies than not to think at all; better for them to climb new trails, and stumble over error if need be, than to ride forever in upholstered ease in the overcrowded highway. It is a primary duty of a teacher to make a student take an honest account of his stock of ideas, throw out the dead matter, place revised price marks on what is left, and try to fill his empty shelves with new goods.[2]

It is, however, possible and necessary that such intellectual awakening be brought about with patience, considerateness and pedagogical wisdom.

There is one further consideration with regard to the class-room utterances of college and university teachers to which the committee thinks it important to call the attention of members of the profession, and of administrative authorities. Such utterances ought always to be considered privileged communications. Discussions in the class room ought not to be supposed to be utterances for the public at large. They are often designed to provoke opposition or arouse debate. It has, unfortunately, sometimes happened in this country that sensational newspapers have quoted and garbled such remarks. As a matter of common law, it is clear that the utterances of an academic instructor are privileged, and may not be published, in whole or part, without his authorization. But our practice, unfortunately, still differs from that of foreign countries, and no effective check has in this country been put upon such unauthorized and often misleading publication. It is much to be desired that test cases should be made of any infractions of the rule.[3]

In their extra-mural utterances, it is obvious that academic teachers are under a peculiar obligation to avoid hasty or unverified or exaggerated statements, and to refrain from intemperate or sensational modes of expression. But, subject to these restraints, it is not, in this committee's opinion, desirable that scholars should be debarred from giving expression to their judgments upon controversial questions, or that their freedom of

---

2. President William T. Foster in *The Nation*, November 11, 1915.

3. The leading case is Abernethy vs. Hutchison, 3 L. J., Ch. 209. In this case where damages were awarded the court held as follows: "That persons who are admitted as pupils or otherwise to hear these lectures, although they are orally delivered and the parties might go to the extent, if they were able to do so, of putting down the whole by means of shorthand, yet they can do that only for the purpose of their own information and could not publish, for profit, that which they had not obtained the right of selling."

speech, outside the university, should be limited to questions falling within their own specialties. It is clearly not proper that they should be prohibited from lending their active support to organized movements which they believe to be in the public interest. And, speaking broadly, it may be said in the words of a non-academic body already once quoted in a publication of this Association, that "it is neither possible nor desirable to deprive a college professor of the political rights vouchsafed to every citizen."[4]

It is, however, a question deserving of consideration by members of this Association, and by university officials, how far academic teachers, at least those dealing with political, economic and social subjects, should be prominent in the management of our great party organizations, or should be candidates for state or national offices of a distinctly political character. It is manifestly desirable that such teachers have minds untrammeled by party loyalties, unexcited by party enthusiasms, and unbiased by personal political ambitions; and that universities should remain uninvolved in party antagonisms. On the other hand, it is equally manifest that the material available for the service of the State would be restricted in a highly undesirable way, if it were understood that no member of the academic profession should ever be called upon to assume the responsibilities of public office. This question may, in the committee's opinion, suitably be made a topic for special discussion at some future meeting of this Association, in order that a practical policy, which shall do justice to the two partially conflicting considerations that bear upon the matter, may be agreed upon.

It is, it will be seen, in no sense the contention of this committee that academic freedom implies that individual teachers should be exempt from all restraints as to the matter or manner of their utterances, either within or without the university. Such restraints as are necessary should in the main, your committee holds, be self-imposed, or enforced by the public opinion of the profession. But there may, undoubtedly, arise occasional cases in which the aberrations of individuals may require to be checked by definite disciplinary action. What this report chiefly maintains is that such action can not with safety be taken by bodies not composed of members of the academic profession. Lay governing boards are competent to judge concerning charges of habitual neglect of assigned duties, on the part of individual teachers, and concerning charges of grave moral delinquency. But in matters of opinion, and of the utterance of opinion, such boards can not intervene without destroying, to the extent of their intervention, the essential nature of a university—without converting it from a place dedicated to openness of mind, in which the conclusions expressed are the tested conclusions of trained scholars, into a place barred against the access of new light, and precommitted to the opinions or prejudices of men who have not been set apart or expressly trained for the scholar's duties. It is, in short, not the absolute freedom of utterance of the individual scholar, but the absolute

---

4. Report of the Wisconsin State Board of Public Affairs, December 1914.

freedom of thought, of inquiry, of discussion and of teaching, of the academic profession, that is asserted by this declaration of principles. It is conceivable that our profession may prove unworthy of its high calling, and unfit to exercise the responsibilities that belong to it. But it will scarcely be said as yet to have given evidence of such unfitness. And the existence of this Association, as it seems to your committee, must be construed as a pledge, not only that the profession will earnestly guard those liberties without which it can not rightly render its distinctive and indispensable service to society, but also that it will with equal earnestness seek to maintain such standards of professional character, and of scientific integrity and competency, as shall make it a fit instrument for that service.

II

PRACTICAL PROPOSALS

As the foregoing declaration implies, the ends to be accomplished are chiefly three:

First: To safeguard freedom of inquiry and of teaching against both covert and overt attacks, by providing suitable judicial bodies, composed of members of the academic profession, which may be called into action before university teachers are dismissed or disciplined, and may determine in what cases the question of academic freedom is actually involved.

Second: By the same means, to protect college executives and governing boards against unjust charges of infringement of academic freedom, or of arbitrary and dictatorial conduct—charges which, when they gain wide currency and belief, are highly detrimental to the good repute and the influence of universities.

Third: To render the profession more attractive to men of high ability and strong personality by insuring the dignity, the independence, and the reasonable security of tenure, of the professorial office. The measures which it is believed to be necessary for our universities to adopt to realize these ends—measures which have already been adopted in part by some institutions—are four:

A. *Action by Faculty Committees on Reappointments.* Official action relating to reappointments and refusals of reappointment should be taken only with the advice and consent of some board or committee representative of the faculty. Your committee does not desire to make at this time any suggestion as to the manner of selection of such boards.

B. *Definition of Tenure of Office.* In every institution there should be an unequivocal understanding as to the term of each appointment; and the tenure of professorships and associate professorships, and of all positions above the grade of instructor after ten years of service, should be permanent (subject to the provisions hereinafter given for removal upon charges). In those state universities which are legally incapable of making contracts for more than a limited period, the governing boards should announce their policy with respect to the presumption of reappointment in the several classes of position, and such announcements, though not legally enforceable, should be regarded as morally binding. No university teacher of any rank should, except in cases of grave moral delinquency, receive notice of dismissal or of refusal of reappointment, later than three months before the close of any academic year, and in the case of teachers above the grade of instructor, one year's notice should be given.

C. *Formulation of Grounds for Dismissal.* In every institution the grounds which will be regarded as justifying the dismissal of members of the faculty should be formulated with reasonable definiteness; and in the case of institutions which impose upon their faculties doctrinal standards of a sectarian or partisan character, these standards should be clearly defined and the body or individual having authority to interpret them, in case of controversy, should be designated. Your committee does not think it best at this time to attempt to enumerate the legitimate grounds for dismissal, believing it to be preferable that individual institutions should take the initiative in this.

D. *Judicial Hearings Before Dismissal.* Every university or college teacher should be entitled, before dismissal[5] or demotion, to have the charges against him stated in writing in specific terms and to have a fair trial on those charges before a special or permanent judicial committee chosen by the faculty senate or council, or by the faculty at large. At such trial the teacher accused should have full opportunity to present evidence, and, if the charge is one of professional incompetency, a formal report upon his work should be first made in writing by the teachers of his own department and of cognate departments in the university, and, if the teacher concerned so desire, by a committee of his fellow specialists from other institutions, appointed by some competent authority.

---

5. This does not refer to refusals of reappointment at the expiration of the terms of office of teachers below the rank of associate professor. All such questions of reappointment should, as above provided, be acted upon by a faculty committee.

APPENDIX B
1940 STATEMENT OF PRINCIPLES ON ACADEMIC FREEDOM AND TENURE*

The purpose of this statement is to promote public understanding and support of academic freedom and tenure and agreement upon procedures to assure them in colleges and universities. Institutions of higher education are conducted for the common good and not to further the interest of either the individual teacher[1] or the institution as a whole. The common good depends upon the free search for truth and its free exposition.

Academic freedom is essential to these purposes and applies to both teaching and research. Freedom in research is fundamental to the advancement of truth. Academic freedom in its teaching aspect is fundamental for the protection of the rights of the teacher in teaching and of the student to freedom in learning. It carries with it duties correlative with rights.

Tenure is a means to certain ends; specifically: (1) Freedom of teaching and research and of extramural activities and (2) a sufficient degree of economic security to make the profession attractive to men and women of ability. Freedom and economic security, hence, tenure, are indispensable to the success of an institution in fulfilling its obligations to its students and to society.

ACADEMIC FREEDOM

(a) The teacher is entitled to full freedom in research and in the publication of the results, subject to the adequate performance of his other academic duties; but research for pecuniary return should be based upon an understanding with the authorities of the institution.

(b) The teacher is entitled to freedom in the classroom in discussing his subject, but he should be careful not to introduce into his teaching controversial matter which has no relation to his subject. Limitations of academic freedom because of religious or other aims of the institution should be clearly stated in writing at the time of the appointment.

(c) The college or university teacher is a citizen, a member of a learned profession, and an officer of an educational institution. When he speaks or writes as a citizen, he should be free from institutional censorship or

---

* Reprinted, with permission of the American Association of University Professors, from *Policy Documents and Reports* 3 (AAUP, 1984) (without Interpretive Comments). In the interest of historical accuracy, this Appendix does not reflect the changes adopted in 1989 and 1990 to remove gender-specific references in the text.

1. The word "teacher" as used in this document is understood to include the investigator who is attached to an academic institution without teaching duties.

discipline, but his special position in the community imposes special obligations. As a man of learning and an educational officer, he should remember that the public may judge his profession and his institution by his utterances. Hence he should at all times be accurate, should exercise appropriate restraint, should show respect for the opinions of others, and should make every effort to indicate that he is not an institutional spokesman.

Academic Tenure

(a) After the expiration of a probationary period, teachers or investigators should have permanent or continuous tenure, and their service should be terminated only for adequate cause, except in the case of retirement for age, or under extraordinary circumstances because of financial exigencies.

In the interpretation of this principle it is understood that the following represents acceptable academic practice:

1. The precise terms and conditions of every appointment should be stated in writing and be in the possession of both institution and teacher before the appointment is consummated.

2. Beginning with appointment to the rank of full-time instructor or a higher rank, the probationary period should not exceed seven years, including within this period full-time service in all institutions of higher education; but subject to the proviso that when, after a term of probationary service of more than three years in one or more institutions, a teacher is called to another institution it may be agreed in writing that his new appointment is for a probationary period of not more than four years, even though thereby the person's total probationary period in the academic profession is extended beyond the normal maximum of seven years. Notice should be given at least one year prior to the expiration of the probationary period if the teacher is not to be continued in service after the expiration of that period.

3. During the probationary period a teacher should have the academic freedom that all other members of the faculty have.

4. Termination for cause of a continuous appointment, or the dismissal for cause of a teacher previous to the expiration of a term appointment, should, if possible, be considered by both a faculty committee and the governing board of the institution. In all cases where the facts are in dispute, the accused teacher should be informed before the hearing in writing of the charges against him and should have the opportunity to be heard in his own defense by all bodies that pass judgment upon his case. He should be permitted to have with him an adviser of his own choosing who may act as counsel. There should be a full stenographic record of the hearing available to the parties concerned. In the hearing of charges of incompetence the testimony should include that of teachers and other scholars, either from his own or from other institutions. Teachers on continuous

appointment who are dismissed for reasons not involving moral turpitude should receive their salaries for at least a year from the date of notification of dismissal whether or not they are continued in their duties at the institution.

5. Termination of a continuous appointment because of financial exigency should be demonstrably *bona fide*.

APPENDIX C
JOINT STATEMENT ON RIGHTS AND FREEDOMS OF STUDENTS (1967)*

PREAMBLE

Academic institutions exist for the transmission of knowledge, the pursuit of truth, the development of students, and the general well-being of society. Free inquiry and free expression are indispensable to the attainment of these goals. As members of the academic community, students should be encouraged to develop the capacity for critical judgment and to engage in a sustained and independent search for truth. Institutional procedures for achieving these purposes may vary from campus to campus, but the minimal standards of academic freedom of students outlined below are essential to any community of scholars.

Freedom to teach and freedom to learn are inseparable facets of academic freedom. The freedom to learn depends upon appropriate opportunities and conditions in the classroom, on the campus, and in the larger community. Students should exercise their freedom with responsibility.

The responsibility to secure and to respect general conditions conducive to the freedom to learn is shared by all members of the academic community. Each college and university has a duty to develop policies and procedures which provide and safeguard this freedom. Such policies and procedures should be developed at each institution within the framework of general standards and with the broadest possible participation of the members of the academic community. The purpose of this statement is to enumerate the essential provisions for student freedom to learn.

I

FREEDOM OF ACCESS TO HIGHER EDUCATION

The admissions policies of each college and university are a matter of institutional choice provided that each college and university makes clear the characteristics and expectations of students which it considers relevant to success in the institution's program. While church-related institutions may give admissions preference to students of their own persuasion, such a preference should be clearly and publicly stated. Under no circumstances should a student be barred from admission to a particular institution on the basis of race. Thus, within the limits of its facilities, each college and university should be open to all students who are qualified according to its

---

* Reprinted, with permission of the American Association of University Professors, from *Policy Documents and Reports* 141 (AAUP, 1984).

admissions standards. The facilities and services of a college should be open to all of its enrolled students, and institutions should use their influence to secure equal access for all students to public facilities in the local community.

II

IN THE CLASSROOM

The professor in the classroom and in conference should encourage free discussion, inquiry, and expression. Student performance should be evaluated solely on an academic basis, not on opinions or conduct in matters unrelated to academic standards.

A. Protection of Freedom of Expression

Students should be free to take reasoned exception to the data or views offered in any course of study and to reserve judgment about matters of opinion, but they are responsible for learning the content of any course of study for which they are enrolled.

B. Protection against Improper Academic Evaluation

Students should have protection through orderly procedures against prejudiced or capricious academic evaluation. At the same time, they are responsible for maintaining standards of academic performance established for each course in which they are enrolled.

C. Protection against Improper Disclosure

Information about student views, beliefs, and political associations which professors acquire in the course of their work as instructors, advisers, and counselors should be considered confidential. Protection against improper disclosure is a serious professional obligation. Judgments of ability and character may be provided under appropriate circumstances, normally with the knowledge or consent of the student.

III

STUDENT RECORDS

Institutions should have a carefully considered policy as to the information which should be part of a student's permanent educational record and as to the conditions of its disclosure. To minimize the risk of improper disclosure, academic and disciplinary records should be separate, and the conditions of access to each should be set forth in an explicit policy statement. Transcripts of academic records should contain only information about academic status. Information from disciplinary or counseling files should not be available to unauthorized persons on campus, or to any person off campus without the express consent of the student involved except under legal compulsion or in cases where the safety of persons or property is involved. No records should be kept which reflect the political activities or beliefs of students. Provisions should also be made for periodic routine destruction of noncurrent disciplinary records. Administrative staff and faculty members should respect confidential information about students which they acquire in the course of their work.

IV

Student Affairs

In student affairs, certain standards must be maintained if the freedom of students is to be preserved.

A. Freedom of Association

Students bring to the campus a variety of interests previously acquired and develop many new interests as members of the academic community. They should be free to organize and join associations to promote their common interests.

1. The membership, policies, and actions of a student organization usually will be determined by vote of only those persons who hold *bona fide* membership in the college or university community.

2. Affiliation with an extramural organization should not of itself disqualify a student organization from institutional recognition.

3. If campus advisers are required, each organization should be free to choose its own adviser, and institutional recognition should not be withheld or withdrawn solely because of the inability of a student organization to secure an adviser. Campus advisers may advise organizations in the exercise of responsibility, but they should not have the authority to control the policy of such organizations.

4. Student organizations may be required to submit a statement of purpose, criteria for membership, rules of procedures, and a current list of officers. They should not be required to submit a membership list as a condition of institutional recognition.

5. Campus organizations, including those affiliated with an extramural organization, should be open to all students without respect to race, creed, or national origin, except for religious qualifications which may be required by organizations whose aims are primarily sectarian.

B. Freedom of Inquiry and Expression

1. Students and student organizations should be free to examine and discuss all questions of interest to them, and to express opinions publicly and privately. They should always be free to support causes by orderly means which do not disrupt the regular and essential operation of the institution. At the same time, it should be made clear to the academic and the larger community that in their public expressions or demonstrations students or student organizations speak only for themselves.

2. Students should be allowed to invite and to hear any person of their own choosing. Those routine procedures required by an institution before a guest speaker is invited to appear on campus should be designed only to insure that there is orderly scheduling of facilities and adequate preparation for the event, and that the occasion is conducted in a manner appropriate to an academic community. The institutional control of campus facilities should not be used as a device of censorship. It should be made clear to the academic and larger community that sponsorship of guest speakers does not necessarily imply approval or endorsement of the views expressed, either by the sponsoring group or by the institution.

C. Student Participation in Institutional Government

As constituents of the academic community, students should be free, individually and collectively, to express their views on issues of institutional policy and on matters of general interest to the student body. The student body should have clearly defined means to participate in the formulation and application of institutional policy affecting academic and student affairs. The role of the student government and both its general and specific responsibilities should be made explicit, and the actions of the student government within the areas of its jurisdiction should be reviewed only through orderly and prescribed procedures.

D. Student Publications

Student publications and the student press are a valuable aid in establishing and maintaining an atmosphere of free and responsible discussion and of intellectual exploration on the campus. They are a means of bringing student concerns to the attention of the faculty and the institutional authorities and of formulating student opinion on various issues on the campus and in the world at large.

Whenever possible the student newspaper should be an independent corporation financially and legally separate from the university. Where financial and legal autonomy is not possible, the institution, as the publisher of student publications, may have to bear the legal responsibility for the contents of the publications. In the delegation of editorial responsibility to students, the institution must provide sufficient editorial freedom and financial autonomy for the student publications to maintain their integrity of purpose as vehicles for free inquiry and free expression in an academic community.

Institutional authorities, in consultation with students and faculty, have a responsibility to provide written clarification of the role of the student publications, the standards to be used in their evaluation, and the limitations on external control of their operation. At the same time, the editorial freedom of student editors and managers entails corollary responsibilities to be governed by the canons of responsible journalism, such as the avoidance of libel, indecency, undocumented allegations, attacks on personal integrity, and the techniques of harassment and innuendo. As safeguards for the editorial freedom of student publications the following provisions are necessary.

1. The student press should be free of censorship and advance approval of copy, and its editors and managers should be free to develop their own editorial policies and news coverage.

2. Editors and managers of student publications should be protected from arbitrary suspension and removal because of student, faculty, administrative, or public disapproval of editorial policy or content. Only for proper and stated causes should editors and managers be subject to removal and then by orderly and prescribed procedures. The agency responsible for the appointment of editors and managers should be the agency responsible for their removal.

3. All university published and financed student publications should explicitly state on the editorial page that the opinions there expressed are not necessarily those of the college, university, or student body.

V

OFF-CAMPUS FREEDOM OF STUDENTS

A. Exercise of Rights of Citizenship

College and university students are both citizens and members of the academic community. As citizens, students should enjoy the same freedom of speech, peaceful assembly, and right of petition that other citizens enjoy and, as members of the academic community, they are subject to the obligations which accrue to them by virtue of this membership. Faculty members and administrative officials should insure that institutional powers are not employed to inhibit such intellectual and personal developments of students as is often promoted by their exercise of the rights of citizenship both on and off campus.

B. Institutional Authority and Civil Penalties

Activities of students may upon occasion result in violation of law. In such cases, institutional officials should be prepared to apprise students of sources of legal counsel and may offer other assistance. Students who violate the law may incur penalties prescribed by civil authorities, but institutional authority should never be used merely to duplicate the function of general laws. Only where the institution's interests as an academic community are distinct and clearly involved should the special authority of the institution be asserted. The student who incidentally violates institutional regulations in the course of his off-campus activity, such as those relating to class attendance, should be subject to no greater penalty than would normally be imposed. Institutional action should be independent of community pressure.

VI

Procedural Standards in Disciplinary Proceedings

In developing responsible student conduct, disciplinary proceedings play a role substantially secondary to example, counseling, guidance, and admonition. At the same time, educational institutions have a duty and the corollary disciplinary powers to protect their educational purpose through the setting of standards of scholarship and conduct for the students who attend them and through the regulation of the use of institutional facilities. In the exceptional circumstances when the preferred means fail to resolve problems of student conduct, proper procedural safeguards should be observed to protect the student from the unfair imposition of serious penalties.

The administration of discipline should guarantee procedural fairness to an accused student. Practices in disciplinary cases may vary in formality with the gravity of the offense and the sanctions which may be applied. They should also take into account the presence or absence of an honor code, and the degree to which the institutional officials have direct acquaintance with student life in general and with the involved student and the circumstances of the case in particular. The jurisdictions of faculty or student judicial bodies, the disciplinary responsibilities of institutional officials, and the regular disciplinary procedures, including the student's right to appeal a decision, should be clearly formulated and communicated in advance. Minor penalties may be assessed informally under prescribed procedures.

In all situations, procedural fair play requires that the student be informed of the nature of the charges against him, that he be given a fair opportunity to refute them, that the institution not be arbitrary in its actions, and that there be provision for appeal of a decision. The following are recommended as proper safeguards in such proceedings when there are no honor codes offering comparable guarantees.

A. Standards of Conduct Expected of Students

The institution has an obligation to clarify those standards which it considers essential to its educational mission and its community life. These general behavioral expectations and the resultant specific regulations should represent a reasonable regulation of student conduct, but the student should be as free as possible from imposed limitations that have no direct relevance to his education. Offenses should be as clearly defined as possible and interpreted in a manner consistent with the aforementioned principles of relevancy and reasonableness. Disciplinary proceedings should be instituted only for violations of standards of conduct formulated with significant student participation and published in advance through such means as a student handbook or a generally available body of institutional regulations.

B. Investigation of Student Conduct

1. Except under extreme emergency circumstances, premises occupied by students and the personal possessions of students should not be searched unless appropriate authorization has been obtained. For premises such as residence halls controlled by the institution, an appropriate and responsible authority should be designated to whom application should be made before a search is conducted. The application should specify the reasons for the search and the objects or information sought. The student should be present, if possible, during the search. For premises not controlled by the institution, the ordinary requirements for lawful search should be followed.

2. Students detected or arrested in the course of serious violations of institutional regulations, or infractions of ordinary law, should be informed of their rights. No form of harassment should be used by institutional representatives to coerce admissions of guilt or information about conduct of other suspected persons.

C. Status of Student Pending Final Action

Pending action on the charges, the status of a student should not be altered, or his right to be present on the campus and to attend classes suspended, except for reasons relating to his physical or emotional safety and well-being, or for reasons relating to the safety and well-being of students, faculty, or university property.

D. Hearing Committee Procedures

When the misconduct may result in serious penalties and if a penalized student questions the fairness of the disciplinary action, he should be granted, on request, the privilege of a hearing before a regularly constituted hearing committee. The following suggested hearing committee procedures satisfy the requirements of procedural due process in situations requiring a high degree of formality.

1. The hearing committee should include faculty members or students, or, if regularly included or requested by the accused, both faculty and student members. No member of the hearing committee who is otherwise interested in the particular case should sit in judgment during the proceeding.

2. The student should be informed, in writing, of the reasons for the proposed disciplinary action with sufficient particularity, and in sufficient time, to ensure opportunity to prepare for the hearing.

3. The student appearing before the hearing committee should have the right to be assisted in his defense by an adviser of his choice.

4. The burden of proof should rest upon the officials bringing the charge.

5. The student should be given an opportunity to testify and to present evidence and witnesses. He should have an opportunity to hear and question adverse witnesses. In no case should the committee consider statements

against him unless he has been advised of their content and of the names of those who made them, and unless he has been given an opportunity to rebut unfavorable inferences which might otherwise be drawn.

6. All matters upon which the decision may be based must be introduced into evidence at the proceeding before the hearing committee. The decision should be based solely upon such matters. Improperly acquired evidence should not be admitted.

7. In the absence of a transcript, there should be both a digest and a verbatim record, such as a tape recording, of the hearing.

8. The decision of the hearing committee should be final, subject only to the student's right of appeal to the president or ultimately to the governing board of the institution.

ACADEMIC FREEDOM AND CHURCH-RELATED HIGHER EDUCATION: A REPLY TO PROFESSOR MCCONNELL

JUDITH JARVIS THOMSON* AND MATTHEW W. FINKIN**

As the American academic profession emerged at about the turn of the century, it adopted for itself a principle of institutional neutrality: professors should be free to teach, conduct research, and publish so long as they adhere to a professional standard of care. But that assertion confronted the stark fact that a significant number of denominational institutions placed doctrinal constraints on their faculties' teaching, research, and publication. The profession's approach, ultimately embodied in the 1940 Statement of Principles on Academic Freedom and Tenure, was to provide that: "Limitations of academic freedom because of religious or other aims of the institution should be clearly stated in writing at the time of the appointment."[1]

This seemingly simple proposition has proved vexing both in terms and in operational effect.[2] Read in light of the history of the profession's engagement with the issue, the "limitations clause" contains at least two elements. First is a refusal to distinguish a limitation that derives from a religious commitment from one that derives from any "other aim." All institutions that exist to propagate a predetermined truth were viewed by the profession as "proprietary" in the moral sense. Even the acceptance of a single gift by an otherwise free institution for the purpose of controlling the teaching in the chair thus endowed was held by the AAUP's Committee A on Academic Freedom and Tenure to take the institution "out of the class of colleges and universities in the accepted meaning of these terms and place it in the class of those engaged in propaganda activities"[3]—such as the Rand School of Social Science, dedicated to the exposition of socialism.[4] Second and consequently, the AAUP insisted that all such institutions be clearly distinguished from institutions where no limitations were imposed; and it adopted accordingly an exacting requirement of

---

*Laurance S. Rockefeller Professor of Philosophy, Massachusetts Institute of Technology.
**Professor of Law, University of Illinois.

1. Reprinted in 53 L & Contemp Probs 3 (1990). This provision was later characterized as a "concession to historical and practical circumstances." Fuchs, *Intellectual Freedom and the Educational Process*, 42 AAUP Bull 472, 475 (1956).

2. See generally Report, *The "Limitations" Clause of the 1940 Statement of Principles*, 74 Academe 52 (1988).

3. Report of Committee A for 1920, 7 AAUP Bull 9 (1921).

4. Report of Committee A for 1921, 8 AAUP Bull 56 (1922) (elaborating upon the observation of the prior year).

institutional candor requiring the precise limitation to be in writing at the time of appointment.

Professor Michael McConnell of the University of Chicago Law School takes issue with the AAUP's treatment of the limitations clause, which, he claims, has de facto repudiated *any* limitation.[5] Whatever the strength of that claim, and it has some,[6] Professor McConnell's critique goes much further than questioning the AAUP's faithfulness to the text, for he argues for "a modification"[7] in the profession's theory of academic freedom: the academic profession "*should* uphold the free exercise rights of religious institutions"[8] that impose such restrictions; the profession, represented by the AAUP, "ought to value"[9] the religious freedom that undergirds such limitations. His critique should not pass without comment.

I

Professor McConnell gives three reasons for exempting religious institutions from the obligation to allow for academic freedom. Two are consequentialist. The first addresses itself to the consequences for intellectual life of a refusal to condone such constraints:

> [R]eligiously distinctive colleges and universities make important contributions to the intellectual life of their faculty, their students, and the nation, and secular academic freedom in its unmodified form would lead quickly to the extinction of these institutions . . . . [10]

The other addresses itself to the consequences for religious freedom of a refusal to condone them:

> [T]he extension of secular academic freedom to religious institutions . . . would subvert the ability of religious communities to maintain and transmit their beliefs, and thus undermine religious freedom.[11]

McConnell's third reason is not consequentialist: this argument alleges an incompatibility between a refusal to condone such constraints and "the" underlying rationale for academic freedom:

> [T]he insistence on a single model of truth-seeking is inconsistent with the antidogmatic principles on which the case for academic freedom rests . . . . [12]

---

5. McConnell, *Academic Freedom in Religious Colleges and Universities*, 53 L & Contemp Probs 303 (1990) [hereinafter McConnell].

6. Metzger, *The 1940 Statement of Principles on Academic Freedom and Tenure*, 53 L & Contemp Probs 3, 36–38 (1990).

7. McConnell, supra n.5 at 304.

8. Id at 316 (emphasis in original).

9. Id at 318.

10. Id at 312. To analogous effect see Laycock & Waelbrock, *Academic Freedom and the Free Exercise of Religion*, 66 Tex L Rev 1455, 1458 (1988) ("[F]rom a societal perspective, pluralism and the search for truth may be more helped than hindered by distinctive institutions forcefully representing each of the country's many religious traditions.").

11. Id at 312.

12. Id.

The academic profession is in no position to ignore consequentialist arguments for or against academic freedom. The 1940 Statement itself justifies the entitlement to academic freedom on consequentialist grounds: it says that "[i]nstitutions of higher education are conducted for the common good," that "[t]he common good depends upon the free search for truth and its free exposition," and that "[a]cademic freedom is essential to these purposes." [13] If it should turn out that academic freedom for all academics is not in fact essential to these purposes—or, more strongly, that academic freedom for all academics is in fact positively inimical to these purposes—then the document's own justification fails.

The document's consequentialist ground for academic freedom is often expressed in a metaphor: truth is most likely to be discovered in a free marketplace for ideas.[14] McConnell's first consequentialist reason can be thought of as the claim that the marketplace for ideas needs regulation if it is to serve the purpose it is valued for—thus truth is most likely to be discovered in a marketplace for ideas which is so regulated that certain options do not disappear, are not, so to speak, driven out of the market.

Now our own view is that religiously distinctive colleges and universities do make important contributions to intellectual life. And we think it possible that those contributions could not be made—or anyway could not be so effectively made—by any other social organizations or agencies than the religiously distinctive colleges and universities. But three things seem to us to be in doubt.

In the first place, we doubt whether their making those contributions requires them to limit the academic freedom of their faculties. Professor McConnell asserts that requiring those institutions to provide their faculties with "secular academic freedom in its unmodified form would lead quickly to [their] extinction." This seems to us false on its face. It is also an insult to the religions which those institutions represent, for it presupposes that the religions themselves are intrinsically so far unattractive or implausible that the faculties at those institutions cannot be expected voluntarily to advance the denomination's educational ends, and that they will do so only if they labor under the threat of discharge for doctrinal infidelity. Indeed, there is a curious incoherence in McConnell's argument. How can one think that the common good requires the continued presence in the marketplace for ideas of bodies of belief whose academic institutional representatives would "quickly" disappear but for the availability of that *in terrorem* technique?

A weaker claim would have been more plausible and less insulting, namely, that requiring those institutions to provide their faculties with "secular academic freedom in its unmodified form" would place the institutions at risk of extinction—given a good governance system, in which the faculty has a voice as to the institution's aims. This brings us to our second doubt. What needs showing, after all, is not merely that it conduces to the common good that there be religiously distinctive institutions of higher education, but that their con-

---

13. Reprinted in 53 L & Contemp Probs at 407 (1990).
14. J. Milton, *Areopagitica* (1644); J. S. Mill, *On Liberty* (1859).

tribution to the common good is sufficiently great to justify them in coercing their faculties in order to place themselves beyond the risk of extinction.

Another way to put the question is this. From any viewpoint, the existence of religiously distinctive institutions conduces to the common good; does the existence of religiously distinctive institutions maintained in existence by coercion conduce to the common good? We are not convinced that it does.

Professor McConnell explicitly describes the consequences for intellectual life that would issue from the disappearance of the religiously distinctive colleges and universities. He says:

> Given the antireligious character of modern academic culture, *serious* religious scholarship would be in danger of extinction if it were not for particular institutions in which it is valued and protected. It is no coincidence that the rise in religious particularism has occurred most prominently in institutions connected with perspectives (evangelical and fundamentalist Protestantism, conservative Catholicism) that consider themselves most ruthlessly suppressed in the secular academy.[15]

So perhaps he would respond to our question in this way: that there should continue to be "*serious* religious scholarship" is of sufficient importance to intellectual life to warrant the use of coercion by those institutions in order to insure against their own extinction.

We think it unquestionable that much serious religious scholarship is engaged in at the religiously distinctive colleges and universities. We think it also unquestionable that much serious religious scholarship is engaged in at institutions which, whether religiously distinctive or not, do not coerce their faculties. Religious thought has made and continues to make significant contributions to other disciplines, as Professor McConnell's jurisprudential examples illustrate;[16] not only Reinhold Niebuhr, but also Robert Bellah in sociology (at the University of California at Berkeley) and Glenn Tinder in political science (at the University of Massachusetts at Boston) come immediately to mind. We suspect, however, that policing a faculty for credal conformity is unlikely to create a climate in which the very best religious scholarship will emerge. To McConnell, this suspicion may seem no more than an expression of faith, based upon a secular measure of scholarly worth. But to us, it seems historically justified.

In sum, then, we have raised two doubts about McConnell's first argument for an exemption for the religiously distinctive institutions: while we grant that they contribute to intellectual life, and thereby conduce to the common good, we doubt whether they need to use coercion in order to remain in existence,

---

15. McConnell, supra n.5 at 315 (emphasis added).

16. Professor McConnell says: "That theology speaks usefully to jurisprudence can be seen through such works as . . . [citing three such works] on different subjects from disparate theological perspectives." McConnell, supra 5, n.35 at 315. One of the authors he cites teaches at the Cardozo Law School of Yeshiva University, which imposes no limit on academic freedom; the others hold positions in public universities.

and, second, we doubt whether it conduces to the common good that they continue to exist at the cost of using coercion.

Our third doubt comes out as follows. Might it not be asked whether the religiously distinctive institutions really are special in the respect McConnell points to here? The religiously distinctive institutions do, as we said, make important contributions to intellectual life; could the same not be said of institutions distinguished by their commitment to a particular body of political or social or economic doctrine? (Compare, for example, the Rand School of Social Science, which we mentioned earlier; compare also the Henry George School of Social Science.) In some views, perhaps McConnell's, the religiously distinctive institutions make a *more important* contribution to intellectual life than do other doctrinally committed institutions. Our third doubt is whether it is open to the American professoriate—through its organized voice, the AAUP—to take a stand on the substantive question whether they do. As we noted at the outset, the 1940 Statement declined to distinguish religious from "other aims," and we greatly doubt that the AAUP is so much as institutionally competent to make such judgments.

There is room here for an argument to the effect that it is not religion, but doctrinal commitment generally that is special. That is, it could be argued that while institutions with different kinds of doctrinal commitment differ in the degree to which they contribute to intellectual life, that is neither here nor there, and that what matters is the contribution to intellectual life that issues from the sheer diversity itself.[17] Such an argument does not invite the academic profession to take a substantive stand on which doctrinally committed institutions make more important contributions to intellectual life; it invites the profession only to agree on the important contribution made by variety.

Analogues of our three doubts remain, however. In the first place, we doubt whether the continued existence of variety requires condoning limitations on the academic freedom of the various faculties. Second, while we think variety on any view conduces to the common good, we doubt whether variety maintained by coercion does. Third, it remains questionable whether the academic profession should take a substantive stand on the differential contributions made by institutions with doctrinal commitments as opposed to institutions with other aims. For why is *doctrinal* commitment to be thought special?

Professor McConnell concedes that if religion is viewed primarily as a body of doctrine, then the claims he makes for an exemption for the religiously distinctive institutions could be generalized to lend weight to an exemption for institutions with other kinds of doctrinal commitments as well. But religions, he says, are more than bodies of doctrine: they "are also communities of believers with mutual ties of loyalty and common purpose."[18] And second, religious colleges do more than transmit belief: "they raise up leaders and members of the tradition and communion of the faith."[19] But neither of these

---

17. Cf Laycock and Waelbrock (cited in note 10).
18. McConnell, supra n.5, n.38 at 316.
19. Id.

is unique to religion and religious colleges. The history of American higher education is in good measure a history of constituencies creating institutions to serve their special needs. For example, the "labor colleges" of the twenties and thirties, notably Brookwood Labor College and Commonwealth College, were intensely communitarian—in the latter, the students and faculty lived in a remote rural setting and were required to share an enormous amount of manual and farming labor to sustain themselves—and they existed in part to educate a leadership for what the founders had the faith to believe would be the coming workers' millennium.[20]

Indeed, neither is special to doctrines and doctrinally committed institutions. Many colleges with no doctrinal commitments are communities of people with mutual ties of loyalty and common purpose. And as Professor McConnell recognizes, developing communal leadership has been a function of traditional black colleges as well as of others catering to special constituencies. Many black colleges, women's colleges, and other "special interest" colleges combine both features.[21]

Accordingly, there is room for a still more general argument, to the effect that it is neither religion, nor doctrinal commitment generally, but any commitment at all that is special—thus that any institutional aim at all would justify limitations on the academic freedom of the faculty. We say there is room for this argument, but we think it plainly has no weight; indeed, the AAUP rejected the claim that a college's openly declared obligation to the local community allowed it to require its faculty to refrain from the expression of views offensive to the community.[22] It is not for no reason that McConnell's defense of limitations on academic freedom is an effort to fix on grounds for thinking religion special; an argument to the effect that the common good is served by a policy under which just *any* institutional aim justifies coercion of the faculty would be an absurdity.

It cannot be denied that declaring this argument absurd is taking a sub-

---

20. See generally R. Altenbaugh, *Education for Struggle: The American Labor Colleges of the 1920s and 1930s* (1990); R. Koch & C. Koch, *Educational Commune: The Story of Commonwealth College* (1972). The labor colleges did not seek accreditation, give examinations, or award diplomas as these were antithetical to the cooperative, egalitarian, noncompetitive society they hoped to create. Some "graduates" of Commonwealth, however, were accepted into the graduate programs of mainstream universities.

21. McConnell addresses himself in a footnote to the fact that an argument similar to his own can be made for institutions with certain nonreligious commitments:

A similar argument can be made for other distinctive colleges, such as single-sex colleges, and may well have merit in those contexts as well. But our society is morally and perhaps constitutionally committed to eradication of differences based on gender (and other distinctions of an invidious character). It is not committed to eradication of differences based on religion; to the contrary, it is committed to preservation of pluralism and diversity in matters of religion. Religiously distinctive institutions thus stand on a different footing.

McConnell, supra n.1, n.30 at 313. We think this dubious on several grounds. In the first place, gender-distinctions are no more "invidious" than religious distinctions are. Second, while our society is committed to eradication of certain differences *based on* gender-distinctions, so also is it committed to eradication of similar differences based on religious distinctions. Third, it is not at all clear to us that our society is committed to eradication of all gender-distinctive schools on the very ground that they are gender-distinctive: social opposition to gender-distinctive schools is selective, and always rests on further features of the objectionable schools beyond the sheer fact that they are gender-distinctive.

22. *Academic Freedom and Tenure: Lincoln College*, 50 AAUP Bull 244 (1964).

stantive stand about the common good. We think that the drafters of the 1940 Statement did take this substantive stand; but we also think that they were obviously right to take it—in any case, we know of no remotely respectable argument that sheds doubt on it.

II

Professor McConnell's second consequentialist argument to the effect that religion is special is that

> the extension of secular academic freedom to religious institutions . . . would subvert the ability of religious communities to maintain and transmit their beliefs, and thus undermine religious freedom.[23]

There are constitutional protections for religious freedom, but private agencies such as the AAUP should go "[b]eyond the legal limits of the Constitution"; they should "uphold the free exercise rights of religious institutions and need not be limited to the narrow conception of those rights expressed in" constitutional law.[24]

Why should the AAUP go beyond constitutional law in upholding the free exercise rights of religious institutions? What McConnell offers by way of reason is not the ringing consequentialist claim he began with—namely, that extending "secular academic freedom to religious institutions" would undermine religious freedom—but rather that

> [t]he AAUP purports to speak in the name of the academy, and not as a mere partisan for a particular faction or point of view. Its pronouncements regarding academic freedom carry weight among academics and the public in large part because it is seen as objective. Such an association has a moral responsibility to respect the rights of religious bodies, even if those bodies entertain *an understanding of knowledge contrary to that of the majority of the AAUP*.[25]

This reason does not appear to be consequentialist. The gravamen of this argument against the enforcement of "secular academic freedom" thus turns out to be, not the bad consequences for religious freedom of enforcing it, but rather that enforcing it constitutes an exercise of partiality—a choice of one understanding of knowledge in preference to another.

McConnell's second consequentialist argument to the effect that religion is special therefore collapses into his third argument, which is not consequentialist. We turn to that third argument shortly. However, we think it pays to stress that it cannot be any surprise that this collapse took place. Religious freedom

---

23. McConnell, supra n.5 at 312. The proposition is dubious on its face. It assumes that religious communities require colleges and universities, as we commonly understand such institutions, in order to transmit their beliefs. But that is not self-evident. There are several hundred "Bible colleges" which transmit Christian denominational beliefs without moving in the orbit of higher education. Orthodox Jewish belief is transmitted in yeshivas and Talmud Torahs that do not call themselves "colleges." And some denominations maintain the faith by eschewing any education beyond the early grades.

24. Id at 316–317.

25. Id at 317 (emphasis added).

cannot in any sane conception of it include the freedom to use just any means at all for the propagation of religion; the means must themselves be acceptable. The ringing claim that enforcing "secular academic freedom" would undermine religious freedom therefore survives a second look only if it is supported by an argument to the effect that refusing to grant "secular academic freedom" constitutes an acceptable means. It is this claim that McConnell's third argument is intended to make a case for.

III

McConnell's own initial summary of his third argument was this:

> [T]he insistence on a single model of truth-seeking is inconsistent with the antidogmatic principles on which the case for academic freedom rests . . . .[26]

What is that model? It is often expressed in the metaphor we pointed to earlier: truth is most likely to be discovered in a free marketplace for ideas. Without the metaphor: truth is most likely to be discovered when research and the exposition of its results are unfettered.

It is quite clear that this model of truth-seeking does animate the central AAUP declarations on academic freedom. The 1940 Statement says that "[t]he common good depends upon the free search for truth and its free exposition" precisely because of the drafters' belief that truth *is* most likely to be discovered when research and the exposition of its results are unfettered.

McConnell says, however, that there is another model of truth-seeking, another understanding of knowledge, or more precisely, of the way in which knowledge is most likely to be arrived at. He says: "The older religious, or dogmatic, tradition also had its theory of knowledge."[27] According to that theory, "truth is only partially discernible through human efforts; indeed, the products of human effort, being a manifestation of a fallen nature, should always be tested against divine authority; . . . [and] truth is imparted to humanity, at least in part, through divine agency . . . ."[28] According to that theory, truth is most likely to be discovered when research and the exposition of its results are constrained by religious authorities.

In short, the AAUP "is seen as objective" by academics and the public, but in imposing a requirement of freedom in research and exposition—in imposing the requirement that institutions provide their faculties with what *it* calls "academic freedom"—it merely displays its partiality for its own favored model of truth-seeking. Candor would be better served by admitting that what *it* calls "academic freedom" is only one conception of what conduces to the common good; that conception is more properly called "secular academic freedom." According to the other theory of truth-seeking, what conduces to the common good is not secular academic freedom but rather doctrinally constrained

---

26. McConnell, supra n.5 at 312.
27. Id at 313.
28. Id at 313–314.

academic freedom. And, McConnell says, "[r]eligious colleges and universities should not be shy to admit that their understanding of academic freedom differs from that of the AAUP."[29]

Indeed, there is an internal inconsistency in the AAUP's demand that all institutions of higher education adopt its own model of truth-seeking and therefore provide their faculties with "secular academic freedom." If one believes that unfettered research and exposition conduces to the common good, how can one fetter institutions which have a different conception of truth-seeking and thereby of what conduces to the common good?

We have laid all this out at some length because we think it should be looked at closely. It has a superficial appeal, but we think there is less in it than first meets the eye. For what exactly is McConnell's objection to the partiality the AAUP displays in opting for its own favored, nonreligious—that is, non-constrained—model of truth-seeking? Is he inviting his readers to reject the nonreligious model in favor of the religious model? Surely not. One would expect something from him in the way of argument for the correctness of the religious model if that were his intention, whereas what he offers is merely the fact that it represents an "older tradition," that it has a long history.

Is he inviting his readers, more weakly, to suspend belief in the nonreligious model? Does the sheer fact that the religious model has a long history call for suspension of belief in the nonreligious model? We think that an odd idea.

Is he inviting his readers, more weakly still, to feel less confidence in the nonreligious model? Does the sheer fact that the religious model has a long history call for diminished confidence in the nonreligious model? Suppose we feel complete confidence in a certain theory, and then learn that an incompatible theory has a long history. It is very plausible to think we should feel some diminution in confidence in our own theory, pending assessment of what there is by way of evidence for the incompatible theory. (That is exactly what the nonreligious model of truth-seeking calls for.) But what if assessment of the evidence brings forth nothing we can regard as counting against the theory we began with? Are we nevertheless to continue to feel diminished confidence in it?

It should be noticed, moreover, that this consideration works in both directions. If proponents of the nonreligious model should feel diminished confidence in their model because the religious model has a long history, so also ought proponents of the religious model feel diminished confidence in their model because the nonreligious model too has a long history.[30]

We are inclined to think that what concerns McConnell is not in fact belief but something else. What he has in mind emerges from the following:

---

29. Id at 317.

30. The idea of academic freedom can be traced as far back as the trial of Socrates, but it began to take on modern form in the right claimed by theologians at the University of Paris in the twelfth and thirteenth centuries to study, teach, and dispute about works proscribed by Church authorities. R. Hofstedler & W. Metzger, *The Development of Academic Freedom in the United States* ch. 1 (1955). Such proscription, in the words of Godfrey of Fontaines, hindered "inquiry into knowledge of the truth." Id at 32.

> It would be a mistake to dismiss the religious understanding as mere obscur-antism. Its presuppositions regarding the pursuit of knowledge differ substantially from those most of us in modern academia share, but they have an integrity and a coherence. Whether they are right or wrong is not susceptible to proof; this is ultimately a proposition of faith. But the same must be said of the scientific method that underlies academic freedom. Neither religious nor rationalist methodology can be "proven" from an objective standpoint. Both systems of thought claim to be self-validating, in that practitioners of both believe that their results are so compelling that one who engages in them will be compelled to assent to their validity.[31]

There is no such thing as "proof" of the correctness of either model of truth-seeking: choice of one in preference to the other is "ultimately" a matter of "faith." The fact (assuming it a fact) that choice of one in preference to the other is a matter of faith is no reason for disbelieving, or even for feeling diminished confidence in, the correctness of one's choice. But—we take McConnell to think—it does bear on the acceptability of taking certain *actions* pursuant to one's choice. So we take his objection to the partiality the AAUP displays in opting for its own favored model of truth-seeking to lie, not in the fact of its preference for that model, not even in the fact of its imposing *a* preference on all institutions of higher education, but rather in the fact of its imposing a preference on all which it has no "objective" ground for but merely accepts on faith.

Is it a fact that choice of one model in preference to the other is a matter of faith? McConnell is presumably right in thinking that neither can be proved. Does it follow that choice of either rests merely on faith? Isn't there an available middle ground? Isn't it possible that a person should have good reason for his or her choice of model? Many people certainly *think* they have good reason—objectively good reason—for choosing the nonreligious model, consisting in the advances that were made by scientists and other scholars when released from their fetters. We are sure that McConnell would reject that thought out of hand, however, and we suggest that what is at work in him is a deep epistemological skepticism, which would say that their having that thought merely shows their faith in scientific method. But deep epistemological skepticism is decidedly not entitled to pass itself off as an obvious truth.

This is not the place for an extended discussion of skepticism, however, and let us therefore concede it: let us suppose McConnell is right, and that the choice of one model in preference to the other really is a matter of faith. What then? McConnell concludes that it is unacceptable for the academic profession (acting through the AAUP) to impose its choice on those who make the other.

What calls for attention is what this *imposing* consists in. Nothing in the profession's writ has ever insisted that proponents of the religious model of truth-seeking give up their belief in it. A commitment to the free marketplace for ideas requires a commitment to their freedom to hold that belief and to propagate it. But an entirely free marketplace for ideas is one thing and an

---

31. McConnell, supra n.5 at 314.

entirely free arena for action quite another. What the AAUP regards as objectionable, and makes use of such powers as it has to condemn, is not the holding of the belief, or the propagating of it, but the coercion of a faculty in its name.

Consider an analogy. Suppose that we accept a moral code which forbids actions of a certain kind and you a different moral code which permits them. Many people regard belief in a moral code to be merely a matter of faith. (The skepticism at work in them may well be merely moral skepticism, which is shallower than McConnell's.) Suppose they are right. It does not follow that we must refrain from using such powers as we have to prevent you from engaging in those actions. For even if our belief that they are wrongful rests merely on faith, our belief is precisely *that* they are wrongful. No doubt we may not prevent you by illegitimate means; we hope it is clear that we are not offering a justification for (as it might be) the firebombing of abortion clinics. No doubt it is arguable that it is permissible for us to intervene only if your actions are "other-regarding"; that is, it is arguable that we must leave you to your victimless sins, however sinful we may think them. But the idea that our hands are tied by the sheer fact that our moral code rests on faith is a confusion. No one is entitled to freedom from intervention just on the ground that a moral code forbidding the action rests on faith.

So also for the coercion of a faculty in the name of the religious model of truth-seeking. No institution is entitled to freedom to coerce its faculty just on the ground that belief in the nonreligious model rests on faith. To have chosen the nonreligious model is to believe that it conduces to the common good that institutions of higher education not coerce their faculties, and therefore to believe it wrongful for them to do so. The wrong is by definition not victimless; and, despite Professor McConnell's accusations of "forcing"[32] or "imposing"[33] secular academic freedom to the point of institutional "destruction"[34] or "annihilation,"[35] the means the AAUP uses are not themselves illegitimate, consisting as they do in making the wrongs public (with painstaking care for factual accuracy), censuring such institutions as engage in them, and warning prospective members of the institution of what they will face if they join it.

---

32. Id at 303, 316.
33. Id at 305.
34. Id at 303.
35. Id at 316. Professor McConnell's claim of institutional "annihilation" is predicated upon the institutions' accepting the profession's position. But these institutions are perfectly free to go their own way. Suffice it to say, the more intensely sectarian the institution the more impervious it is to any rebuke from outside.

Library of Congress Cataloging-in-Publication Data
Freedom and tenure ln the academy / William W. Van Alstyne, editor.
"Previously published as volume 53, no. 3 of Law and contemporary
problems journal, summer 1990. New material . . . by William Van
Alstyne . . . Judith Thomson and Matthew Finkin"—T.p. verso.
Includes bibliographical references.
ISBN 0-8223-1333-2 (cloth : acid-free paper)
1. Academic freedom—United States. 2. Freedom of speech—United
States. 3. Teachers—Tenure—United States. I. Van Alstyne,William W.
KF4242.F74   1993
342.73'0853—dc20
[347.302853]   92-40982 CIP